The Ecology of the
Ancient Greek World

The Ecology of the
Ancient Greek World

Robert Sallares

Cornell University Press

Ithaca, New York

First published 1991 Cornell University Press

Library of Congress Cataloging-in-Publication Data

Sallares, Robert
    The ecology of the ancient Greek world / Robert Sallares.
        p.   cm.
    Includes bibliographical references and index.
    ISBN 0–8014–2615–4 (alk. paper)
    1. Ecology—Greece—History.   2. Human ecology—Greece—History.
    3. Agricultural ecology—Greece—History.   I. Title.
    QH151.S24   1991
    304.2′0938—dc20   90–55920

Printed in Great Britain

Contents

Preface   vii
Chronology   ix

I. Introduction   1

II. Demography   42

   1. The state of the art   42
   2. Population size, density and carrying capacity   50
   3. Human bones, mortality and life expectancy   107
   4. Natural fertility and family limitation   129
   5. Age class systems   160
   6. Social and economic aspects of family structures   193
   7. Disease   221

III. Agriculture   294

   1. Introduction   294
   2. Patterns of land use in Attica   295
   3. Olive production in ancient Attica   304
   4. The extent of the cultivated area of Attica   309
   5. Shifts in the balance between different cereals   313
   6. Previous views on the origin and spread of naked wheats   316
   7. More problems relating to *semidalis*   323
   8. Sowing seasons and distribution patterns of naked wheats   326
   9. Explanation of shifts in balance between cereals   333
   10. Cereals other than naked wheats in Attica   361
   11. Greece and Egypt   368
   12. Cereal yields   372

IV. Conclusions   390

Notes   420
Bibliography   505
Supplementary bibliography   573
Index   576

Preface

This is my first book. It is a synthesis of ancient history and biological or physical anthropology, two subjects which I first studied as an undergraduate. My main aim is to try to show that it is useful to combine subjects like these, which may seem to have little connection with each other. I hope that the reader will be convinced of this whatever he or she may think of any of the arguments employed on points of detail. Indeed the book covers such a wide range of intellectual problems and proposes so many controversial solutions to these problems that it would be unrealistic to expect anyone to agree with everything written here. Much more could be written about virtually every topic mentioned in this book than I have had space for, and I hope to discuss at greater length many of the issues raised here in future publications. Greek names have generally been transliterated, but in a few cases the more familiar anglicised forms have been retained.

My chief debts are as follows. I am grateful to Colin Haycraft for accepting such a long manuscript from a new author, and to Deborah Blake for editing it efficiently. The initial stages of the research presented here were financed by a Department of Education and Science Studentship, and the ultimate stages by a British Academy Postdoctoral Fellowship. It could not have been started without Paul Cartledge as postgraduate supervisor. In these days of concern about Ph.D. completion rates, very few supervisors in any university would have given, as he did, a graduate student the latitude required to perform the kind of research contained in this book. John Davies and Peter Garnsey made helpful comments on the thesis which was the remote and exceedingly primitive ancestor of this book, and the latter has also given me a great deal of assistance subsequently. Steve Hodkinson commented on parts of the manuscript. I also wish to thank Geoffrey Lloyd for benevolence and support down the years. Needless to say none of these people is responsible for any of the views expressed. My greatest debt is to my parents, to whom the book is dedicated.

Cambridge, August 1990   J.R.S.

Chronology

Date	Period	Authors etc.	Personalities/events
2200 BC	EHII (end)		Arrival of proto-Indo-Europeans in the Aegean
2000	EHIII		
1800	MH		
1628			Eruption of volcano on Santorini
1600	MM	Linear A	Minoan palaces on Crete
1400	LHIIIA-B	Linear B	Mycenaean palaces on mainland of Greece
1200	LHIIIC		Collapse of Mycenaean world
1100	Submycenaean		Period of migrations
1000	Protogeometric		Colonisation of Ionia
			Use of iron technology becomes widespread
900	Geometric		
800		Homer	Greek colonisation in Mediterranean begins
750	Late Geometric		Population growth
700	Archaic	Hesiod	'Hoplite revolution'
650	Protoattic	Lyric poets	Colonisation of Black Sea
600		Homeric Hymns	Reforms of Solon at Athens
550	Black figure		Persian empire
			Peisistratid tyranny at Athens
500	Red figure	Pindar	Reforms of Kleisthenes at Athens
	Classical	Gortyn Lawcode	490, Marathon, Miltiades
		Aiskhylos	480, Salamis, Themistokles
450		Herodotos	Athenian empire, Kimon
		Thucydides	Peloponnesian Wars
		Hippokrates	430-427, epidemic at Athens
		Euripides	Alkibiades, Lysander
		Aristophanes	403, Aigospotamoi
400		Xenophon	Spartan empire, Agesilaos
		Lysias	Corinthian War
		Plato	371, battle of Leuktra
		Isaios	Second Athenian League
		Isokrates	Epameinondas
		Middle Comedy	362, battle of Mantinea
350		Aristotle	Philip II of Macedon
		Demosthenes	Alexander the Great
		Aiskhines	Lykourgos at Athens
		New Comedy	Lamian War
		Theophrastos	Demetrios of Phaleron
300	Hellenistic	Menander	Period of the Diadochoi

		Epicureans & Stoics	280, Celtic invasion of Greece
		Zenon 'archive'	Period of the Epigoni
		Theokritos	Chremonidean War
		Philokhoros	262/1, Antigonos Gonatas conquers Athens
200			Second Punic War, Hannibal
			Achaian and Aitolian Leagues
			Macedonian Wars
150		Cato, Polybios	Greece under Roman rule
			Jugurtha, Marius
100		Poseidonios	
		Philodemos	Athens revolts during Mithridatic Wars, Sulla
		Cicero	Caesar, Crassus, Pompey
		Diodoros Siculus	Antony & Cleopatra
1 AD	Early Roman	Strabo, Virgil	Augustus
		Columella, Varro	Tiberius, Claudius, Nero
		Pliny the Elder	79, Pompeii destroyed
		Dioskorides	Vespasian
100		Plutarch	Trajan
		Pausanias	Hadrian
		2nd Sophistic	Epidemic in reign of Marcus
		Galen	Aurelius strikes Athens
200		Athenaios	Septimius Severus
			Elagabalus
	Late Roman	SHA	267, Heruli sack Athens
300		Lactantius	Diocletian
		Eusebios	Constantine
		Ammianus Marcellinus	
		Oribasios	Julian the Apostate
400			378, battle of Adrianople
500	Byzantine & mediaeval		Alaric sacks Athens

I

Introduction

Since many different strands of argument dealing with subject matter which may be rather unfamiliar to many readers have to be woven together in this book, it may be helpful to begin by indicating how it came to be written. I started work as a postgraduate student with the modest idea of producing a thesis to replace that of Gernet (1909) on the grain supply of classical Athens. Gernet's research was the standard treatment of its subject until the recent publication of Garnsey (1988), although Gernet's book is in many respects completely out of date by now. He believed that Attica could only feed a small proportion of its population and that the balance of the food requirements of the classical population came from external sources through trade. This thesis has exerted an influence on subsequent scholarship out of all proportion to the intrinsic merits of the arguments deployed by Gernet. Isager & Hansen (1975), Ste. Croix (1972) and Finley (1985a) are examples of more recent books which bear the imprint of Gernet's ideas.

The main problem raised by Gernet's book is that of the relationship between the population and the land. This question urgently demands reappraisal, following Garnsey's lead. Gernet was writing before population studies in the shape of modern historical demography and population biology had developed as academic subjects. Furthermore his knowledge of agriculture and land economy was very limited even by the standards of the first quarter of the twentieth century. The other available synthetic works on these subjects, such as Jardé (1925), Gomme (1933), and Jasny (1944), although good by the standards of their own time, are also all out of date to a greater or lesser extent. With the proliferation of academic publications in recent years, there have appeared many publications on various aspects of the population and agriculture of the ancient world. In my opinion, however, much of the recent output is only of mediocre value.

The reason for this is that most ancient historians who have taken an interest in these matters have failed to appreciate fully that population studies and agriculture are subjects in their own right with a vast technical literature. It is only by fully exploiting these bodies of technical

1

literature that our understanding of the ancient world in these respects can be advanced far beyond the level attained by Gernet or Jardé, for example. It would be senseless to criticise scholars who lived and worked in the first half of the twentieth century for not exploiting research which had not yet been carried out in their time, but scholars working today have no such excuse. The desire to exploit fully relevant technical literature explains the occurrence in the bibliography to this book of many references to articles in periodicals such as *Nature* and *Science* whose pages are unfamiliar to the vast majority of students of classical antiquity. It is proposed here to carry out an inquiry into the main problem raised by Gernet in entirely new terms.

At an early stage of research it became apparent that the idea that Attica in particular and more generally classical Greece as a whole may have been able to produce all or most of the food required to sustain the human population could not be dismissed as easily as Gernet dismissed it. From this point onwards the research presented in this book came to focus on the relationship between agricultural production and the human population within the boundaries of the mainland of ancient Greece in the first millennium BC. Considerations of space prevented extensive treatment here of the question of the significance of grain imports to Greece from other regions to which Gernet himself attached such great importance, although I may return to this question in future publications. However, in the course of this book a new model concerning the relationship between the population and the land in classical Greece will be put forward which is radically different from Gernet's.

Progress in historiography may be made first by exploiting new sources of information and secondly by asking questions which did not occur to earlier scholars. The first avenue is relatively insignificant in ancient history, although in this book the results of the intensive archaeological surveys which have proliferated in Greece recently will be used to reach conclusions concerning population dynamics in ancient Greece which were unattainable only twenty years ago. It will also be suggested that classical archaeologists could take much more interest than they have done so far in collecting plant remains and animal bones and other raw data for environmental history. However, the exploitation of a previously untouched database in the form of British parish registers has played a fundamental role in the development of historical demography as an academic subject. The results obtained therefrom furnish much food for thought for ancient historians, as will be seen later.

On balance the second avenue plays a greater role in this book. Foucault (1970) showed brilliantly how the development of thought in early modern Europe revolved around the formulation of new ideas or concepts and their integration into new systems of thought in which ideas were related in new ways. A new concept entails analysis of a new network of causal relations. David Hume argued that necessity is in the mind rather than in the objects, in other words a psychological association. Other philosophers have put forward different interpretations of causality, but it remains true that, even if causes do exist as Kant supposed, they generally are not visible to direct human observation. Even the most traditionally minded classical scholars have seldom been able to avoid asking questions involving mental associations of phenomena which were alien to the way of thinking of the ancient Greeks, even though the training of classicists hardly encourages them to consider questions which are not directly suggested by the words of a text. For example, whenever ancient Greek 'literature' or 'religion' is studied one is asking questions involving a pattern of thought which never occurred to anyone in antiquity, notwithstanding Aristotle's book on 'poetry', *peri poiêtikês*, for example, as these words cannot be translated into ancient Greek. 'Literature' is a concept formulated for the first time in early modern Europe, as Foucault correctly stressed, while ancient Greek expressions such as *theôn timai* or *thrêskeia* are an extremely inadequate equivalent of the modern concept of 'religion'. Conversely the ancient Greek language included concepts such as *polis*, whose content is so alien to anything in the experience of people living in modern industrialised countries that it cannot be translated into modern Indo-European languages. We shall return to *polis* later.

'Economy' is another concept much used by modern scholars which cannot be translated into ancient Greek.[1] This book will focus on a set of ideas associated with another modern concept derived etymologically from the same ancient Greek word *oikos* ('household') as 'economy', but very much less frequently mouthed by ancient historians. This concept is 'ecology'. It was coined ('Ökologie') by a German, Häckel, a disciple of Charles Darwin, in 1866.[2] Thus it cannot lay claim to great antiquity, perhaps a reason why hardly any classical scholars have taken any interest in it. However, understanding of the classical world can only be advanced by asking questions about it which were not asked in antiquity. An American scholar, J. Donald Hughes, is about the only classicist to have made the ecology of the ancient world the focus of his research. No disrespect for the intrinsic merits of his little book (1975b) is intended by the statement that it has not grabbed the attention of most ancient historians. One professional ecologist, Paul Colinvaux (1980), has also attempted to apply ecology to ancient history, in an interesting but rather different manner from that proposed in this book. Again his work is not familiar to most classicists.

Why does the study of historical ecology or palaeoecology matter? Two kinds of answer may be given to this question. The first is that in an age of increasing government pressure on British universities to make academic research more relevant to the concerns of everyday life outside the gates of universities, questions which fall into the domain of ecology as popularly conceived are steadily attracting increasing public interest.

One only has to think of the great Dust Bowl in the USA in the 1930s, which inspired John Steinbeck's *The grapes of wrath*, or of the pollution caused by the use of the insecticide DDT after the Second World War which inspired Rachel Carson's *Silent spring*, or more recently of the concern stemming from nuclear pollution from Chernobyl, or of the effects of acid rain, or of the potential threat to life caused by the appearance of holes in the earth's ozone layer resulting from the use of chlorofluorocarbons in aerosols, or of the AIDS epidemic, or of the possible consequences of the greenhouse effect.

The American ecologist Paul Sears described ecology as a 'subversive' subject because it challenges many of the presumptions of modern civilisation, for example that modern technology puts mankind beyond the reach of nature, or that continuous economic growth in the future is in fact desirable or even possible. This assumption underlies the economic policies of both capitalist and communist governments, but it is inherently unlikely, unless the process of controlled nuclear fusion is mastered at some time in the future.[3] The study of historical ecology may be justified on the grounds that the roots of many current problems lie in the past, which may help to instil an appreciation that what is done today may have far-reaching consequences for our descendants.

The second answer to the question raised above is simply that the concerns of ecology are in fact fundamental to understanding the course of history in general (and so the present) and ancient history in particular, irrespective of whether or not any particular phenomenon of the distant past has any practical consequences for the present or future. Indeed I would go so far as to assert that any ancient historian who has not immersed himself or herself fully in the problems of ecology can have, at best, only an extremely limited comprehension of the course of history in classical antiquity. It is hoped that the reader will agree that this proposition has been fully substantiated when the end of the book is reached, although it is acknowledged that the claim is a large one.

Ecology as an academic subject is rather different from the image of it which environmentalists such as the 'Greens' in West Germany or the members of the Greenpeace movement attempt to convey to the general public. Many of the preoccupations of these movements are with pollution of the inanimate environment, for example radioactive discharges from the Sellafield nuclear reprocessing plant in north-west England, which is now becoming a star tourist attraction. In universities the study of the surface of the earth as an inanimate environment is generally consigned to geographers, the rocks below to geologists, and the air above to meteorologists. A couple of ecologists have offered a definition of the 'environment' of an animal as 'everything that might influence its chance to survive and reproduce', but the word 'environment' has a less specific meaning in popular usage, 'the surroundings'.

Perhaps not all, but most professional scholars who regard themselves as ecologists are interested primarily in living organisms, as may readily be seen by glancing through the articles in volumes of periodicals such as *Ecology* or the *Journal of ecology* for example. Naturally account has to be taken of the physical environment inhabited by the living organisms under study, but it seems fair to say that a physical environment which did not contain any living organisms would not be of interest to most ecologists, beyond ascertaining why it could not support life. The most commonly encountered definition of ecology as an academic subject is that it is the study of the distribution and abundance of populations of living organisms in relation to their environment, or words to that effect. It is this definition of ecology which will be adopted in this book. Aristotle observed that the *life of animals centres on obtaining food and on reproduction*. This is also a good description of much of the subject matter of ecology as an academic subject, so long as the dictum is applied to all living organisms, not just to animals. Aristotle's biological works do not leave the smallest shred of doubt that he would have taken a great interest in the modern science of ecology if he could have read some of the literature it has spawned.[4]

The field of inquiry is wider than that of historical demography because we shall be considering not only human populations but also populations of plants and animals upon which mankind depended in classical times as well as populations of bacteria, fungi and viruses which subsisted upon men, plants and animals. Some ecologists tend to interpret their subject in an essentially synchronic manner, seeing its task as explaining how equilibrium is maintained in ecosystems which are basically in equilibrium (analogous to functionalist social anthropologists who build their studies of human societies around the assumption that all institutions function so as to maintain the existing state of affairs, and are then unable to explain social change). This is particularly true of ecologists who are interested primarily in the present and so in very short time-scales, rather than the past. As this book is concerned with history, a diachronic perspective is essential and so a dynamic evolutionary approach to ecology is preferred here. There is no need to make the assumption that we will be dealing with a system in equilibrium at the start of this book. Rather such a point, if true, would need to be established through empirical inquiry. According to the van Valen (1973) hypothesis, living organisms are never perfectly adapted to their environment because the environment (animate and inanimate) is always changing. Natural selection works ceaselessly to try to maintain a living organism's adaptation to its environment.

Another frequently encountered definition of ecology is that it is the study of rates of flow of energy between different levels of food chains, a branch of thermodynamics. Such a definition is not as alien to a study of agriculture in antiquity as may be supposed at first sight, when it is recalled that the purpose of agriculture is after all to transform a larger proportion of the energy contained in living organisms in the environment into a form in which it may be consumed by man. However the subject be defined, it is important to bear in mind that in the pursuit of knowledge for its own sake there is no need to make any assumption that any particular state of affairs is more desirable than any other state. The 'Greens' believe that a lower rate of energy use per caput in the modern world is more desirable than a higher rate because it is conducive to a more stable environment, but this is a political judgment of a kind which is not necessary or desirable in the course of academic research.

In theory if not always in practice, ecology is par excellence a subject for scholars who are synthesisers on a large scale. The field of inquiry of this book delineated above, even though it is a conceptual unity, requires excursions into history, agriculture, botany, zoology, demography and many other subjects too. In short it requires the crossing of interdisciplinary boundaries on a massive scale. In particular it has been found necessary to cross frequently the 'frontier' between the humanities and the sciences. This arbitrary division of the field of learning into two disconnected halves is the most sacred cow of the entire British educational system. Current government policy is predicated on the assumption of the divide between the humanities and the sciences, as illustrated by the constant attempts to divert resources from the humanities into science and technology. In my opinion the divide between the humanities and the sciences has no rational foundation. It is accepted in Britain today because it happens to exist. Nevertheless it should be remembered that the current system of education in Britain is in many respects of very recent origin. There is no reason whatsoever for regarding it as hallowed by tradition. Until 1854 undergraduates were not allowed to *take* the Classical Tripos in Cambridge unless they had *passed* the Mathematical Tripos, in an age when such combinations of subjects were not unusual. The aim of this book is to illustrate the contributions to knowledge that may be made today by such combinations of disciplines.

There is no intelligent justification for the divide between the humanities and the sciences. It may be as well to repeat the philosophical arguments for this point of view, if only very briefly. The German philosophers Windelband and Rickert argued long ago that what separates art from science is not the existence of two separate bodies of subject matter, with no possible overlap between them, but the application of two different methods of investigation to subject matter that may well be susceptible to investigation by *either* method. To give a concrete illustration of this principle which is relevant to the subject matter of this book, the great epidemic which struck Athens in 430 BC may be studied as a unique historical event, unparalleled in the experience of people like Thucydides and Sokrates who lived through it. This is how historians usually consider it. Alternatively it may be studied as a particular example of a class of events, namely epidemics, whose course tends to follow certain forms which may be quantified. This is how a mathematical epidemiologist would want to analyse it.

The unity of this book is provided by a set of subject matter, namely the evidence for a group of populations of living organisms interacting with each other in a particular geographical environment during a particular period of history. That particular subject matter happens to be susceptible to investigation by the techniques both of the historian and of the scientist. This is the epistemological justification for the constant crossing of the divide between the humanities and the sciences which the reader will encounter in this book. An alternative way of considering this philosophical problem was provided by Sir Karl Popper, but it leads to a similar conclusion, which is what matters here. Popper argued that all 'scientific' discoveries are derived from hypotheses which cannot be proved absolutely even if they are right, but may be *falsified* if they are wrong. He went on to argue that scholars in the sciences and the humanities both depend on their imagination to devise hypotheses. This conclusion, like that of Windelband and Rickert, destroys the idea that there is a chasm between the humanities and the sciences which cannot be crossed. Aristotle, in the midst of a mass of studies devoted to human ethics, morality and politics, still found time to emphasise the pleasures that may be obtained from the study of plants and animals. This book seeks to recover, in a modern form, the Aristotelian project of a unitary approach to the whole existing corpus of knowledge.[5]

A number of philosophers and scientists have argued that philosophies of science based on physics as the classic experimental science are inappropriate for biology, because biology is fundamentally different from physics in several important respects: (1) biology has a historical dimension but physics does not; (2) living organisms possess in their genes a plan for governing their whole future development, a characteristic lacking in the subject matter of physics in the inanimate world; 3) phenomena in biology can often be explained with hindsight but rarely predicted, in contrast to classical physics, because most phenomena in (population) biology are only intelligible in terms of nonlinear dynamics, generating mathematical equations that are very difficult to solve. Gould (1989) argued that sciences like palaeontology and ecology have more in common with history than with physics.

Most of the phenomena discussed in this book are theoretically capable of expression in the shape of mathematical equations and models. McCullagh (1984) has argued recently that historians make much more use of 'statistical' inferences than is generally recognised, but only in a special and rather restricted sense of assigning a proportion of objects which belong to one (reference) class to another (attribute) class. In contrast, most of the phenomena discussed in this book may be expressed in a purely numerical form. Nevertheless the reader will find a paucity of quantitative arguments in the rest of this book. The reason for this is that there is a chronic and largely irremediable shortage of quantitative data for the ancient world. Not one of the dozens of scholars who have written articles on the great epidemic of Athens in 430 BC has considered its progress in purely mathematical terms, even though similar events in recent times may be and have been considered in this way. There is plenty of interest at the moment in developing models to predict how the AIDS epidemic is going to develop. The absence of the data required to formulate equations to express the development of the epidemic of 430 BC in a mathematical shape has deterred scholars from even considering what *form* such equations might take, if indeed anyone has ever considered the problem in these terms before.

The shortage of quantitative data from antiquity raises an obvious objection to an attempt to hybridise humanities and sciences, namely that science relies on the exact specification of parameters in quantitative terms permitting attempts at the experimental falsification of the predicted consequences of previously conceived hypotheses, and that any arena in which quantification is impossible inevitably falls outside the domain of science. To specify a practical illustration of this problem, it could be argued that the absence of raw data permitting the empirical determination of mortality and fertility rates for classical Greece prevents the profitable extension of historical demography backwards into the classical period. The following claim has been made recently: 'In the end, demography without numbers is waffle, an amiable kind of social natural history.'[6] The answer given here to any critic who raises this objection to the current enterprise falls into two parts.

A hint of the first part of the answer was given in the last paragraph but one. The most general models of the biological sciences have the function of predicting the *form* that possible solutions to problems may take, rather than facilitating the immediate solution of problems in numerical terms. It is maintained here that the importation of models from the biological sciences may advance understanding of population dynamics in antiquity in the sense that it may enable us to understand the form or shape taken by population processes in antiquity, even if the evidence does not exist to quantify the parameters that one might wish to quantify. It would be foolish to forget that Darwin's *Origin of species* is almost entirely devoid of arguments of a quantitative nature.

It will be argued that there is good evidence that the determinants of certain important demographic parameters in ancient Greece, e.g. (average) age of first marriage, were qualitatively different from the determinants of the same parameters in early modern Europe, and that appreciating this is an important contribution to the historical demography of Europe, even if the actual parameters cannot be quantified. The riposte may be made to the sentiment of the quotation in the last paragraph but one, as Caldwell (1982) has argued, that the emphasis on quantification of demographers working on early modern and modern Europe (or on societies in other parts of the world of European origin) has prevented them from understanding the demography of non-Western societies, e.g. in the Third World, because of a failure to realise that the social determinants of demographic parameters in non-Western societies are *qualitatively* different from those of Western societies. This point is a fundamental starting point for research into the demography of ancient Greece because the ancient Greek *polis* was not a modern Western society either.

The second part of the answer to the question raised above concerning quantification is that the idea that experimentation is the essence of science, separating it from the humanities, is a caricature of a substantial slice of what normally passes for science. The only dividing line that can be used to mark off those areas of academic research in which experimentation may assume a fundamental role is a temporal one, namely that their subject matter lies in the present or future, rather than in the past. Astronomy is a special case. As a historian, I have always envied astronomers because the finite magnitude of the speed of light travelling to earth from faraway bodies means that today they may observe with the naked eye events which actually happened in the distant past.

In other subjects, as soon as a switch to qualitatively similar subject matter located in the past is made, then controlled experimentation becomes impossible for all the reasons that are sadly familiar to historians, namely the patchy nature of surviving evidence, uncertainty whether the evidence that happens to survive records all the important features of the phenomenon under investigation, the impossibility of ascertaining the exact context in which the event of interest occurred, the possibility of displacement of finds from their original context in the case of archaeological (palaeontological) material, etc. For example, plant-breeders developing new varieties of wheat today to feed mankind in the future naturally rely on practical experimental techniques, but as soon as one turns to consider the evolutionary history of wheat in the past, one finds that it is a topic often shrouded in dense fog, in spite of a large volume of research, because it is impossible to carry out experiments on unique evolutionary events which occurred in the past under circumstances which cannot now be ascertained precisely.

The evolutionary history of living organisms is as unique as the political history of human societies. There is no sign of the dinosaurs evolving again after their extinction about sixty million years ago. It is as difficult to state with certainty what caused the extinction of the dinosaurs, to prove for example that an asteroid collided with the earth causing climatic change, or that volcanic eruptions caused the climatic change instead, or that climatic change disrupted the balance between the sexes in creatures with a temperature-dependent mechanism of sex determination, as three current theories maintain, as it is to state what were the causes of the Peloponnesian War.

Later on we shall have occasion to discuss living organisms which exhibit cyclical fluctuations in population size, but this does not contradict the point made here about the uniqueness of the process of evolution. It all depends on the length of the temporal period under consideration. Perhaps 99 per cent of all the species that ever existed in the history of the earth have become extinct. Thus short-term stability and patterns are always resolved into long-term instability. The sciences with which the research contained in this book is principally concerned face essentially the same epistemological problems as are faced by conventional historians. One can only proceed in these sciences by adopting the hypothesis which explains the largest volume of evidence employing the most simplifying assumptions, at least provisionally until another hypothesis of still wider explanatory power is proposed, as it is generally impossible to verify or disprove hypotheses by carrying out experiments in which any or all of the experimental conditions may be modified at will. It is necessary to assume the basic metaphysical axiom of uniformitarianism, namely that the laws of nature do not vary over time, as a guide to what could have happened in the past.

At this point it may be of interest to return to the humanities and consider how the student of human societies in the past may strive to circumvent the impossibility of carrying out experiments on past societies. In order to achieve this end the method of comparative research, which was exploited brilliantly by Max Weber, was devised as a form of indirect experimentation. It is analogous in certain respects to the use of the null hypothesis in scientific research as a means of verifying the importance of a phenomenon under investigation by showing that in its absence a set of data is statistically significantly different. Most classical scholars have tended to denigrate comparative research in historical sociology. Let us take the views of Robin Seager as a typical example of the attitude of traditionalists:

> In fact Cartledge provides a lucid analysis of the reasons why normal Greek slave-owning states were not plagued by risings and why Sparta was different. The traditionalist may still, however, be left wondering why this exposition need be formulated in terms of a demonstration that an American model is useless for Greece, but then, as far as the traditionalist can see, being found irrelevant is the sole function of models ...[7]

No one can possibly accuse the traditionalist of being far-sighted. This kind of attitude amounts to saying that because the ancient Greeks were not identical to any other society that has ever existed in history, it is not profitable to take into account evidence from any other society in attempting to interpret the distinctive features of ancient Greek society.

It depends on an understanding of the nature of comparative research whose inadequacy can scarcely be exaggerated. Seager appears to assume that comparative research necessarily must involve a search for similarities between different societies, and if they cannot be found, then the enterprise is worthless. This is not so because the best comparative research, like that of Max Weber, or Marc Bloch, or the article of Cartledge (1985) which Seager was struggling to criticise, is centred around a search for patterns of significant *differences* between societies. The philosophical reasons why this is a more rewarding approach than looking for similarities were given by John Stuart Mill (1973), who showed that the method of difference is a more powerful analytical technique than the method of similarity.

In Chapter II.5 below it will be argued that the social structure of the ancient Greek *polis* differed from all later societies in European history, including Rome, in ways which had the effect of making the demography of ancient Greece qualitatively different from all demographic patterns that have been observed in the subsequent course of European history. The position adopted in this book is that Greece and Rome should not be assimilated to each other as societies, and the method of difference is an invaluable tool for tracking down the different courses of Greek and of Roman history in antiquity. At the same time, I do not believe that the ancient Greeks were quite as unique as Seager, for example, may suppose. There are two areas of the world, namely East Africa and Papua New Guinea, in which social anthropologists have studied societies which exhibit striking resemblances to the ancient Greek *polis* in respect of socio-political organisation and consequently in respect of demographic patterns, as will be seen in the next chapter.

No more will be said about methodology in this introduction. We must turn now to consider some general features of the ecology of the Mediterranean in antiquity. It is essential to start by picking up the point made earlier about the importance of conceptualisation in history. The Latin word *agricultura*, the root of the modern word 'agriculture', means literally 'cultivation of the land'. Its ancient Greek equivalent *geôrgia* has a similar meaning. For most, if not all, modern scholars doing research into agriculture in antiquity the word 'agriculture' still bears the same connotations that *agricultura* had in antiquity. However, giving a different conceptual content to the word may give it additional explanatory powers. An approach to a different conceptual content may begin with the observation that agriculture is not a uniquely human activity.

For example, the leaf-cutter ants of the genus Atta in the western hemisphere and termites in Africa farm fungi. It has also been shown that other species of ants enter into mutualisms with flowering plants, dispersing seeds and fruits and so facilitating propagation of the plants, protecting plants from their enemies, and feeding essential nutrients to plants, imitating the activities of human farmers. In return the ants receive rewards produced by the plants, especially food and nesting sites. Another interesting parallel is provided by the fact that artificial pollination of plants by ants, although of potential importance, is not significant in practice, just as most crops grown by humans are not artificially pollinated by farmers either. Both plants and ants achieve increases in evolutionary fitness through these mutualisms. Some species of ants also tend aphids and caterpillars for their sugary secretions. This may be interpreted as animal husbandry in miniature.

The lesson to be drawn from ant-plant mutualisms is that farming the land is not the essence of agriculture. The land is not a key element in the equation, and indeed is not strictly necessary for farming at all, as shown by the modern development of aquaculture. The essence of 'agriculture' is rather a relationship between two populations, one plant and one animal, in which the animal helps to spread plant genotypes with characteristics attractive to itself, in the process increasing its own evolutionary fitness. The symbiotic relationship facilitates growth of both populations. This sharply differentiates it from predation or parasitism, which shade into each other, in which one of the species involved benefits while the other is adversely affected, and from commensalism in which one partner benefits and the other is unaffected. It is this definition of agriculture which will henceforth be employed in this book.

The evolutionary relationship between the animal and the plant population is not strictly a case of co-evolution, because the two populations are unequal in that most of the genetic characteristics of the animal population, be it ant or human, are not tied to the relationship between them, whereas many of the genetic characteristics of the plant population have evolved as a consequence of the development of the symbiotic relationship between them. At first sight the ants may appear to be a rather isolated instance of mutualism. However, the recent trend in ecology has been to emphasise strongly that many different species of living organisms participate in mutualistic relationships with other species from quite different taxa. This means that human agriculture is simply the most familiar example of a biological phenomenon which is extremely widespread in the world of nature. As another instance of this phenomenon an important economic pest of the domesticated olive tree in the Mediterranean, namely the olive fly (*Dacus oleae*), may be mentioned. Its larvae depend on a species of bacterium, which the female fly carries around with it, for digesting olive oil, although the bacterium does not seem to need the fly for its continued existence.[8]

In the course of the development of agriculture alternative plant genotypes with characteristics antagonistic to a possible partner animal population tend to fall by the wayside because of their lower evolutionary fitness. This happens especially under difficult environmental conditions, for example at the limits of a plant's normal geographical range. Many plants contain poisonous chemicals which function as a chemical defence system against predators and competitors, because plants cannot move around to escape their enemies and rivals.[9] Krochmal & Laurentiades (1955) listed 185 species of poisonous plants found in Greece alone, a significant cause of mortality amongst livestock in Greece. Other plants contain potent chemicals which nevertheless could be useful to man. For example, a chemical compound which is a precursor of aspirin (acetylsalicylic acid) may be obtained from the bark of the white willow tree (*Salix alba*). These reservoirs of powerful chemicals in plants provided the basis for pharmacy in antiquity, and ancient Greek medicinal recipes were by no means always without efficacy, as was argued well by Riddle (1985).

The domestication of the crops cultivated by human farmers in the distant past in many cases involved loss of these chemical defence systems against predators and competitors. This happened not because men in the Neolithic or in classical antiquity possessed the knowledge or technology necessary to tamper with plant biochemistry by means of genetic engineering, as modern scientists do, but simply as an entirely natural process of competition between different evolutionary strategies with different reproductive rates, leading inevitably to the extinction of the form with the lower reproductive rate. From an ecological point of view, plants which in symbiosis with man had evolved loss or reduction of their chemical defence systems (making themselves palatable to man) and of the energy costs associated with maintaining these systems should have been capable of higher productivity than wild plants which retained these systems, but only so long as man was able to keep predators away from such plants. This is one aspect of the changes in plant productivity associated with the development of agriculture. Even wheat may once have had chemical defence systems directed against certain animal predators, as a chemical found in wheat produces coeliac disease in a small proportion of humans who cannot tolerate gluten. Aretaios described coeliac disease in antiquity.[10]

Such developments do not require any human consciousness or understanding of what was going on. A lack of consciousness does not prevent ants cultivating fungi and plants, either, and selecting features which they find attractive. In the view of agriculture in antiquity adopted here, no important role is assigned to technological progress. In this respect it is necessary to part company with K.D. White, whose two most important books are entitled *Roman farming* and *Greek and Roman technology*. These two titles reveal a very significant association of thought which merits extensive consideration. Suffice it to say that White's lifelong research interests indicate that he thinks that 'progress' in agriculture (as he would define it) in antiquity could only have been qualitatively similar to progress in the modern world, i.e. technological in nature. It is an anachronistic assumption, retrojecting distinctive characteristics of the modern world into an interpretation of the past in a way which to me irresistibly recalls Rostovtzeff's retrojection of the class struggles of Russia and the USSR in the period 1910-1930 into his monumental social and economic histories of the Hellenistic world and of the Roman empire.

Similarly Boserup's investigations (1965 & 1981) of the relationship between human population growth and technological progress are flawed because of a misjudgment of the importance of technological progress in most societies in the past. Only a few mechanical devices which can be dignified with the name of 'technology' were invented in classical antiquity. They cannot quite be enumerated on the fingers of two hands, but not many hands are needed to list them. Either one is or is not impressed by the handful of new pieces of technology invented by the Greeks and Romans as the sum total of technological progress in 1500 years of history. Like Finley, for example, I am not impressed by the evidence for technological progress in antiquity, and it may be added that the minuscule developments discussed by Amouretti (1986) are not impressive in the order of things either (see Chapter III.9 below on iron). As a consequence Finley saw the ancient economy as essentially static, going nowhere.

I differ from Finley, however, in believing that there were very significant developments in agriculture in antiquity as a consequence of unconscious mutual interactions between human populations and plant populations of the kind mentioned in the previous paragraph. These developments will be the main subject of Chapter III below. It is a mistake for a modern scholar to infer that no change was occurring simply because the members of the society under study did not perceive change. Aristotle thought that nearly all possible discoveries had already been made by his time, in the fourth century BC.[11] This book proposes what may be termed an evolutionary biological model of change in antiquity, in opposition to what might be called the technological model of change in the past which is much more familiar to historians. In other words, the ancient Greek *polis* will be considered as an ecosystem, a biological community inhabiting a particular environment.

One of the main theses of this book is that the economic basis of Greek and Roman civilisation in the first millennium BC was provided by a new and more productive agricultural system, permitting human population growth. What was new about it was not that there was any great technological progress – a false perspective – but that a whole range of new crops, especially the olive, vine and the modern types of wheat, besides a host of other plants of lesser significance, either were domesticated or else enormously expanded their geographical range. Viewing agricultural development in classical antiquity in this perspective explains why the classical economies of Greece and of Italy were able to support larger populations than their Bronze Age or

Neolithic predecessors, accounting for the population growth revealed by the recent intensive archaeological surveys. It simultaneously explains why beyond a certain point – when the potential of the new crops had been fully exploited around the Mediterranean – no further progress was possible. This accounts for the eventual stagnation whereby the Roman empire was unable to produce the surplus necessary to increase its army beyond a certain size, in order to repel the barbarians in late antiquity. The fact that other scholars are doing research on the olive in antiquity, besides considerations of space, has induced me to focus on cereals as an example of this phenomenon, since they have been neglected in recent research. The fruits of the ensuing labours will be presented mainly in Chapter III below.

Increases in agricultural productivity are an essential prerequisite for economic development. Kerridge (1967), Vries (1984) and Wrigley (1987) all emphasised the importance of this theme. There would not have been an 'Industrial Revolution' in England if there had not been an 'Agricultural Revolution' first raising agricultural productivity to the point where a diminished number of farmers could produce enough food to feed large urban work forces employed in the nascent factory system. Equally it may be argued that throughout history a certain level of agricultural productivity has always been necessary for the existence of any complex civilisation, i.e. highly stratified society, in which not all the social strata are engaged actively in the process of primary production. In the course of European history it was in the first millennium BC in Greece and in Italy that complex civilisation arrived to stay on a permanent basis. This may be taken as an indication that it was in the first millennium BC that for the first time agricultural productivity in Europe reached levels that were high enough to sustain highly stratified societies, even though they are low by modern standards.

A few words need to be said about the predecessor of classical Greek civilisation, namely the Mycenaean world of the second millennium BC, even though this book's main focus is on the first millennium BC. The economic base of the Mycenaean states was impoverished in the sense that it rested on a small range of what on the whole were rather primitive crops. The primitive husked wheats emmer and einkorn were still important crops and had not yet been ousted from Mediterranean agriculture by the naked wheats which are used to make bread and other cereal products today. That shift in the crop balance reached its climax in the classical period, for reasons that will be examined in Chapter III below. Similarly the Mycenaeans were not yet making extensive use of the domesticated olive tree and seem to have relied on oil from wild olive trees for their perfume industry. Even the textile industry revealed by the Linear B tablets from Pylos may have depended on the wild flax species *Linum angustifolium* rather than on the now familiar species of domesticated flax, *Linum usitatissimum*. A number of other crop plants that reached the Mediterranean in classical times were not yet available to the Mycenaeans.

It would be going too far to claim that the Mycenaean states collapsed because their economic base was incapable of supporting them, or at least the demands made by the ruling class, as several other important factors undoubtedly played a role, e.g. the movements of the 'Sea Peoples', great earthquakes which wrecked the palaces, etc. However, the weakness of the agricultural economy may have been a contributory factor in the breakdown of the Mycenaean world. Before returning to the first millennium BC it may be as well to take this opportunity to make the point that by concentrating on that period this book does not mean to imply that the ecological changes to be described in that period were necessarily any more profound than those that occurred in, say, the second millennium BC or the first millennium AD. If one were to focus on either of those two periods, it might well be possible to piece together a story equally as striking as the one told here, but that would require other volumes. Evolution is a never-ending process.

A detailed analysis of the developments in agriculture in the first millennium BC outlined above requires consideration of the movement of populations into new geographical regions and of crop evolution. To speak of migration to new habitats, first of all, requires definition of ecosystem boundaries. This leads on to some difficult problems regarding definition of the geographical boundaries of the area covered in this book. I began by concentrating on Attica, the part of classical Greece for which there is the most evidence in respect of literary and epigraphic sources, although there is unfortunately from Athens hardly any of the kind of archaeological evidence for environmental history that would be of particular interest here. Eventually it became clear that in certain important respects the human population histories of Attica and of other *poleis* in Greece in the first millennium BC exhibited shared significant features which made it legitimate to argue that the populations of the various *poleis*, in spite of restrictions on intermarriage and interbreeding between them, developed historically in accordance with ecological patterns which transcended the political boundaries between the various *poleis*, for reasons that will be given later on. Thus the scope of the work had to be enlarged, with the consequence that the reader will find, for example, a fair amount about Sparta as well as about Athens in Chapter II below.

Plant populations set even more difficult problems of definition of ecosystem boundaries. Greece is a small part of a much larger biogeographical region, the Mediterranean, which in spite of countless local variations possesses a well known climatic regime which will be defined in Chapter IV below. Many plants which grow well in Greece consequently may grow equally well in southern Italy or southern Spain, for example. However, it would be a mistake to assume that, because a plant is capable of flourishing around the entire Mediterranean, it follows that it always has grown around the entire Mediterranean. Most of the wild ancestors of modern crop plants had small populations in very restricted geographical regions, because large, dense populations covering extended areas create great opportunities for predators and parasites and are rare in the absence of human interference. The wild olive tree, for example, probably occupied semi-arid coastal areas in the eastern Mediterranean as its principal natural habitat, and the extension of the range of the domesticated version from the Levant, where it was first domesticated, further inland and westwards to embrace the entire Mediterranean was a development of the first millennium BC in the main. The Mediterranean Sea itself, a remnant of the ancient Tethys Sea which in bygone geological epochs separated Europe and northern Asia from Africa and southern Asia, is a barrier to the movement of other terrestrial living organisms without man, although it is an important vehicle for human communications.

To understand the ecological history of classical antiquity it is necessary to go back to the Quaternary Ice Ages. Greece itself was not actually covered by glaciers, having a cold and dry steppe climate in the lowlands. However, temperatures fell as the climatic zones familiar to us today were pushed southwards – and also down the sides of mountains – and compressed towards the equator. There was no season of drought as there is today. Peak monthly rainfall occurred in summer. The modern Mediterranean climate did not exist in southern Europe during the last glaciation. The Ice Ages created an ecological vacuum in Europe, at least in respect of the living organisms which are familiar in temperate and Mediterranean climates today. When they retreated for the last time (if we are not merely in an interglacial period at present), a process of filling in of the vacuum commenced. Some important components of this process occurred in the first millennium BC. The prior existence of the vacuum helps to explain why the Greeks and Romans were able to push the olive tree and various other plants into regions where they could grow successfully but did not yet occupy.

The distribution of the olive tree today is often used to define the boundaries of the Mediterranean as a climatic zone, but it would be foolish to assume that the two have always coincided in the past. The northward shift of climatic zones following the end of the last Ice Age back to the positions they currently occupy was accompanied by the desiccation of the Sahara and the Arabian desert, and consequently the isolation of the Mediterranean wild olive, the oleaster, from the rest of its relatives in Olea, a genus of tropical or sub-tropical plants which inhabit sub-Saharan Africa and southern Asia. In other words the southern frontier of the Mediterranean was closed off at the same time as the northern frontier was opening out. There is another still more powerful argument against the assumption that the area covered by Mediterranean climate and the distribution of the olive tree have always coincided. The evergreen trees and shrubs of the Mediterranean evolved millions of years ago in a geological epoch when the region had a *quite different* climate from that of the Mediterranean today. In fact the olive tree is not optimally suited to the modern Mediterranean climate (see Chapter III.3 below)[12].

What all this amounts to saying is that when human farmers began to be active in the Mediterranean for the first time in the Neolithic, they did not encounter an ecological community of plants and animals that was fully settled. In studying the ecological history of classical antiquity we are studying the later stages of the formation of the ecological community of Europe which later on in the early modern period was to conquer much of the rest of the world, a process well described by Crosby (1986). The process involved the creation of a new ecological community, rather than merely the shifting of a community latitudinally, because the evidence of palaeoecology shows that in the Ice Ages plants and animals did not just have different geographical distributions from their present-day ones but also lived in ecological communities which were not identical to modern ones.

It is the fact of shifting populations which creates the difficulty of boundary definition. This problem is not unique to the present inquiry, but is an attribute of all ecological phenomena. Thus although the main concern of this book is with the area that is now called Greece, inevitably it will be necessary frequently to consider what was happening in other areas, first in order to trace the history of species which were arriving in Greece from elsewhere, and secondly in order to draw on the evidence from other areas occupied by species also found in Greece which provide better evidence of their activities than is available from Greece itself. A mundane reason for widening the net is that unfortunately very little research in palaeobotany, palaeozoology and related subjects has been carried out on classical Greek sites. This is owing to the nature of classical archaeology in the past as essentially art history, parallel to ancient history as exegesis of literary sources whose study is often prescribed more because of their literary than because of their historical value. It is a view of the scope of both classical archaeology and ancient history which is rejected firmly here.

For the aforementioned reasons it is impossible to write an ecological history of ancient Greece based solely on evidence drawn from Greece alone. Still less is it possible to consider meaningfully the ecology of any particular region of Greece in isolation. Ultimately research encompassing the whole world may be the only research capable of yielding truly significant results. Two examples drawn from opposite ends of history will serve to illustrate this point. First, Braudel (1981) undoubtedly highlighted a fundamental problem in his discussion of why it was that massive human population growth commenced roughly simultaneously during the modern epoch in China and in Europe, at the end of the 'Little Ice Age' of *c.* AD 1500-1800, in spite of the vast cultural differences between these two areas. Secondly, there is the equally tantalising problem of why plant and animal domestication commenced roughly simultaneously at the end of the last glaciation, certainly in the Middle East and in the western hemisphere, and possibly in other regions as well (e.g. tropical Africa, China, south-east Asia). Both of these phenomena may have been ultimately dependent on worldwide climatic changes altering environments (see Chapter IV below for further discussion). This book has more restricted aims on the whole and does not attempt to follow Braudel's 'total history'. One might draw a comparison here with Finley's argument (1981b) that it is useless to study individual cities in antiquity – only research into distinctive characteristics of the ancient city as a type of city is worth doing. Be that as it may, it is worth spending some time considering possible avenues of migration into the eastern Mediterranean.

Diffusionism or migrationism has pejorative connotations among some historians and prehistorians at the moment. In fact it has almost become a term of abuse in certain quarters. However, there are very powerful reasons why this concept must play a fundamental role in a book on palaeoecology, and, it may be added, in history and prehistory in general. In the Middle East, where agriculture began in the Old World, both mutualistic and antagonistic interactions between man and the other living beings, plants, animals and micro-organisms studied in this book have been going on for longer than anywhere else (the shortage of species of domesticated animals in the western hemisphere had important consequences for human disease evolution). Because competition has been more intense there for a longer period of time than anywhere else, the resulting living beings were generally more competitive than living organisms which had evolved in less competitive conditions in more isolated regions elsewhere. The effects of this became apparent most dramatically during the early modern period, when the living beings which reached the Americas and later Australia from Europe after Columbus were often able to overwhelm the indigenous flora and fauna of those continents.

This book is concerned with an earlier period of history and the invasion of Europe itself, especially Greece, by living organisms from elsewhere. With the retreating ice sheets in the north, the Atlantic on the west, and the advancing Sahara in the south, it was inevitable that the main avenue of immigration was always from the east. For example, Turrill (1958) observed that the flora of the Peloponnese is influenced heavily by immigration from the east, but shows little evidence of immigration from any of the other three cardinal points of the compass. The Orient was much less affected than Europe by the Ice Ages, and so came to constitute a reservoir from which species which had been eliminated from Europe in the glacial periods could be brought back to

Europe by man or migrate back under their own steam. Huntley & Prentice (1988) showed that as recently as *c.* 4000 BC the Mediterranean was appreciably cooler in the summer (or, alternatively, had higher summer rainfall) than it is now and that at that time typical 'Mediterranean' vegetation was largely absent from southern Europe and was confined to the Middle East. Before concentrating on the east, however, it is as well to consider those living organisms which could have approached Greece from the west, north and south in antiquity.

Very little originated from western Europe that is of any interest here. The rabbit (*Oryctolagus cuniculus*) is native to the Iberian peninsula. It was unknown to classical Greek authors, such as Aristotle, and was perhaps still rather unfamiliar to the inhabitants of the eastern Mediterranean as late as the time of Galen. The hare (*Lepus europaeus*) existed instead in classical Greece. The available evidence concerning some aspects of the rabbit's expansion of its geographical range in antiquity is of interest as an illustration of the population dynamics of an invasion of a new environment and will be considered later on in this chapter. One plant of some economic importance was native to Spain, namely esparto grass (the modern species *Lygeum spartum* and *Stipa tenacissima*), a plant that was still wild in antiquity. Gathering, rather than cultivation, of it for its fibres was initiated by the Carthaginians according to Pliny. It also occurs in North Africa.[13]

Finally, another plant should be noted, the opium poppy (*Papaver somniferum*), whose wild ancestor (*P. setigerum*) is native to the western half of the Mediterranean basin. It was certainly present in the Aegean in prehistory, although it is absent from early archaeological sites in the Middle East. Varieties of poppy found in Greece and the southern Balkans contain an exceptionally high proportion of morphine. The cultivation of the poppy in the Mediterranean today is restricted for obvious reasons. It flourishes in south-east Asia as a source of drugs and furnishes a good illustration of a crop which is now chiefly cultivated far from its centre of origin as a result of man's activities.[14]

The list of immigrants to the eastern Mediterranean from the north is only slightly longer. The various species of millets associated with European agriculture are native to east Asia and spread across Eurasia and down into the Mediterranean in the Neolithic. More will be said about them in Chapter III.10 below. The only important plant which spread southwards in classical times was hemp (*Cannabis sativa*), then chiefly valued as a source of fibres. However, the Scythians also inhaled the fumes of burning hemp. Herodotos knew that they cultivated it in south Russia. Textiles made from hemp have been found at Gordion, the capital of Phrygia in Turkey, dating to the eighth century BC.[15]

Among animals the horse (*Equus caballus*) was domesticated on the steppes of south Russia in the fourth millennium BC and its subsequent spread may be associated with the dispersal of the Indo-Europeans. The domesticated horse is not currently attested in Greece until the second millennium BC. There is only very scanty evidence for the presence of wild horses anywhere in the Balkans in the period following the end of the last Ice Age, although earlier they had been widespread all over Europe, and they were entirely absent from the Middle East. The spread of the domesticated horse created the possibility of large-scale nomadism as an economic system. This was a very important ecological development, another symbiosis or mutualism, which occurred in the main in the first millennium BC, according to Khazanov (1984), but considerations of space forbid discussion of it here. The association of man and horse led to the evolution of the common cold (ancient Greek *koruza*), as the rhinoviruses which are the most frequent cause of this familiar ailment are common to man and horse. It is a density-dependent disease which could not have existed before the Neolithic in its present form.

Our brief survey of the north may be concluded by mentioning the domesticated mouse. It has been suggested that the fact that field mice construct miniature houses of their own for shelter in the harsh winter on the Russian steppes was a pre-adaptation for life in human habitations. However, the earliest finds of mouse (*Mus musculus*) come from Middle Eastern archaeological sites. Species of wild mice do indeed still exist in the Mediterranean. The species characteristic of the western Mediterranean (*Mus spretus*) has never developed a domestic form, showing that the domesticated mouse is an invader from the east or north-east, rather than the product of endogenous evolution there. Field mice were important pests of cereal crops in antiquity. Their population dynamics are also of great interest (see Chapter II.2 below).[16]

The south is much more interesting than the west and north. Sub-Saharan Africa, the centre of early hominid evolution, has always had an extremely rich and varied flora and fauna. There was much that potentially could have come to the Mediterranean from Africa. However, the available evidence suggests that nearly all living organisms found the Sahara, which had become a desert by *c.* 2000 BC, an invincible obstacle in classical times.[17] Such living organisms as did reach the Mediterranean from sub-Saharan Africa in antiquity seem to have been forced to adopt a very circuitous route, passing from east Africa via south Arabia to India, and then back across the Middle East to the Mediterranean.

There are seven important crops not native to the Mediterranean but known in classical antiquity concerning which there is uncertainty whether they originated in India or in sub-Saharan Africa. Sorghum is the best candidate for a crop indigenous to Africa. There are very extensive populations of wild sorghum in the Sudan in the territory of the ancient kingdom of Meroe, the earliest civilisation of tropical Africa, close to an area where the zones of European and of tropical agriculture overlap. This leaves open the possibility of stimulus diffusion from Egypt to explain the origins of African agriculture alongside its animal husbandry, which in the form of animals such as sheep in the Sudan certainly depended on diffusion from Egypt. However, as yet there is no definitely dated palaeobotanical evidence for cultivated sorghum antedating the first millennium BC from Meroe or from anywhere else in sub-Saharan Africa, although there is earlier evidence from India. Future excavations will probably unearth earlier evidence from Africa. Moreover sorghum has been discovered on a site in Oman dating to the middle of the third millennium BC, providing the link between Africa and India. Classical descriptions of a cereal which we may recognise as sorghum associate it with India rather than with Africa. Sorghum was probably not cultivated anywhere in the Mediterranean in antiquity. The spread of the durra varieties into North Africa and the Mediterranean took place in the mediaeval period from India. Before leaving sorghum it should be noted that grains of it from Meroe in the third century AD are smaller and morphologically more primitive than the sorghum which is cultivated in the same region today. This is the first piece of evidence presented in this book for cereal evolution in antiquity. It is a topic about which much more will be said in Chapter III below in connection with European cereals.[18]

The second crop of interest here is rice. The species of domesticated rice (*Oryza sativa*) which originated in south-east Asia or south China is very well known. It may not be quite so well known that there is a second species of cultivated rice (*Oryza glaberrima*) which is native to west Africa. The question arises whether the Greeks had any knowledge of African as well as of Oriental rice. Rice is ideal for farming the swamps and wetlands around the Mediterranean, such as the Po valley in Italy or the Valencia region of Spain. It is a much more productive crop than wheat or any other European cereal and is in fact a significant crop in the Mediterranean today. Rice yields in Mediterranean environments are higher than anywhere else in the world because summer hours of daylight for photosynthesis are longer in the Mediterranean than in the tropical regions generally associated with rice cultivation.

Oryza sativa had spread from south-east Asia to the Indus Valley civilization in northern India by *c.* 2000 BC. The Harappans exploited it as a summer crop which complemented the winter crops of wheat and barley already cultivated in the Indus Valley, but the Greeks and Romans failed to take this step. In the first millennium BC it certainly was cultivated in regions of the Middle East which were later incorporated into the Roman empire. It is mentioned in Assyrian cuneiform texts dating to the seventh century BC. It probably reached Anatolia, where very primitive forms of it still exist, in the Hellenistic period. Strabo mentions its cultivation in Palestine in the first century BC, also attested by the Jewish Mishnah and Talmud in Roman times. It was cultivated in the Huleh marshes in the Jordan valley. The Greeks who accompanied Alexander the Great to India became familiar with it, providing Theophrastos with his knowledge of the plant. Earlier Sophokles had mentioned it in his play *Triptolemos*, recounting the story of how the hero had distributed the various cereals to the peoples of the world at Demeter's behest, following the return of Persephone from the underworld.

Thus there is no doubt that rice was available in classical antiquity. There are even some extraordinary palaeobotanical finds of rice in the Mediterranean. The German excavators turned up a solitary grain of rice in an LHIIIC level at Mycenaean Tiryns, dating to the twelfth century BC, the earliest evidence for rice so far west as Greece. However, the Argolid is very dry in summer and Mycenaean agriculture otherwise gives the impression of being rather unsophisticated. It seems outside the bounds of reasonable probability that rice was cultivated in Greece in the second millennium BC. The grain of rice from the palace of Tiryns was an exotic import brought by long-distance trade, alongside the melon of which remarkably early finds have also been made at Tiryns. Tiryns was still on the coast in the Bronze Age and functioned as the port of Mycenae. A substantial quantity of rice was discovered in a Roman army camp in Germany dating to the first century AD alongside other foodstuffs such as olives and figs which could not have been grown anywhere remotely near the locality in question. There is no doubt that rice was at least occasionally transported further west in the classical period, besides being cultivated in the Middle East.

However, there is no evidence that rice was actually cultivated anywhere west of the Middle East in classical antiquity, even though it was available. This failure to exploit the most productive crop available shows that the Greeks and Romans never made the leap necessary from labour-extensive dry farming of wheat and barley, crops native to semi-arid lands, to the very different mentality required for labour-intensive wet-rice cultivation in swamps. Artificial irrigation works of the kind necessary to keep a paddy field permanently under water for rice were virtually unknown in the Mediterranean in antiquity. This was true even of Egypt, where agriculture relied mainly on the annual cycle of variations in the height of the Nile, flood-basin agriculture that was only suitable for European crops, not for genuine swampland plants like rice. (In the vicinity of major Egyptian cities there was some permanent irrigation of gardens, which depended on perennial supplies of water from underground sources.)

Bonneau (1971) showed that the taxation system of Pharaonic times, which supplied the essence of the Ptolemaic and Roman taxation systems, depended on measuring the annual rise of the Nile as a means of assessing production. Butzer (1976) rebutted the well known theory of Wittfogel (1957) that the development of the ancient Egyptian state depended on control of irrigation works that were essential for agriculture in Egypt. However, it remains true that the earliest civilisations developed in great river valleys, as also in Mesopotamia and in the Indus Valley, not in areas depending on rain-fed agriculture such as Europe. This was because agricultural productivity was higher in such areas, with their larger and more dependable water supply for crop growth. Geography and biology were more important than institutions, *pace* Wittfogel, and it is clear again that considerations of agricultural productivity are of paramount importance in economic and state development.

Our conclusion must be that the Oriental rice was known but not exploited in Greece in classical antiquity. Chevalier argued that the west African species of rice was also known in classical times because Strabo appears to mention it, but the manuscript text of Strabo at this point is corrupt. Moreover rice is an unlikely inhabitant of the hinterland of Cyrene, which is desert and was desert in antiquity, as Strabo makes clear. Archaeological evidence is now available for the cultivation of west African rice at Jenne-jeno in the Middle Niger region dating to *c.* 250 BC. There is a scholarly controversy about the question whether *O. glaberrima* is really an independent species or whether it may be a late evolutionary offshoot of *O. sativa*, which spread through the Mediterranean and into Africa in the Middle Ages. Even if *O. glaberrima* is not descended from *O. sativa* and instead evolved from African wild rices which were isolated from their relatives in south-east Asia by continental drift after Africa separated from Eurasia (except in the Sinai area), there is no good evidence that it was known to the Greeks or Romans in antiquity. Rice, like sorghum, did not succeed in crossing the Sahara. A survey of the north-western corner of the Indian Ocean dating to the first century AD states that rice, together with sugar cane, was exported from India to entrepots on the coast of modern Somalia by ships which hugged the coast of Iran and Arabia and then, after the discoveries of the mariner Hippalos, sailed straight across the ocean following the north-east monsoon. That rice was transported such a long way suggests by itself that it was not cultivated in north-eastern Africa, even though sea transport was considerably cheaper than land transport.[19]

The third plant on our list of African/Indian crops is sesame (*Sesame indicum*). As in the case of sorghum, cultivated sesame is attested in India before it is attested in Africa, but most of the wild relatives of sesame live in sub-Saharan Africa, although a possible wild progenitor has been found recently in India. The early history of sesame is still not entirely clear. It is made more difficult to elucidate by the fact that it was used and stored in such a way as only rarely to give rise to carbonised remains on archaeological sites. Characteristically, classical authors associated it with India and indeed it was already known to the Mycenaeans and Minoans in the second millennium BC. Like rice and sorghum, sesame may have come to the Mediterranean from sub-Saharan Africa in antiquity but does not appear to have done so. More will be said about sesame in Chapter III.10 below.[20]

The bottle gourd (*Lagenaria siceraria*) is the fourth member of the list, a plant prized more as a source of containers than as a source of food. It is unique, being the only crop plant to have been present in Eurasia, the western hemisphere and New Guinea in pre-Columbian times. Possibly ocean currents dispersed its seeds, which are resistant to prolonged immersion in sea water, or alternatively it might have achieved a very widespread distribution before the continents assumed their present positions as a result of continental drift. Africa has been proposed by botanists as its most probable centre of origin, but again classical sources associate the bottle gourd with India, not with Africa. More will be said about it and related plants in Chapter III below.[21]

The last three items may be dealt with briefly. Most of the range of the wild water-melon (*Citrullus colocynthis*) occurs within sub-Saharan Africa, and some botanists have suggested that domesticated water-melon (*Citrullus lanatus*) developed from the wild variety of the Kalahari desert. However, there is no evidence for agriculture in southern Africa in the pre-Christian era, and as there are outliers of its distribution in the Middle East, it is possible that water-melon evolved into a crop there rather than in sub-Saharan Africa. Again we shall return to melons in Chapter III below. Rather similar remarks may be made about the cowpea (*Vigna unguiculata*), an important leguminous plant characteristically associated with tropical African agriculture today but which also occurs in a range stretching from the Middle East via India to China. It could have been domesticated first in the Middle East or in Egypt. Alternatively, it is possible that future archaeological excavations may bring to light one day evidence for early cultivation of both water-melon and cowpea from the general vicinity of modern Sudan.[22]

Finally, there is cotton, a plant occurring as different species in both the Old and New Worlds with an extremely complicated evolutionary history which must be passed over here because it is only of peripheral interest to the Graeco-Roman world. Suffice it to say that wild Old World cotton species and the most primitive domesticated Old World cotton species (*Gossypium herbaceum*) seem to be native to sub-Saharan Africa, and there is some palaeobotanical evidence for its occurrence in the Sudan in the pre-Christian era. However, the range of the main species of domesticated Old World cotton (*Gossypium arboreum*) is associated with southern Asia, especially India. Once again the Greeks associated it with the east rather than the south. Herodotos knew that those Indians who were subjects of the Persian empire used garments made from 'wool' which grew on trees. Theophrastos had heard of cotton cultivation in India and on Bahrain in the Persian Gulf, thanks to the knowledge acquired by Alexander's expedition. He called it *to dendron eriophoron*, the 'wool-bearing tree', and the absence of a specific name for it in Theophrastos suggests that it was a novelty to him. By the time of Pliny Latin had picked up the word *gossypium* from an Oriental language, and

Pliny had heard of cotton in Africa. According to Assyrian records, king Sennacherib introduced cotton to Assyria in 694 BC. The species of cotton discussed above have all now been virtually abandoned as crops and replaced by American species introduced to the Old World after Columbus which produce a longer lint. All of these seven crops seem to have passed between Africa and India in a way which bypassed the Mediterranean, by sea along the coast of south Arabia.[23]

Sub-Saharan Africa contributed very little directly to Mediterranean agriculture in antiquity, if contributions which only reached the vicinity of Greece via India and the Middle East are excluded from consideration. Durum wheat, emmer, barley, Mediterranean weeds such as oats, together with the plough reached the highlands of Ethiopia probably from south Arabia in the first millennium BC at the latest, but there was no contact with the very different environment of tropical Africa. Certain living organisms successfully made the journey from the Great Lakes region of East Africa down the Nile Valley to Egypt. The origin of the Nile itself was a source of controversy in antiquity. In many respects the Nile in its present form is of recent origin, since its upper parts may not have existed until less than 12,000 years ago.[24] The plants of significance here belong to the genus Cyperus. First there is papyrus (*Cyperus papyrus*), which spread down the Nile Valley to Egypt. It has been suggested, probably incorrectly, on the basis of the ambiguous evidence of wall paintings that papyrus was cultivated in the Aegean in the Bronze Age, but if so it certainly had disappeared by classical times. Secondly there is chufa (*Cyperus esculentus*), a plant with edible tubers, which is also native to East Africa.

Among diseases there is bubonic plague, which has a centre of distribution among wild rodents in East Africa and was regarded as endemic to north-eastern Africa at the time of the pandemic of the sixth century AD (more on plague in Chapter II.2 & 7 below). Secondly there is schistosomiasis, a scourge of Egypt in antiquity but confined there by the snails which transmit it. Malarias of other primates evolved in Africa and spread to Asia and to hominids in the very remote past. However, most present-day human diseases are descendants of micro-organisms which preyed on animals domesticated in the Middle East in the Neolithic period, especially the sheep, goat, cow and dog, as well as the horse from south Russia. In spite of the rich abundance of micro-organisms in tropical Africa, it is only now that a disease originating in Africa is receiving attention in Europe again with the spread of AIDS. This retrovirus can only be traced as the cause of a recognisable human disease back to central Africa in the 1950s. It has recently been suggested that both the human and the simian viruses may have been around for a very long time and have evolved from a common ancestor which preyed on the common ancestor of primates and hominids. In that case it would only be the virulence of the human virus(es) which has changed recently.

However, this hypothesis is rejected by other scholars.[25]

The balance sheet suggests that the Sahara was a formidable barrier in antiquity. Thus the Mediterranean ecosystem was entirely isolated from that of tropical Africa. In this context the voyage of exploration of the Carthaginian Hanno to west Africa and the alleged circumnavigation of Africa by Phoenicians working for the Egyptian pharaoh Necho, if it actually took place, were of no lasting significance, in spite of Hanno's discovery of the gorilla. The use of the domesticated camel for crossing the desert awaited the rise of Islam for its full exploitation. In the final stages of the last 'Pluvial' period the inhabitants of the Sahara preferred to use oxen, and then horses as aridity increased, as a means of transport. It was probably only in classical times, when the Sahara was approaching its modern extent, that they turned to exploit the camel on a substantial scale. During the last 'Pluvial' period the region of the Sahara was so humid that Lake Chad expanded to the extent that it is regarded by palaeoecologists as having been a sea rather than a lake at that time. Under such conditions camels must have been rare in the Sahara, even though finds of camel bones indicate that they never disappeared entirely from the region. Probably their geographical distribution was pushed southwards, as the areas of equatorial Africa which are covered by tropical rain forest today were much more arid during the last glaciation.

Rock paintings in the Tassili plateau in the Sahara depict small horses, which were used by the Garamantes to draw four-horse chariots. These small, light horses belonged to the earliest wave of diffusion of the domesticated horse, like the small horses of Iron Age western Europe and of classical Greece. They produced the fine light Numidian cavalry which played such an important role in the victories of Hannibal in the Second Punic War. This cavalry force was probably a recent innovation in Hannibal's time. However use of the horse as a means of transport, as a relic of the preceding cooler and wetter period, does not seem to have resulted in any significant ecological interchanges across the Sahara between the Mediterranean and tropical Africa.[26]

This survey of the southern frontier of the Mediterranean ecosystem may be concluded by mentioning the one and only living organism to range freely across the Sahara in classical antiquity. It is naturally the exception which proves the rule, namely the desert locust (*Schistocerca gregaria*). It is recorded that an utterly devastating attack was launched on the Roman province of North Africa by locusts in 125 BC. Such episodes are quite plausible and have occurred in recent times. Pliny also provides evidence for locust depredations in Cyrene, and because swarms can fly long distances and rest by floating on the sea when tired, they can also reach Europe, even as far north as Britain. In 1988 locusts were reported to have crossed the Atlantic from Africa to the West Indies. There is evidence for locust incursions into Sicily and Italy in antiquity and even to the island of Lemnos, an Athenian cleruchy in the Aegean. Pausanias mentions a legendary epidemic of locusts in Attica. However, it is possible that locusts in the Aegean originated in the Arabian desert rather than in the Sahara.

Aristotle misunderstood the ecology of the locust. He thought that the spread of locusts was exacerbated by dry weather, but recent research shows that on the contrary it is rain in the desert which leads to hatching of locust eggs on a large scale in order to take advantage of vegetation growth following the rain. The desert locust regularly migrates across the Sahara to take advantage of different seasons which are favourable for breeding on the north and the south sides of the desert, but it only swarms in occasional exceptionally good years when the increasing population is coming close to eating up its food supply and a shift in its hormonal balance incites gregarious behaviour. Columella, striving to make use of everything, recommended locusts as food for young peafowl, while the Parthians and some African tribes regarded locusts as delicacies.[27]

The population density of most species of living organisms decreases in the vicinity of the desert. This may seem, and is, an exceedingly elementary observation. Nevertheless it is still worth making because some scholars have forgotten it in considering some of the most discussed texts regarding cereal yields in classical antiquity, which relate to regions close to the desert. It raises theoretical problems to which we shall return in Chapter III below concerning the consequences of the reduction in population density for intraspecific competition within populations.[28]

Elimination of west, north and south as significant channels of immigration leaves us with the east. The Fertile Crescent and Anatolia were extremely important centres of origin of many domesticated plants in their own right, besides providing the entry point to the Mediterranean for plants from further afield, Iran, India, China and sub-Saharan Africa. In contrast, *c.* 1000 BC the rest of the Mediterranean, to the west of those regions, was impoverished with regard to the diversity of crops available. Certain plants had not yet evolved the characteristics which make them valuable today. For example sugar beet (*Beta vulgaris*) is a major crop in Greece today, but it has only acquired its present high sugar content over the last century or two, owing to plant breeding. The beets known in antiquity were not sweet, while sugar cane (*Saccharum officinarum*), a native of New Guinea, was not cultivated in the Mediterranean until the Middle Ages, and so the ancient Greeks had to rely on honey as a sweetener.[29]

Certain other plants which are indigenous to the Mediterranean were evolving into proper crops during classical antiquity. The three notable examples of crops which could be indigenous to the Balkans are grass pea, lupins and oats. Bitter vetch is a crop whose cultivation was largely restricted to the southern Balkans and Anatolia in antiquity and may also be indigenous to the region. Much more will be said about crop evolution, including the four crops just mentioned, in antiquity in Chapter III below, but here the emphasis henceforth will be on immigration rather than evolution.

Columella and Pliny both remarked that many plants which were not native to Italy had been introduced to that country. Pliny went on to interpret the movement of useful plants as one of the benefits of the *Pax Romana*. He also observed that the Latin names for fruit trees were generally of Greek derivation, indicating that the Romans had obtained these trees from the Greeks, who had themselves obtained many of them, or at least the technique for cultivating some of them, from further east. Indeed Pliny remarks that from the time of Pompey onwards the Romans even used to parade captured exotic trees in triumphal processions. They also fought a battle against the Jews to defend the balsam trees of Judaea, a valuable source of revenue, which were imperilled by the revolt of AD 66-70. He noted that a type of cherry tree, which had been introduced to Rome by Lucullus during the Mithridatic Wars, had spread to Britain by his own time, although it was not yet well acclimatised to central Italy. Vitellius' introduction of the pistachio tree to Italy is another instance.

Pliny also regarded such trees as peach (*malum Persicum*), walnut (*nux iuglans*), almond (*amygdalis*), chestnut (*castanea*), myrtle (*myrtus*) and cypress (*cupressus*) as exotic to Italy because of their foreign names in Latin. Trees such as apple (*Malus pumila* or *domestica*), pear (*Pyrus communis*), plum (*Prunus domestica*), sweet and sour cherry (*Prunus avium* and *P. cerasus* respectively) and pistachio (*Pistacia vera*) all appear to have entered cultivation for the first time in the first millennium BC, even though archaeological evidence shows that the fruits of related wild species had been gathered from a much earlier date. Palynological evidence may also be cited to support the archaeological and literary evidence. With so many different lines of argument available which support each other, there is no doubting the reality of the situation. The carob tree (*Ceratonia siliqua*) is an example of a tree which existed in antiquity in Syria, Ionia, Knidos and Rhodes according to Theophrastos, but has only spread widely in the last few centuries owing to human destruction of natural vegetation.

Many of these trees depend for successful cultivation on the technique of grafting. The fact that all those species of tree which require grafting entered cultivation at roughly the same time, long after their wild ancestors were well known to farmers, suggests that the technique of grafting only became known in the eastern Mediterranean in the first millennium BC. It may have been derived from China. It evidently acquired a considerable mystique for the ancients, who used it to try to produce many hybrids which are quite impossible. Pliny also hints that there were religious obstacles to grafting certain species together. Such attitudes, which are reminiscent of the Hebrew prohibition on crop mixtures (see Chapter III below), may help to explain the late acquisition of the technique of grafting. This had considerable implications for the history of olive cultivation in antiquity because, although the domesticated olive tree may be propagated vegetatively in many different ways, grafting a cultivated scion onto an existing wild stock is the most rapid method of propagating olive trees.[30]

The movements that Columella and Pliny had in mind were often relatively easy, insofar as any migration from the eastern Mediterranean to Italy and on to Spain remains within the same climatic zone. When the Romans tried to move Mediterranean plants to northern Europe they had less success. A number of exotic plants which were not suited to Britain were brought there by the Romans, the lentil (*Lens culinaris*) being one well-documented example. However, insects were often more flexible than plants, and most of those species which live on cereal products stored by man established themselves in Britain in Roman times, especially the grain weevil (*Sitophilus granarius*), a very significant cause of losses in storage.[31] Northern Europe was a quite autonomous region of the Roman empire, with distinctive crops and agricultural techniques of its own suited to a different environment. In fact there is very little to be learnt about agriculture in the northern regions of the Roman empire from surviving literary sources. Wild plants also found it hard to move across the northern boundary of the Mediterranean climatic zone and thrive. Most of the weeds of cereal fields in the Middle East did not succeed in following the primitive cereals carried by the earliest farmers across Europe in the Neolithic period.[32] This serves to emphasise once again that as far as plants are concerned only east to west migration was really important.

The Greek language exhibits different strata which clearly illustrate the gradual acquaintance of the Greeks and their ancestors with new groups of plants. When the proto-Greeks entered what is now Greece from the north, they found that the indigenous inhabitants were familiar with many plants characteristic of the Mediterranean which were unknown in their homeland, for example *erebinthos* 'chickpea' (a plant of particular interest as its wild ancestor is definitely native to Anatolia), *bussos* 'flax' (*Linum angustifolium*), *elaia* 'domesticated olive', *kissos* 'ivy', *olunthos* 'wild fig', *hyakinthos* 'hyacinth' (various plants), *narkissos* 'narcissus', *akanthos* (various plants), *kerasos* 'cherry', *kuparissos* 'cypress', *minthos* 'mint'. These plant names, which probably belonged to languages of the Anatolian branch of the Indo-European family, were absorbed into the developing Greek language. Theories that the proto-Greeks actually originated in Greece itself (the model of autochthonous origins popular among prehistoric archaeologists) are unsatisfactory and should be dismissed because (*inter alia*) they fail to take account of this kind of evidence. More generally such theories ignore the fact that a very substantial proportion of the words in the Greek language have no etymology in Greek. This can only be explained in terms of the proto-Greeks having fused with the speakers of one or more other languages.[33]

Also in prehistory there was a group of early loans from Semitic languages, e.g. *sêsamon* 'sesame', *kuminon* 'cummin' and *semidalis*. We shall have very much more to say about the last word, used in connection with wheat, in Chapter III below. Loans in this category may have reached Greek either indirectly from Indo-European languages of the Anatolian group or from the undeciphered language of the Linear A tablets on Crete. Much of the Greek vocabulary for vines also appears to be of Semitic origin, or at least to go back to a common 'Mediterranean' linguistic heritage also embracing the Anatolian Indo-European languages. This is an extremely important finding as it suggests that this vital branch of Greek agriculture owed its origins to diffusion from the Levant or perhaps Anatolia, at least of ideas if not necessarily of the actual plant.[34]

This book maintains that migrations of living organisms from the Middle East exercised a great influence on Greece as an ecosystem. However, it will not be argued here that Greek society was derived from the Middle East, for the reason that Greek social and political institutions cannot be derived from those of any known society in the ancient Orient. Indeed the principal thesis of this book is that the transformation of Greek society which culminated in the classical *polis* was a consequence of ecological changes resulting from contact with Middle Eastern societies that were quite different. It will also be suggested briefly that Rome underwent a similar transformation from similar ecological causes, but because archaic Roman social structure was different again from that of the Greek world, the final product was yet again different.

In the course of the first millennium BC other plants were brought to Greece from the east and then taken on to Italy. It has recently been suggested that there were two main periods of introduction of new crops, namely the Persian Wars and the Hellenistic period, but it is preferable to think in terms of a process that was continuing, with occasional changes of tempo, most of the time.[35] The sheer scale of this process and the effect it had on classical agriculture is demonstrated by the data collected by André. He showed that no less than *42 per cent* of all the plants mentioned in Columella's *De re rustica* have Greek names, and it is important to bear in mind that Columella only mentions crops that were of economic significance. The comparison of Columella and Cato shows that the Greek influence increased with the passage of time. In the face of such a mass of evidence, it is perverse to deny, as Roman historians are sometimes wont to do, that Greek agriculture and agronomy exercised a quite overwhelming influence on Roman agriculture and agronomy.[36]

There is no space here to run through all of these crops and only the most important will receive any discussion in this book. It has already been shown that Roman arboriculture was *entirely* dependent on Greek influence. In fact the spread of arboriculture in the Mediterranean was one of the most important ecological developments of the first millennium BC. Before moving on to the olive and vine, a few more brief observations on plant immigration to the Mediterranean must suffice here. Citron and at the end of antiquity other citrus fruits, melon, peach, apricot, lucerne and taro may be mentioned as further examples of plants which entered the Graeco-Roman world during the first millennium BC.[37] In the mediaeval period another group of crops was spread through the Mediterranean by the Arabs. Rice, sorghum, cotton and sugar-cane have already been mentioned, and others were discussed by Watson (1983). After Columbus another very important group of crops arrived from the western hemisphere. They included maize, now the most important cereal in the Balkans, tomato, the most widely cultivated vegetable in modern Greece, tobacco, squash, pumpkin, potato and prickly pear cactus. The latter is now ubiquitous in the Mediterranean.[38] The discovery of Australia by Europeans led to the importation of the eucalyptus tree.

Some crops which were cultivated in the Mediterranean in the first millennium BC are no longer cultivated there. These include most notably papyrus in Egypt, shrub-trefoil in Greece, the primitive flax species *Linum angustifolium* and the mysterious *silphion* of Libya. The point of this balance sheet, which does not claim completeness, is simply to stress that the range of crops cultivated at the dawn of classical history was very different from the range of crops grown in the Mediterranean today. Finally it may be noted that new crops are still being developed from the wild resources of the Mediterranean. Crambe (*Crambe abyssinica*) is an example of a wild plant which may be on the verge of becoming a crop, as it has great potential as a source of erucic acid, a fatty acid sought for various industrial applications.[39]

The olive tree and the vine are such an integral part of Mediterranean farming that it is easy to fall into the trap of thinking that this has been the case throughout history, but then no one would guess from its role in the modern Italian diet that the tomato only arrived in the early modern period. Columella and Pliny, examining the testimony of earlier writers, both observed that the geographical range of olive and vine cultivation in the Mediterranean had expanded enormously by their own time. Pliny noted that Theophrastos' statement that the olive tree was restricted to coastal regions no longer appeared to be valid. He contrasted Fenestella's opinion that olive cultivation did not exist in Italy, Spain or North Africa in the reign of Tarquinius Priscus with the situation in his own day, when olive cultivation was not only practised in these regions but had spread far inland. Vallet (1962) used the disappearance of the SOS amphorae, which probably had served as containers for the export of Attic olive oil to Etruria, *c.* 600 BC, and the simultaneous appearance of Etruscan ceramics used as containers for perfumes made locally, presumably from locally produced olive oil, as evidence to support Fenestella's statement.

Diodoros Siculus stated that Akragas in Sicily became rich in the fifth century BC by exporting olive oil to Carthage, as North Africa was not yet planted with olive trees, although another passage of the same author indicates that olives and vines had been planted in the hinterland of Carthage by the time of Agathokles, a century later. Pliny believed that the commercial importance of fine Italian wines was no older than the Late Republic, from the middle of the second century BC onwards. Justin states that the Greeks introduced olive and vine cultivation to Gaul. As another example of the spread of viticulture a speech attributed to Demosthenes in the fourth century BC suggested to an Athenian jury that the idea that wine could be produced in the Pontos was incredible, but palaeobotanical evidence shows that viticulture commenced in the Crimea in the Hellenistic period.[40] The evidence for Greece itself will be reserved for Chapter III.3 below.

The full weight of such evidence from literary sources has not always been appreciated by scholars, perhaps because of uncertainty concerning the validity and accuracy of information about, for example, early Republican Rome provided by the surviving sources whose authors lived hundreds of years later. However, the gist of the picture given by these literary sources is increasingly being corroborated by the quite independent evidence of palaeobotanical research. For example, work recently carried out by the British School at Rome has shown that olive and vine cultivation in central Italy indeed did commence during the Etruscan period, confirming Fenestella's statement. Palynological evidence suggests that the olive tree was rare in southern Europe during the last glaciation and only survived in small refuges in Spain, Sicily and the south Balkans, perhaps also in south Italy. As the climate ameliorated, the oleaster spread naturally in the south Balkans, and independently northwards to France from Spain by 1000 BC. During the first millennium BC olive pollen became widespread all over the Mediterranean, reflecting the dissemination of its cultivation.[41]

Taking into account the steadily increasing volume of evidence which points in this direction, it is reasonable to affirm that the triad of crops which characterises modern Mediterranean agriculture, namely the olive, vine and the modern types of wheat, was not inherited by the Greeks and Romans from their Bronze Age predecessors living in the same areas but was in the main a product, an innovation, of the first millennium BC, except in the Levant. The third element of this agricultural revolution, namely the spread of cultivation of the modern types of wheat, will be the main subject of Chapter III below, while unfortunately there will be no space to discuss most of the literally dozens of other crops whose Greek names in Latin indicate that the Romans acquired knowledge of them from the Greeks.

The literary sources cited above demonstrate that the Greeks and Romans were aware of changes in the crop balance which occurred in classical antiquity, and we shall see in Chapter III below that this is also true in regard to wheat as well as olives and vines. However, it is very interesting to consider not only their knowledge of the facts of these changes, but also their understanding of the causes of these changes. Columella reported the belief of Saserna (first century BC), which was based upon the astronomical theories of Hipparchos (second century BC), that the spread of olive and vine cultivation had been made possible by an amelioration of the climate, permitting the spread of these crops into regions from which they had previously been excluded by cold winters. In principle climatic change was the correct explanation. However, the details were not understood in classical antiquity. After the last Ice Age the whole year became warmer, not just the winter, and it was the development of the summer drought which provided the principal distinguishing feature of the Mediterranean climate.

However, there is another possible explanation for the spread of cultivation of such crops which was not understood at all in antiquity, namely biological evolution under domestication. In some regions local varieties of wild vine or olive may have been domesticated during the classical period. This is the very clear conclusion of the research on the Crimea mentioned above, where finds of tools etc. for viticulture were made in abundance, but the actual palaeobotanical remains reveal vines that in the Hellenistic period were still morphologically very similar to the local varieties of wild vine which exist there today. Demosthenes, or rather the unknown author of the speech in question, did not understand the evolutionary process of domestication. Such processes resulted in a substantial increase in the productivity of Mediterranean agriculture in classical antiquity. However, this fundamental consequence of these ecological changes was not understood in antiquity any more than their causes were. For example, Galen thought that the olive had very little nutritional value (see Chapter II.7 below). Our conclusion must be that what was going on was to a very substantial extent an unconscious process whose causes and consequences were generally not understood in antiquity, although there was some dim awareness of these ecological changes. Galen had much more in common with the ant than he would have supposed.

This question of the significance, or lack of it, of human intentions merits some attention. The Greeks and Romans were aware of a number of what nowadays may be called 'ecological' problems in the popular sense of the word. For example the philosophical argument from sentiency invoked by modern advocates of vegetarianism was debated in antiquity. Vegetarianism seems to me to lack rational foundations because man, like all other animals, is unavoidably a member of a class of organisms which have evolved dependence upon other living organisms, whether plant or animal, for their sustenance.[42] As an example of consciousness of environmental pollution, there was some awareness of the deleterious effects of lead poisoning in antiquity, a phenomenon which today is suspected of causing deterioration of the mental faculties of children, especially from the cooking utensils used by the Romans and perhaps also by the Athenians. The latter had available very large quantities of lead as a by-product of the Laurion silver mines. An excessive intake of lead cannot have done anyone any good in antiquity, although its effects on human reproduction in Rome have doubtless been exaggerated by some scholars.[43]

Deforestation is another well worn theme of Mediterranean environmental history. Plato postulated it for Attica. His thesis still has supporters, but the weight of expert opinion is now inclined towards minimising its scale and consequences. The Mediterranean was cooler/wetter in the Neolithic period than it is today, providing more favourable conditions for perennial vegetation. It is possible that some deforestation has occurred since then as a result of the development of the summer drought, but that had nothing to do with human activity. (In passing, as an interesting corollary to a small episode of deforestation in antiquity, ecological research has shown that the construction of the Via Cassia *c.* 171 BC close to the Lago di Monterosi in Latium in Italy altered the drainage of water into the lake and so the lake's supply of nutrients, leading to the well known ecological phenomenon of lake eutrophication.) In classical antiquity and today the existence of the summer drought, restricting plant growth for part of the year, means that Mediterranean forests are not as lush as those of temperate regions in northern Europe and of tropical regions.

The summer drought also means that annual plants which complete their lifecycle in between two dry seasons have evolved into a much larger percentage of the flora in the Mediterranean than in tropical and temperate regions. Mediterranean perennial plants require special adaptations to survive the summer drought. A recently studied example is oregano, the perennial species of which exhibits seasonal dimorphism, with large leaves in winter and small leaves in summer, to reduce evaporation of water. The most striking of all adaptations to the summer drought is the requirement of some Mediterranean plant species for periodic *natural* fires as a way of destroying old vegetation and rejuvenating themselves. However, the number of species of perennial plants with such adaptations is too small to elevate them to the same status that perennial plants possess in temperate and tropical forests. Palynological evidence suggests that the pine forests, including the Aleppo pine (*Pinus halepensis*) forests which cover about a quarter of Attica today, have actually been spreading over the last few millennia, confounding the view that human activity in the Mediterranean has always resulted in deforestation.[44]

Some awareness was also shown in antiquity of what would now be called ecological problems in terms of the scientific definition given earlier. The works of Geoffrey Lloyd are the best guide to ancient scientific thought. Here we may mention for instance Empedokles (fifth century BC), who put forward the idea, revived by Herbert Spencer in the last century, of the 'survival of the fittest'. However, Empedokles did not conceive of evolution as a continuous process or understand that it is not just survival, but differential reproduction, which matters. The slogan's relevance to a correct understanding of evolution has been steadily eroded by much recent research, especially modern ideas about the frequency of mutualistic interactions between individuals of different species, about neutral mutations and about the overwhelming prevalence of genetic polymorphisms in all natural populations, all still in the context of natural selection acting on the individual.

To take another example, Dikaiarchos put forward the idea that human societies had passed from a dependence on animal husbandry to agriculture. He proposed on a priori grounds a unilineal chain of development which is unacceptable in the light of modern research for several reasons, foremost among which is that animal breeding is generally only practised in sedentary farming communities. A great interest was taken in antiquity in the plants and animals upon which men depended for their livelihood, and this interest did lead to thoughts about the nature of domestication. However, theorists like Theophrastos, to whose views we shall return later on, failed to understand it as a dynamic process of evolutionary symbiosis between different populations. A utilitarian interpretation prevailed, holding that domesticated plants and animals existed for man's benefit. It is perhaps best expressed in the views of the Stoics, especially Khrysippos, who influenced Cicero.[45]

However, despite their evident interest in nature – an interest that was unavoidable in societies in which most adult males were farmers – the understanding of ecological phenomena displayed by the ancient Greeks and Romans was extremely rudimentary and we would not make much progress if we were to restrict our inquiry to reporting views explicitly stated in ancient sources. One example, relevant to the main subject of Chapter III below, will have to suffice here. Lucretius, an exponent of the atomic philosophy, wrongly denied the possibility of plant hybridisation, the way in which the wheat which the Romans ate and many other of their crop plants evolved.[46] The objective of the present book is to explore 'wie es eigentlich gewesen' in classical antiquity, not ancient interpretations of what happened, although the reader will have surmised that my views on methods of historical inquiry and the nature of knowledge are rather different from those of Ranke.

In that respect this book is quite different from that of Hughes (1975b).

Hughes treated ecology in antiquity in the traditional mode of inquiry of classics and devoted plenty of space to the question 'What were the attitudes of ancient peoples towards nature?' This book does not set out to investigate that question. The emphasis of most ancient historians on the conceptual world of antiquity is an inevitable consequence of the fact that virtually all of them are trained in university faculties whose main raison d'être is classical literary criticism. That is one of the two prime reasons for the backwardness of ancient history as a subject. The highly subjective process of the evaluation of artistic merit which is the essence of literary criticism is irrelevant to historiography, while there is no good reason why historians should restrict themselves, as so many ancient historians have done down the years, to studying the conceptual world of the members of the society under study. The other reason is the cult of positivism and inductivism, a sterile and outdated philosophical system which is incapable of making any significant contributions to knowledge. It will be necessary in the course of this book to stress time and time again that the great ecological developments of antiquity were not understood or planned by anyone alive at the time and often were barely perceived in antiquity. Such developments could not be appreciated if the focus of the current investigation were to be exclusively on the 'mentalité' of ancient Greece.

There are many reasons why ecology as a field of academic inquiry did not emerge in antiquity. Such notions as a Lamarckian belief in the inheritance of acquired characteristics, mistaken ideas concerning the respective contributions of the two sexes to the progeny in sexually reproducing organisms, a belief in the fertility of many mammalian hybrids (not assisted by the absence of the Linnaean concept of 'species' – itself now outdated in the light of recent research in population genetics), and a belief in the spontaneous generation of some types of living organisms, all of which are to be found in various ancient sources, certainly did not help the development of ecology.[47]

However, the most fundamental reason of all for the lack of comprehension of ecological phenomena in antiquity was probably the lack of suitable concepts to structure the investigation. The very word 'population', as used by scientists, cannot be translated into ancient Greek or Latin. The history of the development of this concept in early modern Europe was elucidated by Foucault. It is a statistical concept. Attic orators writing speeches for use in the law courts of Athens in the late fifth and fourth centuries BC by clients who were short of witnesses to support their stories made very extensive use of arguments from probability (*eikos*), but it was never quantified in antiquity, preventing the development of anything akin to ecology or economics, that other major modern concept derived from ancient Greek *oikos*. King Archidamos II of Sparta was fined for marrying a short woman, on the grounds that she would procreate kinglets, not kings. Evidently the

Spartans did not understand that children tend to regress to the mean of the population as a whole, even if their parents represent extremes.

What is in question here is not merely the importance of employing quantitative rather than merely qualitative arguments. It would be wrong to state that ancient science was entirely qualitative in nature, because of such achievements as Eratosthenes' measurement of the circumference of the earth in the third century BC. However, the ancients did not discuss *emergent* properties of groups of members of classes not possessed by any individual member of a class, e.g. mortality and fertility rates and population density. This made the development of mathematical population biology impossible. Practical historical demography tends to confine itself to rates or frequencies rather than to probabilities in the strict sense of the word, but even that stage was not reached in antiquity.[48]

So far in this book little has been said about population dynamics as such. We have concentrated on migration, mainly of plants. Mankind benefited from plant migration, except when weeds were involved, but the Greeks were the prey, rather than the beneficiaries, of other migrations from the east. Considerable space will be devoted to the ecology of diseases in antiquity in Chapter II.7 below. Here the great epidemic which struck the Roman empire in the second half of the second century AD may be mentioned as an example: it started in Mesopotamia and moved westwards to Gaul. Animals also moved around. For example, the peacock was brought to Greece for the first time in the fifth century BC. Finally, the ancient Greeks themselves engaged in very wide-ranging migratory movements. It is therefore appropriate to finish this introductory chapter by considering briefly the ecology of invasions of new environments by living organisms. Elton (1958) is the standard textbook on this subject. He observed that in recent times such invasions have been especially associated with man's activities, conscious or unconscious. In bygone geological epochs they were most noticeable in connection with the separation and joining of continents, as for example when south America was rejoined to north America by a land bridge after a long separation, leading to the ecological event called 'the Great Interchange'.[49]

To introduce this topic to anyone not already familiar with it, ecosystems are required whose boundaries may be delimited more closely than is the case with a region such as mainland Greece, a small chunk of a much larger continental landmass. Fortunately the islands of the Mediterranean in antiquity offer outstanding examples of relatively isolated ecosystems. They were already used for this purpose over forty years ago by Charles Elton, one of the founders of the modern science of ecology.[50] We may begin here with one ancient source which he did not consider. Hegesandros of Delphi recorded the interesting titbit of information that in the reign of Antigonos Gonatas of Macedon in the third century BC, a single breeding pair of hares was introduced from the island of Anaphe to the neighbouring minute Aegean island of Astypalaia. A population explosion of hares (*Lepus europaeus*), which did not previously exist on Astypalaia, promptly occurred there. Faced with this unexpected problem, the inhabitants of Astypalaia consulted the oracle at Delphi (now relegated to dealing with such mundane matters, after the heady days of intense involvement in international politics earlier in its history), which advised them to hunt the hares with dogs. The introduction of the hare to Astypalaia is said to have been carried out deliberately by the people of Anaphe as retaliation for the prior introduction of the partridge from Astypalaia to Anaphe, which caused an epidemic of partridges there.

This tale illustrates the fundamental ecological principle that migrations of a species into new habitats may be followed by very rapid population growth because competitors may be absent in the new environment, permitting adaptive radiation into new habitats from which the migrating species is excluded by other species in its old environment. In addition the predators or parasites (including diseases) which customarily prey on the migrating species in its old environment may be absent from the new environment. This is especially common on islands where the equilibrial population density of predators, which is always much lower than that of their prey, tends to be so low as to expose them to a high probability of extinction. Such very rapid growth from an initially very low population density tends to follow the 'logistic model' of population growth, about which more will be said in Chapter II.2 below in connection with human population growth in archaic Greece. We are concerned here with successful episodes of migration. MacArthur & Wilson (1967) discussed the demographic characteristics of successful colonising species, especially their high intrinsic rate of natural increase. Theophrastos wrote a book about such episodes of very rapid increase and decrease of animal populations in which he devoted a lot of attention to mice and locusts, judging by the summary of Photios which is unfortunately all that is left of it, the only book written by an ancient author about a topic in population biology.[51]

Eventually the rate of population increase in the new environment will start to diminish as the new arrivals consume their food supply to the point where it begins to have difficulty replenishing itself. The increasing population density of the emigrants may also create very favourable conditions for the evolution of new predators or parasites to attack it or for their entry from neighbouring ecosystems. Theophrastos attributed the collapse of field mice populations after episodes of rapid growth to disease epidemics, while Aristotle connected their demise with adverse climatic conditions in the form of heavy rainfall. The history of the rabbit in conjunction with man's activities is of interest here. Strabo, writing in the first century BC, records that a single breeding pair of rabbits was introduced from Spain to the Balearic islands. That single pair was the starting point of a population explosion which seriously threatened the livelihood of the farmers there.

That Strabo's account need not be exaggerated is shown by more recent experiences. For example, after their introduction in modern times a number of small Pacific islands were virtually stripped bare of vegetation by rabbits, which then died of starvation, while the introduction of the rabbit to Australia seriously reduced the profitability of animal husbandry there. The inhabitants of the Balearic islands appealed to Rome for help and asked for a new homeland. However, the problem was tackled by introducing to the Balearics the Libyan ferret, a predator which proved to have a partiality for rabbits and brought the problem under control, saving the local farmers. This is an elementary instance of biological warfare. Similarly in Australia sheep farmers were saved by a more sophisticated application of biological warfare, namely the introduction of myxomatosis, a disease of south American species of rabbits of the genus Sylvilagus. The population of the European rabbit introduced to Australia had no previous experience of this disease and no innate immunity to it and was rapidly reduced.[52]

The examples of the hare and of the rabbit quoted above were inextricably bound up with human activity and it is for that reason that they are well documented, but such invasions of new environments may also occur without any intervention by man. How frequently invasions of isolated island ecosystems will occur is determined by their distance from neighbouring continental landmasses. On all the Mediterranean islands immigration tends to be faster than evolution *in situ* because of their proximity to mainland Europe, Asia and Africa. Even so their flora and fauna are often distinctive. For example, at least 10 per cent of the flora of Crete and of Cyprus are endemic species which occur nowhere else on earth. Crete is a good example of an island in which an equilibrium (under present climatic conditions) in the number of plant species appears to have been reached, with immigration and extinction rates being in equilibrium, in accordance with the arguments of the seminal work of MacArthur & Wilson (1967). In contrast, on the Galapagos islands, which are further away from the mainland of south America, evolution *in situ* tends to be faster than immigration. Speciation as a result of the adaptive radiation of very occasional migrants onto the Galapagos islands provided Darwin with the raw material from which to construct *The origin of species*, although the importance of the finches to his thought has been exaggerated.[53] Invasions of new environments are not just a feature of island ecology and do occur on continents as well, but the situation there is generally more complicated.

The very rapid population growth that often follows emigration to a new environment is only an initial phase in the population history of the migrants. Eventually they will have to evolve a certain level of integration with populations of other species in the new environment. In the case of the rabbit in Europe and in Australia in the twentieth century AD, varieties of the myxomatosis virus which exhibited avirulence came to prevail over the initial virulent varieties which killed rabbits too effectively and rapidly to secure safely their own transmission to new hosts, because the main vector of the virus (in Australia) is a mosquito which only feeds on living rabbits. In addition the rabbits themselves evolved innate genetic resistance, and in Europe they tended to develop social habits such as a more isolated instead of a more communal way of life which restricted opportunities for disease propagation. As a result rabbit populations have started to increase again over the last thirty years or so. The latest information is that rabbits in Australia appear to have developed immunity to even the most virulent strains of myxomatosis which exist at the moment.

However, this population growth may in time create opportunities again for the evolutionary success of new virulent forms of the pox virus which causes myxomatosis. Moreover fluctuations in rabbit numbers cause fluctuations in the population density of the plants which they eat. There is no a priori reason for supposing that the various populations will ever reach a state of perfect equilibrium with each other. Instead it is not inconceivable that a pattern of long-term crude cyclical fluctuations may be set up. The thirty or so year period of observations which has elapsed since the introduction of myxomatosis to Australia and Europe is far too short a timescale for us to be able to say what might happen in the long run. We shall see in Chapter II.2 & 7 below that some diseases do exhibit massive fluctuations stretching over periods of centuries and millennia.

Elton showed that fluctuations are the *normal* state of affairs in many populations of living organisms, epitomised by Aristotle's discussion of the increase and decrease of a mouse population which Elton used as the starting point for his book on animal population fluctuations.[54] Ramifications of such ideas in population biology will play a very large role in the discussion of human demography in ancient Greece in Chapter II below.

II

Human Demography

1. The state of the art

The demography of the ancient Greek world is a poorly developed subject, which has been treated by even the best of scholars in a way that lacks methodological sophistication. As an indication of the state of the subject, consider the following quotations from two leading scholars, who have only been singled out here, needless to say, because of their eminence:

> The demographic structure of Greece in the fourth century BC was basically the same as the demographic structure of the early Roman empire ... the demographic structure of the Mediterranean world in the early centuries AD resembles the European demographic structure c. 1500-1750.[1]

> It is important to stress that we are dealing with a fundamentally unchanging demographic situation throughout Greek and Roman history that was beyond human controls.[2]

Opinions such as these are the product of the natural tendency of classical scholars to regard Graeco-Roman society as homogeneous and uniform. After all, no scholar would be comfortable with the thought that his chosen subject is not a well defined unity. In the case of ancient history, in comparison with mediaeval or modern history, the assumption of uniformity over colossal stretches of both space and time is made easier by the shortage of sources in which one could hope to find evidence to question that assumption. Research which assumes continuity as a way of filling in gaps in the evidence is intellectually less demanding than research which does not make that assumption. The latter path, the hard one, is the one followed in this book. The justification for it, as will be argued, is that the available evidence, scanty as it is, is sufficient to demonstrate that opinions like those quoted above are entirely without foundation, so long as the supposed demographic uniformity of the ancient world is regarded as a state of affairs which requires proof, not assumption. Biraben (1979) observed that very many scholars have assumed a steady and regular pattern of population growth as a means of filling in gaps in the evidence for badly documented periods or regions, but evidence from those periods of European and Chinese history which are well documented shows considerable fluctuations in the rate of increase in the past, contradicting the assumption.

The state of population studies of the Roman empire is no better than that of classical Greek demography. The vastly greater size of the Roman empire relative to even the largest Greek *polis* (Sparta or Syracuse) permits us to make an elementary but nevertheless fundamental point even more starkly in the case of Rome than in the case of Athens. However, it is as relevant to classical Greece as it is to the Roman empire. In scholarly discussions of Roman demography, the assumption of uniformity over huge expanses of time and space is commonly made. This is a very dangerous assumption. For example, it has been shown that in London in the late sixteenth and early seventeenth centuries AD there were significant differences in mortality and fertility between different *parishes*, within a single city, at a time when London was certainly smaller than the city of imperial Rome and perhaps not much bigger than Periklean Athens.

Taking that as a standard of comparison, there is no reasonable a priori argument, let alone any evidence, for supposing that the population of the *city* of Rome in antiquity behaved as a demographic unit. For all we know, the demography of the imperial court, so long as it was based in Rome, may have been quite different from that of the *insulae*, the ancient equivalent of high-rise apartment blocks, in which the urban *plebs* lived. We shall see later that such differences may have occurred within the much smaller town of Athens in antiquity (section 7 below). Yet historians go on attempting to generalise about demographic patterns across the whole Roman *empire*, from Morocco to Germany, Britain to Egypt, and Spain to Armenia. The first major objection to the assumption of uniformity is quite simply that empirical evidence from more recent and better documented periods of history indicates that in pre-industrial societies in general demographic patterns tended to exhibit great variability, even over very short spatial distances and temporal periods. The fact that Europe was more politically unified during the time of the Roman empire than she ever had been before or has been since is irrelevant to population history, when set against the diversity of living standards and physical environments encompassed within the Roman empire.[3]

The second objection to the assumption of uniformity, of 'a fundamentally unchanging demographic situation' as Finley put it, is no less devastating. Following the work of Lotka and Volterra on mathematical models of predator-prey interactions, it has long been known to ecologists that interacting populations within an ecosystem *may* exhibit cyclical fluctuations, and no population of any living organism exists in isolation in the real world (see section 2 below). The stability of human populations in developed countries in the twentieth century is historically a very exceptional state of affairs. There is no particular reason for supposing that the current situation will last for ever and that nature has finished with us. This is shown by AIDS, which already is forcing actuaries working for life insurance companies to revise their tables in western countries. The current stability of the populations of developed countries must certainly not be extrapolated to the past. Scientists, e.g. Ruffié (1982), regard it as axiomatic that populations are transient structures whose characteristics can only be defined at a particular point in time. The assumption generally made by classical scholars of uniformity of population structure in the Graeco-Roman world is not only highly improbable in the light of the empirical conclusions of historical demographers working on more recent periods of history, but is inherently unsatisfactory if theoretical considerations of population biology are taken into account.

At this point we need to pick up again the point made in Chapter I about opinions differing as to whether living organisms or physical environments constitute the main subject matter of ecology. The book which, more than any other, drew the attention of historians to the Mediterranean in the past as a topic for 'environmental' studies, in the broadest sense of the word, is of course Braudel's *magnum opus* (1949, Eng. tr. 1972) on the Mediterranean in the time of Philip II of Spain. This is a great book by a great scholar. Braudel's main theoretical idea was that time moves at different speeds. He coined the notion of 'la longue durée' to designate the slowest type of movement, the almost static nature of the Mediterranean as a physical environment which imposed inescapable shackles on the range of human action in the past. He also emphasised long-term climatic change as a driving force in history. From the point of view of historiography, it is interesting to note that Braudel was writing *The Mediterranean* at roughly the same time that Charles Elton, for example, one of the founders of the modern science of ecology, was absorbing the theoretical ideas of Lotka and Volterra and realising that populations of living organisms may tend to fluctuate, regularly or irregularly, even in physical environments which are completely *static*. This implies that alterations of the physical environment, e.g. climatic variations (as distinct from variability), cannot be regarded as essential prerequisites for population changes, although they will of course complicate matters if they occur.[4]

As was observed in Chapter I above, the ecology of the Mediterranean in antiquity was a postscript to the last Ice Age, and may be a prelude to the next one. However, the fact that massive climatic changes have occurred in the past, forcing massive changes in the distribution and abundance of many species of living organisms, should not be allowed to obscure the equally important fact that population fluctuations need not be tied to such changes in the physical environment. It is necessary to recognise that population fluctuations may be caused in many different ways. Braudel was not in touch with the origins of modern population biology. Even if, for example, the question of the Younger Fill is ignored (Chapter III.12 below), and for the sake of argument the postulate of the stability of the Mediterranean as a physical environment in historical times is accepted, it would still be illegitimate to infer stability of populations of living organisms in the Mediterranean from the stability of the physical environment. The value of the kind of arguments deployed by Braudel is in fact rather limited as far as 'ecological' research is concerned, in the strict sense of the word, if the period of study is going to be restricted to as short a span as a single human generation, as *The Mediterranean* was. One of the main theses put forward here is that it is possible to interpret the ecological history of the Mediterranean as a dynamic process of constant, continuing evolutionary change if we focus on changing populations of living organisms, rather than on the static – within a human lifespan – physical environment.

This approach is fortified if we remember, employing a much longer timescale than Braudel's, that the Mediterranean in any case is not a stable environment in the long run. The present Mediterranean climate, characterised by cool, wet winters and hot, dry summers caused by the flow of currents in the eastern Atlantic, is regarded by palaeobiologists, e.g. Raven (1973), as a transient climatic system which has only developed during the disturbed conditions of the Ice Ages and is not expected to outlive the immediate aftermath of the Ice Ages. If the regular summer rainfall which existed prior to the Ice Ages were restored, it is to be expected that a large proportion of the modern Mediterranean flora of annual plants which evolved during the Ice Ages would become extinct, as conditions become more favourable for perennial plants. Conversely the olive tree, which is often and wrongly identified with the Mediterranean, may well survive the demise of the Mediterranean climate because it is not perfectly adapted to that climate (see Chapters III.3 & IV below). However, for the time being, the focus here will be on short-term population fluctuations which are independent of long-term shifts in the climate.

The starting point of the line of argument of this book is that theoretical population biology should lead us to consider the possibility of fluctuations not only of human populations but also of populations of all other living organisms in Greece and elsewhere in the Mediterranean in antiquity. As has already been seen in Chapter I and will continue to be seen in the rest of the book, there is abundant evidence to vindicate this line of argument. The evidence for relative population changes provided by intensive archaeological surveys in Greece makes it clear now that the entire course of conventional political history depended on a cycle of massive population fluctuations (section 2 below). The periods in which the Greeks were at the height of their powers (the fifth and fourth centuries BC and the Late Helladic period) were periods of relatively large populations. The periods of obscurity or political and military weakness – deficiencies often interpreted by ancient historians in purely moralising terms – such as the Hellenistic period and the 'Dark Ages' after the collapse of the Mycenaean world, were marked by population levels that were relatively considerably lower. This is the reason why no history of ancient Greece, even one addressed exclusively to political and military history, which does not take account of demography can be regarded as satisfactory.

The evidence for population fluctuations over time may be used to construct a periodisation of ancient Greek history that is very different from the conventional one. It is also much more intellectually satisfying because it permits the possibility of explaining the succession of the different temporal periods in *causal* terms, in stark contrast to the current division of ancient Greek history into Archaic, Classical and Hellenistic periods. This framework has no rational foundations. The fact that it is still widely employed by scholars can only be ascribed to inertia and a reluctance to engage in hard thought. It is nevertheless worth devoting a little space to the traditional scheme of periodisation to expose its deficiencies. The terms 'archaic' and 'classical' were originally borrowed from art history. As is well known, the unearthing on the Acropolis of Athens of the sculptures damaged by the Persians in 480/479 BC once afforded a convenient means of linking a turning point in art history with a well dated and documented event in political history. However, the synchronism is no longer valid, because Snodgrass (1980) has argued convincingly that the changes which differentiated 'archaic' from 'classical' art (in art historical terms) were already under way by *c.* 520 BC.

The other divide, between the classical and the Hellenistic periods, is equally unsatisfactory. The term 'Hellenistic' is not even a term borrowed from art history, like the other two, nor did it originally even primarily refer to the situation in mainland Greece like the other two terms. It was coined by J.G. Droysen in the last century to designate the amalgam of Greek and Oriental cultures which he thought developed in the Orient after the conquests of Alexander the Great. His vision of the mingling of cultures was a mirage which never existed, as was well shown by Préaux (1965). In short, the traditional periodisation of Greek history is a mess. The terms 'archaic' (before 480 BC), 'classical' (480-323 BC) and 'Hellenistic' (after 323 BC) are retained in this book, but solely as chronological markers. As they are entirely devoid of explanatory value, a new periodisation of ancient Greek history is required. It is proposed here that there were two crucial epochs in Greek history in the first millennium BC, in the eighth and the fourth centuries. They will be called the 'r' and the 'K' periods of Greek history respectively, for reasons to be explained later.

It was observed above that the course of conventional Greek history was tied inextricably to the population history of Greece. Colinvaux (1980) has attempted to delineate an ecological theory of the causes of war in general and applied it to antiquity. However, this path will not be followed here. Instead the focus will be on questions of distribution and abundance. As the rest of this book will not be concerned with the subject matter of conventional historiography to any great extent, it may just be noted here that numbers were vital for success in war, since innovative commanders such as Epameinondas were rare, at least until war became the preserve of professional soldiers rather than of part-time citizen militias. The Spartan empire collapsed because a shortage of manpower prevented her from making up the losses of a single battle, at Leuktra in 371 BC, as Aristotle noted. The large citizen body of Athens was her principal qualification to be a leading protagonist in the struggle for hegemony in the classical period, while the small size of Oropos and Plataia next door condemned them to be pawns in the game, not to mention the tiny island-state of Seriphos, the exemplar of an insignificant *polis*. Delbrück's arguments, turning Herodotos upside down, that the Greek forces outnumbered their Persian opponents in both the land and the sea battles of the Persian Wars deserve to be remembered more frequently than they are. They are not disproved, but merely supplemented, by recent research emphasising the technical superiority of the Athenian trireme. Nor should Diodoros' opinion on the high population density of Persis compared to the other satrapies of the Persian empire, a potent factor behind the earlier Persian success at empire building, be forgotten.[5]

The manpower concentration in a small area, facilitating easy mobilisation of a large force, together with the fact that in Greek *poleis* the degree of participation of the adult male population in the army and navy could approach 100 per cent in principle, while the degree of participation of the subject peoples in the Persian armed forces was very low for the most part, provide the real, sociological explanation (discussed by Andreski (1968)) of how it was that the Greeks, in fact only a part of them, were able to resist the Persian onslaught successfully. It is possible to go still further and argue that the attack from the Orient failed because it happened to come at a time when Greece was overflowing with manpower. If it is permissible to indulge briefly in speculation as to what might have been, it is arguable that if one of those powerful Assyrian monarchs of the eighth century BC, say Tiglath Pileser III, had chosen to send his armies westwards to the Aegean he would have had a better chance than Xerxes and Darius of conquering Greece, not because the Greeks would have fought any less bravely in the eighth than some of them did in the fifth century, but simply because in the former period they did not have the same manpower resources.

Nobody today literally believes Herodotos' account of the size of Xerxes' army, but this particular piece of fiction still leads historians astray when they come to consider the pseudo-problem of 'why the Persian empire became enfeebled in the course of the classical period'. Herodotos would have us believe that the Persian kings could count on the services of unlimited numbers of soldiers from subject populations. It is much more probable that the Persians were never able to rely on such troops in any numbers, because they failed to assimilate the peoples they defeated in the way that the Romans did (see section 5 below), resulting for example in the endless revolts of Egypt. As a result they had to dissipate their own manpower resources over an enormous area to keep it all quiet and were then unable to undertake any concerted action on the periphery of the empire. The Seleucids inherited this structural problem from the Achaemenids, and the vigour of the first Seleucid kings was no more able than the vigour of Cyrus to set up an imperial system that was capable of surmounting such structural problems in the long run.

The argument in the previous paragraph simply serves to illustrate the elementary but fundamental point that numbers only become significant if set in a structural framework which explains the interplay of forces that regulate the numbers and their effects on other bodies. Beloch (1886) discussed the evidence for population sizes in ancient Greece, largely relying on bits of evidence for the size of Greek armies, in a book yet to be superseded in its field. More recently, Finley, for example, derided the 'numbers game' on the grounds that the sources are not good enough to permit us to discover the numbers in ancient history. Criticism of this kind misses the point. The size of a population considered in isolation at a point in time is a parameter which is of no significance and has little meaning because data on size alone say nothing about the balance of mortality and fertility which regulates changes in size. In ecology, population size only becomes of real interest when it is combined with area to yield data for population density, in which form it becomes useful for biological models of carrying capacity to be considered later on. Even if literary and documentary sources were good enough to give us some reliable estimates of the sizes of the population of one or more *poleis* at particular points in time, or even of the Roman empire, that alone would not constitute a worthwhile population history. There is no intention whatsoever here of traversing again the ground covered by Beloch. Rather the aim is to see what light can be shed on the interplay of forces which regulated human populations in ancient Greece.[6]

Plato's *Laws* provides some of the elements for a model of the population of Athens in the fourth century BC. He considered the possibility of both overpopulation caused by an excessively high birth rate and underpopulation caused either by a decrease in the birth rate or an increase in the death rate due to war or disease as problems that his 'second-best' (after that of the *Politeia* or 'Republic' – a horrible translation) *polis* on Crete might encounter. His proposed remedies were birth control methods, although infanticide is not specifically mentioned, and then the removal of the surplus population by the dispatch of colonies in the former case, to avoid problems arising from a shortage of land, *stenochôria*. In the latter case he prescribed honours for multiple procreation, followed by the creation of new citizens from among foreigners, *xenoi*, in the last resort.

Overpopulation emerges, in our terms, as a strictly economic problem to begin with, which could then have political ramifications. Underpopulation, in contrast, engendered the purely political problem of maintaining enough adult male soldiers to deter aggression by other states. Plato did not consider the idea that underpopulation could have been desirable, through increasing the average area of land available per caput, because the functions of the ideal *polis* could not be restricted to what would now be called 'economic' problems. It is also significant that he did not consider the possibility that the average length of life could change, but took into account changes in fertility and catastrophic mortality (e.g. in epidemics and disastrous military defeats). Plato also shows that ancient authors could conceive of population fluctuations in much shorter temporal periods than the secular and millennial changes revealed by the archaeological record for Greece (section 2 below).[7]

Plato's comments also raise a very important set of questions concerning the relationship of population to agricultural production and to the land. He regarded a decrease in the birth rate without any obvious calamity as a cause as a distinct possibility, and so presumably would have rejected Malthus' famous thesis, in the first edition of his essay on population, that populations could be expected to increase at a geometrical rate and inevitably outstrip food production, which increases at an arithmetical rate, until decimated by disaster. Moreover Plato's horizons evidently did not encompass the possibility of endless technological advance to feed a steadily increasing population within a circumscribed territory, as in Boserup's utopian interpretation of the historical relationship between population growth and agricultural technology, even though Plato did regard Crete as densely populated at the time.

This serves to remind us, first, that a constant dialogue between theory and empirical evidence is always necessary, and secondly that, as Hume observed, it is impossible to separate the inquiry concerning causes from the inquiry concerning facts. There are no invariable factors in population studies, almost by definition as one is always dealing with aggregates of individuals. Moreover an intelligent approach to epistemology would deny the possibility of ascertaining 'facts' in the absence of preconceived ideas or concepts. Plato had no doubt that the nexus between population and food production was critical for the stability of the *polis*. Most ancient historians unconsciously follow Plato and assume that they can recognise 'overpopulation' when they see it, although in demography the question of whether this term is meaningful, and if so, how to define it, is a thorny problem. It will be necessary to consider how accurately Plato's model of demographic trends and their causes and consequences fits the other evidence which can be pieced together from ancient Greece. A start will be made in the next section with a consideration of population size, density and carrying capacity, leading to a reconsideration of 'overpopulation' in ancient Greece.[8]

2. Population size, density and carrying capacity

Ancient historians are accustomed to lament the inadequacy of the literary and documentary sources for population sizes in classical Greece and indeed in all other parts of the ancient world as well. However, classicists are not quite as badly placed vis-à-vis students of more recent periods of history in this respect as may be supposed. A recent authoritative book on urbanisation in early modern Europe offered the opinion that 'the new technical sophistication of demographic history has not enlarged substantially the available stock of knowledge about historical urban populations' (sc. with respect to their size).[9]

This is because the techniques of family reconstitution used by historical demographers of early modern Europe, which depend on linking baptisms and burials to marriages in parish registers and similar types of document, may be applied most easily to isolated rural communities which are relatively unaffected by migration. Such techniques are difficult to apply to large cities whose populations required continuous immigration on a considerable scale from the countryside for their very survival. This problem led Wrigley & Schofield (1981) to exclude London from their *magnum opus* on early modern England, even though R. Finlay (1981) was studying early modern London in this way with some success at the same time. Furthermore labour-intensive family reconstitution techniques are more useful for estimating vital rates than measuring large absolute sizes.

As a result historians of mediaeval and early modern Europe still have to rely to a considerable extent on estimates – guesses may be a better word – of population sizes found in literary sources in much the same way that ancient historians do. Such sources are often unreliable even when they claim to be reporting census returns.[10] In the case of ancient Greek history we generally only have estimates, collected by Beloch (1886), of the sizes of military forces, rather than of total population sizes. These estimates are usually only for individual *poleis*, not for Greece as a whole. The only exception is the statement of Justin that Philip II of Macedon reckoned the military forces potentially available to his 'League of Corinth' for use against the Persian empire as 200,000 infantry and 15,000 cavalry, excluding the Macedonians themselves. The origin of this tradition is unknown. If (quite a big 'if') it is anywhere near the truth, and given that Athenian hoplite armies, for example, actually deployed in the field in the fourth century BC never seem to have included more than about half of the adult male citizen population at the most at any one time, then by any reasonable extrapolation the total 'citizen' (adult and child, male and female) population of Greece, excluding Macedon and the still hostile Sparta, should work out at around a couple of millions, in very rough terms.[11]

Of course such a late source and such a method by itself gives little ground for confidence in the result. Probably all that can safely be drawn from it is an order of magnitude, namely that the population of Greece in the latter half of the fourth century BC was closer to 2×10^6 than to 2×10^5 or to 2×10^7. This order of magnitude is certainly similar to the size of the population of Greece towards the end of the nineteenth century AD. Later on, other arguments of a quite different kind will be used to strengthen this analogy. It is undoubtedly what lies behind Finley's observation that 'the Graeco-Roman world was more urbanised than any other society before the modern era' (at least in Europe), although his hypercriticism with respect to the ancient sources led him to ignore the demographic background to this process of urbanisation.[12] There can hardly be a simpler illustration of how partial and incomplete his concept of the 'consumer city' is as an explanation of what was going on in antiquity. The population of Greece as a whole was larger in the fourth century BC than it was in any other period of history, until about a hundred years ago, as will be seen below.

In the case of Athens, scattered data on military forces may be used to discuss the population of Athens during the *Pentêkontaëtia* (480-430 BC) and the Peloponnesian War in the fifth century BC, as has been done by Patterson (1981), for example. For the fourth century it is also possible to use our knowledge of the Athenian constitution, which for example required a population of a certain size in order to meet the requirements for filling the Athenian council, the *boulê*, to estimate a minimum size for the citizen population in that period, as in M. Hansen (1985), R. Osborne (1985) and the numerous articles of Ruschenbusch cited in the bibliography. At an early stage of research, I too spent a considerable amount of time contemplating the sources used by all the authors mentioned above. However, for the purposes of this book I decided not to review the ground covered by these authors, for two reasons.

First, there is a strict limit to the amount of useful information that may be extracted from the fragmentary surviving sources. Secondly, population size is by itself a parameter of little interest (see section 1 above). Instead the emphasis here will be on new approaches, which are desperately needed to revitalise the historical demography of the ancient world. Hereafter more interest will be taken in Athens than in any other part of Greece, although the line of argument is equally applicable to the rest of the country. However, there is one literary source which must be tackled before moving on to new methods, because acceptance of its veracity would contradict some of the conclusions to be reached later on. It may be regarded as a case study to illustrate how difficult it is to extract useful information from ancient authors. This source is the information given by Athenaios concerning the census of Demetrios of Phaleron carried out in Athens towards the end of the fourth century BC. It was an exceptional event which sets more problems than it solves. The state of the text means that its date is unknown – perhaps 317/316 BC at the start of Demetrios' reign as (effectively) tyrant, or alternatively 309/308 BC during his tenure of the office of eponymous archon, or possibly during his tenure of the office of 'lawgiver', *nomothetês*, if he in fact held that title, which is not certain. The name of Athenaios' source is also uncertain. Athenaios gives it as Ktesikles, about whom nothing is known. However Jacoby noted that Diogenes Laertios calls the book's author Stesikleides. Most important of all, Athenaios does not state the purpose of the enumeration. If it was intended to count all of the inhabitants (*katoikountes*) of Attica it omitted all the female relatives and male children of the (male) citizens. If intended to determine which members of the old citizen body fulfilled the thousand drachmai property qualification for full political rights introduced by Demetrios, as Jacoby suggested, it would have been pointless to enumerate metics and slaves.

Hansen has recently followed Beloch in arguing that the census was intended to ascertain the available military manpower and that the figures for resident aliens (metics) and slaves are derived from different kinds of sources. However, it is not clear that Demetrios, who was not a popular ruler judging by the fragments of Demochares, would have contemplated placing weapons in so many hands when he was not prepared to entrust many former citizens with full political rights. In any case it is certain that by the middle of the fourth century BC not only men eligible for hoplite service but also thetes eligible for naval service were enrolled on the *katalogoi*. This creates the possibility that the 21,000 citizens enumerated by the census – presumably a round figure – could have embraced the bulk of able-bodied Athenian males in the age classes 18-59 (? – another bone of contention), even if Hansen is right to interpret the census of Demetrios as an *exetasmos* to assess military manpower.[13]

Hansen's assumption regarding the proportion of Athenians who underwent ephebic training is arbitrary. Moreover it is not certain that the military institutions of democratic Athens survived the 'reforms' of Demetrios, as none of the surviving ephebic inscriptions can be securely dated to his period of power. It is also arguable that Hansen underestimates the extent to which participation in the institutions of the *polis* of Athens was legally compulsory or very strongly encouraged by the force of public opinion. Athens was a small-scale 'face-to-face' society (P. Laslett) in which a citizen could hardly hope to escape the prying eyes of his neighbours indefinitely. For example, a rich man who tried to evade performance of the liturgy of the trierarchy would be likely to end up in the law courts sooner or later under the *antidosis* procedure, under which he could be challenged to either perform the liturgy or else exchange his property for that of another man. This would make it possible to lower Hansen's estimate of the size of the citizen population in the fourth century BC. The Athenians were certainly aware of conflicts between public and private interests, but the balance lay heavily on the side of duties to the *polis*, not on the rights of the individual against the *polis*, for reasons to be examined in section 5 below, in essence the absence of an absolute monarchy before the development of the classical democracy.

Whether the census of Demetrios was designed to assess military manpower, or whether it was merely a total population count by a ruler who thought of himself – or at least liked to portray himself – as restoring the *polis* after a period of troubles – an interpretation which cannot yet be excluded – the 21,000 adult male citizens can only be a minimum figure for the adult male citizen population of Athens during the fourth century BC. In the former case at least those who were unfit for military service would presumably not have been recorded, while it is probable that the total citizen population had been reduced in any case by the calamities of the Lamian War and the succeeding years. It is not known how many Athenian citizens died during the naval battles of that war. All that can be said in conclusion is that it is likely that the Athenian citizen population (adult males) fell in the range 20-30,000 throughout the fourth century, and Hansen's research has made it more probable that it lay generally towards the upper rather than the lower end of that range. However, Hansen's book has scarcely advanced our *understanding* of the demography of classical Athens beyond the singularly uninformative level provided by those ancient literary sources which give 30,000 as the stock number of Athenian citizens, with 20,000 being mentioned only slightly less frequently.[14]

The possible parallels for a military census from other Greek *poleis*, Rhodes and Megalopolis, cannot prove anything about Demetrios' census, but do serve to cast severe doubt on the credibility of Athenaios' statement, as preserved in the manuscript tradition, that the census of Demetrios enumerated 400,000 slaves in Attica. The need to discuss this statement is the principal reason for this brief digression into the conventional subject matter of ancient history. It is vitally important for the following reason. Louis Gernet (1909) accepted its veracity and consequently came to the conclusion that the classical Athenian population was so large and exceeded the productive capacity of the territory of Attica to such an extent that most of the people who lived in Attica must have been living off imported grain, not off grain actually grown in Attica. His interpretation has had colossal influence. Even Finley accepted that perhaps two-thirds of the grain consumed in Athens was imported, and M. Hansen is currently defending a basically similar opinion.[15]

However, if the very flimsy base for Gernet's theory is rejected and the existence of a huge slave population more than twice as numerous as the free population is rejected, then a quite different interpretation becomes feasible, namely that the total population of ancient Athens was sufficiently small for most of the people in Attica most of the time actually to live off cereals that were grown in Attica. The importance of grain imports would be severely reduced quantitatively. It is this latter interpretation which will be the focus of attention in this book. The intention is to fit the population history of ancient Greece into the framework which prevailed across the still largely agrarian societies of Europe in the early modern period, as shown by Galloway (1988), in which demographic fluctuations were closely related to fluctuations in domestic agricultural production and grain prices via the Malthusian positive and preventive checks. Accordingly it is necessary to clear the way by disposing of Athenaios on slaves in Attica.

It is a refractory text as far as the traditional methods of classical philology are concerned. Dreizehnter's (1972) suggested emendation of the text of Athenaios yields a more plausible result as far as the number of slaves in Attica is concerned. However, it does not explain the similarity in order of magnitude of Athenaios' information on slave numbers in Athens, Corinth and Aigina, derived from different sources. Canfora (1983) has demonstrated that the text of Athenaios is sound, but this does not make it any more credible. There are many reasons why the 400,000 slaves of Athenaios should be dismissed. David Hume listed ten of them, which will not be reviewed again here.[16] Instead the focus here will be on the possible functions of slaves in the Athenian economy. Ste. Croix (1981) was right to state that the most important question to ask is what the slaves were doing. Those scholars who maintain that Athens had a large slave population have failed to address this question in a satisfactory manner.

As far as agriculture is concerned, the labour-intensive cash crops cultivated in modern Greece such as citrus fruits, tomatoes and tobacco were not available in Greece in antiquity. The only crop grown in antiquity which needed a high labour input was the vine. It was certainly cultivated in Attica for local consumption. However, Athenian wine was not of high quality and there is no evidence that it was ever exported in antiquity. The most important crop plants in Attica were olive trees and cereals. Both require small labour inputs per unit area relative to modern cash crops, and this means that they fetch lower market prices. This is also true of grain legume crops. Not only do all three require low labour inputs, but those low labour inputs are very unevenly distributed across the year. A considerable amount of labour is needed for certain operations, especially harvesting, which it is not profitable to maintain on the land during the rest of the year, whether the labour be slave or free, in plough agriculture. Mediterranean agriculture has always depended in the past and still does so today on the availability of a supply of seasonal wage labour to supplement small permanent labour forces on those farms which were too large to be worked by a peasant with the additional labour provided by his wife and children. The largest single component of the total labour input was needed during harvesting, and labour of that kind was generally hired and probably mainly free.[17]

There is no necessary contradiction between accepting that the number of slaves in classical Athens was substantially smaller than the number of free inhabitants and accepting that the propertied class depended on slave labour, as Ste. Croix (1981) insists, with the important proviso that this is true only insofar as permanent labour forces are concerned, rather than part-time seasonal labour. Thus there is no reason why we should not accept that the *ergatai* or labourers of Ischomachos in Xenophon's *Oikonomikos* were slaves, in spite of the doubts of E.M. Wood (1983). In fact that is how Xenophon's text was interpreted in antiquity, as shown by the commentary of Philodemos. However, the Epicurean philosopher made the revealing comment that the overseer (*epitropos*) and the workmen need not be slaves, suggesting that Xenophon's position is partly an ideological stance. This may be compared to his reduction of the diversity of status groups in Lakonia mentioned in his account of the conspiracy of Kinadon in 399 BC to the straightforward slave-free dichotomy presented in his idealised treatment of the Spartan constitution in his *Lakedaimoniôn Politeia*.[18]

It has been argued by Jameson (1977/8) that smallholders could have maintained a slave or two each to raise agricultural productivity. Our literary sources such as Xenophon and Hesiod all took extensive plough agriculture for granted, using the Mediterranean ard. However it is conceivable that they were merely expressing upper-class attitudes and that smallholders worked the land in a different way, by hand with a hoe instead of using a plough with oxen or mules. Intensive cultivation of land by hand is often more productive per unit area than extensive plough agriculture mainly because of more effective weed control. There were no chemical weedkillers in antiquity. However, although hand cultivation may be more productive per unit area than plough farming, that does not necessarily make it the preferred option. Hand cultivation requires much higher labour inputs than plough farming. A man guiding a plough can cultivate a much larger area of land than a man working with a hoe, which is likely more than to make up for the lower productivity per unit area of plough cultivation. In a society which values leisure, farmers might well wish to minimise labour inputs and so prefer extensive plough cultivation to intensive hand cultivation, even though the plough may well give lower yields per unit area than the hoe (though not lower total production if the space available is not restricted).

The question of the role of slavery is relevant here because theoretically slaves could be made to do the extra work required for hand cultivation with the hoe. However, it is not clear that the increase in productivity per unit area would be so great as to justify the cost of maintaining a slave as an extra consumer of food on a small farm. Our main discussion of agricultural productivity in ancient Attica will come in Chapter III.12 below. All that need be said here is the following. Hesiod observed that in setting up a household it was necessary for a man to obtain a 'wife' (see section 6 below for the Greek word here) and an ox for ploughing. Aristotle made a comment on Hesiod which is very important in considering whether or not it is likely that smallholdings would have had slaves on them. Aristotle explained Hesiod's line by saying that for a 'poor' man (*penês*), i.e. a man who had to work for a living, not a beggar, the ox took the place of a slave. This is very significant because it indicates that as far as Aristotle was concerned the boundary between slaveowners and non-slaveowners came higher up the social scale than the boundary between those who could afford to maintain animals for ploughing and those who couldn't. Aristotle would not have accepted the hypothesis that smallholders who could not maintain animals for ploughing would have had a slave instead. Moreover he presumably thought that there were farmers who were sufficiently well to do to be able to maintain animals for ploughing, but who were not rich enough to own slaves.[19]

The theory that slaves were used on smallholdings should be rejected. This does not affect the principle that smallholders who could not afford to maintain animals for ploughing would have had to rely on the hoe instead. There is no evidence that using slaves could raise agricultural productivity on a smallholding sufficiently to justify the maintenance costs even with the extra labour they would have provided. Nor is there any good a priori argument for supposing that smallholdings were actually self-sufficient, creating the possibility of other forms of dependency apart from slavery. In early modern Attica the poor supplemented their income by engaging in seasonal wage labour on the lands of the rich, in particular by helping with the olive harvest. This is presumably at least partly what the *hektêmoroi*, a group of dependent sharecroppers, were doing in archaic Attica before Solon's reforms and the later institution of pay for performing public duties during the classical democracy (see section 6 below).[20]

Nearly all agricultural systems in Europe before the Industrial Revolution were characterised by low labour inputs and consequently a lot of rural underemployment, at least at certain times of the year. Consequently attempts to explain historical change or development in early European agriculture in terms of declining marginal returns on increasing labour inputs are vain, *pace* Boserup (1965). The only exceptions to this rule were rice and sugar cane cultivation in parts of the Mediterranean in the mediaeval period. In mediaeval England, a working day in agriculture is said to have ended at *noon*. In a region with a high population density and an agricultural system with a considerable degree of underemployment, such as that of classical Greece, the limiting factor is land, not labour. If a farmer wishes to maximise his level of production under such circumstances, the primary problem is to maximise crop yields per unit area, not to maximise labour productivity throughout the year. This is the most elementary economics. That is why we should pay more attention to the effects of the spread of new crops, discussed in Chapter I above, and less attention to the employment of masses of slave labour on the land, in research on agriculture in antiquity. The orator Isaios mentions an Athenian who doubled the value of his estate by planting fruit trees on it.[21]

One other major sector of the Athenian economy which employed slave labour on a significant scale may be mentioned here. The best recent study of the Laurion silver mines, by Conophagos (1980), has argued that even in their period of maximum exploitation in the fifth century BC the mines would not have required more than about 11,000 workers in all. Conophagos' work is authoritative because as a mining engineer he has specialist knowledge of the subject not possessed by other writers on the Laurion mines. His estimate drastically reduces earlier estimates of the number of slaves employed in the mines, for example those of Lauffer. Conophagos also pointed out that a substantial proportion, about 40 per cent, of the mineworkers would have had to be *skilled* craftsmen to process the ore on the surface, another noteworthy contribution to the subject. The elaborate arrangements made for recycling water used in processing operations were necessary because of the aridity of the climate which also affects agriculture there. For what it is worth, Xenophon's advice to the Athenians to purchase 10,000 slaves to work the mines *c.* 360 BC when there was little activity there, closely corresponds to Conophagos' estimate of the labour force required.

Furthermore it is possible that the importance of Laurion silver production may have to be downgraded still further. Conophagos based his estimates of total silver production partly on old estimates of the volume of coinage minted by Athens in each period. However, some of these are probably overestimates too. T.V. Buttrey has shown that most coins conventionally classified as fourth-century Attic tetradrachms were actually minted in Egypt and elsewhere in the Middle East to pay Greek mercenaries and may have nothing to do with Athens (the origin of the silver is still unknown). This conclusion enables us to make sense of Xenophon's belief that the value of silver would never drop, no matter how much of it the Athenians produced and released into circulation. Such a result, which is not predicted by any branch of modern economic theory, is only explicable in the context of an economy in which the volume of coinage in circulation was far too small to cover the total value of the volume of transactions. (Athens minted no coins with a value low enough to make them suitable for retail trade before the fourth century

BC, showing that even during the fifth-century empire most buying and selling proceeded on the basis of barter.) As far as the Hellenistic 'New Style' coinage is concerned, Giovannini (1978) has argued that the new Athenian coinage of the second century BC was made by melting down a medley of older denominations which ceased to be manufactured and used at the same time as the 'New Style' coinage was issued. If correct, this would mean that there was not necessarily any upsurge at all in silver production in Attica in that period, as Conophagos implicitly accepted. Adding all this up, the claim made by the orator Hypereides that there were 150,000 slaves in the Laurion mines becomes absolutely incredible.[22]

Slavery is a topic which would require a large book for an adequate treatment, not a few paragraphs, but space only permits a very brief statement here of some of the reasons for rejecting the idea that there were huge numbers of slaves in classical Attica. The father of Demosthenes, who was surely exceptional in having none of his wealth in the form of agricultural land, is said to have owned 52 or 53 slave craftsmen, skilled labour again. This was perhaps a third of the value of an inheritance which left his son, the orator, a *hêgemôn* of a symmory charged with paying *proeisphora*, one of the hundred richest men in Athens. He also owned a few domestic servants. If it is assumed for the sake of example that each of the 300 members of John Davies's 'liturgical class' owned fifty slaves, then the Athenian elite would have owned in all just 15,000 slaves, a tiny proportion of Athenaios' 400,000.

This shows once again that substantial slaveholdings on the part of rich Athenians are not incompatible with the view of A.H.M. Jones that there were no more than about 20,000 slaves in the Athens of Demosthenes in all. The evidence about the family circumstances of Demosthenes, taken alongside Conophagos' conclusions on the composition of the Laurion mine labour force, suggests strongly that the way to make slavery pay in classical Athens was to invest in skilled, and so expensive and scarce, labour, not in unskilled labour. This very important conclusion does not appear in most treatments of ancient slavery. It puts the possibility of *profitable* slaveholding beyond the reach of poor Athenians. As evidence of the importance of skilled labour in the economies of the various Greek *poleis*, the argument of Burford (1969), namely that shortages of skilled labour were a fundamental constraint on the speed of temple building at Epidauros in the fourth and third centuries BC, should be noted.[23]

The impossibility of accepting the existence of so many slaves in such a small territory as Attica leaves the problem of explaining how the tradition embodied in Athenaios arose. Fortunately the problem is easily solved. Canfora (1983) was right to observe that all that the numbers of slaves given in Athenaios for Athens, Aigina and Corinth have in common is that they are extremely high. Aristotle provides us with the motive for such exaggeration on the part of ancient authors by stating that the masses, *hoi polloi*, judged the greatness of a *polis* by its *poluanthrôpia* or populousness, including slaves. He himself thought that only the number of citizens should be taken into account. Delbrück (1913), a model of critical analysis, furnished a beautiful analogy for the type of analysis that needs to be applied to Athenaios. Just as throughout history it has been an invariable practice for the victors in war to claim that the vanquished enemy forces were much larger than their own forces, in order to emphasise the magnitude of their achievement, so it may be inferred that it was normal in antiquity to exaggerate the number of people subject to a *polis* to emphasise its power and magnificence.[24]

Athenaios' evidence on slaves may be rejected safely. Later on in this chapter an attempt will be made to fit slavery in classical Attica into a structural framework, as part of a model to define the parameters which governed the size of the population of Attica in antiquity, without claiming to be able to ascertain its exact size at any point in time. The line of argument in the preceding paragraphs is not intended to suggest that Athenaios has no value at all, if the whole passage is interpreted as it ought to be, not as assorted evidence for cliometric history but as evidence for ideology. Athenaios begins by discoursing on numbers and functions of slaves in various Greek *poleis* in the classical period. He then draws a contrast with the (alleged) current situation in imperial Rome in his own time, asserting that *every* Roman owned ten thousand or twenty thousand slaves, not for production purposes as the Athenians did in the Laurion silver mines, but simply for display, to show that they were individually wealthy enough to maintain so many slaves in idleness. It would be silly to take this as serious evidence for population history, in spite of the evidence of late Roman sources such as Olympiodoros for the wealth of Roman senators, but it does constitute a perfect example of the phenomenon of *conspicuous leisure* which might have come straight from the pages of Veblen's *theory* of the leisure class. To break up that whole section of Athenaios on slavery into little pieces and then discuss them in isolation, as Canfora (1983) does, is to overlook the pattern of thought which gives Athenaios' collection of quotations on slavery its unity.

As far as the particular numbers of slaves in the text are concerned, I find no difficulty whatsoever in believing that they were all simply *invented* by one or more persons unknown. As evidence that ancient authors were guilty of still greater exaggeration, we need only recall the growth of the legend of the size of Xerxes' army, which expanded to the 1.7×10^6 given by Herodotos in the space of less than forty years, when there must have been still some men alive who knew the truth, that the Persian army had only been a tiny fraction of that size. It was probably considerably larger than the army of any individual Greek *polis*, but not larger than the forces of all the Greek allies put together. For a very instructive treatment of similar exaggeration elsewhere in the ancient

world, it is necessary to turn to the Bible, where the estimates of the size
of the Israelite population seem to be wildly inflated because the results
of the censuses were misunderstood in later generations. The Arab
historian Ibn Khaldoun, probably the first scholar to think about rates of
population growth, and writing in the aftermath of the Black Death,
argued that the data given in the Bible implied an impossible rate of
increase for the Israelite population. He wrote a devastating critique of
the massive population sizes mentioned in the Bible, which should be
read by all ancient historians who believe in the myriads of Xerxes' army
or the hordes of slaves of Athenaios.[25]

To sum up, it may be assumed that the Athenian population of adult
males and their relatives fell in the range 100,000-120,000 in the fourth
century BC, extrapolating from the fragmentary evidence for the number
of adult male citizens. There is no trustworthy evidence regarding the
number of slaves at any time in the classical period, but reasons for
preferring a low to a high guess have been given above. Finally, there
were the free resident aliens, *metoikoi*, about whose numbers little can be
said beyond repeating the 10,000 recorded by the census of Demetrios.
They included independent women paying the *metoikion* tax on their own
account and so probably do not require a high multiplier. Furthermore
metics were not allowed to own land in Attica, except by a special
honorific grant of the privilege of *gês enktêsis*, and the *phialai
exeleutherikai* inscriptions (dedications by manumitted slaves) suggest
that over 80 per cent of metics were attached to the urban demes of
Athens and to the Piraeus. It is likely that most of them had to buy grain,
which could have been imported, in the market to feed themselves. In
other words the metics, however numerous they were, are unlikely to
have been a big drain on the agricultural production of Attica.

For the purposes of this book an estimate for the total average
population of Attica in the fourth century BC of 150,000 people will be
adopted, allowing 30,000-50,000 slaves and free aliens on top of the
citizen population. The focus here is on the fourth rather than the fifth
century, because the aim of the exercise is to consider the population that
could be supported by Attica on her own, without the additional resources
provided by an empire. It is freely admitted that the discussion so far of
the Athenian population contains its fair share of guesswork. It may
seem that no real progress has been made. Is the study of the
demography of the ancient world a dead end? It will be suggested below
that there is a path forward, but pursuing it requires a new approach and
the forsaking of the traditional methods of classical philology.

The intensive archaeological surveys which have proliferated in Greece
over the last fifteen years or so provide a different type of evidence for
ancient demography. These surveys attempt to find and list all the
archaeological sites occupied by humans in each historical period in
selected areas chosen for sampling purposes. They provide a picture of

shifts in settlement patterns which has the virtue of embracing rural areas as well as urban centres – literary sources usually say little about the countryside – and also is capable of covering long temporal periods. Again, ancient literary sources more often than not do not do this, and when they do, their judgments were not based on any hard evidence such as data for censuses. On the debit side, there are indeed problems in extrapolating estimates of population size and density from data on settlement numbers. For example, the logical possibility that a reduction in settlement numbers in a region may reflect a concentration of the population into a smaller number of larger centres and so not indicate a real decrease in the total population always needs to be considered.

It is also difficult to assess the population density of urban centres in the past in absolute terms because human population density exhibits such great variability even in the modern world. Thus it is difficult to have much confidence in the stock figures often used by prehistoric archaeologists, e.g. 200 people/ha. It is hardly encouraging, for example, that after two centuries of research on Pompeii, estimates of the size of the population of that well-known town still differ by a factor of about three, because of unresolved problems such as whether or not Pompeian houses generally possessed an upper floor as well as a ground floor, which affects evaluation of average household size. It hardly needs saying that far more is known about Pompeii than about any prehistoric archaeological site. (Pompeii, incidentally, as an ecosystem terminated and preserved by a sudden catastrophe, should offer very favourable opportunities for palaeoecological research.) However, Jongman (1988) has recently adduced convincing arguments in favour of estimates of the size of the population of Pompeii towards the lower end of the scale of suggestions. He effectively did this by emphasising the environmental carrying capacity of the territory, a path which will also be trodden in this section.

It is also the case that the bigger the urban centre, the larger the possible margin of error and the greater the discrepancies between rival interpretations tend to be. For example, estimates of the size of the population of imperial Rome vary all the way from the very low 200,000 suggested by J.C. Russell (1985), who discusses these problems of Roman demography, to seven-figure guesses proposed by various other scholars. Fortunately there was no monstrosity like Rome in ancient Greece that would require detailed consideration here. However, even after taking account of all these caveats, it is arguable that the intensive archaeological surveys do permit an evaluation of relative changes in population size and density in ancient Greece on a regional and secular basis which is of value for demographic purposes. It is worth sketching out the resulting pattern without attempting to quantify the changes.

The disintegration of the Mycenaean world was accompanied in most regions of Greece, except for a few remote areas such as Achaia which

seem to have served as havens for refugees, by a very sharp fall in the
population. This was accompanied by the complete abandonment of a
large majority of all known Late Helladic sites. The well-known estimate
of a decline in the number of occupied sites from 320 in the thirteenth
century BC to 130 in the twelfth century to just 40 in the eleventh century
speaks for itself. Some of them, such as the Mycenaean palace site at
Pylos, were abandoned for ever and almost all knowledge of them was lost
to later generations of Greeks, as we can see from Strabo's inability in the
first century BC to locate the site of the palace of Pylos correctly. The
picture given by the Dark Age Homeric Catalogue of Ships simply does
not correspond to the geography of the Mycenaean world, *pace* the
desperate attempts of some scholars to prove a correspondence, as shown
by the comparison of the catalogue with the LHIIIB political geography of
Messenia revealed by the Linear B tablets. Other sites were eventually
reoccupied after the lapse of a substantial period of time, but there was
usually a break in that subsequent occupation levels did not respect the
Mycenaean layout. This is most significantly true of religious
sanctuaries.[26]

A process of filling in of the landscape commenced slowly in the tenth
and ninth centuries BC in all regions of Greece. In the eighth century BC
there is a sharp increase in the number of settlement sites, tombs,
artefacts and evidence of human activity of all kinds. This is the period
which was termed the r period of ancient Greek history in section 1 above.
The rate of increase slowed thereafter, but nevertheless the peak
settlement density was not reached until the fourth century BC. It was
higher at that time, the K period of ancient Greek history, than in any
other period of history until the modern epoch of population growth which
commenced in Greece in the first half of the nineteenth century AD. In the
Hellenistic period the settlement density decreased, slowly at first in the
third century BC, and then rapidly thereafter, to descend to a new low in
the early Roman imperial period. There appears to have been a
resurgence in settlement numbers in at least certain parts of Greece in
the late Roman and early Byzantine periods, but in general the
population of mediaeval and early modern Greece was smaller than that
of classical Greece in the fourth century BC.

This pattern is reasonably well established now, and it seems unlikely
that future surveys will alter it drastically. The first observation that
needs to be made about it is that the similarity of the results obtained
from surveys in different parts of Greece justifies generalising across the
whole of the country, as was done in the previous paragraph. For
example, the results of the Cambridge/Bradford Boiotia expedition and
the team who have been working in the southern Argolid are virtually
identical. The results from other regions, such as Messenia, Arkadia and
Phokis, are broadly similar albeit less detailed. As far as Attica is
concerned, no intensive archaeological survey has been carried out there,

and unfortunately the increasing urbanisation around the modern conurbation of Athens makes a survey in the vicinity of the city almost impossible. However, the general impression gained from glancing at the settlement maps for Attica in Petropoulakou & Pentazos (1973) is that the settlement history of Attica in antiquity was broadly similar to that of other regions of Greece. Athens herself did not distort population patterns in other regions of Greece in classical times in the way that she does today, attracting migrants from all quarters.[27]

However the population fluctuations delineated above are to be explained, any explanation that is to have any validity must take account of the fact that the observed demographic trends transcend the political boundaries between individual *poleis* in ancient Greece. The correct explanation must not be couched in terms specific to any particular *polis*. This is a methodological point of the most fundamental importance. At the same time the correct explanation must make some allowance for the small-scale variations in demographic parameters characteristic of pre-industrial societies which were noted in section 1 above. It will be argued below that these fluctuations in population size and density can be interpreted as a unitary ecological process which laid the framework for the whole of ancient Greek history in the first millennium BC.

However, before coming on to this, a number of problems connected with the pattern established above must be discussed briefly. Archaeological sites are usually given a relative dating based on pottery styles (radiocarbon dating is too imprecise to be useful in this particular context). The pottery styles may receive an absolute dating if synchronisms can be established between art styles and reliably dated historical events, but such synchronisms are rare and become scarcer the further back one goes. Consequently the duration of the period of use of certain styles is hard to ascertain. The kind of uncertainties that may arise in relying on pottery styles for absolute dating are graphically illustrated by the great volcanic eruption on Thera. It was once generally placed in the fifteenth century BC, but several different scientific dating techniques now concur in indicating a date of *c*. 1628 BC for the eruption, according to Baillie & Munro (1988). Fortunately the degree of uncertainty is less in the first millennium BC, with which we are concerned here.

This problem of the absolute dating of pottery styles affects the dating of the population peak, which may be limited to the fourth century BC or extend into the third century until as late as *c*. 240 BC depending on one's dating of the black-glazed ware in use at the time. Such problems are even more acute for the 'Dark Ages' and the Archaic period. The 'Submycenaean' ware in use in Attica at the end of the Mycenaean period was largely contemporaneous with LHIIIC pottery elsewhere in Greece, according to V. Desborough (1964). Similarly the 'Protoattic' pottery style which marks the transition from Late Geometric pottery to fully developed Attic black figure pottery is so scarce, as is the corresponding pottery in the Argolid, that it should be regarded as marking an ephemeral stylistic development of very short temporal duration, rather than signifying a significant population decrease after the period of growth in the eighth century. The end of the Late Geometric phase has been placed conventionally c. 700 BC because of synchronisms between Greek pottery imported to the Levant and political events there.

The flimsy nature of the evidence has been emphasised by Francis & Vickers (1985), who argue that Middle Geometric pottery was still in use c. 720 BC. If their theory that Greek chronology should be downdated accordingly is correct, it would mean that the phase of population growth leading up to the fourth-century peak would have to be fitted into a shorter period of time, implying a higher average annual rate of increase. Beyond this, chronological refinements of this kind would not make any significant difference to the qualitative arguments to be used in this book. Since I am not sufficiently familiar with the relevant archaeological evidence, I refrain from expressing an opinion on this question. Since it has become conventional to talk about the eighth-century renaissance, as, for example, in the volume in which Snodgrass (1983a) was published, this habit is followed here.[28]

Unfortunately pottery styles raise other problems which go beyond mere adjustments to chronology. P.J. James et al. (1987) have exploited the chronological uncertainties regarding the Early Iron Age to argue that the whole concept of 'the Dark Ages' is a mirage. They suggest that the transition from the Bronze Age to the Iron Age should be drastically downdated, not only in the Aegean but also across the entire Middle East as well. Conversely Anthony Snodgrass has recently brought to the fore as an interesting intellectual problem the question of why the Dark Ages lasted such a long time.[29] There is no doubt that James et al. (1987) are going too far in denying that there ever was a 'Dark Age'. All recent archaeological research in Greece has emphasised the completeness of the break at the end of the Mycenaean period. Similarly there is no doubting the reality of the upheaval caused by the overthrow of the Bronze Age kingdoms of the Hittites and of Arzawa in Anatolia, or the destruction of Ugarit in Syria, or the attacks of the 'Sea Peoples' on Egypt, even if Egyptian sources exaggerate the scale of the onslaught, or the reality of the 'Dark Ages' at the end of the Roman Empire as an analogy if the very concept of 'Dark Ages' requires salvation.

However, it is still possible that adjustments to the accepted chronology may have to be made. Downdating it by a generation or two would not make any difference to the line of argument adopted in this book. In section 5 below it will be shown that the long duration of the Dark Ages was a direct consequence of the socio-political structures of the time in Greece, which acted in such a way as to restrict population growth. Two other problems should be mentioned briefly here. I. Morris

(1987) has challenged the archaeological evidence from Late Geometric cemeteries for rapid population growth in that period. His line of argument should be rejected, but discussion of the reasons why is deferred until section 3 below. The other problem is the 'aceramic hypothesis', i.e. the idea that a region may have had inhabitants who are archaeologically invisible because they did not use pottery. This idea has some validity (see section 3 below), but it does not contradict the conclusion that there was a low population density in periods for which surveys find little evidence. It is a direct consequence of the inability of a thinly scattered population to produce the economic surplus necessary to support a complex division of labour and specialist craftsmen. Indeed Carneiro (1967) showed that on a cross-cultural basis population (community) size is closely correlated with indices of social complexity such as the presence or absence of craft specialisation.

The intensive archaeological surveys suggest that the population of ancient Greece as a whole was not static, but experienced a series of alternating phases of increase and decrease, producing troughs and peaks in turn in settlement numbers, in other words, a crudely cyclical pattern. It will be argued below that it is possible to elucidate in detail the factors which governed that part of the cycle on which this book will concentrate, namely from the Dark Age trough to the peak in the fourth century BC. However, first of all it is necessary to discuss the concept of a 'population cycle' and of 'population fluctuations' in some detail. In Chapter I above it was noted that populations of a number of different species of animals have been shown to exhibit periodic fluctuations. Moreover it has been proved statistically that these patterns are not just random fluctuations but true cycles, i.e. they exhibit recurrent large fluctuations around a constant size at relatively regular time intervals. Four-year and ten-year cycles are particularly prominent in the relevant body of scholarly literature. The most well-known animals in question are small mammals such as lemmings. Most of the research in question has been done in Arctic environments, which have the virtue of containing relatively small numbers of species compared to warmer climates and so are relatively simple ecosystems, like the islands discussed in Chapter I above, facilitating research. Unfortunately, although the ecosystems in question are relatively simple, the population phenomena are still extremely complicated in absolute terms. There is no unanimity among scholars as to how these fluctuations should be explained, especially regarding the timing of the periodicity of the cycles, even though their reality is universally accepted now.

They were originally studied in connection with the Lotka-Volterra two-population models of prey-predator interactions, of which several variants are possible. For example, it has been argued that these small mammal populations were regulated by larger mammals which preyed on them, or that they were regulated by the abundance of the vegetation

upon which they lived, or that they were regulated by disease epidemics
(cf. Theophrastos in Chapter I above). Although cyclical fluctuations of
two species in tandem can be produced under experimental conditions it
is now widely acknowledged that such models of prey-predator
interactions cannot explain the observed cycles of small mammal
populations, because they are so oversimplified that they do not
reproduce the conditions of nature accurately. Nevertheless the
Lotka-Volterra models were the foundation of modern population biology.
More recently, a number of other explanations have been offered. For
example, some scholars have laid stress on the role of limiting nutrients
in the food supply, rather than the total number of calories available, as
the restriction on growth. Others have pointed to the possibility of stress
syndromes terminating episodes of growth once a critical population
density has been reached. Another possibility lies in the mathematical
properties of a logistic equation with a time lag incorporated, which may
generate a cycle with limited periodic fluctuations. Also of interest is the
suggestion that the cyclical fluctuations depend on the possibility of
migration from permanently occupied habitats to other occasionally
occupied habitats which act as population sinks. Later on we shall take
some interest in these last two hypotheses.[30]

The reader may be wondering what the relevance of all this is to human
demography in ancient Greece. Population cycles are not only
characteristic of small mammals in northern Eurasia, but are also
characteristic of human populations in the very same part of the world.
The peoples in question provided the periodic eruptions of pastoral
nomads which have exercised such a profound influence on history, from
the Scythians and Cimmerians in the first millennium BC via the
barbarian migrations, for example the Huns of Attila, besides many other
tribes, which destroyed the western Roman empire, to the Mongols of
Jenghis Khan, who built the largest empire in history. The historical
record in Europe shows a succession of such episodes of nomadic
movements from the Eurasian steppes reaching back to the dawn of
European history. Moreover Chinese historical records suggest that the
migration episodes towards western Europe were synchronised with
similar movements into east Asia. It is likely that the picture of cyclical
state formation by invading nomads and subsequent collapses portrayed
by Ibn Khaldoun for North Africa in the mediaeval period reflects similar
cycles of human population fluctuations. Population movements, such as
those of the Toltecs and Aztecs, from the semi-arid regions of northern
Mexico into the heart of Mesoamerica in the pre-Columbian period
furnish a parallel case of a cyclical pattern of population movements out
of a region with a semi-arid environment in the western hemisphere.

Khazanov (1984), the first full-scale study of pastoral nomadism,
rightly emphasises the cyclical nature of the population movements in
Eurasia, arising as a consequence of phases of population growth. It is

likely that the dispersal of the Indo-Europeans from south Russia or eastern Europe to Greece and elsewhere was the earliest episode in this cyclical history. However, they were probably not true nomads in the sense that they moved slowly relying principally on the ox for transport purposes, while later true nomads such as the Mongols completely abandoned the ox in favour of the faster moving horse. Historians generally have treated individual episodes in these cyclical histories, for example the Celtic attack on Rome in 386 BC or their invasion of Greece and Anatolia in 280 BC, which the Greeks liked to believe was repelled by Apollo from Delphi, as unique historical events.[31]

Some prehistoric archaeologists, concerned by the lack of explanatory theory behind the way such population movements and migrations tended to be handled in the past by historians and the older generation of archaeologists, have gone so far as to pretend that humans did not move around in prehistory and to focus instead on models of autochthonous or endogenous development of prehistoric societies. As Anthony (1985) observed, the types of explanation currently in vogue in prehistoric archaeology are fatally flawed because they do not take any account of the historical record which shows that such migrations have occurred periodically throughout recorded history. Slavs and Albanians in the mediaeval and early modern period followed the migrants of antiquity southwards into Greece. More fundamentally, such explanations are fatally flawed because they show a lack of understanding of *Homo sapiens* as a biological species. Man's most distinctive characteristic is his ability to move into new ecological niches and to learn how to survive and reproduce in new habitats. *Homo sapiens* displayed an unparalleled ability to migrate, for example by colonising the Americas and Australia, which earlier species of hominids had not occupied. In the case of ancient Greece, migration was a demographic factor of fundamental importance, as a means of relieving population pressure on the land.

The third major flaw of theories of endogenous development is that their proponents have failed to recognise that a knowledge of modern ecology makes it possible to treat episodes of migration, such as those from the Eurasian steppes under discussion here, as parts of a recurring pattern which is amenable to scientific research. The old-style diffusionism and migrationism advocated by Gordon Childe, for example, was an easy target for the 'new archaeologists' in the 1960s because of the lack of a firm theoretical foundation. However, it remains true that migrations are frequently attested in every part of the world as soon as documentary evidence becomes available. The migrations of the Polynesians in the Pacific are the most remarkable case of all. Modern research in demography and population biology now makes it possible to offer sophisticated explanations for the population instability which accounted for human migrations in the past and to explain why such instability was the norm, rather than the exception. This is one of the aims of this book.

This means that it is not necessary to treat the events of say, 386 or 280 BC, as unique or random historical events any more than we need consider the epidemic of Athens in 430 BC as unique (see Chapter I above). Rather they may only be understood when considered as cases of expression of a pattern. In fact Colinvaux has given an explanation of the cyclical population fluctuations and consequent migrations of Eurasian pastoralists in terms of modern ecological theory, starting from the observation that human populations fluctuate in those marginal environments in the same way that populations of small mammals do in the same regions. Space only permits attention to be drawn to his analysis here. The very arrival of proto-Indo-Europeans in the country now called Greece, probably towards the end of the third millennium BC, may be explained as part of a phase of an ecological process which has governed the history of human populations in Eurasia for millennia. The Roman reaction to this process was quite remarkable. As they became weary of defending their empire constantly against new barbarian tribes, some of the Romans at least, as Synesios of Cyrene suggests, refused to believe that new tribes were arising on the Eurasian steppes and instead concluded that the old tribes were merely changing their names to try to confuse the Romans! A quite extraordinary denial of reality.[32]

It is possible to move, this time intellectually rather than physically, from northern Eurasia to Greece by another route which is also of considerable interest. The regions of Eurasia in question are rather marginal environments, with alternating short warm summers and long cold winters. The cycles of small mammal populations which are characteristic of these regions are not observed readily in, for example, temperate regions such as Britain or in tropical regions in which the climate does not exhibit such a high degree of seasonality, and also considerably less interannual variability. Thus the kind of population cycles in question are characteristic of highly seasonal environments. However they cannot be explained directly in terms of the changing seasons because the duration of a small mammal cycle is generally longer than a single year, and incidentally also longer than the individual animal's average lifespan in the wild, as were the phases of the human population cycles in Eurasia in the past. Nor can they be correlated with climatic cycles as such because climatic cycles of the required periodicities have never been observed empirically.

What is going on instead is that by means of natural selection highly seasonal environments induce a particular kind of reproductive behaviour in living organisms which is geared to taking maximum advantage of short favourable seasons which only appear at intervals that may be more or less regular depending on the particular climatic regime in question. This kind of reproductive behaviour is characteristic of what ecologists call 'r species', i.e. species which tend to grow at a high intrinsic rate of population growth, generally abbreviated to 'r' (i.e.

exponential growth rate of a population with a stable age distribution and stable age-specific vital rates increasing in an unlimited space – a mathematical abstraction). It favours very rapid population growth and is inherently liable to population collapses when the short good seasons come to an end. Moreover a high degree of seasonality tends to synchronise periods of reproduction and also of mortality. The periodicity of cycles is probably related in some way to average generation length.

In the early modern period the Eurasian pastoralists had extremely high birth rates, high death rates especially in respect of infant mortality and a slow rate of population increase on average. Nevertheless the extremely high birth rates enabled their populations to increase rapidly if environmental conditions were favourable over a number of years. Moreover the low population density of pastoral nomads created a scarcity of density-dependent diseases. These two factors meant that nomadic populations generally had considerable potential for population growth. In modern times, the populations of central Asia, following their enforced sedentarisation and collectivisation in the early years of the history of the Soviet Union, have been growing extremely rapidly to such an extent that they are now threatening to outnumber in years to come Russians of European origin, who currently monopolise places on the Politburo. This situation, which the Russians may well come to regret, is a consequence of the traditional demography of nomadic populations in Eurasia. The same demography explains the tidal waves of barbarians who eventually swept away the western Roman empire and in still earlier millennia the dispersal of the proto-Indo-Europeans. Returning now to living organisms in general, in contrast to the 'r species', the 'K species' characteristic of more stable, e.g. tropical, environments, are adapted to slow population fluctuations around the relatively invariant carrying capacity, 'K', of their territory.[33]

All these basic principles of ecology are as relevant to the Mediterranean as they are to northern Eurasia because the Mediterranean too is a highly seasonal environment. Aristotle and Theophrastos took an interest in population fluctuations of types of animal which ecologists now describe as 'r species' (see Chapter I above). The reader will recall that the field mouse, another small mammal, and the locust figured prominently in the ancient discussions. Unfortunately there is a shortage of research on the ecology of small mammals in the Mediterranean comparable to that which has been carried out in northern Eurasia, although some relevant research has been undertaken in Mediterranean environments in other parts of the world, such as California and Australia. For this reason it is not clear if the Mediterranean populations exhibit cycles with regular periodicity, or whether they may instead merely undergo large random fluctuations. However, there is no doubt that the seasonal Mediterranean environment selects the same kind of reproductive behaviour found in northern Eurasia.

The same ecological principles are equally applicable to plants. Annual plants form an unusually high percentage of the total flora in the Mediterranean (see Chapter I above). Besides the numerous herbs and flowers, the most significant component of the Mediterranean flora as it has been modified by man consists of the cereals which provide the bulk of the food consumed by humans there. Cereals are r species par excellence, opportunists which commence growth in the autumn to obtain a head start over other annual plants which do not begin their lifecycle until the following spring, complete their lifecycle rapidly in the spring and early summer and devote a large part of their resources to the seeds, the reproductive parts of the plants, in order to maximise the chances that a new generation will survive predators and the following winter. The large investment in the reproductive effort makes cereals eminently suitable as a highly productive source of food, but many of the problems that continually beset agriculture flow from the fact that man strives to turn what are in nature essentially opportunist or fugitive species into dominant species, effectively a climax vegetation, over huge areas of land. This is not their natural role or ecological niche.

The seasonality of the environment means that crops have to be harvested in one season and stored to cover the next twelve months (at least) until the next harvest. This by itself creates the necessity of production surplus to immediate consumption requirements, an essential precondition for the development of a complex stratified society in which not all strata of society are engaged constantly in primary production. All major ancient civilisations originated in highly seasonal environments, not for example in tropical regions such as New Guinea which produce root crops, like the sweet potato, that can be sown and harvested all the year round, creating no need to think about the future.[34]

The point of the discussion above is to accustom the reader to the idea that the natural environment of the Mediterranean selects a type of reproductive behaviour in all living organisms, both plant and animal, which is conducive to phases of rapid population growth and subsequent population collapses, characterised by a high degree of instability. The aim is to wean the reader away from the idea, implicit in the quotations on the first page of this chapter, that stability of populations in the Mediterranean is normal and to be expected. In fact the same argument can also be extended to micro-organisms, whose transmission from host to host is very substantially influenced by seasonal changes in environmental conditions. These have the effect of averting any tendency towards damping down of oscillations of epidemic patterns. The interaction between man and measles may be a good empirical example of a Lotka-Volterra prey-predator cycle. The emphasis of the writers of the Hippokratic corpus that diseases followed the seasons had a very firm factual foundation in the epidemiological environment of ancient Greece, to which we shall return in section 7 below.[35]

The kind of cycles of plants and animals and micro-organisms to which attention has been drawn so far are rather short in temporal duration, but not all cycles are necessarily so short. A prime example of great historical importance is provided by the plague bacillus (*Yersinia pestis*) (see section 7 below). It is only by considering the historical record over the last two millennia that it becomes clear that plague, a species of bacteria with an average generation length of two hours, has moved in over two thousand years through just four phases of intense activity marked by onslaughts on man, each of one or more centuries in duration, and each separated by long periods of inactivity. The kind of human population fluctuations that we are interested in are also on the whole to be measured in terms of centuries. However, if they are reckoned in terms of rate of change per generation, they may be as rapid as the small mammal fluctuations considered above. A human population which rises or collapses in four generations, i.e. a century or a little longer, may be experiencing a rate of change per generation as fast as that of a lemming population which passes through its cycle in a few generations, over a four-year period. Furthermore fluctuations stretching over millennia rather than centuries are also conceivable. Scholars are now increasingly favouring the hypothesis that the so called 'Dutch Elm Disease' (*Ceratocystis ulmi*), which is currently active, was responsible for a large decline in elm pollen across Europe in the fourth millennium BC observed in pollen cores. It is not matched by similar shifts in the abundance of the pollen of other trees, ruling out climatic change as the explanation.[36]

Time-lags in a population's response to its own changing situation and/or over-compensating reactions in density-dependent processes may generate an enormous variety of patterns of fluctuation in population density. We should take note here of a recent development in population biology, namely the systematic study of *chaos*, which is now being quantified. It has been shown that very simple non-linear deterministic equations of the type generally encountered in biological models may generate chaotic fluctuations which appear to be random at first sight. Moreover very slight differences in the initial conditions may produce quite different patterns of population evolution. The mathematical models of chaos have the virtue of explaining the periodicity of population cycles of small mammals. All the other theories encounter difficulties trying to explain the periodicity. Thus it is now possible to devise explanations for population fluctuations without any reference whatsoever to external factors. However, it would be quite wrong to ignore all external factors. In palaeoecology, for example, it is obvious that the beginning of a glacial period in high latitudes in the northern hemisphere tended to drive populations of living organisms in certain directions, making life easier for organisms that thrive in cold conditions and more difficult for organisms that thrive in warm environments. It is clear that population fluctuations of living organisms cannot be explained *solely* in terms of *their own* mathematics. (This is true, notwithstanding the fact that the Ice Ages themselves, of which seventeen or eighteen are now known, give all the appearances of being a series of deterministic chaotic fluctuations in the earth's weather.) Accordingly it is legitimate to go on exploring external factors which may tend to push chaos in a certain direction.[37]

Because there is no way of knowing in advance what to expect at the beginning of an empirical study of any given population, arguments from analogy with other populations cannot prove anything. They are merely instructive in illustrating the range of possibilities which must be considered. For this reason the rest of this chapter will be devoted to elucidating the specific factors which governed the observed fluctuations in the case of human populations in ancient Greece. It would be easy for a critic of this book to adduce examples of historical human populations which did not fluctuate wildly, exhibiting properties tending towards a steady state instead. Just to mention two, ancien régime France in the period 1500-1800 AD, which furnished the material for what Emmanuel Le Roy Ladurie called 'l'histoire immobile', and Japan before its opening up to western influence in the middle of the last century, may be noted. Those cases do not prove that the analysis offered here is wrong, but merely that the factors involved in the context of ancient Greece were different from those affecting early modern France and Japan. To anticipate what is to follow, it will be argued in section 6 below that ancient Greek populations lacked the self-regulating mechanisms that kept population fluctuations in early modern Europe within limits.

As far as the ancient Greeks themselves were concerned, instability and cyclical patterns of development were facts of life which underlay all ancient political theories concerning the development of states and political constitutions. The state was likened to a living organism which experiences rapid juvenile growth, matures and then slowly decays and dies. This favourite analogy of ancient political theory was flawed, but nevertheless had a certain element of truth in it. As was observed in Chapter I above, the concept of a 'population' did not exist in antiquity. A fluctuating population would have offered a much better analogy to the state than the developmental stages of an individual organism, first because it may continue to exist indefinitely, unlike any individual organism, and secondly because it is arguable that population fluctuations often did underlie the rise and fall of states in antiquity. For example, Sparta was laid low by *oliganthrôpia*, while Hannibal's Carthage was quite unable to match the ability of Rome to raise army after army, making military disasters ultimately inconsequential. The relationship between abundance of human resources and power in antiquity was expressed most forcibly by one of the writers of the Hippokratic corpus, who said that the number of men whom someone could feed determined that individual's power.[38]

It is convenient to commence consideration of the factors determining population fluctuations in ancient Greece by looking at the peak, which was reached in the fourth century BC. Our hypothesis, broadly speaking, is that the population of Greece in that period had reached the limits set by the carrying capacity of the land and so was unable to expand any further. I initially arrived at this idea in the following way. If the 21,000 adult male citizens of Athens recorded by the census of Demetrios of Phaleron are quadrupled to take account of adult women and children of both sexes, assuming parity in the sex ratio (discussed in section 4 below), a citizen population density of 35 people per km^2 is obtained. The area of ancient Attica is estimated at 2400 km^2, excluding the adjacent territories of Oropos and Eleutherai which were sometimes under Athenian political control but had inhabitants of their own of non-Athenian origin. This result is almost *identical* to the level of population density which Jardé estimated could be supported by the land of Greece on average, namely 36 people/km^2. This remarkable conclusion has not been emphasised by other scholars because of a tendency, already rightly condemned in antiquity by Aristotle in his comments on *poluanthrôpia*, to lump together all social strata in scholarly discussions of the population size of classical Athens. It is exceedingly important to consider not only the size and density of the whole population but also to break it down into different social strata and functional groups.

It is necessary to ask if this equation is just mere coincidence or whether it has in fact a very profound significance for our understanding of the demography of classical Athens. It raises the tantalising possibility that the population of Athens in the fourth century BC was the size that it was, not through chance, but because that size of population was the maximum number of people that the land of Attica could support, i.e. its environmental carrying capacity. It was noted earlier that the 21,000 citizens listed in the census must be taken to be a minimum figure only for the size of the citizen population, however the census be interpreted. This need not invalidate the hypothesis proposed here because there is no doubt that Jardé seriously underestimated the proportion of Attica that may be cultivated (see Chapter III.2 below for the details). Thus it is possible to raise our estimate of the carrying capacity of Attica, even while acknowledging that cereal yields were very low (see Chapter III.12 below). For the time being, the reader may forget the numbers in the previous paragraph and simply keep in mind the qualitative idea, as a heuristic tool.[39]

'Carrying capacity' is an important but tricky concept, like population cycles, which requires discussion before we go any further with our analysis of ancient Greek demography. The term is used in two quite different ways by scholars. Both ideas will be exploited here, but it is important to appreciate the differences between them and to keep them separate. For anthropologists and historians, carrying capacity is generally regarded as a property of the environment, i.e. the number of people who can be sustained by a given territory, exemplified by the recent studies of L. Gallo (1984b) and Garnsey (1988) for classical Attica. In this sense, it was christened 'Cc' by Dewar (1984). Calculations of it assume that the productive capacity of the area in question is/was not changing nor capable of improvement. On the other hand, for ecologists, carrying capacity, generally symbolised by 'K' in this context, is a property of a *population*, not of a piece of land, essentially the population density at which fertility and mortality rates are equal and the population is in equilibrium. Besides these two fundamentally different concepts masquerading under the same name, we shall also have to consider the attack of Boserup (1965) on the utility of carrying capacity in the context of agrarian economics.[40]

Let us begin with ecological carrying capacity, henceforth K. Ecological theory maintains that a small population of a living organism introduced into a suitable new environment will at first increase exponentially, as natural selection programmes all living organisms to maximise evolutionary fitness. As the population increases it will gradually encounter more and more environmental resistance to continued growth as the available resources are used up. The rate of increase will diminish gradually until density-dependent intraspecific competition brings fertility and mortality to the equilibrial population density, K. This is the essence of the Verhulst-Pearl logistic equation in its differential form, which makes this conclusion easily comprehensible:

$$\frac{dN}{dT} = rN\frac{(1-N)}{K} = rN\frac{(K-N)}{K}$$

It is a model of growth relating the rate of increase to the population density. Like all models, it is so oversimplified that it is unlikely to represent any real population accurately, but it has nevertheless been a very fruitful source of further research in ecology. In practice K is always likely to have many different components. Real populations experience a time-lag before their response to their own changing circumstances becomes effective, by which time their demographic parameters will again be different, requiring further response. Depending on the value of r, this process may set up a cycle of fluctuations with stable limits. A very high value of r may generate deterministic chaos. In a highly seasonal environment like the Mediterranean, K varies with the seasons, stimulating evolution of food storage by animals and, it may be surmised, by humans and hominids in semi-arid environments. For many living organisms under such conditions density-dependent conditions are probably only involved in the determination of the winter lows, with the summer peaks being determined by density-independent factors. For humans in ancient Greece the spring before each harvest was the hungry season of the year, as Alkman noted.

Even shorn of these refinements, the logistic equation in its simplest form has been attracting interest again recently in historical demography, because it predicts the current size of the British population more accurately than other methods, starting from the data available in the last century. In principle the equation has predictive value because K may be calculated from data for population density and rate of increase. It is worth considering how the ancients tackled such problems. Aristotle rightly stated that all animals, even individuals of a single species, are in constant competition with each other for food. He thought that if enough food were provided, then even wild animals would live happily together with man. He did not realise that, if a quantity of food surplus to current needs were provided, the animals would increase their reproductive rates until the surplus was all used up and so would always be in competition with each other.[41]

Greece in the nineteenth century AD provides an admirable example of a case where the logistic model may be applied profitably. After this has been demonstrated, it will be suggested that what happened in Greece in the last century constitutes in certain respects a good analogy for the development of ancient Greek populations from the Dark Ages to their peak in the fourth century BC. In the course of the nineteenth century AD Greece went from being a very thinly populated country, at the time of the Napoleonic Wars before the War of Independence, to a country which could not produce enough bread to feed its own population and had to resort to imports of cereals, experiencing massive population growth in the process. It is possible to calculate population density from the data of Greek censuses from the middle of the last century and to correlate increasing population density with the development of cereal imports. In this way the loss of self-sufficiency in cereal production and the responses which this drew from the population of Greece may be examined. In 1880 Greece, excluding Thessaly, Macedonia and Thrace which had not yet been incorporated into the modern Greek state, had a population density of about 32.5 people/km^2 at the time when cereal imports were just about starting to become necessary in order to feed the increasing population. This suggests that Jardé's estimate of Cc for Greece, derived from micro-economic considerations, was not too far removed from the truth, although we shall see later how it may be refined. Jardé's treatment of this topic, which is still of great interest, effectively lumped Cc and K together, but it is better to keep them quite separate for analytical purposes.[42]

As regards the responses to this situation, initially the Greeks cut one level out of the food chain of which they were the summit and so reduced energy losses, in ecological terms, by going over from animal husbandry to arable farming. McGrew (1985) argued that before the War of Independence a larger proportion of the relatively small population of that time made their living from animal husbandry than from arable farming, because the lowlands were largely abandoned to the Turks. Returning to arable farming did not solve the problem because it merely permitted further population growth in what was a 'natural fertility' regime (see section 4 below) in which voluntary family limitation was not practised on any great scale. It should be emphasised that the rate of increase in the Balkans in this period was fast, of the order of 2 per cent per annum on average, as fast as anything experienced in Europe during the last couple of centuries. The second major response was to increase the cultivated area by fully exploiting the lowlands which had been neglected in the preceding historical period, but this response obviously had its limits too.[43]

The third major response to population growth was the introduction of new and more productive crops. As the population density increased the average area of land per person dropped, to the point where many farmers could not make ends meet by concentrating on the traditional subsistence crops of cereals, olives and legumes. They turned instead in the second half of the nineteenth century to cultivating the currant vine, a cash crop the sale of whose products could buy more wheat than a smallholder could actually grow himself. The success of the currant vine in that period depended on two factors which were exogenous to Greece itself. In fact in antiquity it was known but not appreciated. Theophrastos only mentions its cultivation in connection with the Troad in north-west Asia Minor. In the second half of the nineteenth century the accidental introduction from North America of the aphid *Phylloxera vitifolii* (= *vastatrix*), a relatively harmless predator of American species of vine, devastated the vineyards of France and other parts of western Europe, which consisted of susceptible European vines of the species *Vitis vinifera sativa*. As a result vineyards in Greece, which have traditionally produced low quality products, gained access to a large international market. This is another example of the ecological invasions discussed in Chapter I above, and *Vitis vinifera* no longer exists in most of Europe as an independent species because of it. Secondly there was a demand at the time in Britain and other industrialising countries for currants.

The spread of the currant vine in Greece was inextricably tied up with population growth in exactly the same way in which it is argued in this book that the spread of olive cultivation was connected with demographic processes in Greece and elsewhere in the Mediterranean in the first half of the first millennium BC. The only difference between them was that the currant vine was a cash crop, while the olive in antiquity was more of a subsistence crop. The currant boom did not last in Greece because eventually the French vineyards were restocked with European vines grafted onto American root-stocks which are less susceptible to Phylloxera than the European species, the French imposed hefty customs duties on Greek currants, and Phylloxera has subsequently spread to

Greece too. However, it has only spread slowly in Greece, apparently being less suited to the environment there. Again the currant vine was only a temporary solution to the problems raised by population growth, which were exacerbated in the 1920s by the large numbers of refugees from Turkey who arrived in Greece.[44]

The fourth major response of the Greeks was large-scale emigration, first to the rapidly growing conurbation of Athens, the main recipient of grain imports, and secondly to other countries, especially the United States, as the first three responses had not prevented population growth and a point was reached where people had no alternative. There were no significant developments in agricultural technology in Greece in the nineteenth century which could have increased the productivity of the basic subsistence crops. It is argued here that all of the four responses mentioned above, shortening of the food chain by cutting out one trophic level (herbivorous animals), increasing area under cultivation, introduction of new crops, and emigration also occurred in ancient Greece, and that significant technological innovation did not occur in ancient Greece any more than it did in Greece in the last century, strengthening the analogy between the two situations. Of course there were differences between them as well which will be discussed later on.

If the population of ancient Greece had been trapped in that country, then eventually a Malthusian subsistence crisis of the kind studied by Meuvret in particular among the French Annalistes, might have ensued. The size of the ecological niche was fixed and further reproduction could not have pushed population density beyond K *permanently*. From ancient Egypt there are records of episodes of mass starvation. Presumably peasants in the Nile valley, with desert on either side, had nowhere to go if the Nile flood was either too high or too low, reducing agricultural production and causing famine. Similarly in ancien régime France and Japan, mentioned above, the relative stability of population size may have been connected with the fact that the bulk of the population had nowhere to go, however bad times were. As Finerty (1980) showed, it may be demonstrated mathematically that the availability of routes for emigration from a densely populated region may create fluctuations and a population cycle in that region.

This is probably the best explanation for the rapid increases and decreases of field mouse populations in cereal fields in antiquity (see Chapter I above). A cereal field offers a huge store of attractive food at harvest time for mice, which permits massive population growth, but only for a limited time. During the rest of the year, especially the summer when the bare soil is parched by the sun and the winter when it may be very wet, an arable field is not a good place for mice to survive, let alone multiply. As a result they require permanent homes in other environments which allow survival all the year round, but happen to be unfavourable to massive population growth, and the sharp population fluctuations are caused by periodic short-lived migrations to cereal fields at harvest-time.

In both antiquity and the last century, the human inhabitants of Greece, never far from the coast, always had emigration as an option. This is why very little is heard about starvation as a cause of death in ancient Greece, in spite of the population pressure on the land revealed by the intensive archaeological surveys for the fourth century BC. More recent research by the French Annalistes has tended to emphasise that few people directly die from starvation, even in a subsistence crisis, and that disease is usually the proximate cause of death, although malnutrition increases susceptibility to certain diseases. Emigration may well save individuals, but it does not stabilise the population by bringing fertility into equilibrium with mortality and the size of the ecological niche.[45]

The situation in modern Greece was eventually stabilised by a combination of two more innovations of the twentieth century. First cereal productivity was sharply boosted by the advent of chemical fertilisers before the First World War, by the introduction of modern techniques of plant breeding from more developed countries after the First World War and finally in the 1960s by the introduction of the new wheat varieties of the 'Green Revolution' (see Chapter III below), making Greece once again a producer of cereal surpluses. However, all these developments, which were exogenous to Greece herself and obviously impossible in antiquity, might not have solved the problem of feeding the population in the long run if it had not been for the second major innovation, in the same way that it may be argued that the new crops of the first millennium BC did not alter individual well-being in the long run because the population simply expanded till it reached a new equilibrial population density, K.

Population growth in Greece in this century has been restrained by the spread of deliberate voluntary family limitation, principally by means of coitus interruptus and of abortion which have brought down the birth rate to below replacement levels. It is estimated that each married woman in Greater Athens in recent times has had nearly *four* abortions on average. If this is compared to the constant demands in Britain for further restrictions on the availability of abortion, it is clear that there are no absolute moral values in these matters, but only extreme cultural relativity, a conclusion which may also be drawn after the discussion of ancient Greek homosexuality in section 5 below. The simple logistic equation assumes the absence of voluntary family limitation, whose introduction in a human population should complicate the mathematics.[46]

This digression on modern Greece has served to show how in the nineteenth century the population rose to a plateau beyond which it could not expand any further, to consider the responses to increasing environmental resistance to population growth, to establish that carrying capacity is a useful concept in the specific context of the environment of Greece and to point out the similarities between ancient and nineteenth-century Greece. In the same way in antiquity a decreasing growth rate following the eighth-century spurt is indicated by the intensive archaeological surveys, until the peak level of population density was attained in the fourth century BC, interpreted here as the carrying capacity of the country following the spread of the new crops of the first millennium BC. We must move on now to the second concept of carrying capacity, Cc, and show that the results obtained using it are roughly equivalent to those using K in the case of ancient Greece. It was observed above in the case of nineteenth-century Greece that Jardé's estimate of Cc is supported by correlating changing population density, a fundamental component of the logistic equation, with the development of wheat imports.

Presented below are estimates of Cc for Attica. The area of Attica is taken as 2400 km², of which 15 per cent is assumed to have been cultivated with cereals each year, i.e. 360 km². Three possible average yields per unit area are used, namely 600, 500 and 400 kg/ha. The total production is assumed to be 75 per cent barley and 25 per cent wheat. The weight of barley is taken to be 64 kg/hl and wheat 77 kg/hl. One *medimnos*, the Greek dry measure of volume, is about 0.52 hl. Average consumption of 5 *medimnoi* per caput per annum is assumed. The penultimate line gives the population density which could be supported by the average yield in question. The last line gives the Attic harvest of 329/8 BC as a percentage of the total production calculated here for each of the three possible average yields. All these figures are discussed in Chapter III below, and are rounded here so as not to give an excessive appearance of accuracy:

Yield (kg/ha)	600	500	400
Total production (kg/ha)	21.6×10^6	18×10^6	14.4×10^6
Wt. of barley (kg)	16.2×10^6	13.5×10^6	10.8×10^6
Wt. of wheat (kg)	5.4×10^6	4.5×10^6	3.6×10^6
Volume of barley (hl)	2.5×10^5	2.1×10^5	1.7×10^5
Volume of wheat (hl)	7.0×10^4	5.8×10^4	4.7×10^4
Volume of barley (*med.*)	4.8×10^5	4.1×10^5	3.3×10^5
Volume of wheat (*med.*)	1.4×10^5	1.1×10^5	9.1×10^4
Total volume (*med.*)	6.2×10^5	5.2×10^5	4.2×10^5
Number of people fed	124,000	104,000	84,000
Pop. density (people/km²)	52	43	35
329/8 production	59%	70%	88%

No allowance has been made for fodder crops, as animals probably were pastured mainly on fallow land and in the hills and were not well nourished at the best of times (see Chapter III.4 below). Similarly no explicit deduction is made in the table above for cereal losses from: (1) pests, both in the field and in storage from stored products insects (see

Chapter I above); (2) plant diseases (see section 7 below); (3) losses during milling. However, such losses may be assumed to be accounted for by low yield estimates. Nevertheless such causes of losses should not be underestimated. Generally barley produced higher yields in the past than wheat, but whole barley before processing is less nutritious than whole naked wheat. The table above skims over all these questions, to which we shall return later on.

The question of how the estimates in the table above compare with estimates made by other scholars deserves attention. L. Gallo accepted Jardé's estimate of the proportion of Attica that was cultivated in antiquity, but thought that Jardé's cereal yields were too high. It may be agreed that Jardé's estimated yields are on the high side (Chapter III.12 below). However modern Greek data leave no room for doubt that Jardé seriously underestimated the proportion of the land of Greece that may be farmed (Chapter III.2 below). This becomes more and more important the lower the estimates are on the scale of possibilities (also relevant to cereal yields). For example, increasing the evaluation of the cultivated area of Attica from Jardé's 10 per cent to the 15 per cent suggested above increases the size of the population that may be sustained by fully 50 per cent, but increasing the size of the cultivated area from, say, 40 per cent to 45 per cent would only increase the potential population by about 11 per cent. I am in wholehearted sympathy with the re-evaluation of the cultivable area of Attica by Garnsey (1988), raising Jardé's estimate. It is suggested here that we should think in terms of a rather low yield extracted from a larger area than Jardé allowed for. The table above shows that even with low yields per unit area the Cc of ancient Attica might have been higher than Jardé judged possible.[47]

In any case, the congruence of these estimates of possible population density in the fourth century BC with the population densities attained in modern Greece towards the end of the nineteenth century AD cannot be overemphasised. In the latter case the population density was stabilising as a consequence of increasing environmental resistance to population growth after a period of very rapid increase (it had more than doubled in just over forty years). In an animal population such a process – the unfolding of a population history which might be summarised in the logistic equation – would be marked by decreasing fertility and increasing mortality until the two reach equilibrium. In the human population in question it was marked, eventually, by decreasing fertility, as was noted above, but emigration, which is a more rapid response than changes in fertility in any case, took the place of decreases in mortality, because humans can change their niches and other species of animal cannot. This is a fundamental adjustment which has to be made to make the concept of K relevant to human populations like those of Greece. The intensive archaeological surveys suggest that after a period of extremely rapid population growth in the eighth century BC, which may be compared in scale, rate and duration to that of the mid-nineteenth century AD, the rate of increase tapered off afterwards as environmental resistance to the growing population increased, just as it did in Greece in the second half of the last century, until a peak population density was reached in the fourth century BC. One of the major theses of this book is that the meaning of that peak is that it signified K as far as human populations in ancient Greece were concerned, after the spread of the new crops of the first millennium BC. This line of argument is applicable to all the regions of Greece that have been surveyed so far, and it is probable that it is valid for the whole of the country.

The concept of K is very well grounded in modern ecological theory. Nevertheless there are scholars outside the biological sciences who deny the validity of the concept of carrying capacity in the case of human societies. In particular there is the school of thought in land economy inspired by the work of Ester Boserup. She postulated that agrarian societies tend to respond to population pressure, which she regarded as an independent variable, by means of technological innovations, by which she meant in particular reductions in the length of the fallow period. She maintained that such developments are always accompanied by higher labour inputs and so would never be pursued willingly unless there was no alternative. Like any other theory, the attempt should be made to falsify it by means of comparison with relevant empirical evidence. In the case of Greece, it fails this test. Periods of even very rapid population growth in Greek history have never been accompanied by significant *endogenous* developments in agricultural technology, neither in the last century nor in antiquity. She also made the mistake mentioned in section 1 above of assuming steady growth in population, whereas in reality populations fluctuate up and down. Furthermore it may be argued that Boserup has superimposed illegitimately in a developmental framework a series of quite independent agricultural systems which in reality are generally tied to particular ecosystems and cannot be transferred at will by humans to different environments.[48]

Boserup's first stage in this developmental framework is the long-fallow shifting cultivation characteristic of tropical regions. This system is essential in tropical regions because tropical soils contain very low reservoirs of organic matter and essential plant nutrients and require periods measured in decades to regenerate that small reservoir after it has been exhausted by two or three crops. Shifting cultivation is very inefficient as a means of transforming the biomass of tropical rain forest into a form in which it may be consumed by man. The proportion of the available land that can be cultivated is very small. This keeps human population density at a very low level, restricting the development of complex stratified societies, even though the yield may be high relative to the labour input. The shortage of nitrogen in tropical soils forces concentration on a root crop such as cassava whose protein content is very low, leading to malnutrition in the consumers. In addition, in tropical Africa the cattle used to pull the ploughs for European short-fallow farming are very vulnerable to the disease trypanosomiasis. Thus it is not surprising that the inhabitants of tropical sub-Saharan Africa took no interest in the short-fallow plough agriculture characteristic of Europe in pre-modern times. It was impossible there regardless of the population pressure.

Boserup suggested that long-fallow shifting cultivation was also characteristic of the earliest European agriculture in the Neolithic, but this idea is increasingly and correctly being rejected by European prehistorians. Leaving land fallow for decades in Europe is simply unnecessary because differences in the environment make it possible for nitrogen-fixing bacteria to accumulate larger reservoirs of nitrogen in European soils and at a very much faster rate than in tropical soils. Therefore it has always been possible to cultivate a much larger proportion of European lands in the form of *permanent* farms under a short-fallow system. Prehistorians now emphasise the cultivation of permanent farms by hand with the hoe in the European Neolithic. In this context the research of Paul Halstead on Neolithic Greece merits attention.[49]

Hoe cultivation of permanent farms requires a high labour input. Moreover the area of land which can be cultivated in this way by one man is small. Horticultural systems may or may not be highly productive, depending on the crops grown, the availability of fertilisers, and other considerations. On balance the economic productivity per unit area of the farming system of Neolithic Europe was probably low, although it could still have sustained a higher population density than African shifting cultivation because a larger proportion of the available land could be farmed at any one time. The smallness of the area that could be cultivated per man probably entailed concentration on the most productive crops available. This may be one reason for the importance of emmer amongst the wheats and barley in early European agriculture. The development of plough agriculture in Europe made it possible for one man to cultivate a much larger area of land, raising economic productivity and total production per labourer (although probably lowering productivity per unit area). At the very same time, the adoption of the plough sharply *reduced* the labour input required per unit area. Undoubtedly this was the reason for the success of the plough in Europe.

Contrary to Boserup, the shift from the hoe to the plough in Europe was accompanied by a reduction in labour inputs, and it probably did not make much difference to the length of fallow periods. The spread of the plough transformed European agriculture. Because of this, I do not believe that the arguments developed successfully by Halstead for Neolithic Greece are applicable to Greece in the first millennium BC Chirassi (1968) attempted to trace a number of Greek myths, involving plants whose names are etymologically non-Greek and so presumably were adopted by the Greeks from the indigenous pre-Greek inhabitants of the country, back to a prehistoric farming system based on horticulture which preceded classical agriculture based on the plough. In a sense this provides the ideology that corresponds to Halstead's archaeology. The plough is first attested in Greece *c.* 2000 BC in the form of a sign in the Minoan hieroglyphic script, although there is archaeological evidence for its use in central Europe much earlier.

The lower labour inputs required for plough farming meant that it was always the *preferred* option in the classical period, explaining the attitude of Hesiod. However, it was always possible that a smallholding might be so small that its owner could not afford to maintain animals to pull the plough, forcing him to use the hoe instead. (Or, on steep Greek hillsides, the gradient and contours of the land alone might exclude the plough.) Pliny described a garden at Rome as a poor man's farm. The low labour inputs required for plough farming go a long way towards explaining the spatial and sexual division of labour in ancient Greece typified in Xenophon's *Oikonomikos*. The labour of women was not required in the field for most of the year, except especially perhaps at harvest-time, permitting them to stay (or be confined, depending on one's point of view) indoors and concentrate on housework, especially the labour-intensive activity of food preparation. However, on smallholdings where animals could not be maintained and the hoe had to be used, much more labour outdoors from women would probably have been needed, and it is physically easier for women to use a hoe than a plough anyway. So it was that women of the lower classes could not be confined entirely indoors by magistrates like the *gunaikonomoi*, as Aristotle noted with regret.[50]

Reviewing briefly the other stages of Boserup's 'continuum' of land-use patterns, irrigation agriculture of the type required for Oriental wet-rice cultivation requires swampy areas, or at least extremely heavy rainfall collected by irrigation works, and was not practicable in most of pre-industrial Europe. Annual cropping and still more so multicropping in rainfed-farming regions in Europe generally depend on large inputs of chemical fertilisers and were not feasible in most areas before the development of the modern chemical industry, certainly in Greece (see Chapter III.12 below). Moreover Boserup did not consider the importance of arboriculture in Mediterranean agriculture from classical times onwards, providing perennial crops which circumvent the whole question of fallow periods. Each of her stages of land-use is inseparably tied to a distinctive ecosystem. They do not constitute a genuine developmental scheme in which any stage could develop into any other in any geographical region depending on changing population density treated as an independent variable.

However her data on the maximum population density associated with each stage are still of interest, so long as it is realised that they are in reality different values of K for human populations in different ecosystems which cannot be transformed into each other. She found that about 60 people/km^2 is the maximum population density associated with the short-fallow plough agriculture characteristic of pre-industrial Europe (including countries on average more fertile than Greece). In that context the possible population densities suggested for Attica above, albeit low by modern standards, are indicative of a crowded land. The eparchy of Attica, excluding Greater Athens, had a population density of 60 people/km^2 in 1961. Finally, we should recall that, as far as ecologists are concerned, K is an attribute of a population, not of a physical environment, and populations are transient structures. Ecologists calculate K empirically at a particular point in time, or over a short temporal period, and do not pretend that generalisations can be made about it covering extended temporal periods, because populations and environments are not stable in the long run. This sidesteps the issue raised by Boserup about long-term progress making it impossible to ascertain sustainable population density in absolute terms. Of course K was higher after the spread of the olive and vine and the other new crops of the first millennium BC than it had been beforehand, but that does not invalidate the concept. K is subject to natural selection which tends to increase it.[51]

The discussion so far has sought to elucidate the significance of the peak in settlement density revealed by the intensive archaeological surveys for Greece in the fourth century BC. I hope that it is clear to the reader now why the fourth century BC was termed the K period of ancient Greek history in section 1 above. One important fixed point has been set up in our reconstruction of demographic history in the first millennium BC. It is now time to return to the Dark Ages to explain the other key point in the model, the r period in the eighth century BC. After the catastrophes at the end of the Mycenaean civilisation, Greece was very thinly populated in the period *c.* 1200-800 BC. This low point in Greek demographic history was not fortuitous or the outcome of random processes, any more than the peak in the fourth century was.

To anticipate sections 5 & 6 below, it will be argued that the low population density of the Dark Ages was the consequence of a type of socio-political organisation, an age class system, which acted in such a way as to restrain human reproduction very directly. Over most of Greece the beginning of the process of the transformation of these age class systems into the *poleis* of the classical period was accompanied by the breakdown of the socio-political controls on human fertility inherent in these systems. This *explains why* the phase of extremely rapid population growth in the eighth century BC to which Anthony Snodgrass has rightly drawn attention occurred.[52] The question of why most of the age class systems of Dark Age Greece broke down into an attenuated form in the eighth century BC will be tackled more fully in Chapter IV below. Suffice it to say here that the prime role may be ascribed to agricultural intensification caused by the spread of the new crops discussed in Chapter I above. This facilitated higher levels of production and larger surpluses and so made possible increasing differentiation of the population into rich and poor on the basis of wealth. In turn this created the possibility of alternative principles of social stratification and political organisation which gradually undermined the traditional form of solidarity of the Dark Age age class systems. Thucydides in his *Archaiologia* said that the early Greeks did not plant fruit trees. Great significance should be attached to this statement, which is largely supported by palaeobotanical and palynological evidence, as far as mainland Greece is concerned.[53]

It is an interesting question where the idea came from. There was a period of intense Oriental influence on the Greek world, marked especially by the so called 'Orientalising' style of Greek pottery and earlier by the adoption of the alphabet from the Levant by the Greeks, at a date which is the subject of current controversy. Now the Levant was undoubtedly one of the most important centres of early farming and the place where the olive tree, for example, was first domesticated. It is possible that the classical Greek interest in arboriculture, which they passed on to the Romans, was another legacy of this period of Oriental influence. There is no direct evidence that may be cited in support of this idea, but it is suggested here that it is the most plausible answer to the question. After the Persian Wars the Greeks, except for Herodotos, became oblivious of the Oriental influences on their early development, influences which perhaps ultimately owed their origin to links between the Aegean and the Levant created in the migration period at the end of the Mycenaean civilisation.

Leaving aside the topic of social transformations in the eighth century BC for further consideration later on, let us return to the question of population growth in that period. It will be clear from what has been said already that the mechanism for initiating rapid population growth in the eighth century BC was quite different from the causal factors in the nineteenth century AD. In the latter case what happened quite simply was that the Greeks, who had retreated into the highlands during the last century of Ottoman rule, recovered the lowlands – besides of course their freedom – in the War of Independence. That effectively gave them new territories which were more productive than the highlands, and the Greek population expanded until the productive capacity of the lowlands was under full exploitation, at which point population growth ceased, at a new and higher value of K, as we have seen already. However, that does not mean that the two episodes of population growth are not closely comparable as regards scale, rate and duration of growth. They occurred in broadly the same physical environment in the context of a predominantly farming population using primitive agricultural technology and relying on the same major crops, cereals, olives and vines. Consequently similarities are only to be expected, and indeed the two episodes of rapid growth look very similar. At this point it is necessary to clear away an unfortunate misconception which has surfaced in classical scholarship.

This misconception is the belief that pre-modern human populations were incapable of achieving high intrinsic rates of natural increase. In fact it has been accepted by scientists from Charles Darwin onwards that all individuals of all known species of living organisms are led by natural selection to attempt to maximise evolutionary fitness and *Homo sapiens* is no different from any of the others in this respect. Furthermore well documented cases of rapid human population growth before the development of modern medicine are well known to demographers. Greece in the last century is indeed such a case, but there are others as well. In the United States the rate of natural increase of the *white* population never dropped below 2 per cent per annum averaged out over a decade during the decades from 1800 to 1860, after taking account of immigration from Europe and elsewhere. In the decade 1800-1810 it averaged 2.92 per cent per annum, the highest point reached in those six decades, and comparable to many Third World countries today. The demographic history of French Canada was very similar, with crude birth rates of 60/1,000 being attested, the highest crude birth rate ever recorded. On the basis of the Canadian evidence, Henry & Vincent (1947) concluded that Malthus and Darwin were right to maintain that a human population is capable of doubling in about twenty-five years.

The comparison with the totally static population at home in France proves that the fact that the French who stayed at home did not increase their population size is in no way whatsoever a reflection on their biological capabilities. It is of course a reflection on their environment, i.e. they occupied an ecological niche of a fixed size which was already filled. All this occurred before the development of penicillin or antiseptics or any other product of modern medicine. It is widely agreed by scholars that no significant role may be attributed to modern medicine in explaining population growth in the early modern period. *Homo sapiens* has not changed his characteristics as a biological species significantly in recent millennia, and there is no reason for supposing that man was incapable of doing two thousand years ago anything that was within his biological capabilities two hundred years ago. It has been argued that even hunter-gatherers expanded very rapidly, to colonise the whole of the Americas, when man first reached those continents, and studies of the colonisation of small islands in modern times have also revealed rates of natural increase comparable to those achieved in North America in the last couple of centuries.[54]

Thus there is no good argument for rejecting on a priori grounds the thesis of Snodgrass that the population of Attica expanded very rapidly in the eighth century BC, or dismissing the possibility that the expansion of the Athenian population during the *Pentêkontaëtia* was again another phase of substantial population growth. These episodes of rapid growth were both of short duration, about fifty years or so, but that again is not a good reason for denying their reality. What we are considering in the eighth century is a situation in which the population was able to expand into a vacuum, or at least land that was very thinly populated. Archaeological evidence indicates that much of Attica was uninhabited in the period *c.* 1100-950 BC. The small population that remained after the Mycenaean collapse was concentrated in Athens, presumably exploiting the surrounding plain, and a handful of other small settlements. There was virgin land available, and the breakdown of social controls on fertility permitted the Athenian population to expand rapidly until that land was fully occupied. In fact this is another example of an ecological invasion of a new environment, of the kind discussed in Chapter I above. The phases of fast exponential growth at the beginning of such invasions, however small the initial invading population and however large the territory to be occupied, always tend to be of short duration for the elementary reason that populations growing at a geometrical rate of increase grow so rapidly that any territory, no matter how large, is bound to be overrun in a short period of time, after which growth must taper off and eventually cease, at the value of K empirically attained.

The best illustration of this comes from the Americas after Columbus. A few horses introduced by the early settlers escaped into the wild. They had the whole of the Great Plains of the USA (which expanded as European colonists started to chop down the post-glacial forests) and the pampas of Argentina to occupy, and no predators or natural enemies to hold them up. An extremely high rate of natural increase was attained. Within fifty years there were herds of literally millions of wild horses in the Americas. By that time, the Americas were already crowded with wild horses, and increasing intraspecific competition for food made further population growth more and more difficult. The European settlers of the time noted that the average age of first reproduction of a mare increased and the interval between births also increased. Classical authors also noted that the rate of reproduction and vitality of animal populations depended on the richness of the pastures available. Similarly, the very rapid human population growth in the USA and Canada mentioned above is to be explained in exactly the same way. It was expanding into what was effectively a vacuum as far as a farming population was concerned (Indian hunter-gatherers had a low population density) – the great rush to the West.[55]

Snodgrass argued that the Attic population grew by 4 per cent per annum during a sixty-year period, corresponding basically to Late Geometric II, basing his estimate on numbers of graves. This estimate may be somewhat on the high side. However, there is no good a priori argument for supposing that the Athenian population was physically incapable of achieving rates of natural increase of the order of 2-3 per cent per annum during that period. There is one aspect of this process of

expansion which deserves particular emphasis because of its historical
singularity and because it serves to stress the point that what is in
question is an invasion of a vacuum or quasi-vacuum.

The growth of the Athenian population took the form of the expansion
of an 'urban' population outwards into the surrounding countryside,
which helps to explain the political unity of classical Attica. It is abusing
the word 'urban' to speak of urban centres in Greece in the eighth century
BC. After all Athens merely consisted of a handful of villages, or still
better, hamlets, which in the course of the archaic period gradually
coalesced into the town now called Athens and were then granted
political status, as the urban demes, by Kleisthenes in 508/7 BC. The
pattern of development of Corinth and other classical towns was similar,
while those regions described by Aristotle as *ethnê* continued to be
organised in terms of villages (*kata kômas*) even in the classical period.
However, the process of the growth of the populations of nucleated
settlements and their expansion outwards to occupy the surrounding
countryside is still extraordinary because it is without parallel in those
later periods of European history which have been studied in detail by
historical demographers. The cities of early modern Europe all depended
on immigration from more scattered but healthier rural populations not
only to grow but also to maintain themselves, for their very existence.
Urban centres in the past were intrinsically unhealthy and offered a
favourable environment for density-dependent diseases (see section 7
below). This was also true of the later stages of antiquity.[56]

Finley drew attention to the colossal growth of the population of
Hellenistic Alexandria. In this case, the required rate of natural increase
does exceed the biological capabilities of *Homo sapiens* by a long way, and
there is no doubt that immigration was the main factor responsible for
the growth of Alexandria. The population of Athens, by way of
comparison, did increase about 45 times in the period *c.* 1800-1920 AD,
but this was largely due to immigration, even though the population of
Greece as a whole did increase rapidly during the same period. One
ancient source provides the key to understanding the situation in
Alexandria. The *Letter of Aristeas to Philokrates* speaks of masses of
peasants migrating from the *chôra* to Alexandria and indicates that the
Ptolemies tried, evidently unsuccessfully, to prevent it, because it was
leading to a drop in agricultural production and so to a diminution in the
Ptolemies' tax revenues, as the consequence of the drop in the rural
labour force. A papyrus shows that the emperor Caracalla also tried to
prevent migration to Alexandria during the Roman empire.

The letter ought to be the classic text on the 'consumer city' of
antiquity. It shows that there were significant structural constraints on
economic development, rooted in low agricultural productivity, besides
the cultural constraints emphasised by Finley, even in Egypt which was
famed for fertility. Alexandria was possible because of the Nile, along

which grain could be transported to the overgrown city from the entire length of the valley. However, Finley was wrong to say that Alexandria was unique. There was another instructive example in antiquity, namely Rome. The fact that slaves and freedmen formed such a large proportion of the population of imperial Rome, as funerary inscriptions suggest, indicates that immigration, including the forced importation of slaves, was the principal means by which the urban population was maintained and grew, as in Alexandria. The social composition of the *plebs urbana*, reviled in Juvenal's *Satires*, was largely the consequence of demographic factors, alongside the Roman custom of placing new citizens from servile backgrounds in the four urban tribes.[57]

If we return to Athens now, it is clear that the increase of the Athenian population in the first half of the first millennium BC and the increase of the populations of Rome and Alexandria in the second half of the first millennium BC involved fundamentally different models of what Vries (1984) termed 'demographic urbanisation'. The Athenian population expanded from a small nucleus into surrounding territory that was largely empty, until the available cultivatable land was occupied. Alexandria and Rome, in contrast, became very large cities because of immigration from rural areas. In the first case, increase of the 'urban' population depended on the availability of a vacuum in the surrounding countryside. In the second case it depended on the continued growth of an already existing rural population.

Because the rate of growth of Rome and Alexandria depended on the rural population, the increase of these urban populations did not entail any corresponding expansion of the urban economy. This is why, when scholars try to collect evidence for urban economic activity and for goods produced by the populations of Rome and Alexandria, a blank inevitably is drawn, leading to the concept of the 'consumer city'. Instead, if the city of Rome for example can be said to have had a function in the Roman empire, it can only have been the following: people migrated there, failed to reproduce themselves and died young. In effect Rome acted as what animal ecologists term an (internal) 'population sink', absorbing and disposing, very efficiently it might be added, of excess population in the countryside and in this way contributing to the stability of the Roman empire. In the same way the mere existence of London reduced the rate of increase of the English population as a whole in the early modern period. The demography of Athens, then, was fundamentally different from that of Rome, and indeed from all the cities of early modern Europe. It must be stressed yet again that it is wholly illegitimate to generalise across the whole ancient world, as classical scholars are in the habit of doing.

Just to emphasise once again the reproductive capacity of the human species in favourable circumstances, A.J. Coale, an eminent demographer, by combining the age pattern of co-habitation of the inhabitants of the Cocos Islands with the age-specific fertility rates of the Hutterites, the two fastest-growing modern human populations known to demographers, and relating the results to model life tables, has shown that crude birth rates of 63/1,000 with a life expectancy at birth (e^0) of 20 and 53/1,000 with an e^0 of 53 are possible, and he reckons that still higher rates are conceivable. The differences in fertility induced by restricting marriage (see sections 5 & 6 below on this in ancient Greece) and their potential effects on population growth in the context of similar levels of e^0 have been well illustrated by another eminent demographer, N. Keyfitz. He showed that modern Madagascar had in 1966 a crude birth rate of 46/1,000 and a crude death rate of 25/1,000 (rounding the numbers), a population growth rate of about 2 per cent per annum. e^0 was 37 for males and 38 for females, which was similar to its values in Sweden *c.* 1800 AD. However, because Sweden's demographic system forced a late age of marriage on both sexes, the Swedish population only had a crude birth rate of 31/1,000, yielding a rate of natural increase of only about 0.5 per cent per annum.

After the breakdown of social controls on fertility (see section 5 below), there was no barrier to rapid population growth to fill the largely empty Attic countryside from Athens, or the southern Argolid from the Argos plain, to give another example. Taking account of the conclusions of these demographers, it is quite possible that at the start of the Late Geometric II period the Athenian population could have exhibited for a few years a crude death rate of *c.* 25-30/1,000, a crude birth rate of *c.* 55-60/1,000, combined with a life expectancy at birth of 35-40, yielding a rate of natural increase of about 3 per cent per annum and showing that the thesis of Snodgrass is perfectly plausible.[58]

It is worth listing at this stage the factors responsible for population growth in Attica and elsewhere in Greece in the eighth century BC. Firstly, there was the possibility of expansion into a quasi-vacuum, an ecological invasion of a new environment. Secondly, there was the breakdown of the social restrictions on fertility imposed by the age class societies of the Dark Ages (section 5 and Chapter IV below). Thirdly, the initially very low population density meant that there was low mortality from those diseases which are density-dependent (section 7 below.) Fourthly, the new crops of the first millennium BC raised the carrying capacity of the land (Chapter I above and Chapter III.3 below). Fifthly, those new crops also helped to improve the nutritional status and health of the population, which was also conducive to population growth (section 7 below). Adding all this up, it would indeed be surprising if the population of Greece in the eighth century BC had *not* increased very substantially. Leaving aside those causal factors which have not yet been examined exhaustively for treatment in later parts of this book, it is time to run through again the evidence provided by the intensive archaeological surveys to put some flesh on the bones of the description of the data given earlier on.

In the period *c.* 950 – *c.* 800 BC the archaeological evidence indicates slow population growth starting from an extremely low population density. The 'Ionian migration', the colonisation of the Aegean coast of Turkey, was probably the result of this earliest phase of growth.[59] In the eighth century BC the surveys and the other available archaeological evidence indicate that the rate of natural increase reached a peak. In the seventh century BC, a poorly documented period, the rate of increase across Greece as a whole decreased sharply, but nevertheless growth did continue because the surveys generally indicate that the peak settlement density was not reached until the fourth century BC. Although it is impossible to quantify this picture accurately, it still bears a striking qualitative resemblance to the sigmoid-shaped curve found in all textbooks on ecology in discussions of the logistic equation in its integral form, in which the rate of natural increase reaches its highest levels at intermediate population densities and then slows down and ceases at K. The hypothesis of this book is that the demographic history of most parts of Greece from the Dark Ages to the fourth-century peak may be described by the logistic equation as a reasonable approximation. (Sparta and Crete are excluded from this generalisation because they retained the socio-political controls on fertility which broke down elsewhere in Greece in the eighth century BC, and this violates an assumption required for the logistic equation – see sections 4 & 5 below.)

Athens did not participate in the external colonisation of the eighth century BC because she was colonising her own hinterland, which was large by the standards of Greek *poleis*. The same was true of Argos, while Sparta solved her problems by conquering the more fertile territory of Messenia. Other Greek *poleis* ran out of land more rapidly and turned to colonisation to solve their problems, because after the breakdown of socio-political restrictions on fertility a high birth rate continued even when they had reached the environmental carrying capacity of their territory, Cc. In section 4 below it will be argued that Greek populations from the Dark Ages through to the fourth-century peak possessed what is termed by demographers a 'natural fertility' regime, i.e. voluntary family limitation by couples was not practised to any great extent. A few observations on Greek colonisation are in order here.

First, its scale can hardly be overemphasised, covering the coasts of Sicily and southern Italy in the eighth century BC and then adding the south coast of France and the north-eastern corner of Spain, Cyrenaica and the shores of the Black Sea in the seventh and sixth centuries. Secondly, it is admitted that the initial colonising expeditions were often very small, as in the case of Cyrene. Nevertheless individuals probably followed the original expeditions. Certainly in the fifth and fourth centuries BC for which there is more evidence individual migration occurred on a very substantial scale. Accordingly it is likely that the demographic impact of the eighth-century colonies as a whole had a very considerable impact on removing surplus population from Greece, albeit only temporarily because of the lack of restrictions on fertility. Thirdly, the fact that such small expeditions were so frequently successful alone suggests that the target areas were themselves very thinly populated, i.e. they were quasi-vacuums. Accordingly the colonists were able to manifest the same kind of population growth in their new habitats that their relatives had been achieving back home in Greece, until they reached values of K empirically attainable in their new environments.

Fourthly, there is the interesting question of why Greek colonists always clung to the coast and never penetrated far inland. It has long been a topic of controversy amongst ancient historians as to whether they were primarily interested in obtaining land for farming or in acquiring good locations for carrying on sea-borne trade. The answer to this question becomes clear when it is realised that the Greeks were not merely exporting human beings. They also took with them the crops with which they were familiar. In other words they were not merely founding new colonies, but creating new ecosystems modelled as closely as possible on those at home. In the eighth century BC the olive tree, whose natural habitat was in coastal semi-arid regions, was becoming a fundamental component of the Greek crop complex. This explains why Greek colonisation in the Mediterranean was confined to the coast. The colonists, who often chose sites which did not have good harbours (e.g. Khalkedon in preference to Byzantion, or Selinus in Sicily), were indeed primarily interested in acquiring land for growing crops, crops which were suited to coastal regions.[60]

An ancient historian, J.L. Myres, wrote an article of some interest many years ago about population fluctuations in antiquity, including the demographic background to archaic Greek colonisation, which is little known even to classical scholars, or at least rarely cited. Shortly afterwards, he was criticised by Carr-Saunders, author of an influential early work on historical and anthropological demography, for attributing the colonisation of the archaic period to the fact that 'population had overtaken the means of subsistence ... The idea of population catching up the means of subsistence and bringing about a crisis followed by migration is the product of an altogether unhistorical view of the matter.' In other words he sought to deny the reality of the population fluctuations and periods of rapid growth emphasised by Myres, alongside the present author. Carr-Saunders attempted to develop a theory that populations strive to control themselves by means of voluntary family limitation to achieve an optimum population density, contra Malthus, correlating population density and the productiveness of industry.

His book, although influential at the time, is now seen to be out-dated. First, much of the anthropological evidence he used is of dubious value. Secondly, he was writing just before Lotka & Volterra introduced the idea of population cycles and founded modern population biology, which has now been taken into a new dimension by research on deterministic chaos. Thirdly, he was writing a long time before Louis Henry, one of the founders of historical demography, discovered that many historical populations possessed 'natural fertility' regimes, i.e. there was little or no voluntary family limitation. Fourthly, and this is what requires the most emphasis here, he made an elementary conceptual error frequently made by scholars who are not experts in population biology, namely that of confusing regulation of *family* size with regulation of *population* size, i.e. treating them as synonyms.

The modern scientific position is that an individual of any species of living organism may engage in regulation to achieve an optimum *family* size for reproductive purposes to maximise evolutionary fitness. However, no individual of any species ever engages in regulation of population size, in accordance with the principle that natural selection always acts on the reproductive success ('fitness') of individuals, never on that of groups. This rules out the type of theory developed by Carr-Saunders, namely that individuals regulate their own families in order to achieve an optimum population density, and is the reason why his criticism of Myres is completely without justification. The reader should bear this in mind upon reaching the discussion of the Greek population as a natural fertility population in section 4 below.[61]

There are other features of the r period in the eighth century BC to which attention should be drawn. Even the subject matter of philology, the backbone of classics in the past, did not escape the influence of demographic processes. The disappearance of the scribes who used the Linear B syllabary in the Mycenaean palaces was one consequence of the population collapse and ensuing collapse of craft specialisation at the end of the Mycenaean period. In the Dark Ages the Greek language itself underwent radical change. Out of the proto-Doric and Mycenaean dialects, the only dialects of Greek which existed in the second millennium BC, there developed the assortment of dialects of the classical period which are familiar to classicists, including Arkadian, Cypriot, Attic, Ionic, North-west Greek and Aeolic. These developments have to be understood in the context of the disintegration of the cultural homogeneity of the Mycenaean civilisation, running parallel to the replacement of the cultural *koinê* of LHIIIB pottery by the heterogeneous LHIIIC styles. The collapse of the Mycenaean world was followed by independent linguistic innovations within very small isolated populations in the Dark Ages, which then grew and radiated outwards in the eighth century and came as a result in closer contact with each other, eventually leading to the disappearance of all the other dialects (bar the Lakonian version of Doric, which has lasted to the present day in the form of the Tsakonian dialect of modern Greek) in favour of the *koinê*, based on Attic, from the fourth century BC onwards. This process up to the fourth century BC may be compared to the situation in New Guinea in modern times, where rapid population growth has been accompanied by the development of between 700 and 1,000 'languages' – very many closely related – among the proliferation of tribes on that island. The history of the Greek language itself is a by-product of demographic history, in the period in question.

Archaeological evidence indicates that after the eighth century BC growth continued, but at a much slower rate. The decrease in the rate of natural increase is attested more directly by osteological evidence, which shows that the average age of death increased from the archaic period to the classical period. Demographically the fact that the age distribution pattern of the population was becoming older suggests that fertility was decreasing, in accordance with increasing environmental resistance to further population growth (see section 3 below). Population growth within a territory of fixed dimensions will be accompanied by a reduction in the area of land available per person. There is evidence from Third World countries today that this eventually leads to increased mortality and lower fertility among smallholders as they struggle to make ends meet. In Attica the increasing pressures on smallholders culminated in the crisis which was resolved, at least temporarily, by the reforms of Solon in the early sixth century BC. Many poor Athenians, who had been forced to take loans from richer neighbours and were subsequently unable to repay those loans, were forced to work for their creditors, who needed labour to work their own farms, and hand over five-sixths of the produce. In such circumstances it is not surprising that parents were forced to sell children whom they could not maintain, as Plutarch states. This passage should be noted both as evidence for the absence of voluntary family limitation in the sense of birth control and for the fact that infanticide is not mentioned, in connection with the discussion in section 4 below.[62]

Solon abolished the status of the *hektêmoroi* (see section 6 below) by means of the *seisachtheia*, the cancelling of existing debts and the prohibition for the future of loans contracted on the security of the human body. However this legal reform did not solve the underlying structural problems caused by population pressure within an increasingly crowded territory. The tyranny of Peisistratos, who was supported by the *diakrioi* or *huperakrioi*, 'men of the hills' or 'men beyond the hills' – probably farmers on marginal land – in the mid-sixth century BC indicates that agrarian discontent continued. It was in the same century that Athens began to take an interest in external colonisation, for the first time.[63]

By the late archaic period and the reforms of Kleisthenes *c.* 508 BC the Athenian citizen (adult male) population had probably grown to around 30,000, which was already a stock figure for the size of the citizen body by the early years of the fifth century BC. As Peter Garnsey has noted recently, there is *no* direct evidence, either literary or archaeological, for Athenian grain imports in the archaic period. In the absence of evidence to the contrary, it may be presumed that the Athenian population was not far removed from self-sufficiency as late as the early fifth century BC. Estimates of sustainable population density like those made earlier make the assumption of equal division of agricultural land. Of course, given marked heritable variability in human fertility and a system of partible inheritance of property, there were bound to be rich and poor, and so individuals in any given generation who were struggling to survive, even if the density of the population as a whole was roughly equivalent to the environmental carrying capacity, Cc (see section 6 below).[64]

There followed the Persian Wars and the acquisition of an empire by Athens after 480 BC. It is beyond the scope of this book to consider in detail the evidence for the size of the military forces fielded by Athens during the *Pentêkontaëtia*, 480-430 BC, as evidence for the size of the citizen population. Suffice it to say that there is no doubt that the Athenian citizen population had increased from 30,000 to at least 50,000 by *c.* 450 BC and perhaps as many as 60,000 by the start of the Peloponnesian War, a doubling in about fifty years or a rate of natural increase of about 1.4 per cent per annum. This only applies to the *adult* population. It implies that the population as a whole more than doubled because population growth affects infant and juvenile age groups more than it affects adult age groups. In recent years several Greek historians have asserted, on the basis of inappropriate parallels from early modern Europe which had a fundamentally different demographic system in any case, that only rather slow population growth (<1 per cent) was possible in human populations in the past. Consequently the expansion of the Athenian citizen body in the *Pentêkontaëtia* is sometimes now attributed to block grants of citizenship to aliens.

As far as grants of citizenship are concerned, complicated questions arise which can only be dealt with in a summary manner here. Space only permits me to assert that there is no evidence, and indeed no probability, that the Athenians ever devised a policy of systematically sharing the profits of empire with non-Athenians. Human nature has never been so altruistic. (The Romans, who did make extensive grants of their version of citizenship, had a quite different social structure from the Greeks – sections 5 & 6 below.) Nor is it certain that any of the few securely attested block grants of citizenship, such as those to the democrats on Samos and to the Plataians, which all occurred in exceptional circumstances, actually led to the permanent integration of substantial numbers of aliens into the Athenian citizen body.

As regards the possible rate of natural increase, the interpretation which invokes mass enfranchisements rests on a lack of understanding and knowledge of demography. The white populations of the United States and Canada, which originated from those very same European countries which are cited as 'evidence' for the impossibility of high intrinsic rates of natural increase in the past, increased at a phenomenal rate, comparable to that of many Third World countries today. This demonstrates that there is no a priori reason why the populations of European countries such as Britain which provided the nucleus of the white population of the USA could not themselves have increased at the same phenomenal rate, *if they had had spare land available into which they could expand*, i.e. if they had not faced a carrying capacity barrier to further population growth. This is the nub of the matter.[65]

During the *Pentêkontaëtia* the Athenians took over substantial chunks of land all over the Aegean from enemies and disaffected allies and sent colonies to cities that were already established on the shores of the Black Sea. Such places as Skyros, Potidaia, Aigina, Naxos, Andros, Melos, Brea, Khalkis, Eretria, Neapolis, Hestiaia, Skione, the Chersonese, Astakos, Amisos and Sinope were affected. The Athenians also sponsored Panhellenic enterprises such as the colonies of Amphipolis and Thurii. The consequence of the intense military activity was that the area of land available to the Athenians was no longer 2,400 km² (and the areas of the older cleruchies of Lemnos, Imbros and Salamis which were in Athenian hands before 480 BC), but a much larger territory. In addition it is clear that many Athenian citizens somehow exploited the fear of Athenian power to secure substantial landholdings for themselves in the Aegean outside the colonies listed above. Athenian landgrabbing clearly so alienated the other Greeks that when the Athenians in the fourth century BC tried to reconstitute their empire as a league of free states, the 'Second Athenian League' under their leadership, they were forced to give an undertaking that no Athenian citizen would be allowed to obtain ownership of land in any of the allied states by purchase or by mortgage or by any other means. There is no need to look any further to explain the population growth of the *Pentêkontaëtia*. The Athenian population simply behaved in the same way that any population of any species of living organism under a natural fertility regime (see section 4 below) would be expected to behave in similar circumstances, as the white settlers of the USA did, and as the population of Greece itself did in the last century. It increased to occupy the new lands which had become available.

The mortality rate of the epidemic of 430 BC relative to the whole population was about 25-35 per cent according to Thucydides. As it is certain that a substantial proportion of the population was not infected (there was a second epidemic in 427 BC), the mortality rate amongst those who actually contracted the disease was substantially higher. Yet Thucydides also indicates that the Athenian population had recovered by the time of the Syracusan expedition fifteen years later, continuing the growth during the *Pentêkontaëtia*. It is easy to calculate that such a recovery, i.e. a population losing about a quarter of its members suddenly and recouping the losses in just fifteen years, requires an annual growth rate of about 2 per cent per annum (a view which will be significantly refined in section 7 below). The fact that rates of natural increase of the order of *c.* 2 per cent per annum were attainable at a time when Attica was densely populated, even after the ravages of the epidemic, strongly suggests that in the Dark Ages, when much of Greece was virtually uninhabited, Greek populations should have been capable of still higher rates of natural increase, because in the logistic equation the growth rate is inversely proportional to the population density.[66]

The Athenian population of the *Pentêkontaëtia* increased to fill the additional lands which the Athenians had laid their hands on, one way or another, all around the Aegean. The *hypothesis* to speech VIII of Demosthenes, by Libanios, tells us quite explicitly that the Athenians used their cleruchies to turn poor thetes into hoplites. It is wrong to assume that all those Athenian hoplites who were still resident in Attica actually owed their hoplite status to land which they possessed in Attica. Undoubtedly there were many Athenians like the Eutheros who was interrogated by Sokrates. It is not necessary to invoke colossal grain imports from areas which were not 'owned', or at least possessed, and exploited directly by Athenian citizens in order to explain how the citizen population was fed in the *Pentêkontaëtia*. Peter Garnsey pointed out recently that there is *no* explicit evidence for *regular* grain imports to Athens during that period, barring exceptional events like the gift from Psammetichos in Egypt. Some scholars, such as M. Hansen, still argue that the population of classical Attica largely depended on grain imports for its survival.

It must be stressed that it was the perception of the ancient Greeks themselves that *c.* 430 BC grain produced in Attica itself was a very important contribution to the total volume of cereals consumed by the inhabitants of Attica annually at about that time. Two quite separate illustrations of this point may be given. At the beginning of the Peloponnesian War many Greeks had reckoned that the Spartan strategy of invading Attica to disrupt agricultural operations there would bring the Athenians to their knees in one, two or three years. The fact that they turned out to be wrong does not indicate that Attica was fundamentally different from the rest of Greece. It merely shows that they had not considered the possibility, which the 'Old Oligarch' ruefully acknowledged, that the Athenians would be able to use their seapower to bring in massive grain imports from the Black Sea and elsewhere to make up for lost agricultural production in Attica. This strategy was probably put into effect *for the first time* during the Peloponnesian War, perhaps not until the Spartan occupation of Dekeleia in 413 BC on a large scale, if V. Hanson (1981) is right to minimise the damage caused by the earlier Spartan incursions.[67]

The second illustration is very interesting because it comes from a quite independent source and has nothing intrinsically to do with the Peloponnesian War. Diodoros Siculus gives information on the epidemic of 430 BC which is rarely cited but extremely valuable, although Diodoros is a late author, because it is derived from sources other than Thucydides (cf. Diodoros' use of the Oxyrhynchus Historian, 'P', a better authority than Xenophon for late fifth- and early fourth-century history). Diodoros states that in the winter preceding the epidemic there was very heavy rainfall. The poor quality of the grain reaped at the subsequent harvest in Attica was attributed to the deluge, and the severity of the epidemic in the summer was widely attributed to the poor quality of the available grain, i.e. in modern terms, we might think of malnutrition reducing the human body's defence mechanisms against disease. Whether or not this explanation is medically plausible will be discussed in section 7 below.

All that matters here is that the explanation only makes sense on the assumption that most of the inhabitants of Attica resident there in the summer of 430 BC were actually eating cereals grown in Attica in that very same year, which had been reaped shortly before the epidemic struck. It is the very same assumption found in Thucydides. Diodoros gives mortality figures for adult male citizen soldiers for the epidemic which are not identical with but nevertheless close to those of Thucydides, namely over 4,000 hoplites and 400 cavalrymen (4,400 and 300 respectively in Thucydides). Diodoros, unlike Thucydides, gives a figure for mortalities among the rest of the population, speaking of more than ten thousand, *free and slave*, an estimate which is surely too low. Two further pieces of evidence that the Athenian population was very closely tied to the land of Attica at about the time of the Peloponnesian War should be noted. First there is Thucydides' statement that most Athenian citizens had always lived in the rural demes and were unhappy about having to abandon their homes to take refuge in Athens in the early stages of the war. Secondly, after the end of the war, there is the information transmitted by Dionysios of Halikarnassos from Lysias, namely the proposal about citizenship made by Phormisios which suggests that about 5,000 Athenian citizens at the most (a quarter to a sixth of the total) did not own any land.[68]

Hansen's collection of sources for Athenian casualties in the course of the Peloponnesian War does serve to illustrate the scale of their losses. The fact that they were able to press on with the war year after year, regardless of those losses, alone suggests that the Athenian citizen population was capable of achieving, and actually was achieving, very high fertility rates. Nevertheless in the last decade of the war manpower shortage began to be felt. Strauss (1987) argued that the thetes who manned the triremes suffered proportionately higher casualties than the hoplites because most of the major battles in the final stages of the war occurred at sea. He went on to suggest that this weakened the radical democracy in the aftermath of the war. A decree is said to have been passed permitting each Athenian citizen to procreate children with another woman besides his own wife, a probable reflection of an imbalance in the sex ratio which had arisen because of male casualties in the war (see section 4 below on the sex ratio). Such children probably had certain legal rights, but not full citizenship. Sokrates took full advantage of this decree, but modern philosophers are not keen on drawing attention to his bigamy. Such measures proved to be in vain, and the Athenians lost their empire at the end of the war and with it the means of feeding 60,000 rather than 30,000 citizens.[69]

The loss of her empire brought Athens back into the mainstream of ancient Greek demographic history. The rest of Greece attained the highest population density reached in pre-modern times in the fourth century BC according to archaeological survey data. The ancient Greeks themselves also thought that their country was more densely populated in the fifth and fourth centuries BC than it had ever been before. Both Aristotle and Thucydides believed this in relation to the archaic period. However Thucydides preferred to put the emphasis for the lack of major wars in earlier periods of Greek history on the shortage of money and resources for undertaking action in those periods, obviously influenced in his historical interpretation by the strategy of Perikles which was devoted to accumulating reserves of strength for Athens. Demosthenes reckoned that Greece was more densely populated in his own time than she had been at the time of the Persian Wars in the previous century.

In the terms of Aristotelian political theory, that population growth was implicated in the increasing democratisation of Greece. Archaic Greek societies lacked absolute monarchies or other forms of government which could exercise a monopoly of force, and Greek soldiers had to provide their own weapons. This excluded the poor from hoplite service but at the same time worked against tyrannies or dictatorships. Aristotle noted that the larger the population of a *polis*, and so the larger the number of self-financing warriors, the harder it was for any small group to acquire a monopoly of force and seize and maintain political power, which caused an inclination towards more democratic forms of government. In the light of this analysis it is not surprising that Athens and Syracuse, the two *poleis* with the largest citizen populations, went furthest along the road towards democracy. Aristotle's own view that the development of the Athenian democracy was a matter of historical contingency does not fit very well with his emphasis elsewhere in the *Politics* on the political consequences of the size of the citizen body. However, it may be explained partly by the fact that he did not appreciate the democratic system. It forced him to flee for his life from Athens to Khalkis, shortly before his death. Aristotle's perspective shows a fascinating divergence from modern political theory, because it has become a 'truism' nowadays that *increases* in population density are correlated with increases in social stratification.[70]

In our interpretation the fourth century peak was K, i.e. the population density at which mortality had finally caught up with fertility after the period of growth which commenced in the Dark Ages. This, too, is

corroborated by Aristotle, who observed that the populations of Greek
poleis were not increasing or decreasing very much in his own time,
although they were larger than they had been in the archaic period.[71]
Although the size of the ecological niche determined population size in
the case of each *polis*, nevertheless fertility was not under control,
because the Greeks had a natural fertility regime which lacked the
self-regulatory mechanisms characteristic of north-western European
populations in the early modern period (see sections 4 & 6 below). As a
consequence there was a steady stream of Athenians who regarded
emigration as the only solution to their problems. In spite of their
promises at the inception of the Second Athenian League, the Athenians
soon returned to their bad old habits of grabbing other people's land.
Samos was the most notorious case, and Alexander's 'Exiles Decree' of
324 BC forcing the Athenians to return Samos to the Samians drove
Athens into the Lamian War in 323 BC. The evidence for Athenian
interest in colonisation in the fourth century is very impressive, even
though the citizen population was smaller than it had been during the
Pentêkontaëtia.[72]

Similarly, there is a substantial amount of evidence in this period for
individual migration, which often led to mercenary service. The
demographic consequences of mercenary service should not be
underestimated. It has been suggested that mortalities among Swiss
mercenaries in the early modern period mopped up 35-40 per cent of the
natural increase of the population of the Swiss cantons. The 'Ten
Thousand', including Xenophon, who supported the Younger Cyrus' bid
for the Persian throne, are only the most well-known case in the classical
period. There is no doubt that mercenaries were already leaving Greece
in the archaic period to serve in Egypt and elsewhere. Also worthy of
mention are the more than ten thousand Greeks who assembled at
Corinth in response to Timoleon's call to repopulate Sicily in the 340s
BC.[73]

Finally, there was the exodus to the Orient after the conquests of
Alexander the Great. The reality and magnitude of this phase of
emigration is no longer open to question after the excavation of Seleucid
settlements in places as far flung as Aï Khanoum in Afghanistan and
Failaka in the Persian Gulf. It is a case of recent archaeological research
confirming statements by ancient authors about demographic trends
which used to be widely disbelieved by historians who focus on literary
sources. One episode of early Hellenistic colonisation is of particular
interest as far as Athens is concerned. In 309/8 BC a considerable, but
unfortunately unspecified, number of Athenians sailed to Cyrene to join
the ill-fated expedition of Ophellas with Agathokles of Syracuse against
Carthage, in order to escape *ta kaka*, 'the evils', of life in Greece. The fact
that Ophellas appears to have regarded these Athenians as non-
combatants suggests that they were thetes, unaccustomed to hoplite

service, i.e. emigration was mainly of interest to the poor. This particular venture also demonstrates clearly that men who migrated took their wives and children with them. It was not only adult males who emigrated.[74]

It is now time to put a twist in the tail of the story so far. The fourth-century peak settlement density has been described as K. In fact populations in practice require time to respond to their changing circumstances. Once K is reached it will take time for fertility rates to be reduced to the level appropriate to K, and while that adjustment is taking place the population is likely to overshoot K to reach a population density which cannot be maintained. Thereafter a decline is inevitable as mortality exceeds fertility until K is reached. However, yet again a period of adjustment will be needed during which the population density will drop below K. If the time-lags involved are sufficiently large, then it is possible to demonstrate mathematically that a stable limit cycle may be set up. These phenomena of time-lags and of the momentum of population growth are very important in considering the situation in Third World countries today. It has been shown that on average if age specific birth rates were to drop immediately (in 1971) to bare replacement levels, then the final population size of the average Third World country would be about 1.6 times its current size; if the response is delayed fifteen years, then final population size would be about 2.5 times current size. In the case of European countries with slowly increasing populations the final population size may be expected to be about 1.2 times its current size, which is still a sizeable overshoot.[75]

It is not suggested here that ancient Greek populations were increasing *in the fourth century BC* at anything like the pace set in the Third World today, although they probably were in the eighth century. However, their response to their changing circumstances could not have been instantaneous. The consequence of this is that it is inherently probable that the maximum population density recorded by the various archaeological surveys for the fourth century BC and especially the age of Alexander represents an *overshoot* of K, the equilibrial population density. Some empirical evidence for this may be found in osteological studies (see section 7 below), which indicate that at the time of the maximum population density attested by the surveys the health of the population had already started to decline. In Third World countries today the declining size of landholding associated with population growth is often correlated with deterioration in nutritional indices, exactly as predicted by Malthus, which may be expected eventually to have demographic consequences. Human beings are able to tolerate a moderate degree of chronic malnutrition without dying immediately, although their resistance to infection may be impaired. Because of this, it is only possible to specify a band of values for K, rather than an exact value.[76]

The fourth-century overshoot had the further important consequence that a subsequent decrease in the population density of Greece was inevitable. That decrease is empirically attested by the archaeological surveys which suggest that the population of most areas of Greece decreased considerably in the Hellenistic period, a process which accompanied *pari passu* the declining importance of Greece in international affairs. This gives us a basis on which to construct an explanation of the decrease of the population of Hellenistic Greece. It is necessary to explain why the population density did not recover in antiquity to its fourth-century level. This will be achieved in section 4 below by arguing that the fourth-century overshoot induced the widespread adoption of voluntary family limitation measures such as infanticide. In essence, the thesis of this book is that the period of unrestricted growth between the eighth and the fourth centuries was an interlude in between two quite different systems of fertility control which restricted population growth before the eighth century, in one case, and after the fourth century, in the other case.

The fourth-century peak was a Malthusian crisis, in which population growth outgrew the means of subsistence, explaining the mass emigration to the Orient after Alexander. It is interesting that it was in this very same period that the Greeks began to think about the Malthusian positive checks of famine, disease and war. Dikaiarkhos wrote a book, no longer extant, on the causes of man's destruction, which was probably influenced by Aristotle's surviving summary discussion of the question in the *Meteôrologika*. Both argued that more men had been destroyed by war and revolution than by any other type of calamity, although they also acknowledged the destructive consequences of disease and famine. They did not live to witness the collapse of the population of Greece shortly afterwards which might have induced them to revise their opinions. Both lived in an unstable ecosystem in which biological phenomena did not interact in such a way as to produce a 'steady-state' system. That is the most fundamental reason why the desire of Aristotle and Plato for a steady-state ideal *polis*, with a fairly constant population, was truly utopian in character.[77]

It is interesting to compare Greece to Egypt, a much more fertile land because of the water and silt supplied by the Nile. If the total cultivatable area of Attica is taken to be 40 per cent of her territory, at the most (Chapter III.2 below), then our assumed 150,000 total population for fourth-century Athens yields a population density of about 156 people per km^2 of farm land. This may be compared to the figures for population density per km^2 of cultivated land in Egypt which have been suggested of 135 for the Delta and 240 for the Nile valley and the Fayoum *c*. 150 BC, and 90 and 180 respectively in the second millennium BC. It is clear that Greece had to support a population burden of a similar magnitude with inferior natural resources. Consequently it is not surprising that many

Greeks chose to emigrate to Egypt in the Hellenistic period, even though Egyptologists often regard Egypt as a country in which cultivatable land was in short supply. As in other phases of colonisation, the Greeks took their favourite crops with them. For example, they introduced varieties of garlic from Lycia in Asia Minor and chick-pea from Byzantion. But they could not always grow their favourite crops successfully in a different environment.[78]

It is worth considering briefly how these general considerations of demographic processes in the fourth century BC may be applied to one small corner of Greece which has been the object of intensive research in recent years, namely the southern Argolid. The survey data indicate that there was a decrease in the number of sites from over 100 in the fourth century BC to about 20 in the late Roman period. That is in spite of the fact that alluviation – the deposition of the Younger Fill – was going on in Hellenistic and post-Hellenistic times which might be expected to have obscured traces of earlier sites. Most notably, an entire polis, Halieis, was abandoned in the early Hellenistic period. Although the data are very interesting, the type of *explanation* for these changes offered by the scholars working in this region is judged here to be unsatisfactory, first because it is an explanation for population changes which does not take any account of strictly demographic phenomena, such as momentum of population growth, and secondly because it ignores important testimony in classical literary sources as to what was actually going on in the region in question. The scholars connected with the southern Argolid survey hypothesise that the prosperity of the region was connected with the buoyancy of international trade, especially in respect of olives and olive oil, the region's main products, and interpret the population decline in the Hellenistic period as a result of a downturn in international trade.

Now it may be granted that the olive tree was indeed a major crop in the area in the fourth century BC. Palynological evidence indicates that this was a development of the early first millennium BC. Secondly, it is acknowledged that fluctuations in agricultural production are intrinsically bound up with the well-being of the population in an agrarian society. H. Forbes explains how a very good olive harvest led to an upsurge in the marriage rate in modern Methana, because people acquired the money to be able to pay for the necessary ceremonies. In antiquity Aristotle cited an *euetêria*, a good year for the fruits of the earth, as a factor liable to lead to political change in an oligarchy because more people could meet the property/wealth qualification for citizenship. Nevertheless the question may be raised of whether the olive tree in antiquity was essentially a cash crop or a subsistence crop. I incline towards the latter view (see Chapter III.3 below), but it is not necessary to discuss that question in detail at this juncture.[79]

Much more important here are those ancient sources which indicate that the whole region and its surroundings were in the throes of a

Malthusian crisis in the fourth century BC, in the period immediately preceding the population collapse. Classical sources say very little about the area, but what they do say is highly significant. First, a passage in Isokrates indicates that the region of Troizen was regarded as extremely unhealthy, so unhealthy in fact that a group of Athenians were afraid to visit the place because of the danger of contracting lethal diseases. Until recently the Troizen plain was heavily infested with malaria, but that is not necessarily the only possibility.

Secondly, Theophrastos tells us that people who drank the wine of Troizen became sterile. It is not utterly inconceivable that the local wine may have contained a chemical which impaired human reproduction, since Greek wines usually contained herbal products which were added to flavour them, and plants often contain potent chemicals (see Chapter I above). However, it is perhaps safer merely to assume that the inhabitants of Troizen were as enthusiastic about the drink of Dionysos as the rest of the Greeks, and to draw the inference that the local population was perceived to have a fertility problem, i.e. it was struggling to reproduce itself, a problem which probably had nothing at all to do with the local wine.

This inference is confirmed by a fascinating text of Aristotle, which states that the women of Troizen customarily married at such an early age that their first pregnancies were very difficult and had a high rate of maternal mortality. This passage, to which we shall return in section 4 below, makes sense in the light of modern research in demography and medicine. It has been shown that women who marry and become pregnant before the age of seventeen have more difficult first pregnancies, because physical maturity of the pelvis occurs later than the ability to ovulate, and run a higher risk of maternal mortality than women who marry after reaching that age. Furthermore, because the reproductive organs are likely to be damaged by a pregnancy before the female body is ready for it, even if maternal mortality is avoided, the total fertility of women who marry before the age of seventeen over their whole reproductive lifespans has been shown to be *lower* than that of women (e.g. those of Sparta) who marry afterwards.

Adding all this up, our picture of fourth-century Troizen is of an unhealthy, disease-ridden place in which the women were having difficulty reproducing the population. In that context, the fact, recorded by the archaeological survey team, that the population of an adjacent region collapsed shortly afterwards is hardly surprising. It is also worth remembering that Asklepios, the hero who developed into the god of healing in the classical period, had his most important sanctuary at Epidauros, in the same region. It has been observed that *Asklêpieia*, sanctuaries of Asklepios, were often situated in unhealthy regions, and this may have been true of his most important cultic centre as well. The reason why *Asklêpieia* were usually located outside cities (except· in

Athens) was discussed in antiquity. It may now be explained in terms of rites of passage and primitive initiation rites (see section 5 below). Needless to say, none of this has anything at all to do with the olive tree, although Theophrastos thought that it had something to do with the vine, probably incorrectly. The population of the region had exceeded the equilibrial population density, K, and was facing the inevitable crash afterwards. The problems of the southern Argolid had nothing at all to do with international trade. Palynological evidence indicates a reduction in the extent of arable cultivation in the southern Argolid in the course of the Hellenistic period. Such a decrease in agricultural production could be as much an effect as a cause of a human population decrease.[80]

On the whole it is wise to reject the possibility of reductions in agricultural productivity as an explanation for the population decrease of the Hellenistic period. If changes in soil fertility and so in agricultural productivity were the root cause of the population decline in Hellenistic Greece, then one would expect to observe significant differences between regions with different potentials for agriculture, for example between Boiotia and the southern Argolid, but such differences are not observed in practice. The Roman agronomists debated the idea that the earth had become exhausted through over-production. Columella rejected it on the grounds that the earth could always be replenished with manure. However, modern research has shown that not even manure is needed to maintain indefinitely a certain, albeit low, level of production of cereal crops. In the climatic conditions of the Mediterranean, with the summer drought which inhibits regeneration of the soil's organic matter by nitrogen-fixing bacteria, experiments have demonstrated that a gap of a year between crops, on a cereal-bare fallow rotation system, is sufficient for the bacteria to produce enough nitrogen to ensure yields of a few hundred kg/ha in alternate years even on poor land. Thus it is not to be expected that this rotation system, which was common in classical Greece (Chapter III.12 below), would have resulted in average yields ever dropping below a certain level. However, annual cropping without manure or artificial fertilisers rapidly leads to catastrophe in the Mediterranean.

In Britain, in contrast, the absence of the summer drought helps nitrogen-fixing bacteria to do their work more rapidly. Experiments at the Rothamsted Experimental Farm have demonstrated that in a system of annual cropping in Britain without manure or fertilisers average annual cereal yields of about 400 kg/ha may be maintained indefinitely. There is no particular reason, then, for supposing that population pressure in fourth-century Greece would have caused cereal yields to plummet towards zero, although it must be remembered that the average area of land available per person was decreasing. However, some scholars argue that soil erosion was taking place after the classical period, leading to the deposition of the Younger Fill. The physical disappearance of the soil would affect crops. This is a large topic which cannot be discussed here (see Chapter III.12 below for one or two comments).[81]

Problems similar to those of the southern Argolid were encountered all over Greece. On the small but interesting island of Keos, to which we return later on (section 5 & Chapter III.12 below), the *tetrapolis* of the fourth century was reduced to a two-*polis* system in the course of the Hellenistic period. Moreover there was a reduction in settlement density within the two *poleis* which survived, suggesting that their populations were diminished too, even after synoikism with the two which lost their independent identities. Again, it will be seen later on that Keos, like the southern and eastern Argolid, was facing a Malthusian crisis in the fourth century BC. Strabo tells us that in Arkadia by Roman times there had been a switch from arable farming to animal husbandry, which can only mean a reduction in the human population density with the addition of another trophic level to the food chain increasing energy losses. This piece of information may be connected with research on Mantinea, one of the most important *poleis* in the region, showing that it was very densely populated in the fourth century BC. Again it may be inferred that the population had climbed to a level in the fourth century BC which could not be sustained in the long run.

It should also be noted that decreases in rural settlement densities were accompanied by reductions in the size of neighbouring urban centres as well. This is illustrated by survey work in the urban centres of Thespiai, Askra and Haliartos, and also more impressionistic research on Thebes a little further afield, which should be set beside the results of the rural surveys of the Cambridge/Bradford Boiotia expedition. Finally, it is noteworthy that in Thessaly, the most fertile region of Greece, palynological research suggests that there was a reduction in the extent of arable farming in Hellenistic and Roman times compared to the classical period. A drop in human population density would have been an almost inevitable concomitant of such a development. Plutarch, commenting on the depopulation of Roman Greece, stated that the entire country in his own time could scarcely have raised the 3,000 hoplites available to classical Megara, a small *polis*.[82]

Not all was gloomy in Hellenistic Greece, however. The less well developed regions of Aitolia and Achaia flourished in that period and were overflowing with manpower. Pausanias noted that the Aitolians excelled in the number of young men they had in the early third century BC, explaining their political and military power at the time. They applied it enthusiastically in the cause of self-enrichment through piracy and pillage. Pausanias ascribed the growth of the power of the Achaians to the fact that they had suffered less from disasters in wars and from the great epidemic of 430 BC than any of the other Greeks. His interesting opinion on the long-lasting effects of the great epidemic will be considered in section 7 below.

Similarly Crete, like Aitolia and Achaia, had an excess of manpower and accordingly entered the fray in the Hellenistic period. All these three regions appear to have been backward compared to the rest of the Greeks in respect of both political development and of demographic history. Coincidence or not? In section 5 below it will be shown that the slow population growth in Crete in the archaic and classical periods was connected inextricably to the slowness of her political development. Although we are not so well informed about Aitolia and Achaia, it is possible that the same kind of explanation is valid for them as well. Because some regions of Greece were experiencing population growth in at least the early and middle Hellenistic period, it was still possible for the great Hellenistic monarchs in the Orient to encourage emigration to their kingdoms from Greece.[83]

How does Athens fit into all this? There are no detailed survey data from Attica. The Athenian bouleutic system, which required a population of a certain size in order to provide a suitable number of eligible citizens each year, was maintained throughout the Hellenistic period and into Roman times, after the size of the *boulê* or council was increased from 500 to 600 in the late fourth century BC. This may be a sign that the population decrease in Hellenistic Attica was not as rapid and as dramatic as it was in some other parts of Greece. In ecological terms, Hellenistic Greece was characterised by a smaller biomass and a lower total fixation of solar energy, as Boyden put it. Fowden (1988) has recently shown that there was a resurgence of human activity in Attica during the late Roman period, as in various other parts of Greece. However, that particular cyclical peak was not sustained any more than the peak in the fifth and fourth centuries BC was. Census returns for late mediaeval and early modern Athens show that the population then was substantially lower than even the low estimate of the fourth-century BC population advocated in this book. In that respect Attica was no different from the rest of Greece. The arguments of this section have rested mainly on archaeological survey data and on classical literary sources. In the next section another very interesting type of evidence, namely human bones, will be considered. It sets special technical problems and so demands separate treatment.[84]

3. Human bones, mortality and life expectancy

Ancient historians are in the habit of approaching the problem of life expectancy in antiquity by adopting a model life table on a purely a priori basis, usually for an e^0 of 25 years, in order to circumvent the shortage of firm data. This procedure may be of some use for teaching purposes as a means of illustrating what a typical pre-industrial population looked like to those who are unfamiliar with literature in historical demography, but beyond that it seems to me to have no value. It cannot help us to understand the reasons for any of the considerable changes in the size and density of any of the populations of ancient Greece described in the previous section. Furthermore, the assumption of the validity of a single demographic model over a geographical area the size of the Graeco-Roman world over a period of many centuries not only has no explanatory value but is positively misleading. It is the aim of this book to convince the reader of this point.

Any given age distribution pattern at any point in time, the essence of a life table, may be produced by a wide variety of combinations of age-specific mortality and fertility rates. In addition it is impossible to calculate the rate of natural increase from empirical age distribution data, because data on fertility as well as on survivorship are required. As the comparison of Sweden and Madagascar in section 2 above showed, almost identical values of e^0 may be associated with very different levels of fertility and so with very different rates of natural increase. The a priori assumption of an e^0 of 25 (or any other value) is of *no help whatsoever* in discussing possible rates of natural increase in antiquity. This is why it was not considered worth adopting a life table in the discussion of population growth in ancient Greece in the previous section.[85]

For those who are not satisfied with the patently unsatisfactory procedure mentioned above, it is necessary to try to find actual evidence which may be used to construct a life table. In the absence of census data, the bones of the ancient Greeks themselves constitute the main type of evidence with the potential to expand our knowledge. One characteristic of classical Athens that may be of advantage to us is that the Athenians insisted that everyone who died had to be buried, including slaves. Not to do so offended their religious beliefs. Sophokles' tragedy *Antigonê* revolves around the theme of the duty of kin to bury the dead. Moreover it was a public duty which ultimately had to be enforced by the local deme magistrate, the *dêmarchos*. The aftermath of the naval battle of Arginousai in 406 BC, leading to the condemnation of the victorious Athenian generals, resulted from their failure to collect the corpses of those killed in the battle from the sea, according to the account of Diodoros Siculus perhaps derived from the Oxyrhynchus Historian. (Xenophon gives a divergent account, as so often, emphasising instead the failure of the generals to save those who were still alive.)

In the case of Athens the duty of burying the dead probably simply involved piling earth over a corpse. It may be presumed that slaves at least did not receive grave goods or tomb markers, making their places of burial harder to identify. The Athenians even claimed that they buried the bodies of the hated Persians killed in the battle of Marathon, but Pausanias noted that no burial mound for the Persians was visible. Again what is in question is disposal of corpses under the ground without any indication of the burials being left on top of them. However, accessories such as grave goods are irrelevant for the purposes of palaeodemography, except insofar as the inquiry is directed at a particular status group. All that matters is that skeletons were buried, preferably in locations which offered favourable pedological conditions for preservation. Inhumations are obviously more useful than cremations. Unfortunately osteological research for demographic purposes is still in its infancy as far as ancient Greece is concerned. For a long time the late J.L. Angel was almost the only scholar working in this field, but more research is being done now by other scholars.[86]

On p. 110 below the reader will find a life table based on the age distribution pattern of mortality given by Angel for his largest collection of skeletal material, for Greece in the period *c.* 650-350 BC, i.e. the period in which population growth was gradually decreasing after the r period of the eighth century. Unfortunately the evidence does not come from a single site, as Angel lumped together adult skeletons from Athens and Corinth and infant and juvenile skeletons from Olynthos to obtain a sufficiently large sample to permit the application of statistical tests for significance.

The life table is for males only. An equivalent table could be constructed for the females in Angel's collection, a considerably smaller sample and so statistically less satisfactory, although demographers generally prefer to work on data for females to obtain values for various demographic parameters. Weiss (1973) lumped together Angel's data for males and females to obtain a larger collection of evidence. However it is judged preferable here to separate them because of the possibility of differences between the sexes in respect of life expectancy. The equivalent table for females would only duplicate most of the methodological points to be made below, which are also applicable to Angel's studies of skeletal material from other periods of Greek history.

The life table has been constructed according to the principles prescribed by Weiss, except that in calculating the probability of death, Q (X), for ages 15 and above the simplifying assumption has been made of linear changes in survivorship across five-year age intervals, instead of calculating annual probabilities of death. Of necessity it is based on deaths, in contrast to the family reconstitution methods of historical demographers which take data on births as their starting point. It is also a summation of the experience of many different cohorts. The absence of the necessary documentary evidence makes it impossible to follow the life history of any particular cohort.[87]

It is easy to discern in both Angel's raw data for the age distribution of mortality and in the ensuing life table reasons for questioning whether his collection of skeletons is a fair sample of a real population. The problems are comparable to those faced by palaeoecologists working on prehistoric animal populations. The sex ratio of Angel's collection is far removed from the value close to parity (about 105:100) observed in all well documented human populations. The sex ratio in antiquity will be

Life table

Column	(1)	represents	age
"	(2)	"	the *number of individuals*, D(X), dying in each age interval in Angel's sample
"	(3)	"	the numbers of column (2) expressed as *percentages*, D(X), for ease of further calculation
"	(4)	"	*survivorship*, l(X), starting with an initial cohort of 100. It is found by subtracting the proportion who died in the previous age interval
"	(5)	"	Q(X), the *mortality rate* for each age interval. It is determined by the equation $Q(X) = 1 - \dfrac{l(X + n)}{l(X)}$
"	(6)	"	the *total years lived in age interval X* by all individuals who enter that interval, L(X). For age intervals 0-1, 1-5, 5-9 & 10-14 it is calculated by the equations given by Weiss (1973) 37. For other age intervals it is calculated by the equation $L(X) = 5 \times (0.5 \times [l(X) + l(X + 5)])$
"	(7)	"	the *total years to be lived* by those reaching age X until all are dead, T(X). It is calculated by the equation $T(X) = T(X - n) - L(X - n)$
"	(8)	"	*life expectancy* at age X, E(X). It is calculated by the equation $E(X) = \dfrac{T(X)}{L(X)}$
"	(9)	"	the *age distribution* of the assumed stationary population, C(X). It is calculated by the equation $C(X) = \dfrac{L(X)}{E(0)}$
"	(10)	"	the age distribution pattern of a model population chosen for comparative purposes, namely Weiss MT:22.5--50.0
"	(11)	"	another model population, namely Coale & Demeny (1983) Model West level 1 (males) for a zero rate of increase
"	(12)	"	the same model as in column (11), but for a rate of natural increase of 0.5 per cent

(1)	(2)	(3)	(4)	(5)	(6)	(7)	(8)	(9)	(10)	(11)	(12)
0	22	26.83	100	0.268	83	2443	24.4	3.4	4.1	4.0	4.5
1	9	10.98	73.17	0.150	264	2360	32.2	10.8	13.0	10.7	11.8
5	5	6.01	62.20	0.099	295	2096	33.6	12.1	14.4	11.5	12.4
10	2	2.44	56.10	0.044	274	1801	32.1	11.2	13.0	10.9	11.5
15	1	1.22	53.66	0.023	265	1527	28.5	10.9	11.3	10.2	10.6
20	1	1.22	52.44	0.024	259	1262	24.1	10.6	9.4	9.4	9.5
25	3	3.66	51.22	0.072	246	1003	19.6	10.1	7.8	8.5	8.4
30	8	9.76	47.56	0.206	213	757	15.9	8.7	6.4	7.6	7.3
35	3	3.66	37.81	0.097	180	544	14.3	7.4	5.2	6.6	6.2
40	7	8.54	34.15	0.250	149	364	10.7	6.1	4.2	5.6	6.1
45	12	14.63	25.61	0.572	91	215	8.4	3.7	3.4	4.6	4.1
50	3	3.66	10.98	0.334	45	124	11.3	1.8	2.7	3.7	3.2
55	0	0.00	7.32	0.000	37	79	10.8	1.5	2.1	2.7	2.3
60	4	4.88	7.32	0.667	24	42	5.7	1.0	1.5	1.9	1.6
65+	2	2.44	2.44	1.000	18	18	7.4	0.7	1.7	2.1	1.7

considered in the next section. Suffice it to say here that the highly skewed sex ratio could cast doubt on either Angel's criteria for sexing skeletal remains, or on the representativeness of the sample, or on both. In general, physical anthropologists appear to be satisfied that their techniques for sexing complete skeletons with a well preserved pelvis, which offers the most distinctive features for sex diagnosis, are highly accurate, as is indicated by double blind tests. As a result the highly skewed sex ratios, with a large predominance of males, which are commonly found in palaeo-osteological research, are viewed with equanimity. However, these sex ratios are demographically implausible and certainly not attested in well documented human populations. In the case of classical Athens, there is no evidence for voluntary family limitation methods biased against the female sex, nor in fact any evidence for voluntary family limitation at all (see section 4 below).

There is a strong likelihood that differential preservation is being observed. The gracile bones of females are less likely to be preserved than those of males. Moreover even during life the bones of women start to become brittle and lose mass, while retaining their structure, at an earlier age on average than those of men, owing to osteoporosis. It is possible that this phenomenon was more important and commenced earlier in life in historical populations than in well nourished modern Western populations which provide the standards used by physical anthropologists. The problem of differential preservation of bones of the two sexes rules out use here of one of the methods used by historical demographers to assess the plausibility of data for a population, namely the evolution of the sex ratio with age. Furthermore, it is possible that this progression was distorted in historical populations in any case by the effects of maternal mortality (see section 4 below).[88]

Other problems readily catch the eye. It is not to be expected that no individuals would die between the ages of 55 and 59 in any large real population. In addition the probability of death at age 15 is lower than the probability of death at age 10, which fits one of Weiss's rejection criteria, since age classes 10-14 are usually the healthiest segment of a population. However, it is quite possible that both of these problems might be consequences of stochastic factors when each age interval contains such a tiny number of mortalities. In general Angel's skeletal series gives the impression of too many individuals dying in the age range 15-45 in relation to both the numbers of deceased infants and juveniles put together and of adults dying above the age of 45. It is a very common feature of skeletal series that they seem to contain hardly any old people. This is a consequence of the methodological problems of relating biological age to chronological age, as humans cease growth in their late teens today (perhaps in the mid twenties in less well nourished historical populations), after which time it becomes harder to differentiate them.

Angel's methods are open to criticism for not using multivariate statistical techniques in his determinations of skeletal age. Sattenspiel & Harpending (1983) pointed out that the very low average adult age of death given by Angel yields birth rates so high that it is likely that he underestimated this statistic, although the birth rates in question *are* physically possible (section 2 above). His mortality data do display on a graph the distorted U-shaped mortality curve typical of populations with a low life expectancy at birth, after smoothing employing the elementary method of three-way moving averages.[89]

The only way of assessing the plausibility of Angel's mortality data as a basis for constructing a life table is to compare it to models devised by modern demographers. These models fall into two categories. The first group, e.g. Coale & Demeny (1983), uses mathematical extrapolations from modern populations with high life expectancies at birth to predict the demographic patterns of hypothetical populations with low life expectancies at birth. This procedure, when applied to the past, assumes that human populations have been similar in all important characteristics throughout history, an assumption which is likely to be broadly correct, but may nevertheless be invalid for certain details. For example, it is probable that life expectancies of women in the reproductive age groups were lower than those of men in the same age groups in historical populations, contradicting the widespread modern pattern of females having higher life expectancies at all ages (see section 4 below). Moreover it is dangerous to assume that such models necessarily express all the possibilities. The more recent United Nations models have shown that age at death patterns in developing countries systematically deviate from the modern European patterns used by Coale & Demeny. This is very significant because it is arguable, as we shall see, that the demographic structures of ancient Greece were in many respects closer to those of Third World populations than to those of modern European populations.

The other approach is to construct models on the basis of a very wide range of evidence for pre-modern populations, including osteological evidence, as has been done by Weiss (1973). This alternative procedure may seem more appropriate at first sight, but some scholars reject it precisely because it relies on actual evidence of a kind which may be biased or distorted by observational error, in view of the problems discussed above. Certain scholars dismiss bones altogether as a source of information for demographic purposes, but this is going too far. It is necessary to strive to improve the techniques available at the present time, instead of just giving up. To some extent attempting to differentiate these two categories of model life tables is splitting hairs, because the results are not dissimilar. This alone suggests that bones are not entirely without value for demography.[90]

In the life table above, the last three columns contain the age distribution pattern of selected model life tables which may be compared to the age distribution pattern derived empirically from Angel's mortality data, presented in column (8). However different life tables are juggled around for comparison purposes, problems always arise. For example, life tables that fit the empirical data closely for infant, juvenile and mature adult age intervals invariably have substantially larger proportions of individuals above the age of 50 than is revealed by Angel's data. Similarly model life tables that approximate the proportions of individuals in age intervals above 50 in the empirical data suggest that there are too few infants and juveniles in Angel's sample.

It is possible to go beyond these purely qualitative assessments and use statistical tests to investigate the relationship between the data and model populations. The chi-square test for goodness of fit was employed for this purpose, with some of the cells being lumped together to avoid expected frequencies of less than about five in any of them. In fact good correlations between the empirical data and some of the models which were tested did emerge. For example the Coale & Demeny table in column (11) above yielded a chi-square value of about 3.632, significant at the 95 per cent level with the eleven cells and ten degrees of freedom in the test, while the age distribution pattern of column (12) – the same Coale & Demeny life table but shifted for a rate of increase of 0.5 per cent, yielded a chi-square value of about 2.934, significant at the 98 per cent level. In general somewhat better correlations were obtained from the Coale & Demeny tables, based on modern data, than from the Weiss tables, which are based on evidence from ancient populations. For example, the Weiss table in column (10) above gave a chi-square value of about 5.490, significant at the 80 per cent level.[91]

These correlations indicate that Angel's data are not devoid of value for population history. However, they only give a very general impression of mortality in ancient Greece. Many of the model life tables are very similar to each other, which means that different life tables may give very similar degrees of correlation to the same empirical data. The fact that all human populations have a similar age-specific structure of vital rates and so a built-in similarity to each other explains the unusually high probabilities obtained above, which fall on the opposite side of the table of chi-square values to that upon which statistical analysis usually focuses (P = 0.05 or 0.01). The methodological problems mentioned earlier should not be forgotten either. In spite of the closeness of these statistical correlations it is still probable that Angel underestimated the average adult age of death and allowed for too few elderly people.

The prolonged growth of ancient Greek populations until the fourth century BC, as manifested in the archaeological surveys and in extensive external colonisation, suggests flourishing populations in which birth rates generally exceeded death rates. In the first half of the first millennium BC at least, mortality was probably at intermediate levels rather than at the extremely high levels generally presupposed by ancient historians. Accordingly it is preferable that we should think of a life expectancy at birth in the thirties in Greece in that period, as has been well documented for England most of the time in the early modern period by the Cambridge Group for the History of Population and Social Structure, rather than accept the value of about 25 which is currently favoured by most ancient historians. In the reasonably well documented family of Ausonius in late Roman Gaul, at least one man survived past the age of eighty in each generation. Average life expectancy at birth in this family was 44 for males, 33.7 for females and 39.2 for both sexes combined.[92]

There are other fundamental problems as well. In particular it is debatable whether the emphasis that ancient historians have allotted to life expectancy, to mortality and to trying to construct life tables on the basis of flimsy evidence is really justifiable. This is not just because, as Finley probably would have insisted, the evidence is simply not good enough. There is another, more weighty reason. Even if one finds any of the statistical correlations above impressive, all that has been established is that life expectancy at birth in classical Greece was low rather than high, just as it was in all societies before the modern period. The fact that life expectancy at birth has been on the low side throughout most of history, if considered alongside the evidence for population fluctuations, alone suggests that mortality is not the key to demographic history (making all due allowances for events such as the Black Death). In Italy, for example, life expectancy at birth for both sexes was no higher than 35 in 1880 AD, and it was also in the thirties in Greece in the middle of the last century. In fact a good case may be made on both theoretical grounds of population biology and on empirical evidence from historical demography that fertility was a more important variable than mortality in historical populations.

In the Darwinian theory of evolution natural selection works primarily on differential reproduction. Evolutionary success is not a matter of survival alone but of successful reproduction. As far as human populations are concerned, it is well known to demographers that changes in fertility, which have their greatest impact on infant and juvenile age groups, have more profound effects on the age structure of a population than changes in mortality, which tend to produce proportionate effects on all age groups. A sudden increase in fertility is the single most disruptive type of demographic event, with longer-lasting effects than a great epidemic, for example. We shall see in section 5 below that this is exactly what happened in Greece in the eighth century BC, after the breakdown of the socio-political controls on human reproduction imposed by the age class systems of the Dark Ages. Moreover historical populations and modern primitive populations exhibit very wide differences in fertility under natural fertility conditions (section 4 below). Wrigley & Schofield (1981) concluded that changes in fertility, expressed via shifts in the average age of marriage and so of admission to the breeding population, were the critical factor in the demography of early modern England, permitting an effective response (dilatory homeostasis) to changing circumstances. It will be argued in this book that fertility, not mortality, was the crucial variable in ancient Greece too, although the mechanisms were quite different from those of early modern England. To that extent the focus of ancient historians on life expectancy is misguided.[93]

Subsequent sections of this book will concentrate on fertility, but there is one aspect of it which requires discussion here in the context of bones. Angel attempted to measure fertility directly from female skeletons, by estimating the average number of births per woman from scarring on the pelvic bones. This method is judged by other workers in the field to be too subjective to yield reliable results. However it is still possible to use skeletons as evidence for fertility by using the average age of death to investigate fertility instead of mortality. An untoward emphasis on life expectancy has characterised most research in human palaeo-demography based on osteological studies, but some recent work has begun to alter this situation in a way which has implications for Angel's data too.

The life table above was constructed on the simplifying assumption of a stationary population. It is only by exploiting the most important feature of such a population, namely that life expectancy at birth is equal to the average age of death, that it is possible to derive the age structure of a population from data on age at death. If the population under study is not stationary, then average age at death systematically deviates from life expectancy at birth. In particular population growth under constant mortality results in a decrease in the average age of death, which drops below life expectancy at birth, as infant and child age groups with high age-specific mortality rates (in pre-modern populations) come to form an increasingly larger proportion of the whole population. Conversely a falling rate of increase owing to lower fertility with constant mortality results in an increase in the average age of death as those young age groups decline as a proportion of the whole population, and life expectancy at birth drops below the average age at death.

Palaeo-demographic research on the transition to agriculture at the start of the Neolithic period, for example, has shown consistently a decrease in the average age of death. This is not evidence for a deterioration in living conditions causing a drop in life expectancy, as has often been supposed by scholars. It is evidence for the sharp rise in fertility that was made possible by the sedentarisation of Mesolithic hunter-gatherers and their metamorphosis into farmers, possessing a much larger food supply which facilitated population growth. That provided the kick for the expansion of farming across Europe, a process probably not dissimilar to the expansion of the populations of the European colonists of North America.[94]

In contrast, Angel's data for the period *c*. 650-350 BC suggest that the average age of death reached its maximum in ancient Greece in that period. Combined with the knowledge from the archaeological surveys that the population was growing in that period, albeit more slowly than in the eighth century BC, this should be interpreted not as evidence for increasing life expectancy at birth, but as evidence for decreasing fertility. This accords perfectly with the arguments in section 2 above that the rate of increase decreased in the archaic and classical periods after the r period of the eighth century, suggesting reductions in fertility, in accordance with the logistic equation.

The important consequence of all this for longevity is that the fact that a life table could only be constructed out of Angel's data on the assumption of a stationary population, an assumption made in respect of a population which according to other types of evidence was certainly not stationary, indicates that the life table is not an accurate reflection of the true level of life expectancy. This is why the 98 per cent correlation with the age distribution pattern of the Coale & Demeny life table for an 0.5 per cent rate of natural increase given in column (12) in the table above is a statistical artefact. To the extent that the life table constructed from Angel's data is accurate, the similarity with the model would be a case of two populations with similar age distribution patterns which however were in reality being produced by different combinations of vital rates.

Information about nutritional status may also be derived from bones. For example, it is now possible to investigate the relative proportions of plant foods and of meat in the diet, and the role of legumes in the diet. However, little research along these lines has been accomplished so far in relation to ancient Greece (see section 7 below).

A brief digression from the topic of bones is in order at this point to consider what literary and documentary sources have to say about longevity in ancient Greece. The maximum lifespan attainable by man is about 110 years. This has probably not changed significantly since *Homo sapiens* first evolved. Progress in modern times has only served to increase average life expectancy at birth, pushing it into the seventies, not to increase the longest possible duration of life. In antiquity too Solon and Aristotle regarded the human lifespan as approaching seventy years. However, this statement must be interpreted as referring to a notional estimate of the likely possible length of life for a person who survived infancy, because evidence from cemeteries in classical Greece indicates high infant mortality and so a life expectancy at birth which was much lower than seventy. Similarly 'three score years and ten' was regarded as the duration of life in Tudor England, although parish records show that not many Englishmen at that time survived past the age of sixty. Seventy marks the 'limits of David' in the Bible, although hardy individuals might reach the age of eighty.

Aristotle thought that it was not wise to delay too long starting to have children because one would not (live long enough to) obtain much in the way of reciprocal benefit (from their caring for their parents in old age). This text also illustrates the characteristic Greek view of interpersonal relations, even within the nuclear family, as founded on *charis*, interpreted strictly as the necessity of making an equivalent return for services received and nothing at all to do with Christian 'charity'. It is this attitude towards social relations from which Strepsiades' son Pheidippides is portrayed as an ungrateful deviant in Aristophanes' *Clouds*.[95]

Of course some people lived longer than seventy years. Lucian in his work *Makrobioi*, 'Long-lived men', drew up a long list of famous Greeks who were supposed to have reached or exceeded eighty years of age. A large measure of scepticism is appropriate when considering such claims, especially in regard to philosophers who were alleged to have led virtuous lives. Even more scepticism is in order in consideration of lifespans of the order of 100-150 years frequently claimed on Roman funerary inscriptions. Greeks in the classical period seldom recorded age at death on tombstones. Consequently there is no need for us to enter the quagmire of the debate among Roman historians regarding the utility or otherwise of data from funerary inscriptions for demographic purposes. Pliny states that the Roman census of 74 AD in Italy had recorded as a matter of admitted fact the existence of three individuals in one region of the country who were about 140 years old. It would be a mistake to take too seriously the efficiency of the bureaucratic organisation of the Roman empire. Similar claims of exceptional longevity in certain modern populations, e.g. in Soviet Georgia, are generally dismissed by demographers. Nevertheless it is likely that a few individuals would have reached the age of about 100. The Attic orators mention two men who lived to the ages of 96 and 95 respectively. These claims are probably reasonably accurate because of the records of Athenian citizens kept in the deme registers.[96]

However, such individuals were doubtless the exception rather than the rule. Life expectancy at birth was low because of high infant mortality. Infant mortality is a topic on which it is very hard to obtain any reliable information. It is totally ignored in the discussions of family histories in the Attic orators (see sections 4 & 6 below). As far as archaeological evidence is concerned, it is always possible that deceased infants may not have received formal burial. Moreover their thinner bones are less likely to be preserved than those of adults anyway. However, in those classical Greek cemeteries which seem to represent a population with a full age structure about 50 per cent of all the burials seem to be of infants and juveniles. Aristotle mentioned a custom in part of the ancient Greek world, also recorded from other societies, of not naming infants until seven days after birth because of the danger of infant mortality. However in Athens infants seem to have been named after ten days, at the *dekatê* ceremony. Such customs permit infanticide, because the newly born infant does not yet have a social personality, but it would be wrong to infer from that possibility that infanticide was necessarily very common (see section 4 below). It is simply a recognition of the risks to the new born. It is impossible to generalise about infant mortality because it has varied very widely in history, like fertility, even though choice may play a role in the case of fertility.

In the classical period, as population density increased, density-dependent diseases encountered more favourable circumstances for their transmission and propagation, and towns became larger and less healthy, infant mortality may have been significantly higher than it was in the Dark Ages. Thus the high infant mortality of the K period of the fourth century BC does not rule out massive population growth in the r period of the eighth century BC. Moreover the lengthy average duration of breastfeeding in ancient Greece would have reduced infant mortality, because of better nutrition and the transmission of antibodies in breast milk (see section 4 below). In scholarly research on 'the demographic transition' in modern European history from high vital rates to low vital rates the fundamental and much debated problem arises of whether a fall in mortality, especially high infant mortality, was an essential precondition for the adoption of voluntary family limitation on a large scale and the fall in fertility which led to the average family having two children. Unfortunately demographers have not reached a consensus on this question, on which quite contradictory opinions have been expressed in recent scholarly literature.[97]

Before leaving the topics of mortality and life expectancy it is necessary to consider the possibility that different status groups may have had different vital rates. Pliny noted that disease epidemics sometimes affected one social class more than another. Of particular importance for ancient history is the question of whether slaves had demographic patterns different from those of the free population. It is very hard to draw any firm conclusions from the scanty available sources as to the extent to which slaves in classical Athens were permitted to have a normal family life and to breed. However, slaves were characteristically *barbaroi*, non-Greek aliens, and there is no doubt that forced immigration was the principal factor determining their numbers in Athens. Their standard of life was probably generally worse than that of citizens and free aliens, in spite of the comments of the 'Old Oligarch' about the impossibility of visually distinguishing poor citizens from slaves on the streets of Athens and the fact that some of them were allowed to earn money on their own account as *chôris oikountes*, living and working outside the master's home. Importing adult slaves was always cheaper than breeding them, and the slave population probably did not reproduce itself.[98]

The question of slave reproduction has attracted more attention amongst historians of the Roman empire than amongst classical Greek scholars. Although the Roman empire is not the subject of this book it is perhaps still worth devoting a paragraph to exposing the deficiencies of some of the erroneous opinions which have been expressed on this question. Students of ancient slavery inevitably have drawn comparisons between slavery in antiquity and in the USA before the American Civil War, and such comparisons have been extended to the demography of the two sets of slaves. However, the analogy is invalid. The slave population of the USA did maintain itself and increase after the supply of slave imports was cut off, but to understand this it is essential not to abstract arbitrarily the slaves from the total environment in which they lived. The Negro slave population managed to increase in an environment in which the free white population was also increasing at a phenomenal rate comparable to that of Third World countries today. This was possible because they were effectively filling a vacuum. In other words both whites and Negroes lived in an environment which offered unusual opportunities for massive population growth. The fact that the slave population increased as well shows that they reaped some of the benefits of living in that extraordinarily favourable environment, but not as large a share of the benefits as the free white population, which had a higher life expectancy at birth and increased more rapidly. Thus the demographic performance of the slaves was inferior to that of their masters, even in the USA. The inferior condition of slaves there has now been illustrated by the physical anthropological research of Kelley & Angel (1987), showing that the skeletons of Negro slaves often display stress fractures presumably caused by excessive hard physical labour. Unfortunately no similar research has yet been carried out in relation to ancient history because of the difficulty of identifying slave burials.

If we return to the Roman empire now, it is plain that unless it is believed that the population of the Roman empire *as a whole, slave and free*, was expanding into a vacuum, it is illegitimate to transfer the slave demography of the USA to the Roman empire. We shall not find a Roman historian who reckons that the Roman empire was a vacuum, and so the analogy is inappropriate. Consequently the slave population of the Roman empire probably did not reproduce itself in the long run, one of the factors behind the gradual transformation of the slave societies of antiquity into the feudal societies of mediaeval Europe. However, it would be wrong to generalise across the whole of antiquity in respect of demographic patterns. In Greece, for example, there were periods of low population density, for example in the Dark Ages and in the late Hellenistic period in which slaves, if there were any, could have multiplied alongside their masters.[99]

There is one other type of evidence from classical Athens for life expectancy which may be compared to the osteological evidence. This is the evidence for the ratio between the ephebes and the arbitrators (*diaitêtai*), which was analysed by A.H.M. Jones. He used Burn's models based on Roman funerary inscriptions, which are now regarded as unsatisfactory for demographic purposes by some scholars. However, this criticism only affects the shape of Jones's survivorship curve, not the potential value of the ephebe-arbitrator ratio itself. This ratio should give us a measure of life expectancy at about age twenty, *if* the numbers of ephebes and arbitrators can be ascertained reliably. An essential precondition is that all, or at least the vast majority, of ephebes who survived to the age of fifty-nine actually became arbitrators. It is known that failure to serve as an arbitrator after progressing through the forty-two annual military age classes brought the penalty of *atimia*, effectively disfranchisement in the fourth century BC, unless a citizen liable for such service happened to hold a magistracy during the year in question or was abroad at the time.

After taking into account the substantial number of known magistracies in fourth-century Athens, the number of *diaitêtai* must be regarded as a minimum estimate of the number of survivors to age fifty-nine out of each cohort. There is also the question of cleruchs and colonists in the fourth century BC. There must have been some Athenians who served as ephebes, or perhaps in the earlier institution of *peripoloi*, before the Lykourgan period, and then left Athens permanently and so did not become arbitrators later, even if they lived to fifty-nine. There is no reason for supposing, as Ruschenbusch did, that any of the known cohorts of arbitrators had been decimated by epidemics. The particular reasons that Gomme gave for regarding these totals as too low should also be dismissed, because he relied on inappropriate modern census data for his demographic analogies.[100]

The average size of an annual age group of ephebes is probably the most firmly established element of Athenian demography in the fourth century BC. L. Gallo (1980a) rightly drew attention to an important passage of Demosthenes which shows that the orator regarded the average size of a *hêlikia* or annual age group of Athenian *stratiôtai*, 'soldiers' (in this case clearly hoplites), as 500 men, probably having in mind recently enrolled *hêlikiai*. This confirms the estimates of 450-500 men each year reaching the age of about twenty derived from the ephebic inscriptions by several scholars, even though M. Hansen has recently discussed a little evidence that some annual age groups of ephebes may have numbered as many as 600 men.

There would inevitably have been stochastic fluctuations in the size of cohorts. One of our problems is that although the Athenian citizen population as a whole was large enough to have had a fairly regular age distribution pattern, nevertheless it is only possible to try to infer that pattern from fragmentary evidence relating to subdivisions of the population such as tribes which were small enough for chance to have had very significant effects. In any case the text of Demosthenes destroys the theory of Pélékides that the surviving ephebic inscriptions just happen to represent cohorts of below average size. It also knocks down Ruschenbusch's interpretation by showing that the 500 members of a *hêlikia* were specifically hoplites, not all Athenians including the numerous thetes.[101]

A basic problem in considering whether or not the number of ephebes was relatively stationary from year to year is that no source explicitly states the criteria which determined eligibility for hoplite service in classical Athens. I share Ste. Croix's doubts about the statements of our sources regarding the requirements for membership of the Solonian 'classes' (*telê*). There is no doubt that at least half of the Athenian citizens never became ephebes, because 500 or even 600 men at the age of twenty simply cannot be reconciled with a total (slowly growing) citizen (adult male) population of 20-30,000 in any plausible age distribution pattern. Nevertheless the sources do give the impression that *all* Athenians were expected to become ephebes, pass through the age class system and end up as arbitrators. This must have been an expectation that many Athenians never fulfilled, because hoplites had to provide their own weapons and armour, and the poorer Athenians could not have afforded the expense.

The crucial text of Demosthenes also shows that the reform of the *ephêbeia*, inspired by Epikrates, which is often supposed to have taken place *c.* 336 BC, did not alter in any way the number of hoplites that Athens had at her disposal. It was probably merely a financial measure which transferred the cost of military training from private individuals to the public treasury (with a spear and shield for each ephebe). In spite of Hansen's doubts, the old interpretation that only would-be hoplites became ephebes is preferable. Probably the number remained fairly static, although it depended on the wealth of individuals, because in a fixed territory with static agricultural productivity and a system of partible inheritance which hindered property accumulation, the number of Athenians with the requisite level of wealth did not fluctuate very much.[102]

Nevertheless the combined testimony of Demosthenes and the ephebic inscriptions of the Lykourgan period suggests strongly that whatever the precise determinants of eligibility/liability for hoplite service were, there was a very substantial measure of stability in the size of the Athenian ephebic (hoplite) body in the fourth century BC. Cohorts born in the 370s BC were yielding about 500 men aged twenty *c.* 351 BC, when Demosthenes made his speech, while the cohorts born in the 350s and 340s BC produced age groups of 450-500 men aged twenty in the Lykourgan period. The number of arbitrators aged fifty-nine is not so well documented. One complete inscription dating to the Lykourgan period lists 103 *diaitêtai*, which is supported by another fragmentary inscription. On the other hand Ruschenbusch has tried to reconstruct another inscription so as to give a total of about 170 arbitrators in the first half of the fourth century BC. However, this represents a cohort born during the Peloponnesian War and it is probably wise not to compare it to the evidence from the Lykourgan period.

If we take 475 as the average number of ephebes and compare it to the 103 on the one surviving complete inscription from that period, the ratio between them gives a value for adult life expectancy at age twenty which fits Weiss MT:25.0--55.0, yielding a life expectancy at birth of about 23 years, assuming a stationary population to simplify matters. This life table yields a chi-square value of 5.534 in relation to the age distribution pattern of Angel's skeletal population. However, it is unwise to make much of it. Reasons have been given for believing that both the osteological evidence and the ephebe:arbitrator ratio provide us with underestimates of the true level of life expectancy.[103]

After the fourth century BC there is little concrete evidence for life expectancy in Greece until modern times. Patlagean estimated that half of the males who reached adulthood were dead by age thirty-nine and half of the adult females by age thirty-four in the Byzantine empire, which included Greece, but these assessments were made on the basis of funerary inscriptions which are probably not a reliable source of demographic information. Laiou-Thomadakis (1978) adopted a model life table on a priori grounds for an interesting study of peasant families in northern Greece in the late mediaeval period. No research has been carried out on the historical demography of early modern Greece comparable to that performed so far for England, France, the Nordic countries, and potentially Italy as well.[104]

So far the focus has been on aggregate characteristics of the osteological evidence such as average age of death. It is also of interest to consider variations in the age structure of skeletal populations and differences between cemeteries. Here careful consideration has to be given to the theories advocated by I. Morris (1987). These ideas require extensive criticism, but their positive aspects are noteworthy as well. Morris rejects the arguments of Snodgrass for massive population growth in the eighth century BC, claiming that the cemetery data from different periods are not comparable because they represent different age structures. Instead he maintains that the observed changes must be correlated with the political history of Attica and represent shifts in the sections of the population which were entitled to formal, archaeologically visible, burial. The following quotation gives the essence of his argument insofar as demographic problems are concerned:

Comparing the total number of Protogeometric to Middle Geometric graves with those of Late Geometric is not a valid procedure, since in Late Geometric II over half the burials are of sub-adults, while in Early Geometric to Late Geometric I less than one-tenth are children. As a result, the rather improbable 4% per annum population growth suggested by Snodgrass is reduced (Morris (1987) 72).

It was explained in detail in section 2 above why very substantial population growth in the eighth century BC was not 'rather improbable' at that particular historical juncture. Morris hugely underestimates the extent of the variability exhibited by well attested populations in history. Thus on p. 57 he cites the opinion of C.M. Cipolla that 'any agricultural society ... tends to adhere to a definite set of patterns in the structure and movement of birth and death rates'. Cipolla's statement is indeed correct, but it is reasonably certain that he did not intend the illegitimate inference which Morris has drawn from his statement. What Cipolla meant is that, for example, age-specific birth rates tend to follow a similar pattern in all natural fertility populations, so that if the patterns are plotted on a graph, they all look rather similar as regards the shape of the curves (see section 4 below).

However, from the correct observation that the age-specific *structure* of vital rates tends to be similar in all traditional populations, Morris seems to have jumped to the quite false inference that the *absolute values* of vital rates were similar in all pre-modern populations. This is simply not true, especially as regards fertility. The great achievement of Louis Henry was to show that traditional populations exhibited very great differences in fertility levels even in the complete absence of voluntary family limitation. It is now reckoned by demographers that average completed family size in populations which do not practise any form of family planning whatsoever may vary from as few as four to conceivably as many as seventeen or eighteen children. Such differences in fertility are naturally fundamental in any consideration of possible population growth. On a sufficiently large scale they will lead to very significant alterations in the age structure of a population.[105]

Morris's disbelief in the possibility of substantial variations in the age structures of historical populations is based on an inadequate acquaintance with literature in demography. This vitiates the line of argument of his whole book. From the point of view of logic, the argument against Snodgrass in the quotation above is an example of completely circular reasoning, because by making the initial incorrect assumption that traditional populations did not exhibit wide variations in fertility and so in age structure, Morris has ruled out the possibility of rapid population growth at the outset. In other words he commenced by assuming what he was attempting to prove, namely that the population of Attica did not increase very rapidly in the eighth century BC. Let us see how this works in detail.

Morris states that infants are barely represented in Early Geometric-LGI cemeteries. It is true that they are under-represented. Infant burials (age group 0-1) might be expected to have comprised 20-25 per cent of all burials in a *stationary* population with the kind of levels of life expectancy at birth (in the thirties) suggested in this section. However, as has already been noted, the rate of infant mortality has varied widely in the course of history. There is no reason for supposing that the rate of infant mortality was the same in the classical period, with its high population density, as it had been in the Early Geometric period, with its low population density. Attica may well have been a healthier place to live in in the earlier period, because of the scarcity of density-dependent diseases then (section 7 below), including several which prey on infants in particular in large populations. In any case it must be stressed that the levels of infant mortality indicated by even classical cemeteries would not necessarily have been an obstacle to rapid population growth, as the white population of the United States had an infant and juvenile mortality rate of about 50 per cent, but still doubled every twenty-five years or so.

The crux of the debate, however, rests on the interpretation of the changes that occurred in the eighth century BC. Morris claims that the shift in the age structure of the cemeteries in Late Geometric II relative to earlier periods means that the cemetery data for the different periods are incommensurable and so cannot be used as evidence for massive population growth simply by assessing the number of tombs in each period to give an indication of population size, as Snodgrass did. This is where Morris's analysis takes a critical turn in the wrong direction, because by wrongly refusing to admit the possibility of variations in fertility rates and so in the age structure of historical populations, he has wrongly excluded the possibility of rapid population growth *ab initio*. If a population starts to grow rapidly, the number of adults does eventually increase, but the numbers of infants and juveniles increase much more rapidly, leading to a much lower average age for the entire population, a much younger age distribution pattern, and a younger average age of death (not identical to life expectancy in a population which is not stationary) because infants, with their relatively high mortality rate, come to form a steadily larger proportion of the whole population.

This is the state of affairs in many Third World countries, such as Mexico, today. Such changes may occur very rapidly indeed. If people in Britain today abandoned contraceptive measures en masse, with the ensuing very rapid population growth the age structure of the British population would come to resemble that of Mexico in a very few decades and old age pensioners would soon form a much smaller proportion of the population once again. (To feed such a population Britain would have to cut one trophic level out of the food chain, reducing energy losses, by abandoning meat consumption in favour of bread.) There is no intrinsic reason why similar phenomena could not have occurred in the distant past, if the newcomers could be fed. It should also be emphasised that fertility has a much more powerful influence on the age structure of a population than mortality. Britain is full of old age pensioners today because of low fertility (two children per family), not because of high life expectancy at birth.

Empirically such a phase of increased population growth should be reflected in cemeteries in the archaeological record in the form of a younger age distribution pattern of the skeletal population, with a substantially higher representation of infants as a proportion of all burials. The number of infant burials ought to increase much faster than the number of adult burials, and the two must be considered together. It is wholly illegitimate to argue, as Morris implies, that Snodgrass's postulated growth rate can be reduced by considering adult graves *only*. That would be to treat one age group, the one which increases *most slowly* in a growing population, in isolation from the rest of that population.

The archaeological record reveals that infant and child burials increased from *c*. 10 per cent of all known burials in Late Geometric I to *c*. 50 per cent of all burials in LGII. The total number of burials of deceased of all ages increased rapidly in the latter period, sevenfold in fifty years according to Snodgrass. This shift in the age distribution pattern of mortality is precisely in the general direction of what is to be expected if a population with a low life expectancy (not rock bottom) relative to modern Britain, for example, enters a phase of rapid natural increase. As a formal refutation of Snodgrass and as an exercise in logic, Morris's line of argument is a failure. Not only is it a failure as a refutation, but Snodgrass is entitled to claim that the evidence for the shift in the age structure of the Athenian population from LGI to LGII, as presented by Morris, actually supports his own (Snodgrass's) point of view in principle.

These qualitative points may be quantified by examining model life tables. If Coale & Demeny (1983) Model West (the best documented model) mortality level 7 (females) is considered, it will be seen that the stationary population has a life expectancy at birth of 35 (within the range for early modern England which is the best documented pre-modern population), an average age at death also of 35 for the whole population (51.64 for those who passed the age of 5), and crude birth and death rates both of 28.57. 19.95 per cent of the population is in the age groups 1-9, which Morris classed as infants and children, and those infants and children contribute 35.67 per cent of the mortalities. If the same population, with the same underlying level of life expectancy, is considered for a rate of natural increase of 3 per cent, a very rapid rate, it will be seen that the average age of death drops to 13.84 for the entire population (36.37 for those who survived past the age of five), the crude birth rate increases dramatically to 59.93 (matching the French Canadians) and the crude death rate increases slightly (because of high mortality amongst infants and children aged 0-5, the most rapidly increasing segment of the population) to 29.93. 36.33 per cent of the population is distributed in age groups 1-9, which now contribute 68.22

per cent of the total deaths in the population.

Obviously it is impossible to insist that any of these details are applicable to Late Geometric Greece. They merely illustrate possibilities, which Morris has ruled out on a priori grounds. Equally it would be wrong to put too much emphasis on the precise data from the cemeteries. However there is no doubt that rapid population growth produces a sharp increase in mortalities (and so burials) of infants and children as a proportion of all mortalities (and burials). The cemetery data from Late Geometric Attica in fact support Snodgrass's thesis of rapid population growth. This thesis, applied to Greece as a whole, is immeasurably strengthened by the intensive archaeological surveys recording not just tombs but settlements and evidence for human activity of all kinds, and by the evidence for external colonisation. The analysis proposed here also mops up the misguided demographic ideas of Camp (1979), whose imaginative but unsound hypotheses about great epidemics and famines in Attica in the seventh century BC will be dismantled in section 7 and Chapter IV below.

The rest of the historical period studied by Morris may be dealt with briefly. He is right to say that it is implausible that there was a great decline in human activity in Attica in the seventh century BC on the basis of the shortage of archaeological evidence for that period currently available. Probably the chronology, which is based on pottery styles, requires modification (see section 2 above). Morris is right to draw attention to the fact that the number of burials in Attic cemeteries increases substantially *c.* 500 BC and to connect this development with the reforms of Kleisthenes in Athens. However this is only part of the explanation. As was shown in section 2 above, the evidence for the Athenian population in the fifth century BC again indicates a phase of rapid population growth with rates of increase of the order of 2 per cent per annum for many years. Although Kleisthenes may have given a new significance to Athenian citizenship and to the criteria required for it (e.g. being able to point out the graves of citizen parents), that is by no means the only possible explanation for the substantial increase in the number of burials in the fifth century BC. Of course the explanations in terms of political developments and population growth are not mutually exclusive.

This leads on to consideration of Morris's ideas on the social structure of the ancient Greek *polis* and its links with population history. These ideas are in certain respects unsatisfactory. This is not intended as a criticism of Morris, but rather as a comment on the limitations of the archaeological evidence upon which he primarily relied. There are strict limits as to how far it is possible to reconstruct political and social structures, ideology and religion, on the basis of archaeological evidence. Nevertheless Morris's approach does contain the germ of a very valuable idea, which he did not pursue anywhere near far enough.

Morris equates the right to 'formal burial', by which he cannot really mean any more than a type of burial that happens to contain durable material artefacts likely to survive for archaeologists to find them, with full membership of the community. He argued that formal burial was limited to a restricted age and rank group. The concept of 'rank' adds nothing to the analysis, and will not be considered any further here. However the concept of age as a principle of social organisation, age class organisation as it may be termed, is indeed fundamental to understanding the social organisation of the ancient Greek world (see section 5 below). Morris does not justify his belief in the importance of age class organisation in great detail. His view may have been influenced by the important unpublished thesis of Whitley (1987). Neither Morris nor Whitley, both archaeologists primarily interested in material remains, not in written sources, familiarised himself with the abundant mass of evidence for age class organisation to be found in ancient Greek literature, or with anthropological evidence for age class societies in other parts of the world and so with the consequences of age class organisation.

On the basis of ancient written sources and modern social anthropology, it is possible to pick out three important points in respect of which Morris's analysis is unsatisfactory. First, although Morris emphasises age class organisation, he also persists in describing Athens as a society whose social structure was based on kinship. This is a fundamental misconception. In fact age and kinship are radically different, and mutually contradictory, principles of social organisation, and often do not coexist in the same society. There is no evidence in the extant written sources, from Homer and Hesiod to the fourth-century Attic orators, that Athens or any other Greek *polis* ever possessed a social structure based on kinship. This assertion will be justified in section 6 below.

Secondly, Morris equates formal burial with *full* membership of the community. The arguments of Morris and Whitley that burial patterns in Protogeometric Athens were regulated by the socio-political organisation are valuable and should be accepted (section 5 below). It is characteristic of age class societies that members have different rights and duties at each stage of their lives corresponding to different stages of the age class system, but that does not mean that any of them are not full members. The fact that if a person died at a particular age at which he or she was not entitled to receive formal burial that person did not receive such a form of burial does not prove that that person was not a full member of the community.

This point may be exemplified by ancient Sparta, which merits more attention than the handful of comments devoted to her by Morris. The provision of grave goods was prohibited in Sparta, except for a perishable purple cloak and olive leaves which were placed with the corpse. The two kings received special honorific forms of funeral, while men who died in battle and probably also women who died in childbirth were permitted to have their names inscribed on memorials. However that does not mean that men who died from, say, natural causes, instead of in battle, and so were not eligible to have their names recorded on a memorial, were not full members of the Spartan *polis*. It is evident from literary sources that all Spartiates who passed through the Spartan system of education, the *agôgê*, became *homoioi*, 'equals' (the precise significance of this word is considered in section 5 below), regardless of how they eventually died. Thus Morris's assumption of an antagonistic relationship leading to social conflict between those who received formal burial and were full members of the society and those who did not receive such burial and were not full members is a false dichotomy. It is also worth observing that there is no evidence that any *polis* ever had legally defined status groups called *agathoi* and *kakoi*, as Morris claims.

Sparta is the one Greek *polis* in which there is written evidence that burial was still regulated in the classical period in accordance with the dictates of the socio-political organisation of an age class society. In view of that it may seem surprising that Sparta does not figure more prominently in Morris's book, in spite of his focus on Attica, because of his thematic interests. However it is not really surprising that Morris neglected Sparta, because Sparta is the case which illustrates more starkly than any other the limitations of archaeological evidence, upon which Morris primarily depends. The Spartan system forbade the deposition of grave goods with the corpse. The accuracy of Plutarch's account seems to be validated by the scarcity of finds of Spartan burials so far.[106] Obviously a society which lays down the regulation 'thou shalt not put objects in the ground' is of singularly little interest to the average archaeologist. (They must be grateful that there have not been many more such societies – perhaps there were in prehistory after all, and it is just that archaeologists are not trained to consider such provocative possibilities!) It was in relation to Sparta that Thucydides made what is still the most penetrating observation ever made on the limitations of archaeological evidence as a means of reconstructing a society. He said that no future visitor to the ruins of Sparta and Athens, if they were to be deserted, without knowing any more about them, would ever imagine that Sparta had once been as powerful as Athens, and so would overestimate the power of Athens.[107]

It is only from literary sources that it is possible to understand the social structure and political organisation of the Spartan *polis* which regulated what Morris calls 'formal' burial. It is worth drawing attention to another fundamental archaeological problem upon which the very same Spartan customs, as described by Plutarch, shed light. This is the old question of the lack of evidence for the Dorian invasion. There is no space to discuss here the reasons for the collapse of the Mycenaean civilisation, and it does not matter for current purposes whether the Mycenaean palaces were or were not destroyed by the Dorians (see

Chapter I above). However, an interest will be taken later on in this book in some of Anthony Snodgrass's other ideas which are relevant to the possibility of the Dorians moving around in Dark Age Greece after the Mycenaean collapse, namely the idea of the significance of pastoralism in Greece in that period and of the mobility of Dark Age Greek populations. The idea that populations, except in Attica, were not sedentary in the Dark Ages was put forward by Thucydides, but is not received enthusiastically by many archaeologists nowadays, because of the influence of the school of thought in prehistoric archaeology whose hostility to the idea of human population movements in the past was criticised in section 2 above. However, Spartan burial customs present a satisfactory explanation for the lack of archaeological evidence for the Dorian invasion. In view of their prohibition of grave goods it is hardly surprising that there is little evidence for the Dorian invasion, given the emphasis allotted by so many archaeologists to tombs. A mobile population would not be expected to leave behind much trace of itself anyway. The Celtic migration into the south Balkans and Anatolia in 280/279 BC, which is well documented in literary sources, has left hardly any trace in the archaeological record.

So much, for now, for Dark Age Sparta. The third mistake in Morris's account of ancient Greek social organisation provokes the most fundamental criticism of his book made here, because it destroys his attempt to divorce social and political history from demographic history, to relegate population growth to being what he terms an 'oblique' manifestation of the *polis*. Although Morris emphasised the importance of age class organisation, he did not realise that such a type of social organisation may regulate not only burial customs and rituals, but also all other facets of social organisation, including important demographic parameters. In section 5 below it will be argued that the age class societies of Dark Age Greece acted in such a way as to restrict human reproduction. The weakening of those social systems in most parts of Greece in the eighth century BC, which is manifested in funerary customs in Attica by the shift from the homogeneity of Protogeometric assemblages to the heterogeneity of Late Geometric assemblages, also implied the disappearance of socio-political restrictions on human fertility. It was that which permitted the rapid population growth in Late Geometric Greece correctly emphasised by Snodgrass and wrongly denied by Morris. We shall now leave mortality to concentrate in the next two sections on fertility and controls on fertility, the most important demographic parameter in ancient Greece.

4. Natural fertility and family limitation

Angel's research on skeletal populations suggests that adult women had a lower average age of death than adult men. The modal ages of death of adult females and males fall in the age intervals 35-39 and 45-49 respectively for the period *c*. 650-350 BC, indicating that the death of the average adult woman occurred before menopause in ancient Greek populations. In the previous section it was argued that Angel underestimated average age of death and life expectancy at birth for both sexes. Nevertheless his data raise interesting questions about the evolution of the human sex ratio and about the validity of extrapolations from modern to ancient populations. In all developed countries today female life expectancy is higher than male life expectancy at all ages from birth onwards. This may also be true from conception onwards and so more male than female foetuses end up as spontaneous abortions, but this is more controversial. As a result model life tables based on data from modern populations, e.g. Coale & Demeny (1983), simply project the experience of countries such as Britain since about AD 1870 onto their mathematical extrapolations for populations with low life expectancies at birth, assuming higher life expectancies for females at nearly all ages.[108]

Data from developing countries give a rather different picture. Life expectancy at birth is higher for females than for males almost everywhere. However in many Third World countries excess female mortality has been found in two age groups, namely 1-4 and 15-45. The excess mortality among young female children may be ascribed to such factors as a tendency to wean females earlier than males, resulting in a loss of immunological protection against diseases from maternal antibodies at an earlier age, and to sex-differential nutrition, which is probably widespread on a cross-cultural basis. Male ancient Greek writers thought that women needed, and so received, less food than men. This was the case everywhere except in Sparta. Although they are often criticised by modern scholars for discriminating against women in this way, it must not be forgotten that women are smaller than men on average (sexual dimorphism). The long-term trend in hominid evolution has been towards a reduction in sexual dimorphism. Moreover the two sexes have different metabolic rates. Nevertheless the average difference in energy requirements between the sexes is smaller than the average difference in size between them because a smaller body has a higher ratio of surface area to volume, resulting in higher heat losses and so a need for a proportionately greater calorific intake. Female mortality may have been higher than male mortality in the 1-4 age group in ancient Greece for these reasons, but no definite evidence is available on this point.[109]

The excess female mortality found in various modern populations in the 15-45 age group, i.e. the reproductive age group, also sets interesting problems. It is tempting at first sight to explain it in terms of maternal mortality, which was undoubtedly higher in the past than it is today in developed countries. The Hippokratic corpus describes in detail a number of cases of deaths among pregnant women, for various reasons, and among women who had recently completed a pregnancy, owing to puerperal fever. Aristotle thought that women who worked hard gave birth more easily than those who were inactive. Pregnancies in which the foetus did not present itself head first were especially liable to end in disaster. In Attica the clothes of women who died in childbirth were dedicated at the temple of Artemis at Brauron, while women who died in childbirth in Sparta had the privilege of having their names recorded on funerary monuments. However, it is impossible to quantify maternal mortality in ancient Greece from such evidence, interesting as it is. Even among hunter-gatherers such as the !Kung Bushmen in southern Africa, maternal mortality is rare. Recent research on better-documented periods of history suggests that the rate of maternal mortality may not have been so high in historical populations as has generally been supposed. For example, the average woman had a 6-7 per cent chance of dying in childbirth during her reproductive career in early modern England. The rate of maternal mortality in ancient Greece need not have been any higher than this level.[110]

There is another good reason why maternal mortality is not a convincing explanation of excess female mortality in the reproductive age groups. Such excess mortality is observed in the two fastest-increasing populations known to demographers in the world today, namely the Hutterites, a religious sect often used by demographers as a paradigm for a population increasing almost at r, the intrinsic rate of natural increase, and the inhabitants of the Cocos-Keeling islands. In spite of the excess female mortality deduced from life table analysis, maternal mortality is rare amongst the Hutterites, who enjoy the general standard of living of the United States. The fact that women have a lower life expectancy than males in the age group 20-60 in this rapidly increasing population must be explained in a way which is related to a very large number of pregnancies but is nevertheless not dependent on maternal mortality. The Third World populations with excess female mortality in the reproductive age groups are also populations which are increasing rather rapidly.

The correct explanation for this phenomenon seems to lie in medical research which has shown that the female body's immunological defences against diseases are suppressed during pregnancy, especially the final three months, in order to avert the possibility that the mother's defences might turn on the foetus. In other words, any disease that happens to infect a woman during pregnancy is likely to find a more favourable terrain to begin its career than in the same woman outside pregnancy, even if the disease has nothing intrinsically to do with pregnancy. In a population with very high fertility the average woman's immune system is likely to be depressed for several years, giving diseases of all kinds (including the likes of malaria, tuberculosis, smallpox, influenza, plague and breast cancer) plenty of opportunity to strike. Procopius noted that plague was almost invariably fatal for pregnant women during the great epidemic at Constantinople in the sixth century AD. Weakening of the body's natural defence mechanisms is the reason for excess female mortality in the reproductive age groups in high fertility populations. The reduced fertility of populations in modern developed countries has transformed this state of affairs by reducing the period of increased susceptibility to disease.[111]

Aristotle is the only classical source to comment on sex-differential life expectancy. He thought that men lived longer on average than women, and added the very important observation that it was women who had had several pregnancies in particular who had shorter lifespans. This exactly parallels the situation in the modern populations discussed above. Similar statements appear in literature on early modern Greece in the r period of the last century. Aristotle was an extremely intelligent and shrewd observer who made many other observations of value for demographic and ecological purposes (and errors as well, but no one is perfect – see Chapter IV below on the importance of his biological works).

Some scholars dismiss his testimony on the grounds that he was biased against women and was merely expressing an attitude of male superiority. Criticising Aristotle for not sharing modern ideological assumptions about the equality of the sexes does not advance our understanding of the ancient world in any way whatsoever. The participants in the recent philosophical debate about whether Aristotle's biology was sexist have failed utterly to comprehend, for example, that Aristotle's recommendations concerning the ages of marriage of men and of women were a product of the historical development of classical Greek society out of the Dark Age age class systems, a type of socio-political organisation which exercises a rigid control over such matters. All that is to be learnt from perusing the literature in this modern philosophical debate is that scholars who attempt to interpret the views of ancient philosophers without first understanding the social environment which moulded their attitudes are unlikely to be making contributions to knowledge (see Chapter IV below). As far as purely biological problems are concerned, variance of reproductive performance is greater among males than among females, and this may be connected with differing degrees of variance between the sexes in other attributes, including intellectual ability.[112]

Even though Aristotle was a male chauvinist and his statement about sex-differential longevity was an a priori argument not based on statistical data, that statement was still probably correct because insofar as it concerns the reproductive age group it accords with the demographic patterns of modern high fertility populations. One of the authors of the Hippokratic corpus noted that women who became ill during pregnancy tended to have miscarriages or difficult deliveries. Sometimes in the cases in the Hippokratic corpus it is difficult to tell the difference between a natural miscarriage and an induced abortion. However several cases in which a pregnant woman had a miscarriage or abortion are described, and it is possible that deliberate termination of a pregnancy during illness sometimes occurred, in order to help the mother. The lower average age of death for adult women than for men found by Angel probably reflects a reality of excess female mortality in a high fertility population in ancient Greece. Since, however, such excess female mortality in the reproductive age groups is found in the *fastest* growing populations known to demographers in the modern world and is actually a consequence of their high fertility, mortality of this kind is not an impediment to very rapid population growth. Thus it would be quite wrong to use Angel's data as an argument against the possibility of rapid population growth in antiquity.[113]

The sex ratio of the skeletal populations from ancient Greece is heavily skewed in favour of males by differential preservation. However Aristotle and Plato, who made the only explicit references to the sex ratio in the corpus of surviving classical Greek literature, took it for granted that women constituted half, or nearly half, the population. This strongly suggests that classical Greek populations were not significantly affected by selective female infanticide. Indeed Pausanias even records that in the town of Patrai in Roman times women outnumbered men by 2:1. However this was evidently an exceptional state of affairs brought about by an unusual concentration of textile workers in a town which specialised in manufacturing clothes from the fine *bussos* of Elis, a type of flax (see Chapter III below).

It is worth reviewing briefly the factors which determine the evolution of the sex ratio of a cohort with increasing age. In modern low fertility populations women always live longer than men on average, although they suffer more from chronic autoimmune diseases such as arthritis. The reasons for greater female longevity are not known ·in detail, although they are probably connected with Darwin's sexual selection which acts mainly on males. It is a case of the sex with the higher variance in reproductive performance suffering a higher mortality rate because of more intense sexual competition for mates. In any event, the consequences of greater female longevity for the sex ratio are clear. Natural selection produces equal parental investment in children of both sexes, as was argued by the leading geneticist R.A. Fisher, and more males are born because they have a lower life expectancy at birth. The differences in life expectancy between the sexes then lead to a gradual evolution of the sex ratio with increasing age in a cohort. There is no evidence that the population of classical Athens did not follow this natural pattern. However many ancient historians have supposed that the sex ratio in classical Greece was heavily skewed by selective female infanticide. This view will have to be demolished after some reflections on fertility in ancient Greece.[114]

The maximum possible reproductive capacity of the individual human female is vastly greater than the average completed family size of even the fastest-growing populations known to demographers. The present author has come across records of two women in the United States who had 27 and 32 children respectively in the first half of this century, while there are two women in Britain today who are said to have 22 children each. Pliny states that Eutychis, a woman of Tralles in Asia Minor, had thirty children, of whom twenty survived her, while two poems (perhaps not trustworthy) in the *Greek Anthology* mention women who gave birth to 29 children. Even populations like the Hutterites, who had a growth rate of 4.13 per cent per annum at the time of study, did not average more than about nine children per woman. Thus the average rate of reproduction is always far below the theoretical maximum possible rate of natural increase, i.e. the rate of increase that would apply if each woman in a population had 32 children. This is true of all species of living organisms (cf. Chapter III.12 below on wheat).

Theoretically this may be explained in terms of natural selection for an optimum family size under competitive conditions (cf. the attempt of MacArthur & Wilson (1967) to define fitness in terms of K rather than r). It is essential to consider carefully the factors which restrain human reproduction. Charles Darwin observed correctly that the difficulty of gaining subsistence (food) was the main check on population growth, expressed in civilised nations, by which he meant Victorian England, by restraints on marriage. This was also true of ancient Greece. However we shall see in section 5 below that the precise mechanism by which marriage was restrained at the dawn of European history in ancient Greece was quite different from that of Victorian England. For the time being, the focus will be on other factors.[115]

A fundamental concept here is the idea of 'natural fertility', on the basis of which Louis Henry performed important research. This concept is easily misunderstood. It means that there is no deliberate attempt on the part of individuals or of couples to limit the number of births. Historical demographers verify its existence in a population by means of statistical techniques applied to reconstituted families, showing that reproductive behaviour is not altered by each subsequent birth. In other words the validity of the idea does not depend on the existence or absence of historical literary sources claiming that voluntary family limitation was being practised. Nor does natural fertility imply or require any conscious thought whatsoever among the members of a 'natural fertility population'.

In the absence of suitable quantitative data for the application of statistical techniques, ancient historians have always relied in discussing the possibility of voluntary family limitation in antiquity on attempting to generalise from anecdotal literary and documentary sources, the worst possible kind of evidence. For example there is the infamous letter of a man in Roman Egypt to a woman, apparently his wife, asking her to rear an expected infant should it turn out to be male, but expose it if it turned out to be female. It is not known whether or not the woman obeyed her husband, nor how typical they were of the population of Roman Egypt in holding such attitudes. In a similar episode in a work of fiction the wife did not obey her husband when she gave birth to a girl.

It is inevitable that ancient historians will continue to argue on the basis of anecdotal literary sources so long as the vast majority of them are trained in university faculties whose main raison d'être is classical literary criticism. However it is methodologically the wrong way to investigate a problem of this kind, when the subject of interest is the aggregate behaviour of a whole population, not the behaviour of individuals who may be atypical. No historical demographer would dream of taking statements by Shakespeare as serious evidence for the demography of Tudor England in the way that certain classical scholars have used bits of ancient Greek tragedy as evidence for the quantitative significance of infanticide in classical Greece. In fact the abundant evidence for aggregate behaviour found in English parish registers shows irrefutably that the marriage pattern described in Shakespeare's Romeo and Juliet is fiction. Ancient historians must reckon with the possibility that the works of Aiskhylos, Sophokles and Euripides too are just fiction and untrustworthy sources for a historian.[116]

No faith is put in such sources here. A better approach is to do what little can be done with respect to inferring reproductive behaviour from family reconstitution for classical Athens. The Attic orators provide us with details, not by any means complete, of a few rich families in classical Athens. Such a small and biased sample is far from entirely satisfactory. In particular the Attic orators *never* mention infant mortality (see section 6 below). Archaeological evidence shows that there was substantial infant mortality, perhaps of the order of 25-30 per cent or so as at Olynthos, and so all estimates of family size made from such literary sources must be evaluated accordingly. Nevertheless the small sample of rich Athenian families is of interest because historically the rich have always been the *first* to adopt voluntary family limitation measures on a large scale, as has been shown for early modern England, France, Switzerland and Italy. This is partly because some of the motives for high fertility among the poor in pre-modern societies, such as the need for children to provide support in old age and the desire for extra labour in a peasant family, do not apply to the rich, as we shall see later, and partly because, as Colinvaux put it in ecological terms, the niche of a rich man is larger and more expensive to fill than the niche of a poor man. Accordingly the rich always have a greater interest in family limitation than the poor and inevitably are less numerous than the poor. Accordingly it is to be expected that if family limitation had been practised by any segment of the Athenian citizen population, it would have been by the rich.[117]

In the speeches of Isaios there are instances of families of two sons and two daughters, a son and four daughters, three sons and two daughters, three sisters, another instance of two sons and two daughters, two sons

and four daughters, and five sons. A speech of Lysias mentions a family of
two sons and two daughters. The speeches of Demosthenes include cases
of three daughters and one son (with the wife then having two more sons
by a second husband after the death of her first husband), four sons and
one daughter, three sons and one daughter, and two sons and two
daughters (by two different wives). These are only those born who
survived to adulthood, or at least well past infancy, in these well-to-do
families.

All this information comes from forensic speeches, most of which were
delivered in cases of patriline discontinuity (discussed further in section 6
below) in which rival claims to the right to inherit an estate legally were
being made. In other words a man had died intestate without a
recognised son as his heir, or in the absence of a son had adopted an heir,
and the validity of the adoption was contested. In either case the history
of the family had to be discussed. It is remarkable how many large
families are attested in such circumstances, which would not be expected
to be a good source of evidence for large families. The evidence from the
Attic orators suggests, first, that rich Athenians were quite happy for
their property to be divided between several children under the partible
inheritance system, and secondly, that they were as happy to have
daughters as to have sons. If rich Athenians behaved in this way, it is
very likely that poor Athenians did so as well.[118]

If the line of argument here is correct, then there should be evidence
that the prevailing social values of classical Athens were hostile to the
idea of voluntary family limitation. Such evidence does exist, but it is the
end point of our argument rather than the starting point because
normative statements in literary sources have no quantitative
significance. Engels correctly observed that there is virtually no evidence
for infanticide in classical Athens and Aristotle recognised that there
would be popular opposition to the idea. Literary sources suggest that
poluteknia, the attribute of having many children, was regarded as a
desirable quality in fourth-century Athens, with reference to children of
both sexes.

This social norm developed several centuries before the classical period
at a time when the population density was very low. It entailed the
absence of an important potential brake on population growth. The
population growth of the first half of the first millennium BC eventually
led to severe pressure on the environmental carrying capacity of the land
and made it steadily more and more difficult for people to regard
poluteknia as a desirable quality. I believe that this eventually resulted
in a genuine shift in social mores in the course of classical antiquity,
explaining why there are many references to infanticide in sources of the
Hellenistic and Roman periods, but not in classical Athenian literature.
More on this later on.[119]

For the time being, however, we must concentrate on natural fertility.

If the classical Athenian citizen population was not practising voluntary family limitation on any significant scale, the Athenian population was a natural fertility population. This is an essential requirement for the application to it of the logistic model of population growth, discussed in section 2 above. Knowing that it was a natural fertility population unfortunately does not tell us anything about the actual levels of fertility prevailing at any particular time, because natural fertility populations exhibit enormous variations in average family size, as Henry discovered.

For example average completed family size of four to five has been observed amongst the Dobe !Kung bushmen of the Kalahari desert in south Africa and among the Gainj, a tribe of Papua New Guinea, to be contrasted with the nearly nine of the Hutterites. Much higher values are theoretically possible, if unlikely in practice. The populations of early modern Europe generally fell in between the extremes represented by the Hutterites on the one hand, and the !Kung and the Gainj on the other, but tending towards the lower end of the scale (five-six). On the other hand the population of the United States as a whole perhaps averaged about eight children per family, below the level of the Hutterites.

Such variations naturally affect the possibility of population growth. In the case of ancient Greece, the evidence for rapid population growth in the period from the eighth century BC onwards suggests that fertility was high rather than low, and is itself another argument against the idea that voluntary family limitation was widespread in archaic and classical Athens. By making various assumptions about infant mortality and other factors, Corvisier suggested that women in ancient Greece had to bear 4.6 children each on average to reproduce the population, in between the Gainj (4.3) and the Dobe !Kung (4.7). However this estimate only represents a minimum. The actual level could easily have been substantially higher in many *poleis* in many periods. An interesting passage of Theophrastos suggests that different parts of Greece were thought to have different fertility rates.[120]

Many factors may conspire to produce a very low total fertility rate in a natural fertility population. For example, among the Gainj late menarche (reported to be at the age of twenty, an extraordinarily late age) and marriage, long intervals between marriage and first pregnancy (about five years, again extraordinarily long), a high probability of widowhood at later reproductive ages, low effective fecundability and prolonged lactational amenorrhoea (mean birth intervals of four years) all combine with near-universal marriage, a low prevalence of primary sterility, no evidence for contraception or for venereal diseases affecting fertility and no divorce to produce a total fertility rate of only 4.3 children per woman. These are the types of factors which must be taken into account in research on fertility in ancient Greece. The most important factor of all is undoubtedly breastfeeding producing amenorrhoea. Knodel (1977) calculated that the difference between short and long periods of breastfeeding could make the difference between a woman bearing 7-8 or 12-13 children on average under natural fertility conditions. It is here that we shall start.

A few sources from antiquity give information on the duration of breastfeeding. Unfortunately none of them refers specifically to Athens, but the periods are always long, extending from over one to four years. The average duration of amenorrhoea is increased as the average duration of breastfeeding increases, but at a slower rate, and a contraceptive effect is produced. Aristotle paid some attention to lactation and noted that it tended to prevent conception. This contraceptive effect appears to be caused, however, not so much by the mere act of suckling as by a high daily frequency of suckling. The contraceptive effect of lactation is often reinforced in pre-modern societies by the avoidance of sexual intercourse until the child is weaned. Galen recommended abstention. In Athens a speech of Lysias suggests that a mother with a young child slept in a different room to her husband. Prolonged lactation increases birth spacing, but also reduces infant mortality because of greater immunological protection to the child from the mother's antibodies. Modern research suggests that the market demand for female labour may affect the average duration of breastfeeding. Accordingly it may be expected that in classical Athens, in which the ideal of the sexual division of labour was that women should be housewives and not go out to work, besides the fact that the agricultural system required low labour inputs, the average duration of breastfeeding would have been long rather than short. However poor women who had to work for a living may have had higher fertility rates as a result.[121]

One of our best sources for breastfeeding in antiquity is Soranos, a doctor of Roman times who made recommendations for wet-nursing. He recognised that the breast produces more milk if suckling is more frequent. However he advised wet-nurses not to breastfeed at all times day and night and not to allow the child always to suckle just because it cries. The demographic consequences of such advice, if followed, are likely to be a shortening of the period of amenorrhoea and a probability of becoming pregnant again more rapidly in the case of a mother who is having coitus. Soranos was writing for the Roman upper classes who employed wet-nurses, although moralising authors of the Roman period advised upper-class women to breastfeed their own children, as it was thought that the characteristics of the mother would be transmitted through her milk. The mere employment of wet-nurses should have increased fertility amongst Roman upper-class women by ending periods of post-partum amenorrhoea quite rapidly, exposing them to the risk of becoming pregnant again.

A wet-nurse, Eurykleia, is mentioned several times in the *Odyssey*. In classical Athens it is not clear how widespread wet-nursing as a form of wage labour may have been. One passage in the Demosthenic corpus claims that many, presumably poor, Athenian women had resorted to it in a period of general hardship. The *phialai exeleutherikai* inscriptions mention manumitted slaves who worked as wet-nurses in Athens in the fourth century BC. The methods of infant feeding and care used in Sparta attracted attention from a wider audience. Apparently the Spartans did not use the swaddling clothes that were in widespread use elsewhere in Greece, as shown by terracottas. Plato considered the regulations that would be necessary for infant care in his ideal *polis*.

The use of human milk is assumed by our literary sources. It is not clear to what extent animal milk was also used, although vessels for animal milk have been found on archaeological sites. The Jewish Talmud mentions the direct suckling of the udder of animals by human infants, but not the consumption of bottled animal milk. Animal milk cannot be preserved for long in the heat of the Mediterranean (except as cheese). The low frequency of the allele(s) controlling production in adults of the enzyme lactase, required for digestion of lactose, in the modern populations of southern Greece and Italy suggests that consumption of animal milk in adulthood was rare in the past in these areas (see section 7 below). Soranos also states that rickets in infants, caused by vitamin D deficiency owing to insufficient exposure to sunlight, was especially characteristic of Rome, that unhealthy city. However it was not unknown in Greece as well, where it was associated with the use of swaddling clothes. Soranos also advised wet-nurses to eat fine white leavened loaves of bread wheat, about which much more will be said in Chapter III below.[122]

Prolonged breastfeeding by spacing pregnancies even in the complete absence of voluntary family limitation, was the most important factor reducing the average number of children per woman to a level a long way below the theoretical maximum in all pre-modern populations. After about six months of lactation the supply of breast milk starts to decrease even with frequent suckling, and other types of food are usually added to the infant's diet. However modern experience among Australian Aborigines shows that breast milk alone may be adequate for at least the first nine months, if not longer, and it becomes gradually richer during the first few months. Quantity of milk is not the only nor even necessarily the most important factor. Soranos recommended the introduction of soup, eggs, diluted wine and crumbs of bread at six months of age. His recommendation to give wine to children at such a young age is particularly noteworthy. Similar advice is found in the Hippokratic corpus and in Rufus of Ephesos, but Aristotle rejected it.

Nevertheless continuing lactation, especially if combined with restrictions on sexual intercourse between wife and husband, may easily spin out birth intervals to three or four years on average. Amenorrhoea was the usual situation for women in the reproductive age group in historical populations. It is now often thought that the inventors of the modern contraceptive pill erred in designing a product that would mimic the menstrual cycle, instead of the natural condition of amenorrhoea. However, the ancient Greeks, like other pre-modern populations, generally had an interest in increasing fertility, for reasons to be discussed below. As a result amenorrhoea was sometimes regarded as an undesirable condition. The Hippokratic corpus contains passages devoted to folk remedies intended to induce the return of the menstrual cycle. The demographic consequences of a reduction in the average duration of lactation would be a reduction in birth spacing, permitting a larger average completed family size, but also an increase in infant mortality.[123]

Before considering the other factors which influence fertility, we must explain why high fertility was desirable in archaic and classical Greece. First, it is essential to remember that the populations of Third World countries are expanding rapidly today because people in general want to have more children. Only the most totalitarian states, such as China, can attempt to curb this natural human desire, and then only with extreme difficulty. In Papua New Guinea four main reasons have been ascertained for having large families: (1) children support their parents in old age; (2) more children bring in more income; (3) the family will be happier; 4) the family will have greater status and strength. Other motives may also be found in ancient Greek literature, such as the desire to avoid patriline discontinuity and the wish to have descendants to perform the burial rites.[124]

The first of the motives in New Guinea is arguably the most important of all, and is equally relevant to ancient Greece. Historical populations and modern Third World countries do not have welfare states or complex social security systems providing old age pensions. Classical Athens was exceptional in providing pay at the expense of the *polis* for poor disabled citizens who could not work for a living. However even there it is clear that children had to maintain their elderly parents, by law. This was intended to be the main source of support for the elderly. In a population with high mortality amongst infants and young children, it is necessary for parents to have several children to ensure that one or two of them survive to old age to support their parents. It has been suggested that this is the single most important motive for high fertility in Third World countries.

In ancient Greece, the obligation of children to support their retired parents is one of the commonest themes in the surviving corpus of literature. The obligations of children to their parents are parodied in Aristophanes' *Clouds*. Classical scholars have not realised its demographic consequences, or the fact that it is a major reason for massive population growth in developing countries today. Hesiod, who enjoyed grumbling about the state of the world, or at least the condition of Askra in Boiotia, complained that it was characteristic of the miserable Iron Age that children did not support their parents. His testimony shows that this important motive for high fertility was already of importance to the Greeks *c*. 700 BC, at the end of the r period.

In Athens the obligation of children to support their parents was enshrined in law, as in all other Greek *poleis*. Solon is said to have exempted illegitimate children from this obligation, to punish adultery, as well as sons whose fathers had not taught them a trade, and sons whose fathers had hired them out as male prostitutes (a phenomenon to be distinguished carefully from the institutionalised homosexuality discussed in section 5 below). In all other circumstances, failure of a son to support his parents was a serious offence, which incurred such penalties as a prohibition on speaking in the assembly. Children who maltreated their parents faced *atimia*, disfranchisement, in the classical period. Those who had received this punishment were re-enfranchised in the desperate circumstances after the battle of Aigospotamoi, before the surrender of Athens to Lysander. The fact that parents desperately wanted to have children to support them in old age shows that adults had a *reasonable expectation of reaching old age*. This militates against the view frequently expressed by ancient historians that life expectancy was extremely low (see section 3 above).[125]

Theoretically, the importance of the need to have children for support in old age as a motive for high fertility may be reduced by the availability of other forms of social insurance. For example, it has been argued that adults who live in extended families will have less need of children for this purpose than adults who live in nuclear families. In section 6 below it will be argued that the nuclear family was indeed characteristic of the social structure of Athens at the familial level, with an admixture of three-generation families but no laterally extended families. The implication of this is that ancient Greek family organisation favoured high fertility to a greater extent than, for example, such family forms as the Slav *zadruga*, a very complex extended family form found in the Balkans from the mediaeval period onwards.[126]

The second motive for high fertility emphasised by demographers researching on Third World populations relates to the economic benefits that the availability of additional labour may confer on a family. Caldwell (1982) argued that there are only two types of fertility regime: (1) where there is no economic gain to individuals from restricting fertility; (2) where there is economic gain from restricting fertility. His analysis is closely related to Chayanov's (1966) theory of the peasant family, in which the largest families are the richest families because they have a larger labour force and so are able to cultivate more land. Both theories function better in the context of a thinly populated region with a low population density in which additional land is readily available, such as Russia for which Chayanov's model was designed, or the areas of sub-Saharan Africa characterised by shifting cultivation in the past, in which Caldwell specialises. Neither theory works so well in the context of a densely populated region in which all available land that may be used for farming is already being exploited and agricultural productivity is static. However, this motivation for high fertility may still have some effect under such circumstances if privately owned land is available for leasing. For example, in classical Athens the property of minors whose father was dead could be leased out by the guardian until they came of age. In effect this second motive for high fertility is likely to have a powerful influence during an r phase of a population's history, but once the following K phase is reached, then it should cease to be influential.

This is exactly what we find in the case of Greek history. Hesiod expressed the opinion that more sons could easily bring extra wealth to a family. However he was also attracted by the contradictory notion of avoiding estate subdivision, which was bound to ensue if a man had more than one son surviving his death, under the partible inheritance system characteristic of ancient Greece. By the fourth century BC, a K period, a diametrically opposed opinion prevailed. Aristotle thought that having several children inevitably led to poverty. He was writing at a time when Greece was overcrowded with people and no spare land was available, and emigration was the main response to poverty. The fourth-century peak population density was not sustained. After further ups and downs, in the first half of the nineteenth century AD after the War of Independence, another r phase, literature on Greece again affirms that having a large family was a pathway to prosperity, a state of affairs which did not last for long, as was shown in section 2 above. The importance of this motive for high fertility has been correlated with changing population density in the course of Greek history.

In the logistic model, as applied to Greece between the eighth and the fourth centuries BC, the decreasing importance of this motive provides a mechanism for translating increasing competition for resources with increasing population density into decreasing fertility and so a decreasing rate of natural increase of the population, even given constant life expectancy at birth. However, the first motive continues to operate even at high population densities, because people always need support in old age, regardless of the population density. Moreover emigration as a response to population pressure encourages social conservatism because it does not necessitate any changes in the reproductive behaviour of those who stay behind. For these two reasons it took a long time for an interest in voluntary family limitation to develop in Greece, in spite of the population pressure from the time of Hesiod onwards.[127]

The desire for extra labour as a motive for high fertility is influenced not only by population density but also by the precise requirements for labour of different agricultural systems. For example, Caldwell argued that children are profitable to their parents from a very early age in sub-Saharan Africa, but diametrically opposed conclusions have been reached for south-east Asia. The traditional shifting hoe cultivation of root crops of sub-Saharan Africa is quite different from the wet-rice cultivation of south-east Asia. The two systems differ in every respect, including their labour requirements. Different conclusions may be appropriate for different geographical regions regarding the profitability or otherwise of children to their parents. In the case of ancient Greece, which had an agricultural system that required a low labour input for short-fallow plough cultivation, with ploughing being an activity unsuitable for young children, children were probably of less economic value to their parents than in the hoe cultivation of sub-Saharan Africa. As a result having a large family because of the economic benefits that would flow to the parents during their active working lives was probably a motive for high fertility of less importance in ancient Greece than the need to have children to provide support in old age.[128]

Caldwell (1982) also argued that changes in the direction of intergenerational wealth flows accounted for the demographic transition to low fertility in the populations of modern developed countries. In other words instead of wealth flowing from children to parents as in pre-modern societies making it profitable to have many children, parental expenditure on children began to exceed the return as the cost of education steadily mounted, resulting in a desire to reduce fertility. We shall see in section 5 below that the strong forms of age class organisation in ancient Greece indeed followed the pattern which Caldwell postulates as typical of the populations of non-developed countries. Agapitidis (1969), discussing fertility decline in modern Greece, argued that children in Greece are now perceived as a burden because of the cost of education, instead of a help in farming as they used to be. In antiquity Diodoros Siculus argued that the population of Egypt was so large because the cost of bringing up a child until the age of maturity was only twenty drachmae.

Another important line of argument employed by demographers, derived this time from Cain (1982), maintains that it is often *mothers* in developing countries who desire to have *sons* (contrary to the hypothesis held by some classicists of husbands imposing selective female infanticide on their wives), because sons are better able than daughters to help their mothers in a society characterised by marked sexual inequality. This too is relevant to classical antiquity, because Plutarch states that mothers wanted sons for this very reason. An argument which follows on from mothers' preference for sons is that the rate of natural increase is likely to be maximised when mortality is at intermediate levels and the parents wish to have at least one son to survive them. This again is a plausible scenario for classical Athens. Finally as a motive for high fertility in Athens the call of Perikles in Thucydides' Funeral Oration to the Athenian women to bear more children should be mentioned. It is perhaps unlikely that people took any more notice of what politicians say about how they should order their private lives in antiquity than they do today, but Perikles' call was logical in that extra manpower could help to maintain the Athenian empire and at the same time be fed from the profits of empire.[129]

The argument so far has been intended to demonstrate that the same motives for high fertility which underlie population growth in the Third World today also operated in ancient Greece. The implication is that there is no rational foundation for supposing that infanticide was widespread in classical Athens. Infanticide will be discussed a little further on, but first a range of other factors which influenced fertility in ancient Greece must be considered. Above all fertility is a function, first, of the duration of the phase in a person's life when reproduction is possible, and, secondly, of the duration of the portion of that phase during which the person is admitted to the breeding population.

Classical sources generally state that puberty commenced in both sexes at about the ages of thirteen or fourteen on average. This is a quite young age relative to both well documented 'primitive' societies in the modern world (e.g. the Dobe !Kung and the Gainj) and to certain populations in early modern Europe. However, the onset of puberty is heavily influenced by nutritional status. It is conceivable that the statements found in classical sources only refer to the upper classes and their entourage, as Aristotle rightly states that luxurious living accelerated puberty. Moreover the placing of puberty at age 13-14, i.e. at the end of the second seven-year phase into which the human lifespan was divided in ancient arithmological theories, may simply be an a priori argument intended to accommodate human development within the framework of these theories. The reader will appreciate the ultimate origins of these theories after digesting section 5 below. It is also noteworthy that attempts were made employing herbal drugs to delay the onset of puberty in the case of handsome male slaves for paederastic purposes. In fact keeping the slave badly nourished would have done the trick.[130]

In any case variations in the age of menarche in women only have a minor effect on fertility. Moreover menarche does not immediately permit the possibility of conception, because a period of adolescent sterility follows the beginning of menstruation in most women, owing to the fact that large-scale production of two hormones which are both necessary for successful ovulation does not commence simultaneously. Aristotle expressed a belief in adolescent sterility on a priori grounds. In addition the possibility of conception at a young age does not mean that pregnancy is necessarily likely to be successful (see section 2 above on Troizen). At the other end of the reproductive period, ancient sources placed menopause at about age 45 for women, occasionally 50, and the cessation of reproduction at age 65 for men, sometimes 70. The data for menopause do not differ significantly from the figures for modern populations, although nutrition may have a minor effect on the age of menopause. Thus the duration of the reproductive period in ancient Greek populations was not significantly different from modern populations. Both menarche and menopause are now thought to be initiated by hormonal changes in the brain, and menopause is not simply a question of the ovary's running out of eggs.[131]

Two more important pieces of evidence that classical Greek populations were natural fertility populations should be mentioned at this point. Xenophon recommended that men should delay marriage until about the age of thirty, when sexual desire was less strong, in order to avoid having too many children. Clearly there is an interest in family limitation here, but it is equally clear that Xenophon does not conceive of the possibility of voluntary family limitation measures taken by the couple *within* marriage. The only way he could think of to reduce the number of children likely to be procreated in marriage was to *delay* marriage. Malthus made exactly the same assumption in his famous essay on population. The only way that Malthus could foresee to reduce the numbers of the poor was to prevent them marrying and so breeding. He could not visualise voluntary family limitation measures being employed by couples on a large scale. Malthus's assumption has been confirmed by the research of the Cambridge Population Group, which has shown that the population of early modern England as a whole was indeed a natural fertility population. The fact that Xenophon shared Malthus's assumption suggests that he would have regarded the Athenian population as a natural fertility population, if he had possessed the concept of natural fertility. For Xenophon, the purpose of marriage was procreation. He added that men could satisfy their sexual desires in other ways, by which he meant male paederasty and female prostitution.[132]

The second crucial text comes from Aristotle in a fascinating passage on Crete. He states that the age class systems of the Cretans segregated men from women in an attempt to control the birth rate, at a time when it is clear from other types of evidence that the population of Crete as a whole was actually increasing. The sexual desires of the men were certainly catered for by institutionalised male paederasty, while the women appear to have been left to their own devices, which may well mean lesbianism. This conjuncture of circumstances again shows that such populations could grow. However it suggests that they did so in the virtual absence of effective voluntary family limitation measures at the *individual* level, since otherwise segregation would not have been thought to be necessary. Aristotle's information suggests that the Cretans shared Xenophon's and Malthus's assumption about the prevalence of natural fertility behaviour among married couples. The extraordinary demography of Crete and the closely related demographic system of Sparta will be discussed in much more detail in section 5 below. Our conclusion at this point is that natural fertility in ancient Greek populations from the eighth to the fourth centuries BC was yet another factor making feasible prolonged population growth. However it must be remembered that natural fertility populations need not have high fertility levels and need not be increasing rapidly.[133]

If contraceptive measures are not being taken, then the frequency and timing of coitus also have a major influence on fertility. Judging by a fascinating passage of Lucretius, some people in antiquity also thought erroneously that the position adopted during coitus affected the probability of conception. Lucretius thought that women were most likely to conceive after intercourse in the manner of four-footed mammals. There does not appear to be any parallel in Greek literature for this statement, but it may throw light on the fact that vaginal penetration from the rear is portrayed more often than vaginal penetration from the front in Attic vase paintings. This would also cast doubt on the claim of Sir Kenneth Dover that many of these vases are depictions of heterosexual anal intercourse. Aristotle correctly believed that women may conceive in any position.

There is hardly any evidence on frequency of coitus from ancient Greece. It is doubtless an aspect of human behaviour about which it is difficult to obtain reliable statistical information for any period of history, or even the present day. All that we have is the law of Solon prescribing that the husband of an *epiklêros*, an heiress, had to have sexual intercourse with her at least three times a month. This is an extremely low frequency of coitus for young adults and low for most adult age groups, judging by surveys of sexual behaviour in modern populations. If the husband had combined the legal minimum frequency of coitus with the recommendations made by classical writers regarding the timing of coitus within the menstrual cycle, then the poor *epiklêros* would have had virtually no chance of becoming pregnant, if that had been her desire!

Those recommendations, which were made to improve the chances of procreation, had the opposite effect, because the position of ovulation within the menstrual cycle was not understood in antiquity. Ancient authors recommend intercourse for the purpose of procreation either just before or after menstruation. They may be forgiven for this mistake, as a modern textbook on demography states that many couples in the United States today are misinformed regarding the timing of ovulation within the menstrual cycle. Doubtless this is true of other modern populations as well. To the extent that the ancient recommendations were followed in practice, couples relying on such advice would de facto have been employing the rhythm method of contraception, although it was not understood as such in antiquity. The question of why concealed ovulation evolved is a thorny problem, frequently discussed by sociobiologists. In other mammals and some other primates oestrus signals the onset of ovulation. Burley (1979) suggested that concealed ovulation arose by means of natural selection to counter a conscious tendency by females to avoid conception and pregnancy through abstinence from intercourse around the time of ovulation. In other words she suggested that concealed ovulation served to increase fertility against a conscious human desire to decrease it. However, humans in classical antiquity interpreted female menstruation in the same way as other primates interpret oestrus, i.e. as heralding the onset of ovulation. Consequently sexual intercourse immediately before and after menstruation was recommended for the purpose of procreation. Evidently this would defeat natural selection if the Burley hypothesis were correct. Moreover, fully developed consciousness probably does not have as long an evolutionary history in hominids as concealed ovulation. Kinsey et al. (1953) found that women tend to prefer intercourse around the time of menstruation.

The answer to this problem probably lies in a different direction. Since concealed ovulation is an alteration of the reproductive system it is likely to have purely demographic consequences. It is better to try to explain the phenomenon in terms of the effect of these consequences on evolutionary fitness before we resort to conscious behavioural explanations. We must distinguish between the maximum possible completed family size and the optimum completed family size for maximising child survivorship. As women are continuously receptive to coitus, in principle they may have a very large number of children, but in practice under primitive conditions the vast majority of women could not possibly bring up twenty or thirty children successfully. If they tried to do so, inevitably the rate of child survivorship to adulthood would be extremely low. Accordingly it is arguable that concealed ovulation evolved by natural selection to counter the effects of continuous receptivity to coitus, by *reducing* fertility from a theoretical maximum to a much lower level in practice that was optimal for child survivorship, in accordance with the general mammalian tendency towards increased parental investment in offspring which is carried to its furthest extent in humans. Continuous receptivity to coitus was more important for pair bonding in hominids than concealed ovulation, particularly after the evolution of consciousness, because in the monkey *Cercopithecus aethiops* concealed ovulation is associated with promiscuity.

If this hypothesis is correct, then the recommendations of ancient Greek authors regarding the timing of coitus within the menstrual cycle were treading in the footsteps of the path followed by natural selection. Logically the interpretation of the demographic transition in early modern Europe given by Caldwell (1982) goes still further along the same path, as increased parental investment in educating their children accompanied a reduction in fertility. However at that point along the path culture took over from biology, and increased parental investment in children no longer involved strictly biological change. The extraordinary effectiveness of nature's stratagem of concealed ovulation is shown by the fact that the ancient Greeks had no certain knowledge of the length of the gestation period in humans. Aristotle was led to believe that man was the only animal with a variable gestation period.[134]

If voluntary family limitation measures were not being practised on any substantial scale in Greece from the eighth to the fourth centuries BC, as is argued here, then the determinants of admission to the breeding population were of crucial importance as regulators of fertility levels. Age of admission to the breeding population is the most important of all human demographic parameters. The problem then is to ascertain average ages of first marriage for both sexes and investigate the determinants of these marriage patterns. Before moving on to marriage, however, a few observations are in order on natural sterility.

A small proportion of both sexes is sterile in each generation throughout the normal reproductive years, perhaps about 3-5 per cent. In addition the sterility rate gradually increases with age, slowly until the 35-39 age group and then rapidly thereafter, in the case of women. Men of course have fertility problems as well. Sterility may be induced by damage to the female reproductive organs, either during pregnancy or induced abortion. The fact that the latter was an important cause of acquired sterility was well known to the authors of the Hippokratic corpus. In addition many diseases may cause damage to human reproduction. Suffice it to say here that venereal diseases were probably fairly insignificant as causes of acquired sterility in classical Greece, but on the other hand malaria and tuberculosis, both of which may affect fertility as well as mortality, were rampant in the fourth century BC (see section 7 below).

Besides diseases, Aristotle believed that obesity reduced fertility. He noted that many marriages were infertile, but many of the people involved then had children with different spouses. Childlessness was a good reason for divorce in ancient Greece. Remarriage was freely permitted for both sexes, minimising the demographic consequences of sterility and also of mortality among spouses. However, rates of remarriage in classical Athens may have varied according to social class. Remarriage of both spouses tends to reduce the proportion of childless women by about 50 per cent. Those who were still unlucky could only invest their faith in a visit to a sanctuary of the god of healing Asklepios, who was called on frequently to deal with problems of infertility. Certain causes of acquired sterility which are curable today were not curable in antiquity.[135]

For those not afflicted by sterility, age of marriage was a crucial determinant of fertility levels and patterns. Ancient literary sources agree in recommending a late age of first marriage for men, around the age of thirty or sometimes even later. It is not necessarily sensible to take all such recommendations at face value, since normative statements are not identical to ontological or existential statements. For example, it has been suggested that when Aristotle recommended that men should marry at about the age of 37, he was simply recommending the age at which he had married his own wife, Pythias. He suggests that men married at an early age in some parts of Greece. The evidence suggests that that was the case in Crete, Troizen and Ephesos for example. However the meagre available evidence does suggest that men married considerably later than women on average in classical Athens and Sparta (see section 5 below), at about thirty. Delaying marriage and procreation for the purpose of obtaining legitimate heirs in this way could have been the product of many different factors, including socio-political imperatives, economic pressures, and cultural attitudes, which will all have to be considered later on. It is not implied that the achieving of sexual gratification was delayed in the same way.[136]

In contrast all available evidence suggests that in all *poleis* women married for the first time at a much younger age, before the age of twenty. B. Shaw (1987) suggested that it occurred at about eighteen in the Roman empire, in which case the marriage pattern which Hajnal postulated for Mediterranean Europe in the early modern period would already have been in place in Roman times. However it is dangerous to generalise about a region the size of the Roman empire, or even just the western half of the empire as Shaw did, in respect of demographic patterns.

The evidence of literary sources for Greece suggests that the average age of first marriage for women varied from *polis* to *polis*. For example Aristotle's information about the difficulties of first pregnancy in Troizen suggests that women there indeed married at an early age, certainly before seventeen at which age these difficulties tend to be diminished. Similarly Xenophon clearly believed in very early marriage for women and reflected the situation in classical Athens, where orphan girls were assimilated to *epiklêroi* and had to be found a husband from the age of fourteen. However other sources, including Hesiod (but see n. 137 for doubts about his evidence) and Aristotle, provide evidence for first marriage of women (or at least Aristotle's own wife) at about the age of eighteen, while Plutarch suggests that it took place at about seventeen on Keos. In Sparta marriage for women may have been delayed until eighteen or even about twenty. In any case, marriage of women in their teens creates the possibility of very high fertility rates, which tend to be reduced in practice by extended periods of lactation spacing out births.[137]

The determinants of average age of first marriage for both sexes will be fully explored in sections 5 & 6 below. Here it is only necessary to consider the effects on fertility of a pattern of first marriage at about thirty for men and fifteen to twenty for women. Such a pattern does not maximise fertility, but rather inherently tends to reduce it, because women approaching the peak of their reproductive powers are joined in marriage to men whose reproductive powers, expressed in terms of coital frequency, are already waning. Such research as has been undertaken on these matters indicates that a large number of acts of coitus are required on average for conception to take place, especially if the menstrual cycle is not understood as in antiquity, given that conception may only be possible for 12-24 hours in each menstrual cycle. The earliest research in this field suggested that as many as two or three hundred acts of coitus may be required on average, although more recent studies have substantially reduced this estimate. Decreasing age-specific fertility rates of women with rising age are caused in part by the declining sexual powers of their usually older spouses. Even Xenophon appreciated this, in an elementary manner. It is a mechanism for decreasing fertility levels which does not require any conscious thought on the part of the spouses and so does not contradict the idea of natural fertility behaviour within marriage.[138]

The marriage structure of classical Athens, with marriage at a very late age for males and a very early age for females, was a power structure in which husbands were entitled to exercise authority over their wives by virtue of their greater age, the fundamental principle of social organisation of the *polis*. Aristotle appreciated this fully. He stated that marriage was a type of 'friendship' in which one party is superior to the other. He drew an analogy between the relationships of husband and wife, father and son, elder and junior, and in general ruler and ruled. All four of these power relationships depended on the principle of differences in age to confer legitimacy on the superior party in the relationship. The type of analysis proffered by Aristotle is sometimes denounced as a blatant example of male chauvinism. In a way it is, because Aristotle undoubtedly believed in the superiority of the male over the female. However it is also a very powerful sociological analysis of how the power of the male over the female in marriage was derived from the most basic principles of social organisation of the *polis*. The raison d'être of the marriage patterns of the *polis* was to arrange the balance of power between the sexes in accordance with its fundamental principles of social organisation. Restraining fertility was not the *purpose* of this marriage pattern, but it was an important unintended *effect* of it, about which much more will be said in section 5 below.[139]

Under such circumstances variations in age-specific nuptiality may have a very substantial impact on fertility and may also take effect more rapidly than variations in age-specific fertility itself. Henry found that the average completed family size for a series of natural fertility populations which he studied was 8.42 children for women who married at the age of twenty, but only 6.25 for women who married at the age of twenty-five. In other words, each year of delayed marriage tends to reduce average completed family size by about 5 per cent. Evidently a lowering of the average age of first marriage can create the potential for very substantial population growth, *ceteris paribus*, and a very high average age of first marriage for both sexes did impede population growth in early modern England and France.

These two countries differed from their North American colonies principally in this respect, as first marriage for both sexes took place at a much younger age on average in North America. That is the difference between the slow rate of increase of the English population and the almost stationary French population on the one hand, and the very high rates of natural increase displayed by the colonists on the other. Similarly some rather impressionistic literature on Greece in the first half of the nineteenth century AD speaks of *both* sexes frequently marrying then in their *teens*, a state of affairs which is conducive to the possibility of maximising fertility. Greece in the early nineteenth century AD was like North America, a thinly populated land with spare capacity. Early marriage, without the need to work for a long time to accumulate the resources to support a family, was a realistic option just as it was in North America. The marriage pattern of classical Athens and Sparta (late marriage for males, early marriage for females) lay in between that of early modern England and France (late marriage for both sexes) and that of North America and Greece at the time of the War of Independence (early marriage for both sexes). Accordingly it is to be expected that the fertility of classical Athens also lay at intermediate levels. The determinants of age at marriage are of the most fundamental demographic significance (see sections 5 & 6 below).[140]

It is time to return now to the question of voluntary family limitation, especially infanticide, in ancient Greece, which has been emphasised by many ancient historians, in spite of the fact that there is no evidence for it in classical Athens. The arguments which have been deployed in favour of the importance of infanticide in classical Greece rest on a long string of methodological errors. First, there is the failure to treat separately sources dating to different periods. For example, it has been claimed that 'exposure can be discussed as a general phenomenon of Greek society not bound to any one period of Greek history'. This is just bad historical method, compounded by the illusion that populations are static and do not vary significantly over time. It is striking that almost all of the sources on infanticide collected by Eyben (1980/1) date to the Hellenistic or Roman periods. It must be stressed that evidence from, say, Roman Egypt, such as the infamous letter mentioned earlier, is not evidence for classical Greece.[141]

Secondly, there is the misuse of comparative methods in history. Quoting a long list of other societies in which infanticide is alleged to have been widespread proves nothing for classical Athens if it cannot be established on the basis of evidence from classical Athens that infanticide actually occurred there. In section 5 below, where parallels are drawn between Greece and East Africa and New Guinea, the reader will notice that care has been taken to establish on the basis of classical sources that the phenomena under consideration actually occurred in ancient Greece. Furthermore, the most powerful applications of the comparative method in history depend in any case on finding patterns of significant differences between societies, not similarities, as will be seen in the contrast of

Greece and Rome in sections 5 & 6 below (cf. Chapter I above).

Thirdly, there is the abuse of anecdotal sources. For example, the famous fragment of Poseidippos is almost meaningless in the absence of the context, like all fragments of Greek comedy and tragedy. I recall reading somewhere once that all reconstructions of the plots of plays of the New Comedy made by classical scholars on the basis of fragments have been shown to be incorrect in *every* case in which further evidence was subsequently discovered. This serves to emphasise what a subjective process literary criticism is. Tales of abandoned children probably appealed to the poets of the New Comedy in the early Hellenistic period because they provided a story with an unhappy beginning to arouse the sympathy of the audience, to which the poet could add a happy ending.[142]

Fourthly, the failure to comprehend fundamental elements of population biology merits a more extended discussion here. Scholars who believe in the importance of infanticide in many historical and primitive human populations generally make the fundamental conceptual error of treating regulation of *family* size and regulation of *population* size as synonyms, concluding that if family regulation is being practised, it proves that the population as a whole is being regulated and stabilised. In fact many biologists believe that regulation of family size may be practised by any individual of any species of animal. However the aim of such regulation is always to achieve the optimum family size for maximising survivorship of children. In other words regulation of family size is an instrument for maximising evolutionary fitness. Natural selection always works on individuals, never on groups. Colinvaux put it most strikingly with his argument that infanticide is a device for boosting human population growth, however paradoxical this may seem. This argument puts a dagger in the heart of a huge volume of entirely misconceived literature on infanticide. It goes back, however, to the research of Lack, who showed that in birds natural selection acts so as to produce an optimum family size, reflected in the size of clutches of eggs. If the amount of food that a bird can collect is limited, laying a large number of eggs is likely to lead to very high infant mortality. A smaller clutch of eggs means more food per infant bird, a higher probability of survivorship, and so creates the possibility of a faster rate of population increase.

Colinvaux proposed that the human family should be interpreted as a clutch of births built up sequentially, and so subject to natural selection as regards family size. Clearly voluntary family limitation need not lead to population *stability*. In a review of the problem of population stability in ecology, Connell & Sousa (1983) concluded that it is more appropriate to think in terms of population persistence within stochastically defined limits rather than in terms of stability. As regards high infant mortality and neglect of infants by parents, Clutton-Brock et al. (1989) suggested that in deer lactation is much more costly than gestation. Consequently it may be advantageous to produce more young than can be reared and then reduce the number of offspring to an affordable level, possibly explaining why juvenile survival in these mammals declines more rapidly than fertility with increasing population density and pressure on resources. In humans the gestation period is longer and birth is more difficult than in other mammals. As a result it makes sense for women to be able to restrict the number of gestations as well, even though lactation is more expensive than gestation in energetic terms in women too.

In pre-modern human societies in which breast milk is the main source of food for infants and continues to provide a degree of immunological protection for young children even when it is supplemented by other foods, it is not easy for a woman to provide adequately for two children simultaneously. If she becomes pregnant again and gives birth within a year and a half of a previous birth, the risk of mortality for the first child is increased by over 50 per cent in many Third World countries today. Similarly the chances of death are substantially increased for the second child as well. If the mother attempts to feed and bring up both of them, they *both* have an increased risk of mortality. In such a situation, it is a reasonable hypothesis that infanticide of one infant, or better still (from the viewpoint of evolutionary fitness) abortion of one pregnancy at an early stage, increases the probability that one of the two infants will survive. This is a theoretical reason why abortion should be a more productive strategy than infanticide. Ethical considerations are irrelevant here.

Anthropological literature provides plenty of evidence for infanticide in two circumstances which are particularly relevant to this scenario. Both occur among the Dobe !Kung Bushmen, for example. First, killing or exposure of deformed or weak infants is common in primitive societies, as in ancient Greece and Rome. It is a waste of the mother's energies to attempt to bring up infants who would be unlikely to make a genetic contribution to the next generation anyway. Secondly, in many primitive societies it is customary for one of a pair of twins to be killed or exposed, because a mother cannot produce enough milk for two infants at the same time. These two cases are congruent with the explanation of voluntary family limitation as a mechanism for *increasing* child survivorship and so the family's contribution to the next generation, i.e. the evolutionary fitness of the parents. The Jewish Talmud recommended that a mother who had twins should suckle one herself and hire a wet-nurse for the other, but presumably many poor people in antiquity could not have afforded to hire a wet-nurse.[143]

Other mistakes are frequently made in this field. Some categories of well known evidence from antiquity, such as the inscriptions from Hellenistic Miletos, are inherently tendentious because of the fairly small sample of families. The probability of fluctuations in the sex ratio is inversely proportional to population size. Moreover, the mercenaries listed on these inscriptions (some with their families) hardly constitute a homogeneous population, which is necessary for meaningful demographic analysis. However, it should not be forgotten that mercenary service itself probably had significant demographic consequences in ancient Greece (section 3 above). It is sometimes forgotten by classical scholars that infant mortality was high in the past, and populations with low life expectancy at birth whose members sought to restrict themselves to very small families would simply not have survived in the long run.[144]

So far it has been argued that high fertility was desired in classical Athens for very good reasons, voluntary family limitation, including infant exposure, was not widely practised, and the demographic significance of infanticide is in any case frequently misunderstood by scholars imagining that it serves to regulate population size. This line of argument is not intended to deny that awareness of infanticide or indeed of other effective methods of family limitation existed, but to argue that the mentality of classical Athens was hostile to the idea of family limitation as such.

In this respect the position advocated here is diametrically opposed to that of Himes, the author of the standard textbook on the history of contraception, who asserted that the desire to prevent conception was common, but knowledge of effective techniques for doing so was restricted. His book, written before demographers discovered the significance of natural fertility in historical populations, should now be regarded as unsatisfactory. Its significance is illustrated by the case of China, for example, where infanticide, directed especially at females, was once believed (e.g. by Ping-ti Ho) to have been prevalent in the past. However recent research suggests instead that the traditional Chinese demographic structure was characterised by a natural fertility regime with a low level of fertility.

Dickeman argued that in societies in which it occurs, infanticide is 'a normative, culturally sanctioned behaviour'. In this sense infanticide or exposure of normal infants was not important in classical Athens as a means of family limitation, as there is no evidence for it. However, literary sources indicate that deformed infants were often exposed, for example in Sparta (see section 5 below) and Rome. But even this category of infanticide did not necessarily always happen. Bräuer & Fricke (1980) studied the skeleton of a woman from Geometric Tiryns who suffered from spina bifida, complicated by thalassaemia, but still survived until the age of 18-21.[145]

Besides infanticide, abortion should not be underrated as a possible means of family limitation. It may be more dangerous, outside a modern hospital, to the mother than giving birth and then exposing the child, but human beings customarily do many things that are dangerous (e.g. smoking cigarettes) in modern times. The recent experience of the populations of countries such as Greece herself, the Soviet Union and other communist states in eastern Europe, and Japan after the Second World War demonstrates incontrovertibly that it is perfectly feasible for abortion to be used on a very large scale as a means of regulating family size, with women averaging four to six abortions each in the course of their reproductive lifespans. It was noted earlier that the Hippokratic corpus speaks of pregnant women in classical Greece having abortions or miscarriages if they fell ill. Another fascinating case in the corpus unmistakably shows a woman having abortions one after the other as a means of family limitation, just as so many women have done in modern Athens during the last generation or so. Prostitutes also frequently resorted to abortion.

Aristotle envisaged that there would be opposition to infanticide as a method of family limitation in his ideal *polis*. He considered that abortion would be more acceptable, so long as it was carried out before the foetus acquired sensory perception, which in his opinion occurred during pregnancy. It was widely considered that the foetus was not a living organism with a mind of its own at conception. The Hellenistic Stoic philosopher Khrysippos argued that the foetus was like a plant so long as it was in the womb, and only acquired a soul and the sensory perception characteristic of animals when it emerged into the open air. Attitudes of this kind, which vary greatly from society to society, served to legitimise abortion. It is quite possible that if an Athenian woman became pregnant with a child she and her husband did not want, abortion was the first option considered, rather than infant exposure after birth.

Little is known about the legal status of abortion in classical Greece. A late source states that both Lykourgos and Solon prohibited abortion, but there is no other evidence for this. A fragment of Lysias suggests that abortion was a crime in Athens, but only in the special circumstances of a woman's being pregnant at the time of her husband's death, in which case the unborn child would eventually have had an inheritance claim on the estate. In other words the abortion was a crime against the husband, rather than the foetus. It is dangerous to generalise from this fragment. Cicero mentions a similar case in Miletos in which a woman was condemned for having an abortion and so depriving her husband of an heir. Further evidence for the clear-cut distinction made between a pregnant woman and the foetus she was carrying comes from the fact that many Greek *poleis* had a law that convicted pregnant women could not be executed until they had given birth. The oath contained in the Hippokratic corpus forbade doctors from assisting an abortion. However, the oath may be a Pythagorean text of the late fourth century BC and is not closely connected to the rest of the corpus. The Pythagoreans reckoned that the foetus was an animal from conception onwards.[146]

Abortion has probably been underrated by ancient historians as a means of family limitation in antiquity. The line of argument in this section is not intended to deny that anyone ever practised family limitation in classical Athens, but merely to maintain that it was rare, even though techniques for doing so were well known. The hypothesis of natural fertility involves a consideration of aggregate behaviour. Even if a few individuals or couples sometimes practised family limitation, the population as a whole would still have largely exhibited the statistical characteristics of a natural fertility population if the majority did not do so.

Aristotle mentions some contraceptive techniques, including the application of lead ointment or olive oil in the vagina. Marie Stopes, one of the founders of modern family planning, experimented with olive oil and concluded that it was 100 per cent effective as a contraceptive. Its messiness results in its failure to be used widely nowadays, even though it does not share the potential side-effects of the chemicals introduced by the pill into the female body, or cause the physical damage that may result from the use of mechanical intra-uterine devices. Moreover it acts as a lubricant. One of the authors of the Hippokratic corpus stated correctly that in order to increase the chances of conception men should avoid hot baths before coitus. Again this knowledge could have been exploited for contraceptive purposes.[147]

Very little is heard about coitus interruptus in classical sources, even though it was the principal method of contraception used during the demographic transition in the countries of early modern Europe, and has also played an important role alongside abortion in modern Greece. It is only mentioned in a fragment of the poet Archilochos, if the papyrus has been interpreted correctly. Possibly the unnatural intercourse between Peisistratos and his wife, the daughter of Megakles, was coitus interruptus (but more probably anal intercourse). A rabbi in Israel in Roman times raised the possibility of using coitus interruptus as a means of preventing pregnancy while a mother was breastfeeding a child. However, the story of Onan suggests that coitus interruptus was in general deprecated in Israel, because the purpose of marriage was procreation, as in Greece.

It is probable that no interest was taken in coitus interruptus in ancient Greece because procreation and pleasure were separated into different relationships. As Xenophon said, marriage was for the purpose of procreation, while men could satisfy their sexual desires in other ways. It will be shown later on that in the age class systems of the Greek *polis* marriage and sex were privileges/duties acquired at different stages of the human lifespan. Consequently procreation and pleasure, which today may be kept separate within the same relationship by means of the pill or other contraceptive techniques, were in classical Greece kept separate by being allocated to different relationships. It is in this context that the famous statement of an Attic orator distinguishing the roles of 'wife, mistress and prostitute' must be considered. In such a situation there was little room for coitus interruptus.[148]

Golden (1981) made an ingenious attempt to infer an imbalance in the sex ratio in Athens, which he hypothesised was counteracted by selective female infanticide, from the consequences of a 'marriage squeeze'. Unfortunately his theory is beset by problems, many of which have already been pointed out by other scholars. The focus here will be on the two most fundamental difficulties which play the greatest roles in undermining Golden's theory. Owing to age- and sex-specific differences in life expectancy, it is to be expected that women in their teens should have considerably outnumbered men aged about thirty or so in the marriage market. 'Marriage squeezes' do indeed occur, but it is likely that there were two significant consequences which were not considered by Golden. Our sources never explicitly comment on bachelorhood *per se* in classical Athens and universal marriage for both sexes is assumed as a norm, although there were recalcitrant individuals in Sparta who had to be compelled to marry (see section 5 below). This is another feature in respect of which the demography of Athens was different from that of countries like Britain and France in early modern Europe.

It was fashionable for women to marry as soon as possible after menarche in Athens and most of them appear to have done so in the eyes of our sources. However, the people mentioned in the Attic orators, for example, belonged overwhelmingly to the upper strata of Athenian society. Strictly all that the bulk of the available sources tells us is that women who belonged to rich families had no trouble finding husbands, which is hardly surprising. The same was also true of remarriages. However, the scanty sources which explicitly refer to women from poor families in Athens certainly do envisage the possibility that a woman who had little or nothing to offer by way of dowry might have difficulty finding a husband.

There was a law attributed to Solon which stated that the nearest kinsman of a thetic *epiklêros*, an heiress of a man in the lowest property class, had to either marry her himself or else provide her with a dowry to look for another husband. It is not known how effective the law was, but presumably some women still had difficulties because there is no other way of explaining the existence of the category of the *pallakai*, women who were given to a man in a type of union which had a lower status than dowry marriage in classical Athens (see section 6 below). If it were at all common in practice for women to have difficulty raising a dowry for marriage, and it might well have been if thetes constituted anything like half the citizen population as is generally thought by ancient historians, then Golden's carefully constructed theory would collapse like a pack of cards. Charles Darwin, commenting on Theognis, observed that an emphasis on wealth as a desirable quality in the selection of a spouse, a habit denounced by the poet, interferes with the proper action of sexual selection, an important component of his theory of evolution.[149]

The second way of accounting for the imbalance in the sex-ratio of

marriageable age groups does not even require invoking the possibility
that some women did not marry or at least experienced difficulty finding
a husband. It revolves around the simple and well-documented idea that
when the older husband of a younger woman dies, the woman is removed
from the pool of married women for a *period of time*, while she is in
mourning and looking for a second husband, perhaps a year or so. At any
point in time a certain proportion of all women in the reproductive age
groups are likely to be either widowed and not yet remarried, or
alternatively divorced and not yet remarried, which was also possible in
classical Athens. This proportion of women may well be large enough to
account entirely for the imbalance in the sex-ratio of marriageable age
groups of the two sexes. Research in a number of Third World countries
where women marry at a fairly early age on average has shown that they
spend about two-thirds of their reproductive years (15-45) in matrimony,
about a quarter living singly before marriage, and the rest (nearly 10 per
cent) in the widowed or divorced state.

Furthermore in Athens women who already had sons when their
husbands died may have concentrated on bringing up the sons to take
over their father's *oikos*, household, which would have prevented them
seeking remarriage even if they were still in their reproductive years. A
combination of these factors permits us to account for the problem of the
consequences of the marriage-squeeze without invoking selective female
infanticide, which is completely unattested in classical Athens, as a
means of balancing the sex-ratio of marriageable age groups of the two
sexes.[150]

To round off discussion of the sex-ratio, it is important to note that any
disproportions between males and females in literary sources such as the
Attic orators must be completely disregarded as evidence, because
although quite a number of large families are attested, as was noted
earlier, nevertheless the total family sizes given by the orators are much
too small to reproduce a population with low life expectancy at birth (see
section 6 below). Censuses in modern Greece continued to underreport
women by as much as 10 per cent until well into the twentieth century
AD. Accordingly we should not be surprised that women are not fully
represented in literature produced by men for a predominantly male
audience in classical Athens, in a society in which it was appropriate in
public discourse not to refer to respectable women by name.[151]

The sources collected by Eyben (1980/1) provide far more evidence for
infanticide in the Hellenistic and Roman periods than they do for
classical Greece, although unfortunately there is little that refers
specifically to Hellenistic and Roman Athens. The most famous piece of
evidence comes from Polybios, commenting on Boiotia in the Hellenistic
period. He stated that members of the upper classes were attempting to
restrict themselves to one or two children each to save wealth for
consumption during their own lifetimes and to prevent estate subdivision

under the partible inheritance system. This resulted frequently in patriline discontinuity if the one or two children were carried off by disease or war. Other members of the upper class were avoiding marriage and procreation altogether. Polybios used this pattern of behaviour to explain population decline and so decreasing agricultural production in Boiotia. He noted that the population was decreasing even though there had not been any major epidemics (see section 7 below) or any heavy mortality in war. He does not make it clear how far down the social scale family limitation was being practised.

The archaeological evidence from the Cambridge/Bradford Boiotia survey shows unequivocally that the population of Boiotia indeed did collapse in the course of the Hellenistic period. This conjunction of different types of evidence makes it probable that Polybios, for all his moralising, was describing a real phenomenon. The pattern of reproductive behaviour he describes was certainly very different from that of Athenians in the classical period, judging by the Attic orators. It fits the pattern found empirically for the demographic transition in early modern Europe, in which family limitation always started among the rich and later spread to the poor. It has also been found empirically in modern times that once family limitation practices start to spread through a population, fertility rates tend to drop very steeply to below bare replacement levels, as in modern Greece for example, and do not begin to recover until very low rates have been reached. This is probably relevant to understanding the situation in Hellenistic Greece. In addition it has also been shown, in a famous study of the parish of Colyton in early modern England, that family limitation measures adopted during a Malthusian subsistence crisis may continue to be employed after the immediate need for them has passed.[152]

As was argued earlier, the best way of explaining this development is to hypothesise that the population density overshot K in the fourth century and the early Hellenistic period, as cohorts already born that were too large for the conditions of the moment entered the reproductive ages. Natural selection then favoured family limitation in order to produce a smaller average completed family size, the optimum family size in those circumstances. Family limitation to attain optimum family size would not have maintained population density at that particular juncture, but would instead have decreased it in the direction of K. As K was approached, reached, and then passed on a downward trajectory, owing to the delay in the reaction to the population's own changing circumstances, optimum family size varied accordingly, decreasing but eventually starting to increase again, accounting for the population decline in the Hellenistic period and the subsequent resurgence in the late Roman period. As the available manpower decreased in the Hellenistic period, the Greek *poleis*, even when banded together into leagues with federal institutions, ceased to be significant powers on the international stage.

This type of explanation does not require invoking any degeneracy on the part of Greeks in the Hellenistic period. Patterson asserted that 'the view that exposure only became prevalent in the Hellenistic period goes hand in hand with a view of the essential decadence of Hellenistic Greeks'.[153] This is nonsense. By adopting infanticide Hellenistic Greeks were tackling rationally a problem which their classical ancestors had failed to get to grips with. The Attic New Comedy, with all due reservations about relying on fragments, stresses the misfortunes (at a time of high population density) of poor men marrying and having children. Polybios describes the rational response to that situation which was eventually adopted. That is not degenerate behaviour. This may be an unpalatable conclusion to any modern scholar who objects to infanticide or other forms of family limitation on ethical, moral or religious grounds, but no historian who assigns a privileged status to his or her own morality is ever going to understand the past. The reproductive behaviour of Hellenistic Boiotians was denounced by Polybios because it entailed a reduction in military manpower and so a weakening of the power of the state. His line of reasoning was similar to that of Plato, who could not consider the idea that a lower population density might be economically beneficial for individuals because the state was more important than the individual to his way of thinking (see section 1 above).

In this section sexual and reproductive behaviour has been considered at the level of individuals and couples. This is the whole story as far as the societies in modern and early modern Europe which are familiar to historical demographers are concerned. However it is only half of the story as far as ancient Greece is concerned, because in ancient Greece the socio-political organisation of the *polis* could act to regulate important demographic parameters in a way unparalleled in later periods of European history. Plato and Polybios were right to think that ultimately the *polis*, in its pristine state, should have and in fact did override the desires of individuals. The development of an individualistic form of reproductive behaviour, emphasising voluntary family limitation, in Hellenistic Greece was merely one aspect of the transformation of the *polis* into a quite different type of society. It is to this aspect of the historical demography of ancient Greece that we must turn our attention now.

5. Age class systems

In recent times some European states have pursued pro-natalist policies. For example Mussolini's Italy imposed a tax on bachelors and introduced family allowances to make having children financially attractive. It has been argued that the propaganda of the fascist government significantly delayed the spread of interest in family planning in Italy. According to Hammond & Walbank (1988), 'between 1944 and 1972 Albania trebled its population by setting targets for the production of children, village by village, and by imposing the capital sentence on any form of contraception'.

Similarly in antiquity Philip V of Macedon forced the Macedonians to procreate children and to rear them all, as a response to a shortage of manpower for military purposes attributed to continual wars over several generations. Modern European states have not followed policies designed to have *restrictive* demographic effects, for example to restrict birth rates or to regulate age of marriage for the two sexes, apart from prescribing a minimum age before which marriage is forbidden. However, restrictive demographic policies exist in other parts of the world today.

China, with its compulsory family limitation policies to restrict the growth of a population which has already surpassed the thousand million mark, is the most notable example. Since China alone accounts for at least 20 per cent of mankind, determination of family size by the state is a phenomenon familiar to a substantial minority of the human race today, even though such forcible regulation of demographic patterns in a restrictive manner by the state has not been a feature of mediaeval or modern European history. However, there is abundant evidence that there were periods and places in the history of ancient Greece in which the socio-political organisation of the *polis* attempted to regulate various aspects of human social behaviour in a restrictive manner which had profound demographic consequences.[154]

Max Weber raised the problem of the historical individuality of the Greek *polis*, which is of fundamental significance for the present inquiry. What were the specific features of the *polis* as a socio-political organisation which significantly differentiate it from other types of society? The answers which have been given to this question in the past are generally unsatisfactory or incomplete. For example the frequent translation of the word *polis* as 'city-state' does not differentiate Athens and Sparta in any way from Renaissance Venice and Florence or from modern Monaco and Liechtenstein. Rather than resort to such a profoundly misleading and unsatisfactory translation, the word has been left untranslated in this book, although the pages which follow will attempt to elucidate its true meaning. Equally, in my judgment, the two best-known attempts at a sociological analysis of ancient Greek society, namely the Weberian and Marxist models, are both inadequate. It is necessary to explain the reasons for this conclusion because they shed a great deal of light on the question of the historical individuality of the Greek *polis* and are very relevant to human demography.

However surprising this may seem in the light of the manifest differences between them, both the Weberian and the Marxist models insofar as they have been applied to the ancient world suffer from the same basic defect. They are both so preoccupied with specifying differences between industrial societies in general and pre-industrial societies in general that they do not pay sufficient attention to significant differences between various categories of pre-industrial societies. Let us take Weber first. He emphasised three factors in his research on antiquity, which have been stressed again recently by Finley: (1) the economic character of 'the ancient city' as a 'consumer city', rather than a centre of production; (2) the political character of the citizen body of the ancient city as a warrior society, 'eine Siedlungsgemeinschaft vor Kriegem'; (3) status. It cannot possibly be maintained that any of these features was unique to the ancient Greek *polis* and was not equally characteristic of a huge variety of other pre-industrial societies. Ancient Mesopotamian, Indian and Chinese cities, not to mention ancient Rome or Aztec Tenochtitlan, were all consumer cities just as much as classical Athens or Sparta, in the sense that they were inhabited by, amongst others, an urban elite which lived as a rentier population off taxes or tribute exacted from the surrounding countryside.[155]

The same point is applicable to the concept of a warrior society. At an early stage of research, I too was impressed by this idea. After all, 'war' was so frequent in ancient Greece that it was taken for granted as the natural subject matter for historiography. It scarcely required any analysis or explanation as a category of phenomena in its own right. Peace (*eirênê*) was more often than not the diversion of affairs from their usual state. It seems intuitively obvious that military organisation must have been a predominant aspect of social organisation under such circumstances. However, upon second thoughts, doubts began to creep in. This was partly a consequence of reflection upon the ancient sources, which stress that in spite of the endless battles, the ancient Greek citizen soldier remained a part-time amateur warrior who did little training for war and had a limited amount of time to devote to it, after performing the necessary tasks on his farm.[156] Indeed the sheer lack of professionalism of citizen militias and the seasonal constraints on their ability to engage in campaigns created a demand for mercenaries who did not share these problems. The Spartans in the classical period were exceptional for their devotion to preparation for war, and even their highly ritualised preparations are most notable for their simplicity and naïvety.[157]

Doubts also arose in my mind as a consequence of reflections upon the nature and logic of scientific inquiry. War was a constant feature of life not just in ancient Greece, but equally in the ancient Near East and in Italy and everywhere else in antiquity too. For example, the narrative books of the Old Testament are filled with accounts of bloody conflicts, more often than not inspired by Yahweh, while the closure of the doors of the temple of Janus at Rome to signify peace was an exceedingly rare event in Republican Rome. It is impossible to use a factor which is common to several societies to explain differences between those societies, for instance to answer such fundamental questions as why Rome was able to assimilate, one by one, all the peoples she conquered to create an empire spanning most of the then known world, while Athens and Sparta were utterly unable to do anything of the sort, or why ancient Greek 'religion' was so different from the uncompromising monotheism of

Judaism. Yet a satisfactory analysis of ancient Greek society ought to be able to answer such fundamental questions. The Weberian model, although not incorrect as far as it goes, does not in fact go very far and is of strictly limited explanatory value. Classical Athens was a consumer city and a warrior society, but those conclusions do not solve the problem of the historical individuality of the ancient Greek *polis*.

In my opinion, Weber fell into the very same trap that so many ancient historians employing the traditional methods of classical philology have fallen into. Although he did not write a narrative history of any war or wars in antiquity in the way that most ancient historians do, Weber was induced by the omnipresence of war in the literary sources for ancient Greece to attribute to military organisation a greater role in sociological analysis than it deserves. By stressing shared attributes of the societies of antiquity which differentiate them all from all later European societies, instead of looking for patterns of significant differences *between* the various societies of antiquity, Weber did not fully exploit the potential of the method of comparative social analysis which he himself did so much to establish. Weber has exercised a greater influence on the research presented in this book in respect of his theoretical methodology of comparative research than in respect of his substantive conclusions about ancient Greece and Rome.

Let us move rapidly on to Marx, as developed and interpreted by Ste. Croix (1981), since Marx himself wrote little directly on antiquity. The fact that production is a very widespread human activity does not allow one to infer that the development of production has had to follow a unilineal course in history, any more than it can be inferred from the fact that all populations of all species of living organisms are constantly evolving that the evolution of life forms has followed an inexorably pre-determined path since the origin of life. Nor are there any good a priori reasons for assuming that changes in production in the past were always, or even often, the consequence of human awareness of economic self-interest. The development of a new agricultural system in classical antiquity with a higher level of productivity occurred in the context of an almost complete absence of consciousness in all strata of society of the changes that occurred, their causes and their consequences.

Let us furthermore acknowledge the obvious, namely that 'class struggles', disputes over the distribution of wealth and control over its means of production, were frequent in antiquity, in Greece, Rome and indeed everywhere else. Admitting that the statement – 'the history of all hitherto existing society is the history of class struggles' – is of any validity may seem a surprising path for a critic of such theories to take. However it is undoubtedly the most rapid way of ascertaining the *limits* of class struggle theories as a mode of explanation. The very ubiquity of class struggles lays them open to the same charge made above against Weber's main ideas, namely that their explanatory value is inevitably restricted as a direct consequence of their ubiquity. If it is argued that Periklean Athens and the early Roman empire were both slave societies and claimed that this mode of exploitation is *the most important* feature of their respective social organisations, or if the Helots of Messenia and Lakonia are assimilated to mediaeval serfs, as Ste. Croix does, then it becomes impossible to explain any of the very obvious differences between Athens and Rome, or between Sparta and the feudal societies of mediaeval Europe. Ste. Croix's conceptual framework is as incapable as Weber's of answering the fundamental questions posed above of the differences between Greek and Roman imperialism and of the relationship of Greek and Jewish ideologies to their respective social organisations.

I am happy to accept that the 'propertied class' in classical Athens, to use Ste. Croix's term, depended on slave labour insofar as *permanent* labour forces on farms and in 'manufacturing' enterprises were concerned (see section 2 above for the role of slavery in agriculture). Nevertheless that conclusion leaves us very far from comprehending the essence of the Greek *polis* as a social organisation. Class, like Weber's status, is merely one out of several possible principles of social organisation. Their relative importance is a matter of debate. It will be argued below that there is a third principle of social organisation which brings us much closer than either class or status to appreciating the historical individuality of the ancient Greek *polis*. This third principle, unlike class and status, happens to have very major demographic consequences, which justifies the lengthy treatment of it below – consequences qualitatively quite different from the association of higher mortality with poverty commonly found in research on modern populations.

Aristotle in the *Politics* believed that nature had provided age and sex as methods of organising the *polis* and ordering the hierarchy inherent in any structure. He regarded *age* as the fundamental principle of internal organisation of the *polis* in its pristine state.[158] This is a convenient starting point for our discussion of the *polis* as an *age class system*. Versions of this theory have indeed been proposed before by Henri Jeanmaire in very important publications and also more briefly by the Israeli sociologist Eisenstadt.[159] However, developments in both ancient history and the social sciences over the years since the publication of their works make possible important modifications to their ideas. Of particular relevance to this book is the fact that neither Jeanmaire nor Eisenstadt considered the demographic implications of age as a principle of social organisation.[160]

Furthermore, because of hostility to comparative research among most classicists (see Chapter I above), the idea of age class organisation has had very little influence on mainstream Anglo-Saxon historiography of the classical world. However, scholars belonging to other cultural traditions, such as Brelich (1969), Calame (1977) and Polignac (1984), have attached due significance to it. These scholars were primarily interested in ancient Greek religion and in interpreting works of literature – Alkman's poetry, in Calame's case. While it is acknowledged that age class organisation does have a religious dimension, this is not what makes it interesting in the context of the research presented here, as will be seen. In opposition to Brelich and Calame who stressed the idea of initiation, which is merely one possible expression of age as a principle of social organisation, stress is laid here instead on age itself because it opens up new vistas of investigation.

Previous discussions of age class organisation have tended often to devote more space to Sparta and to Crete than to Athens, as it is apparently in the former two cases that this principle played a more important role. It will be suggested here that this is a misapprehension and that Athens was a society based on an age class system just as much as – and in the same ways as – Sparta and the many *poleis* of Crete were. However, it is convenient to start with the cases which are likely to be accepted more readily and run through the evidence for Sparta and Crete, drawing attention to demographic aspects of the system in particular and drawing parallels with Athens and with ethnographic evidence where appropriate.

The Spartan lawgiver Lykourgos is said to have attached the greatest importance to *paideia* as an object to which the legislator should pay attention. The word 'Lykourgos' is used here as a form of shorthand for the earliest institutional complex of Sparta. It is unlikely that he ever existed. The idea of Jeanmaire that behind the legend lay the reality of a face on a mask at an initiation ceremony remains far and away the most original and penetrating solution proposed so far to the problem of his significance. Like the hero Lykourgos, 'the man who keeps the wolf away', in Sparta, in Athens the god Apollo Lykeios presided over the Athenian adult male citizen body. These two cultic figures probably originated in institutional nexuses that were once very similar. A second preliminary point is that translating *paideia* as 'education', or as 'culture' ('Kultur') as Werner Jaeger did, gives a far too narrow sense. It signifies the process of socialisation in its entirety, embracing many aspects of life which are completely outside the domain of the educational systems of modern countries.[161]

For Lykourgos, the starting point in arranging *paideia* was the supervision of marriages and births, *tous gamous kai tas geneseis*.[162] Straight away this takes us into the context of a society in which marriage and having children are not matters of individual choice, but are privileges and duties regulated by the socio-political organisation. Newly born children were judged by the eldest men in each tribe, *hoi presbutatoi tôn phuletôn*, as to whether they were suitable for raising. This may have been primarily intended in the classical period to weed out infants with obvious physical defects at birth. However it is not inconceivable that in the earliest stages of Spartan history it was a mechanism for eliminating children who had been born outside socially approved heterosexual relationships. In any case family limitation was not a family prerogative in Sparta.[163]

Beyond the age of seven Spartan parents were not allowed to feed and educate their children as they wished, because the children were taken away and put into groups of age mates, the 'herds', *bouai* or *agelai*.[164] On Crete the name *agelai* was given to an age grade not entered until the age of seventeen.[165] In their teens the age classes of Spartan boys passed through a complicated sequence of age grades, whose details cannot be discussed here for want of space. The competition to steal cheeses from the altar of Artemis Orthia, which was originally an age class contest and later developed into the flogging of boys to amuse Roman tourists, fits into this part of the Spartan age class system. Graf (1979) argued that rituals analogous to those for Artemis Orthia at Sparta were performed in the cult of Artemis Tauropolos at Halai Araphenides in Attica.[166]

In Sparta at the age of twelve boys became involved in paederasty, their lovers being young men, *neoi*.[167] The principle was the same but the timing yet again different on Crete, where youths only entered into institutionalised paederastic relationships after emerging from the *agelai*. The best known *erastês-erômenos* pair in Spartan history are Lysander and Agesilaos, who exceptionally for a Spartan king passed through the *agôgê*, the sequence of age grades, as he was only the younger son of Archidamos by a second wife.[168] Greek homosexuality was always structured so as to involve two individuals from different age groups. This is the key to understanding it. Sir Kenneth Dover wrote that 'we must assume that homosexuality satisfied a need not otherwise satisfied in Greek society and try to identify that need. It was the need for personal relationships of an intensity not commonly found within marriage or in the relations between parents and children or in those between the individual and the community as a whole.'[169] This is the right question but the wrong answer. An approach to a better answer may be obtained by considering how paederasty could have fitted into the ideal *polis* as portrayed by Aristotle and Plato (the Plato of the *Phaidros*).

Erastai were characteristically *young* men.[170] In the ideal *polis* – and originally, it will be suggested later on, in historical *poleis* as well, men were not permitted to marry and procreate legitimate children until a particular age, which varied from 25 to 37 in utopia and doubtless varied historically as well.[171] The point is that the problem was not that adult men were trying and were often unable to form satisfactory sexual relationships with 'citizen' women, as Dover supposes. The problem was rather that below a certain age which was well past sexual maturity adult males were prohibited by custom or law from marrying and forming a permanent legitimate sexual relationship with a 'citizen' woman. This is the 'need', to use Dover's term, or function that paederasty originally existed to fulfil as far as the young adult male *erastês* was concerned.

The structuring of sexual roles by age is a classic example of the way in which an age class system may govern the personal lives of the members of the society in question. Boys had to play a passive role, like women, within a homosexual relationship, young adult males played the active role in the same homosexual relationship, while having the right to marry a 'citizen' woman and to procreate legitimate children was theoretically the prerogative of a still older age grade of adult men. The boys received group membership as a consequence of undergoing the rite de passage, *inter alia*, while the *neoi* received a measure of sexual gratification. Nevertheless in both Sparta and Crete it was not the handsomeness of the boy that was supposed to attract the *erastês*, but his courage and valour.[172] In the earliest phases of Greek history it was a group activity in the sense that it was compulsory for all males upon reaching a certain age. The Spartan ephors are said to have fined a citizen who failed to choose an *erômenos*.[173]

In other *poleis* such as Thebes and Elis homosexuality had become a matter of individual choice by the classical period, and pleasure was what counted. Nevertheless it is highly significant that in the case of Thebes the prominence of paederasty is explicitly attributed to the Theban lawgivers, *nomothetai*, suggesting that it had once been institutionalised there too. Indeed Plutarch shows that paederasty was part of the rituals marking initiation into adulthood at Thebes just as it was on Crete.[174] In Athens as well by the fifth century BC paederasty had become a matter of individual choice for the likes of Sokrates and Alkibiades or earlier for Aristogeiton and Harmodios. However, there are indications in Solon's laws and poetry that it may have been institutionalised in Athens as late as the early sixth century BC. It is an important pointer to its origin that sexual roles were still structured according to age even in fifth-century Athens.[175]

Dover argued that paederasty declined in fourth-century Athens, but this apparent shift may simply be a consequence of changes in the nature of our sources. The manufacture and use of painted pottery, one of Dover's principal sources of information for earlier periods, ceased during the fourth century BC for unknown reasons. The contrast between homosexuality in Aristophanes and heterosexuality in Menander may be quite misleading, as Menander may have been the only poet of the New Comedy not to include any homosexual themes in his plays.[176] Such lawcourt speeches as Aiskhines I and Lysias III suggest that it was still perfectly respectable for an Athenian to admit in public to involvement in a paederastic relationship after the Peloponnesian War, so long as the accepted etiquette was observed. In interpreting the evidence of the Lysias speech, the crucial point is that the defendant-speaker thought that the jury might take offence at his behaviour not on the grounds that it was wrong under any circumstances, but because by his own admission he was in the *wrong age group* for such behaviour.

In classical Ionia paederasty was actively discouraged. This is doubtless not just a consequence of Persian domination of Ionia at that time, as the sources suggest, but a development from the situation in the Homeric epics, written in the Ionic dialect, where paederasty is not made explicit. Nevertheless relationships such as that between Patroklos and Achilles probably do conceal a paederastic relationship similar to the pairs of *erastai-erômenoi* which made the Theban Sacred Band such a formidable fighting force in the fourth century BC. By the second century AD the process of the transformation of the *polis* into a quite different type of society was drawing to a close. This process altered the role and social acceptability of paederasty. Soranos regarded paederasty as an inherited mental disease. The only inference to be drawn from his remarks is that Rome and Greece were quite different as regards social structure. It is illegitimate to generalise across the whole Graeco-Roman world as regards social structure. As evidence of the demographic significance of age class organisation in Ionia, at Ephesos the age class of boys aged sixteen had to meet the age class of girls aged fourteen with a view to arranging marriages.[177]

Over the course of time a single institution, originally common to all the Greeks, developed in a variety of different ways in different *poleis*. All these ways are variations on the theme of the structuring of sexual roles according to age within an age class system. Other kinds of variation in details are also possible. Theoretically the sexual desires of young adult males denied access to proper marriage within an age class system may be satisfied by access not only to adolescent boys but also to adolescent girls outside marriage, within the confines of an age class system. Most of the Greeks in the classical period, including the Athenians, rigidly prohibited 'citizen' women from having sexual relations with men before and outside marriage. Solon prescribed that a father or brother acting as guardian of an unmarried girl who was found to have had sexual intercourse with a man could sell her into slavery. In the fourth century BC such a girl would probably have suffered the penalty of being unable to secure a husband afterwards, a severe penalty. In such a situation young adult men had to content themselves with paederasty, as they had no chance of a permanent legitimate sexual relationship.[178]

However, such a state of affairs is by no means common to all the age class societies known to anthropologists. In some of the African age class systems, for example, young adult men, while being denied access to the privilege of marriage and procreation of legitimate children, may nevertheless have sexual relations with young women before the latter get married, or sometimes even while the women are married (to other men) and outside their marriage.[179] Customs of this kind are conducive to the spread of AIDS and other venereal diseases in several African countries today. The number of births as a consequence of such relationships is generally small because of adolescent sterility after menarche, and such infants as are born outside marriage are denied legitimacy and may even be exposed in the African societies.[180] The ancient sources do provide evidence for such patterns of sexual behaviour in antiquity in various regions. They characterised Macedonia, Thrace and Illyricum for example. The custom of pre-marital sexual intercourse in these regions may suggest a scarcity of venereal diseases in antiquity (see section 7 below).[181]

Sparta differed from most of the other *poleis* in the classical period in that husbands could share their wives with other men. This was probably a development from a prior situation in which all the members of an age class had collective rights of access in certain circumstances to all the women married to members of that age class. In the case of Sparta we can see the two methods of solving the problem of the allocation of sexual rights to *neoi*, namely (1) male paederasty, and (2) sexual relations with women outside marriage proper, co-existing with each other. In such a situation it is quite correct to affirm, as Plutarch did, that adultery was unknown in Sparta. In Sparta it was also possible for an older man to bring in a younger man to have sexual intercourse with the older man's younger wife and so procreate an heir for himself. Similarly Plutarch indicates that in archaic Athens an heiress, *epiklêros*, could have intercourse with her husband's next of kin for the purpose of procreating a male heir to her father's *oikos*, if her husband was impotent. Clearly Athens was once not dissimilar to Sparta in this respect.[182]

Since heterosexual intercourse is essential for procreation, the regulation of access to sexual rights by the socio-political organisation must have profound demographic consequences. As Bernardi aptly put it, 'age class systems have the effect of a birth control plan'. The most detailed study available of the demography of a modern age class society suggests that the social system may have had quite extraordinary demographic effects.[183] Aristotle thought that the purpose of paederasty and of the segregation of men and women on Crete, the most isolated region of ancient Greece and the one in which the original institutional complex survived longest, was to prevent population growth by reducing coital frequency and so the birth rate.[184]

It is unlikely that anyone ever consciously planned it that way. The origins of classical Cretan and Spartan society must be set in a time in the Dark Ages when the population density was very low, judging by the recent archaeological surveys (section 2 above). This makes Aristotle's explanation of the original function of paederasty quite anachronistic. It was rather a case of unintended effects of social action. Archaeological evidence suggests that the population of Crete did not fully experience the r phase of the eighth century BC on mainland Greece. Instead the population of Crete increased slowly for a long time. Moreover it was still noticeably growing in the third century BC at a time when the populations of the various regions of mainland Greece had already overshot K and so stopped increasing. This suggests that the age class systems of the Cretan *poleis* in fact did slow down the rate of population increase on Crete in the first half of the first millennium BC relative to the *poleis* of mainland Greece.[185]

The Spartans on the other hand from the fifth century BC at least, if not earlier, found their ambitions (not shared by the Cretans) of political hegemony in Greece endangered by a grave shortage of manpower, *oliganthrôpia*, for military purposes, at least in respect of the Spartiate citizen body if not in respect of the total population of the agglomeration of different status groups in Lakonia and Messenia.[186] One of the causal factors, emphasised by Hodkinson (1986), was that the mechanics of the inheritance system favoured property concentration. Fulfilment of the requirements for full citizenship entailed regular and substantial contributions in kind (and coin too) to the common messes, *sussitia*, by Spartiates from their own (*de facto* if not *de jure*) property, in addition to the requirement of having passed through the *agôgê*.[187] Conversely on Crete the *sussitia* were supported by public funds, a more sensible measure in Aristotle's opinion.[188] To tackle the problem of *oliganthrôpia* the Spartans discouraged bachelorhood and set up incentives for marriage such as parading young unmarried girls naked in front of the *neoi* to incite sexual desire. They also awarded privileges to fathers of three sons, a measure which in any case would have done little more than reproduce a population with low life expectancy at birth.[189]

However, the entire Spartan social system in the classical period, simply because it was a system which in its ideal form by restricting access to marriage and procreation had the unintended effect of restricting population growth, was very ill suited to combating *oliganthrôpia*. The Cretan age class system, which was undoubtedly closely related to the Spartan one and was believed in antiquity to be ancestral to the Spartan system (though it is more probable that they had both equally inherited certain principles of social organisation which had earlier been common to all those who spoke the Greek language, *pace* Huxley (1971)), had the effect of *restricting* population growth by reducing the rate of natural increase. The Cretan system produced results diametrically opposed to what the Spartans needed in the fifth and fourth centuries BC in order to maintain their military manpower. Solving Sparta's problem of *oliganthrôpia* would have required much more radical reforms than anyone envisaged at the time, certainly more radical in principle than Lysander's scheme of making the kingships into elected magistracies for his own benefit. A social revolution would have been required.

The problem of Spartan *oliganthrôpia* originated as the consequence of the operation of an inheritance system which favoured property concentration within a population governed by a socio-political organisation which itself tended to restrain population growth, and hit by demographic catastrophes. Invoking such historical contingencies as the earthquake of *c.* 465 BC as the explanation for Spartan manpower shortage, as Figueira (1986) did, is inadequate by itself because research in historical demography, such as Le Bras (1969), shows that populations which are otherwise buoyant tend to recover rapidly from such catastrophes. The demographic effects of the structure of the socio-political organisation of Sparta explain why the Spartiate population struggled to *recover* from such contingent events in the long run.

The customs described in the sources as responses to *oliganthrôpia*, such as the stigma attached to bachelorhood, need not have had anything whatsoever to do with manpower shortage in the earliest stages of Spartan history. Their interpretation as responses to manpower shortage was a late interpretation which reveals not their original raison d'être but the internal contradictions of the Spartan social system, which was unintentionally geared to restricting population growth. Baxter & Almagor put forward the following line of argument, which clearly has analogies in Spartan customs, in respect of the East African age class societies: 'as a set (sc. class) advances in seniority its members are more likely to be married, but while only a few are married those few are anomalous in that they cease to be equal with their age-mates by the very fact of having a wife. This inequality is partially evened out by permitting sexual access to wives. When the majority of a set is married then the anomaly ceases and the pressure is transferred to the bachelors to get a wife. A consequence is that age mates prefer to keep their marriages in step.' This passage shows clearly how a stigma on bachelorhood may be explained without any reference to manpower shortage.

It also furnishes a good illustration of how an age class system may function in practice in an informal way in the absence of written laws and a state police organisation to enforce them. Sparta lacked written laws even in the classical period and had only unwritten customs. The social structure of the Greek *polis* developed in an essentially non-literate setting, paralleling in this respect the age class societies in East Africa and New Guinea which are familiar to anthropologists. Probably neither military organisation, the purpose of the social system in the eyes of classical observers such as Aristotle and Xenophon, nor manpower shortage, its principal perceived shortcoming in the classical period, played any role whatsoever in the genesis of the Spartan social system several centuries before.[190]

Female homosexuality also occurred in Sparta according to Plutarch. Again it was structured on the basis of age, between unmarried girls, *parthenoi*, and older married women, *gunaikes*.[191] A mature Spartan woman could have had both a husband and a paederastic relationship with a young Spartan *parthenos*. However, ethnographic evidence indicates that in age class societies the age class system is essentially a way of organising the male half of the population and is never as well developed amongst women.[192] Aristotle noted that Plato was the only lawgiver to have recommended *sussitia* for women.[193] Nevertheless there are traces of the formal division of women into age grades in ancient Greece, for example in Elis. The age class organisation of Spartan girls described by Calame (1977) did not extend beyond puberty or marriage into adult life.[194]

The passage from boyhood to adulthood in both Sparta and Crete was marked by important rites of passage, in the Cretan case by the ritual abduction of the initiand by an *erastês*, and in Sparta by the famous *krupteia*. Jeanmaire's analysis of the latter institution, comparing the murder of Helots to the ritual head-hunting of primitive peoples, is undoubtedly correct in its essentials.[195] The alleged purpose of the institution, given by classical authors as a preparation for war, is senseless, as the discipline required for successful service in the rigid hoplite phalanx is quite different from the tactics of the 'guerrilla warfare' in which the *kruptoi* might seem to have been involved. In its deepest significance, the *krupteia* was a temporary withdrawal from the rest of society during the transition between two stages of life and a temporary inversion of adult norms. Insofar as the military explanation has any validity at all, it must relate to a time before the institution of the hoplite phalanx in the seventh century BC. However, it is open to serious doubt whether the military explanation, which was espoused by Aristotle, has any validity at all for Dark Age Sparta and Crete.[196]

Bernardi observed that the military function is just one out of many possible functions of such a system, which may in principle serve to regulate the distribution of any or all social rights and duties. It is a serious conceptual mistake to equate *social* organisation with the much narrower field of *military* organisation, as Weber did. Bernardi argued that the militarism of the Zulus, to whom ancient historians have been wont to compare the Spartans, was quite exceptional among the African age class societies in precisely the same way that it is clear to ancient historians that Sparta was exceptional in ancient Greece for her devotion to warfare. In fact the militarism of the Spartans and Cretans originated in a particular set of historical circumstances, the 're-institutionalisation' (Cartledge and Finley) of the seventh and sixth centuries BC, motivated by the need to keep watch on subject serf populations, the enemy within.[197]

Poleis such as Athens, Thebes and even a Peloponnesian *polis* such as Elis which did not have any Helots to keep in place, had no need for the militarism of classical Sparta and Crete. Nevertheless, because there is no good reason for regarding the military function as the most important function of an age class system, there is no good reason for modern scholars to regard Sparta and Crete as better examples of age class systems than Athens and Thebes. Although Aristotle concluded that

Lykourgos was a bad lawgiver because the Spartans ultimately lost their empire, did not know how to enjoy peace, and equated courage with the totality of virtue, this did not in any way alter his opinion that age and sex categories were the natural way of organising the *polis*. Similarly, although Plato criticised the militarism of Sparta in the *Republic* and *Laws*, he is said to have adopted Lykourgos' laws as a model for a constitution. The reduced place allotted by Aristotle and Plato to military objectives, beyond the requirements of self-defence, and so to imperialism within the confines of the age class system of the ideal *polis* exactly parallels Bernardi's argument that military organisation is not the essence of age class systems.[198]

The military interpretation of the third *rhêtra* of Lykourgos, namely that the Spartans should not make war on the same enemy continuously in order to prevent the enemy acquiring experience of war, is also a late anachronism. Antalkidas used this dictum to criticise Agesilaos after Sparta's calamities in Boiotia in the 370s. Ethnographic evidence makes it plausible that it was originally a rite of passage in which a new age class of *neoi* had to prove itself by making war on an enemy whom their ancestors had not fought and defeated, in a context in which war was a highly ritualised business.[199] Before leaving the topic of van Gennep's 'rites de passage' from one status to another, it is important to bear in mind that virtually all societies have rites of passage of one kind or another. However it is only a highly specific form of social organisation, an age class system, in which *ideally all* social rights and duties from birth to death and all life stage transitions are regulated on the basis of age by society as a whole and not left to individual choice. I hope that it is clear by now why Weber's description of the *polis* as a warrior society is an inaccurate description.

At the next stage in the cycle of age grades after leaving the *bouai* or *agelai* and spending a couple of years as *paidiskoi*, or in some cases *kruptoi*, Spartans and Cretans became eligible for membership of the *sussitia, suskania, andreia* or *phiditia*, according to the varying terminology for the common messes.[200] An age class system may regulate access to food just as it may regulate access to sexual relations. Not only Spartan adults but also boys had a fixed diet prescribed for them by Lykourgos, intended to make them lean and tall, while in the Cretan messes old men received larger portions of food than young men. Caldwell (1982) suggested that in pre-industrial societies in general economic benefits tend to flow from the young to the old and that the direction of the intergenerational flow of wealth has been reversed in modern industrial societies. An age class system may well formalise and intensify this trend.[201] Xenophon noted that in other *poleis* men dining together tended to be of the same age (*hêlikes*), but Lykourgos introduced mixed *sussitia* at Sparta, access to which depended on the approval of all the existing members.[202]

Regulating access to food is merely one possible function of an age class system. It would be quite wrong to use the fact, noted by Aristotle, that *sussitia* on the one hand and *phratriai* and *phulai* on the other hand were alternative methods of subdivision of the citizen body of the *polis*, to deny that Thebes and Athens, for example, were age class societies on the grounds that they did not have *sussitia*.[203] Only a minority of the African age class societies have or had anything comparable to the Spartan and Cretan *sussitia*. Aristotle regarded *sussitia* as a very widespread institution, no doubt correctly, and stated that he shared the *communis opinio* that they were a good idea. Unfortunately he did not fulfil his promise to explain why, at least within the surviving corpus of his work.[204]

The *sussitia* were a platform for group political activity in the Dorian *poleis*. In the third century BC Gortyn in Crete was ripped apart by a civil war between younger and older men, *neôteroi* and *presbuteroi*. In Sparta the revolutionary plans of Agis were liked by the *neoi* but not by most of the *presbuteroi*. He attempted to revive decaying institutions such as the *sussitia* to take advantage of the feelings of the young men. On a more tranquil note, it may be recalled that the Spartan *neoi* wished to make war on Athens *c.* 479 BC after Sparta had lost the leadership of the war against Persia, but were dissuaded from doing so by Hetoimaridas, a member of the council of elders, the *gerousia*. Later on the Spartan assembly which debated whether or not to start the Peloponnesian – or from their viewpoint the Athenian – War decided on war. Here again a division between younger men with no previous experience of war and older men appears to have played an important role in the debate.[205]

Plato mentions episodes of revolutionary social conflict, *staseis*, in the *sussitia* and *gumnasia* in various other *poleis*, about which nothing else is known. He also made the tantalising statement that conflicts between younger men who had grown up at home and the older soldiers returning from the Trojan War were at the root of the troubles that afflicted Heroic Age Greece after that war. Plato's historical information is usually deprecated, but I have a hunch that if only we were better informed that particular statement might turn out to be of fundamental importance. It certainly brings to mind the episode of the Spartan *Partheniai* who were forced to leave Sparta to found Tarentum in Italy, when older men who had been absent during the First Messenian War returned to Sparta to reclaim their position there.

A noteworthy point about that war is that the decision of the Spartiates at war in Messenia not to have sexual relations with their wives until they had won the war is more easily understandable in the context of a social structure which imposed substantial restrictions on heterosexual intercourse anyway, even under normal circumstances in peacetime. The children who were born from the Spartan women at home during the war (their fathers being of uncertain social background) were denied legitimacy and a share in the conquered land of Messenia by the older men upon their return home. Clearly they had been born outside approved sexual relationships between Spartiate men and women. Furthermore it is not known whether or not they actually passed through the *agôgê*, while the war was in progress and the Spartiates were away. Although the details of what happened are obscure, the whole episode serves to stress the point that family organisation was very heavily influenced by the socio-political structure of the society as a whole. Children who had not been born and brought up in socially approved ways could not expect any share in the benefits of full Spartan citizenship.[206]

Classical Athens did not have *sussitia*. Nevertheless even in the classical period informal age classes still played a role in political conflict, most notably at the assembly which made the fateful decision to dispatch the Syracusan expedition. In that debate the *neoi* supported the ambition of Alkibiades, while the *presbuteroi*, who would have been in a minority anyway in a population with low life expectancy at birth and whose numbers had been still further reduced by the differential age-specific mortality rates of the epidemic of 430 BC (see section 7 below), supported the caution of Nikias.[207]

Such age groups were constituted on an informal basis in classical Athens. However, the Theseus legend and archaeological evidence for Dark Age burial practices indicate that Athens too may once have had a formal age class system (see below). In the archaic period conflicts formally organised on age class lines may have been as important in Athens as they undoubtedly were in Sparta and Crete. The reason for thinking this is that in the earliest well documented event in Athenian history, Kylon was supported by a fraternity of age-mates, *hetaireia tôn hêlikiôteôn*, in his attempt at a coup d'état, according to Herodotos. Following Lévy's downdating of this event to *c.* 597/6 BC, it now appears plausible that Solon's reforms, traditionally taken as the starting point for the development of the Athenian democracy, were an attempt, not altogether successful in view of Peisistratos' subsequent tyranny, to pick up the pieces in a society which had been convulsed along age class lines. Aiskhines' statement that Solon (and earlier Drakon too) had legislated for the various age grades (*hêlikiai*) in succession suggests that such concerns were indeed not far from Solon's mind. In the aftermath of the Kylonian conspiracy the purification of Athens by Epimenides required a human sacrifice. A boy called Kratinos was chosen as the victim, and his *erastês* Aristodemos committed suicide to follow him.[208]

In classical Athens access to political office was still regulated according to the principle of age, e.g. thirty for eligibility for service on the council, *boulê*, and for jury service, forty for the right to become a *sôphronistês* of the ephebes, fifty-nine for the office of public arbitrator, *diaitêtês*.[209] In the assembly it was those over the age of fifty who were asked by the herald in order of age if they wished to speak, while those below the age of thirty were apparently not allowed to speak at all.[210] Similarly in Sparta men below the age of thirty had to keep away from the market-place, the *agora*. More generally, the fact that in Sparta any man could chastise any boy for misbehaviour is an expression of the power structure of an age class system.[211] In an age class system there is no age as one moves through life at which a *complete* set of political rights and duties is suddenly granted. As Bernardi put it, 'distribution and the differentiation of power among the classes are a peculiarity of the system. No form of power is suddenly achieved, nor can it be obtained simultaneously with other forms; rather it is gradually distributed in turn through succession.' It will be argued later on that this observation is of the most fundamental significance for understanding the nature of 'citizenship' in the Greek world and how it differed from citizenship in Rome.[212]

One of the things men had to do during the peak of life, *akmê*, was to marry. On Crete those who emerged from the *agelai* at the same time had to go simultaneously through marriage ceremonies, although they did not lead their very young wives home until they were old enough to do the housekeeping.[213] In that isolated region of Greece, where an age class system best preserved its original traits into historical times, the timing of marriage was not left to individual choice but was determined by the socio-political organisation. The same was undoubtedly once true of Sparta, as Lykourgos is said to have prevented men from taking a wife, in the Spartan manner by a ritual display of force, whenever they felt like it. Forcible abduction of brides is also found as a motif on Attic vase paintings.[214]

The Spartan husband, after marriage, did not actually live with his wife until he reached the age of thirty. Until then he had to visit her secretly, as he was required to sleep with his age mates, *hêlikiôtai*, among the *neoi*. This is the key to understanding what was going on. Originally in Sparta the right to marry and so to procreate legitimate children probably belonged to men in a particular age grade, but not the youngest adult age grade. This is indicated by the existence of a group of unmarried men, *agamoi*, involved in the organisation of the *Karneia* festival. The explanation given by our sources, namely that Lykourgos wished to reduce the frequency of intercourse between husband and wife to make the offspring more vigorous, is a false explanation. However, it shows that Spartan paederasty was thought to have the same effect in reducing coital frequency, with implications for birth rates, that Aristotle believed it had on Crete. By the classical period, as Sparta was beset by *oliganthrôpia*, it may be hypothesised that the restrictions imposed by the original system were weakened, so that there is no evidence in the classical period for a minimum age of marriage for men, but only for a maximum age by which they had to marry.[215]

In an age class system control of marriage and the right to procreate legitimately is the most fundamental aspect of the entire socio-political organisation, controlling as it does the reproduction of the entire population. Pollux states that never marrying was an offence in many *poleis*. The regulation of age of marriage for both sexes which we find in the ideal *poleis* of Aristotle and Plato was not a product of fertile imaginations in ivory towers such as the *Peripatos* and the Academy. It was a product of reflection upon the historical development of a particular type of social organisation possessed by the ancient Greeks but never, for example, by the Anglo-Saxons. This explains why determination of age of marriage by the state has never been a feature of English history and thought and consequently why Anglo-Saxon historical demographers have neglected to study such possibilities.

The statement of P. Roussel – 'Quant au mariage, la date tardive qui lui est d'ordinaire assignée, ne permet guère, dans les institutions des philosophes, de lui attribuer quelque influence régulatrice' – is as devoid of insight into both demography and sociology as it possibly could be. In the classical period in Athens age of marriage was a matter of individual choice, or rather her father's or other *kurios'* (guardian's) choice in the case of a woman. Such evidence as there is suggests that Athenian men, unlike the Cretans for example, tended to marry late (see section 4 above). The complicated determinants of marriage patterns in classical Athens will be discussed in section 6 below. However, it is suggested here that one of the reasons for late average age of first marriage for males in classical Athens was that it was a legacy from an earlier period of history in which marriage had been regulated in this way by the socio-political organisation of Athens.[216]

Men were liable to military service outside Attica for forty years after completing their service as ephebes, when they were confined within the borders of Attica. However in practice men above the age of fifty or perhaps even forty do not seem to have been called on to serve, at least in the fourth century BC. Similarly in Sparta the period of eligibility for active military service spanned the same forty-year period. The particular age grades involved, lumped together, were equivalent to the Homeric *laos*, the community of men who in their function as warriors followed a chief to war.[217] The Athenian annual age grades, *hêlikiai*, for hoplite service, were all named after eponymous heroes, giving them an existence of their own independent of any particular individual or age class (group of age mates). Consequently it is quite correct to regard them as a succession of formal age grades through which each age class had to pass. Men in these forty age grades comprised the essence of the *polis*.[218]

Aristotle, concentrating on the political dimension of an age class system, observed that boys and old men, *paides* and *gerontes*, were not 'citizens' in the fullest sense of the word, which he regarded as signifying the right of access to political and judicial offices.[219] It would be more accurate to say that by virtue of having reached particular stages in an age class system, these particular groups had particular privileges and duties. Hesiod put it concisely – *erga neôn, boulai de mesôn, euchai de gerontôn*, 'deeds are the business of young men, advice of middle-aged men, prayers of the elderly'. His verse could easily be extended, neglecting the metre, to attribute a distinctive role to the *paides*, boys, as well.[220] Aristotle's focus in the *Politics* on the distribution of political power by age, although extremely penetrating, is in its own way as misleading, because one-sided, as the emphasis of some modern historians on the military aspects of the Spartan age class system. The distribution of political power and of military functions are just two out of the many possible functions of an age class system, such as regulating access to food and sex.

After serving as public arbitrators at the age of fifty-nine for a year, men became *gerontes* in Athens. This was equivalent to retirement and the age at which sons took over the management of the estates of their fathers. However, men above the age of sixty were certainly not barred from political activity. It is worth stressing that service as an arbitrator was compulsory. There was nothing optional about the age class system in classical Athens in those domains of life in which it had an active role, even though its scope was smaller than in contemporary Sparta and Crete. After 'retirement' parents had to be supported by their sons, as daughters had usually moved away after marriage to live in their husbands' homes. This was a very powerful motive for high fertility (see section 4 above).[221]

In certain other *poleis* becoming an old man created the possibility of access to a very important locus of political power, namely membership of the *gerousia* or council of elders. Theoretically anyone over the age of sixty could be elected to it. However, in Sparta, Crete and Elis Aristotle indicates that candidature in practice was restricted to members of certain families or rather patrilines. The thirty Spartans on the *gerousia*, including *ex officio* the two kings who were not necessarily over the age of sixty, were exempt from rendering an account of their tenure of their office. This privilege enabled them to accept bribes freely, according to Aristotle. The *gerontes* in the Cretan councils of elders were also thirty in number, another sign of the very close relationships between the Spartan and Cretan constitutions. It is very significant that the Cretans called their councils of elders by the name of *boulê*, 'council', alone, implying that there was no popular council encompassing the whole citizen population, as in archaic Chios or classical Athens.[222] This recalls the fact that the Homeric *basilêes* who met in council were equated with the *gerontes*, or at least were drawn from among them.[223] The Greek council was originally a council of elders. It is likely that this was as true of the Athenian *Areiopagos* as it was of the councils in other *poleis*. Some people regarded the Spartan *gerousia* as an oligarchic feature, according to

Aristotle, but this was only possible in a period when in some cities the role of old men was not preponderant.[224]

The precise details of the role of old men may diverge between different age class systems as much as they do so for younger age grades. In Athens old men played a respectable but passive role as recipients of assistance, whilst in the Dorian *poleis* some old men at least had a very important political role throughout the classical period. For the sake of completeness we must mention one part of Greece, namely the island *tetrapolis* of Keos, where old age was a pronounced disadvantage, to put it mildly, even without taking account of the infirmities which usually accompany old age. On Keos there was a law that men above the age of sixty had to commit suicide by drinking hemlock so that there would be enough food left for the rest of the population.[225]

Recent archaeological survey work on the island shows that the proportion of land which was terraced and so presumably cultivated in the classical period is much larger than the proportion of the island which is covered with good soil today. It is possible that the Keans artificially extended the cultivated area by covering rocks with soil in the same way that the people of Aigina are said to have done, rather than that massive soil erosion has occurred since antiquity. In any case it is clear that the population of classical Keos was struggling to survive at the very limits of the carrying capacity of its territory. Strabo also mentions that during a siege by the Athenians, probably having in mind events that occurred in the fourth century BC during the Second Athenian League, the people of Keos voted that all those above a certain age should be put to death to conserve food for the rest, after which the Athenians lifted the siege. Marriage on Keos was also regulated by the socio-political organisation. There were public festivals at which *parthenoi* danced and played before prospective suitors.[226]

Aristotle compared *basilikê archê*, the type of rule characteristic of kings, to the rule of a father over his child, and spoke of rule *kata presbeian*, according to age, as its distinguishing feature.[227] For Aristotle the type of kingship characteristic of early Greece, as opposed to the absolute monarchs of the Orient such as Persian kings of kings or Egyptian pharaohs, was to be comprehended in the context of a social organisation in which age was a guiding principle. This deserves the utmost stress. Aristotle explained lucidly where the principles of the distribution and rotation of power among the citizens which characterised the *polis* came from. He stated that nature, by making every man young and then old, had provided a basis whereby each and every member of the *polis* could be ruled and then rule – *archomenos kai archôn* – in the course of his life (women of course didn't come into it). Carlier, in his recent study of royalty in Greece, affirmed that 'les *poleis* de l'époque classique ont inventé un tout autre système politique dans lequel chaque citoyen est tour à tour gouvernant et gouverné', instead of the royalty which he discerned in Dark Age Greece. This is a classic example of putting the cart before the horse.[228] It is only in the context of the prior existence of the *archôn kai archomenos* principle that the Heroic and Dark Age kings, who were *awarded fixed* privileges by the people and assimilated to *gerontes*, make sense.[229]

It is necessary to digress briefly at this point to comment on Jeanmaire. His thoughts on Homeric kings led him to insist on a parallel between Homeric/Dark Age Greek societies and feudalism in mediaeval Europe. This is undoubtedly the least satisfactory aspect of his *magnum opus, Couroi et courètes*. As Carlier (1984) emphasises, early Greek kings *received* privileges from the people and did not themselves award, for example, *temenê* to other individuals, as mediaeval kings did. Moreover, recent anthropological research on age class societies shows that they have nothing whatsoever to do with feudal societies, as they put the accent on the relationship between *groups*, while feudal relationships link *individuals*, e.g. the king and each of his barons. However, it is easy to drop Jeanmaire's parallel with feudalism in its entirety without affecting in any way his main and still very valuable insights into the importance of the principles of age and sex organisation in ancient Greece.

Carlier collected a fair amount of scattered evidence for kings of one kind or another in Dark Age Greece, although the traditions concerning Attica are rather ephemeral. The main problem in considering monarchy in the Greek world is not so much the absence of kings, as Drews (1983) thought, but rather to explain why absolute monarchies of the Oriental type, whose legitimacy was generally accepted by their subjects, were alien to the ancient Greek world. It was the age class systems of early Greece, in which was inherent the principle of the distribution of fixed *quotas* of power, which made possible the particular kind of restricted kingship attributed to early Greece by Aristotle and Thucydides. The African age class systems are essentially acephalous polities. However, in certain cases such as the Zulus powerful monarchs did arise as a product of historical contingencies, by a process which may not have been unlike Aristotle's analysis of the dual Spartan monarchy as a pair of hereditary lifelong generalships originally awarded by the Spartan people as a reward for the acquisition of territory.[230]

'The distribution and rotation of power have emerged as the main social and political characteristics of age class systems.'[231] The contrast between the equal but potential right of all the individuals in a particular age grade at a given time to share in all the privileges and duties allotted to that age grade and the allotment of different sets of rights and duties to different age grades unmistakably recalls the contradiction between Aristotle's emphasis on the equal potential right of all members of the *polis* to hold all the political and judicial offices and his simultaneous emphasis on the need for a rotation of offices, which could not be held by everyone at the same time. Aristotle thought in terms of the rotation of individual offices between individuals, not in terms of the rotation of sets of rights and duties between age groups, because the original age class system of Athens, in which he was writing, had long since been weakened by the fourth century BC. However, the formal rotation of groups was still very important then in Sparta and Crete.

Interpreting Dark Age Greek societies as age class systems enables us to comprehend immediately many features of the classical *polis* which appear as novelties in relation to contemporaneous and earlier Near Eastern societies. Such features include the fact that *absolute* monarchy as an institution was alien to the ancient Greek world, the non-hereditary nature of classical Greek political organisation as reflected by the use of election and sortition as methods of allotting political offices (with the use of the lot being a means of ensuring that everyone stood an equal chance of success), and the insignificance of kinship groups as a principle for the *internal* organisation of the *polis* (see section 6 below).

The notions of the distribution, rotation and limitation of power which are inherent in age class systems cut two ways. On the one hand the system makes possible the distribution on fixed terms of qualities such as the power to judge lawsuits, conduct sacrifices or lead the army in war – all attributes of Homeric and Dark Age kingships – to particular age grades or rather to individuals chosen from among the membership of those particular age grades at a given time. The tenure of kingship in Dark Age Sparta and Crete was probably held for a certain period of time only and subject to the rotation of the age classes (see below).

On the other hand the notions of the distribution, rotation and limitation of power according to fixed rules contain within themselves the seeds of a possible progression towards democracy. An age class system need not be democratic in the sense of one man, one vote. It may theoretically assign power to men over, say, the age of sixty. Such a system would not be considered democratic today nor would it have been so regarded in Athens in Aristotle's time. As Carlier observed, voting is not mentioned in the Homeric epics.[232] Nevertheless such a system contains certain tendencies which are essential for any successful democracy because of the theoretical equal access to the appropriate rights of the members of each age class. Aristotle said that many people described the Spartan system as democratic because *paideia* and the *agôgê* were the same for rich and poor alike in each age grade (*hêlikia*). They were indeed 'equal', but in terms of a principle of social organisation, namely age, which has not played a significant role in Western democracies which have arisen since the French Revolution, with its slogan of 'liberté, egalité et fraternité'.[233]

One modern school of thought in the social sciences, exemplified by Foner (1984), emphasises the inequality that arises out of the attribution of different rights and duties to different age grades. This ethnocentric viewpoint – the outcome of the modern definition of equality, namely that everyone of a common status (e.g. 'adult citizens') should have the same rights and duties *at the same time* – is a great barrier to understanding the genesis of democracy from age class organisation in ancient Greece. In an age class system men are equal because they have equal rights and duties at each stage of their lives. The temporal dimension is crucial to understanding the difference between ancient and modern democracy.

In the Spartan sense of 'equality' the Athenians in the classical period could not possibly be described as *homoioi* because they were not subjected to the same treatment in each age grade and differences in wealth inevitably resulted in great differences in the lifestyles of rich and poor in classical Athens. The incipient democrat in a slightly more modern sense, say Ephialtes in Athens, was the person who thought to himself, 'Power at the present time is not distributed as widely as it could be. Let us extend its distribution to a larger proportion of the population.' Ephialtes, probably acting on behalf of Perikles, secured the abolition of the judicial powers of the *Areiopagos*, except in cases of homicide and some other sacred matters, and handed them over to juries in law courts drawn from the entire citizen population, except those under the age of thirty. It was the very same idea of the *distribution of power* inherent in an age class system which made possible both the attribution of fixed privileges to Homeric kings by the people and the wider distribution of power to the people in a classical democracy such as Athens.[234]

Considered in this perspective, the abolition of the monarchies described by Carlier as characteristic of Dark Age and Homeric Greece did not require an intellectual revolution of the kind that would have been needed to abolish for example the *office* of Pharaoh in Egypt, where the monarch was a god on earth, or at least went to join the gods after his death. Herodotos observed that the Egyptians could not live without kings.[235] Abolishing the office of Pharaoh would have required a cataclysm in the ideological superstructure of the ancient Egyptian state. In contrast abolishing the *basileiai* of Agamemnon or Odysseus or, in a historical setting, of the Temenid kings of Argos in the fifth century BC, simply required the redistribution of certain units of power in a society in which the very idea of the regular distribution of rights and duties (between different age grades), thus excluding absolute monarchy, was *already* a well established principle. The word 'already' requires the utmost stress here. If its historical origin is considered in these terms, classical Greek democracy did not in fact represent such an enormous leap forward *relative to what had gone before* as is generally supposed by classical scholars.

Similarly the tyrannies of archaic Greece were another reaction to the same principles of social organisation. The would-be tyrant was the person who wished to break out of the limits of the distribution of power set by an age class system to his own personal advantage, expressing *hubris* by going too far. This is clear in Athens too in the case of Kylon, who persuaded his age mates to help him to improve his own, and presumably also their, position. The very concept of the tyrant only makes sense given the *prior* existence of ideas concerning the regular distribution and rotation of power. It was an idea that could hardly have been intelligible in absolute monarchies such as Persia or Egypt. Homeric kingship, archaic tyranny and classical democracy are all readily comprehensible as three different reactions to a single set of principles of social organisation, namely those of an age class system, which lie at the roots of Aristotle's analysis of the *polis*. Modern philosophers have failed dismally to understand the *historical* roots of the set of ideas which formed the starting point for all subsequent Western political theory.

Having made one link between kingship in early Greek history and age class systems, another link between the two may be made by a different route. A number of sources connect kingship with eight-yearly rituals, cycles or age groups. Worthy of mention here is the ritual of the Spartan ephors watching the sky for meteors once every eight years to see if a king had sinned, the reform of the laws once every eight years by Minos in Crete, and the legend of Theseus in Attica.[236] Such details are recorded for both Dorian and Ionian *poleis*, suggesting that they were once common to all the Greeks. Censorinus said that many festivals in Greece, such as the Pythian Games at Delphi, had once been celebrated at intervals of eight years.[237] Jeanmaire correctly suggested that all these rituals at intervals of eight years or so were all originally rites of passage at the periodic transition of new age classes into the first adult age grade. It is probable that originally Greek 'kingship' was strictly integrated into age class systems. Jane Harrison conceived the germ of this idea a long time ago. Either a new king had to be appointed every eight years or so or at least his powers had to be renewed periodically.[238]

Eight-year age classes are widely attested ethnographically. Quite what the magic of the number 'eight' is in this context, beyond being 2^3, is uncertain. George Thomson argued that eight-yearly festivals were associated with the return of the sun, moon and stars to their original positions once every eight years, a phenomenon used to link the solar calendar, essential for the operations of the agricultural year, with the lunar calendar originally used by the Greeks.[239] The phases of the moon indeed did play a role in determining the timing of various agricultural operations in antiquity, and are still regarded with awe by modern Greek peasants.[240]

Thomson's argument may be part of the truth, but there is another possible explanation, proposed by Jeanmaire. He argued that the duration of the period between the formation of new age classes was related to the size and density of the population. For example initiation rites dating to *c.* 1000 BC, when Greece as a whole and Attica in particular were very thinly populated, would have been widely spaced in time.[241]

The long period of time between the formation of new age classes in Dark Age Attica, a plausible interpretation of the significance of the dispatch of seven *Kouroi* and seven *Korai* once every seven years to Minos on Crete, correlates neatly with the archaeological evidence for a small population. The low population density permitted a considerable emphasis on animal husbandry within the economy (cf. Chapter III.12 below), and ethnographic evidence shows that age class societies often have a significant pastoral component to their economies, completing the circle. The utility of age as a principle of social organisation for pastoralists and for farmers practising shifting subsistence horticulture is that it is completely independent of territory.[242]

As the population of Attica and indeed of the rest of Greece grew in the Late Geometric and Archaic periods, age classes formed once every eight years or so became unsatisfactory and disappeared (see Chapter IV below) and, as may be inferred from Censorinus, the periodicity of many Greek festivals was altered accordingly. Because age class systems have demographic effects, it is inevitable that changes in the details of the system, or the disappearance of such a system in its entirety, will have notable demographic consequences. By the fifth century BC Athens only had *annual* age classes which did not have any regulatory effect on marriage patterns.

The interpretation of Greek social organisation proposed here is quite compatible with the view that the tribes (*phulai*) of many classical *poleis* were a late development, and not a feature of the earliest stages of their history. Aristotle regarded *phulai* and *sussitia* as alternative methods for the internal subdivision of the citizen body of the *polis*. Tribes such as those introduced by Kleisthenes at Athens towards the end of the sixth century BC were probably a late innovation to take the place of an earlier all-embracing age class system which had broken down by then. Similarly Brelich rightly argued that the classical Athenian laws on education attributed to Drakon, Solon and Kleisthenes by our sources already governed individual, rather than collective, education and so had governed the transition from the *paideia* of a fully fledged age class system to the rather different educational system of the attenuated age class system of classical Athens.[243]

An important recent doctoral thesis by A.J.M. Whitley devoted to mortuary practices in Dark Age Attica and Crete, by investigating how different categories of grave goods are correlated statistically with the age and sex of the deceased as determined by physical anthropologists, has shown that in Athens in the Protogeometric period the nature of the grave goods deposited in a tomb is linked closely with the age and sex of the deceased. Thus arguments for the importance of age class organisation in the Dark Ages need not depend any longer solely on extrapolation backwards from fragmentary literary sources of later date – the path taken by Jeanmaire and Brelich and by me so far in this section – but may now be substantiated by material evidence dating directly to the Dark Ages. The same thesis also showed that in Knossos on Crete in the Subminoan period (roughly coeval with Attic Protogeometric) the form of the grave assemblage was also closely correlated to the age and sex of the deceased. The subsequent changes were less marked on Crete than in Attica. This is another manifestation of the influence of age class organisation continuing into the Hellenistic period on all aspects of life on Crete. The different rates of change in Attica and in Crete of socio-political structures which had direct demographic effects is directly related to the different patterns of population growth exhibited by Attica and by Crete.[244]

Some consideration, of necessity brief owing to the scarcity of documentary sources and the lack of archaeological research of the kind mentioned in the previous paragraph, must be paid to the other end of this course of historical development. Besides the parallel with feudalism in mediaeval Europe, the other unsatisfactory aspect of Jeanmaire's classic book *Couroi et courètes* is his insistence on unbroken continuity from the Mycenaean period to later periods of Greek history. Jeanmaire wrote his book before the decipherment of Linear B, with its revelation of an Oriental-style palace bureaucracy unparalleled in later periods of Greek history, and he could not have been aware of the results of the many recent archaeological surveys showing that there was a collapse in the size of the population of most parts of Greece at the end of the Mycenaean period.

Many features of archaic Greek society, including the basic elements of age class organisation, probably did have antecedents in the Mycenaean period, although unfortunately there is little to be learnt from the Linear B accounts about Mycenaean social structure.[245] Nevertheless it is only prudent to assume that a traumatic shock affected Greek societies at the end of the Mycenaean period, creating the conditions for what Mendenhall termed 'retribalisation' and the prevalence of societies that were either acephalous or only weakly centralised (compared to those in the Near East), existing under conditions of a low human population density conducive to transhumant pastoralism as a significant component of the economy and to age class organisation. Given the absence of literary sources before Homer and Hesiod, there is little more that can be said at the moment.[246]

Age class systems do not merely govern access to material necessities such as food, vital physical activities such as sexual intercourse, and the distribution of political power, but also create a symbolic order governing the values and ideology of such societies. The ideological component of age class systems is very important for their successful functioning because they usually do not have police forces or other agencies for maintaining law and order. In Sparta ritual activities such as the organisation of choirs at festivals were organised in accordance with the age class system.[247] In the context of all the other manifestations of the Spartan age class system which have already been described this may seem a relatively trivial detail. However, the organisation of ritual activities on the basis of age is by itself sufficient to constitute an age class system, as in Bernardi's 'choreographic model'.[248]

Lack of space here prevents any extended discussion of the ground covered by Jeanmaire's studies of ancient Greek religion. Suffice it to mention his demonstration that the god Dionysos was the *neos*, initiate, par excellence (although the evidence of the Linear B tablets now indicates that Dionysos was around in the Greek world much earlier than Jeanmaire thought), and his convincing arguments that the myth of Demeter and Kore celebrated in the Eleusinian Mysteries and other Athenian festivals such as the rites of Artemis at Brauron were rites of passage. Brelich extended Jeanmaire's research in many interesting ways, most notably by showing how the Athenian rites performed by girls in the guise of *arrhêphoroi, aletrides, arktoi* and *kanêphoroi* once could have been stages in an age class system for women in Athens, even if the details remain obscure and the subject of continuing debate. Burkert has confirmed the view that rituals such as initiation into the Eleusinian Mysteries were rites of passage conferring group membership on the initiand. There was no question of access to an afterlife or anything of the sort. Finally, the research of Lincoln on the Eleusinian Mysteries also merits a mention. He argued on the basis of a cross-cultural study of women's initiations that both men and women generally have a role to play in them, explaining why both men and women were eligible for initiation into the Eleusinian Mysteries in the classical period. Kore's disappearance into the underworld and her return as Persephone was the original initiation of a woman, re-enacted during the Mysteries.[249]

It is always instructive to correlate archaeological and documentary evidence, and doing so yields a rich harvest in the field of religion, ideology and art too. Recent archaeological research has stressed the importance of the construction of extra-urban sanctuaries, often situated on frontiers, as a component of the development of the *polis* in the eighth century BC. Athens had sanctuaries of this kind in places like Brauron, Halai and Eleusis. These extra-urban sanctuaries were the site of initiation ceremonies at which the young men were spatially separated from the rest of their own society for a time. Van Gennep (1960) emphasised the importance of spatial separation during a rite of passage. In the course of antiquity such rites tended to lose their original significance. By the sixth century BC the myth of Demeter and Kore was already being erroneously interpreted in certain quarters as an agricultural festival. Shifts in the meaning of such festivals in the course of the archaic period should be linked with the disappearance of the type of age class system indicated for Dark Age Attica by the Theseus legend. However, the fact that during the Greek colonisation of the

Mediterranean in the eighth century BC extra-urban religious sanctuaries continued to be built, as argued by Polignac in the case of Sicily, instead of being incorporated into the nascent urban centres, suggests that in that century the initiation rites of the age class societies of Dark Age Greece were still flourishing.[250]

It is also worth raising the tantalising possibility that certain developments in art styles from the archaic to the classical periods, such as the abandonment of the manufacture of the rigid erect frontal facing archaic marble *kouroi* and *korai* statues, whose *social* significance should not require any explanation by now, may not have been just a matter of art styles changing (in this case towards an increased expression of naturalism) in splendid isolation, as if such a thing were possible, but may well have been a consequence of a changing social order. The fact that it can be shown that these statues had a variety of functions in the later stages of their history should not be allowed to obscure the strong possibility that when they were first manufactured they were integrally related to the rituals of age class systems. In connection with the lack of naturalism of these archaic statues, it is not irrelevant to remember that the physical beauty of the young man was not a factor to be taken into account as far as Lykourgos and Minos were concerned. Similarly, in explaining the fact that the archaic Athenian *korai* statues are draped, unlike the *kouroi* statues, it is necessary to bear in mind the fact that the Athenians did not parade their *parthenoi* naked as the Spartans did. The Spartans, unlike the Athenians, did dedicate bronze figurines of naked girls in their sanctuaries.

However objects of art alone cannot tell us when an idea first developed. The *kouros* statues began to be manufactured in archaic Greece in the seventh century BC, but the concept of the *kouros*, as it appears in classical Greek myths which are connected with initiation rites, undoubtedly existed centuries, perhaps even millennia, earlier. The word underwent different but regular transformations in all the various Greek dialects which enable philologists to deduce that it was present in *the original* dialect of Greek, even preceding the division into Mycenaean and proto-Doric which had occurred by the time of the Linear B tablets. This permits the tentative conclusion that the concept of the *kouros*, and with it age class organisation, already existed amongst the proto-Greeks in the first half of the second millennium BC, long before anyone thought of depicting it in marble.[251]

Just as ancient Greek social organisation took the differentiation of people by age as its guiding principle, so Greek religion, the ideology corresponding to that social structure, was centred in essence on the symbolisation of the major events of the human lifespan, especially the transition from childhood to adulthood. The prevalence of initiation myths in Greek religion, such as the Demeter-Kore myth, can only be understood in the context of age class systems similar to Bernardi's 'initiation model', in which the basic principle of class recruitment is the social recognition by those who are already classified as adults of the biological changes which mark the advent of adulthood.[252]

Even in classical Athens the members of a deme, when examining a candidate for admission to the deme, had to decide if the candidate possessed the physical features characteristic of adulthood, and if not the candidate was returned to the ranks of the *paides*. The *boulê* then reviewed all those admitted by the demes to check that they satisfied the age criterion, besides being of citizen descent on both sides. Plato in his ideal constitution only recommended a physical examination at the time of marriage, to assess the suitability for producing children of aspirants to the privilege of marriage, to be carried out with males stripped naked and females stripped down to the navel.[253] Plato thought that children should be registered as citizens *at birth*. This at first sight trivial reform would have entailed a social revolution in an age class society. It shows that Plato did not understand the historical origins of the society he lived in.[254]

Ancient Greek religion cannot be understood without a proper understanding of the nature of Greek society any more than Greek art can. As it revolved around symbolising the major events of the human lifespan in this world, ancient Greek religion had nothing whatsoever in common with Judaism and its proselytising sect, Christianity. It was because ancient Israelite society, which may be classified as what social anthropologists call a segmentary society, was quite different in structure from ancient Greek society that its religion/ideology was quite different as well and was utterly incomprehensible to committed pagans. The same differences in social structure explain why institutionalised paederasty was alien to the world of ancient Israel. As age class systems faded away from the Greek world in the course of the first millennium BC, Greek religion became an ideological superstructure which had lost its material foundations in the shape of the social structure to which it had originally corresponded. It thus became devoid of meaning. This helps to explain why so many pagans were an easy prey for the missionaries bringing the new promise of an after-life made by Christianity.[255]

Membership of the community of full citizens in the Greek *polis* was not ascribed at birth, in spite of Plato, but above all at an initiation ceremony at the transition to adulthood which took various forms, ranging from a gentle examination before the members of one's father's deme in classical Athens to the hardships of the Spartan *krupteia* or the eroticism of Crete. 'Citizenship' in the ancient Greek world was not ascribed at birth and cannot be equated with the modern concept of 'nationality'. Nor did initiation into adulthood give the initiate a *complete* set of political rights, as occurs upon attainment of the age of majority in modern democracies, but only a selection which gradually increased with time and passage into older age grades. In Sparta no one apart from the kings (or those who had been high princes) who had not passed through the *agôgê* had any share in the rights of 'citizenship'. The basic idea here is relevant to the nature of 'citizenship' in all the other *poleis* as well. 'Citizenship' in the *polis* could only be fully acquired, or rather *experienced* in its totality, by passing through the entire human lifespan from birth to death and undergoing all the stages of *paideia*. The totality of that experience could not be conferred on an alien at any particular instant in time.[256] This is the fundamental reason why imperial Athens, Sparta and Thebes all found it impossible to extend their 'citizen' bodies to incorporate the other Greeks whom they defeated and conquered in war. Aristotle intuitively and correctly felt that defining a citizen as the son of ancestors who were citizens, for one or more generations, was an inherently unsatisfactory way of comprehending the nature of 'citizenship', *politeia*, in ancient Greece. However, his own definition, namely that the *politês* was a person who was eligible for political and judicial office, is also unsatisfactory because he made the same error of mistaking a part for the whole which he imputed to the Spartans. Aristotle picked out and isolated the function of what we may now call an age class system of distributing political power as if it were the *only* function of such a system. The analysis put forward here also explains why ancient Greek religion could *never* have been a *proselytising* religion, unlike Christianity.[257]

Xenophon described the essential features of an age class system, dressing up Sparta in Persian clothes in the *Cyropaedia*. He describes clearly the potential access to new rights and duties acquired as each successive age grade is reached and the peer competition between members of each age class, with the inherent conflicting tendencies of hierarchy between different age grades and equality within age classes. Some scholars might object on the grounds that Xenophon's description (and also Ephoros' account of Crete) is utopian in character. The most fundamental reason for dismissing such an objection is that if Xenophon and Ephoros had been engaging in speculative political theory, then it is only to be expected that their constructions should be extremely unrealistic in nature, given that utopias tend to be diametrically opposed to reality, more or less by definition. However, comparison with the findings of modern social anthropology suggests that the principles of social organisation described by Xenophon and Ephoros constitute the foundation for a perfectly realistic and feasible type of society. Moreover, Xenophon was not a radical theoretical sociologist seeking to draw up a blueprint for an alternative society, but an arch-conservative. His idealised view of how the Spartan system was supposed to work coincides in its essentials with Aristotle's analysis of the distribution and rotation of power in the *polis* according to age.[258]

As was pointed out long ago but is not emphasised sufficiently in most books on ancient history, the early Romans did not have categories based on age as a principle of social (as distinct from purely military – the *iuniores* and the *seniores*) organisation.[259] Instead they had unilineal descent groups, the *gentes*, on which see section 6 below. Consequently the Roman conception of 'citizenship' was quite different from the Greek one. At the beginning of the process that was to lead to the development of Roman jurisprudence, the Romans were able to conceive of citizenship as a package of rights and duties which could be conferred on an alien all at once, because they lacked any notion that rights and duties should be obtained gradually by passing through a succession of age grades. The contrast between Greece and Rome in this respect is a prime example to confirm Eisenstadt's hypothesis that the way in which age is incorporated into the social structure is bound up inextricably with the way in which citizenship is achieved and maintained.

Age and seniority were indeed important in Rome, but they were expressed in Roman social structure in a fundamentally different way from the Greek method which has been under scrutiny so far. The Romans possessed the institution of *patria potestas*, linking child to father in a way which gave the father the power of executing his own child. This method of incorporating age into the social structure linked individuals on a purely familial basis, not age classes comprising individuals who need not be related to each other at all, and consequently did not have the demographic consequences of the Greek method. The Romans were aware that the concept of *patria potestas* had no parallel in the Greek world.[260]

This difference in social structure between Greece and Rome is arguably the most important single fact in ancient history, because it explains why Rome was able to assimilate all the peoples she conquered in order to create an empire spanning most of the then known world, while Athens and Sparta were utterly unable even to step onto the same path. Such conclusions cannot be reached by assimilating all the societies of antiquity to each other, whether it be in the form of the 'consumer city' or the 'slave mode of production' or any other catch-all concept, but only by contrasting them rigorously using the method of comparative analysis of institutions.[261]

Eisenstadt's otherwise admirable contrast between Greece and Rome has one drawback. He depended entirely on secondary literature for his knowledge of ancient Greece and so inevitably had to interpret the 'facts' as they were presented to him by his secondary sources, which suffered from one severe defect. They took the *genos* of Fustel de Coulanges seriously. Consigning Fustel's *La cité antique* to the wastepaper basket – it can only be of interest now as a best-forgotten episode in the development of modern historiography – enables us significantly to deepen and sharpen Eisenstadt's contrast between Greece and Rome and furthermore to turn the course of historical development around and argue that Greece and Rome, originally very different, were tending to *converge* during the first millennium BC, instead of Eisenstadt's idea that two societies with similarities early in their history were *diverging* from each other in that period. This problem will be discussed again in section 6 below.

If 'Greek society' and 'Greek religion' have been discussed so far as unitary conceptions, to which some scholars might take exception, it is because of my belief that certain elementary principles of social organisation were shared by all the Greeks without exception and underlay all aspects of life in every *polis*. The distribution and rotation of political power by age, one of the most important features of an age class system, was shared by both Athens and Sparta, as well as a religion and ideology which symbolised and legitimised what was culturally defined as the single most important step in the course of the human lifespan, namely initiation into adulthood. The concept of an 'age class system' is an ideal type, like Weber's 'consumer city' or Marx's 'slave mode of production', but only more discriminating in this particular case and so more valuable for the ancient historian because it differentiates Greece from Rome, while the other two concepts lump them together.

There is no reason why instances of the ideal type should not differ in details. At this point it is perhaps worth rejecting in advance the objection that differences in detail make generalisation impossible. If the more than 150 constitutions of other *poleis* written by Aristotle's followers were still extant, besides the one on Athens, it would be possible to compare and contrast them all and arrange them into a series of sub-types according to which aspects of social life were organised according to the age principle in each case, in exactly the same way that Bernardi has done for the African societies. In this perspective the presence of *sussitia* in Sparta and their absence from classical Athens, for example, is a non-essential detail, not a fundamental principle.

Much of this section may seem to the reader to have had little or nothing to do with demography. However, in order to establish the validity of the idea that the ancient Greeks possessed a particular type of social organisation which had considerable demographic consequences, especially in respect of marital timing and coital frequency with effects on age-specific fertility patterns and rates, it was necessary to explore the whole range of manifestations of age class systems. As firm evidence of the demographic significance of marriage control, the situation in modern China should be considered. Chesnais & Hong (1986) argued that the Chinese government's raising of the minimum age of marriage for men to twenty-two and for women to twenty has contributed about 20 per cent of the total fertility decline there recently (the rest coming from the restriction to one child per couple).

The main conclusion of this section is that during the first millennium BC the various societies in ancient Greece developed from socio-political systems which had marked demographic consequences into systems which did not have any such consequences. The timing of this development varied from *polis* to *polis*. Sparta, for example, disintegrated in the course of the third century BC. (Indeed she flourished during the Roman empire thanks to Roman tourism, but the archaic and classical social structure had disappeared.)[262] In the case of Athens the course of history is more uncertain, because by the fifth century BC, the first century to yield a significant amount of surviving written evidence, Athens was not a society in which the age class system had notable demographic consequences. But it is reasonable to hypothesise that she once had been such a society because ethnographic evidence shows that nearly all types of age class system imply such demographic functions. Moreover there is now archaeological evidence suggesting that Athens indeed was firmly organised as an age class system in the Protogeometric period. Ephesos in Ionia definitely had age class organisation of age of marriage for both sexes. As the Ionians migrated to Anatolia from Attica in the Dark Ages according to one strand of tradition, this piece of evidence enables us tentatively to trace back the social organisation of Ephesos to Protogeometric Attica. Ephesos proves that regulation of age of marriage by the age class system was not a feature possessed by the Dorian *poleis* only. A special mention should be reserved for Crete. Those Cretans who, in the first century BC formed part of that mass of pirates in the Mediterranean which had the nerve to fight the might of Rome assembled by Pompey and the effrontery (with hindsight) to kidnap Julius Caesar, had the sociological distinction of being products of the last society in European history to be organised as an age class system.

To round off this section, having considered Finley and Ste. Croix, Weber and Marx, on the characteristics of the *polis*, it is appropriate to consider the view of the dichotomy between the ancient and the mediaeval world proposed by another leading scholar, a historian of the world in the early modern period, Fernand Braudel.[263] Braudel noted, quite correctly, that town and country were unified in ancient Greece and drew a contrast with the closed city of the mediaeval world. So far so good. But his explanation of the difference between them is not so convincing. He thought that as towns had only just come into existence in ancient Greece (after the Dark Ages) there had simply not been enough time for them to develop their own trade and industry and a distinctive civic organisation. The real reason for the unity of town and country in ancient Greece is that the citizen body of the *polis* was regulated according to a principle of social organisation, namely age, which was independent of territory. Ultimately I disagree with all five of the scholars mentioned above concerning the role of economics in history. The ancient Greek *polis* owed its historical individuality to principles of social organisation which cannot be subsumed under the category of economics. The course of European history cannot be reduced to economics.

6. Social and economic aspects of family structures

This section concentrates on social and economic aspects of the family in ancient Greece. The initial question must be how complete are the families described in our sources. Families of two, three or four children are mentioned not infrequently in the Attic orators (see section 4 above). Similarly epigraphic sources suggest that many families on Hellenistic Delos had at least three or four children. However populations with values for life expectancy at birth similar to those discussed in section 3 above require average completed family sizes of four to five children just in order to reproduce themselves. This elementary fact suggests that the families described by the Attic orators as apparently complete families were too small to reproduce the population.

The orators simply omitted children of both sexes who died as infants (infants who died before receiving a name at the *dekatê* ceremony presumably were never recognised as socially accepted members of the family) and juveniles. Similarly Klein (1932) showed that dead infants are usually not portrayed in vase paintings. The orators also omitted adult females who had left their father's household to get married before the time of the court case in question. In the well-known family described in Isaios XI and (Demosthenes) XLIII, Bouselos *ex Oiou* is said to have had five sons, a family size which, if complete, would only just be large enough to reproduce such a population on average. In fact the mathematical probability of having five sons and no daughters is quite low. The odds are that Bouselos also had daughters who married into other patrilines and did not play any role in the events pertinent to the orators' cases, because they could not inherit any of the property that was at stake in this long-running legal wrangle. Furthermore these five sons all reached adulthood. There is no telling how many other sons, and daughters, who did not survive infancy and early childhood Bouselos and his wife may have had. The complete family size of this couple may have been more like ten or fifteen than the five mentioned by our sources. Bouselos evidently did not share the preoccupations of the Greeks of Polybios' time with family limitation.

This is not to deny that the orators are a useful guide to those individuals, especially males, who reached adulthood. What is in question here is the validity of using literary sources as a *birth register*. Demographic factors must be taken into account in considering to what extent it is likely that the literary and epigraphic sources upon which J. Davies (1971) relied, the most important compilation of data on Athenian families by a modern scholar, are giving us complete records of births in the families in question. Raepsaet (1973) assumed parity in the sex ratio in order to extrapolate total family size from the number of sons mentioned, in order to surmount the tendency of the sources not to name females. This procedure yielded an average of 2.65 children per marriage in Isaios, much too low to reproduce such a population. It is only valuable if one thinks in terms of literary sources as providing information only on those children who reached adulthood, in which case the Athenian population was reproducing itself in the fourth century BC and probably increasing slowly.[264]

The number of children per family is highly skewed even in natural fertility populations. The main reason for this is that there is a substantial inherited genetic component to human fertility, just as there is to longevity. Not only is survivorship of children to adulthood low in populations with a low life expectancy at birth, but the distribution of those survivors between families is also highly skewed. In each generation about 10-20 per cent of all marriages fail to leave any children at all surviving the husband's death and about another 20 per cent of all marriages only leave female children surviving the husband's death. This is not inconsistent with the absence of voluntary family limitation because the chances of children outliving their parents are much lower in populations with high mortality in infancy and early childhood than in modern populations. This may explain the Greek habit of often giving a son the name of his paternal grandfather. As a result high fertility is required to maximise the chances of parents having surviving children to look after them in old age. The phenomenon of patriline discontinuity is common to all well-documented pre-modern populations.[265]

One very important passage of Aristotle indicates that ancient Greek populations behaved in the same way. After speaking at length about the dangers inherent in people having several sons who would inherit small portions of property (in the circumstances of the high population density of the fourth century BC), leading to poverty and possibly social conflict (*stasis*), Aristotle suddenly stated that the frequency of families altogether without sons was high enough to keep the populations of existing *poleis* more or less stationary (at K). His ideas on population in *Politics* book II have been persistently misunderstood by modern scholars through their failure to realise that he was describing two *complementary* aspects of a single population, which theoretically could have been quite stationary. Aristotle's comments exemplify the pattern so familiar in historical demography, namely the co-existence within a single population in each generation of a significant minority of families ending up with two or more surviving sons with another significant minority of families ending up with no sons at all to survive their father. The word *ateknia*, 'childlessness', here refers to male children only, as Aristotle was debating with Plato the question of regulating the number of citizens (*politai*), technically excluding women. Nevertheless the same pattern of statistical distribution of variation within a population applied as well to women, in whom Aristotle was not interested at that particular point.[266]

A significant minority of all biological patrilines inevitably became extinct in each generation under such conditions. It is quite plausible that, say, 40-50 per cent of all patrilines became extinct in Athens in the course of the fourth century BC. However the magnitude of this phenomenon would have been sharply reduced during phases of rapid population growth, and so larger average completed family size, as in the r period of the eighth century BC. In cases of a man dying without surviving male heirs patrilines could be maintained as socially recognised descent lines by legal devices such as adoption, but *de facto* social mobility was inevitable, even when adoption took place. The longest-lived families known to us, such as the priestly Eteoboutadai, had to resort to adoption to try to ensure social continuity, not always successfully. Posthumous adoption was also possible, although not compulsory, as a means of preserving a patriline for social purposes. The rules governing it are left in great obscurity by our sources.

The bilateral kindred was the basic unit of the Athenian kinship system. It was possible to inherit property via both male and female relatives, but a woman could not be *kurios*, i.e. legally in charge, of the property base of a household (*oikos*). Moreover, the paternal grandfather of the children of an heiress (*epiklêros*) was surely the father of the husband of the *epiklêros*, not the father of the *epiklêros* herself. This implies that the *oikos* of a man may have disappeared if he did not have any male children surviving his death and had not adopted a male heir, barring posthumous adoption. It has been suggested plausibly that the function of the epiklerate was not to preserve patrilines, but to ensure that every heiress, whether rich or destitute, found a husband. In any case, some men would have died fairly suddenly through war or disease even in the age groups of early adulthood in classical Athens, before they had given up hope of having children of their own or probably even married, if there was a tendency to delay first marriage for males till about the age of thirty or so. Consequently it is unlikely that legal devices such as adoption did succeed entirely in solving the problem of the maintenance of patrilines as biological entities.[267]

There was evidently a great desire to perpetuate family lines. To tackle the problem of patriline extinction Solon invented the legal device of a will to permit a childless man to retain ownership of his land during his lifetime and transfer it to a chosen heir on his death, without having to alienate it during his lifetime or die and leave his property to be divided up amongst his relatives. Solon is also said to have allowed a childless man to adopt an heir *inter vivos*, as an alternative.

If the emphasis of Athenian law by the early sixth century BC upon patriline preservation, at the expense of the interests of collateral relatives, and the consequent exclusion of laterally extended family units are taken together with the mathematical impossibility of vertically extended families constituting more than a minority of all families in a population with low life expectancy at birth, it is obvious that the isolated nuclear family was the numerically predominant component in the family structures found in Attica in Solon's time. In fact it is very likely that the atomic social structure of the Boiotia of Hesiod, who advised that neighbours were more likely to be a source of assistance than kin living far away and recommended that witnesses should be used even in transactions with one's own brother, was characteristic of Attica as well by Solon's time, and indeed probably much earlier too.[268]

There was an admixture of three-generation families arising from the duty of children to support their parents, as it is clear that retired parents at least sometimes continued to reside with a child. A surviving parent was more likely to be a mother than a father because of the differential in ages of marriage between men and women. However, three-generation families were always less numerous than nuclear families. Moreover their character was fundamentally different from the stem family systems (Le Play's 'la famille souche') familiar to historians working on mediaeval and early modern European history, because three-generation families in ancient Greece were associated with partible inheritance, in contrast to the custom of primogeniture commonly found in later periods of European history.

Primogeniture was inconceivable in ancient Greece because under age class organisation all individuals in the same age class, or more broadly speaking in the same generation, have potentially equal privileges and duties. Plato did dream up the idea that only one son should inherit his father's *klêros*. However, Aristotle defended partible inheritance against him on the grounds that no one was left destitute in existing *poleis*, in contrast to what would have happened in the ideal *polis* of Plato's *Laws*. It was not assumed in antiquity that a vertically extended family was conducive to social harmony and stability. An interesting passage in the corpus of the Attic orators states that where there is a father and adult sons and perhaps also grandchildren, there are bound to be many divergent wishes, because young and old people do not act or speak in the same way.[269]

The evidence of the Attic orators also suggests that it was not usual for two married couples in the same generation to reside under the same roof. This situation is analogous to that described for early modern England by Laslett (1983). Sometimes brothers did decide not to divide up their father's estate, but even so they did not live with their wives in the same house. Decisions by brothers not to divide the estate of their deceased father often appear in the orators in such contexts as a decision by one of the brothers not to marry for the time being, or to travel abroad e.g. as a merchant. Burch (1970) showed that even under conditions of quite rapid population growth the average number of adults per household never exceeds three in a nuclear family system and rarely does so in a stem family system (his calculations assumed universal marriage of all females at an average age of twenty). It follows that even the demographic conditions of the r period did not radically disturb this picture of rather small families in each household, which we find in Hesiod, *Works and Days*. The population growth of the eighth century BC increased the number of families more than it increased the average size of families in respect of the number of adults per household, although the number of children increased very substantially.[270]

The household was called *oikos* in ancient Greek. As defined by Aristotle it referred to all those who shared day-to-day life. The Athenians had a concept of the *oikos* as a property unit (including slaves) which could be considered independently of its male master, as in the phrase *oikos erêmos*, recalling the *ostal* of Le Roy Ladurie's Montaillou. However, the fact that an *oikos* could be thought about independently of the man at its head does not imply that a living master did not have absolute control over his own *oikos*. There is no evidence that the *oikos* was in any way subject to the control of a wider descent or kinship group at any time prior to the classical period. For example, the plot of the *Odyssey* would be unintelligible if the suitors had been encroaching on part of the property base of a unilineal descent group rather than on the estate of an individual, namely Odysseus, exercising full control in theory over his own property. This leads on to the vexed question of kinship systems in ancient Greece and the significance of the term *genos*.[271]

Recent research, especially by Bourriot (1976) and D. Roussel (1976), has utterly discredited the picture drawn by Fustel de Coulanges of the Attic *genos* as a corporate kinship group. Fustel simply attempted to apply to ancient Greece the characteristics of the ideal-type of 'primitive society' which was dreamed up by the major social anthropologists of the last century, an idea dismantled by Kuper (1988). In fact the ancient Greeks *never* (and not just in the classical period) had any corporate groupings of kin (either exogamous or endogamous), such as the unilateral descent groups found in many 'primitive' societies known to anthropologists. Claude Lévi-Strauss has described the Athenian kinship system as an 'undifferentiated system', with no intrinsic mode of filiation or descent, which was oriented predominantly towards the patrilineal rule, but in which incest prohibitions were more strict on the maternal side. He thought that the Athenian kinship system had to be analysed in terms of the exchange of women and the relative strengths of wife-givers and wife-takers within an alliance.

It is instructive to review a few of the numerous mistakes made by Fustel de Coulanges before going on to explain why forms of social organisation in which corporate kin groups play an integral role were alien to the world of the Greek *polis*. His analysis of the Greek *genos* rested on a fallacy which has had a tenacious grip on modern scholarship, namely that the development of the classical Greek *polis* involved a transition from kinship to politics, to put it crudely. This fallacy depends on another fallacy, namely that kinship is the *only* principle of social organisation available to 'primitive' societies, and so the Greeks must have been a kin-based society before they developed elaborate political systems such as the classical Athenian democracy. In fact age class organisation is an alternative method of organising 'primitive' societies which has still been widespread in the world in recent times. There is no reason whatsoever for supposing that it is any less ancient than kinship as a principle of human social organisation, because human beings have been young, matured and then grown old for just as long as they have had relatives.[272]

Because of his grossly inadequate knowledge of the Greek language and the sources for ancient Greek history, Fustel de Coulanges assumed that the word *genos* had a technical meaning whenever it appears in our sources. In fact, as Bourriot rightly pointed out, the word in its most general sense signifies a 'type' or 'kind' and may be applied to any group at any level of any classification scheme, as in Aristotle's biological works, where it is illegitimate to translate it by modern concepts such as 'species' or 'genus'. Accordingly it must not be assumed that the word has a special legal or technical meaning whenever it occurs in the context of familial organisation.

Fustel also failed to observe important yet elementary distinctions in anthropological terminology, namely the distinctions made by W.H.R. Rivers between *descent* (group membership), *inheritance* (of property) and *succession* (to office). He persistently mixed up *descent groups*, which do not require any particular man to have an heir surviving his death in order to ensure *group* continuity, with *patrilines*, which do require the incumbent in each generation to have an heir surviving his death if the patriline is to continue to exist in the next generation. All the characteristic defining attributes of unilineal descent groups, such as group names distinct from the names of individual members, a legal personality as a group, common ownership of property, etc. were absent from ancient Athens. There are many contexts in which 'patriline' is the best translation of the word *genos* when it occurs in relation to human beings, but it never signifies anything like a unilineal descent group.

Maintenance of patrilines through blood descendants is a biological improbability in the long run, as it is a statistical phenomenon. It is silly to imagine that the pattern of land ownership could have remained static down the generations anywhere in archaic Greece, as Fustel's interpretation required, because changes in the ownership of land caused by patriline extinction undoubtedly occurred, as Solon envisaged. Inalienability of land, the ideal of political theorists and legislators, was a dream that could never have been realised, because the absence of a legal concept of sale applicable to land could not do away with the facts of demography, as Plato found to his chagrin when drawing up the *Laws*, discussed below.[273]

Fustel's inadequate knowledge of ancient history also led him to generalise unwisely from Rome and to assume that the Greeks must have had descent groups comparable to the Roman *gentes*, membership of which was signified by the *tria nomina* system of nomenclature. Fustel was formally writing in opposition to German scholars of the time (the middle of the last century), but nevertheless he shared some of their assumptions in the intellectual atmosphere then prevailing. The context was the development of comparative philology, the discovery that the Indo-European languages were all related, the conclusion that they were all descended from a single ancestral language presumably spoken by a single people, and the consequent assumption that Rome, the best known early Indo-European society, could safely be taken as a model for all other early Indo-European societies. Accordingly Fustel foisted Roman social organisation onto Greece.

Later on other historians, including one as eminent as Marc Bloch, attempted to extend the Roman system to the early Germanic peoples as well. Again recent research has demonstrated that, as in the case of the ancient Greeks, Germanic kinship systems were based on a bilateral kindred. There were no *gentes* among the early Germans any more than there were among the Greeks. Thus the social structure of archaic Rome and of other groups of speakers of Indo-European languages of the Italic language group, which shared the *gens* system of personal nomenclature in a binomial form in the Early Iron Age (at least by the seventh century BC according to inscriptions from central Italy), far from being a paradigm for Indo-European societies in general, as it was taken to be by Fustel de Coulanges and German scholars in the last century, now appears to have been atypical of early Indo-European societies, or at least not shared by the Germans and Greeks.

Evidently after the break-up of the original Indo-European society, the various segments followed independently different paths, both geographically and in respect of the development of social institutions. It is probably impossible now to decide what the primaeval Indo-European society looked like. However, Germanic, Baltic and Slavic sources are much more likely to give us a glimpse of it than Greek, Latin or Hittite literature, as the latter group of peoples were probably all heavily influenced very early in their history by contact with speakers of non-Indo-European languages. The tripartite ideology ascribed to the proto-Indo-Europeans is not prominent in ancient Greek literature, in contrast to the legends about early Rome, as interpreted by Dumézil. This contrast may be explained in terms of the dominance of age class organisation in Greece, which wholly overshadowed the tripartite ideology.[274]

By the time in the late Republican period from which significant literary sources have survived, it is clear that the members of Roman *gentes* had ceased to act as corporate groups in any meaningful way. However, the mere existence of the binomial nomenclature (the *cognomen*, the third name, did not appear until the time of the Second

Punic War), with a name of a *gens* signifying group membership added to a personal name (*praenomen*), suggests that unilineal descent groups were once a fundamental feature of Roman social organisation in the period of the kings. The early Romans had unilineal descent groups but did not have social categories based on age as a principle of social (as opposed to purely military) organisation.[275]

In contrast the Greeks did not need kinship groups, because age and sex provided satisfactory alternative principles for the internal structuring of the *polis*, as Aristotle knew full well. Not only did they not need kin groups as a method of socio-political organisation, formal kin groups would have interfered with age class organisation, and vice versa, because age and kinship are two quite different principles of social organisation. Eisenstadt (1956) argued that a formal age class system is incompatible with a strong lineage system. He postulated that membership (i.e. citizenship) of age class systems could not be determined by membership of kin groups because of the particularistic nature of kin groups. He went on to argue that a nonkinship, nonparticularistic allocation of social roles, as in age class systems, entails either that status differentiation and social stratification depend on occupation roles, political power, wealth and personal qualities (not on ethnic ties, personal relations or kin relations), or that they depend on an individualistic achievement orientation. The latter possibility is relevant to considering how the world of the Homeric heroes in the *Iliad* and *Odyssey* may be interpreted in the context of age class organisation.

Relying on secondary sources as he did, Eisenstadt was aware of the evidence for strong forms of age class organisation in classical Sparta, but was also influenced by modern literature derived from Fustel de Coulanges which emphasised the *genos* as a descent group in archaic Greece. Accordingly he thought that the development of the elements of age class organisation seen in classical Sparta represented a late divergence from a family- and kinship-based social structure common to Greece and Rome. Jettisoning Fustel's aberrations enables us to strengthen Eisenstadt's contrast between Greece and Rome. It is clear now that Greece and Rome were originally very dissimilar as regards social structure – differences which are obscured by the way in which ancient history is taught in university faculties which emphasise the sharing of a common body of literature among an elite at a rather late stage in the Graeco-Roman period – but underwent a process of convergent development in the course of the first millennium BC.

This happened partly because of Greek cultural influence on Rome. However there was a more fundamental reason, namely that Greece and Rome underwent a similar process of ecological development which created new principles of social organisation, based on wealth, that were able to compete successfully in the long run with both unilineal descent groups in Rome and age class organisation in Greece (see Chapter IV below). By the fourth century BC at least some of the Greeks classed Rome as a *polis*, a state with a constitutional form of government excluding absolute monarchy.[276] The demographic significance of all this is that age class systems regulate the timing of marriage, which has enormous demographic consequences, whereas kin-based social organisation tends to regulate marital alliances, which do not have any demographic consequences. It follows that the demography of Dark Age and archaic Greece was fundamentally different from that of archaic Rome.

In Greece age class organisation not only made complicated kinship systems redundant but also exercised a great influence on Greek kinship terminology. Most of the Greeks had kinship terms such as *kasignêtoi* and *kasioi* which were used to designate not only siblings but also first cousins and sometimes other kinsmen. The Athenians were exceptional in not using these particular terms by the classical period. However Homer, Herodotos and Eustathios show that these words were in use among the Ionians, who were regarded as closely related to the Athenians, suggesting that they had earlier been employed by all the Greeks, not just by speakers of Dorian dialects. All those relatives who belonged to the same generation received the same kinship term, under the influence of generational thought patterns. This is a case of what social anthropologists, from L.H. Morgan onwards, have called classificatory kinship systems, in which the generation is the main method of classification, sometimes being subdivided according to sex and/or lineage. Anthropologists have generally discussed such systems as part of the topic of 'kinship'.

However, this is a misunderstanding of the situation, as may be seen clearly in the case of ancient Greece, because generational terminology is an expression of age class organisation, which is a distinct principle of social organisation, quite separate from kinship. Age class systems may easily group together people who have no close (biological) blood relationship nor even any fictive kinship link. Under such circumstances it is wrong to describe kinship as the primary principle of social organisation. Similarly certain words which are interpreted by comparative philologists as derived from roots that referred to, say all the female members of a joint family or 'clan' in proto-Indo-European society, such as the archaic Greek word *eor*, may be interpreted more plausibly as generational terms that developed their meaning under the aegis of age class organisation. If this interpretation is correct, then the idea of 'clans' among the proto-Indo-European ancestors of the Greeks should be abandoned by philologists, just as ancient historians are increasingly ditching the concept of the *genos* as a corporate descent group.[277]

By the fifth century BC the Athenian kinship system had lost generational kinship terms which were still in use in Sparta, for example. This accords with the fact that age class organisation only existed in an attenuated form in classical Athens, in comparison to the strong forms which still dominated Sparta and Crete in the fourth century BC. Vartigian described the Athenian kinship system as an Eskimo-lineal kinship system, i.e. cross-cousins were equated with parallel-cousins (*anepsios*, fem. *-a*) and contrasted with siblings, while both types of uncle and aunt (*theios*, fem. *-a*) were equated and contrasted with father and with mother respectively in the first ascending generation from ego. The abandonment of generational kinship terms, together with the complete absence of unilineal descent groups, left the Athenians in the classical period with a bilateral kindred which was slanted towards the patrilineal side as regards inheritance rights.[278]

This brings us back to the meaning of *genos* in Attic sources. In a loose sense it often signified patriline, especially if immediate female descendants of males in the line are included. It was noted that Perikles was descended from the Alkmaionidai via the female line. However, in the Attic orators *genos* also has a technical sense, signifying all the relatives (*sungeneis*) in the *angchisteia*, a person's collateral relatives extending as far back as and including second cousins, i.e. collateral patrilines stretching back three generations anterior to ego to the great-grandfather (*propappos*) as common ancestor. These two concepts have frequently been described by scholars as 'descent groups' or 'families', a description which inevitably carries the suggestion of corporate action on the part of the members of the group. However that description is false because it fails to observe the terminological distinction between *descent*, denoting membership of groups whose existence is independent of that of any particular individual, and *inheritance* of property.

The *genos* in its technical legal sense and the *angchisteia* were not descent groups but sets of rules delimiting those collateral relatives of a dead ego who had rights of inheritance to his estate, in the absence of direct heirs. (In the archaic period in Attica the law of Drakon on homicide suggests that these sets of rules were also used in the organisation of feuds to determine who was responsible for avenging a murdered man, in the absence of a developed judicial system.) This is why virtually the only context in which *genos* in its legal sense and *angchisteia* occur in classical literature is in cases in the Attic orators in which the inheritance of an estate was disputed. The failure of Fustel de Coulanges to distinguish effectively between group membership and inheritance rights and to distinguish between descent groups and patrilines set the stage for the development of the myth of the Greek *genos* as a corporate descent group.[279]

On a cross-cultural basis groups of kin stretching across four generations are extremely widespread. For example they occur in societies as diverse as ancient Greece, Rome, the ancient Celts, ancient Israel, modern Turkey, etc. The reason for thinking in terms of four generations (including ego), rather than say, three, five, six or any larger number of generations, is quite simply that four generations of a patriline is the maximum number of generations that are likely in practice to have members living *simultaneously* who would consequently be able to put in a claim of inheritance rights upon the death of ego without surviving heirs, because of the biological characteristics of *Homo sapiens* such as longevity and age at which reproduction may commence. (Five simultaneously living generations are theoretically possible but never common in a population with low life expectancy at birth, and would be expected to occur more frequently in the female line than in the male line when women marry at an earlier age on average than men.)[280]

I. Morris (1987) described these four generation groups as 'descent groups', when in fact they were only sets of rules governing inheritance rights. This point affects his interpretation of Greek social structure based on burial groups in cemeteries (see section 3 above). It is not surprising that most burial groups terminated after about four generations, because biological patrilines have a high probability of extinction and the memory of ancestors tends to fade after about four generations of oral tradition. The burial groups do not supply any evidence for the existence of corporate descent groups, implying a kin-based form of social organisation, in any period of Athenian history in the first millennium BC.

Sons were emancipated from the control of their fathers (but not from such legally enforceable duties as feeding their parents) at the age of eighteen in Athens, which did not have anything like the Roman *patria potestas*, with the result that there was no legal basis for enforcing corporate action by the members of a four-generation *genos*. Nevertheless a man's relatives within his *angchisteia* would still have claimed his property after his death in the event of his dying intestate, without recognised children or with an adopted heir who could be challenged, regardless of how much they had disagreed with him during his lifetime. This may be surmised frequently in the speeches of Isaios, the leading speechwriter for lawsuits of this kind in Athens in the fourth century BC.[281]

The absence of exogamous descent groups, or anything else of the kind, meant that Athenians were able to marry very close relatives or non-relatives as they wished. Endogamy was certainly widespread, and was probably practised chiefly as a means of avoiding alienation of property in the form of dowries. Although marriage between full siblings was prohibited in classical Athens, it was legal for a brother to marry a half-sister by a different mother. Neither in ancient Greece nor in Rome were there extensive degrees of relationship within which sexual relations were defined as incestuous, as there have been in the Christian societies of Europe since the early mediaeval period. Goody (1983) gave a fascinating but controversial explanation of the genesis of the modern very broad definition of incest in terms of the desire of the Christian church to lay its hands on property. Incest is subject to far-ranging cross-cultural variability, as are attitudes to paederasty and abortion, for example. Very narrow limits on the range of relationships defined as incestuous may well have been appropriate to 'primitive' societies in the distant past, and to small scattered groups of Greeks in the Dark Ages, because wide-ranging incest prohibitions may have very substantial demographic consequences for very small populations.[282]

However endogamy was by no means compulsory and does not imply the existence of endogamous descent groups. It was simply a matter of convenience for some people. The evidence for the Athenian liturgical class amassed by John Davies (1971) suggests that the richest Athenians frequently took spouses from other demes, often distant demes, not from their own deme. As there were 300 citizens in this category, comprising the richest Athenians, at any one time during most of the fourth century BC (400 in the late fifth century), who were scattered over 139 demes, i.e. just over two a deme on average, it must often have been impossible for a man rich enough to meet Davies's criteria for inclusion in this category who was looking for a wife to find a woman of marriageable age and of suitable status in his own deme, even with extremely narrow limits on incestuous relationships. Rich Athenians preferred to seek a spouse from an unrelated family of equal status in another deme, rather than a family of lower status in the same deme. In practice considerations of descent imposed virtually no constraints, barring marriage between full siblings, in the direction of either exogamy or endogamy on the marital alliances that Athenians sought to build in the fourth century BC. Judging by Hesiod this also applied to archaic Boiotia. The conclusion reached here is that kinship was *never* a significant principle of social organisation in the Greek *polis* at any time in the first millennium BC.[283]

Ancient writers were well aware that the interaction between the demographic phenomena of patriline discontinuity and the inheritance system had important consequences for the stability of the *polis* by posing the dilemma of choosing between two different and potentially disastrous 'strategies of heirship', in Goody's terms. A man could sire several children to maximise the chances of his patriline continuing to exist after his death (besides having a source of support in old age), incurring the risk that several children might actually survive to adulthood and end up inheriting small portions of property under partible inheritance, leading to downward social mobility, poverty (relative if not absolute), and possibly *stasis*. Alternatively he could restrict the size of his family voluntarily to maximise the chances of one or two children retaining his own position in the hierarchy of society, thereby running the considerable risk that his children might die before him, leading to patriline extinction.[284]

Both strategies had advocates in antiquity. Hesiod advocated the second strategy, and Hellenistic Boiotians actually followed it, according to Polybios, while the Athenians described in the fourth-century orators adhered to the first strategy. Any population with low life expectancy at birth which followed Hesiod's advice of having one son would fail to reproduce itself. This was the fate of the Hellenistic Boiotians. However, if the population had overshot K (see section 2 above), the optimum family size at that particular time was indeed too small to maintain the current population size. Polybios did not understand this. The Cambridge/Bradford Boiotia survey suggested that the population of Hesiod's patch of Boiotia increased sharply during the archaic period, indicating that Hesiod's advice was not widely followed in his own time. Clearly reproductive behaviour in Boiotia changed dramatically from the time of Hesiod to that of Polybios. Nevertheless many scholars have interpreted sentiments such as those of Hesiod as evidence that families were small in antiquity. The problems of demography, with its scientific base, are a field in which the limitations of the 'philological method' may be exposed very clearly. It was argued in section 4 above that classical Athenians generally chose the first strategy. This had very important consequences for the distribution of the Weberian triad of wealth, status and power.[285]

In classical Athens the influence and prestige which provided the possibility of access to political power flowed directly from *ploutos*, wealth, without the additional requirement of holding a title or office as in the aristocracies of the states of early modern Europe. The top stratum of classical Athenian society was not defined in the same way as the aristocracies of the absolutist states of early modern Europe, nor was it defined in the same way as in Rome, where wealth did not automatically turn an *eques*, knight, into a senator, or in Sparta, where membership of the *gerousia* was probably confined to certain families in practice in the classical period. Moreover the Athenian upper class was most certainly not an *aristokratia* as that word was used by Greek philosophers, in the sense of 'rule by the best men'.

Discussions of 'aristocracy' in ancient Greece by modern scholars have often been vitiated by a failure to discuss what the word means. For example Donlan attempted to delineate a *distinctive* 'aristocratic ideal' in ancient Greece. However he was forced to acknowledge that 'those who are not members of the wealthy upper class, unable to resign themselves to a position of social inferiority, could only assert that they themselves possessed the qualities proclaimed by aristocrats as exclusively their own'. This amounts to admitting that in fact there was only one set of social values in fourth-century Athens shared by everyone, not two competing ideologies. Of course most people did not attain the goals of that value system, giving rise to prejudice and envy. The brilliance of Demosthenes' speech XVIII (*On the crown*) as a piece of oratory is shown by his success in exploiting the Greeks' wholehearted love of wealth to disparage Aiskhines for his alleged poverty, while at the same time managing not to attract envy of his own more favourable personal circumstances from poorer Athenians in the jury.[286]

All closed elites in history have failed to reproduce themselves. The aristocracy of early modern England was vulnerable to the consequences of Hesiod's strategy, as a closed circle of titleholders will inevitably fail to reproduce itself over time. However it was not decimated by the other strategy of having many children, one of whom would inherit his father's title. In Athens both strategies decimated the ranks of the richest stratum of society, Davies's liturgical class, since partible inheritance caused the relative pauperisation in the next generation of a family in which two or more sons survived their father's death. Consequently patriline discontinuity regarding the performance of liturgies, which depended on wealth, should have been much greater than the high degree of discontinuity found in the early modern English aristocracy.[287]

It has been calculated that in a population with an average completed family size of 5.5 children, 36.8 per cent of marriages would end up with just one son surviving his father's death (the only situation guaranteed to ensure continuity of the patriline within Davies' liturgical class), 25.1 per cent would end up with two or more sons surviving their father's death, 23.6 per cent with only one or more daughters surviving their father's death, and 14.6 per cent with no heirs at all. The latter three situations could all remove a patriline from the liturgical class. These calculations exclude the proportion of all marriages that would have been sterile in any case (see section 4 above). The incidence of men having no surviving children at all on their deaths, only daughters surviving, and enough sons to divide the inheritance in such a way as to leave all of them outside the liturgical class, could have accounted for anything up to about 60 per cent of all 300 patrilines in the 'trierarchic class' in each generation. The extreme discontinuity in patriline performance of liturgies that Davies found, even between his two best documented generations, H and I, covering the last two thirds of the fourth century BC, was not simply a consequence of deficiencies in the sources or of the hazards of politics thinning out the ranks of politicians. It was above all a consequence of the interaction of demography, the Athenian inheritance system and the precise way in which Davies defined the stratum of the richest Athenians.[288]

Such a state of affairs implies a very high level of social mobility. Not surprisingly, attitudes to newly acquired wealth are a constant theme in our sources. Aristotle formally discussed it as a rhetorical *topos*. He said that those who had long been rich seemed to deserve it, because that which was old seemed to be natural, while those who had recently become rich possessed something which did not traditionally belong to them, and so lacked the experience to use it correctly. *Nemesis*, righteous indignation, was a just reaction towards *neoploutoi*, the newly rich. The poets of the Old Comedy were interested in new wealth. Demosthenes, our main source for fourth-century Athens, refrained from using the word, according to Libanios. This might tell us something about the history of Demosthenes' own patriline, whose wealth was probably exceptional in not being based on ownership and exploitation of agricultural land. However, the rhetorical *topos* certainly occurs elsewhere in the speeches of Demosthenes. It is frequently found in the other Attic orators.[289]

The next problem relates to reference group theory. Who felt *nemesis* towards *neoploutoi*, those who were already rich or the poor who had lost one of their brethren? Aristotle said that *phthonos* ('envy'), an inferior cousin of *nemesis*, was felt between equals, which fits in with the assumption that all surviving literature, bar Hesiod, was produced by or for the wealthy. The *neoploutos* concept expressed the resentment of those who were already rich at the arrival of competition. Ideology did not fully correspond to reality. The *archaioploutoi*, those whose families had long been rich, could never have been a closed monolithic group. Discontinuity and instability constituted the *de facto* state of affairs in classical Athens revealed by Davies (1981). I prefer to go still further and insist that classical Athenian society and democracy developed out of a type of social organisation based on an age class system in the Dark Ages which was ideally non-hereditary in nature. The Greek *polis* in its pristine form was a form of socio-political organisation which did not stress inheritance, because ideally rights and duties were acquired with passage through successive age grades, as in the Spartan *agôgê*, not by inheritance from one's parents.[290]

Wealth did circulate widely in classical Athens, mainly through the vagaries of the inheritance system, but also through mechanisms such as conspicuous consumption. However, it did not circulate to any significant extent via the market. We may agree with Finley (1952) that land was not a commodity and there was no genuine land market in classical Athens. There is no reason for questioning the historicity of the activities of Ischomachos' father, which must date to the first decade of the Peloponnesian War, but only involve economic activity of a windfall nature. It is not utterly inconceivable that the Periklean strategy of abandoning Attica during the war did encourage an atmosphere in which people were more willing to sell land, as Fine (1951) argued, even though the extent to which the Athenians were deprived of the use of Attica during the Peloponnesian War has been exaggerated by scholars in the past, as has the originality of Perikles, the essence of whose policy must date back to the time of Themistokles.[291]

However, our sources have nothing whatsoever to say about the possible origins of the sale of land in the initial phase of the Peloponnesian War. What is said is quite different. Thucydides states that during the epidemic of 430 BC Athenians cooped up in Athens became rich suddenly through inheriting the property of dead relatives (see section 7 below). Obviously people would have died anyway and their property would have been inherited by others, even if there had not been any epidemic at the time. The increased mortality of the epidemic merely accelerated a continuing process, which might be expected to have had considerable momentum of its own in any case. The principal way in which a man could become rich in classical Athens was through inheritance, by no means necessarily from his father. This is what ought to be expected in a society in which land was the main component of wealth but was not integrated into a market economy as a factor of production subject to a proper factor market. However, this interpretation does not imply the existence of a *stable* hereditary plutocracy.

The population growth of the eighth century and archaic periods reduced the area of land available per person on average. However, it did not fragment landholdings if the inheritance system found in Athens in the classical period was already in operation, in which women received mobile goods as a dowry, excluding land, leaving a unilineal inheritance system as far as land was concerned. The transition from abundance to scarcity of land occurred during the seventh century BC. Solon's *seisachtheia* is testimony to its consequences. Population growth is a very powerful cause of landlessness. A proportion of all property holdings ceased to be viable in each generation owing to division of the paternal inheritance between two or more sons, the opposite side of the coin to patriline discontinuity. In a stationary population these additional sons would ideally have ended up inheriting land from men other than their fathers who died without leaving any surviving sons, or marrying heiresses, resulting in no change in the average size of landholding. However in an increasing population many sons would have failed to find a suitable niche in each successive generation.

An increasing number of Athenians in each generation had to look to richer neighbours for assistance or employment as sharecroppers, entering into debt bondage from which they were henceforth unable to escape, as their creditors needed to control their labour in order to work their own fields. The *hektêmoroi*, regarded as equivalent to *pelatai*, i.e. men who on account of poverty approached neighbours for employment (tantamount to slavery), were forced to hand over a very large proportion of the produce of the land they worked, namely five-sixths (rather than the one-sixth often assumed), because it was not in their creditors' interests that they should be able to repay their debts. The smallness of the share of the crops retained by the *hektêmoroi* suggests that they essentially only contributed their own labour, while seed grain, oxen, ploughs and other tools etc. were supplied by the owners of the land. There is no reason for doubting that the *hektêmoroi* indeed had to hand over five-sixths of the crops, in accordance with the etymology of the word, because there are ethnographic analogies for similar customs in Italy in antiquity and in Mediterranean and Middle Eastern lands in recent times. In Greece in the nineteenth century AD there were sharecroppers who had to hand over half of the produce. These sharecroppers were able to make a reasonable living on fertile land, but it was impossible to make ends meet on land that only produced, say, a 3:1 or 4:1 yield:seed ratio. The same was true in archaic Attica, as population growth forced people to exploit marginal land. Plutarch states that parents were forced to sell their children into slavery.[292]

When a sufficiently large proportion of the population had fallen into the grip of debt bondage, there was a serious danger of *stasis*. However, the exact timing of the political crisis was probably a consequence of the conspiracy of Kylon, as Lévy (1978) argued, because the split in the Athenian propertied class made possible the freeing of the *hektêmoroi*. Solon solved the problem temporarily by cancelling existing debts and forbidding loans secured on the person in the future. Athenian families which possessed more land than they could work themselves, having lost control over their labour force, turned to imported slave labour to meet their requirements for permanent labour forces, as opposed to temporary seasonal wage labour at harvest time.

Homer, Hesiod and Solon provide evidence that thetes, landless labourers, could be hired on a yearly basis in archaic Greece, a custom also found in recent times in that country. However, such employment was assimilated to slavery after the spread of chattel slavery. In spite of Solon's reforms, the problem of Athenians who were landless or possessed non-viable property holdings continued to exist on the same scale as before, providing a fertile terrain for the development of the plans for tyranny of Peisistratos. The food that might previously have gone to a poor Athenian in a similar situation to Hesiod's *thês* was now more likely to go to a barbarian slave. Appian described an analogous situation in late Republican Italy, where the rich preferred to use slave labour on farms instead of free men who were liable to be called up for military service.[293]

From Solon's time onwards a section of the Athenian citizen population became interested first in external colonisation and expansion and secondly in grain imports and after 480 BC in pay for performing public duties to enable them to buy imported grain. In other words, the fact that classical Athens was a grain-importing country was not just a consequence of the size of the population in absolute terms, but also of the *structure* of the economy and society of classical Athens. The most important determinant of the number of slaves in classical Athens was the quantity of labour required to perform the annual tasks (except harvesting) on that proportion of all property holdings which were too large to be worked by the unaided labour of a peasant family. That quantity of labour was not enormous because cereal cultivation in the Mediterranean has traditionally been very labour-extensive, insofar as property holdings large enough to sustain animals for ploughing are concerned. In this way it was possible for a proportion of the citizen population of fourth-century Athens, which was excluded from permanent employment on the land, to be interested in grain imports, even though that citizen population as a whole was so small that it could probably all have been fed from the territory of Attica itself, in the absence of slaves.

The role of slavery as the principal form of permanent labour employed by the propertied class in classical Athens had very important demographic consequences, whose significance becomes apparent if a contrast is drawn with early modern England. The most extraordinary feature of English history is surely that long before the Industrial Revolution a system of wage labour had developed in which a substantial proportion of the working population spent years of their lives employed as servants by the wealthier members of the community, to accumulate the resources to set up an independent household, without any loss of social status. Having accumulated the necessary resources they were then able to leave 'domestic' service (including farming etc.) and enjoy a social status that was not necessarily inferior to that of their former employers. Domestic service of this kind created the preconditions for the permanent employment of wage labourers on a large scale in the nascent factory system during the Industrial Revolution. In most societies in history, including ancient Greece and Rome, working for another man for one's living on a long-term basis was regarded as equivalent to slavery. Mediaeval feudalism was probably an essential interlude between ancient slavery and modern capitalism by creating a form of labour relations in which serfs had obligations to lords but were not totally under their control, unlike chattel slaves.

In early modern England the engagement of a substantial proportion of all persons in domestic service during young adulthood played an absolutely fundamental role in what had become a self-regulating demographic system, because it provided a means of relating economic opportunities, especially in regard to obtaining food, to fertility and mortality levels. If mortality rose, for example during an epidemic, economic opportunities improved (e.g. labour became scarcer and so better paid), leading to a shortening in the period of service needed to earn the money to set up a new household, a lowering of the average age of first marriage as a result, and so higher fertility permitting population growth. On the other hand difficult economic conditions caused an increase in the average age of marriage, as people had to work for longer to acquire the resources for a new household, leading to a decrease in fertility. It was a homeostatic system in which demographic conditions were tied inextricably to economic conditions, the relative ease or difficulty of making a living. A remarkable degree of stability was the result. The system depended, first, on both sexes engaging in domestic service and having their average ages of first marriage regulated in this manner, secondly, on the social acceptability of domestic service as an activity which did not incur any loss of social status, thirdly, on the belief that it was necessary to acquire the economic resources to support a family before marrying, and fourthly, on the existence of a natural fertility regime in which average completed family size was directly related to age at marriage.[294]

Classical Athens was quite different. The fact that permanent wage labour in the service of another man was not an acceptable way of living, in a society in which chattel slavery was widespread, entailed the complete absence of the crucial link between economic conditions, age at marriage and so fertility in the English demographic system. It follows that classical Athens did not have a self-regulating demographic system. Although slavery was widespread in history, it has only occurred on a large scale in a few societies. In antiquity slavery as a concept could only be defined in opposition to freedom. Neither concept was very meaningful in an absolute monarchy like Pharaonic Egypt. In Greece the development of chattel slavery as an institution went hand in hand with the political developments which culminated in the classical democracies, as Finley rightly argued. However he did not perceive that the nature of citizenship, giving political rights, in the classical *polis* was integrally bound up with the historical development of age class systems in ancient Greece. This line of thought leads us to the conclusion that the development of mass chattel slavery in classical Greece cannot be explained in terms of economic factors as prime movers. It is only explicable as a *consequence* of the changing influence over time of age (as a principle of social organisation completely independent of *economic* factors), which gave rise to the idea of the distribution of political rights across the (citizen) population and in doing so permitted the development of the concept of slavery understood in antithetical terms to the liberty of the citizen. In ancient Greek the word *pais*, 'child' (any age up to adulthood, but excluding infancy), was applied frequently to slaves during adulthood. This was a result of age class organisation, because the inferior status of slavery had to be assimilated to a junior age group.

Before leaving the topic of slavery, it is worth considering Aristotle's thoughts on the subject. Aristotle proposed the theory that slavery was natural, or in other words there existed some humans who were suited by nature to being slaves. He regarded the slave as an instrument of action (*praxis*), not of production (*poiêsis*), which he envisaged as the domain of hypothetical robotic tools and machinery. The ultimate criterion of the natural slave was psychological rather than physical in the sense of outward appearance, since he maintained that the natural slave did not possess all the faculties required for critical reasoning. Aristotle's theory of natural slavery has been lambasted by modern philosophers, who judge it to be morally repugnant. However, the arguments of modern philosophers are no better than those of Aristotle, because there is an important sense in which slavery is natural, even though Aristotle's detailed arguments about slavery as natural for barbarians are incorrect. Aristotle's concept contains the germ of a very important idea.

It is necessary to turn to modern biology to justify this perhaps at first sight startling conclusion. In the world of the social insects there are species of ants which specialise in raiding the nests of other species of ants to steal their pupae. The captured young ants, when they mature, are then brought up to do all the necessary work in the nests of their captors. Thus it is factually correct to say that slavery is natural in the sense that it has been produced in nature by natural selection, although this does not mean that any species has any characteristics that make it especially suitable for slavery. However, slavery is rare in the world of nature just as it is rare among men, in the sense that there have only been a handful of societies in history that can be accurately described as slave societies. Probably this is because groups of men or other animals who allow themselves to be enslaved are unlikely to persist as independent groups in the long run. Also we have just seen that the development of chattel slavery in ancient Greece was consequent upon the historical development of a particular form of socio-political organisation. It could not happen in any society chosen at random.

Slavery is most certainly not a phenomenon unique to *Homo sapiens*. Among ants there are a series of intermediate stages in between pure predators and specialised slave-makers. This appears to confirm Darwin's theory that slave-making evolved gradually out of predation. Returning to classical Athens, insofar as slavery was the characteristic form of relationship between two individuals, one of whom was permanently working for the other, we may conclude that the social relations of production in classical Athens had not transcended the forms of relationship found in the world of nature. (It is also worth remembering here that the Helots were enslaved by the Spartans as a group and were not subject to individual slave-owners.) This conclusion is another piece in the jigsaw, which when complete will enable us to comprehend the ancient Greek *polis* in terms of biological models.[295]

The lack of a homeostatic mechanism, short of invoking the Malthusian positive checks, for readily adjusting natural fertility to mortality and the environmental carrying capacity of the land was the fundamental reason why emigration was an ever-present phenomenon, in fact a demographic parameter of fundamental significance, in ancient Greece, and indeed elsewhere in the ancient world. Isokrates in the fourth century BC urged the potentates of his time to conquer regions outside Greece in order to accommodate the surplus population of Greece, which was then at an all-time high in the pre-modern period according to archaeological survey data. That was the background to the conquest of the Persian empire by Alexander the Great and the subsequent massive influx of Greeks and Macedonians to the Orient, as far as Afghanistan and India. Similarly Aristotle records that the Carthaginians kept their lower classes happy by dispatching colonies every so often and so relieving population pressure. Many of the Italic peoples practised on occasion the custom of a *ver sacrum*, sacred spring, whereby all living creatures, including humans, born in a designated period were dedicated to the gods and were forced to leave their native land, so effectively relieving population pressure. The fundamental role of emigration in the demographic systems of antiquity also explains why the models of autochthonous origins currently favoured by prehistoric archaeologists are devoid of intellectual coherence.[296]

The statement that demographic systems in ancient Greece were not self-regulating of course does not imply that they were completely unregulated. The two most important constraints which have been emphasised so far were the food supply, reflected in the carrying capacity of the land, which imposed absolute limits on population size and density, and the age class systems of Dark Age Greece. Age class systems may have very powerful demographic consequences by controlling age at marriage for both sexes, affecting coital frequency and fertility, and also by segregating the sexes even after marriage. However, that alone does not make for a homeostatic system if age at marriage and the consequent level of fertility is not determined in accordance with the environmental carrying capacity of the territory occupied, so that they may be altered in response to changing economic conditions as they were in early modern England (the power of the market as a distributive mechanism! – raising the question of the extent to which the ancient economy was a market economy, which cannot be discussed here for want of space). Age of marriage and so fertility must be capable of being varied to meet changing conditions in order to create a homeostatic system. In the interpretation proposed in this book, the demographic consequences of age class organisation in ancient Greece were unintended effects of human action, whose primary aim was the allocation of sexual rights and duties among different age grades on a hierarchical basis, as part of the distribution of all privileges and duties according to age. It follows that age class systems in ancient Greece did not necessarily create stable homeostatic populations.

This is clear in the case of classical Sparta, where the logical response to *oliganthrôpia*, manpower shortage, would have been to make both sexes marry in their teens and to stop discouraging men younger than thirty from having sexual intercourse with their wives. However the Spartan age class system, which had demographic effects but was not designed for demographic ends, evidently did not permit such flexibility, and so *oliganthrôpia* felled Sparta. The idea that Sparta once was a populous and stable social system which was gradually corrupted and so degenerated is a theme of Spartan history which has had an excessively long lifespan in historiography, stretching from antiquity right up to the present day, and mortality is long overdue. Sparta *never* had a stable demographic system at any time in the first millennium BC, neither in the time of Lykourgos nor in any later period. The conclusion of the line of argument presented here is that instability was an inevitable product of human population dynamics in Greece in the first millennium BC. This is why the opinion of Finley and M. Hansen (cited in section 1 above) that demographic systems were static in antiquity should be dismissed – a point that would surely not have been lost on Plato who set himself a fruitless task as lawgiver attempting to devise mechanisms to stabilise the population of the ideal *polis*.

The population pressure which led to emigration also created demographic pressure on the inheritance system. One motive for brothers to leave paternal estates undivided, in a world of private property in which the essence of justice was 'possessing what was one's own', was surely to maintain farms large enough to support animals for plough agriculture. A failure to divide inheritances in the classical period should not be interpreted as a relic of an older system of joint ownership of property. Plato tried to tackle the problem of the formation by partible inheritance of farms that were too small to be viable on their own by proposing that in his second-best *polis* on Crete only one son should inherit his father's property, regardless of how many sons the father had. He suggested that other sons should be allotted the *klêroi* of citizens without male heirs by adoption, or, if a balance could not reached in this way, forced to emigrate from the 'ideal' *polis*! Such ideas were alien to the social organisation of the Greek world, because of the equality of age mates in age class systems.

Plato's projected system was inherently unworkable because families could not be restricted to one son and one daughter as he wished. An average completed family size of about five children was necessary to reproduce the population. The statistical distribution between families of those sons who outlived their fathers made it inevitable that a substantial minority of property holdings would be left without male heirs and another substantial minority with too many heirs in each generation. Plato's proposals were stop-gap measures in response to a perennially recurring problem. They lacked the flexibility of the market, which Plato wished to banish from utopia as far as possible. Plato's analysis of the demographic problems faced by the Greek *polis* (see section 1 above) was accurate in many respects, but he did not understand that a self-regulating homeostatic demographic system could not be achieved within the age class system that was to constitute the framework of utopia.[297]

The two complementary sides of this statistical distribution of variation within a population created the problem of how to connect men who inherited little or no property with property holdings which either lacked heirs altogether or only carried a female *epiklêros*, who would probably not be doing any ploughing on her own. To function effectively a certain amount of social mobility was necessary, i.e. some poor men had to marry rich women and vice versa, in order to smooth out stochastic fluctuations in family size and in amount of property inherited. This problem lies at the heart of Menander's only complete surviving comedy, the *Dyskolos*, especially the final act, in which Sostratos, son of the fabulously rich Kallippides, wishes not only to marry a woman who was daughter of the middling Knemon and half-sister of the poor Gorgias, but also to give his own sister as a bride to the same Gorgias. Kallippides initially resists the idea of so many marriage links to a family so much poorer than his own. Menander's play was not a portrayal of reality but a dream of a utopia in which social harmony would prevail through the free will of all concerned, rather than as the result of the compulsion of the inexorable weight of the laws and their guardians, as in Plato's authoritarian utopia.

The social values of classical Athens, where wealth was regarded as good and desirable by all and sundry, rejected the type of social mobility that was necessary to obviate some of the structural problems inherent in a demographic and inheritance system like that of classical Athens. Plato knew that in his Cretan utopia it would be necessary for rich people to marry poor people and for men who inherited no property to be adopted as the heirs of men lacking male heirs who owned property. However, beyond emphasising the importance of *paideia*, he failed to get to grips with the implications of something else which he knew perfectly well, namely that in reality rich men did not wish to be intimately associated with poor men. It is doubtful that the Demosthenes who took such pride in public in the wealth which freed him from the necessity of working for a living, in contrast to Aiskhines' alleged poverty, would have been as ready as Menander's Kallippides to be convinced of the virtues of an alliance with a poor family formed through one marriage, let alone two such marriages. Marriage was probably not so common a means of social mobility in classical Athens as inheritance, because of the stress on marrying spouses from families of equivalent status. Social mobility was very imperfect in the classical *polis* and many Athenians were forced to emigrate to try to solve their problems.[298]

The interaction of the demographic and inheritance systems created a steady flow of opportunities for personal enrichment. Nearly all the speeches in the Isaios corpus are cases in which the victor – usually unknown to us – either made a significant addition to his own property holding, if claiming to be next of kin to the deceased, or presumably acquired a larger property holding than he had received or could expect to receive from his own father, if claiming to have been adopted as the son of the deceased. No one would have bothered to pay for the services of an Isaios and turn up in court if it were not worth fighting for the property. A very significant minority of adult male Athenians in each generation left only female children as *epiklêroi* to succeed them, creating further opportunities for personal advancement. Furthermore, owing to late average age of first marriage for males a significant proportion of Athenian citizens would have inherited the paternal property at the time of their father's death when they were still below the age of maturity, providing opportunities for guardians to enrich themselves at the ward's expense in the way that Demosthenes alleges happened in his own case.[299]

It is suggested that the surviving examples of inheritance disputes were only the tip of an iceberg, and a significant proportion of all property holdings in Athens, and indeed every other Greek *polis*, were up for grabs, so to speak, in each generation. However, the services of an Isaios would only have been hired if a large amount of property was at stake. The techniques employed in pursuit of such claims by the orators, as was demonstrated admirably by Wyse (1904) in the case of Isaios, are very revealing as to the importance of the hunt for *ploutos*, wealth, by individuals in a democratic *polis* which 'officially' rejected *ploutos* as the *horos*, limit, of eligibility for citizenship.

In a poorly developed legal system in which everything depended on oral testimony it must have been very hard to be certain of proving anything to a jury's satisfaction, even if one were in the right. Combined with the obscurity enveloping the laws on inheritance, this created a situation in which the odds are that the laws were frequently and successfully broken. Such a state of affairs is frequent, indeed normal, in peasant societies, as anthropologists know, but orthodox ancient historians are often curiously oblivious to realities. This is why I believe that an approach which emphasises legal and constitutional technicalities is not the way to understand the society of ancient Athens. Hesiod's *Works and Days* and Homer's *Odyssey* became classics of ancient literature at least partly because they stressed the significance of inheritance disputes in a peasant society that is so obvious in the Athens of Isaios.[300]

In certain circumstances it was possible to go still further than the clients of Isaios did. In Sparta the two kings had jurisdiction over *patrouchoi*, the Spartan version of *epiklêroi*, heiresses. (It should be noted that the legal rights of Spartan women were different from those of Athenian women.) We may be sure that they rewarded their friends and that this offered a simple mechanism for property concentration in Sparta. The obvious way for a rich Spartan to become richer was to marry the richest *patrouchos* he could find. At the same time patrilines became extinct at a steady rate in each generation and some men from large families were forced out of the *homoioi* into the ranks of the inferior *hupomeiones* because of their inability to pay the dues to the *sussitia* required to maintain Spartan citizenship, with no means of regaining their former position. A vicious circle was set up in which the rich became fewer and richer and the poor became more numerous and poorer.

Aristotle's statement that women owned about 40 per cent of the land in Sparta, where they could inherit land in their own names even in the presence of a brother, is not evidence for unusual demographic problems and may be explained easily in terms of patriline discontinuity and Spartan inheritance customs, as has been admirably shown by Steve Hodkinson. The later, historical, segments of the Spartan kinglists also provide good evidence for the difficulties of maintaining patrilines in Sparta. The earlier, legendary, segments of those lists, which show patrilines continuing over many generations without a break, were undoubtedly invented or at least altered later on so as not to leave any breaks in the patrilines.[301]

The real significance of the epiklerate in Athens, which scholars have always struggled to fathom, was that by insisting that an heiress had to marry her next of kin, it acted as a colossal brake on the most important way in which property could be accumulated in Sparta and other *poleis* which did not possess the epiklerate. Alongside the custom of giving dowries in mobile goods, the exclusion of women from inheriting land in their own names in Athens sharply reduced the degree of fragmentation of property holdings in classical Athens, judging by the estates mentioned in the orators, in comparison with modern Greece where it is common for the average three-hectare farm to consist of about fifteen separate plots of about 0.2 ha. each, as a result of untrammelled diverging devolution. This helped to sustain plots of land at a size adequate for plough agriculture.

If these ideas are correct, then it may be predicted that property holdings in Sparta (where women had limited inheritance rights, probably permitting a sister to receive half a brother's share as on Crete according to the Gortyn law code, analogous in this respect to the Shari'a law of Islam which helps to put Spartan women in perspective) should have been more fragmented than in Attica, but less fragmented than in modern Greece. It has been argued that fragmented land holdings in modern Greece reduce the risk of total crop failure, because of the larger diversity of environments encompassed within property holdings, and some ancient historians have extrapolated straight back from the present day to classical times. However all the actual evidence from antiquity suggests that full diverging devolution, which leads to extensive land fragmentation, did not exist in any ancient *polis*. Consequently it is wrong to extrapolate directly from modern to ancient Greek peasants as regards inheritance patterns.[302]

The last topic, but by no means the least important, to be considered in this section is marriage in ancient Greece. The evidence for ages of marriage for both sexes and their demographic consequences was considered in section 4 above. Here the focus will be on some social aspects of marriage in ancient Greece. Aristotle noted that the concept of the joining of a man and a woman in what is now called marriage did not have a name in the Greek language. In this respect Greek followed

proto-Indo-European. Classical sources reveal the existence of a variety
of different possible relationships between men and women, epitomised
by the Attic orator who spoke of men having *hetairai* for pleasure,
pallakai for everyday care of the body, and *gunaikes* for the procreation of
legitimate children and to provide a trustworthy guard for the contents of
the household. These different relationships arose in two different ways.
First, it is characteristic of age class systems that marriage for
procreation and sexual relations for pleasure are kept quite separate.
Secondly, it is arguable that in the course of the first half of the first
millennium BC there was a transition from bridewealth to dowry.[303]

Legitimate marriage in classical Athens occurred when a father
betrothed a daughter to the bridegroom in the customary manner
(*enguêsis*), although there was no public register of marriages. It was an
agreement between two men, the bridegroom and the bride's guardian,
reflecting the difference in age between husband and wife. In our
upper-class sources, such as the Attic orators, the bride generally brought
a dowry consisting of mobile goods to the marriage. Her husband was
legally obliged to maintain her so long as they were married and had to
return the dowry if divorce subsequently occurred. In other circumstances the dowry would eventually pass to the children of the marriage.
However, some poor women, whose male relatives could not afford a
dowry, probably entered relationships with men as *pallakai*, a status less
favourable to the woman than dowry marriage, although it was regulated
by formal terms whose details are unknown (see also section 4 above).[304]

Dowry marriage was probably a recent innovation in archaic Greece
and had to compete with other forms of marriage. Solon and Lykourgos
are both said to have abolished dowries, in the latter case to ensure that
all women could marry. Clearly their laws, if they ever existed, had been
repealed or at least fallen into disuse by the classical period. Similarly
Hesiod advised his readers to look for a *gunê ktêtê*, literally a bought
woman, not a *gunê gametê*, in a very interesting line whose authenticity
is unfortunately not quite certain. The former expression seems to refer
to bridewealth marriage. Aristotle states that the Greeks used to buy
(*ôneomai*) their wives. There are various indications in the Homeric
poems, especially the *Iliad*, that bridewealth marriage was well known to
Homer and was the predominant form of marriage in the society depicted
in the *Iliad*, although the *Odyssey* is not so clear in this respect. The word
eedna also provides conclusive evidence for bridewealth marriage in the
fragments of Hesiod's *Eoiai*.

The question of marriage forms in archaic Greece is a very complicated
and controversial topic. Snodgrass (1974) argued that the data provided
by the Homeric poems in respect of marriage customs and inheritance
patterns were self-contradictory. Accordingly he doubted the historicity
of Homeric society, as presented in the epics. Finley (1978), on the other
hand, attempted to piece together the sources as evidence for a society

based on gift exchange. *The World of Odysseus* assumed a kin-based society as the context for this system of gift exchange (see also Chapter IV below). Lello-Finuoli (1984) expressed the judgment that a kin-based society is not attested in the extant sources. (The institution of *xenia*, guest-friendship, certainly existed, but it was a mode of external relations which is never attested between two members of the same *polis*, and so is irrelevant to the question of the internal organisation of the *polis* in general, and marriage within the *polis* in particular.)[305]

Lello-Finuoli proceeded to give a new interpretation, with which I agree. However, it needs to be set in a broader context. This interpretation accounted for the contradictions noticed by Snodgrass by arguing that at the time of Homer and Hesiod there were two forms of marriage, bridewealth, the older type, and the newer dowry form of marriage, which were in competition. By classical times, dowry marriage had become predominant, at least among the upper classes. However the classical *pallakê* was a descendant of the bridewealth marriage that was the principal type of marriage practised in the society represented in the *Iliad*, whose historicity and coherence as a society need not be doubted.

In general Lello-Finuoli's interpretation of the ancient sources is admirable. The detailed arguments employed will not be reviewed here to save space. However, she did not provide an *explanation* for the rise of dowry marriage in archaic Greece and its eventual triumph over bridewealth. The explanation follows naturally, however, from her observation that bridewealth is characteristic of the societies of sub-Saharan Africa. Conversely, dowry has been characteristic of Eurasian societies in recent times. The societies of sub-Saharan Africa include the age class societies in East Africa. To put the argument in a nutshell, bridewealth marriage is found in Homer and Hesiod because it was appropriate to the social conditions of the age class systems of Dark Age Greece. Dowry marriage, which is suited to the types of social organisation characteristic of later phases of Greek (and in general Mediterranean) history, began to compete with bridewealth marriage and eventually superseded it as part and parcel of the breakdown of the strong forms of age class organisation in ancient Greece during the first millennium BC. This line of argument will be developed further at the end of the last chapter of this book.

The development of marriage institutions in ancient Greece only makes sense, like the development of kinship terminology, if interpreted in the context of the historical development of age class systems in that country. The breakdown of those systems entailed the disappearance of formal restrictions on age at marriage. However, there continued to be strong cultural attitudes derived from those systems which exercised a strong influence on attitudes towards marriage. Here we must take account of Foucault's (1984) powerful argument that the passages in classical Greek literature which recommend that marriage for males should be delayed until a late age were at least partly expressions of an ideology of sexual behaviour. Its essence consisted in *enkrateia*, mastery over oneself, which took time and experience to acquire, not in one's behaviour towards one's wife or sexual companion. The desire for personal independence was important in the ancient world in societies in which chattel slavery and other types of labour bound by non-economic constraints were a regular phenomenon. Such attitudes reinforced the tendency of age class systems to enforce delays before marriage.[306]

Cultural attitudes of this kind were reinforced in Athens by economic factors. Given the shortage of opportunities for making a living from long-term wage labour in classical Athens, the main way of making ends meet, independently of others, depended on acquiring landed property by inheritance from one's father, if he had any. The most important single factor affecting the average age of first marriage for men in classical Athens, at least in the landowning classes, was how old they were when their fathers died, allowing them to inherit paternal property and become fully independent. (It was also possible for a father to hand over part or all of his property to his son during his own lifetime, but it is impossible to say how frequent this was in practice.)

The average ages of first marriage for men in classical Athens and early modern England were probably not dissimilar, but if so it was entirely coincidental, as the factors governing marriage patterns in those two societies were quite different. In particular classical Athens lacked the institution of domestic service which related age of marriage and fertility levels to the economic possibilities for making a living. In a population with low life expectancy at birth, it is likely that if men did postpone marriage until about thirty on average, then less than half of them would have had a father still alive who could have tried to influence their choice of wives.

The effect of differences in economic structures on marriage patterns comes out even more clearly in the case of women. In classical Athens women ideally received a dowry of mobile goods from their fathers after puberty and married. They did not have to wait for their fathers to die to receive a share of the landed property, to which they were not entitled in their own names. Furthermore, there seems to have been virtually no long-term employment of free 'citizen' women as domestic servants working outside their father's homes, barring some wet-nursing perhaps (see section 4 above), in order to raise the resources to found a new household jointly with their husbands. The role of women in agriculture in ancient Greece was insignificant relative to the role they play in, for example, the tobacco cultivation of modern Greece and Turkey, which is carried out entirely by hand and so is eminently suitable for female labour. In such a situation, where female labour is more important in the economy at large (excluding housekeeping), the social status of women appears to rise accordingly.[307]

Conversely in classical Athens women did not play an important role in the economy outside the household and had a lower status, which was exacerbated by the sexual division of labour which is characteristic of age class societies. Accordingly there was no obstacle preventing many women from marrying in their teens, either bringing a dowry or as *pallakai*. In this respect the demography of classical Athens was quite different from that of early modern England and France. However, it presaged Hajnal's Mediterranean family structure in the early modern period in respect of age of marriage, with early marriage for women and late marriage for men. That family structure reflected differences in economic structures between Mediterranean lands and the countries of northern Europe which were moving towards the Industrial Revolution.

It also corresponded to the marriage structure for ancient Near Eastern societies. Roth (1987) suggested that men and women married in the age ranges 26-32 and 14-20 respectively in ancient Mesopotamia. However, there is currently no evidence that ancient Mesopotamia was ever governed by age class systems, the starting point for the development of classical Greek demographic structures, and so we should not assimilate ancient Greece to ancient Mesopotamia in this respect. In Israel in early Roman times very early marriage for men, by the age of eighteen, was recommended. Later the recommended upper limit was raised to twenty or twenty-four, and by the age of Diocletian the opinions of the rabbis had swung towards recommending that marriage should be delayed until thirty or forty.[308]

Classical Athens was at a half-way stage of demographic development. She had ceased to have formal controls on marriage imposed by age class structures, unlike Sparta and Crete. However, she had not developed a self-regulating demographic system in which age at marriage was integrally related to the economic rewards of wage labour in a fully fledged market economy. That concludes discussion of factors affecting marriage and the family. In the next section we shall return to mortality to consider causes of death in ancient Greece and the ecology of diseases.

7. Disease

The maximum possible human lifespan, about 110 years, may be determined ultimately by the inability of cells to divide and so reproduce themselves more than a certain number of times, according to one well-known theory. However, in practice the proximate cause of death is usually ascribed to a disease at post-mortems, if death as a result of violence or accident has not occurred. This leads on to the problem of whether diseases play a crucial role in human demography as a means of population regulation. The beautifully written account of McNeill (1976), building on the insights into disease evolution of earlier researchers such as T. Cockburn (1963), is the most famous exposition of the idea that diseases have been a major factor in determining the course of human history.

Although McNeill's book was widely acclaimed by scholars when it was published, it is open to criticism in respect of one fundamental theoretical problem which he did not discuss. This was put into a nutshell by Colinvaux, who criticised McNeill on the grounds that natural selection operates on differential reproduction. This implies that McNeill's emphasis on mortality as a driving force in human history, however persuasive it may seem, in fact contradicts the theory of evolution. Darwin himself, it may be noted, observed that a new disease often causes a high rate of mortality at first, and also that the meeting of previously isolated human populations often results in the exchange of diseases. However he did not construct a theory like McNeill's implying that diseases have served to constrain human populations throughout history.[309]

This problem is related to the debates in ecology about Lotka-Volterra prey-predator cycles (see section 2 above). The fact that two cycles are correlated does not prove that there is a causal relationship between them, since in logic both cycles may be determined by a third factor, nor does it tell us which is cause and which is effect, when it is suspected that there may be a causal relationship between cycles of two living organisms. It seems to be agreed by many ecologists that predators do not cause oscillations of prey populations, although it is difficult to generalise about these matters. On the whole it rather seems to be the case that when fluctuations of a predator species are correlated with fluctuations of a prey species, the predator is following helplessly fluctuations of its prey which may be happening for quite different reasons, for example deterministic chaos.

To illustrate this point in relation to diseases let us consider measles, still a common disease in Britain today where governments delayed introduction of the vaccination measures necessary to eradicate it, an achievement which has already occurred in the United States. Measles is a mild disease in Britain at the present time, if certain rare brain complications are avoided. However, it is still a major cause of infant mortality in developing countries. The reasons for the difference are not known with certainty. An attack of measles induces lifelong immunity. Measles is the classic example of a density-dependent disease, which requires a host population of a certain size in order to exist indefinitely. This population size is of the order of 350,000 in isolated island populations, or perhaps as many as 500,000 if the population density is very high, although research on cities in developed countries yields slightly lower estimates. In fact it is more accurate to say that a certain birth rate is required, about 300 births a week.

Measles epidemics occur at intervals of about two years, when a sufficient number of new individuals susceptible to infection becomes available. It has been argued recently that epidemics of measles, as well as mumps and rubella, follow a pattern of deterministic chaos. The average age of infection with measles is substantially lower in developing countries than it is in Britain. High fertility in developing countries makes a pool of new susceptible individuals large enough for an epidemic available more rapidly. Although measles achieves a high mortality rate among infants and young children in the Third World and so restrains human population growth to some extent, the frequency of epidemics is actually regulated by human reproductive patterns. This illustrates how measles, as a predator, is merely tracking the reproduction of its prey. It was argued in section 3 above that mortality of women in the reproductive age groups is connected to the level of fertility. Again this shows how disease-induced mortality does not regulate human populations as a prime mover but itself actually depends on the level of human reproduction.[310]

Such problems of cause and effect apply in the case of diseases which are much more dangerous than measles. Even in the case of the Black Death in Europe, it is doubtful that plague actually *started* the population decline. Instead the evidence studied by Postan (1972) suggests that the population of England had reached a cyclical peak about a generation beforehand. Plague merely accelerated a downturn, which had already commenced for other reasons, and so substantially increased the negative rate of increase. As McNeill rightly emphasised, plague did have devastating effects in the short term. However, it is unlikely that plague can continuously depress human populations in the long run (over periods of, say, several centuries), even though the pneumonic and septicaemic forms of the disease are 100 per cent lethal if antibiotics are not administered within twenty hours of infection, because plague is subject to crude cyclical fluctuations of its own, for reasons which we shall explore later on.

Human populations in the past were capable of recovering rapidly from even the worst epidemic. In the village of Eyam in Derbyshire in England, an epidemic of plague produced a mortality rate approaching 50 per cent, according to a recent reassessment, of the entire village population in 1665-1666, a very high mortality rate. Even so, the survivors managed to restore the population to about its former size in a couple of generations without significant immigration to help them. This episode confirms the argument in section 2 above that the populations of early modern Europe were quite capable of growing rapidly if there was vacant land available to be taken up.

Similarly AIDS may produce extremely high mortality rates over the next few decades in Africa, taking account of its very long incubation period of up to about nine years. The length of its incubation period suggests that the common ancestor of the human and simian viruses was an ancient disease adapted to surviving in small host populations (cf. the discussion of varicella below). Shortly before the time of writing this section the President of Zaire said that his country is finished if an answer to AIDS is not found soon. This is too pessimistic an assessment of the prospects in the long run. Even if a cure or vaccine is not invented in the near future, AIDS will probably not decimate human populations indefinitely in the future. The latest research, discussed by Doolittle (1989), suggests that retroviruses cannot remain stable entities in the long run because of the unreliability of their mechanism of reproduction. They can only survive in the long run by being absorbed into the genomes of their hosts, where they cease to be pathogenic. This is perhaps the evolutionary destiny of AIDS. Moreover extreme virulence does not lead to high reproductive fitness in the long run, as shown by the case of myxomatosis. If AIDS were to wipe out the population of Zaire entirely, its reproductive fitness there would be zero. It is improbable that natural selection will produce such a result.[311]

It is perfectly legitimate and interesting to study causes of death, but in view of the understanding of modern evolutionary theory employed here, which puts the accent on differential reproduction rather than mortality, less importance is attached here to diseases as a driving force in human history than McNeill attached to them. Since the development of agriculture in the Neolithic period human populations have tended to increase steadily in spite of cyclical fluctuations and occasional massive setbacks. For example the population of France during the ancien régime, about twenty million people, was three to four times the population of Roman Gaul, according to the estimates of Biraben (1988) and Etienne (1988) in the massive *Histoire de la population française* whose volumes have begun to be published recently. Such evidence suggests that in the long run reproduction has tended to outstrip mortality. The ultimate regulatory factor is not disease but the food supply, as Malthus and Darwin thought. Such increases in population imply increases in agricultural productivity rather than decreases in mortality caused by disease. This is why a chapter on agriculture will follow the present chapter. It is doubtful that diseases, like other predators, are capable of regulating prey populations, so long as the predator's effects on the prey are purely negative, even though some of them are well capable of causing massive short-term decreases. Of course the situation is very different when a predator not only kills its prey but also acts as a propagating agent for it, as in the case of the mutualisms between man and domesticated plants and animals (see Chapter I above & Chapter IV below).

A few words on the scope of this section are in order. To save space, identifications of diseases in ancient literary sources and in palaeo-osteological remains made by earlier scholars are accepted without discussion, where they seem to be acceptable. Above all reference should be made to the *magnum opus* of Grmek (1983) on diseases in the Hippokratic corpus. His book is a product of the Annales school at the École des Hautes Etudes in France, which I admire for supporting a brand of interdisciplinary research that can make great contributions to knowledge and understanding of man. Unfortunately this type of research is not encouraged or supported in universities in the Anglo-Saxon world, as I have discovered in Cambridge.

If there is a criticism of Grmek, it is that his book offers relatively few details about the area in which I am most interested, namely the population biology of diseases and its interaction with human demography. Grmek coined the concept of a *pathocoenosis*, which is modelled on the term 'biocoenosis', coined by the German Möbius and employed in ecological literature written on the European mainland to designate what in English is usually called an 'ecological community'. According to Grmek (1983, p. 15) 'la pathocénose tend vers un état d'équilibre, ce qui est particulièrement sensible dans une situation écologique stable'. The present book sets out to question this assumption of ecological stability in classical antiquity in respect of all living creatures, both large and small. Grmek rightly went on a couple of pages later to discuss 'la dynamique de la pathocénose', but the prevailing impression given emphasises equilibrium rather than instability. The emphasis will be reversed in this section.

Scholarly literature on diseases in antiquity has been so preoccupied with identifying the diseases described by ancient authors that little attention has been paid to disease ecology. It is difficult to identify diseases in ancient sources because the Greeks, being unable to see micro-organisms, often classified individual symptoms as discrete diseases. For example in the Hippokratic corpus fever is described as a 'disease' that accompanies all the other 'diseases'. There are very few names for diseases as such in ancient Greek. The Greeks divided illnesses into two main categories: (1) diseases that affected all men at the same time in a place (*loimos*) and were ascribed to the air that was breathed in, the only discernible common factor; (2) diseases that affected individuals in an area sporadically and were explained in terms of the idiosyncrasies of the diet and lifestyle of individuals. The word *epidêmios* did not bear the meaning of the modern word 'epidemic', namely an increase in the rate of incidence of a disease, but simply designated a disease that happened to be dwelling in the area under consideration. Patients suffering from infectious diseases were not isolated because the authors of the Hippokratic corpus did not believe in contagion. This assisted the propagation of infectious diseases in classical Greece. Plutarch states that it used to be customary for the sick to be placed outside the house so that passers-by with experience of similar cases could offer advice.[312]

Osteological evidence is also available, but there are sampling problems as always. These become obvious when one tries to assess the frequency of, say, tuberculosis, leprosy, malaria or nutritional deficiencies on the basis of bones. Moreover many diseases do not affect bones significantly. Despite these problems, Grmek, and also Corvisier (1985), have made sufficient progress in identifying the diseases active in ancient Greece for it to be possible to bypass in the main the question of identification and concentrate here on disease ecology, the main focus of this section. Some attention will also be paid to nutrition insofar as it affects susceptibility to disease, to population genetics and its relationship to disease resistance, and at the end of the section to plant and animal diseases in antiquity to provide a link to Chapter III on agriculture. Only very recent literature and a few of the most important older articles are cited on topics also covered by Grmek, as it would be pointless to duplicate here all the bibliography available in his book.

Since death in practice is caused by disease (barring violence, etc.), variations in disease ecology cause variations in mortality patterns, accounting for much of the variability of demographic patterns in the past mentioned in section 1 above. For example in Ceylon after the Second World War, according to Gray (1974), the eradication of malaria reduced the crude death rate by 23 per cent and eliminated regional differences in mortality patterns which had existed until then, because of the differing degrees of adaptation of the vector mosquitoes to various micro-environments in the island. Malaria was a very important disease in antiquity, and more will be said about it later on. However, we should start by pointing out a few of the idiosyncratic features of the epidemiological environment of ancient Greece to illustrate the regional variation that is possible.

Ancient authors happen to mention two specific features of the pathocoenosis of Attica. First, Theophrastos states that the Athenians did not suffer from tapeworms (*Taenia solium*), unlike the inhabitants of Boiotia next door. Humans contract tapeworms mainly from pork which has not been cooked properly, and Greek medical writers regarded pork as the best meat to eat. Thucydides states that the Aitolians still ate raw meat in the fifth century BC, one manifestation of the backwardness of that part of Greece which he thought had characterised all the Greeks in earlier periods of history. The writers of the Hippokratic corpus stressed the superiority of cooked over uncooked food, but their precepts about nutrition rested on a priori assumptions that are often wrong, a topic to which we shall return later. The modes of transmission of parasitic worms were not understood in antiquity. This led Aristotle to discuss parasitic worms as examples of spontaneous generation. Cases of individuals suffering from various kinds of worms and other parasites turn up in the records of the sanctuary of Asklepios at Epidauros. Clearly divine guidance was sought, when all that was necessary was to consume properly cooked food and to maintain reasonable standards of cleanliness and hygiene. The example of parasitic worms illustrates how the distribution and abundance of a disease may be linked inextricably to human cultural patterns.[313]

Secondly, Lucretius mentions a disease of the feet which he says was characteristic of Attica. It is difficult to identify the disease in question, but it is usually interpreted as a reference to gout. In any case, like the absence of tapeworms, it serves to stress the point that a small region like Attica may have had a distinctive ecological community of diseases, from which it may be inferred that it may also have had a distinctive mortality pattern. Corvisier (1985) provides a useful discussion of regional differences in disease patterns in ancient Greece. He reached the conclusion that Attica could have been unhealthy, while mountainous regions were the healthiest part of the country. Inevitably the low human population density of mountainous regions inhibited density-dependent diseases.[314]

Greece as a whole differs in various aspects of disease ecology from other parts of Europe. For example cystic hydatid disease, which is mentioned in the Hippokratic corpus and is carried by dogs, reaches its highest known frequency in the lands around the Aegean. In passing, it is worth noting that dogmeat was consumed in classical Greece, although this habit may have disappeared later on in antiquity. To give two more examples, both hepatitis A (infectious jaundice acquired from eating contaminated food) and hepatitis B (associated with liver cancer) reach unusually high frequencies in modern Greece compared to many other European countries. 82 per cent of the Greek population carry antibodies to hepatitis A. Both of these viral diseases display an ability to persist in small, isolated populations in the modern world, indicating a long history, and hepatitis A at least is described in the Hippokratic corpus.[315]

Grmek argued that the distribution of diseases in ancient Greece approximated the log-normal distribution used by the ecologist F.W. Preston to account for the fact that in nature a few abundant species generally co-exist with a much larger number of other species that are much rarer. This argument is probably correct. However, there are several possible reasons why the ecology of diseases may have been unstable over time in Greece in antiquity. First, the massive climatic changes mentioned in Chapter I above would have affected many diseases, and also their vectors in cases where the disease requires a vector. Secondly, the fluctuations in human population density discussed in section 2 above would have affected a number of important diseases which are density-dependent. Thirdly, equilibrium of the disease community could have been disrupted by the evolution of new diseases. Fourthly, there is the very important possibility that micro-organisms may themselves undergo population fluctuations even in the absence of massive climatic change and of changes in host populations in the same way that larger organisms may do so.[316]

Diseases such as measles and smallpox could not have existed anywhere in the world before the Bronze Age because there were no human populations large enough to support them. It is conceivable that such diseases, or ones similar to them, evolved several times in prehistory, but failed to establish themselves until they encountered host populations of a suitable size. Grmek suggested that the population of the Aegean was probably large enough to support density-dependent diseases by the Late Bronze Age. Even if this is correct, the collapse of the human population at the end of the Mycenaean period undoubtedly eliminated any density-dependent diseases which had already become established in Greece. Snodgrass (1983a), discussing Lefkandi, showed how small were the populations of Dark Age Greece even on Euboia, the most prosperous part of the country in that period. Under such circumstances only diseases with special adaptations may have survived.[317]

The pathogens which display the best adaptation to man as a host, in the sense of being able to survive in very small human populations, belong to the herpes family, including such viruses as herpes simplex, cytomegalovirus, and the varicella virus which causes both chickenpox and shingles (herpes zoster). They require no intermediate hosts and can survive throughout the host's lifetime. However, it is not known in detail how varicella, at least, manages to evade the body's immune system for decades. They have been associated with man for a very long time and were active in antiquity. The Hippokratic corpus mentions herpes simplex (HSV-1) and genital herpes (HSV-2). It used to be thought that chickenpox and shingles are not attested in the corpus, although Grmek accepts that two passages refer to the different manifestations of the varicella virus. Moreover shingles is mentioned by Roman authors who borrowed the Greek words *zona* and *zoster* to designate it, also suggesting that it was sometimes called *herpes* in Greek. This proves that the varicella virus was known in the Greek world. It is capable of surviving in a human population as small as eighty.[318]

The other diseases that can survive in small human populations are chronic conditions. Diseases that fall into this category include typhoid fever, which is mentioned in the Hippokratic corpus and can persist in small populations in humans who act as carriers but are unaffected themselves, because of its ability to hide inside human cells. In addition it is able to survive in water, food and even snow for months. The various strains of typhoid fever differ in virulence, a theme to which we shall return. Other chronic diseases adapted to small human populations include amoebic dysentery, trachoma, tuberculosis and leprosy (the last three discussed further below). Obviously many important infectious diseases are absent from this list, even if the inquiry is restricted for the time being to diseases whose primary host is man, excluding zoonoses. F. Black (1975 & 1980) suggested that the advances of modern medicine have only restored the state of health that mankind enjoyed over ten thousand years ago, before human populations became large enough to support density-dependent diseases. This is another reason for concluding that physical anthropologists generally have underestimated average age of death of adults in prehistoric skeletal populations (see section 3 above). The fact that many diseases important in later stages of history were not endemic in Dark Age Greece increased the rate of natural increase attainable in that period. This in turn raises questions about the nature of the various epidemics mentioned in Greek legends and stories about early periods of Greek history.[319]

For example, in the 46th Olympiad the Athenians sent for Epimenides of Crete to purify the city after an epidemic. He is said to have declared that the epidemic had been caused by the pollution incurred by the *polis* in the aftermath of the conspiracy of Kylon (see section 5 above). Camp (1979) drew attention to these tales. They can be accounted for in two ways. Major epidemics occurred in the Near East in the Bronze Age, suggesting the presence of some density-dependent diseases in the region where the world's first urban civilisation developed and where several important animals were domesticated, creating mutualisms with man and bringing him into close contact with the micro-organisms responsible for their own diseases. For example, a disease introduced to Anatolia by Egyptian prisoners of war *c.* 1346 BC ravaged the Hittite population for several years. McNeill (1976) tried to trace the confluence of the disease pools of different geographical regions. Contact alone is not sufficient for a disease to become endemic in a new population exposed to it.[320]

We might discuss here the characteristics that make a disease (or any higher organism) into a successful colonising species, a familiar problem in ecology discussed by MacArthur & Wilson (1967). However, we will just note that the varicella virus, needing a host population of eighty, is many times more likely to be a successful coloniser than measles, which requires host populations of hundreds of thousands in a restricted area. Accordingly diseases like measles, smallpox and rubella probably made many unsuccessful colonising expeditions from their original foci in the Middle East, India or China to other less densely populated regions before they finally succeeded in becoming endemic in peripheral regions. Even at the time of the Roman empire, the population of the lands surrounding the Mediterranean as a whole was sufficiently small for such diseases probably to have had difficulty establishing themselves, except in Egypt and the Middle East.

Estimates of the total population of the Roman empire, for example that of Beloch, tend to be around fifty or sixty million. This would be equivalent to scattering the population of modern Britain over half of Europe, North Africa and a large part of the Middle East. It would have been difficult for density-dependent diseases to become endemic at such low levels of human population density. (Those suggested for Attica in the fourth century BC in section 2 above, relating to a cyclical peak, were not sustained for long and were unrepresentative of the Mediterranean as a whole in antiquity.) Smallpox was introduced several times in the seventeenth century AD but did not become endemic in the European colonies in North America then because European populations in North America, expanding into a vacuum as we have seen, were too small and scattered to support it. Similarly in antiquity smallpox attempted to colonise the Mediterranean several times, most notably c. 430 BC and again in the second century AD during the time of Galen, as will be argued later on. It caused great loss of life in the process, but did not succeed in becoming endemic because the human populations under attack were too small to support it permanently. Some of the legends about epidemics in early periods of Greek history may represent unsuccessful attempts at colonisation by density-dependent diseases arriving from more densely populated regions further east.

Diseases associated with harvest failures and subsistence crises provide the second way of explaining epidemics in Dark Age Greece. In a highly seasonal environment with a high degree of interannual harvest variability, food shortages and on occasion famines occur periodically and may affect even small human populations (see Chapter IV below). The Greek words for famine (*limos*) and epidemic (*loimos*) look and sound similar and may have an etymological relationship, although it is not straightforward. They were sometimes confused in antiquity, as Thucydides shows, and may be confused sometimes in the manuscript tradition of ancient authors. A passage of Theophrastos, which speaks of an otherwise unattested *loimos* at the time of the period of food shortages c. 330 BC, which is well attested in a number of other sources and elsewhere in Theophrastos himself, may exemplify such manuscript corruption. Perhaps the two words are variants on the theme of 'disaster'.[321]

Typhoid fever (*Salmonella typhi*), shigellosis (*bacillary dysentery*), another distinctively human disease, amoebic dysentery (*Entamoeba histolytica*) and other enteric diseases are liable to flourish during times of malnutrition. Herodotos describes a typical example, stating that the fleeing Persian army after the battle of Plataia was struck by food shortage, leading the soldiers to eat unwholesome foods, and was then attacked by dysentery which decimated it. Galen also describes how famines led to disease in Asia Minor in Roman times.

Hesiod was familiar with subsistence crises, even though Boiotia was not as densely populated in his time as it was later on in the fourth century BC, judging by archaeological surveys. There are several signs of this. First, he speaks of famine and disease and the failure of women to bear children as a punishment for wrongdoers. This reduction in fertility was the consequence of famine amenorrhoea. Secondly, he states that the *basileis* did not appreciate mallow and asphodel, famine foods for the poor. Galen states that asphodel (*Asphodelus microcarpus*), which he had seen consumed in famines in his own time, was barely edible. However,

Theophrastos, who was less fussy than Galen, praised the utility of asphodel, saying that its stalk was edible when fried, its seed if roasted, and its tuberous roots made a good meal when chopped up with figs. It was eaten again in Greece during the First World War.

Thirdly, Hesiod says that an idle man would end up suffering from a swollen foot, a sign of famine oedema. Fourthly, he stresses the need to work hard to avoid hunger. Subsistence crises and associated epidemics were ingrained in the oral traditions of early Greece and came to be associated with all important past events, a pattern observed by anthropologists who have studied the development of oral traditions in populations living in a seasonal environment. Accordingly we should reject the historicity of individual episodes of epidemic and/or famine in Greek legends, contrary to Camp (1979), but nevertheless accept that they testify to a pattern of recurring phenomena.[322]

Arrian notes that Alexander the Great had an attack of diarrhoea, which was attributed to drinking bad water. Lucian states that the provision of a proper water supply at Olympia by Herodes Atticus eliminated some diseases there. The Greek custom of drinking wine made liquid refreshment somewhat safer. Giving wine to young children, as recommended by medical writers from the Hippokratic corpus onwards (see section 4 above), may have made their drink healthier. The enteric diseases caused great mortality in the past, especially among children, and still do so in developing countries. On the whole they were ever present, causing continual attrition of human populations rather than massive short-term decreases.

Salmonella is also attested in the Hippokratic corpus. It is not associated with raw egg ingestion in the corpus as it is today because the chicken was still relatively insignificant as a source of food in classical Greece (see below), but salmonella infects many other types of food as well. Certain other diseases which undoubtedly existed in classical Greece, such as malaria and relapsing fever, increase susceptibility to salmonella, probably by weakening the body's natural defence mechanisms. However, the most important member of the constellation of enteric diseases may be infantile viral diarrhoea, caused by the rotaviruses which were discovered in the 1970s and are found in many animals. Young children are especially vulnerable to the rotaviruses and also to shigellosis at the time of weaning, when their diet is changing and they may well be malnourished under primitive conditions. This often produces a secondary peak of mortality at the age of weaning, following long periods of breastfeeding, after the initial peak of infant mortality in the first year of life in developing countries today. It was observed in the Hippokratic corpus that children who had already been introduced to foods other than milk withstood weaning better, suggesting that the secondary peak of mortality also occurred in Greece in antiquity. More evidence for this suggestion will be adduced later on.[323]

The legends of epidemics in early Greek history may be explained in these two ways, without invoking the permanent presence of the major density-dependent epidemic diseases in a land and period of low human population density. In fact diseases like smallpox, measles and rubella are not mentioned in the Hippokratic corpus. It is generally agreed by scholars that they were not endemic in classical Greece. In populations in which they are endemic, such viral diseases generally affect infants and young children, with substantial mortality rates in the past. The survivors tend to be immune for the rest of their lives.

In addition, as Corvisier noted, certain diseases which are mentioned in the Hippokratic corpus, such as diphtheria and mumps, are not described as characteristically diseases of childhood, as they are today, although whooping cough (*Bordetella pertussis*) may already have been a typical childhood disease. Aretaios, who gave the best description of diphtheria to survive from antiquity, regarded it as characteristic of Egypt and Syria, two densely populated regions where it was doubtless able to persist endemically. Diphtheria (*Corynebacterium diphtheriae*) and mumps seem to have appeared in Greece occasionally in epidemic form, afflicting all age groups. Ancient Greek populations were too small to maintain them endemically preying on young children, and so there were large numbers of adults who were vulnerable to periodic attempts at colonisation by all these density-dependent diseases. Scarlet fever is another childhood disease which is not attested in the Hippokratic corpus. However, it is no longer regarded as a distinct entity by modern doctors. As other diseases caused by the group A streptococci which also cause scarlet fever, such as puerperal fever and skin infections like erysipelas, are clearly described in the Hippokratic corpus, scarlet fever may also have occurred in classical Greece, in spite of the lack of evidence.

The shortage of diseases of infancy and childhood in early Greece is another reason why the high infant mortality revealed by cemeteries should be explained in terms of high fertility and rapid population growth from the eighth century BC onwards, not as a consequence of extremely low life expectancy at birth (see section 3 above). Diphtheria, for example, had a case-mortality rate of about 10 per cent in the past. Bernoulli, a pioneer of mathematical epidemiology, calculated in 1760 AD that the universal application of smallpox inoculation would increase life expectancy at birth by about three years. He relied on Halley's life table for Breslau which was one of the earliest life tables. In fact an interest in the demographic consequences of smallpox inoculation played an important role in the development of probability theory in mathematics. Anderson & May (1979) suggested that such diseases slow down but do not stop human population growth. Consequently their absence or inability to persist endemically should increase the rate of population growth, *ceteris paribus*. The reader should recall at this point that the population of Athens expanded *outwards* in the eighth century BC, a demographic feat unparalleled in major urban centres in early modern Europe (section 2 above).[324]

In passing, a few remarks on mumps may be of interest. Hippokrates gave a well known description of an epidemic of mumps on Thasos, in which the disease in males may be recognised above all from the characteristic symptoms of orchitis and swelling of the parotid glands. However, mumps is not a significant cause of sterility in males. It affected young and middle-aged adults as well as children on Thasos. Mumps was not endemic on that small island at the time and could not have become endemic there, as it is a density-dependent disease which tends to disappear in small isolated populations in the modern world. It is not known whether mumps was endemic anywhere in classical Greece, or whether it merely made periodic incursions from the east in the same way that it will be argued smallpox did. In this context it is interesting to note that mumps is related not only to parainfluenza but also to the virus that causes Newcastle disease of poultry, a severe disease of chickens. The ancestor of this particular family of viruses may have preyed on birds or on domesticated animals such as cattle and sheep, which are afflicted by viruses similar to the human parainfluenza virus.[325]

The chicken was a newcomer to Europe in the first millennium BC, yet another participant in the great movement westwards to fill the vacuum left by the last glaciation. It was native to south-east Asia, spread to China in the Neolithic period and then to India by the third millennium BC. It was called the 'Median' or 'Persian bird' by Greeks such as Aristophanes in the classical period when the Persians ruled the Near East. Its exotic character in classical Greece is also indicated by the detail, preserved by Porphyry, that initiates in the Eleusinian Mysteries refrained from eating it. It is first attested in Italy in the sixth century BC at the Greek colony of Paestum.

Towards the end of the first millennium BC the chicken starts to appear on archaeological sites in Britain. Caesar states that the Britons refused to eat the strange new bird, valuable both for its meat and eggs, and kept it solely for pleasure and amusement, showing how a useful new food resource might be neglected in primitive societies merely because it was not part of the traditional diet. According to Columella the Greeks were interested in breeding cocks mainly for fighting, although Diokles of Karystos does mention consumption of chicken. Columella himself preferred to breed domestic fowl as a source of food. Taken alongside the epidemic character of mumps in classical Greece, the westward movement of the chicken may be an example of prey being followed by predator (or a relative thereof) as it migrated. It is also possible that the virus in question passed from man to chicken at some stage, or a similar virus from another domesticated animal to the chicken.[326]

The demographic history of Greece in the Dark Ages provided very favourable conditions for alleles which are usually rare in large populations to reach exceptionally high frequencies. This was caused by the population's passage through a bottleneck at the end of the Mycenaean period, with a drastic reduction in population size and fragmentation of the gene pool, followed by rapid population increase in the eighth century BC under conditions of r selection, in which alleles with a low evolutionary fitness under competitive conditions (at K) may attain high frequencies. This was followed by the operation of the 'founder effect' as small groups of Greeks set off on colonising expeditions. The theory of Cann et al. (1987), namely that all modern humans are descended from one female who lived in Africa about 200,000 years ago, provides the most striking evidence for the importance of founder effects in human population history. Given the significance of emigration in the demographic systems of antiquity, founder effects probably played a very important role in the genetic histories of ancient Greek populations. We may also consider the Samaritans, a highly inbred endogamous group descended from the inhabitants of the kingdom of Samaria, destroyed by Sargon II of Assyria in 722 BC. They had been reduced to a very small population by a couple of centuries ago but have since increased substantially, in the process developing a unique genetic profile. Such developments may easily have medical implications because the genotype determines the body's response to disease.[327]

There is no quantitative evidence for gene frequencies in ancient Greek populations, although advances in molecular biology will probably make it possible one day to study directly DNA from classical antiquity. All that the modern scholar can do at the moment is search literary sources for conditions which, for example, were described as common in antiquity but are rare today. Two possible pieces of evidence for alleles in ancient Greece with frequencies quite different from their modern ones will be mentioned here. First, Behçet's disease, which occurs sporadically in the Aegean today, is described in the Hippokratic corpus in such a way as to suggest that it had an epidemic character in antiquity. This would be an example of a disease common in antiquity which has since become rare, and it is interesting to consider how this could have happened. The aetiology of the disease is complicated and not properly understood. The herpes simplex virus seems to play a role, providing further evidence for its importance in classical Greece. However, modern research also indicates that immunogenetic factors, the body's HLA system, are involved. The epidemic character of this disease in classical Greece may be explained in terms of the allele in question having attained a high frequency, perhaps during the r period of the eighth century. The selective agency of the disease may then have led to a gradual reduction of the frequency of this allele.[328]

The second example is furnished by the small island of Mykonos, where baldness was said to be prevalent. Premature baldness appears to be distinct from late baldness, whose frequency increases with age, as Aristotle noted. It has been suggested that the former is transmitted by a single autosomal dominant gene, a sex-linked character found in both sexes but not expressed in females. The genetics are not completely understood yet, but both types of baldness are inherited and depend on stimulation by androgenic hormones of susceptible hair follicles. On Mykonos the fact that most men were bald can only be explained in terms of the gene for early baldness having attained an exceptionally high frequency in this small, isolated population. Similar phenomena occur in small island populations in modern Greece (see Chapter I above on island populations). For example muteness among females has reached an unusually high frequency on Amorgos and Donoussa. Genetic phenomena of this kind were probably common in ancient Greece.[329]

Some scholars have concluded that inbreeding in human populations leads to increased mortality, for example in the population of the island of Tristan da Cunha, and reduced fertility, for example among the Old Order Amish, a religious sect in North America. It has been suggested recently that inbreeding among the small Spartiate population may have been one of the reasons for its lack of vitality and decline. However, deleterious consequences of inbreeding have not been discovered in all studies of this problem. The fact that something is probable does not mean that it is bound to happen. Moreover a recent review concluded that 'with the exception of incest and families known to carry deleterious recessive mutants, the risks to offspring of inbred unions generally are within the limits of acceptability'. (In evaluating this conclusion in relation to antiquity it must not be forgotten that the definition of incest was much narrower then than it is now.) Accordingly in the absence of direct evidence it is impossible to confirm or falsify the hypothesis that inbreeding adversely affected the population of Sparta.[330]

Other changes in gene frequencies that merit mention here are connected to the evolution of human resistance to malaria. In Greece, the part of Europe that was worst affected by malaria in the past, several genotypes causing deficiency in production of glucose-6-phosphate dehydrogenase, an important enzyme found in most living organisms except plague (*Yersinia pestis*), reach their highest known frequency and radiate out from Greece along geographical lines which correspond to the colonisation of the archaic period and the conquest of the Persian empire by Alexander. This condition creates resistance to falciparum malaria under certain circumstances (discussed in Chapter III.2 below). Such mutations are found in all human populations at low frequencies, but are neutral, or conceivably even disadvantageous, and so do not increase in frequency in the absence of malaria. They only attain high frequencies if the powerful selective force of malaria is active.

The alleles responsible for traits conferring resistance to malaria, such as thalassaemia and haemoglobin S as well as G6PD deficiency, may have started to reach significant frequencies under the uncompetitive conditions of r selection in the eighth century, and subsequently have been maintained under conditions of K selection in dense human populations in which malaria was endemic in classical Greece, having a selective advantage. Sickle-cell anaemia, which occurs in homozygotes for haemoglobin S, occurs with a high frequency in northern Greece today. Grmek suggested that it was introduced to Greece in the first millennium BC. However, the fact that the name 'Ethiopian' occurs on a Linear B tablet from Pylos shows that Negroes could have introduced haemoglobin S to Greece in the second millennium BC. Edelstein (1986) argued that it evolved at least three times independently in the first millennia BC and AD. Mathematical models indicate that it could have reached frequencies similar to modern values in regions where it is found in about forty to fifty generations after its evolution.

The high frequencies in Greece of genetic traits conferring resistance to malaria suggest that the Greeks were well equipped in terms of their genetics to colonise other regions, for example in the Middle East during the Hellenistic period, where malaria was present. This may well have been one of the reasons for the success of Greek colonisation. It may be contrasted with the inability of north Europeans in the early modern period to colonise west Africa, where those who went more than a few yards inland from the coast had an average life expectancy of six months because of their lack of resistance to yellow fever and falciparum malaria.

West Africa is the region where the most striking human adaptation to malaria occurs. Most of the indigenous inhabitants possess the Duffy negative blood group allele which confers almost complete resistance to vivax malaria. It appears that in prehistory this species of malaria was once holo-endemic in west Africa, leading to the evolution of total human resistance which in the end completely drove the parasite out of the region, an example of a human victory over a dangerous disease achieved by means of natural selection. (During the Ice Ages much of what is today tropical rain forest was savanna grassland – a difference in the environment that would have favoured vivax malaria, a species which is better adapted than falciparum malaria to seasonal environments.) Its place was taken by falciparum malaria, which is more dangerous and probably of more recent evolutionary origin. The Mediterranean, a highly seasonal environment since the Neolithic period, has been the main home of vivax malaria since then, and we shall return to it later.[331]

Population growth in archaic Greece permitted an increase in the frequency and severity of tuberculosis (Greek *phthisis*, Attic *phthoê*). Tuberculosis is not highly infectious and is capable of remaining endemic in small populations in a chronic form. However, in early modern Europe it caused its worst ravages in crowded towns, according to a general pattern of differential disease morbidity and mortality rates in town and country which will be considered later. Urbanisation led to the congregation of genetically susceptible individuals.

The epidemiology of tuberculosis is unique among diseases in that it characteristically affected young adults, especially women, in populations in which it was endemic in the past, in addition to the mortality peaks in infancy and among older adults found in many diseases, for example smallpox. The particular vulnerability of women in the reproductive age groups to tuberculosis is a consequence of pregnancy-mediated depression of the body's defence mechanisms against disease. J. Russell (1985) attempted to exploit this distinctive feature, which was observed in antiquity, to trace fluctuations in the incidence of tuberculosis via fluctuations in young adult mortality in historical populations. The writers of the Hippokratic corpus make it clear that tuberculosis was rampant in classical Greece, often as an acute rather than a chronic disease. One of them even states that it was always fatal. Corvisier pointed out that the high frequency of tuberculosis, besides other pulmonary and respiratory infections, in the Hippokratic corpus refers to northern Greece, with its cooler environment. However, it was common enough in Attica as well.

In constructing their model life tables, Coale & Demeny (1983) explicitly refused to take into account documentary evidence from populations in periods and regions in which tuberculosis was common, because they regarded it as a factor which would distort their idealised models. This means that in fact none of their life tables provides appropriate models for any historical population, including those of ancient Greece, in which tuberculosis was frequent. The incidence of tuberculosis could help to explain the excessive mortality among young adults relative to both children and older adults which was observed in Angel's skeletal samples for ancient Greece (see section 3 above). It must be considered carefully, alongside the other possibilities of under-representation of infant mortality and underestimation of average age of death of older adults, in research on skeletal populations.[332]

By selectively killing adults, especially women, in the reproductive age groups, tuberculosis has a restraining effect on human reproduction. It also has a minor effect on fertility, even when mortality is avoided, in cases of genital tuberculosis, when sterility sometimes occurs. This particular type of tuberculosis is often asymptomatic, and sterility attributed to tuberculosis is mentioned in antiquity only in one surviving source, of late Roman date. There is plenty of evidence for pulmonary tuberculosis in ancient Greece. The Hippokratic corpus also mentions the skeletal lesions such as Pott's syndrome which may be produced more frequently by bovine tuberculosis than by human tuberculosis. The course of evolution of human tuberculosis, a very old disease which existed in ancient Egypt, is unclear. It may have been connected to (or at least occurred at the same time as) the domestication of cattle during the 'secondary products revolution' of Sherratt (1981) in the Late Neolithic period, even though bovine tuberculosis only occurs among domesticated, not wild, bovids. Grmek suggested that human tuberculosis evolved in Africa. However, it should be noted that tuberculosis was found to be almost unknown in tropical Africa by the first European explorers in the early modern period.[333]

Bovine tuberculosis was common in countries like early modern Britain and France before the process of pasteurising milk was invented. However, it was probably relatively infrequent in southern Greece in antiquity, where little milk was consumed by adults (except as cheese). The frequency of lactose intolerance in southern Greece and Italy is high today, as it is in non-European populations in which adults did not drink milk in historical times. There was little pressure for natural selection to increase the frequency of the one or two alleles responsible for the conservation in adults of the ability to make the enzyme lactase. The ancient Greeks possessed a stereotyped image of nomads such as the Scythians who did drink a lot of milk as adults. This suggests that a high frequency of lactose tolerance had already evolved or was evolving in classical times in pastoral societies in northern Eurasia. Presumably its frequency decreased along biogeographical lines from north to south, parallel to changes in the frequency of milk consumption by adults. This particular example of natural selection at work is diametrically opposed to the case of malaria in which the frequency of resistant genotypes increases from north to south.[334]

Natural selection should have produced similar clines in allele frequency along biogeographical lines in the course of time irrespective of where the human population actually came from. In other words it is irrelevant whether the Proto-Indo-Europeans originated in eastern Europe/south Russia or alternatively in Greece/Anatolia/Armenia as suggested (in my opinion wrongly) by some scholars (C. Renfrew and R. Drews – the divergence between their views alone shows how shaky the foundations of the whole hypothesis are). Nevertheless Ruffié & Sournia (1984) have shown that the patterns of frequency of various blood groups in European populations may be correlated with the spread of the Indo-Europeans from the east over pre-existing non-Indo-European populations.

The frequency of tuberculosis has probably varied considerably in the course of history. In the last century it declined exponentially in Europe even before the rest cure, which was first advocated by Alexander of Tralles at Constantinople in the sixth century AD, began to be employed systematically. This is one facet of the puzzle of the apparent decline in infectious diseases in the early modern period *before* the development of modern medicine, a puzzle upon which McKeown (1976) expended his energies. It is probably a false problem, or a bad question, at least in the terms in which it is usually put, because the underlying assumption is that diseases did restrict human populations in the past but somehow ceased to be able to do so during the Industrial Revolution.

In contrast the reality is that they were probably never able to regulate human populations in the long term in the distant past. 'The modern rise of population', to borrow the title of McKeown's book, was made possible by increases in agricultural productivity, raising K, and improvements in living standards and nutritional status increasing resistance to diseases. R. & J. Dubos (1953) argued that selective elimination of susceptible individuals increased resistance to tuberculosis, a hypothesis suggested by studies of twins. However, it is improbable on statistical grounds that this phenomenon can explain the modern decline of tuberculosis on its own. Among women at least, the decrease in fertility during the demographic transition reduced vulnerability to diseases like tuberculosis, providing at least a partial explanation for their decline in terms of human population dynamics.

At the other end of the early modern period, several scholars have reached the conclusion that tuberculosis was increasing in frequency at the end of the mediaeval period. They sought to explain in this way the disappearance of leprosy, an important disease in mediaeval Europe which is closely related to tuberculosis. Tuberculosis and leprosy have similar antigenic properties, creating the (unproven) possibility that infection with one may give some protection against subsequent infection from the other. There are two other similar systems of antigenic cross-protection which are relevant to our inquiry. First, dengue and yellow fever are mutually exclusive. This helped to keep the scourge of the white man in west Africa out of the Mediterranean in the past. Secondly, plague is mutually exclusive with yersiniosis, a disease of animals whose spread in modern times may explain the disappearance of plague in Europe, according to some scholars (but see below). The spread of tuberculosis may have been related to the decline of leprosy. However tuberculosis was extremely frequent in classical Greece, while leprosy was absent and began to spread in Europe in Roman times, and tuberculosis was seemingly less prevalent in mediaeval Europe, although it must be said that the evidence is extremely poor. It is more probable that tuberculosis has displayed cyclical behaviour of its own in the course of history that is not related to leprosy, increasing by becoming epidemic rather than endemic and acute rather than chronic in periods of rapid population growth and urbanisation such as the archaic period in Greece and in early modern Europe, followed by subsequent declines.[335]

Leprosy is the most certain example of a disease which entered the Graeco-Roman world from outside in the course of the first millennium BC. This was made possible by population growth and increasing intensity of communications over long distances. It has been suggested that the army of Alexander the Great brought leprosy back from India. However, it is more likely that the disease had long been endemic in the Middle East by the classical period, as Grmek thinks. It is extremely difficult to tell the difference between leprosy and non-infectious skin diseases (e.g. psoriasis) in early sources, for example in the Bible. This is an acute problem because a disease like psoriasis has probably existed in hominids and all their mammalian ancestors for many millions of years, if the explanation, propounded by R. Harper (1975) developing one of Darwin's ideas, of it as a *reversion* to a skin type characteristic of reptiles is correct.

Aretaios gave the best ancient description of acute lepromatous leprosy, the most severe form of the disease. It is a disease of the peripheral parts of the nervous system. Authors dating to the Roman period discuss leprosy as a new disease which was not known to their classical predecessors. Rufus' citation of early Hellenistic sources shows that leprosy existed in Egypt in the third century BC, a conclusion confirmed by the recent discovery of palaeo-osteological evidence for leprosy from the Dakleh oasis dating to the second century BC. It was common by Roman times in the Middle East, but rare in Italy. It is not clear how frequent it was in Greece. The authors of the Roman world reached the conclusion that new diseases could not be evolving and decided that their predecessors must have failed to notice 'new' diseases such as leprosy. However, they evidently felt uncomfortable about such an improbable conclusion. This is another illustration of the prevalent belief in Graeco-Roman society that genuine innovation, whether man-made or natural, was impossible. It recalls the belief that new barbarian tribes were not arising in Eurasia, and the old ones were merely changing their names to confuse the Romans (see section 2 above). Denials of reality of this kind constitute one of the most interesting aspects of the 'mentalité' of the ancient Greeks and Romans.

The epidemiology of leprosy presents many points of obscurity. In populations in which it is endemic, many individuals who contract it appear to have done so without any discernible contact with other cases of the disease. Moreover where it is endemic a large proportion of the whole population possesses antibodies to leprosy without ever having developed the disease, in clinical terms. These observations have led recently to the propounding of two novel hypotheses which have not yet been investigated thoroughly. First, it is suggested that *Mycobacterium leprae* is distributed widely in the *inanimate* environment, and so does not depend on human-to-human transmission. This idea is fortified by the fact that other related bacteria of the genus Mycobacterium are present in the soil, water, insects and other animals. The second idea is that in populations in which it is endemic virtually *everyone* is infected, but in most cases the disease never develops beyond the sub-clinical level. The development of the disease is heavily dependent on immunogenetic factors. It is also assisted by protein-calorie malnutrition.

Until the population biology of leprosy today is better understood, it is idle to speculate on its demographic impact on historical populations and on interactions with tuberculosis. However, as leprosy generally does not cause epidemics and as the clinical disease only occurs sporadically even when it is endemic, its consequences in terms of mortality probably did not match the fear it aroused in the Roman and mediaeval periods. D. Smith & R. Guinto (1978) argued that lepromatous leprosy, but not the milder tuberculoid leprosy, reduces male fertility very substantially by attacking the testicles, and also female fertility to a lesser extent. This provides a mechanism for limiting the incidence of the most severe form of the disease, as individuals who are genetically susceptible to it tend to fail to reproduce themselves and are eliminated selectively from the population. According to this theory there would be no need to invoke any interaction with tuberculosis to explain the decline of leprosy in Europe.[336]

Although the Greeks became aware of leprosy in the early Hellenistic period, the pathocoenosis of Greece at that time still lacked other notable diseases which were major killers in early modern Europe, besides smallpox and measles. Plague, to which we shall return, was certainly not endemic in classical Greece, although there may have been occasional cases arising from contact with animal hosts. Cholera did not spread from its heartland in India to Europe until the nineteenth century AD. It is generally agreed by scholars that there is no evidence for venereal syphilis in classical antiquity (see below).[337]

It is uncertain whether or not influenza existed in antiquity, as certain epidemics characterised by high morbidity but a low case mortality rate, without further details, conceivably could have been mild strains of any one of several diseases. Even if the mortality rate is low, influenza epidemics have a short-term effect on fertility rates because it reduces sperm production in males for a few months after the illness. Like the common cold, which certainly did exist in classical Greece (see Chapter I above), influenza is a density-dependent disease. However, it has the great advantage over measles and smallpox of continuous antigenic drift, overcoming the obstacle to its propagation imposed by acquired immunity. It was probably originally a disease of birds. In recent times, influenza pandemics generally have originated in the Far East and spread westwards, fitting into the general pattern emphasised in this book.[338]

The absence of several important diseases suggests that classical Greece was a relatively healthy place in which to live. Estimates of how healthy the ancient Greeks were depend on how many diseases can be identified in the Hippokratic corpus. Goodall (1934) decided that he could identify several diseases (e.g. relapsing fever, acute poliomyelitis and epidemic typhus) in addition to those which have been discussed here already, and so concluded that classical Greece was an extremely unhealthy place in which to live. In contrast Corvisier emphasised the Greek interest in bathing and hygiene and suggested that the way of life of the Greeks was quite healthy relative to that of populations in early modern Europe. Considerations of space forbid exhaustive consideration of this question here.[339]

Few epidemics made enough of an impact on political and military affairs to be recorded in non-medical sources for classical Greece in the fifth and fourth centuries BC. Armies in the Persian Wars, the Peloponnesian War(s) and the struggles for hegemony in the first half of the fourth century were seldom impeded by epidemics. In this respect classical Greece was quite different from early modern Europe, as shown by the entertaining history of typhus written by Zinsser (1935). However the Hippokratic corpus suggests that small-scale localised epidemics were common enough in the various *poleis* of northern Greece, where Hippokrates worked.

Hippokrates himself is said by late sources to have helped the Greeks to stop a dangerous epidemic which started in Illyria and Paionia and to have ended the great epidemic of Athens. It is uncertain whether these two episodes were supposed to be different parts of the same story. However, there is no good contemporary evidence for these achievements. They were invented by much later authors as the historical traditions regarding the Father of Medicine were engulfed in legend. Herodotos mentions an epidemic which killed 98 members of a choir of 100 young men sent from Chios to Delphi. A treaty between Argos and Sparta during the Peloponnesian War included a clause in which both sides agreed to the possibility of fighting a ritual battle for the disputed territory of Kynouria if neither of them were affected by disease, *nosos*, an example of ritualised warfare originating in initiation rites. However, there is no evidence that either of them was being troubled by disease at the time. The list of major epidemics in fifth-century Greece is very short, with only one large item on it.[340]

The list for fourth-century Greece is also characterised by extreme brevity, even though that particular period is documented better than the fifth century. Besides the Hippokratic corpus, whose most important works span the fifth and fourth centuries, some Greek philosophers did take an interest in diseases. It is not certain whether Demokritos wrote a book on epidemics in the fifth century, but he did write one on fever and coughing illnesses, *peri puretou kai tôn apo nosou bêssontôn*. Plutarch records that Demokritos or one of his disciples devised a theory that epidemics developed as a consequence of the arrival on earth of organisms that cause diseases from extra-terrestrial sources (anticipating Fred Hoyle on AIDS). However, there is no trace of this theory in the surviving fragments of Demokritos. Aristotle wrote a book on the origins of diseases, *peri tôn tôn nosôn archôn*, while Theophrastos wrote about epidemics, *peri loimôn*. Unfortunately none of these works are extant to enlighten us. The main historical sources, Diodoros and Xenophon, do not mention any major epidemics at all in fourth-century Greece. Nor did Demosthenes ever worry about epidemics in Athens. The lightning movements of the armies of Philip II and Alexander the Great were not prevented by disease epidemics.[341]

It is worth contrasting the situation in Greece in the classical period with the situation in the western Mediterranean. Livy and Dionysios of Halikarnassos do mention quite a number of epidemics in Italy dating to the early Republican period. Some of these were associated with subsistence crises of the kind discussed above, while others are described as autonomous epidemics which were not related to crop failure. Part of the explanation for the contrast lies in the different nature of the sources for Greece and Rome. Livy and Dionysios, or rather their predecessors in the annalistic tradition, ultimately depended on the *Annales Maximi*, an annual documentary record of major events kept by the pontifex maximus. It recorded events such as epidemics, increases in the price of grain and eclipses that were not necessarily of interest to literary authors such as Thucydides and Xenophon in Greece, or Cato in Rome, who concentrated on war and politics. Presumably just the bare fact of an event was recorded in the pontifical annals, and it is presumed that most of the wealth of detail about the history of early Rome found in the pages of Livy and Dionysios was invented by their predecessors. Certainly as far as the epidemics are concerned the recorded details are hardly sufficient to permit identification of the disease in question in any of the cases.[342]

Similarly Diodoros mentions some major epidemics that affected Carthage in North Africa and Carthaginian and Athenian armies in Sicily. The occurrence of major epidemics, bearing the hallmarks of the intrusion of density-dependent diseases, in Italy and Sicily in the fifth and fourth centuries BC suggests that the population of these regions had already advanced to the point where it was exceeding the population of Greece, following the spread of arboriculture and the new crops of the first millennium BC, which made possible increases in K. Italy is larger and generally more fertile than Greece. According to the Threshold Theorem of McKendrick and Kermack the introduction of infectious cases into a community will *not* cause an epidemic, in the case of density-dependent diseases, if the population size and density fall below a certain critical value. Above that value an epidemic may result, but the disease may not become endemic if the population size and density do not also exceed another, higher, critical value.[343]

By the mid-fourth century BC the population of the city of Rome was of the order of 50,000-60,000, according to a recent estimate. By then Rome may already have been larger than Athens or any other town in Greece. On the eve of the showdown with Hannibal in the second half of the third century BC the confederation of peoples ruled by Rome was able to field more than 770,000 soldiers, according to Polybios. This compares with the Athenian or Theban citizen armies, which barely exceeded 10,000 each, while the adult male Spartiates would have been outnumbered heavily by a single Roman legion in the mid-fourth century BC. Justin estimated the total manpower resources of the Greek states comprising the 'League of Corinth' which were subject to Philip II of Macedon as just 215,000 soldiers (see section 2 above). The manpower resources of Rome in the Second Punic War could not have been built up suddenly. Population growth in central Italy in the fifth and fourth centuries BC created some of the essential preconditions for the expansion of the Roman empire in subsequent centuries. The fact that more major epidemics are recorded for Italy than for Greece in the fifth and fourth centuries BC, even though Greece is much richer in *contemporaneous* documentary/literary sources, is not just a consequence of the Roman annalistic tradition, but was also a result of population growth in the more fertile country, producing sufficiently large prey populations to support density-dependent predators, at least temporarily.[344]

Nevertheless, the fact that the literary/documentary sources for classical Greece are much better than those for Italy at the same time means that much more is known about the one great epidemic in Greece in that period than about any of the epidemics in Italy and Sicily. It is necessary to consider the great epidemic which began at Athens in 430 BC as a typical example of a 'virgin-soil' epidemic, paying particular attention to its demographic consequences. First of all, however, a few comments about the sources and the identification of the disease in question are necessary. The whole episode will not be called 'the plague of Athens' here because it is extremely unlikely that it was caused by plague.

Thucydides, the main source, hoped that his description of the disease would allow men in the future to recognise it if it should strike again and be aware of the likely consequences. This was the purpose of his 'history' (actually a record of contemporary events) as a whole. In fact his description has been identified with a quite extraordinary variety of diseases by modern scholars, many of which are so dissimilar to each other that there really should not be any possibility of confusing them. The lack of unanimity among scholars has provoked three counsels of despair in recent literature. First, Longrigg (1980) states that one of his colleagues had suggested the possibility that Thucydides' description of the epidemic 'is a purely literary invention for historiographical purposes'! This hypothesis may be dismissed immediately, because there are other sources (see below) that provide pieces of information about the epidemic which are not found in Thucydides. This shows that there were other independent traditions and that Thucydides did not invent the whole episode. Of course he did make up the *speeches* in his 'history', but that does not affect the point at issue here.[345]

Secondly, Langmuir et al. (1985) reacted to the lack of unanimity among scholars by naming the disease 'the Thucydides syndrome' to emphasise its distinctiveness! However, their own attempt to elucidate the nature of this new-fangled entity is methodologically indefensible. They attempted to account for all the symptoms mentioned by Thucydides by postulating the coincidental occurrence of two quite different diseases. This procedure is unsatisfactory because Thucydides does not give the slightest hint that more than one disease was involved. He states that all the other diseases known to the Athenians were inactive at the time when the epidemic commenced. Moreover the authors of the article in question admit that even pandemics of influenza, their first choice, do not produce case mortality rates anywhere near as high as those indicated by Thucydides. (Mercier (1974), another advocate of influenza, overlooked this point.) This forces them to choose a second disease supposed to be at work simultaneously, a virulent staphylococcus, to account for such high mortality rates during the postulated influenza epidemic. Thucydides' emphasis on acquired immunity preventing second attacks rules out the possibility that more than one disease could have been involved, and influenza undergoes genetic recombination rapidly anyway, making acquired immunity relatively ineffective. This whole approach to the problem is quite misguided. Only a single disease is required. According to Dixon (1962) it is unusual for smallpox to occur concurrently with other epidemics, although it may in fact strike individuals already suffering from a wide variety of other diseases. Thucydides indicates that this happened in Athens.

The third counsel of despair is the opinion of Holladay & Poole (1979) that it may not be possible to identify the disease in question with any disease known today. Giving up when faced with a problem is never likely to add to the sum of knowledge. Undoubtedly the text of Thucydides does not match the precision of the case-notes of modern doctors. He did not employ any specialised medical terminology. Some scholars have argued that Thucydides derived the terminology used in his description from certain works of the Hippokratic corpus, especially *Epidemics* I & III and the *Prognôstikon*. Quite apart from the demonstration by A. Parry (1969) that almost all of the words and phrases in question also occur in non-medical writers of the classical period, there are three arguments which are quite decisive against this hypothesis. First, Thucydides' analysis, stressing the role of contagion, as noted by Lichtenthaeler (1965), in the great epidemic while omitting to discuss the environmental conditions prevailing at the time, is quite different in character from the explanations of the causation of diseases given by all the authors of the Hippokratic corpus. It is a perverse method of textual criticism which holds that one of two texts whose respective interpretations are quite different from each other is derived from the other one.

There is also an insoluble chronological problem. The early books of Thucydides' 'history' were written in the first half of the Peloponnesian War, before 411 BC when the text breaks off, even if II.65 suggests that he lived until the end of the war. When writing his account of the epidemic he had not read the Hippokratic works in question, which were not written until the last decade of the fifth century at the earliest. The icing on the cake is provided by Galen, who states quite explicitly that Thucydides wrote 'as a layman for laymen' (*hôs idiôtês idiôtais*). Thucydides did not exploit even the rather limited amount of specialised medical terminology which was available in his own time (probably not much).[346]

The fact that he was not guided by a doctor is not the only reason why Thucydides' description of the epidemic lacks precision. The second reason is that he does not give a *complete* account of everything that happened during the epidemic (or, for that matter, the Peloponnesian War as a whole). Even if we did not have his explicit statement that he was not going to mention many symptoms which occurred in certain individuals, because the disease manifested itself in so many different ways, it would be obvious that Thucydides was a highly intelligent writer who possessed criteria of selection and presented his readers (or listeners?) with a selection of 'facts' which he judged to be important. For example, in describing the revolt of Mytilene from Athens Thucydides chose to emphasise the political reasons for the revolt, while Aristotle, who evidently had other sources of information available, stressed the personal motives of some of the leading politicians in Mytilene. As far as the epidemic is concerned, several other sources yield information which is not available in the text of Thucydides, proving that he chose not to tell his audience everything that he could have told them.[347]

Plutarch tells us that Perikles died in the epidemic, a piece of information which Thucydides did not tell us because of his admiration for the policies of Perikles. The traditions which built up around the figure of Sokrates recorded that he did not contract the disease, a stroke of good fortune attributed to his virtuous lifestyle as a philosopher. Smallpox is not the most infectious of diseases, as we shall see. Thucydides states that the epidemic did not affect the Peloponnese to any great extent and does not give us any details of its occurrence there. However, Pausanias notes that the epidemic struck the *polis* of Kleonai. He also states that the temples of Apollo at Bassae and Pan *Lutêrios* at Troizen were erected by the people of Phigalia and Troizen respectively to thank the god for averting the epidemic, while Plutarch records that all those who came into contact with the Athenian forces attacking Epidauros contracted the disease from them. Again Thucydides tells us that religious measures to try to end the epidemic were of no avail. He does not give any information as to what measures were taken. Pausanias records that the Athenians appealed to Apollo, who put an end to the epidemic, i.e. it happened to end soon after the appeal. As a result the title *Alexikakos*, 'averter of evil', was given to a statue of the god said to have been made by the sculptor Kalamis, whose chronology is disputed. Diodoros, unlike Thucydides, associates the purification of Delos with the great epidemic.[348]

Diodoros Siculus, the most important source of additional information, gives us very interesting details about environmental conditions in the year of the epidemic and a theory about its aetiology which are nowhere to be found in Thucydides. The main modern commentary on Thucydides suggested that Diodoros, or rather his postulated source Ephoros, simply invented the additional information which he presents. This is a feeble argument. Instead it is preferable to apply the very same principle applied to Thucydides and Hippokrates above, and assume that Diodoros represents a different tradition from Thucydides, given that what he has to say about the epidemic is quite different from what Thucydides says.

Diodoros' treatment of the climatic conditions and environmental circumstances prevailing when the epidemic started is very similar to the *katastaseis* or 'Constitutions' found in the books of the Hippokratic *Epidemics*. It is surely how we can only suppose Hippokrates would have attempted to explain the great epidemic himself, judging by the method of explanation used in his surviving authentic writings. Thucydides probably did not read the works of Hippokrates and his disciples, but Ephoros could have read them (or talked to the disciples) in the fourth century BC. Insofar as medical writers exercised any influence at all on historians, that influence is to be observed in the tradition represented by Diodoros, not in the tradition started by Thucydides. Similarly Lucretius' account of the epidemic of Athens, although obviously influenced by Thucydides, also uses terminology for the signs of death derived from the Hippokratic corpus, which Thucydides did not employ.[349]

These are the most important problems directly arising from the sources. Many scholars have compounded these difficulties with an excessive desire for originality, feeling the need to come up with a new identification of the disease in question, often on the basis of the flimsiest evidence, frequently basing the identification on one symptom alone, or alternatively choosing to ignore the absence of references to the most prominent features of the suggested identification. (Only a selection of relevant literature is given in the bibliography.) The suggestion that bubonic plague was responsible falls squarely into the latter category, given that Thucydides does not mention the unmistakable buboes, which occur in most outbreaks of bubonic plague. The hypothesis that measles was responsible, which is based largely on the supposed tendency of victims of this disease to throw themselves into pools of water to relieve the fever during an epidemic in Fiji in 1875, is an example of the former category. It is hardly a feature of measles today in Britain, or even in developing countries where measles is still a major killer of children. The thirst mentioned by Thucydides was a consequence of the intense summer heat as much as of the disease. His failure to describe its characteristic skin rash is the main objection to measles. The vesicular rash predominantly found on the extremities of the body which he does mention is characteristic of smallpox.

The two Littmans (1969) rightly stressed that we must consider the overall description of the disease, and not rely on one symptom to the exclusion of all the other available information. For example, according to Dixon (1962) smallpox may be confused with influenza, scarlet fever and enteric fever in its initial stages, with measles and rubella in the erythematous phase, and with chickenpox in the vesicular and pustular phase of the disease. (Only enteric fever and chickenpox are securely identified elsewhere in ancient sources.) It is only by considering the *whole* course of the disease that a differential diagnosis is possible (in the absence of modern techniques of laboratory analysis). Even then it may be difficult, because fulminating smallpox for example, the most dangerous type of smallpox, has no completely characteristic features to differentiate it from other hyper-acute infections.[350]

We shall content ourselves here with subscribing to the best suggestion made by earlier scholars, namely smallpox. Willan (1821), a learned work little known to ancient historians which is still well worth consulting, discussed the evidence for smallpox in classical antiquity in detail, subjecting Galen in particular to thorough scrutiny. His analysis and conclusions are superior to those of many of the numerous articles relating to the problem which were published in the subsequent 170 years or so. Littré, whose comments on the epidemic in his monumental edition of the Hippokratic corpus are still of interest, noted its similarity to smallpox later in the last century. The resemblance was also noted by Kobert-Rostock (1899, although he mistakenly implicated ergotism as well), Zinsser (1935) and Ebbell (1967), for example. More recently, the two Littmans (1969) considered the parallels between the epidemic and smallpox in great detail. Their convincing arguments will not be repeated here to save space. The conclusion of Littman (1973), namely that the great epidemic in the Roman empire in the second century AD was caused by smallpox, is also accepted here without further discussion.[351]

However, it is worth answering the objections to smallpox that have been made by other scholars. Longrigg (1980) noted that Thucydides does not mention the facial pockmarks. These only appear a few weeks *after* the end of the illness in survivors, in cases of *Variola major*, and so play no role in prognosis. Alivizatos (1950) argued that the Greek word *helkos* originally contained the implication of tissue scarring within its semantic field. Thucydides did not need to mention the pockmarks explicitly. In addition it may be relevant to note that modern Greek peasants tended to refrain from talking about the pockmarks produced by smallpox, before its eradication, because they were felt to be a mark of shame.

Thucydides mentions the symptom in some cases of 'gangrene' of the limbs and extremities. This has been seized upon by advocates of typhus as the cause of the epidemic. However, it is sufficient for now to answer this hypothesis with the conclusion of the expert on typhus, Hans Zinsser, that the symptoms as a whole of the disease do not match those of typhus (see below). In addition there is a perfectly straightforward explanation in terms of smallpox for the statement of Thucydides. Before the advent of antibiotics secondary bacterial infections of the skin lesions created by the centrifugal vesicular rash of smallpox occurred frequently. (Such lesions and secondary infections do not occur in the case of influenza, explaining why the arguments of Langmuir et al. (1985) are much weaker.) As a result even septic complications occurred not only in cases of *Variola major* but even sometimes in cases of *Variola minor*. Page (1953) objected to smallpox because Thucydides does not mention the 'characteristic' backache. However, this is not a regular symptom of smallpox according to Dixon (1962), the most detailed modern treatment of the disease. Thucydides' failure to mention backache in fact would militate as much against typhus as it would against smallpox.

Holladay & Poole (1979) came up with two more objections to smallpox. First, they claimed that Thucydides states that dogs and birds that eat carrion were killed by the disease, and inferred that the disease could not have been smallpox because it does not infect such animals. Thucydides' statement that such animals died is an inference from the observation that they kept away from the corpses of the dead and forsook human company during the epidemic. To anyone who has ever seen even a photograph of a person who has died from severe smallpox, when large parts of the body may become quite black, dogs can hardly be blamed for not fancying such a meal. The sickly smell probably helps to put off dogs, which have a much finer sense of smell than humans. In the last century 'some members of a cannibalistic East African tribe drew the line at eating persons who had died of smallpox', although other members of the tribe did not. It will be argued later on that comments such as those of Thucydides on the relationship of animal and human diseases depended on an a priori belief which is not supported by modern research and so should be completely disregarded wherever they occur in attempting identifications of diseases found in ancient sources.[352]

The second objection of Holladay & Poole refers to the aspects of the epidemic in which we are most interested here, namely its epidemiology and consequences for human demography. It will be argued that the demography of the epidemic fits smallpox very well, strengthening the case presented by the Littmans and the other scholars mentioned earlier. Before concentrating on demography, it is worth reiterating the conclusion reached by the two Littmans, namely that the overall description of the disease resembles smallpox much more closely than it resembles any other known disease, despite the possible objections listed in the previous three paragraphs. Holladay & Poole asserted that the Athenian epidemic, which produced mortality rates of 25-35 per cent among young adult males, could not have been smallpox because in recent times in Europe 85-90 per cent of the deaths in smallpox epidemics occurred in children under the age of five.

The error here is to confuse a situation in which a disease is endemic with a 'virgin-soil' epidemic, in which a disease strikes a population with no recent previous experience of it. In the former case, as in early modern Europe for example, most adults had contracted the disease in childhood, and most of those who survived were immune for the rest of their lives, with the result that the disease was confined mainly to children in practice. This is true of the classic density-dependent viral diseases such as smallpox and measles, but does not apply to chronic bacterial diseases such as leprosy and tuberculosis, nor to the viruses of the herpes family, for the reasons mentioned earlier. However, when smallpox or measles strikes a population with no immediate previous experience of the disease, as in the well documented cases of the epidemics among Amerindians after European contact with the Americas, all age groups are vulnerable, not just children, and very high mortality rates are quite possible in all age groups.

Even measles, which is less dangerous than smallpox, produced a case mortality rate of 27 per cent among those individuals who did not receive medical treatment during a virgin-soil epidemic among a tribe of Indians in Brazil in 1954, contradicting the opinion of Holladay & Poole on the mortality caused by measles. Diseases like measles, smallpox and typhus all tend to be more severe in early adulthood than in childhood because the body's immune system is at its most vigorous then and tends to overreact to attacks. On average smallpox has a case mortality rate of about 30 per cent in an unvaccinated population, averaged across all age groups. For example, a well documented 'virgin soil' epidemic in a village in Japan in AD 1795 produced a morbidity rate of 85.7 per cent with a case fatality rate of 38.3 per cent.[353]

In antiquity in the great epidemics that may be identified as smallpox, namely the epidemic of Athens during the Peloponnesian War and the Antonine epidemic in the time of Marcus Aurelius, large numbers of adults were infected and died. This also applies to the first epidemic in Europe which is widely accepted as having been caused by smallpox, namely the one which struck Gaul in AD 570. The implication is that in all these cases, immediately prior to the outbreak of the epidemic, the disease was not endemic in the population under attack, because if it had been most adults would have been immune as a result of having contracted the disease earlier in life during childhood.

The first undoubted description of *endemic* smallpox in western Eurasia was given by the celebrated Arab physician Rhazes *c.* AD 900. (It is also clearly attested in Chinese sources contemporaneous with the Late Roman Empire.) He also gave the first unequivocal description of measles, accurately differentiating it from smallpox. According to Rhazes smallpox was characteristically a disease of childhood and was seldom caught by adults. He believed that contracting it was inevitable. This situation prevailed in the Middle East from the time of Rhazes until smallpox was eradicated. As Rhazes used older sources, going back to

Aaron of Alexandria who described a smallpox epidemic in that city in AD 622, endemic smallpox in the Middle East may be traced back to the seventh century AD. Galen recognised the disease described by Thucydides as identical with the disease responsible for the Antonine epidemic in the second century AD, and Rhazes in turn recognised the disease responsible for the Antonine epidemic as smallpox.[354]

In passing, attention should be drawn to another mistake made by Holladay & Poole (1979). They asserted that natural smallpox *always* produces lifelong immunity and never strikes a second time, although immunity following vaccination is less certain. Consequently they used Thucydides' statement that second attacks were never fatal when they occurred as another objection to identifying smallpox as the disease responsible for the epidemic in 430 BC. However, the standard modern textbook accounts of smallpox, which Holladay & Poole do not appear to have consulted, state that second attacks of natural smallpox did occur with a low frequency, in about 1 out of every 1,000 cases, although contradictory opinions have been expressed regarding the case mortality rates of second attacks. The frequency of second attacks may have been rather higher than this in practice. Many second attacks may not have been recognised for what they were, partly because of the mildness of many of them, and partly because a mild first attack might have been mistaken for another disease. The mediaeval Arab doctors such as Rhazes and Avicenna believed that second and even third attacks of smallpox were possible.[355]

The epidemiology of the Littmans also leaves something to be desired. The (1984) article propounds a theory that epidemics somehow recur at intervals of thirty or forty years, in order to account for the temporal gap between the epidemic at Athens in 430-427 BC and that at Syracuse in 396 BC. In fact a density-dependent disease is either endemic or it isn't. (Fluctuations in frequency may occur when it is endemic, caused by deterministic chaos, for example, but that does not affect the point at issue here.) If it is endemic then the situation is like that described by Rhazes, in which there is a significant mortality rate among young children all the time, but no great epidemics among adults. (Phenomena such as migration from the countryside to towns – i.e. from areas of low population density to areas of high population density, discussed further below, may complicate the issue.) If the prey population is too small for the disease to become endemic after its introduction, then it will die out. Afterwards the human population is free from the disease until it happens to be reintroduced from outside. This was the state of affairs in antiquity. Ideally it should be possible to express the chances of smallpox's becoming endemic in purely mathematical terms, by using the known demographic characteristics of smallpox and humans to estimate the average survival time before extinction of an immigrant population of smallpox, as a measure of the probability of success of smallpox as a colonising species.

Such an exercise might be very interesting in relation to estimates of human population sizes in antiquity. The population of the Roman empire was small relative to European populations in more recent times in which diseases like smallpox and measles were endemic. A minor but interesting detail here is that the literature on infant feeding of early modern Europe recommended that wet-nurses who had not had smallpox and measles themselves should not be considered for employment. There were no such prescriptions in antiquity, even though in other respects the infant feeding literature of early modern Europe was modelled on Soranos and other classical sources.[356]

If we were to accept low estimates of population sizes, like J.C. Russell (1985), even imperial Rome might have had difficulty maintaining density-dependent diseases in the long run. The same would be true of Constantinople in the Byzantine period according to the conclusions of Bratton (1981). The sizes of the populations of Alexandria, Antioch and Carthage are equally uncertain, but it is possible that there was not a single city in the Roman empire with a large enough population to sustain by itself density-dependent diseases permanently. Of course classical Athens could not do so either. The *epidemic* character of smallpox in classical antiquity is to be explained in terms of human population sizes. The cities of the Graeco-Roman world were large enough for epidemics to occur if a density-dependent disease were introduced from outside, but not large enough for it subsequently to become endemic. The fact that density-dependent diseases like smallpox and measles were not endemic in classical Athens is another nail in the coffin of the ridiculously inflated estimate of the size of the population of Athens made by Gernet (1909).

The difficulty of making themselves endemic encountered by density-dependent diseases in the Graeco-Roman world had the consequence that the Greeks and Romans, not having acquired immunity as a result of experiencing such diseases in childhood in most periods of ancient history, did not have any biological weapons which could be used against other peoples with whom they came into contact. Charles Darwin made the profound observation that the barbarians did not melt away when they came into contact with the Greeks and Romans in the way that the inhabitants of the Americas and Oceania did when they encountered European colonists in the early modern period, a story described well by McNeill (1976) and Crosby (1986). In other words the Romans had no biological answer to the expanding waves of barbarian tribes of pastoralists created by cyclical population movements in Eurasia. This is an important aspect of the history of the decline and fall of the Roman empire.[357]

The analysis presented here is strengthened if we turn to consider the only definition of an epidemic in purely quantitative terms that is extant from antiquity. In the Jewish Mishnah an epidemic is defined as occurring when three deaths occur in the space of three successive days in a population of five hundred adult males. Obviously such an event would be a minor affair, except for the three unfortunate individuals. The major density-dependent diseases could not survive for long in such a small population. This picture of small-scale epidemics is equally valid for classical Greece, where the epidemics of various diseases mentioned by the authors of the Hippokratic corpus as having occurred in various communities in northern Greece were not big enough to leave any mark on the mainstream historical record as portrayed by Thucydides, Xenophon and Diodoros. The Black Death in AD 1347-1348 or the epidemic in Athens in 430-427 BC are scarcely measurable on the same scale. It is an unavoidable conclusion that the mortalities in the legendary epidemics in the Old Testament are enormously exaggerated so as to correspond to the population sizes recorded there, which are generally regarded by Biblical scholars as hugely inflated (see section 2 above).[358]

The point of the discussion in the preceding paragraphs is to emphasise how exceptional the epidemic of 430 BC in Athens was and why it was exceptional. Thucydides indeed states that the same disease had earlier been recorded on Lemnos and elsewhere. However, it could not conceivably have been endemic in such a small population. We must conclude that Thucydides had in mind a short-lived epidemic arising from an unsuccessful attempt at colonisation of Lemnos on the part of smallpox. He did not have a Greek name available for the new disease. In modern Greek smallpox is called *eulogia*, a euphemism which has no antecedents in ancient Greek, at least in that particular sense. Thucydides states that the disease first appeared in the Piraeus, presumably having arrived by sea.

According to Thucydides the epidemic commenced in 'Ethiopia', probably a reference to sub-Saharan Africa in general. It then ravaged Egypt and most of the Persian empire before spreading to Greece. In this connection it may be relevant to note that east Africa was the last region of the world in which smallpox remained endemic before its recent eradication. The evolution of smallpox is shrouded in obscurity, but monkeypox in tropical Africa appears to be its closest relative, although the relationship is not very close. Smallpox may have evolved in sub-Saharan Africa and then spread to Egypt in the Bronze Age, before the Sahara became desiccated, and from east Africa across the Indian Ocean to India. Dupont (1984) poured scorn on historians who accept the reference to 'Ethiopia', on the grounds that the explanation of the origin of the disease in a hot southerly region was merely an a priori hypothesis based on Greek ideas about the types of climatic conditions and geographical environments that favoured particular diseases. Clearly Lucretius in his treatment of the epidemic of Athens was influenced by such ideas, which characterise the Hippokratic treatise *Airs, waters, places*, for example.

However, Thucydides had no precedent for such an event. There is no good reason for doubting his statement, even though scepticism may be in order regarding later historians who took Thucydides as their model and located the origin of other epidemics in 'Ethiopia'. The information about 'Ethiopia' is presented as hearsay. There was probably little or no reliable information available in Athens about what was going on in Ethiopia. However, there was extensive contact between the Greek world and not only the periphery but also the very heart of the Persian empire, as shown by the Persepolis fortification tablets. Consequently there is no reason for disbelieving the information that Egypt and most of the rest of the Persian empire were affected by the epidemic. Egypt was the most densely populated part of the Mediterranean in antiquity and so was the most probable region for epidemics of density-dependent diseases to commence and then spread to other areas. She was already playing this role in the Late Bronze Age, as we have seen, and doubtless continued to do so in the first millennium BC. Evidence has been adduced from studies of skin lesions on mummies and from the second-millennium Ebers papyrus in support of the hypothesis that smallpox existed in Pharaonic Egypt.[359]

Littré was right to stress the magnitude of the geographical area affected by the epidemic because it allows us to rule out most of the identifications of the disease suggested by modern scholars. For example, typhoid fever, which is contracted from infected sources of water or food and is not contagious, may be ruled out immediately, as may diseases such as typhus and tularaemia which depend on arthropod vectors and consequently do not produce epidemics spanning such enormous geographical areas. Only diseases transmitted directly from person to person principally by the respiratory route (mainly inhalation from face-to-face contact) such as smallpox, measles, influenza, chickenpox, and pneumonic plague (active in some parts of Europe in the initial stages of the Black Death) are capable of simultaneous activity stretching across such huge areas.

It is probable, as was suggested long ago, that the epidemic of 430 was carried by sea further west. At Rome the whole period 437-427 BC was dominated by severe epidemics. Unfortunately the chronology of the period is uncertain because different sources assign different lengths to a period of anarchy in the 370s BC. Severe skin pain is cited as a characteristic symptom, compatible with smallpox and fitting the descriptions of Thucydides and Diodoros on the disease in Greece. Livy preserves the detail that the Romans dedicated a temple to Apollo at this time, recalling the contemporaneous Athenian appeal to Apollo recorded by Pausanias. Thus the migrations of smallpox *c.* 430 BC fit into the general pattern of east to west movements of populations emphasised in this book. It subsequently became extinct again in Greece and Italy because what was left of the Athenian and Roman populations was not large enough to maintain it endemically as a disease of childhood. A fortiori smaller urban centres could not sustain it either.[360]

This failed attempt to colonise the Mediterranean was a forerunner of the Antonine epidemic of smallpox, which commenced in Mesopotamia and was transported by the luckless soldiers of the Roman army to Gaul in the second century AD, striking both Athens and Rome again along the way (see Chapter I above). The Antonine epidemic is badly documented. However, Galen was sufficiently impressed by the danger to leave Rome, an act which cannot have done his reputation as a doctor any good, while the author of the *Scriptores Historiae Augustae*, unfortunately not the most reliable of sources, speaks of the dead being carted away in wagonloads. Imprecise as this may be, it nevertheless conveys a similar impression to Thucydides' description of the events of 430-427 BC at Athens, where many of the corpses did not receive formal burial according to the customary procedures.

The hypothesis may be ventured that these two colonising expeditions by smallpox were very similar to each other. Pliny offered the generalisation that great epidemics usually started in the south, probably meaning Egypt, and then moved westwards, always in summer, and never lasting for more than three months. Before leaving the Antonine epidemic, it is worth recalling Willan's (1821) suggestion that inoculation against smallpox was practised during a recrudescence of the Antonine epidemic in the reign of Commodus, and also during what would have been an earlier epidemic of smallpox, in the reign of Domitian. However, it was misunderstood by our source, Dio Cassius, because the technique of inoculation, employing live smallpox virus as it did (unlike vaccination in recent times which uses the related but harmless vaccinia virus), inevitably produced some fatalities. Dio Cassius suggests that intradermal inoculation of smallpox was attempted. This method was widely employed in the Ottoman empire in the Near East in the early modern period, while the nasal route was used in China instead. If correctly interpreted, these episodes would extend the history in Europe of inoculation and of understanding the idea of acquiring immunity artificially much further into the past than has generally been thought.[361]

It would be incorrect to speak of smallpox's exhibiting a cyclical population history in classical antiquity, because there was no intrinsic relationship between these two great epidemics in the sense in which it was argued in section 2 above that human population fluctuations in Greece constituted a roughly repetitive cycle. However, it is possible to state that such episodes of attempted colonisation would be likely to have occurred with a certain frequency and to have had a certain probability of success or failure. In these probabilistic terms it would be legitimate to interpret the two great epidemics as expressions of a single pattern.

It is not certain if smallpox succeeded in establishing itself in the Mediterranean in the second century AD, as it is impossible to identify the epidemic described by Cyprian in the third century AD, which is said to have caused many deaths in the cities of the Roman province of Achaia in Greece. However, recent archaeological survey data suggest that the population of Italy, for example, collapsed at the end of the Roman empire (cause or effect?) in much the same way that the population of Greece collapsed at the end of the Mycenaean period. The consequent reduction in the division of labour and the disappearance of craft specialisation were marked in both cases in exactly the same way by the reappearance of handmade pottery on archaeological sites after long periods during which wheeled ware had been manufactured. In the sixth century AD Italy was very thinly populated, creating unfavourable conditions for density-dependent diseases. When smallpox reappeared in Italy in the early mediaeval period it once again had an epidemic character. It was probably not until the mediaeval period that smallpox became truly endemic in western Europe. The aim of this population history of smallpox in antiquity is to show how in ecological terms it behaved as a predator that was entirely dependent on the availability of its prey, which for other reasons (deterministic chaos?) was fluctuating around the critical population density required for the predator to establish itself permanently. This analysis is very different from the conclusions of McNeill (1976) concerning the role of diseases in human history.[362]

It is necessary to focus now on the epidemic of 430 BC to consider in more detail the demographic consequences of an epidemic. Thucydides states that the epidemic spread from the Piraeus to Athens, where it had its worst effects. Elsewhere, he adds, it caused the most serious damage in the most densely populated places. The standard commentary on Thucydides took this to refer to other parts of the Athenian empire, such as Chios, Ephesos and Byzantion. However, it may well refer to the largest demes in Attica apart from the urban demes, e.g. Eleusis. In any case it was evidently a density-dependent disease. The critical population size required for smallpox to become endemic is smaller than that required for measles, because smallpox remains infectious in a patient for longer than measles does, but it is nevertheless still substantial, of the order of 200,000.

Thucydides states that the epidemic was exacerbated by the crowding of refugees from outlying parts of Attica into Athens, to avoid the Spartan invasion. There were no houses available for the refugees, who had to live in crowded huts within the Long Walls and suffered more severely from the disease. There was a very striking parallel for this pattern of development of an epidemic in modern Athens. In 1927/8, when it was crowded with Greek refugees from Turkey, an epidemic of dengue occurred which infected about 90 per cent of the population. It is transmitted by the *Aedes aegypti* mosquito, which is abundant in modern Athens. However, the mortality rate was low, because dengue is a mild disease among children, although occasionally severe in adulthood. Moreover it has the virtue of giving cross-protection against the much more dangerous yellow fever. There were similar epidemics of dengue in Athens in the nineteenth century.[363]

The differential vulnerability of the permanent residents of Athens and of the temporary refugees in 430 BC leads us on to the general problem of the reproduction of historical urban populations. In general large urban populations in the past were unable to reproduce themselves and depended on continuous immigration for their very survival. Some recent research has suggested that mortality is density-dependent even in modern primitive societies and in quite small nucleated settlements in historical populations. However, the whole question of density-dependent controls on populations of living organisms has been a thorny issue which has given rise to a lot of polemic in ecology during the last few decades. It remains an interesting question why urban populations had difficulty reproducing themselves in the past.[364]

The larger cities become, the dirtier and unhealthier they tend to become as well. It is clear that classical Athens had a waste disposal problem, because refuse collectors, *koprologoi*, existed who had the task of removing rubbish. They sold human manure to farmers for use as fertiliser (see Chapter III.12 below). Classical Athens may well have been better off than many cities in early modern Europe in possessing a mechanism for removing waste systematically. However, living standards and the healthiness of lifestyles undoubtedly varied along social class lines. Vries (1984) gave an interesting twist to the standard position concerning the inability of historical urban populations to reproduce themselves by linking the phenomenon to the frequently observed pattern of differences in vital rates according to social class. Even in modern Britain, in spite of the existence of the National Health Service, the lower classes have lower life expectancies than the upper class. Vries argued that permanent residents belonging to families which had long been established in cities did tend to reproduce themselves in the past, but that immigrants to the towns, who were usually poorer and had lower standards of living, did not reproduce themselves (see also section 1 above).

As far as antiquity is concerned, the description of Thucydides, showing that the refugees were particularly badly affected by the epidemic in 430, suggests that the Vries model of differential demographic performance according to permanency/duration of residence and standards of living in urban populations could also have applied to a town like Athens in antiquity. A fortiori it is probable that the situation was the same in Rome because of its greater size and the greater depth of social stratification in the Roman empire. However, it would be an error to neglect the effects of different levels of population density in town and countryside. In early modern England smallpox was endemic in London, but not in many rural areas. Consequently many individuals who were born in the countryside did not contract smallpox in childhood. If they

migrated to London in adulthood they were liable to catch the disease and
die as a result, while most of those born in London became infected in
childhood and the survivors were subsequently immune as adults. This is
how London was able to kill off large numbers of immigrants. It is a
mechanism which does not involve making any assumptions about the
relative prosperity of permanent residents of towns and migrants.
Similar density-dependent controls may be envisaged for large towns in
classical antiquity in relation to other diseases, for example tuberculosis,
even if smallpox was not endemic even in the largest urban centres.

It is worth noting here that great epidemics may create economic
prosperity for the survivors. The reduction in population size leads to an
increase in the amount of land available per caput, as happened at Albi as
a consequence of the Black Death. Perhaps a similar phenomenon in
Athens helps to explain the decision of the Athenians to accept the first
ever *eisphora* (or the first *eisphora*, a kind of tax, specifically of 200
talents, or the first *eisphora* in the war) in 428 BC. It is well known that
wage rates increased with the decrease in the labour supply caused by the
Black Death. After the great epidemic of bubonic plague at
Constantinople in the reign of Justinian in the sixth century AD the
emperor ordered the prices which had prevailed before the epidemic
started to be re-established. They had doubled or trebled in the space of
three years.[365]

The demographic consequences of the epidemic of 430 BC will now be
examined on the assumption that the disease was smallpox, in an
attempt to show that this assumption fits the circumstances of the
Athenian epidemic very neatly. The general level of mortality when
smallpox strikes a population with no previous experience of it is about 30
per cent, averaged across all age groups. Thucydides states that 1050 out
of the 4000 hoplites in the Athenian army besieging Potidaia perished
after the disease had arrived by sea with reinforcements from Athens, i.e.
about 26 per cent. In all the Athenians lost 4,700 men as a result of the
disease out of their total first-line hoplite and cavalry strength of 14,000,
i.e. about 34 per cent, in the three years 430-427 BC. These data apply to
young adult males.

Thucydides describes malignant confluent (or early haemorrhagic-
type) smallpox, the second most severe type, characterised by the
appearance of vesicles from the fifth day of the disease onwards, with
death frequently occurring from about the sixth day onwards. The main
cause of death may be heart failure, rather than haemorrhages. In
fulminating smallpox, the most dangerous kind, the disease runs its
course until death occurs in four or five days at the most, not allowing
enough time for the vesicular eruption to appear. All the different kinds
of smallpox tend to occur together in the same epidemic, but Thucydides'
description suggests that malignant confluent smallpox was the most
frequent kind. The case mortality rate of malignant confluent smallpox is

about 70-80 per cent. The fact that the Athenian army was able to continue the siege of Potidaia shows that many of the soldiers did not contract the disease at all. In fact smallpox is not the most infectious of diseases, being considerably less infectious than measles and chickenpox. Although almost all members of a population will probably contract it eventually after repeated contact with infectious cases, the chances of picking it up from contact with one infectious case are only about 50 per cent, even if resident in the same household.[366]

The general estimate of 30 per cent mortality across a whole population varies when the population is broken down into age groups. The breakdown is given in the accompanying note. The Athenian soldiers at Potidaia undoubtedly fared relatively well, because smallpox achieves higher mortality rates among infants and older adults than among young adults. In this respect it is similar to many other diseases, but not tuberculosis and venereal diseases which predominantly strike the most sexually active age groups. Children and teenagers aged 5-19 are the least vulnerable age group, while mortality in the age groups 20-29 (the cream of the Athenian army) is estimated by modern medical authorities at 35 per cent.[367]

Thucydides does not tell us anything at all about the groups who should have suffered the highest mortality rates in the epidemic, namely pregnant women, unborn foetuses and infants. More than anything else, this shows how incomplete his account of the great epidemic is. Smallpox, like other diseases, was more dangerous to pregnant women than it was to anyone else (see section 3 above), and the most severe forms of smallpox occurred most frequently in pregnant women. Even if the pregnant woman avoided death, abortion of the foetus was likely. About 75 per cent of all pregnancies in which smallpox was contracted in the first few weeks terminated with miscarriage, while about 60 per cent of pregnancies in which the disease was contracted after the foetus had become viable ended the same way. The prospects for infants were not good either if they contracted smallpox after birth, although transmission of smallpox to the foetus *in utero* was relatively rare.

In the years 430-427 BC the live birth rate should have been depressed and the mortality rate of those infants who were born alive should have been abnormally high. When the male half of the cohorts born in those years reached the age of majority, in the years 412-409 BC, and became eligible for military service, the number of new soldiers becoming available annually was sharply reduced. This probably accounts for the *oliganthrôpia*, manpower shortage, of Athens in the closing stages of the Peloponnesian War as much as the casualties during the Syracusan expedition in 415-413 BC.

However, before this decline set in, the Athenian hoplite strength had experienced a temporary resurgence. Thucydides tells us that the Athenian 'population', i.e. adult males eligible for military service, had *recovered* by the time of the debates concerning the proposal to send an expedition to Sicily. This was why the younger Athenians at least (see section 5 above) were confident that they had the strength necessary to make the expedition a success, and it might well have been a success if the fumbling and superstitious Nikias had not been in command. Anyone who was eligible for military service abroad in 415 BC was at least twenty years old, as ephebes (probably *peripoloi* in the fifth century BC) aged 18-19 only served within the borders of Attica. Accordingly the Athenians who were enthusiastic about the Syracusan expedition were at least five years old when the epidemic started in 430 BC. The key to understanding this situation lies in the fact that in smallpox epidemics it is the age groups 5-19 which suffer the lowest mortality rates. Those Athenians who were 5-19 years old in 430 BC were 20-34 years old in 415 BC and provided the main manpower resources of the Athenian armed forces then. That is how Athenian military strength appeared to Thucydides to have made a recovery relative to the situation after the 34 per cent mortality among all those classified as hoplites in 430-427 BC.

Comparative evidence from more recent times suggests that populations which have suffered a sudden catastrophe do tend to recover rapidly, within a couple of generations. (Section 5 above explained why Sparta was an exception to this rule.) Thus the birth rate probably did accelerate from 426 BC onwards, especially since mortality among girls aged 5-15 in 430 BC should have been relatively low, although there is no explicit evidence. Thucydides may have had in mind children as well when he said that the Athenian population had recovered by 415 BC. However, this would not have been reflected in the size of cohorts reaching the age of liability to external military service until 406 BC at the earliest, by which time the Athenians were almost exhausted, after the condemnation of the generals who won the battle of Arginousai. Smallpox damages the male reproductive organs in survivors in some cases, reducing fertility. This factor may have delayed the recovery.[368]

William McNeill suggested that the Athenians never recovered from the great epidemic. This was not the opinion of Thucydides, although his account requires nuancing to take account of distortions in the age structure of the population created by the epidemic. Pausanias was the end point of one strand of historical tradition, perhaps ultimately starting with Ephoros and the Oxyrhynchus Historian, which did emphasise long-term effects of the great epidemic stretching even into the Hellenistic period. Pausanias thought that the growth of the Achaian League in the Early Hellenistic period was to be explained in terms of its having suffered less from the epidemic and from wars than any other part of Greece (see section 2 above). When Thucydides states that the epidemic had no noteworthy effects in the Peloponnese, this does not mean that the disease was not introduced there. It simply indicates that the population density of the Peloponnese was in general too low for an epidemic to arise from the introduction of infectious cases, as predicted by the Threshold Theorem of MacKendrick & Kermack.

Pausanias also states that the Athenians cited the disastrous effects of the epidemic as a reason for refusing to provide a military contingent to join Agesilaos' expedition to Asia Minor in 396 BC. However, that was probably merely a convenient excuse to evade a duty which the Athenians wished to evade anyway. The numerous Athenian colonies and cleruchies in the second and third quarters of the fourth century BC suggest that Attica was once again overflowing with people, although the population that could be fed without an empire was naturally smaller.

It is a principle of demography that stable (i.e. having constant but not necessarily identical birth and death rates) human populations exhibit the property of weak ergodicity, i.e. they tend to forget historical perturbations of their age structures. This always happens within little more than a century at the most. Moreover it occurred faster in historical populations with high fertility and low life expectancy at birth than it does in the populations of developed countries today. It is unlikely that the age structure of the Athenian population in the age of Demosthenes still displayed any particular characteristics that could be said to have been caused directly by the epidemic. Smallpox became extinct in Greece after the second phase of the epidemic in Athens in 427 BC, since it was not mentioned subsequently by Thucydides nor by any fourth-century writer. Thucydides states that there were two phases, the first lasting for two years and the second for one year, but the disease was present continuously in Athens during the short interval between them.[369]

Before taking our leave of the great epidemic of Athens the evidence of Diodoros Siculus must be considered (see also section 2 above). He emphasised the very heavy rainfall in the previous winter (cf. the heavy rainfall in winter 432/1 BC during the Theban attack on Plataia). His account presumably refers to the first phase (the mortality figures refer to the whole epidemic), even though it is attached to the second phase in the extant text. The rainfall produced poor quality crops and bad food. Moreover the Spartans and their allies had invaded Attica to destroy the crops at the time when the epidemic started. Diodoros' ultimate source thought that malnutrition played an important role in the aetiology of the epidemic. This is not implausible in the case of some diseases, for example outbreaks of enteric diseases associated with subsistence crises. Little is known about the effects of malnutrition in conjunction with smallpox, but it may have little bearing on the course of the disease among adults. However, some of the complications of smallpox, particularly with respect to the eyes, in children may be aggravated by malnutrition (vitamin A deficiency). Thucydides states that the strong suffered as much as the weak during the epidemic. Diodoros' explanation, which was influenced by the kind of thinking which lies behind the Hippokratic corpus, is wrong in this particular case. The occurrence of a bad harvest and a 'virgin soil' epidemic in the same year was coincidental, although it compounded the problems faced by the Athenians. The evidence of Diodoros tells us more about the a priori intellectual reasoning of the Greeks than it does about the causes of the great epidemic. He also states that the etesian (north-east) winds failed to blow, thus explaining the excessive heat which led those who contracted the disease to throw themselves into water. Thucydides does not explain why it was so hot. Smallpox prefers dry rather than humid air. Like many other diseases its transmissibility is affected significantly by seasonal conditions. This is where the evidence provided by Diodoros may help us to understand the spread of the epidemic.[370]

The ecology of smallpox in antiquity has been portrayed here as that of a predator entirely dependent on the abundance of its prey. Of course relations between a disease and its human prey can be much more complicated than this. Thucydides wrote his account of the great epidemic to enable men to recognise it if it should return in the future and be forewarned regarding its likely consequences. This shows some of his limitations as a thinker because he did not consider the possibility that Greek 'society' (a concept which he did not possess) might undergo significant changes in the future, nor the possibility that the impact of a new disease may depend not only on the nature of the disease but also on the character of the society attacked.

For example, Thucydides maintained that smallpox undermined the fabric of society in Athens because people turned to crime as it became apparent that law-abiding citizens were as liable to perish as the lawless. However AIDS today may be having the effect of pushing social *mores* among certain high-risk groups in the United States, for example, in what might be regarded loosely as a more 'conservative' direction, in terms of motivating a reduction in the average number of sexual partners per person. It is by no means inevitable that a new 'plague' will undermine rather than strengthen the fabric of a society, and so there is no general lesson to be learnt from Thucydides' account of the effects of smallpox in Athens in 430 BC. This exemplifies the difficulties faced by any historian who operates with the same explicit purpose as Thucydides did.[371]

It is necessary to focus now on another factor which complicates the relationship between diseases and human populations, namely the possibility of evolutionary variations in the organisms responsible for the diseases. The AIDS retrovirus mutates rapidly because its mechanism of genetic reproduction, relying on RNA rather than DNA as in most other living organisms, is relatively inefficient at reproducing itself accurately. Influenza evolves rapidly by means of genetic recombinations of human and animal influenza viruses, an attribute which helps to defeat vaccination as a preventive measure, as well as acquired immunity after one infection. Smallpox existed in strains of differing virulence. Besides fulminating smallpox and malignant confluent smallpox, which we have already encountered, Dixon (1962) described seven other types of *Variola major*, all with substantially lower mortality rates. (These different types are partly the expression of the host's reaction to the disease, and are not just caused by different strains of virus.) In addition *Variola minor*, a rather distinct virus that was rarely fatal, also existed until the eradication of smallpox from the world in the 1970s. However, all the strains of smallpox were antigenically similar, allowing vaccination to be uniformly effective. For a historian, it is instructive to take plague (*Yersinia pestis*) as an example of the possible consequences of evolution of micro-organisms. Plague did not cause any major epidemics in classical Greece. Nevertheless it was of paramount importance in late mediaeval and early modern Greece, and it is of such interest from a theoretical viewpoint that it is well worth devoting some space to it here.

Plague is primarily a disease of certain species of rodents, in which it is a childhood disease like endemic measles in humans. It also infects other species of rodents, especially rats, which are not so well adapted to it, and it is thought to come into contact with humans mainly through rat fleas, which seek new hosts when their rats die. The ecology of plague is more complicated than that of smallpox because it involves animal hosts and arthropod vectors. The absence of great plague epidemics in classical Greece may be explained at least partially in terms of the absence or scarcity of rats in classical Greece. Littré drew attention to passages in the Hippokratic corpus that may refer to plague, perhaps isolated cases arising from contact with rodents, but there is no evidence for any great epidemics of plague in classical Greece or Roman Italy.[372]

The question of the rat in classical times is shrouded in obscurity because of a grave shortage of palaeo-zoological research on classical archaeological sites which could provide a definitive answer to the problem. Literary sources only mention the word *mus*, which refers to mice of all kinds, both wild and domesticated. However, it is not clear if the same word designated rats as well in antiquity. It is hard to believe that the Greeks would not have differentiated between rats and mice if they had been familiar with both types of rodents, even though in zoological nomenclature the genus Mus encompassed both rats and mice until eighty years ago. The word *mus* is a Proto-Indo-European word which probably antedates the geographical dispersal of the two species of rats. Aelian gives a description of what sounds like *Rattus norvegicus* (the brown rat), swimming across rivers, but locates them in the region to the south of the Caspian Sea.

In recent archaeological excavations *Rattus rattus* (the black rat, although colour is not in fact a reliable criterion for differentiating the two species) is now well documented at Quseir el-Qadim on the Red Sea coast of Egypt, in London, and at Stobi in Macedonia in the early centuries AD. There is an unpublished claim of *R. rattus* in Pompeii dating to the second century BC. The earliest evidence for the larger and more ferocious *R. norvegicus* currently dates to the tenth century AD. Future excavations may force a revision of this statement. The two species of rats fit into the general pattern of post-glacial movements of populations into Europe from Asia that is one of the major themes of this book. *R. rattus* was a forest dweller by nature and so was absent from the steppes of Ice Age Europe. However it is a much more sedentary creature than *R. norvegicus*. *R. rattus* may have been introduced quite early here and there into the Graeco-Roman world from India, travelling on board ships, one of its favourite domains, but took a long time to expand its geographical range because of its innate behavioural tendencies. Grain is its favourite food, and it doubtless began to evolve into a parasite of man sometime after the development of agriculture in the Neolithic period. On balance the scarcity of evidence suggests that rats were not common in classical Greece. The cult of Apollo Smintheus has been thought to be associated with rats spreading plague, but Aelian's description of the animals involved could equally refer to field mice. It has been argued that the cult of Asklepios originated as a Proto-Indo-European cult associated with the mole, which in Greece was transferred to Apollo, and rodents in regions where moles do not occur.[373]

Another complication is introduced by the need to consider the ecology of other diseases associated with rats. Typhus stands out here, because its 'murine' form (*Rickettsia mooseri*), a mild disease as a zoonosis in humans ancestral to the much more dangerous epidemic typhus (*R. prowazeki*), is carried by rats, although it can also infect a wide range of other animals. Fleas act as the vectors of murine typhus, while epidemic typhus is transmitted by human lice and has no animal host, except flying squirrels in the USA. Some scholars have argued that epidemic typhus caused the great epidemic of Athens. 'Gangrene' is the main symptom described by Thucydides which points to typhus. However, its importance in the overall picture of typhus seems to have been overemphasised by the advocates of typhus as the cause of the Athenian epidemic, especially W. MacArthur, since the most recent description of typhus available to the present author merely allots gangrene of the extremities one sentence in a long description of the disease, commenting that it 'may occur'. Furthermore this symptom can be given a perfectly satisfactory explanation in the case of smallpox, as was explained earlier.

On the other hand, the most important features of typhus are either absent from Thucydides' account or are directly contradicted by what he says. This applies above all to its mental symptoms. It produces headache in the early stages as one of its most regular symptoms, followed by mental dullness and occasionally delirium in the acute stage, followed by stupor developing into coma in those cases (about 20 per cent) destined to end in death. Instead Thucydides noted restlessness and sleeplessness as symptoms, with temporary amnesia in the case of some survivors. He also observed diarrhoea in the later stages of the disease in some cases, but constipation is much commoner in typhus. Again in differential diagnosis the appearance and evolution of the rash distinguishes typhus from other diseases, but the (centrifugal) vesicular skin rash mentioned by Thucydides points to smallpox, not typhus. The environmental conditions at the time are also unfavourable to the hypothesis of typhus, which prefers cold climates and usually peaks in winter, while the Athenian epidemic began at the end of spring, a good time for smallpox, and continued into an unusually hot summer. The balance sheet compels rejection of the hypothesis that typhus caused the epidemic of Athens.

The evidence of Brill-Zinsser's disease suggests that epidemic typhus may be able to persist in the human body for many years in certain cases. This property suggests that epidemic typhus may after all have been an ancient disease adapted to small human populations, like the herpes viruses. On the other hand its severity in many cases for both man and the vector louse has suggested to several scholars that epidemic typhus must be of recent evolutionary origin. These lines of argument contradict each other. It is not clear which is correct. There is plenty of evidence that the ancient Greeks were infested with lice, which were regarded by Aristotle as generated spontaneously. Even Agesilaos was bitten by a louse while sacrificing to the gods. Nevertheless the presence of the louse in classical Athens does not prove that epidemic typhus caused the epidemic of 430 BC, even though epidemic typhus probably did exist in antiquity. If typhus had caused the epidemic of 430 BC, it would probably not have become extinct but instead persisted in the population to re-emerge years later as Brill-Zinsser's disease and cause further epidemics. However, no such epidemics are recorded in fifth- and fourth-century sources. In any case the existence of epidemic typhus in classical Greece would not prove that rats were present there as well.[374]

Unfortunately the question of whether the rat was present in classical Greece, even if it were to receive a conclusive answer, may not suffice to explain the ecology of plague there for two reasons. First, Biraben (1975) argued that plague is spread among humans predominantly by the human flea (*Pulex irritans*) and by human lice, rather than the rat flea (*Xenopsylla cheopis*). This thesis, which is extremely controversial among experts on plague, would mean, if correct, that plague epidemics need not be tied to the presence of large numbers of rats living in close proximity to humans. The arguments of Hirst (1953) in favour of the theory that *R. rattus* and its flea *X. cheopis* are of paramount importance in human plague rest on a large volume of practical experimentation and field observation performed during the fourth pandemic in Asia at a time when the aetiology and epidemiology of plague were beginning to be understood. In contrast Biraben's hypothesis that rats did not play an important role in historical pandemics is merely based on an *argumentum e silentio* of historical documents dating to earlier periods when nothing was known about the causes of plague or indeed other diseases. Consequently there is no particular reason why we should expect to find accurate information regarding the genesis of plague in those documents.

In order to carry conviction, Biraben would have to specify in detail the mistakes which he thinks were made in the experiments and fieldwork described by Hirst. As this has not been done, it seems better to accept that rats and rat fleas did play the major role in human plague epidemics, with human fleas playing a minor role, and to conclude that the apparent rarity of rats in the Mediterranean world in the first millennium BC, if it is confirmed by palaeo-zoological research which, will one hopes be carried out in the future, was a major reason for the absence in the first millennium BC of plague pandemics on the scale of the Black Death. However, the rat is not the only factor that we must consider, because there is now evidence for the importance of evolution of plague itself.

In order to approach this evidence it is necessary to consider briefly the historical ecology of plague. It has been argued that bubonic plague caused various epidemics mentioned in the Old Testament. However the Biblical descriptions are too poor to permit definite identification of the disease(s) in question, and the records of mortalities are enormous exaggerations. The earliest plague epidemics that are reasonably well documented took place in Libya, Egypt and Syria in the Hellenistic period. Rufus of Ephesos, an author of Roman times citing Dionysios the Hunchback, who lived in the third century BC, and Dioskorides and Poseidonios, two physicians of the first century BC, provides a clear-cut description of bubonic plague, characterised by buboes, inflammations of the lymphatic glands which appear in the groin more frequently than anywhere else. These epidemics did not spread very far and probably originated in the foci of endemic plague among other rodents which look like original hosts in Cyrenaica, Kurdistan and the Great Lakes region of East Africa.[375]

Thereafter there is no record of plague until the sixth century AD, when bubonic plague suddenly erupted and devastated the Middle East and Europe for about two centuries. Its distribution followed a coastal pattern, probably to be explained in terms of long-distance transport by fleas alone in merchandise as well as on rats on board ships, although it may be an artefact created by the lack of evidence for many inland regions. Procopius' account of its effects on Constantinople in the reign of Justinian is very well known. At around AD 750 plague disappeared rather suddenly from the whole area in which it had been active for two centuries. The suddenness of its disappearance was noted by contemporaries. The caliphs of the Abbasid dynasty, which happened to come to power in the Islamic world at about the same time that plague ceased to be active, exploited its contemporaneous disappearance for propaganda purposes as evidence of divine favour for their dynasty. It is only. very recently that modern scholarship has reached the point at which it is becoming possible to offer an alternative and rational explanation for this phenomenon.[376]

Thereafter plague is not documented for six centuries in Europe. It suddenly reappeared to cause the Black Death in AD 1348, depopulating many regions of Europe and Asia in the process. However, it should be remembered that the population of England, at least, had already begun to decline for other reasons before the Black Death. Plague then caused a series of major epidemics for about three centuries in western Europe. The last major epidemic in Britain was in AD 1665-6 in London and Eyam, after which plague suddenly disappeared in Britain, even though the last epidemic in Eyam was one of the worst of all well documented plague epidemics in Britain. In the Mediterranean and the Middle East, however, plague was endemic until well into the last century. In AD 1678, for example, it killed over a third of the population of Crete, while in AD 1822 it killed about a third of the population of Kea (ancient Keos) in Greece, one of the last major epidemics in Europe. Fleas are said to be sensitive to olive oil, a feature exploited in the past to try to prevent plague. However, the ubiquity of this commodity in Greece did not prevent several severe epidemics.

Recent research on the Ottoman empire has emphasised the importance of repeated plague epidemics as a mechanism for keeping the populations of the regions incorporated in the empire, including Greece, small. However, it was more a case of plague causing short-term setbacks unconnected to each other, after each of which the human population could start to increase again, than of a *constantly* working process of population regulation like that of the demographic systems of north-west Europe at the same time, in which fertility and mortality were integrally and constantly related to economic conditions (see section 6 above). By concentrating on increasing numbers and so maximising evolutionary fitness, rather than living longer, human populations in the past under natural fertility conditions were behaving in accordance with the Darwinian theory of evolution. At around AD 1830 plague started to vanish from the Ottoman empire, as always rather suddenly. The disappearance of plague should be added to the list of factors in section 2 above which facilitated rapid population growth in Greece in the last century. Its insignificance in archaic and classical Greece had the same effect.[377]

The fourth pandemic of plague commenced independently in east Asia in the second half of the last century and spread to various parts of the world. It was encountered by American soldiers in Vietnam, for example. In India plague is thought to have caused several million deaths in the first half of the twentieth century. From about 1950 onwards its frequency started to decline and from 1967 onwards not a single case of plague in humans has been recorded in India. This cannot be attributed to any action taken by the Indian government or to measures in preventive medicine. The sudden disappearance of human plague from India is as mysterious as its sudden disappearance in the Middle East *c.* AD 750 and in Britain after AD 1666, and probably also in north-east Africa in the Hellenistic period.

In general historians have attempted to get to grips with these problems in ways that do not carry conviction. Usually a particularistic approach is adopted in which circumstances unique to a particular region and period are employed to try to explain the disappearance of plague in that particular period and region. The power of humans to manipulate their environment in the past is taken for granted, even though they did not understand it. For example, it has been argued that quarantine measures played a very important role in the disappearance of plague in western Europe in the seventeenth century AD and in the Ottoman empire in the nineteenth century AD, while improvements in housebuilding and construction have also been emphasised. The idea is that the contact between rats and humans, and so the chain of infection, was broken when the latter started living in brick buildings rather than wooden buildings. Biraben (1975) and Post (1977) are two well-known scholars who have argued in favour of such theories forcefully and with a considerable amount of plausibility, the latter with reference to the Balkans in the nineteenth century.

However, theories of this genre are not completely satisfactory because they do not meet the requirements of logic, since they fail to account for the recurring nature of the phenomena under investigation, even though the quarantine theory may well be applicable on a local level in certain cases of plague epidemics. Plague declined in Asia at the same time that it declined over large areas of Europe towards the end of the third pandemic, but there is no evidence for significant improvements in house construction techniques in Asia at that time where many populations were still engaged in pastoralism. Nor have there been significant improvements in housing in India recently, nor are there known to have been any in the Middle East *c.* AD 750 or in classical antiquity.

The pandemics of plague resemble each other in the sense that they all started very suddenly, raged for quite a long time, and then were terminated as rapidly as they had commenced. They look like a cyclical phenomenon, which has been repeated several times, in which populations of plague with certain characteristics increased at a geometric rate once the population reached a certain density threshold, and then crashed equally rapidly when a critical density threshold was reached in a cyclical downturn. In the terms of the device in logic called Occam's razor, an economical explanation of the observed phenomena would have to be repeatable and so not intrinsically linked to circumstances which were unique to any particular geographical region or temporal period.

The makings of an economical explanation of the observed phenomena have begun to emerge from very recent research on plague and its close relatives among bacteria. It has been discovered that certain simple gene mutations may enormously increase or decrease the virulence of bacteria of the genus Yersinia. Research on myxomatosis and rabbits had earlier revealed that there is a trade-off between genetic factors creating virulence and genetic factors that favour transmissibility or infectivity (see Chapter I above). For example, a long period of infection in which the prey is still capable of moving around is more likely to lead to the propagation of the micro-organism to other hosts than a short period of infection leading to rapid death in which the prey cannot move. Thus natural selection in Australia has led to myxomatosis becoming less virulent during the last forty years. A similar phenomenon occurred in relation to smallpox in the last century or so of its existence, as *Variola minor* gradually spread at the expense of *Variola major*, at least partly because patients with mild smallpox were often mobile, facilitating the spread of the virus. Similarly a chance mutation to a highly virulent strain at a time when the prey population happens to be abundant may lead to the temporary evolutionary success of the virulent strain.

Plague itself possesses several different characteristics which create virulence. For example at least two of these permit plague to survive and multiply within phagocytes, while a third inhibits the growth of *Y. pseudotuberculosis*, a related species which gives cross-immunity to plague and by spreading in recent times is thought by some scholars to be connected to the decline of plague in Europe. However, it may in fact have been fluctuating in the past in the same way that plague itself did. *Y. pestis var. antiqua*, probably responsible for the epidemics described by Rufus, possesses the ability to reduce the nitrate ion to nitrite and to ferment glycerol, while *var. mediaevalis*, probably responsible for the Black Death, cannot reduce nitrate, and *var. orientalis*, definitely responsible for the twentieth-century pandemic, cannot ferment glycerol, an anti-freezing chemical that accumulates in the bodies of certain rodents during hibernation. These features are used to differentiate the three main varieties of plague in the laboratory.

Consequently the massive fluctuations of plague down the centuries will probably eventually receive a satisfactory and economical explanation in terms of its own evolution, a ceaseless and probably chaotic process of competition between highly virulent genotypes and easily transmitted or highly infectious genotypes. A corollary of such a theory will be that plague indeed was beyond human control in the past, and that was why it was so terrifying. We may be confident that plague will be active again in the future on a cyclical basis because it still flourishes in wildlife in various parts of the world.

Biraben noted that the virulence of plague among humans often drops substantially in the course of an epidemic, from about 80 per cent case mortality to 50 per cent or less. However, the explanation of this phenomenon was not yet available when he wrote his *magnum opus*. He was right to explain the cyclical recurrence of plague epidemics once every eleven or twelve years or so in France in the third pandemic as a distorted reflection of epidemics among the normal rodent hosts of plague in north-east Africa and the Middle East. Since plague is a density-dependent disease which probably had some difficulty penetrating regions of low human population density during the pandemics, it flourishes at cyclical peaks of the populations of its normal rodent hosts, and then overflows into populations of other species which are not normal hosts, such as rats and man. Elton (1925) argued that plague epidemics at rodent population maxima act as a means of population regulation among the normal rodent hosts. Later he revised his own conclusions, and today it seems more probable that plague as a predator merely tracks population fluctuations of its customary rodent hosts that are caused by deterministic chaos. Nevertheless it remains true that population fluctuations of small mammals in the eastern Mediterranean and Middle East are not merely of academic interest (see Chapters I & II.2 above), as they have been since the time of Aristotle and Theophrastos, but have been of fundamental importance in relation to human population history and the lives and deaths of very large numbers of people.[378]

These aspects of plague evolution and ecology, which account for its instability, provide other reasons, besides the one outlined at the beginning of this section, why diseases should not be invoked as a mechanism capable of permanently and continuously regulating human populations. Two modern examples of this phenomenon merit brief mentions. The classic variety of cholera, which caused great epidemics around the world in the nineteenth century, has been gradually displaced in the twentieth century by a competitor, the El Tor variety, with rather different characteristics. Over the last generation or so, *Staphylococcus aureus*, which causes most infections of wounds today and probably did so in antiquity as well, has exhibited cyclical fluctuations in abundance, and a remarkable mechanism has been proposed to explain this phenomenon. It appears that a continuous process of changing resistance and susceptibility to bacteriophages creates changes in the virulence of the staphylococcus towards man.

In the light of such phenomena, the ancient Greeks were fortunate to live during a period when plague was inactive, while Greeks from the sixth to the eighth and the fourteenth to the nineteenth centuries AD did not have such good fortune. Before leaving plague, it is worth noting how it is affected by climatic variations, which are particularly important in a highly seasonal environment like that of the Mediterranean, a topic to which we shall return shortly. Bubonic plague spreads in late summer as the vector flea requires heat and humidity to lead a long, thriving life, but pneumonic plague, which is spread by airborne droplet infection, is characteristic of cold northern countries, where the droplets have a longer lifespan. Most of the major epidemics of plague in Greek history were outbreaks of bubonic plague.[379]

From plague we move on to another disease that requires vectors and has also played a prominent role in Greek history, namely malaria. W.H.S. Jones collected the abundant source material for malaria in classical Greece and argued that the spread of malaria was responsible for the decline of Greek civilisation. His theory has attracted little favour among classical scholars not only because of Jones's primitive moralising tendencies but also because he invoked malaria as a *deus ex machina* to explain the decline of ancient Greece. The question 'why was malaria spreading in antiquity?' is a perfectly legitimate question for which Jones did not have an answer. The upshot of the eighty years of research since the publication of his books and articles is that it is now possible to give a convincing answer to that question. Nevertheless the hypothesis that malaria played a decisive role in Greek history is still open to question, as part of the theoretical debate mentioned at the beginning of this section.[380]

The ecology of the four different species of human malaria is linked inextricably to climatic conditions. Climatic instability in the lands around the Mediterranean in antiquity provides the mechanism for explaining the gradual spread of malaria in the past. The Hippokratic treatises emphasised the seasonality of the occurrence and frequency of diseases in classical Greece. Autumn was observed to be the most dangerous season of the year, because of the danger of malarial fevers and of tuberculosis. Spring was the healthiest season of the year, and 'fevers' were frequent in summer, but were not so dangerous as in the autumn. Not all fevers were caused by malaria. There are and were many other diseases of greater or lesser importance in the Mediterranean that cause fevers, including for example relapsing fever, undulant fever (brucellosis), dengue and leishmaniasis among important human diseases, as well as rare zoonoses such as three-day or sandfly fever, Mediterranean spotted fever, etc. However, there is no doubt that malaria was the commonest cause of diseases characterised by fevers (*puretoi*) in antiquity. Many passages in the Hippokratic corpus and later medical writers such as Galen clearly describe fevers recurring every two or three days that are characteristic of malaria.[381]

The highly seasonal climate of the Mediterranean influences the ecology of both the species of mosquito which act as vectors for malaria and the protozoan parasites themselves. There are very sharp differences in the size of mosquito populations from season to season. The research of Ross and Lotka, who were pioneers in the study of the mathematical epidemiology of malaria early in this century, showed that a certain mosquito population density is required before a malaria epidemic can start at all. A slight increase above that threshold is all that is needed for the frequency of malaria to increase dramatically. Only a handful of the large number of species of mosquito known to exist are efficient vectors of malaria. The main characteristics of an efficient vector are that the females of the species, the only ones to bite, habitually enter human dwellings and are not deviated from humans by the presence of alternative hosts such as domesticated animals.

In prehistory, before the development of agriculture and large permanent human settlements, man was presumably attacked by zoophilic species of mosquito. It is unlikely that species of mosquito which habitually enter human dwellings evolved before the Neolithic period, even though it is generally accepted that the hominids inherited malaria vertically as they evolved from their pre-human ancestors in Africa (see Chapter I above). The mode of transmission of malaria was not understood in antiquity. Aristotle observed the metamorphosis of mosquito larvae into the adult forms, but he did not have any inkling of the vast multiplicity of species of mosquito, each occupying a quite distinct ecological niche, which has been revealed by modern research and used to explain the observation that in many parts of the Mediterranean in the past large numbers of mosquitoes existed without a trace of malaria. Many of them were incapable of transmitting it efficiently. Indeed the ancient Greeks scarcely differentiated between mosquitoes and gnats.[382]

The low mosquito population density is not the only reason why the transmission of malaria is interrupted in winter in Greece. The parasites themselves require a certain temperature to develop, about 15°C in the case of vivax (benign tertian) malaria, caused by *Plasmodium vivax*, and about 19°C for falciparum (malignant tertian) malaria, caused by *P. falciparum*. Accordingly vivax malaria manifests itself in the summer, while falciparum malaria, which has a longer incubation period in addition to its higher temperature requirements for development, does not reach its peak frequency until the autumn in the Mediterranean. Vivax malaria has always been the most important species of malaria in the Mediterranean since the classical period because its lifecycle is better suited to a highly seasonal climate than falciparum malaria.

However, falciparum malaria is much the most dangerous species of malaria, because erythrocytes infected by *P. falciparum* parasites tend to cling to the walls of narrow blood vessels, thus avoiding the destruction of parasites that would follow passage through the spleen. Consequently it achieves higher population densities in the blood than the other species of malaria do. This explains why the autumn was the most dangerous season of the year in ancient Greece. If the autumn were unusually long, wet and hot the frequency of falciparum malaria would reach unusually high levels at the expense of the other species of malaria. The third species of human malaria, quartan malaria caused by *P. malariae*, is also found around the shores of the Mediterranean, but is not as frequent as vivax and falciparum malaria and is less dangerous. The fourth species (*P. ovale*) does not occur in the Mediterranean. The modern demography of the three species of malaria found in the Mediterranean exactly fits the situation described in the Hippokratic corpus.

The seasonal environment of the Mediterranean creates a distinctive epidemiology of malaria as far as humans are concerned. In those regions of Greece where it occurred in the past, malaria was generally hyperendemic, which means that 50-75 per cent of children and a high proportion of adults show clinical symptoms of malarial attacks such as splenomegaly (this is also a symptom of various other diseases). However, the interruption of malaria transmission in the winter and spring meant that the adult immunity to falciparum malaria found in tropical zones where it is holoendemic (100 per cent of children have enlarged spleens, while adults are not visibly affected) was not created in the Mediterranean, because immunity to falciparum malaria is short-lived and constant reinfection under holoendemic conditions is required to maintain it. Under such circumstances more adults than children may suffer from malaria, whereas in the tropics all those who survive childhood have become immune to falciparum malaria and show no symptoms of the disease for the rest of their lives. The Mediterranean climate prevents malaria from becoming yet another disease of childhood. Interannual climatic variability, doubtless assisted by deterministic chaos, generated periodic epidemics of malaria in the Mediterranean in the past, even where it was endemic.

The effects of malaria on adults explain its prominence in the Hippokratic corpus. In the tropics malaria is responsible for a substantial proportion of infant mortality, but does not have any effects on fertility. However, in the seasonal climate of the Mediterranean malaria may cause a reduction in sperm production in men as well as anaemia and pregnancy loss in women. Infants tend to be of below average weight at birth, a factor which predisposes towards a higher probability of infant mortality, because falciparum malaria parasites congregate in the placenta. The other species of malaria have less significant effects in this respect because they favour peripheral parts of the body. Malaria may also affect the growth of children and play a role in the development of protein energy malnutrition. Infection with malaria weakens the body's natural defence mechanisms against other diseases, for example food poisoning caused by salmonella.

Of course malaria may also kill non-immune adults, especially as a result of blackwater fever, a disease produced by *P. falciparum* which was frequent in Greece but infrequent in tropical regions where adults seldom visibly suffer from malaria. Littré (1872) concluded that Alexander the Great died from an attack of malaria at Babylon. However, the frequency of malaria in Macedonia itself in the fourth century BC is a matter of debate. All that need be said about this here is that the

Hippokratic corpus, a very large source which is strangely neglected by specialists on Macedonian history, shows that all three species of malaria were common in the *poleis* of northern Greece before Alexander's time. However, the vector mosquitoes may have been largely confined to the coast in that period. In the early modern period Macedonia and Epirus were the most heavily infected parts of Greece.[383]

This leads on to the problem of historical fluctuations in the incidence of malaria. Although the ecology of malaria in Greece in the fifth century BC was virtually identical to its ecology in recent times there are still very good reasons for thinking that the incidence of malaria has not been static in the course of history. Zulueta (1973) made the fundamental contribution towards answering the question that W.H.S. Jones failed to answer. The spread of malaria in the Mediterranean was made possible by the environmental changes that followed the end of the last glaciation. During the Ice Ages the most important vector of malaria in Greece in modern times, *Anopheles sacharovi*, could not have endured the cold, since it requires a temperature of 23-24°C in July. However, certain species of mosquito which transmitted vivax malaria in northern Europe in recent times may have existed in the Mediterranean during the Ice Ages. Nor could falciparum malaria itself have survived in southern Europe during the Ice Ages, although vivax and quartan malaria could have endured the cold.

At the end of the last glaciation at the latest, if not before, vivax malaria was driven out of its original home in western and central Africa by the evolution of human immunity and by the disappearance of highly seasonal environments in areas now occupied by tropical rain forest, which tilted the ecological balance in favour of *P. falciparum*. The connections between the various river drainage systems in the Sahara during the last pluvial period, following the end of the last glaciation, probably assisted the spread of the mosquito vectors of malaria, as well as the snails that carry schistosomiasis. Thereafter vivax malaria established its main place of residence in the Mediterranean. *P. falciparum* followed in its tracks, but more slowly, as the climate gradually changed in the direction of the modern Mediterranean climate. As recently as the late Neolithic period the summer in the Mediterranean was significantly cooler than it is today, a factor which impeded the spread of all species of malaria in southern Europe. Grmek, who attempted to criticise Zulueta on this point, wrote his book before the recent research in palaeoecology which reached this conclusion was published. The spread of malaria depended on the dispersal of the vector mosquitoes into the vacuum, a gradual process. Zulueta suggested that the coastal distribution of *A. sacharovi* and of *A. labranchiae*, the most important vector in the western Mediterranean, indicates that the mosquitoes moved around mainly by sea on board ships, from the Middle East in the case of *A. sacharovi* and North Africa in the case of *A. labranchiae*.[384]

The lack of evidence makes it impossible to delineate the chronology of the post-glacial diffusion of malaria in Europe in any detail. In the fifth century BC, the first century to yield a large volume of pertinent extant literary sources, the three species of malaria were already well established in Greece and Italy. Physical anthropologists such as J.L. Angel have attempted to trace malaria in prehistory by investigating porotic hyperostosis and cribra orbitalia, syndromes in which the skull in particular suffers characteristic deformations. Angel believed that porotic hyperostosis was a by-product of thalassaemia, a genetic condition affecting the regulatory genes for the production of haemoglobin chains which confers resistance to malaria. He used its frequency in skeletal remains to argue that the earliest Neolithic farmers in Greece were severely affected by falciparum malaria, whose frequency then decreased until the classical period. Angel maintained that *c.* 300 BC the frequency of porotic hyperostosis again began to increase, suggesting an increased frequency of malaria which could be connected with the decline of ancient Greek civilisation.[385]

Unfortunately recent research has shown that the interpretation of the significance of the changing incidence of porotic hyperostosis is much more complicated than Angel supposed. It has become clear that it is an example of a set of symptoms which may be caused in several quite different ways. An iron deficiency anaemia is always the proximate cause, but such anaemias may arise in several different ways. Besides the anaemias bound up with thalassaemia and malaria which Angel emphasised, iron deficiency anaemias of nutritional origin are equally capable of causing porotic hyperostosis. Moreover there are at least three different aetiologies, by no means mutually exclusive, of nutritional anaemias. First, the diet may be deficient in iron. Secondly, the diet may be adequately endowed with iron, but intestinal parasites may take up most of it for their own use, where infestation with such parasites is common (see above).

Thirdly, the diet may contain an adequate supply of iron, but other chemicals present in the diet may prevent absorption of dietary iron by the human body. This is particularly important in the case of farmers whose diet is based on whole cereals. The aleurone layer of wheat contains phytic acid, which forms insoluble compounds with iron, zinc, possibly calcium and magnesium, and other metallic salts in the diet, preventing the body from utilising them. 10 per cent of bran in bread decreases iron absorption by about 50 per cent. Moreover even the highest quality bread produced in antiquity contained much more grit than modern bread does. This is shown by the fact that bread which was so light that it could float on water was regarded as utterly amazing in antiquity. To remove phytates leavening is even more important than the degree of milling, as about 50 per cent of the phytates are hydrolysed during breadmaking. However, the durum wheat of the Mediterranean was often eaten in an unleavened form in the past (see Chapter III below). It is quite possible for humans on a diet in which whole wheat provides about 70 per cent of the energy intake to suffer from iron deficiency anaemia, even though whole wheat is a rich source of iron. Even today consumption of whole fibre cereals by pregnant women may deprive foetuses of essential elements such as zinc.[386]

Yet another complication is introduced by evidence that porotic hyperostosis as caused by nutritional anaemias may be mainly a disease of childhood, whose effects on bones persist into adulthood long after the actual malnutrition syndrome has ceased to operate. Even so malnutrition in childhood may permanently reduce life expectancy and stature. This would mean that it is illegitimate to conclude that an adult whose skull shows signs of porotic hyperostosis had been suffering from the malnutrition syndrome at the time of his death. Makler (1980) cited evidence from the Hippokratic corpus that bladder stone disease was a common disease among infants and young children, especially males who have greater difficulty passing bladder stones than females, in classical Greece. Attempts were made to remove the stone surgically. It is now found only in Third World countries afflicted by severe food supply and malnutrition problems, especially a shortage of proteins, and indicates inadequate lactation and/or problems at weaning. Makler also suggested that bladder stone disease arose in ancient Greece as a consequence of inadequate diets for children in which barley gruel (*ptisanê*) was the main supplement to breast milk (see Chapter III below on the role of barley in ancient Greece).[387]

The multiple aetiologies of porotic hyperostosis throw severe doubt on Angel's assumption that its frequency may be used as an index of the frequency of malaria. There are two good reasons why falciparum malaria is unlikely to have been prominent in Greece *c.* 6000 BC. First, the climate was still rather cool for it and the vector mosquitoes. Secondly, it is a density-dependent disease which only persists in the human body for about a year after a single infection and is infectious for only about eighty days, although it compensates for these characteristics to some extent by existing in many different immunological strains, so that constant reinfection is possible. In contrast vivax malaria may persist in the human body for about three years and quartan malaria for six or seven years after a single infection, enabling them to survive in smaller host populations. The earliest Neolithic farming populations had extremely low population densities, as they had just ceased to be hunter-gatherers. It is unlikely that falciparum malaria prospered under such circumstances.

In my opinion most of the cases of porotic hyperostosis discovered by Angel in early Neolithic farming populations in Greece and elsewhere should be explained as products of nutritional anaemias rather than thalassaemia. Recent research indicates that the earliest farmers in the

Middle East at sites like Tell Abu Hureyra suffered from malnutrition caused by the changeover from the broad spectrum diet of Mesolithic hunter-gatherers to a very narrow diet consisting mainly of cereals. Whole wheat contains little fat, no vitamins A, C and D and the phytic acid may make most of its iron content inaccessible to humans. Moreover the earliest Neolithic farmers also suffered severe skeletal damage that was induced by the sheer strain of grinding cereals. Angel too found evidence for osteoarthrosis probably caused by excessive hard physical labour in the prehistoric eastern Mediterranean populations which he studied. Angel (1944) also discovered that the degree of abrasion of teeth decreased from the Neolithic to the classical period in Greece, suggesting increasing refinement of cereal products. He concluded that the health of ancient Greek populations increased gradually from the Neolithic to the classical period, judging by various skeletal indices of nutritional status such as stature, although there was a range of variation according to social class. The individuals who were buried in the Shaft Graves at Mycenae were on average about 5 cm. taller than people buried in chamber tombs around Mycenae during the same period.

All this evidence for improvements in nutritional status from the Neolithic to the classical period should be correlated with the decreasing frequency of porotic hyperostosis and cribra orbitalia. Most of the cases of porotic hyperostosis found by Angel in his prehistoric populations relate to infants and young children, which is compatible with the theory of nutritional iron deficiency anaemias in childhood as the cause, and the syndrome is not as severe as in modern cases which are known for certain to have been caused by thalassaemia. The frequency of porotic hyperostosis is very low in Angel's skeletal population for early classical Greece (*c.* 650-350 BC), at a time when all three species of malaria were common enough judging by the Hippokratic corpus. If the hypothesis that porotic hyperostosis basically reflects the incidence of falciparum malaria were accepted, there would be a glaring contradiction between the palaeo-osteological and the literary evidence. Neither Angel nor Grmek has given a convincing explanation of this anomaly. This again illustrates the difficulty of estimating the incidence of diseases on the basis of small skeletal populations. Porotic hyperostosis is rare in skeletons from prehistoric sites in Italy, suggesting that prehistoric Italian farmers were nourished better than their Greek counterparts and/or that falciparum malaria had not yet reached Italy.[388]

If porotic hyperostosis is dismissed as an unreliable indicator of falciparum malaria, the conclusion that it is impossible to assess the distribution and abundance of malaria in prehistoric Greece becomes inevitable. All we can say is that all three species were abundant in Greece by the fifth century BC. Undoubtedly they all remained common in Greece and many other parts of the Mediterranean throughout the rest of antiquity, and throughout the cycle of human population fluctuations described in section 2 above for Greece, as shown by the works of Galen and other writers of the Roman period. Galen states that falciparum malaria was common in Rome in the second century AD. Its demographic characteristics in respect of density-dependence permitted it to remain endemic permanently in Rome. Evidently it was a lethal hazard for adult immigrants who had not been born in a region in which it was endemic, like smallpox in early modern London, while those who were actually born in Rome would probably have been infected in childhood and been more secure for the rest of their lives if they survived that experience of childhood. However, there were doubtless plenty of other reasons why the population of Rome was incapable of reproducing itself, and the level of immigration was sufficient for Rome to remain a great city for centuries in spite of the scourge of falciparum malaria.[389]

This leads us on to the general problem of the demographic consequences of malaria. Ross was a pioneer of modern research on malaria who visited Greece in the early years of this century. He saw the debilitating effects of malaria on many of those who suffered from it and reached the conclusion that the classical Greeks could not have been as active as they were if malaria had been as abundant in classical Greece as it was in Greece around the turn of the twentieth century. His conclusions had a great influence on W.H.S. Jones, who devised his hypothesis about the role of malaria in Greek history shortly afterwards. However, there is one very striking and unshakeable fact about the demographic history of modern Greece which surely casts severe doubt on the whole hypothesis. In the three generations or so before the work of Ross and Jones, massive population growth had occurred in Greece. The rate of increase did decline sharply towards the end of the nineteenth century, the time when Ross and Jones were working. However, this happened because the country had exhausted the possibilities of producing cereals itself and of producing cash crops to raise the money to buy cereals from abroad, not because of malaria. In other words the Greek population in the last century proved itself capable of substantial population growth in spite of the mortality and debilitating effects of malaria.[390]

The situation in Greece in the last century bears an extraordinary similarity to that in classical Greece, where malaria was widespread but the human population still managed to display very considerable powers of population growth, as shown by the Athenian population during the *Pentêkontaëtia*. It is reasonable to conclude that malaria was no more capable of preventing substantial human population growth in the fifth century BC than it was during the nineteenth century AD, even though the mortality which it caused undoubtedly reduced the rate of increase which was feasible. Furthermore it follows that the hypothesis of W.H.S. Jones is fatally flawed. The case of malaria in Greece illustrates the principle that diseases in general did not restrict human populations in the past.

This principle fits perfectly into the framework of the theory of evolution, in which natural selection works essentially on differential reproduction. In the final analysis the death of every individual, usually brought about by the agency of disease, and the passing of each generation are advantageous for the species because they permit genetic recombination via sexual reproduction and so a continuously changing genetic response to constantly altering environmental conditions.

However, it would be a grave mistake to underestimate the power of malaria as an agent of natural selection. Research in population genetics shows that malaria is capable of inducing dramatic changes in the frequencies of various genes in human populations. It is by means of this very process that the frequency of defensive genetic traits like G6PD deficiency, thalassaemia, haemoglobin S (which causes sickle-cell anaemia in homozygotes) and the Duffy negative allele increases and so enables human populations to reproduce themselves in spite of malaria. Ross and Jones did not understand this. A few years after their work, the armies of north European powers fought each other in northern Greece during the First World War. Terrible epidemics of malaria ensued among the foreign soldiers who had no experience of the disease, but not among the local inhabitants, many of whom had inherited resistance to malaria.[391]

If it is accepted that malaria was incapable of regulating human populations in the long run in antiquity, because of the inevitable reproductive success of genotypes resistant to it, and given that malaria undoubtedly was already widespread in the fifth century BC, it may be asked whether there is any particular reason for believing, as Jones did, that malaria had only been introduced to Greece recently at the time of the Peloponnesian War. The hypothesis that it was brought to Greece by the Persians during the Persian Wars in the early fifth century BC has been proposed. Grmek, who seemed to be more impressed by porotic hyperostosis as evidence for malaria in prehistory in Greece than I am, revised the hypothesis of Jones by speaking about a 'reintroduction' of falciparum malaria in Greece in the fifth century BC (after the hypothetical Early Neolithic phase of activity of the disease). However, there seems to be no reason why falciparum malaria could not have been present in Greece during the Dark Ages *c.* 1000 BC just as all three species of malaria were endemic in Greece during the late Ottoman period, another period of low human population density which preceded the phase of population growth after the Greek War of Independence in the last century.

Grmek also argued that the Mediterranean variety of *P. falciparum* is significantly different from the strains characteristic of tropical Africa. He exploited this point to suggest that the Mediterranean variety has existed separately from the varieties of sub-Saharan Africa for a very long time. However, this does not prove that the 'Mediterranean' *P.*

falciparum variety was common in southern Europe during the last glaciation. There is no reason why it should not have been largely confined to the Middle East until after the end of the last Ice Age in the same way that species of plant adapted to the Mediterranean climate were rare in southern Europe during the last glaciation. Malaria certainly gives the impression that its incidence has fluctuated widely in the course of history. For example it was active in the East Anglian fens from the early mediaeval period onwards, and then disappeared during the nineteenth century AD for unknown reasons. Landscape modification owing to agricultural intensification is one explanation that has been advanced. Nevertheless such phenomena suggest that cyclical or irregular fluctuations may be inherent in the ecology of malaria. The protozoans that cause it do not exhibit any great variations in biochemical characteristics for virulence or transmissibility at the infraspecific level analogous to those of the bacilli of the genus Yersinia. However, it is easy to envisage historical developments that may have altered the ecology of the mosquito vectors.

Zulueta (1973) discussed changes in the physical environment that may alter a region's suitability for particular species of mosquito. In Greece many of the most intensely malarial zones in recent times were alluvial coastal plains, for example Marathon in Attica and Thermopylae. These alluvial plains were produced by the deposition of the Younger Fill which in many, but not necessarily all, cases occurred after the classical period. They contain many small pools of brackish water which are the favoured breeding ground of *Anopheles sacharovi*. Such changes in the physical environment may have resulted in an increase in the frequency of this important malaria vector since the fifth century BC. Empedokles is said to have diverted two rivers into another river and so freed Selinous in Sicily from a *loimos*, perhaps malaria, which killed adult citizens and made childbearing difficult for the women. However this tale was questioned even in antiquity and is probably unreliable.[392]

Deliberate innovations by humans have also sometimes led to the spread of malaria in the Mediterranean. For example, the introduction of rice cultivation in the mediaeval period (see Chapter I above) led to an increase in some regions of the frequency of *Anopheles atroparvus*, a zoophilic species of mosquito which took a liking to paddy fields for rice in Mediterranean wetlands as a breeding ground and turned to humans after it had run out of domesticated animals to exploit. This did not happen in south-east Asia or south China, the centre of origin of domesticated rice (*O. sativa*), where the indigenous species of mosquito are not interested in paddy fields. In passing it is worth noting that rice fields produce methane gas, which makes a contribution to the greenhouse effect. Even in regions of rice cultivation in the Mediterranean the frequency of malaria was observed to decrease eventually from the initially very high epidemic levels, as Hackett (1937) noticed. This may have happened partly because natural selection increased the frequency of human genotypes resistant to malaria. Another possible reason is that as a region was developed there may have been a historical succession of different species of mosquito, some suitable and others unsuitable as vectors for malaria, which would parallel the well known ecological phenomenon of plant succession leading up to a climax vegetation. It should be noted, however, that most malaria in Greece and Italy in the past depended on species of mosquito which breed in small pools or streams. It did not depend on large areas of marshland.

Successions of different species of mosquitoes occur annually on a seasonal basis. For example, in Greece *Anopheles sacharovi*, which breeds in the summer, is succeeded by *Anopheles superpictus*, a less efficient but still dangerous vector which breeds in foothill streams in the autumn. It is possible, but difficult to prove, that displacements of one mosquito species by another have also occurred historically on a rather more permanent basis over periods of decades or centuries, perhaps as a concomitant of localised climatic or environmental change. This is the most probable explanation of the fluctuations in the incidence of malaria on a regional basis observed in the course of history. If correct, this may explain the 'reintroduction' of falciparum malaria to Greece in the fifth century BC postulated by Grmek. However, it is equally possible that falciparum malaria had existed in Greece throughout the first millennium BC and perhaps in the Bronze Age as well. In any case, the hypothesis that malaria had a decisive influence on Greek population history does not stand up to critical scrutiny.

Sexually transmitted diseases, the last category of infectious diseases considered here, are of particular interest in demographic research which emphasises the working of natural selection on differential reproduction. There is little evidence for the most serious STDs, especially syphilis and gonorrhoea, in the Hippokratic corpus. However some of the less serious STDs certainly existed in classical Greece. It was noted earlier that genital herpes is mentioned in the Hippokratic corpus. It has minor effects on human fertility, but may cause a severe congenital infection in newborn infants.

Secondly, trachoma (*Chlamydia trachomatis*) is well documented in classical times in its role as the leading infectious cause of blindness. Lucretius observed that eye diseases were characteristic of the Roman province of Achaia, an impression supported by the high frequency of votive offerings of eyes to Asklepios and the inscriptions at Epidauros. Where trachoma is a significant cause of blindness it is usually a holoendemic disease of childhood in which virtually everyone contracts the disease in early childhood. Immunity then develops so that adults do not suffer from the active disease. Nevertheless the damage done in childhood to the eyes persists and may deteriorate into blindness. It is transmitted by flies and cultural practices that permit eye-to-eye transmission. In the modern world it always disappears as an eye disease as the standard of living rises. Constant reinfection is necessary to produce blindness eventually. Homer was the most famous Greek said to have lost his sight because of an eye disease, at least according to one strand of tradition. The very same micro-organism also causes genital infections, including a variety of ocular-genital infections and lymphogranuloma venereum. It may well be the most widespread sexually transmitted micro-organism in developed countries today. As in other diseases pregnant women are the group infected with the greatest of ease. It probably also caused genital infections in classical antiquity, as Grmek argued.[393]

From a theoretical point of view it would have been quite feasible for STDs to exist in classical times even in very small human populations. Their demographic characteristics are very different from those of diseases like smallpox because the average number of sexual partners per person is inevitably much smaller than the average number of incidental contacts per person. Genital herpes never goes away, like the varicella virus. Gonorrhoea, which is a very major cause of infertility in regions in which it is endemic, renders an individual infectious for long periods of time. Moreover it reproduces itself inefficiently, forming new strains which defeat acquired immunity and facilitate repeated reinfection. Consequently gonorrhoea is not a density-dependent disease and could have evolved in the very distant past. However, there is no unambiguous evidence for it in classical Greece in the Hippokratic corpus. Some scholars have attempted to identify it in the Bible and in medical literature dating to Roman times, and it has even been argued (improbably) that gonorrhoea played a large part in the failure of the Roman aristocracy to reproduce itself. In spite of such speculation, there is little evidence for gonorrhoea in the classical world, and it is certain that the frequency of infertility in archaic and classical Greece did not approach the levels generated by gonorrhoea in central Africa today. Major epidemics of gonorrhoea and other STDs which commenced a generation ago paved the way for the spread of AIDS in that part of the world. These phenomena were facilitated by heterosexual promiscuity.[394]

The history of syphilis has been the subject of enormous controversy, which cannot be reviewed here in detail. Suffice it to say that classical scholars, from Littré to Grmek, have generally agreed that there is no evidence for venereal syphilis in the Hippokratic corpus. The view that it was confined to the western hemisphere until after Columbus has been expressed frequently. On the other hand epidemic venereal syphilis is very closely related to a spectrum of nonvenereal endemic human treponematoses, including members characteristic of the Old World. In addition the rabbit, native to Spain in antiquity (see Chapter I above), suffers from its own version of syphilis (*Treponema cuniculi*), which is very closely related to the endemic treponematoses but not transmissible to man, and the baboon in west Africa also suffers from a specific treponematosis. If all the treponematoses were native to the western hemisphere, then the rabbit could only have acquired its variety of syphilis after Columbus, perhaps the most probable answer to the problem. The alternative is that endemic treponematoses are of great antiquity in the Old World.

Endemic nonvenereal syphilis has been identified in various parts of the Balkans, the lands around the eastern Mediterranean, North Africa and Arabia in recent times. It is a disease of childhood like measles, not associated with sexual activity, and does not have any significant effects in terms of either child mortality or subsequent fertility in adulthood. This raises the possibility that syphilis may have existed in classical antiquity, but in this nonvenereal form. If this was the case, then it would have been one of the variety of skin diseases mentioned in classical sources which are very difficult to differentiate and identify. Grmek rejects the idea that endemic treponematoses existed anywhere in the Mediterranean in antiquity, even though he admits their existence in tropical Africa in pre-Columbian times, because of the absence of evidence for syphilitic skeletal lesions on human bones of classical date from the eastern Mediterranean. However, we should not forget how thin is the palaeo-osteological evidence for tuberculosis in ancient Greece, also acknowledged by Grmek. Venereal syphilis frequently causes miscarriage in the initial stages of the disease, and a high proportion of infants born prematurely to syphilitic mothers die. However, its effects on fertility are rather limited and less impressive than those of gonorrhoea, as it does not affect either fecundity or the ability to have coitus. In conclusion, STDs did not play an important role in reducing fertility in ancient Greece.[395]

The nutritional iron deficiency anaemias mentioned earlier introduced the question of the relationship of nutritional status to disease susceptibility. This question requires more systematic treatment now. Angel concluded that the health of the population of Greece started to decline in the late classical and early Hellenistic periods after reaching a peak in the late archaic and early classical periods. It is very interesting that the health of the population had already started to decline at a time when the population density was attaining the highest level achieved before modern times, judging by archaelogical survey data (see section 2 above). This suggests that the Malthusian positive checks were beginning to operate, a finding which fits in very neatly with the biological models of carrying capacity employed in this book. In general malnutrition weakens the human body's ability to resist disease, although the courses of a number of important diseases are scarcely influenced by the patient's nutritional status. Acute starvation, causing famine amenorrhoea in women, does severely reduce fertility, but moderate chronic malnutrition has only minor direct effects on human fertility. Insofar as malnutrition influences fertility it does so principally by means of increasing disease susceptibility, and also to a very minor extent by increasing the average age of menarche.[396]

Judging by evidence for standard rations (see Chapter III below), the diets of adults in ancient Greece were adequate from a calorific viewpoint, but it is quite possible that they were not entirely satisfactory from a qualitative viewpoint. Moreover, it is clear from what has already been said that malnutrition was endemic among young children in ancient Greece, as iron deficiency anaemias, bladder stone disease and rickets (see section 4 above) interacted with the probability of inadequate feeding during prolonged periods of breastfeeding (section 4 above) and diseases of the alimentary system caused by viruses, bacteria and parasitic worms. As regards infant mortality, this complex of circumstances doubtless went a long way towards making up for the shortage of density-dependent diseases of childhood such as smallpox, measles, mumps and diphtheria in the endemic form in which they are characteristically diseases of that stage of life.

Another piece may be added to this jigsaw with the observation that trachoma was by no means the only cause of eye diseases in antiquity. There is also evidence for night blindness, the first stage of xerophthalmia, which is caused by vitamin A (retinol) deficiency. Aristotle noted that it was mainly observed among young children, which is congruent with its epidemiology in developing countries today. Vitamin A deficiency may arise for various reasons. Intestinal infections and parasites reduce absorption of vitamin A. It is a fat-soluble vitamin and a shortage of dietary fat makes it difficult to absorb the vitamin from ingested food. This is a probable scenario in any population which lives off a diet heavily based on carbohydrates from cereals. However, consumption of foods containing fats which have started to turn rancid, for example stale fish, will lead to the destruction of vitamin A. The Attic comic poets mention attempts by unscrupulous fishmongers to sell stale fish in classical Athens.

Moreover the carrot, which is highly valued today as a source of vitamin A, did not possess its present high content of vitamin A precursors in antiquity. Only white carrots, which were correctly not valued as food, existed in antiquity. White carrots do not contain a high proportion of vitamin A precursors, and the red carrot only evolved under domestication in the early modern period in Europe. In addition green vegetables, which contain some carotene but not as much as the red carrot, were not always valued as highly as they are today. For example, one of the authors of the Hippokratic corpus advised ordinary people to eat as few vegetables as possible in winter.[397]

This introduces an interesting problem in relation to a body of ecological theory called (optimal) foraging theory whose relevance to understanding the early history of agriculture will be explained in

Chapter III.9-10 below, namely are humans capable of accurately appreciating the nutritional value of different kinds of food in the absence of the facilities afforded by a modern chemical laboratory? Herbivorous animals cannot do so in respect of most nutrients, except sodium in salt. This means that it is necessary on the whole to think in terms of maximising the net rate of acquisition of all nutrients put together in relation to such questions in ecology as why herbivorous animals choose one patch of food in preference to another, for example. Even with the advantage of consciousness, humans have great difficulty under primitive conditions in understanding the nutritional value of the foods they eat.[398]

Galen furnishes one extraordinary illustration of this point from classical times. He believed that the olive is of very little nutritional value. In the light of modern knowledge his statement is incredible. After all fats like olive oil produce more than twice as much energy per unit weight (38-39 kJ/g) as carbohydrates in cereals (17 kJ/g), not to mention their value in respect of assisting the absorption of the fat-soluble vitamins A, D, E and K from ingested foodstuffs. Even the unrefined olive as it comes straight off the tree has a calorific value roughly equal to that of an equal weight of carbohydrates from cereals. But Galen did not have the facilities of a modern chemical laboratory at his disposal. Consequently he had no way of measuring the heats of combustion of olive oil fats and cereal carbohydrates and proteins. He simply assumed on a priori grounds that firm, solid food like that derived from cereal grains must have a higher nutritional value than soft, mushy food like olives. If considered in these terms, his mistake is quite understandable.

This low opinion of the nutritional value of the olive as food assumes great importance in relation to the problem broached in Chapter I above, namely explaining why olive cultivation took such a long time to spread around the Mediterranean. The question of whether the olive was nutritious was also debated in ancient Israel, although a positive conclusion was reached there. It seems an inevitable conclusion that large quantities of olive oil were consumed by humans in classical antiquity, despite Galen's opinion, and that the spread of olive cultivation raised environmental carrying capacity (see Chapter III.3 below). There were a lot of domesticated olive trees in Greece by the fifth century BC, and even more all around the Mediterranean in the time of the Roman empire. Nevertheless the fact remains that humans did not appreciate the nutritional value of the foods they were eating in antiquity.[399]

Two more illustrations of this point will be given here. The Hippokratic corpus expressed the opinion that highly milled bread was more nutritious than wholemeal bread. A high degree of refining of wheat flour does improve it in certain respects, by removing most of the phytic acid and most of the fats, permitting longer storage of cereal products before they become rancid. It also improves its baking qualities. However, highly refined wheat flours contain less fibre, less calcium and iron, less of several trace elements, less protein and less B vitamins. On balance white bread is less nutritious than wholemeal bread, but this was not understood in antiquity. Throughout history white bread has been preferred to wholemeal bread for social reasons, but wholemeal bread is increasing in popularity now as appreciation of its superior nutritional value becomes widespread.

For the second illustration we must return to Galen, who was extremely suspicious of the value of eating fruit and indeed thought that fruit consumption could cause fevers. Again Galen's views are diametrically opposed to the opinions of modern experts on nutrition, but it is nevertheless interesting that attitudes to fruit consumption analogous to those of Galen occur in some Third World countries today. Diokles of Karystos in the late fourth and early third centuries BC also said that fruits from fruit trees were of little value, but do relatively little harm if consumed in moderate quantities before meals. This shows that Galen was merely repeating an opinion that was widely expressed throughout antiquity.[400]

It would be a serious mistake to assume that the ancient Greeks acted on the basis of knowledge which they did not possess. We must conclude that many of the precepts proposed by ancient dieticians may have had the opposite effect to that which was intended because they were a priori arguments lacking the necessary grounding in rational experimentation. The interaction of diet with other aspects of human ecology in antiquity is a fascinating topic which owing to considerations of space cannot be treated here in the detail it deserves. Future osteological research will probably expand knowledge in this field as modern techniques are brought to bear. For example the strontium/calcium ratio in bones may be used to investigate the relative proportions of foods of animal and of vegetable origin in the diet. Unfortunately there is only room here to mention two further instances of the interaction between diet and disease in antiquity, but these particular cases at least have the merit of introducing two categories of diseases which have not yet been considered.[401]

Heart disease is not prominent in ancient medical literature, undoubtedly because it was difficult to observe. Vivisection of the human body was not practised widely until the era of Herophilos and Erasistratos in Early Hellenistic Alexandria, and it became socially unacceptable again afterwards. This made it difficult to observe heart disease in humans. However, Aristotle tells us that animals were frequently observed to have diseased hearts when they were cut open, and heart disease must have occurred in humans as well. It is a disease of complex multiple aetiologies which increases in frequency with age. Given the argument in section 3 above that adult life expectancy has been underestimated by many scholars working on ancient societies, heart disease was not necessarily very much less frequent in classical Greece than it is in the modern world.

There is only space to mention one facet of the ecology of heart disease in classical antiquity. The ratio between saturated fats and polyunsaturated fats is believed to be a factor conducive to the development of atherosclerosis and heart disease. Comparison of wild animals and of domesticated animals maintained on grassland or on cereal-based diets shows that the ratio of saturated:unsaturated fats in meat is very different in the two categories of animal. Wild animals contain much less fat and a much higher proportion of unsaturated fats than domesticated animals because wild animals which roam woodlands have access there to sources of fats unavailable to domesticated animals kept on grassland or stall-fed with cereals. The different chemical compositions of meat from wild and domesticated animals mean that they have rather different characteristics, which may be noticed easily. Both the Hippokratic corpus and Galen comment on the differences in the taste of meat from wild and from domesticated animals. It may be inferred that domesticated animals in classical times already possessed the particular combination of fats which is conducive to heart disease. Undoubtedly poor people could not afford to eat much meat in antiquity (see Chapter III.4 below). However, the diet of the rich may have been as unhealthy as the diets of people in developed countries today in this particular respect.[402] The situation is complicated by evidence that some unsaturated fats are healthier than others. Some of them may play a role in the aetiology of cancers, the last group of human diseases to be considered here, by acting as cancer tumour promoters, if certain other necessary conditions for the development of cancers are also met. In particular linoleic acid, which is abundant in some cooking oils of vegetable origin such as sunflower oil and corn oil, falls into this category. In contrast oleic acid ($C_{17}H_{33}COOH$), a mono-unsaturated fatty acid from olive oil, and eicosapentaenoic acid from fish, more important than meat as a source of animal protein for many poor people in antiquity, are not cancer tumour promoters. The fact that the frequency of important cancers like breast cancer in Mediterranean countries is fairly low, even though fats comprise a high proportion of the total calorific intake, is explicable in terms of the role of olive oil in the Mediterranean diet. Cancers, especially of internal organs of the body, do not figure prominently in the Hippokratic corpus, for the same reason as heart disease. However, the cancers which are common today were also frequent in antiquity. Galen commented on the frequency of breast cancer. Olive oil also reduces blood levels of low density lipo-proteins, which maintain high cholesterol levels, and maintains blood levels of high density lipo-proteins which remove cholesterol. Consequently olive oil is responsible for the fairly low frequency of heart disease in the Meditérranean.[403]

So much for human diseases. A few brief comments on animal diseases in classical antiquity are necessary now to deal with a problem encountered earlier, namely the relationship between human and animal diseases. The Greeks and Romans took a considerable interest in animal diseases because of their economic importance in animal husbandry. Aristotle and Columella describe the diseases of several animals. Among them we may recognise, for example, anthrax, which probably spread to humans as a zoonosis and was responsible for some epidemics in antiquity. It has been suggested that the major epidemic at Rome in 453/2 BC was caused by anthrax. Virgil described a great epidemic of anthrax (*Bacillus anthracis*) among livestock in the eastern Alps, creating a model description of an animal epidemic which was imitated by later writers. He observed the association of anthrax in humans with consumption of meat from animals killed by the disease and with use of the hair and hides of such animals.[404]

Other animal diseases which struck humans as zoonoses include two particularly associated with horses, namely glanders (Greek *melis*) and tetanus. The latter was not uncommon in the past, and still occurs in developing countries today, as a disease of newborn infants whose umbilicus was covered with unhygienic materials after the cord had been cut. Other zoonoses mentioned by ancient authors include foot-and-mouth disease, bovine tuberculosis, which may have been a frequent zoonosis wherever milk was consumed by adults in significant quantities, and rabies in dogs. Aristotle noted that the bite of a rabid dog does not always produce the clinical disease in humans. This accords with modern experience, which shows that the body's natural defence mechanisms are often able to prevent the rabies virus reaching the central nervous system, and the chances of developing the disease depend on the distance of the bite from the central nervous system. The Roman agronomists appreciated that some animal diseases were contagious. They also understood some elementary principles of density-dependence, observing that epidemics were less frequent in small groups of animals than in large groups and recommending the maintenance of small herds and flocks to reduce the incidence of diseases.[405]

All infectious diseases that usually prey on humans ultimately originated elsewhere in the animal world. Some, like malaria, were inherited vertically by hominids as they evolved from their primate ancestors in Africa. Others were acquired horizontally by humans from other animals at a very much later date. A good example here is measles, descended from the ancestor of modern canine distemper of dogs, and also related to rinderpest of cattle. Domesticated dogs themselves inherited canine distemper vertically as they evolved from wild wolves (see Chapter IV below). Domesticated animals have been a major source of origin of human diseases. It is not coincidence that the dog, which became the first domesticated animal in the Epipalaeolithic Middle East *c.* 10,000 BC, has more diseases that are similar to or identical with human diseases than any other animal. However, the four species of human malaria and measles, for example, evolved into diseases that are adapted to life in human populations and may be transmitted from person to person, with or without an insect vector as the case may be. A very large number of other animal diseases infect humans sporadically as zoonoses, but are not adapted to life in human populations and cannot be transmitted readily from person to person. Consequently such diseases never cause epidemics, no matter how deadly they may be in individual cases. A good example here is rabies, which is almost 100 per cent lethal if the virus happens to get as far as the central nervous system.[406]

The Greeks and Romans noticed that some distinctively animal diseases could be transmitted to humans. They also saw similarities between some animal diseases and some human diseases, for example bovine tuberculosis and human pulmonary tuberculosis. These observations seem to have led them to the conclusion that most diseases were common to humans and to other animals. Aristotle expressed this viewpoint as a generalisation about man, horse and sheep. An ancient commentary on Homer states that all with experience of such matters know that outbreaks of epidemic diseases in humans commence among four-footed animals. It is clear that this belief colours the interpretations given by ancient authors of many of the epidemics that affected humans in antiquity, especially Thucydides' account of the epidemic of Athens in 430 BC, but also some of the epidemics in the early stages of Roman history.

Before comments such as those of Thucydides are taken at face value and used as evidence bearing upon the identification of the micro-organism that caused the epidemic, it is important to consider the validity of the generalisation that underlies all comments of this kind, namely that humans share most of their diseases with other animals. Quite a number of scholars have reached the conclusion that Thucydides' comments on the behaviour of dogs and birds during the Athenian epidemic compel us to search for a disease that infects both animals and humans, and have excluded smallpox from consideration on the grounds that it does not infect other animals, even though virtually all the other details given by Thucydides about the epidemic are compatible with the hypothesis of smallpox as the causative agent.[407]

In fact our conclusion should be that although most diseases in humans that are *adapted to person to person transmission* (as the disease of 430 clearly was, since Thucydides emphasises how contagious it was) exhibit similarities to animal diseases, they are not identical to animal diseases or freely interchangeable with them, because they have evolved alongside man as a specific host. For example bovine tuberculosis (*Mycobacterium bovis*) characteristically causes skeletal lesions as a zoonosis in man, while human tuberculosis (*Mycobacterium tuberculosis*) mainly attacks the respiratory system, because it requires a lot of oxygen. Similarly smallpox was related to cowpox, but the two were by no means synonymous, since smallpox often produced a fatal disease in man, while cowpox, acquired accidentally as a zoonosis or transmitted deliberately for the purpose of vaccination, never produced serious consequences. Smallpox had several other relatives among the orthopoxviruses, for example monkeypox, but none of these other viruses is known to be capable of producing epidemics in humans, although they may be transmitted to humans sometimes, and in the case of monkeypox occasionally from person to person. In the same way the two human AIDS viruses (HIV-1 & HIV-2) are related to the simian AIDS virus (SIV), of which more than one variety is now known, in the sense that all three have a common ancestor, but they are certainly not identical.

Most micro-organisms adapted to animal hosts cannot produce great epidemics in human populations because they are not adapted to person-to-person transmission. (Plague is a rare intermediate case in that it has succeeded in ravaging human populations for periods of centuries but has never become truly adapted to man as a host and endemic in human populations.) This applies to diseases like tularaemia, leptospirosis and glanders which have been suggested as causes of the Athenian epidemic by scholars who have taken Thucydides' comments on dogs and birds at face value. It applies equally to equine encephalomyelitis as the hypothetical cause of the epidemic that struck the Achaians in the Trojan War.[408]

Although the generalisation made in antiquity that most diseases were common to man and other animals contains a nugget of truth, it is unacceptable as it stands in relation to diseases that are capable of causing large epidemics in human populations. It is an a priori belief that just happens to be incorrect in the light of modern knowledge, like the belief that the olive was of little nutritional value. Consequently it is suggested here that statements about epidemic diseases infecting both humans and animals should be disregarded for the purposes of disease identification wherever they occur in ancient sources, *unless* specific details are provided about the means of transmission from animal to man which enable us to identify a particular animal disease infecting humans as a zoonosis. Virgil fulfilled this requirement in the case of cutaneous anthrax. The account of Thucydides does not meet this requirement. This is why his statement about dogs and birds was rejected earlier in this section in favour of the vast bulk of the other evidence he provides which points to smallpox as the culprit. It is striking that Thucydides does not make any reference to the disease of 430 BC affecting large domesticated animals, e.g. the horses of the Athenian cavalry operating around Athens during the Spartan invasion. This is a sure sign that the disease was not epizoötic. His contorted comments on dogs and birds of prey look like a desperate attempt to make the epidemic of 430 BC fit a mental stereotype already established among the Greeks to which it did not in fact conform.

To provide a link to Chapter III on agriculture, this chapter ends with a brief discussion of the epidemiology of diseases of cereals in antiquity, a topic which may seem even more abstruse than most of the other topics covered in this book. However, there is no doubt that its importance was understood in the fifth century BC. Among the benefits to the Athenians of possessing a farflung maritime empire the 'Old Oligarch' listed the fact that in the event of an epidemic striking the crops in a particular region a maritime power could always obtain food from other regions, because such epidemics never affected all regions simultaneously, while a landlocked power was helpless in such a situation, no matter how fertile its own territory was. Epidemics of diseases of cereals, the main crop, did not strike all regions simultaneously because of the great diversity of varieties of each species of cereal cultivated in antiquity and the fact that different strains of each plant disease tend to be highly specific to particular varieties of each species of crop plant. Susceptibility and resistance on the part of cereals, and virulence in the case of invading micro-organisms such as cereal rust, usually correspond on a one-to-one basis at the genetic level. Since domesticated cereals only have a short generation length of less than a year, it is possible to observe readily in them the process of endless competition between the evolution of genetic resistance in plants and the evolution of disease virulence. Such processes undoubtedly also occur in humans but are much more difficult to observe because of the long lifespan of man.

The monocultures of agriculture in modern developed countries, in which enormous areas of land may be occupied by a single variety of wheat for example, create great opportunities for plant diseases because of the large prey populations and the lack of variety in those large populations in respect of genetic resistance to disease. Since monocultures of particular varieties were not employed in antiquity on anything like the same scale that they are today, Orlob (1973) suggested that the scale of losses caused by plant diseases may have been rather lower on average than it is today. He suggested 5-10 per cent of the crop was lost annually. This opinion requires nuancing. No individual strain of a disease could have infected crops in antiquity across such large geographical areas as is feasible today. However, no species of wheat is invulnerable to diseases, and virulent disease genotypes undoubtedly evolved periodically and enjoyed temporary evolutionary success in restricted geographical areas, until the wheat variety under attack evolved genetic resistance. Besides the 'Old Oligarch', the comments of Theophrastos also indicate that epidemics of plant diseases were a frequent problem for farmers.

It is difficult to identify the plant diseases such as *erusibê*, *uredo* and *melumen* which are mentioned in classical sources because the descriptions are devoid of detail. Biblical scholars have also debated the question of whether the *yerakon* of the Old Testament was cereal rust or a human disease. However, palaeobotanical evidence shows that stem rust of wheat, the most dangerous of the three species of wheat rust (genus Puccinia), existed in the Levant in the Late Bronze Age. Accordingly the traditional translation of *erusibê* as 'rust' is perfectly acceptable. Stem rust of wheat may have been particularly significant as a cause of lost production among the durum wheat varieties characteristic of the Mediterranean in antiquity because it tends to flourish in wet springs, in other words in precisely those years in which plentiful spring rainfall might induce the expectation of a good harvest of wheat. Stem rust of wheat is inhibited by dry air, and its association with dew and warmth was noted in antiquity. Strabo states that many cereal crops which had given the prospect of bumper harvests earlier in the season were ruined by rust in Triphylia, on the wet western side of the Peloponnese in Greece. In years of low spring rainfall durum wheats would not be significantly affected by rust in the Mediterranean, but would be liable to the effects of drought instead. Consequently cereal rust epidemics *complemented* inadequate rainfall owing to interannual climatic variability as causes of lost production in ancient Greece.

The cereal rusts offer fascinating illustrations of the complexity of ecosystems. First, the various species of wheat rust have evolved in tandem with the various species of wheat (see Chapter III below on wheat). Baum & Savile (1985) argued that *P. graminis var. graminis*, the largest spored and morphologically most advanced stem rust variety, evolved within the last few thousand years after hybridisation of other rust biotypes on hexaploid bread wheat, following the evolution of that particular species of wheat. Bread wheat inherited a great susceptibility to rust from one of its parents, *Aegilops squarrosa*, and this variety of stem rust doubtless spread in the wake of the spread of bread wheat cultivation in the first millennium BC.

Secondly, the impact of plant diseases may alter the competitive ability of different species of cereals cultivated together as a polyculture. (The importance of crop mixtures in ancient agriculture will be emphasised in the next chapter.) Theophrastos observed that barley was worse affected than wheat by one plant disease, although his remarks apparently were misunderstood by Pliny. Modern research shows that in barley-wheat mixtures barley is the stronger competitor, except in the presence of a specific pathogen, namely barley mildew (*Erysiphe graminis f. sp. hordei*), which equalises the competition between wheat and barley.

Thirdly, the cereal rusts require alternate hosts to survive because cereals are not cultivated in the fields all the year round. In the case of the brown leaf rust of barley (*P. anomala*), species of the genus Ornithogalum, for example Bath asparagus (*O. pyrenaicum*), act as alternate hosts for the pathogen in Attica. Bath asparagus may have been cultivated and eaten in antiquity, and its deliberate propagation by farmers would have had the effect of creating more favourable conditions for the spread of the leaf rust of barley. In the case of stem rust of wheat, its original host was the barberry bush (*Berberis vulgaris*) in Anatolia. Wild grasses, including wheat, were a secondary host, and the present worldwide distribution of wheat rusts is a consequence of the spread of wheat cultivation by man around the world.

It is generally thought that the barberry bush did not achieve a wide distribution in Europe until the mediaeval period. However, Pliny appears to show some knowledge of it. He reckoned that placing branches of the bush in a wheat field drew the rust 'away' from the wheat into the branches. This of course has an element of truth in it, but by disseminating the alternate host the only real effect would be to increase the abundance of the pathogen and so the deleterious effects on the wheat crop. This then is a case in which human intentions had the opposite effect to that desired, a fitting way of ending this chapter, which has stressed that the biohistory of the classical world pursued its own course in spite of attempts by man to modify the environment to his own advantage.[409]

III

Agriculture

1. Introduction

The Mediterranean gives the impression of profound continuity in many aspects of human life stretching as far back in time as historical sources can take us. Rural parts of the Mediterranean are still dominated by the triad of cereals, olives and vines which the Athenian ephebes swore to defend in their oath and which Alkibiades urged the Athenians to regard as the natural boundaries of Attica, although the side-effects of modernisation and urbanisation in Attica have recently advanced to the extent of making direct extrapolation back to antiquity a risky business. However, the degree of continuity on the surface is still such as to make Braudel's idea of 'la longue durée' seem as much a matter of induction from historical sources and from present-day observations as a consequence of abstract considerations of the nature of time. It has certainly inspired attempts to trace continuity not only of the physical environment but also of human cultural patterns in the Balkans down the millennia.[1]

Such attempts are interesting but carry inherent dangers, as similarity in behavioural patterns may simply be the result of groups of people recurrently stumbling upon the same solutions to the same problems without necessarily implying continuity in the transmission of tradition. The most intensively studied community of subsistence farmers in modern Greece practises polyculture just as classical Greeks did, but consists of the descendants of Albanian immigrants into Greece – no kinship with the ancient Greeks there.[2]

Similarly, continuity in the natural environment may also be deceptive. For example, the fact that wheat is the most highly prized cereal in modern as in ancient Greece conceals the equally important fact that over 90 per cent of the wheat grown in Greece today consists of varieties that have been introduced or artificially bred within the last seventy years or so. This may seem insignificant at first sight, but these new and higher yielding varieties have played a significant role in feeding the progeny of the population explosion in Greece over the last 150 years or so by helping to make possible the increases in agricultural productivity that have made Greece as a whole self-sufficient in wheat since 1957. These increases in agricultural productivity have made possible economic development by freeing a significant proportion of the labour force for work outside the primary sector.[3]

One of the main themes of the following study of agriculture in ancient Greece, especially Attica, is that significant changes in the types of cereals cultivated also took place in the past. The second theme is that understanding these changes is indispensable to understanding the land economics of ancient Greek societies. The third theme is that we can only make sense of the crop patterns of classical antiquity by placing them in a very much broader perspective and considering how they fit into the whole of the history of agriculture from the Neolithic revolution right up to the present day.

Section 2 below discusses the modern land use pattern of Attica. In section 3 the role of the olive tree in Greek agriculture is considered. Section 4 focuses on animal husbandry and its relationship to arable farming. Previous scholarly opinions on the history of cereals are reviewed in sections 5 & 6. Section 7 is devoted to *semidalis*. Sowing seasons form the subject of section 8. The longest section, 9, concentrates on wheat evolution in antiquity, and section 10 encompasses other cereals. Some aspects of the expansion of Greek agriculture to Egypt are studied in section 11, and cereal yields round off the chapter in section 12.

2. Patterns of land use in Attica

A start will be made by considering the pattern of land use in modern Attica, as revealed by the 1961 census, with the aim of justifying the estimates of the environmental carrying capacity of ancient Attica in Chapter II.2 above. Two points will be emphasised: firstly, in spite of modernisation the constraints imposed upon agriculture in Attica by the environment are still very strong; secondly, there is no evidence that the ancient economy was of such a nature as to induce changes in producer behaviour comparable to those induced in modern farmers by the tentacles of a capitalist economy. The data on land use presented below relate to the modern eparchy of Attica, excluding the Athens-Piraeus metropolitan area, and the north-west corner of ancient Attica which belongs to the modern eparchy of Megara. Unfortunately modern Greek administrative units do not correspond to ancient Greek political units. Moreover older published census data, antedating the Second World War, are of little use because they lumped together data for Attica with data for Boiotia, including the ecologically very different region of the former Lake Kopais.[4]

A few crops to which an extremely small amount of land was devoted have been omitted from the table. The bulk of the total area of farmland unaccounted for by the data given above was presumably fallow,

Land use in modern Attica

Total area 1,615,300 stremmata (10 str. = 1 ha.), of which 563,300 str. were classified as farm land in 1961 (34.87 per cent)

Crop	Area (str.)	% of total area of farmland	% of area of eparchy
Wheat	101,659	18.05	6.29
Barley	41,272	7.33	2.56
Oats	24,046	4.27	1.49
Rye	1,698	0.30	0.11
Maize	1,094	0.19	0.07
Total cereals	169,769	30.14	10.52
Fodder crops	58,502	10.39	3.62
Total field crops	228,271	40.53	14.13
Spring vegetables	15,940	2.83	0.99
Winter vegetables	6,012	1.07	0.37
Vegetables of various seasons	21,218	3.77	1.31
Total vegetables	43,170	7.67	2.67
Edible pulses	8,882	1.58	0.55
Cotton	1,871	0.33	0.12
Melons	706	0.13	0.04
Citrus fruits	39,400	6.99	2.44
Vines (for wine)	146,891	26.08	9.09
Vines (for table grapes)	1,765	0.31	0.11
Potatoes	4,639	0.82	0.28

although no specific information on fallow was provided. The 765,175 olive trees were to a considerable extent intercropped with the cereals and the legumes. There were also 104,070 dried fruit trees (almonds, walnuts, hazelnuts, carobs, figs, etc.) and 44,374 deciduous fruit trees (apples, pears, peaches, cherries etc.). The nome of Attica as a whole had 49,000 str. of irrigated land. Besides the farm land of the eparchy another 399,700 ştr. (24.74 per cent) of land was classified as pasture land. The enumeration of animals recorded 2,376 horses, 1,948 mules, 5,629 donkeys, 9,091 cattle, 6,506 pigs, 94,362 sheep and 46,313 goats. The fodder crops included vetch, lucerne and clover. Spring vegetables included onions and cabbage, and the heterogeneous category of 'vegetables' of various seasons included leeks, beets, strawberries, asparagus and carrots. The metropolitan area of Greater Athens still included 265,330 stremmata of farm land as late as 1961.

The most striking feature of this modern agricultural system is that it is to a large and increasing extent geared to producing cash crops for an urban market at the expense of the subsistence crops of cereals and olives. This is manifested most notably by the fact that the area devoted to the main cereal, wheat, is smaller than the area planted with vines, to meet the drinking requirements of modern Athenians.[5] Since a litre of wine provides about half of the basal metabolism of a resting man for twenty-four hours and it has been suggested that alcohol may have provided up to 25 per cent of the calorific intake of inhabitants of the Mediterranean in the past, the spread of viticulture in classical antiquity probably did raise environmental carrying capacity substantially (see Chapter I above). Children in antiquity drank diluted wine from the age of six months onwards (see Chapter II.7 above).[6] Nevertheless viticulture demands a high labour input and is risky in terms of the danger of climatic fluctuations affecting yield. It would be foolish to assume that such a high degree of specialisation in viticulture was ever a feature of Attic agriculture before the last couple of generations, in the absence of a large urban market with a purchasing power comparable to that of modern Athens. Indeed Attica ranks second out of 143 eparchies in modern Greece in terms of the proportion of the total cultivated area devoted to vines.[7]

The demand of a huge urban market also manifests itself by the areas devoted to vegetables and citrus fruits. The modern Greek census employs the same threefold classification of vegetables according to their season of planting as Theophrastos did, but some of the species grown today have only arrived in Greece since the end of antiquity, including the tomato.[8] Agriculture in modern Attica increasingly operates on the basis of a symbiotic relationship with a large urban centre which provides both a large effective demand for cash crops and a labour force to meet the requirements of a labour intensive type of agriculture. The essential premise of such a symbiotic relationship is the virtual certainty of being able to purchase from elsewhere the bread to feed both the urban population and farmers who specialise in cash crops.[9]

Following Gernet (1909), most ancient historians have believed that this premise was also valid in classical antiquity, or, in other words, that classical Athens had a reasonable degree of certainty of being able to import very large quantities of cereals each year in order to feed a population whose own territory was nowhere near self-sufficient. It was

shown in Chapter II.2 that a consideration of the carrying capacity of
Attica casts severe doubt upon this interpretation. Moreover the modern
consequence of specialisation by farmers in more profitable but
non-essential cash crops almost certainly did not follow in ancient Attica
as well, where the ideal remained *autarkeia*. This word is untranslatable
into English because it bore the connotations not only of 'self-sufficiency'
in the parlance of modern economics, but also had moral overtones alien
to the modern world, encapsulating the basic attributes of the truly 'free'
man who did not depend on anyone else for his livelihood and was not
subject to the authority of any other private individual.[10]

The purely 'economic' aspects of *autarkeia*, in Polanyi's substantivist
sense, are illustrated very well by Xenophon's *Oikonomikos*. He assigned
priority to cereal cultivation in his discussion of polyculture, a pattern of
farming designed to boost total productivity of all crops put together in a
situation in which a shortage of fertilisers made it impossible to boost the
yields of monocultures to high levels. Xenophon's precepts on agriculture
were already recognised in antiquity for what they were, banal common
sense, by such an unoriginal mind as that of Philodemos. The
pseudo-Aristotelian *Oikonomikos* observed that small Athenian households had to sell their produce immediately and later on buy what they
needed on the market because they did not have a storeroom (presumably
the towers called *purgoi* found on some classical farms in Attica).
Philodemos' attitude suggests that this was not the preferred way of
making a living. He described it as unprofitable, presumably because
market prices were at their lowest immediately after the harvest, when
smallholders and sharecroppers without a storeroom would have been
forced to sell their produce, and then rose gradually during the year.[11]

Attitudes to dependence on the market for daily necessities are also
illustrated by the reaction of the other members of Perikles' household to
his decision to rely on the market for daily requirements. This anecdote is
undoubtedly a reflection of the prevailing attitude towards market places
in antiquity, all the more so if it was invented by a Hellenistic biographer,
as has been suggested.[12] However, the moral and political dimension of
autarkeia was also very important in antiquity. It was the essence of life
in the *polis* for Aristotle, an important theme in Cynicism, as shown by
the work of Teles *peri autarkeias*, and was identified with the principal
virtue of self control by the Stoics. Such philosophers were systematising
a line of thought which had originated by the Homeric age. The emphasis
of these philosophers on *autarkeia* should be taken literally and seriously.
Their opinion is almost infinitely superior to the conclusion reached by
historians in the nineteenth century AD, anachronistically retrojecting
the conditions of Europe during the Industrial Revolution back to
antiquity, namely that a state such as Athens depended for her
prosperity and livelihood in antiquity on international trade.[13]

One important reference to the word *autarkeia* outside the philosophers deserves consideration. Thucydides, in his version of Perikles' funeral oration, regarded Athens as the *autarkestatê polis*, 'the most self-sufficient *polis*'. In contrast Demosthenes stated in the Athenian assembly less than a century later that Athens had to import more grain than any other Greek *polis*. This is paradoxical from the viewpoint of modern economics, because modern scholars are rightly unanimous that the number of mouths that had to be fed in Athens in the mid-fourth century BC was rather less than in the time of Thucydides, but nevertheless in terms of his own set of values Thucydides was right. Athens was 'self-sufficient' in the *Pentêkontaëtia* because she was the hub of what Sir John Hicks (1969) styled a 'command economy', as the 'Old Oligarch' knew only too well, and she had problems achieving 'self-sufficiency' in the fourth century because she had ceased to be the hub of a command economy.[14]

Finley (1985a) correctly observed that the ancient Greeks lacked concepts such as 'productivity' appropriate to an economy with a fully integrated system of self-regulating markets linking together all the factors of production. Even the way the ancient Greeks thought about 'self-sufficiency' was fundamentally different from the way a modern economist would reason about its pros and cons, concentrating on the advantages generated by an international division of labour. Later on ancient concepts of farming productivity will be examined in detail (section 9 below). The modern substantivist 'economic' sense of 'self-sufficiency' was deliberately suppressed in the funeral oration, which Loraux (1981) identified as the quintessential expression of the ideology of the Athenian *polis*. It was subordinated to hierarchical relations of dominance and subordination between the Athenians and their subject allies, within an ideology which attempted to eliminate such relations, inherent in any structure, between the members of the group who shared that ideology. Panegyrics of Greek *poleis* only put such topics as how beautiful the crops were in the forefront of attention during the Roman empire, when the Greeks found themselves on the bottom rung of the ladder of hierarchical relations, following in the footsteps of Xenophon's *Poroi*, which explicitly renounced imperialism as the way to achieve self-sufficiency.[15]

Nevertheless modern historians should not wish to confine themselves to trying to understand what thinking in ancient Greek terms meant to an ancient Greek, nor could Demosthenes ignore the changed reality of his own time, and the modern concept of self-sufficiency still sets very interesting problems for Athenian history. Xenophon's common sense approach to farming did not lead him to consider downgrading cereal cultivation in favour of more remunerative cash crops, as farmers in modern Attica are increasingly doing. The observed differences between ancient and modern practice should make us not only recall that the ancient Greeks lacked a commercial, as distinct from an import, interest, in Hasebroek's terms, but also question the validity of the vital premise mentioned above, as Garnsey (1985) & (1988) has started to do. Finley did not appear to be bothered by the divergence between the ideal of self-sufficiency and the 'reality' of massive grain imports. In this book a new approach to Athens' problems in achieving self-sufficiency in antiquity is outlined, revolving around the concept of carrying capacity.[16]

It is convenient to mention at this point certain other features of agriculture in Attica which may be inferred from the modern land use pattern. Attica is one of the driest regions of Europe and the low average annual rainfall has an obvious impact on the modern agricultural system. This is shown by the very small areas of land devoted to, first, maize and potatoes, two crops from the western hemisphere with a potentially much higher productivity than wheat or barley which helped to support and indeed make possible the expanding population during the early modern period in various parts of Europe but which are not suited to Attica's dry climate; secondly, to irrigated land, even with the assistance of modern pumping technology; and thirdly, to edible pulses.[17]

The inadequate rainfall of Attica prevents the cultivation of leguminous grain crops such as broad (field) beans on a large scale as field crops, rather than garden crops, in rotation with cereals. The broad bean is the least drought-resistant pulse crop. Theophrastos regarded it as a crop which gave a small yield. The fact that Theophrastos discusses legumes alongside cereals in his works on botany does not prove that they were integrated into sophisticated crop rotation systems. He bracketed them together because in his fourfold classification scheme of plants into *dendron* (tree), *thamnos* (shrub), *phruganon* (under-shrub) and *poa* (herb), cereals and legumes both fell into the category of *poa*. A subsidiary reason for considering them together was that they were both *sitos*, i.e. food suitable for breadmaking. Moreover many grain legumes are undesirable preceding crops for cereals in any case, extracting more nitrogen from the soil than they put in, if the crop is harvested.[18] Beans do have a beneficial effect on soil fertility if they are instead ploughed in as green manure, as was the custom in Thessaly and Macedonia, cooler and wetter areas than Attica, in antiquity. However, the crop is then not available for human consumption. Beans were also used as animal fodder.[19]

Pulses contain a good supply of amino acids such as lysine and tryptophan in which cereals are deficient and so in combination with cereals form a balanced diet. However, the higher total proportion of proteins in legumes than in cereals means that the nitrogen requirements of legumes are substantially higher, resulting in lower yields. The ecological mutualism between legumes and nitrogen-fixing bacteria is only advantageous in environments in which plant nutrients are scarce, because it is more expensive in energetic terms for leguminous plants to maintain these mutualisms than to take nitrogen compounds straight from the soil. In rich environments legumes tend to be overshadowed by rapidly growing stronger competitors such as grasses, explaining the problems encountered in repeatedly cultivating legume crops on the same plot of land. The abundance of beans, lentils, chickpeas and other legumes in Mediterranean agriculture is a direct evolutionary consequence of an ecosystem in which plant nutrients are scarce, because of the summer drought.[20]

Under traditional conditions in which fertilisers are in short supply a cereal-food legume rotation system only makes sense if interpreted as a polyculture in which the combined yield of a cereal crop and a legume crop, expressed in either calorific or monetary terms, in successive years is on average greater than the yield of either a cereal crop preceded by bare fallow or the combined yields of two cereal crops without an intervening fallow year or the combined yields of two successive pulse crops. However the yield of the cereal component alone of the cereal-grain-legume rotation is lower than the yield of a cereal crop preceded by bare fallow. The importance of multiple cropping systems in antiquity will be emphasised in this chapter, but in the sense of growing more than one crop on the same plot of land at the same time, not in the sense of crop rotation systems. Even though legumes contain a higher proportion of proteins than cereals, a sufficiency of proteins may be obtained from cereals alone if the consumption level is sufficiently high. This is doubtless one reason for the large cereal rations attested for antiquity.[21]

The disease called favism, a haemolytic anaemia, precipitated in certain individuals in Greek and other Mediterranean populations by the reaction of certain genotypes, which are deficient in the ability to make the enzyme glucose-6-phosphate dehydrogenase, to the ingestion of the beans of *Vicia faba, inter alia*, certainly caused individuals, and possibly even whole communities, to neglect this important source of protein. The field bean contains isouramil, a strong oxidising agent which ruptures red blood cells containing malaria parasites before they have completed their development. Galen records that many people preferred to eat the field bean (*kuamos*) raw. This habit meant that such chemicals were not degraded by cooking, and may have led to the frequency of favism in the past being higher than it is today. The enzyme mentioned above plays an important role in stabilising the cell walls of erythrocytes as part of a biochemical cycle for destroying such oxidising agents. A deficiency in enzyme production confers resistance to falciparum malaria, the most dangerous species of malaria. The parasites of falciparum malaria are vulnerable to oxidising agents in the presence of G6PD deficiency because they habitually complete their lifecycle in internal organs of the body where oxygen is relatively scarce, in contrast to the other species of malaria in humans which mainly dwell in the peripheral tissues of the body.

The frequencies of the various alleles in question, sex-linked characters which protect only heterozygous females who may then play their role in reproducing the population, could only rise to significant levels in areas of field bean cultivation and of endemic malaria. However, excessive bean consumption, causing favism in some individuals in whom the enzyme is in short supply, would have prevented the various alleles responsible for differing levels of enzyme deficiency spreading throughout the entire human population and to some extent discouraged consumption of beans, maintaining a very complicated genetic polymorphism. Pythagoras' injunction against eating beans may well be a consequence of this state of affairs. Some modern Greek villagers still believe that *Vicia faba* beans are harmful to all humans.

The case of the field bean in antiquity furnishes a good example of the complexity of an ecosystem, involving such diverse elements as climatic variations, agricultural techniques, the interaction of different species of plants within crop rotation systems, and the dependence of an evolving plant's suitability or unsuitability for human consumption on the genotypes of potential consumers, which were themselves evolving in response to evolving disease patterns, which themselves depended on the changing distribution of the species of mosquito which act as vectors of malaria in the Mediterranean, in accordance with global climatic variation. Only the small-seeded varieties of *Vicia faba* (*var. microsperma*, field beans) existed in antiquity, and the higher-yielding large-seeded varieties (*var. macrosperma*, broad beans), which are important crops today, did not evolve until the first millennium AD. This is the first instance to be mentioned in this chapter of plant evolution in classical antiquity.[22]

Ancient sources also mention deleterious consequences of excessive consumption of certain other legumes, such as the disease lathyrism, caused by excessive consumption of the grass pea (*Lathyrus sativus*). The Hippokratic corpus mentions illnesses arising from excessive consumption of bitter vetch (*Vicia ervilia*, Greek *orobos*) during a subsistence crisis at Ainos in Thrace in the late fifth century BC. Demosthenes states that the Athenians were reduced to eating bitter vetch during the war with Sparta in the 370s BC. Plutarch records that the Pythagoreans prohibited consumption of *lathuros* (grass pea) and *erebinthos* (chickpea) as well as *kuamos*. The comic poets suggest that grass pea was sometimes eaten in Attica, and Galen says that it was frequently consumed in Anatolia. Grass pea has also been found on prehistoric archaeological sites in Greece. Evidently people sometimes had no option but to eat plants which had retained powerful chemical defence systems (Chapter I above). Nitrogen isotope analysis of human bones, taking advantage of the difference in isotopic ratios of the atmospheric nitrogen fixed by the bacteria associated with legumes and of nitrogen derived from other sources, makes it feasible now to investigate directly the contribution of grain legumes to diets in antiquity, but to my knowledge this technique has not yet been employed in physical anthropology in Greece.[23]

The low rainfall of Attica also makes an impact in that a not insignificant proportion of arable land is still left fallow rather than supporting a leguminous fodder plant as part of a crop rotation system, even though there is no doubt that across modern Greece as a whole the more systematic employment of crop rotation systems including such plants and the use of modern pumps to water them are two of the factors which have led to a very sharp decline in the proportion of arable land left fallow each year over the last two generations. However, water conservation was not the most important benefit derived from leaving land fallow in Greece in the past (see section 12 below). H. Forbes (1985) showed how these recent developments, together with the modern demand for cash crops and the elimination of malaria, have transformed the Troizen plain.[24]

The widespread employment of fodder crops such as lucerne (*Mêdikê poa*), which requires irrigation in a semi-arid climate to give high yields, is a very recent phenomenon, although they were known in antiquity. This is another consequence of the crop evolution that was taking place in antiquity. Lucerne was mainly used for feeding horses in antiquity. The domesticated horse arrived from south Russia in the late third millennium BC in the mountainous areas of Persia and Anatolia to which the primitive diploid form of lucerne was indigenous. It was only then that the cultivated tetraploid forms of lucerne evolved and began to be spread by man. Since it was not yet fully acclimatised to semi-arid lowland areas and only reached Greece at the time of the Persian Wars, lucerne was not a major crop in classical Greece. Travelling in the opposite direction as well, lucerne was brought to China in 126 BC.[25]

To conclude this section, it seems reasonable to suggest that in the pre-modern period the proportion of farm land in Attica devoted to viticulture was never more than a small fraction of what it is today, in the absence of urban demand on the modern scale. This suggestion is strengthened if it is recalled that Athenian wine, which was ignored by Athenaios (book I) in his catalogue of fine wines, was apparently not a connoisseur's delight and is not known ever to have been exported in antiquity. Its probable resemblance to retsina accounts for this.[26]

Similarly, the area devoted to vegetables as cash crops for the same urban market was doubtless much smaller than it is today, as was the area devoted to leguminous fodder crops, for the reasons explained above. Crops such as citrus fruits, potatoes, maize, cotton and tomatoes did not exist in Attica in classical antiquity. Most of the land occupied today by vines, citrus fruits, and a few crops of lesser significance was used to grow cereals and olives in the past. The proportion of Attica that could have been planted with cereals intercropped with olives in the past was about twice as large as the area devoted to the various cereals and fodder crops today (about 14 per cent of the eparchy). The very important question of the incidence of fallow will be discussed in section 12 below.

3. Olive production in ancient Attica

It is necessary to consider the role of the olive tree in ancient Attica, its place of origin according to Herodotos. Pausanias regarded Attica, along with Sikyon, as the district of Roman Greece in which olive oil was most plentiful, but not the best in quality. Again this was a consequence of the low and variable rainfall of Attica. Recent experimental work has confirmed that the olive tree in fact does better under irrigation, which ensures a supply of the water needed during the dry summer before the final maturation of the fruit in order to complete its development, however surprising these results may seem in the light of the traditional association of the olive with dry farming in the Mediterranean. The evergreen sclerophyllous trees characteristic of the Mediterranean today evolved many millions of years ago before the modern Mediterranean climate developed. At that time the climate was warm, with rainfall in summer as well as in winter, and so there was no summer drought as there is today. It is because of this evolutionary history that the olive tree is able to respond to artificial irrigation in the summer (replacing the summer rainfall of millions of years ago), and produce bumper harvests every year, although under dry-farming conditions it only produces a small crop once every two years. This inherited capacity to use water all the year round sharply differentiates the olive tree from plants which really evolved in arid conditions, such as cacti and succulents, and consequently cannot tolerate water all the year round. The olive tree, which prefers summer rainfall and once received it but no longer does so and accordingly is not perfectly adapted to its environment, illustrates beautifully the operation of the van Valen hypothesis to explain why evolution is a never-ending process (see Chapter I above). Aristotle noted that large olive crops were correlated with the swarming of honeybees, caused by spring and summer rainfall good both for olive trees and for flowers for bees.[27]

In fact in modern Greece Attica is a long way from being pre-eminent in olive cultivation, in terms of the ratio of the number of trees to the total area of cultivated land, contrary to expectations aroused by the fame of her olives in antiquity. Olive trees, like cereals a crop that only produces a low income, have lost out to the desire of modern farmers to maximise income by concentrating on viticulture. Moreover the coastal regions which are most suitable for olive cultivation are more profitably devoted to tourists nowadays. Nevertheless the contrast raises some interesting questions.[28]

The olive tree does grow on poor ground where cereals cannot be raised, of which Attica has its fair share, but it undoubtedly only gives good yields on good soils and so does compete with cereals for land, reflected in the practice of intercropping. A lot of recent research in agriculture has shown that in traditional farming systems, in which fertilisers are in short supply and the absence of mechanised equipment means that one important motive for crop uniformity is absent, crop mixtures often yield a higher combined productivity than monocultures of any of the components of the mixture grown under similar environmental conditions. This is because different types of plants cultivated together exploit the environment more fully. Moreover the resulting reduction in the population density of each of the components of the crop mixture also reduces the density of populations of pathogens which might adversely affect the productivity of monocultures. Similarly experiments at the Rothamsted Experimental Farm on grass mixtures have shown that as the yield decreases with lower fertiliser inputs the number of species of grasses which can establish themselves successfully increases. An impoverished environment may well support a larger number of species than a rich environment, in which the strongest competitors become dominant. Under traditional farming conditions in the Mediterranean a mixture of olive trees and cereals or legumes is on average more productive than monocultures of any of these plants. The spread of olive cultivation and of the practice of intercropping in Greece and elsewhere in the Mediterranean in the first millennium BC did cause a real increase in agricultural productivity, besides increasing the quality and variety of the diet.[29]

The natural biological rhythm of the olive tree, with production of a good crop only once every two years, synchronised on a regional basis, is a reaction to the Mediterranean summer drought which is disadvantageous for farmers. The difficulty of practising irrigation in Attica would have affected not only the quality of the fruit as table olives, but also intensified interannual variations in yields as well as affecting the density of plantation of olive trees.[30]

The concentration of olive trees in modern Greece is the result of thousands of years of human activity, and the number of olive trees in Greece as a whole has increased very substantially over the last two generations alone. Ancient sources hint that in some regions of ancient Greece, especially in early periods, olive cultivation was not taken for granted as it is today. It is well known that Hesiod does not mention the olive tree in the *Works & Days*, at least in the text as it has been transmitted to us. Pollen cores suggest that in central Greece incipient olive cultivation was disrupted at the end of the Mycenaean period, while in the southern Argolid it did not commence until the early first millennium BC.[31] In the Peloponnese the Spartans received olive oil as part of the rent in kind paid by the Helots. However, table olives only appeared sparsely on the menu of the *sussitia* or common messes, according to Dikaiarchos, and olive oil was only consumed as part of the subsidiary *epaikla*, according to Persaios. Apparently it was not regarded as a prime item of consumption by the overlords of the Peloponnese. This seems strange, given the suitability of Lakonia for olive cultivation.

However, it should not be forgotten that some ancient authors regarded the olive as having little nutritional value (see Chapter II.7 above).[32]

Nor should the very substantial areas of Greece, including Arkadia and most of northern Greece and Macedonia (barring the coastal strips), in which the olive tree does not grow successfully even today for climatic reasons, be forgotten. The traditions that Peisistratos and Solon were interested in fostering olive cultivation indicate that it was not necessarily regarded as an automatic thing to do even in Attica as late as the sixth century BC. It is arguable that the spread of olive cultivation in mainland Greece and in most of the rest of the Mediterranean was largely a phenomenon of the first, not the third, millennium BC, contrary to C. Renfrew (1972b), and that this addition to the food supply was a not insignificant factor behind the population growth of the first half of the first millennium BC.[33]

As far as the Mycenaean period in the second half of the second millennium BC is concerned, it has been shown that the olives found at Tiryns dating to the LHIII period still bore considerable similarities to wild forms. They exhibit the heterogeneity characteristic of sexually reproducing wild varieties instead of the relative homogeneity of vegetatively propagated domesticated varieties. Moreover it has been argued that the olive oil mentioned on the Linear B tablets was largely the oil of wild olive trees (*Olea europaea var. sylvestris*), which constituted a more suitable base for perfume manufacture. The perfumed oil of the palaces was a luxury product intended for a very restricted social circle. Moreover oil-presses and other equipment for processing olives have not been found on archaeological sites in mainland Greece antedating the Late Bronze Age. Oil-presses are not essential for olive oil production, but only small-scale production is possible in their absence.[34]

Insofar as Renfrew's theory has any validity it must be restricted to Crete. Even there the origin of olive cultivation probably depended on diffusion from the Levant. Finds of olive pollen in sections of pollen cores dating to the Neolithic period in Crete probably represent a refuge of wild trees which survived the last glaciation. This is certainly the correct explanation for all pre-classical olive pollen everywhere in the western Mediterranean, as shown by classical literary sources (see Chapter I above). The same explanation is probably valid for mainland Greece and Crete as well. If the domesticated olive tree was introduced to Crete from the Levant in the fourth millennium BC, Renfrew's systems theory becomes quite useless as a means of explaining the development of the Minoan civilisation, because systems theories cannot predict novelties arising outside the system. The spread of cultivation of the domesticated olive tree to mainland Greece may have been a consequence of the conquest of Crete by Greeks from the mainland in the middle of the second millennium BC.[35]

We ought to be wary of assuming that olive cultivation has always been as important in Greece as it is today. This note of caution applies even more to other parts of the Mediterranean such as Italy and North Africa. The spread of olive cultivation was one aspect of changing ecological patterns in the first millennium BC. The distribution of the olive tree is very closely determined by winter temperatures. These must descend to a certain level to permit initiation of flowering in the following year (vernalisation). This requirement excludes *Olea europaea* from the tropics. However, if winter temperatures are too low the trees are killed by the cold. The proximity of the sea, which acts as a moderating influence on winter temperatures, explains the preference of the olive tree for coastal regions. Thus the distribution of the olive tree is in fact an indicator of the cool but not too cold Mediterranean winter, as was shown by Mitrakos (1982), rather than the Mediterranean summer heat and drought which are much better known to tourists. Theoretically extension of olive cultivation requires selection for increased cold tolerance, a phenomenon observed in many other crop plants, and the Quaternary Ice Ages forced the olive tree to evolve its present level of cold tolerance, up to $-10°C$. The evolution of the domesticated olive tree from its wild ancestor, the oleaster, was not necessarily any slower than the domestication of cereals from wild annual grasses, if we think in terms of generations. The generation length of an olive tree is much longer than that of an annual plant. Consequently the same rate of change per generation translates into very different rates of change per unit time. This is the best way of explaining why the domestication of fruit trees was a much slower process than the domestication of cereals.[36]

The large cereal rations attested in the ancient sources are not implausible on a comparative basis, but only make sense on the assumption that per capita consumption of olives and olive oil was lower than the world record levels achieved by modern Greek peasants. A low level of consumption of olive oil by the Spartans would correlate neatly with the high level of cereal consumption suggested by their contributions to the *sussitia* as a means of attaining the desired calorific intake. Even so the contributions to the messes were so large that a substantial proportion of them was probably destined for long-term storage rather than immediate use.[37]

The very latest techniques available for olive cultivation today require an extra labour input to irrigate the trees in semi-arid regions, but historically olive cultivation has often been very extensive in nature, with little effort being put into it, as is still common among farmers in Crete. It may be wondered whether Perses' (alleged) laziness was not actually more typical of attitudes to work among peasant farmers in ancient Greece than his brother Hesiod's polemical injunctions to work hard, given the absence of the Protestant work ethic. However that may be, Theophrastos provides a very illuminating commentary on the extensive nature of olive cultivation in ancient Greece. He states that it was thought that intensive cultivation of the olive tree would shorten its lifespan. Consequently the Thasians actually welcomed lazy farming by tenants on leased land bearing olive trees.[38]

The strategy enunciated here is that of the subsistence farmer, who was interested simply in conserving his olive trees as a source of food, not in intensifying cultivation solely for short-term monetary gain. Naturally he would rarely have had the security of life necessary to envisage considerably expanding his stock of a tree which requires 5-15 years to produce any return at all, depending on the quality of the attention given to it, and 35-50 years to reach maturity and full production. A fragment attributed to Hesiod by Pliny may indicate that Hesiod was unaware of the technique of grafting, the most rapid method of propagating olive trees.[39] Theophrastos' information goes a long way towards explaining why surviving examples of land leases from ancient Greece sometimes lack clauses requiring the tenant to make improvements to the leased land. This is testimony to the primitive nature of agriculture in ancient Greece, as are the short tenures mentioned in most of the surviving leases. In the Agricultural Revolution that preceded the Industrial Revolution in England very long leases were regarded as essential in order to encourage tenants to improve the land.[40]

There is no doubt that by the classical period there were some estates that specialised in olive production, perhaps even for export. However, Hadrian's law, entitling the *polis* of Athens to purchase up to one third of the annual production of olive oil, is the only source that indicates the size of the surplus that might have been produced in a good year in Roman Athens in the second century AD.[41] The law states that the producers could keep more than two-thirds of the harvest if the state did not need as much as a third in a good harvest year. It also envisages considerable interannual fluctuations in yields, also discussed by Theophrastos. Such fluctuations create the possibility that an individual producer with a surplus in the on years might have had a deficit in the alternate off years and so have to buy olive oil himself, if the surpluses of the on years were largely entrusted to the marketplace. The severity of the problems caused by bad cereal harvests in a region like Attica in antiquity was probably greatly affected by whether or not they happened to coincide with the alternate off years in the olive's biennial cycle.[42]

The natural biological rhythm of the olive tree must have been a motor for inter-regional trade and exchange. Nevertheless, it is important to bear in mind that subsistence farmers in Greece today still respond to this problem, and presumably always have done so, by storing most of the surplus of the on years for the anticipated following off years. This means that the surpluses of on years can be rather illusory if production is on a small scale. The market need not play a significant role.[43]

In our assessment of the economy of ancient Athens, it is important to remember that olives and olive oil, the only product that ancient Athens could have exported in significant quantities, apart from silver in certain periods, are regarded today as a low income crop which often yields a vanishingly small profit margin for its producers.[44] It already had that status in classical antiquity. The Romans did not need to possess the concept of an 'economy' to realise, as Pliny did, that the cost of hiring extra labour at harvest time, which is not required during the rest of the year, makes it extremely difficult to make olive cultivation viable as production of a cash crop for the market. Columella also noted that the olive tree required hardly any expenditure, except at harvest-time. The situation is exactly the same in Mediterranean countries today, where the cost of hiring extra labour at harvest time amounts to up to 80 per cent of the total annual investment required for olive cultivation. 'With the low yields being obtained from the olive groves in Greece, cash production costs should be cut to a minimum.' This is why olive oil production is simply not suitable for the 'slave mode of production'.[45]

That the Athenians relied so heavily on such a crop is evidence for a very low level of development of the agrarian economy. In recent times the development of capitalist agriculture in Europe has generally entailed a shift towards cash crops, which require a high labour input throughout the crop's lifecycle and so fetch a high market price, and towards meat and dairy products. These are much more expensive to produce, because of the higher position of animals on ecological food chains, than the subsistence crops of olives and cereals. In this respect description of the agricultural system of ancient Attica as a primitive agricultural system is justified. Finally, we should note H.A. Forbes's observation that the labour requirements of olive and cereal cultivation do conflict with each other. Farmers might have sown less land in what they expected to be on years for their olive trees. This conflict was probably less severe in the past when biennial fallow was a regular practice. Nevertheless it serves to bring us on to the next topic, namely possible variations in the size of the total cultivated area.[46]

4. The extent of the cultivated area of Attica

The complete absence of literary or documentary evidence for the size of the cultivated area in antiquity is reflected in the diversity of the estimates given by modern scholars, ranging from Jardé's opinion that arable land was about 20 per cent of the total area of Attica (of which half was fallow) to a recent guess that up to 50 per cent of Attica might have been cultivated in antiquity.[47] Moreover more recent experience suggests that the area sown would have displayed interannual variability itself, depending on such factors as the availability of seed grain, war and peace, the availability of animals for ploughing and the amount of time left for ploughing depending on the time of arrival of the autumn rains. Ancient cultivation undoubtedly exceeded present-day limits in some areas. For example, the Dema House stands in an area which has remains of old terracing but is desolate today. Moreover population pressure on the land in modern Greece has declined since the high point in the 1920s owing to migration away from the countryside and higher cereal yields.[48]

However, if the definition of arable land employed in the 1961 census is remembered, which included land of such poor quality that it had only produced a cereal crop once in the five years prior to the survey, and the opinion of the authors of the *Economic and Social Atlas of Greece* that modern cultivation has gone well beyond the limits consistent with conservational land use, the modern area of cultivated land, about 35 per cent of Attica, should be regarded as the maximum possible rather than a minimum which could be very significantly exceeded. The inclusion of the Athens-Piraeus area, dominated by agriculture in antiquity, and the north-west corner of ancient Attica, including the Thriasian plain (excluded from the data for the modern land use pattern quoted above), would probably take the proportion of classical Attica as a whole that was cultivated towards the 40 per cent mark.[49]

The population growth of the archaic period, with a consequent increase in the number of very small property holdings, took the Athenian population towards the limits of the environmental carrying capacity of Attica by the time of Solon. Virgin land was colonised in the archaic period. In the classical period there is virtually no trace of any remaining unoccupied cultivable land in Attica, which fits in with the high population density discussed in the previous chapter. It may also explain why there is no certain evidence in classical Athenian sources for any procedure equivalent to the Roman *usucapio*, whereby occupation of unused land could lead to legal ownership. It is a matter of dispute among legal historians whether or not *usucapio* was permitted in classical Athens. Certain areas of land were not cultivated because they were consecrated to the gods, such as the *Hiera Orgas* on the border between Attica and Megara. The fourth-century BC financier Lykourgos may have boosted Athens' public revenues by leasing out previously uncultivated consecrated land belonging to the *polis* and to demes. Nor is there in Attica any trace of land, at least in the lowland plains, with a legal status comparable to that of Roman *ager publicus*. The usual Greek practice was to rent out public land to specific private individuals. Consequently the absence of common land was another problem for Athenian smallholders. The legal status of mountain pastures is unclear.[50]

Finley used the fact that Athenian honorary decrees for foreigners never awarded pasturage rights to the honorands as evidence that animal husbandry was not important in ancient Attica. However this is surely incorrect, since a quarter of modern Attica is classified as pasture land. Moreover the ancient Greeks themselves were conscious that Attica was better suited to animal husbandry than to agriculture. We must distinguish between sheep and goats, of which Attica can accommodate a considerable number, and larger animals, very few of which can live in Attica, given the shortage of both meadowland and fodder crops.[51]

The paucity of references to shepherds in Athenian literature must be ascribed, first, to the very low level of prestige attached to such an occupation, and secondly, to a powerful ideological tendency to regard sedentary agriculture as the way of life befitting a civilised people, in contrast to animal husbandry which was associated with wild and uncivilised ways of life. This idea is not irrelevant to understanding the autochthony myth of the Athenians, with its contrast between the stationary Athenians and the movements of all the other Greeks in early periods of Greek history. Justin, who used sources favourable to the Greeks, for instance in his treatment of the Lamian War, likened Philip II of Macedon to a transhumant shepherd.[52]

The main occasions for meat consumption in classical Athens were furnished by religious festivals at which meat was distributed from animals sacrificed at public expense. Xenophon made Sokrates describe a man who wanted to eat meat alone, without bread, as a glutton. Only an Athenian who was so wealthy that he need not fear food shortages even in years of bad harvests would have used the produce of land to support animals, beyond the bare minimum required for ploughing, if that same land could produce cereals, because animal husbandry is an extremely costly way of producing food, although its products are very prestigious, for the same reason. Animal biomass is much smaller than plant biomass because of its higher position on ecological food chains and energy losses as food chains are ascended, in accordance with the second law of thermodynamics.[53]

An even more effective way of manifesting superiority and expressing social distance was to raise not useful animals such as cattle and sheep, but useless animals. The useless animal par excellence in ancient Greece was the horse. It was difficult to maintain because of the shortage of suitable natural pastures in most of southern Greece and the scarcity of fodder crops such as oats and lucerne. The horse's dietary requirements are more particular than those of various other domesticated animals because it only has a simple one-chambered stomach, unlike the complex digestive system of ruminants. However the main problem in using the horse in ancient Greece was that the *hippos*, conventionally translated as 'horse', was no larger than a modern pony. This is shown by both archaeological remains and works of art. Consequently it did not have the physical strength necessary to challenge the ox as a draught animal or carry a soldier in heavy armour on its back. It also had limited military value in the terrain of ancient Greece. For it to become a really useful domesticated animal another stage in the evolution of *Equus caballus* was required. Larger-size groups of horses began to evolve in the first millennium BC in Iran (see also Chapter IV below). Consequently *hippotrophia*, horse breeding, was a characteristic of the rich in ancient Greece.[54]

There is still a large predominance of sheep and goats in modern Attica, despite the increased cultivation of fodder crops recently, and the same was doubtless true in antiquity. Jardé's argument that animal consumption must have accounted for most of the grain recorded on the inscription IG II^2 1672 should be rejected, because he failed to take into account the following factors:

(1) farmers with very small plots of land would have cultivated them by hand with the hoe, not with a plough;[55]
(2) farmers could have shared or borrowed oxen from each other, a possibility envisaged by Hesiod;
(3) most importantly, much of the ploughing on light Mediterranean soils, especially the summer ploughing of fallow land, could have been done by mules, not by oxen, using the ard. The Athenians did not need as many oxen as Jardé supposed.[56]

One of the authors of the Hippokratic corpus provides the best testimony to the struggle for survival of cattle and oxen in ancient Greece. He observed that these animals found it difficult to eat grass on fallow fields at the end of the winter, when it was still very short, because of the nature of their jaws and lips. As a result they were so badly nourished that they suffered from a characteristic dislocation of the thigh bones from their sockets at the end of the winter season. To make matters worse, Hesiod recommended halving their rations of fodder during the same season. Horses too had a lean time, judging by Xenophon's recommendations for fodder rations which would not have sufficed to keep them well nourished.[57]

Use of arable land to support animals in semi-arid Attica was restricted to a minimum because of the high human population density. In a wetter and cooler area such as Thessaly, in contrast, cereal crops ultimately intended for human consumption could be used to feed animals because autumn grazing reduces the intense competition between plants in a rich environment and the ensuing excessive production of their vegetative parts. As a result the plants can devote a larger proportion of their resources to seed production. This is impossible in a drier region such as Attica where spring rainfall is generally too low to permit plant recovery after grazing. A mountainous region such as Epirus, which was not suited to arable farming, but possessed extensive pasturage, could support animals of above average size and productivity. However, Attica does not fall into this category.

This section may be concluded with the suggestion that the modern cultivated area of Attica should be taken as the core of the cultivated area in antiquity. However, the best of the pasture land might have sometimes produced a cereal crop under long fallow cultivation and otherwise have provided forage for sheep and goats, alongside fallow land in the core area. It has been estimated that a sheep needs about 938 m² of poor grazing land, probably an underestimate. On this basis the 94,000 sheep in the modern eparchy of Attica would require about 88.5 km² of pasture land, which may be compared with the 399 km² currently classified as pasture land. The sheep of modern Attica are roughly equivalent in number to the palace flock of Knossos on Crete in the Late Bronze Age, which could only have provided enough wool to have clothed about 25,000 people. The Athenians could not have exported wool in antiquity.[58]

5. Shifts in the balance between different cereals

After considering the size of the arable area, it is necessary to get to grips with the fascinating problem of historical changes in the species and varieties of cereals cultivated down the millennia. The data presented in section 2 above show that the main cereal in modern Attica is wheat. This was the case across southern Greece as a whole by 1860, the date of the first modern agricultural census spanning the entire country, when the ratio of the area sown with wheat to the area sown with barley was roughly 3:1.[59] In early modern Attica durum wheat (*Triticum durum*) was cultivated because it was the species of wheat best suited to the climate of Attica, having the lowest water requirement.[60] Since the 1920s the Greek government has encouraged farmers to abandon durum wheat in favour of new, more productive varieties of bread wheat (*Triticum aestivum*), which is very much better suited to bread-making. However, this policy has had its main effects in northern Greece, not in Attica. Selective breeding of the durum wheat of southern Greece produced increases in yields of up to 40 per cent in some areas from 1925 onwards.[61]

Jasny's standard work on the wheats of classical antiquity simply extrapolated from the modern distribution of species of wheat back to antiquity. He asserted that 'the distribution of the several wheats in the classical period is a natural predecessor of the present one'. It is arguable that he made here an assumption whose validity requires demonstration. History is about change over time and plants have a history just as men do. As Le Roy Ladurie said, 'it is mutilating the historian to make him into no more than a specialist in humanity'. The main thesis of the rest of this chapter is that it is possible to improve our understanding of agriculture in the ancient world by replacing Jasny's totally static view of cereals in antiquity with the dynamic perspective provided by evolutionary biology.[62]

The modern predominance of 'naked' wheats, i.e. wheats in which the glumes do not enclose the grains tightly and are easily detached by threshing, suggests that there is no a priori argument why they cannot be cultivated successfully across most of Greece, although the recent striking improvements in yields of both durum and bread wheat are due principally to the introduction of new, more productive varieties and the use of chemical fertilisers.[63] However the ancient sources unquestionably give the impression that naked wheats were much less important in ancient Attica than barley, especially the inscription IG II² 1672 which suggests a wheat:barley total yield ratio across Attica circa 329 BC of about 1:9.3.[64]

Many other sources support this impression. For example, some estates are known which are said to have produced large quantities of barley, but no wheat at all is mentioned.[65] One of Solon's laws prescribed that those invited to dine in the *prutaneion* at civic expense should have food made from barley on ordinary days and food made from wheat as well only on festival days. The victors at the Eleusinian Games received a prize of barley, and the Homeric Hymn to Demeter mentions the cultivation of *kri leukon*, white barley, at Eleusis.[66] References to food made from barley are more frequent than references to food made from wheat in the comedies of Aristophanes, as they had earlier been in Homer as well.[67] A woman's competence to engage in transactions was restricted to one *medimnos* of barley. This was doubtless one of the factors which led Geoffrey de Ste. Croix to propose the idea of a 'barley standard' in archaic Attica, in an unpublished paper unavailable to the present author.[68] Moreover several ancient authors record the tradition that barley was the oldest cultivated cereal in Greece.[69]

Nevertheless all this evidence may be questioned. It has been suggested that IG II² 1672 represents the harvest of a year in which very low or badly distributed rainfall had disproportionately reduced the wheat yield relative to the barley yield. Discussion of this problem will have to be postponed until Chapter IV below except for stating my belief that naked wheats were less important than barley in classical and especially in archaic Attica.[70]

The evidence from the Peloponnese should also be considered. The Helots are said to have paid tribute to the Spartiates in barley rather than in wheat.[71] It would be wrong to fall into the trap of 'le mirage spartiate' and attribute this to a desire for a 'spartan' diet because the rich sometimes contributed wheat to the *sussitia*, showing that at least by the early fourth century BC a cultural preference for wheat existed among the richest of the *homoioi*. It is arguable that if the masters ate mainly barley, then presumably everyone else did so as well.[72] The ancient sources provide a prima facie case that in archaic Messenia, when the tribute was imposed on the Helots, and in Lakonia in the fifth to third centuries BC the most important cultivated cereal was barley, not any kind of wheat. The contrast with the modern situation is even more striking than it is in the case of Attica. The preponderance of wheat in Messenia, a region with a much higher proportion of cultivatable land than Attica, was quite overwhelming even before the introduction of chemical fertilisers and other recent innovations.[73]

It appears then that in the archaic and classical periods in southern Greece barley was the most important cereal and that at some time since then, for some reason or reasons, there has been a shift from barley to wheat as the main cereal. There is nothing a priori implausible in suggesting that such a shift has taken place, since many well documented similar changes have taken place in other parts of the world and other periods of history. To give one well-known example, all the more interesting for being directly analogous to the problem delineated here, Le Roy Ladurie showed that the peasants in Languedoc in southern France consumed barley as a major component of their diet until the fourteenth century AD and then in the space of three generations in the fifteenth century AD wheat completely displaced barley as a human foodstuff.[74]

His explanation of this transformation revolved around the man:land ratio, which he argued changed to the advantage of the survivors after the depopulation which followed the Black Death. This resulted in a significant increase in the amount of land available per person on average and facilitated dependence on wheat, a cereal which was much more vulnerable to the effects of interannual climatic variability in a semi-arid climate. Consequently a family needed to sow more land with wheat than was needed in the case of barley to have the same degree of certainty of being able to make ends meet even in a year of a below average harvest. Later on the recovery of the human population was accompanied by a switch from wheat to rye, an even more reliable crop in much of France.

The parallels to this process in the relevant aspects of the history of Attica are very striking. The ancient sources emphasise the importance of barley in classical Greece, when the population density was very high (see Chapter II.2 above). However, wheat had become the main crop grown in southern Greece by the nineteenth century AD and the population of mediaeval and early modern Attica was much lower than that of classical Attica. In the century AD 1875-1975 the area of land per head of the population in Greece fell considerably in step with the population growth of that period. However, technological innovations such as methodical breeding of cereals (in Darwin's sense) and chemical fertilisers (first used in Greece in AD 1906) together with the rising standard of living and the consequent more powerful expression of consumer preferences have sustained the position of wheat as the main cereal cultivated in Greece.

The problem was exacerbated in the past by the larger area of land that was required in any case because of much lower cereal yields (see section 12 below). The minimum size of property-holding necessary to support a farming family today is only a third or an even smaller proportion of the area necessary to sustain a family at an equivalent standard of living in classical antiquity.[75]

It is suggested here that one of the reasons why barley was the most important cereal in classical Attica was because of the relatively small area of land available per person, and that wheat took over in a period when the population density was much lower. The small mediaeval population of the Peloponnese and Crete was regularly able to produce a surplus of wheat for export, unheard of in classical antiquity, in years of appropriate rainfall. Mediaeval Attica might also have been able to export wheat on occasion, while even Hellenistic Attica had had to spend money on buying foreign grain to meet the extortionate demand for grain of a Roman commander to feed his army.[76] It is very striking that mediaeval historians generally think of Greece as a grain exporting country, while ancient historians usually regard Greece as a land which had to import grain. The difference was not the result of any great improvements in cereal productivity, but of a massive decrease in the population of Greece. The question of surpluses or deficits in cereal production is entirely relative to the size of the population.

Ladurie's work suggests one fundamental methodological principle. We cannot hope to understand an agricultural system simply by studying all aspects of farming, because the choice of crops to be grown could be influenced by an exogenous factor such as population density, which is naturally related not only to the environmental carrying capacity of the land, but also to demographic factors such as the ecology of diseases and deterministic chaos which may have little or nothing to do with agriculture. It is suggested here that an analysis along these lines is relevant to the agrarian history of Attica down the millennia. However, it does not by itself explain all the observed phenomena, because there is plenty of evidence that the production of various types of naked wheat was actually increasing in Greece and elsewhere in the Mediterranean in the course of the first millennium BC during a period when the areas in question were all experiencing a phase of considerable population growth (see section 9 below).

6. Previous views on the origin and spread of naked wheats

The history of durum wheat is fundamental to understanding the agrarian history of Attica. By the onset of the modern period it was the only species of wheat grown in Attica and the main cereal. Ancient historians have followed Jasny in thinking that the same was true throughout antiquity. Recently, however, an Orientalist has challenged this orthodoxy by arguing that durum wheat was not grown in the classical period, possibly evolving during the lifetime of the Roman empire and then only spreading widely in the wake of the mediaeval Arab migrations. In view of this very considerable divergence of opinion it is well worth having a new look at the wheats of classical antiquity to see how recent archaeological and scientific work may affect the interpretations put on ancient Greek and Latin sources by classical scholars.[77]

Jasny identified *semidalis* as the Greek word signifying the flour made from durum wheat, but did not believe that durum wheat was a major crop before the first millennium BC. *Semidalis* indeed does have a relationship with the Orient. It was not originally a Greek or Indo-European word at all, but an Akkadian word which entered other Oriental languages such as Aramaic. It was then borrowed, possibly from the Hittites as intermediaries, by proto-Indo-Europeans when they entered Greece at the end of the EHII period, *c.* 2200 BC, to designate a type of plant and the food made from it. It may be inferred that this plant was native to the Middle East and eastern Mediterranean but not to the region of origin of the Indo-European ancestors of the Greeks. Whatever its identity, the geographical range of the cereal used to make *semidalis* was extensive in the Middle East by the third millennium BC, earlier than Jasny thought. In the classical period comic poets mention export of *semidalis* from Phoenicia to Athens. The word also makes an appearance in comedy as a personal name.[78]

The use of an Akkadian word to signify such a basic item contradicts the strong tendency in prehistoric archaeology to argue that the development of agriculture and civilisation in the Aegean was an independent process. Such loan words are only to be expected because throughout antiquity Greece was constantly receiving new plants and other living organisms from further east. A fitting moment to recall Grierson's brilliant dictum that if the spade cannot lie, this is at least partly because it cannot speak. Nevertheless, although the spade cannot speak itself, it can illuminate the ambiguities of human language by confirming the presence of material objects and natural organisms presumed to have been signified by the surviving words of an ancient language. This is of great potential value in agricultural history, as words signifying cereals are notoriously liable to alter their meanings (illustrated by the case of *zeia* in section 10 below). It is for this reason that we must subscribe to the words of a pioneer in palaeobotany, written over a century ago:[79] 'We must say it frankly, the works which repeat and comment on the ancient authors of Greece and Rome without giving the first place to botanical and archaeological facts, are no longer on a level with the science of the day.'[80]

Unfortunately things are never quite so simple. Whether or not durum wheat was widespread as early as the word *semidalis* is a thorny problem because palaeobotanists have expressed countless changes of opinion in the course of this century, so many in fact that it is an unavoidable conclusion that palaeobotany is not an exact science in the same way that physics, for example, is. The uncertainties in the identification of archaeological specimens of wheat grains are the consequence of several factors:

(1) overlaps in the ranges of variation of various species of wheat in respect of quantitative features such as seed size;
(2) the possibility that modern species of wheat are not identical to their early ancestors as a result of evolution;

(3) distortion of seed shapes and dimensions by carbonisation, which preserves them but tends to make them shorter and rounder;
(4) the possibility of the existence of any particular morphological feature in both tetraploid and hexaploid wheats, as a product of Vavilov's (1922) law of homologous variation;
(5) variations in soil fertility;
(6) the position of the grain in question vis-à-vis other grains in the spikelet;
(7) the impact of various plant diseases if they happen to strike late in the plant's lifecycle.[81]

Jasny relied on early palaeobotanical research which had concluded, for instance, that durum wheat was the main crop in Egypt before Alexander the Great.[82] A later generation of palaeobotanists concluded that these early identifications of durum wheat had been made using unreliable microscopic techniques and that durum wheat did not evolve before the last few centuries BC. At the same time it was concluded that bread wheat had been cultivated from *c.* 6000 BC onwards and had reached remote Britain by the third millennium BC. This school of thought has had a considerable impact on ancient history, especially on literature relating to Hellenistic Egypt to which we shall return (section 11 below).[83]

Other scholars came to the conclusion in the 1970s that it was impossible to differentiate reliably the carbonised remains of tetraploid and hexaploid naked wheats dug up on archaeological sites, unless spikelet fragments, which are rare on archaeological sites, are found. This opened up the possibility that durum wheat might have existed after all in the Neolithic period, without adducing definite proof, and also the possibility that naked hexaploid wheats might not have evolved until a much later stage. Finally the most recent research, employing more sophisticated techniques, focusing on the more distinctive spikelet fragments rather than on the grains themselves and employing electron microscopes, has concluded that it is possible to differentiate bread wheat and durum wheat and that progenitors of both had evolved by *c.* 5000 BC.[84]

It is obvious that all possible hypotheses have found an advocate. The current state of play is that both tetraploid and hexaploid naked wheats existed long before the classical period, but they were not dominant features of the crop pattern in the first few millennia of sedentary agriculture, a role filled by barley and emmer (see section 9 below). This is a paradox which requires explanation.

In general, historians of the Orient do not recognise the existence of durum wheat in the ancient Middle East in documentary sources. Mesopotamian cuneiform texts contain three important words for cereals which are usually translated as emmer, barley and bread wheat.[85]

Similarly, Dynastic Egyptian sources mention a triad of cereals which is probably identical to the Mesopotamian triad, although the crop pattern in Pharaonic Egypt has usually been regarded as idiosyncratic, with naked wheats being entirely absent. However, the identity of the third member of the trinity is uncertain, as it could have been bread wheat, durum wheat or simply a generic term covering all naked wheat, in the light of the controversy in palaeobotany reported above.[86]

The Akkadian word *samidu,* the ancestor of *semidalis*, which is based on a root *se* with the generic meaning of 'grain', is translated, probably incorrectly, as 'the finest flour' (see section 7 below). It is possible that this word did not have the same meaning in Akkadian as in ancient Greek. This is a common phenomenon in agricultural history exemplified by the fact that words that signified millets in mediaeval Italian came to mean maize after Columbus (see section 10 below). The conclusion of this section must be that the identity of Akkadian *samidu* remains uncertain. M.J. Geller's review of Jacobsen (1982) questioned whether the words for cereals have been translated correctly in cuneiform texts, and the problem is even more complicated than he thought. However, the conclusion reached below that *semidalis* was made from a tetraploid naked wheat inclines the balance of probability in favour of the idea that the naked wheats grown in ancient Mesopotamia included tetraploid wheats, contrary to the view of Helbaek.[87]

It is necessary to consider next the arguments of mediaevalists such as Watson (1983) who suggest that durum wheat did not become an important crop before the mediaeval period. The heart of their argument lies in changes in the human diet. Bread wheat (a soft grain with a high water content) is especially suitable for making fine flour for bread, while durum wheat (a hard grain with a low water content) can be reduced easily to semolina particles but cannot be pulverised any further into fine flour with primitive milling equipment. Durum wheat's suitability for making pasta rests largely on the glieden:glutanin ratio among its proteins, while bread wheat's superior breadmaking properties are controlled by genes on the D genome, absent from durum wheat. These features together with the characteristics of the gluten derived from its starch make durum wheat eminently suitable for making the pasta-based foods beloved of modern Italians. The Greek and Roman diet was characterised by bread, for those with sufficient land or money to have access to naked wheat. Pasta-type foods are conspicuous in classical sources only by their absence. After more than a century of speculation about the problem by modern scholars, it remains curious that the Greeks should have simply failed to think of the idea of making alimentary pastes, considering all the inventiveness with regard to cooking and food preparation on display in Athenaios and also taking into account the simplicity of the process of making this type of food. Drying the product is the hardest part of it. Durum wheat varieties with characteristics favoured in antiquity, such as highly vitreous kernels and high average seed weight, have produced the highest yields of semolina in recent times.[88]

The most important reference to a semolina-based food in a classical source is the exception that proves the rule. Pliny discussed the preparation of *alica*, a kind of groats eaten widely in the Roman Mediterranean, especially in North Africa, Italy and Egypt. Semolina particles, called *aphairema* in the Campanian dialect of Greek, were preferred for its manufacture. A type of food prepared by a very similar recipe is still consumed in Tunisia and elsewhere in the Islamic world today, called 'borghol'. Today it is produced from durum wheat, which has indeed dominated agriculture in North Africa during the last few centuries.[89] However, Pliny explicitly states that the *alica* of antiquity could be made from any kind of wheat but was mainly made from 'land-races' of *emmer*. Roman *alica* was indeed similar to Greek *chondros*, which was made from *zeia dikokkos*, probably emmer according to Dioskorides, although Pliny failed to see the connection. Jasny attributed this preference for emmer to primitive milling techniques. However it is not clear that milling techniques in the mediaeval period, when pasta-type foods began to spread, were significantly more sophisticated than those available to the Romans. It is more likely that emmer was preferred because of the intrinsic qualities of its grains.[90]

This piece of evidence lends some support to Watson's thesis, suggesting that perhaps as late as the early Roman empire durum wheat did not occupy the position of dominance in North Africa which it has held more recently. The relative insignificance of durum wheat in classical antiquity postulated by Watson (1983) could explain the absence from the ancient diet of the foods made from durum wheat which are so characteristic of modern Italy. Nevertheless there is no doubt that tetraploid wheats did exist in antiquity. Pasta became more useful after the spread of the chicken across Europe in the first millennium BC (see Chapter II.7 above), as pasta may be used as a means of storing egg products included in pasta-based foods.[91]

Even today varieties of durum wheat differ in their suitability for making semolina-based foods. This applies especially to modern Greek durum wheats, not all of which met EEC standards, upon Greece's recent entry into the European Economic Community. This incidentally helps to explain why pasta-based foods are regarded as characteristically Italian, not Greek, even though durum wheat was the most important species of wheat cultivated in early modern Greece until the 1920s. The hardness of modern durum wheat cannot be significantly altered phenotypically in experiments, although the characteristics of the grain of poulard wheat (*T. turgidum*), in contrast, are influenced by changes in environmental conditions. The traditional Greek durum wheat was hard to mill, required ample moisture in the early stages of growth, and had large seeds. Because it could not be milled into fine flour until the recent arrival of modern mechanical mills in Greece, Greek peasants traditionally have consumed a substantial proportion of their cereals in the form of porridge. Pliny stated that the Greeks preferred barley for making porridge, implying that oats was an insignificant crop in antiquity (see section 10 below).[92]

In passing, it is worth taking account of two other important caveats to Watson's theory. Although the developments he describes were part of the process of filling in the vacuum in Europe left by the last glaciation, his contrast between the backward Greeks and Romans and the progressive Arabs is tendentious because after the spread of Islam by land to India and beyond the Arabs had much greater opportunities for learning about the flora of those regions. It is always tempting to exaggerate the importance of one's chosen subject. Teall (1971) provides an instructive contrast with Watson, denying that Byzantine land economics was backward, without providing any evidence to support his assertion. The scholars who accompanied Alexander the Great certainly were interested in exotic plants and provided Theophrastos with his knowledge of the citron, for example. It grew in Iran and did not become acclimatised to the Mediterranean in the pre-Christian era. Nor were any other species of citrus fruits cultivated there before Christ. Seeds of the citron (*Citrus medica*) were brought to Athens from Persia in the fourth century BC. Citron seeds on a Bronze Age site in Cyprus probably represent an earlier phase of long-distance trade.[93] The ecological history of the classical world is of great significance because in that period links between Europe, Asia and Africa were intensified owing to increased human activity. This applies to plants and diseases and undoubtedly had a greater impact on the masses than the contemporaneous trend towards political unity, emphasised by nearly all ancient historians, following in the footsteps of Polybios.[94]

The second caveat relates to Watson's localisation of the origin of durum wheat in Ethiopia, a country situated at the very edge of the Graeco-Roman world. The great Russian botanist Vavilov, a victim of Stalin's purges, observed in the 1920s that Ethiopia possessed an extraordinary range of varieties of durum wheat, an observation confirmed by more recent work. He suggested that durum wheat evolved there or at least diversified from an early stage of its appearance there, as mountains provide a very favourable environment for the diversification of wheat.[95] Subsequent scholarship has been critical of the idea that Ethiopia was a primary centre of origin of crops grown by man and has placed the origin of naked tetraploid wheats in the Middle East instead. Harlan suggested that the combination of barley and durum wheat found in both modern Ethiopia and Attica goes back several thousand years.[96] As far as Ethiopia is concerned, this idea seems to rest on no evidence, given the shortage of recent relevant archaeological research in that

troubled country. Although cultivation of the indigenous millets, teff and
finger millet, may have commenced as early as *c*. 5000 BC, there is no firm
evidence that any kind of wheat or barley was grown there before the first
millennium BC.[97]

Classical sources only mention barley and 'millet' cultivation in
'Ethiopia' and imply that wheat was entirely absent, although this is
unfortunately not conclusive because by 'Ethiopia' they usually had in
mind the kingdom of Meroe in modern Sudan, not the highlands of
Ethiopia proper which lay just beyond their horizon and are critical for
our enquiry. Unfortunately the durum wheat of Ethiopia does not shed
any light on the durum wheat of Attica. Archaeological evidence shows
that the 'millet' of Meroe in the first millennium BC was in fact mainly
sorghum. This is also the probable identity of the very tall *kengchros* of
Babylonia mentioned by Herodotos. Theophrastos described an un-
named cereal with the characteristics of sorghum encountered by
Alexander's army in India as 'wild barley'. The application of names such
as 'millet' (*kengchros*) and 'wild barley' to sorghum suggests that Greek
authors based in the Mediterranean had never actually seen the plant
themselves. Pliny indicates that a variety of sorghum was imported from
India to Rome during the first century AD.[98]

The dates proposed in recent scholarly literature for the origin and/or
the inception of widespread cultivation of durum wheat range all the way
from the seventh millennium BC to the mediaeval period. It is time now to
consider the relevant classical sources, whose interpretation is a tricky
task because the ancients did not classify plants in the way that modern
botanists do and it is dangerous to assume that any ancient type of wheat
is identical to a type that still exists in the world today. The reader would
appreciate the difficulties involved in identifying cereals described in
classical sources upon comparing these late Greek sources with brief
descriptions of the grains of bread and durum wheat for a layman taken
from a modern textbook on wheat.[99]

Galen states that grains of *semidalitai puroi* were much heavier than
an equal volume of grains of *sitanioi puroi*. Tetraploid wheats are heavier
and more nourishing than bread wheat because they contain a higher
proportion of dry matter in the form of protein. Modern Greek durum
wheats have large seeds. The ranges of variability of the dimensions of
the caryopses of modern varieties of bread and durum wheat overlap,
making the identification of archaeological samples difficult.[100]

The comments on the difficulty of biting the grain of *semidalitês puros*
and the word *diaphanês*, vitreous, with the qualification that the best
wheats had entirely vitreous grains, indicate that a naked tetraploid
wheat is in question, as Jasny pointed out. Only tetraploid wheats can
have completely vitreous grains, although the grains of some hexaploid
wheats may become vitreous on the outside in hot dry climates. Certain
characteristics of modern durum wheat, such as the length and

narrowness of its grains, are not mentioned by Galen or Oribasios. This is doubtless at least partially because the grains of tetraploid wheats were shorter in antiquity than they are today (see section 9 below). The descriptions of *semidalitês puros* in the ancient sources refer to a tetraploid naked wheat related to modern durum wheat but not necessarily identical to it in all respects. Other differences between types of wheat were said to arise from differences in location, soil, rainfall, temperature and other climatic factors. The adaptation of *semidalitês puros* to hot, dry climates also suggests that it was a tetraploid wheat. The descriptions of Galen and Oribasios undoubtedly mingle together species, subspecies and varieties, in the language of modern taxonomy.[101]

7. More problems relating to *semidalis*

Semidalis and its Akkadian ancestor are usually translated as 'the finest wheaten flour', e.g. by Liddell & Scott and in the Loeb edition of Athenaios, presumably because *semidalitês artos* invariably occupies the first place in lists of *artoi* given by classical and Hellenistic Greek sources. It will be argued in section 8 below that the geographical distribution of cultivation of bread wheat was very widespread by the classical period. The question then arises of how *semidalis* could have been used to signify the finest flour, if this word also referred to durum wheat as argued by Jasny, in the simultaneous presence of bread wheat, given that durum wheat cannot be turned into fine flour with primitive milling techniques. 'Fine' is an ambiguous word.[102]

The bread available in classical Athens was regarded as very good quality bread by ancient standards. The demand of the Athenians for top quality bread ought to signify a demand for bread wheat, not for durum wheat.[103] It is wrong to regard *semidalis* as the finest flour. For the reason why classical and Hellenistic Greek authors such as Diphilos of Siphnos and the writers of the Hippokratic corpus classified *semidalitês artos* as the most desirable *artos*, loaf of bread, was that the heavy grains of the tetraploid wheat used to make it were more nourishing than the lighter grains of bread wheat that were employed for making *aleuritai artoi*. Fineness of flour was a criterion of lesser significance for these medical writers than the amount of nourishment obtained. Galen and Oribasios make it clear that *semidalis* flour in bread was not easily digestible and was a coarse flour. This explains the word's survival into modern Greek with the meaning 'semolina', *semigdali*.[104]

The Archbishop Michael Choniates, describing the miserable state of Attica towards the end of the twelfth century AD, regarded the bread available in Attica at that time as wretched, in stark contrast to classical sources which praise the bread of classical Athens. This contrast probably represents the difference between the consumption of bread made from bread wheat imported from south Russia (see section 8 below) and made into *aleuritai artoi* in classical Athens and the consumption of bread made from durum wheat, the major crop in Attica itself in the twelfth century AD.[105]

The low reputation of mediaeval Greek bread survived into the twentieth century AD, alongside the predominance of durum wheat, until selective breeding of bread wheat started in Greece in the 1920s. Very recently the cultivation of durum wheat has begun to be encouraged again, to feed animals this time, not humans.[106] However, *semidalitês puros* was not necessarily a very important item of cereal consumption by humans in classical Athens, because the most important local product was barley and the single most important imported cereal was almost certainly bread wheat from south Russia. As a result of the transformation of the political scenery in late antiquity, mediaeval Athens could not import desirable bread wheat from south Russia and had to consume the inferior bread made from durum wheat, by then the main crop. However, the increased proportion of zinc in Athenian bones of the Byzantine period indicates that the cereals were more highly refined for human consumption in the mediaeval period than in classical times, revealing subtle differences between the diets of classical and of mediaeval Athenians.[107]

Oribasios contrasts *puroi ... sitanioi kai aleuritai* with *semidalitai puroi*. This suggests that the fundamental difference between *semidalitai artoi* and *aleuritai artoi*, used as a pair of contrasted technical terms by medical writers from Hippokrates to Oribasios, was that the former was the more nourishing but otherwise inferior bread made from durum wheat, while the latter was the less nourishing but otherwise superior bread made from bread wheat. The evidence of the lexicographers, who speak of clean *semidalis* and show that it was not wholemeal flour, should be accepted. Similarly a mediaeval Greek poet dating to the twelfth century AD also talks about *aspron semidalaton*, 'white *semidalis*', showing that it was not wholemeal flour.[108]

The classical terminology for milling products is very ambiguous because certain words such as Greek *semidalis* and Latin *siligo* refer both to particular grades of flour which theoretically could be made from almost any plant and to certain actual plants which evidently were generally used to make the grades in question in practice. Even if the word *aleura* strictly only designated a particular grade of flour, finer than *alphita* (generally but not necessarily barley meal), which could theoretically be made from any grain, as Moritz argued, it remains true that the flour made from bread wheat is finer than the flour made from durum wheat with primitive milling technology.[109] Philologists regard the words *aleura* and *puros* as very archaic words that were familiar to the primaeval Indo-Europeans in the regions from which the ancestors of the Greeks migrated to the southern Balkans in the third millennium BC. For example, Greek shares *puros*, 'wheat', with distant I-E languages such as Lithuanian and Latvian. It was probably originally a word signifying some kind of 'grass' in the proto-I-E lexicon.[110]

On the other hand the tetraploid wheat used to make *semidalis* was not native to the regions inhabited by the ancestors of the Greeks because after entering the south Balkans they had to acquire an Akkadian word to signify that particular type of wheat, which originated in the semi-arid zones of the Levant. This wheat was prevented by the climate from reaching the north, where the Indo-Europeans originated. On the other hand, bread wheat, possessing the D genome from the central Asiatic plant *Aegilops squarrosa* (= *tauschii*), is better adapted to a colder climate, as was noticed by Graeco-Roman writers. It unquestionably evolved further north than durum wheat, closer to the homeland of the Indo-Europeans. Vavilov placed its centre of origin in Afghanistan, now thought to have been a secondary centre of diversity like Ethiopia. More recent biological research has placed its origin in Soviet Transcaucasia. Jasny supposed that bread wheat was not as winter-hardy in antiquity as it is today, seeking to explain in this way its association with spring sowing in the classical period. However, it is now generally believed that the hulled hexaploid spelt wheat (*Triticum spelta*) was the earliest hexaploid wheat, because all known varieties of *Aegilops squarrosa* carry the Tg gene preventing free threshing. As spelt wheat is the species of wheat which is best adapted to cold climates, it is likely that bread wheat, which evolved from spelt wheat by mutation of Tg to the recessive allele tg, possessed its winter hardiness from the beginning of its evolution.[111]

The presence of a Semitic word for *semidalitês* (*puros*) in an Indo-European language suggests that the Greeks, or rather their ancestors, first encountered it in a different place and at a different time from the other cereals they were familiar with. Thus it can be seen that comparative linguistics and evolutionary biology interact fruitfully with regard to elucidating the history of wheat. Another stage in the history of *semidalis* is also of interest. The adjective derived from this noun signified the most nourishing *artos* for classical and Hellenistic Greek writers. But for Galen, writing under Roman influence, *semidalitês artos* had lost its position of primacy to *silignitis* (*artos*), which was unknown to earlier Greek authors as he pointed out, being a loan word from Latin. When Jasny wrote his book, it was generally assumed that there were no very significant improvements in cereal-processing techniques during antiquity, with the result that he automatically assumed that if the Romans had a grade of flour and bread superior to anything available in classical Greece, this must have been because the Romans cultivated a species of wheat not known in Greece. This led him to localise the cultivation of bread wheat, used to make *siligo* flour, in central and northern Italy.[112]

However, the Athenians were familiar with bread made from bread wheat imported from south Russia (see section 8 below), even if little or none was grown in Attica itself for climatic reasons. This leaves the question of why the Greeks and in particular the Athenians had no equivalent to the *siligo* flour of the Romans. A few years after Jasny's work, Moritz rightly demonstrated that there were significant developments in food-processing techniques in the course of antiquity, because the Romans used finer sieves than the Greeks to separate off the bran and also used the rotary grain mill, suited to bread wheat, which does not appear to have existed in Greece in the fourth century BC.[113]

Thus the absence of a Greek equivalent for the product of this new technology could be explained purely in terms of innovations in food processing made by the Romans. However, Moritz then went on to accept Jasny's view about the extremely restricted distribution of bread wheat cultivation in classical antiquity. This was no longer necessary. The contrast between the *aleuritês artos* of classical Athens and the *silignitis artos* of Rome was a contrast between a brownish loaf, with a small proportion of the bran removed, and a whiter loaf, with a larger proportion of the bran and detritus removed, but both were made from bread wheat. The contrast is to be explained by improvements in food-processing techniques, rather than by the geographical distribution of the cultivation of bread wheat. However, even the best bread available in antiquity contained much more grit than modern bread, because in classical antiquity bread so light that it could float on water was regarded as miraculous in nature.

The high Roman evaluation of *silignitis artos* was probably related to the spread of the practice of making leavened bread (*artos zumitês*), for which durum wheat is especially unsuitable. Galen recommended a heavily leavened loaf as the most suitable type of bread for most people. In contrast, for example, the absence of bread ovens from the Minoan palaces on Crete in the second millennium BC suggests that unleavened flat cakes of bread cooked on griddles were generally consumed. For this purpose durum wheat is more suitable than bread wheat. The importance of the preference for white bread is also shown by Pliny's statement that chalk was added to *alica* made from emmer to make it white (see Chapter II.7 above on the nutritional value of wholemeal and refined flour).[114]

8. Sowing seasons and distribution patterns of naked wheats

Theophrastos followed Hesiod in stating that cereals were usually sown about the time of the setting of the Pleiades, but said that certain kinds ('three month') of wheat and barley were sown at the end of winter, *purôn te ti genos kai krithôn ho kalousi trimênon*.[115] What does *ti genos* mean here in modern taxonomical terminology? The same imprecision is encountered with the same resulting uncertainties previously met in Chapter II.6 above when considering the use of *genos* as a term signifying elements of social structure or kinship units, the product of poorly developed ideas on defining and elaborating classification systems. However, it is only fair to remember that Theophrastos' books on plants were the work of a pioneer. It is perfectly legitimate for a modern scholar to try to identify the plants referred to by Theophrastos, but this does not mean that Theophrastos himself was attempting to establish a taxonomy in the style of Linnaeus. The important work of Pellegrin (1982) rightly criticised the assumption of many scholars that the intentions of Aristotle in his biological works were similar to those of Linnaeus, a line of argument also applicable to Theophrastos. Theophrastos attempted to improve on Aristotle's surviving biological works, which happen only to refer to the animal kingdom, by questioning Aristotle's teleological explanations of biological phenomena (see Chapter IV below). However, it is still true to say that he was trying to write down a folk taxonomy, rather than produce a reference book which could be said with hindsight to be a precursor of the modern 'Flora Europaea' or of the 'Flora Graeca' of Sibthorp.[116]

In folk taxonomies the 'genus' is generally accorded much greater significance than the 'species'. For example Proto-Indo-European tree names were generic rather than specific in character. This may also be seen clearly, with specific reference to ancient Greece, in a fragment of the comic poet Epikrates making fun of Plato's Academy, where the students were trying to decide to which *genos* the *kolokuntê* belonged, a particularly apt example as modern scholars have not found it easy to interpret ancient texts relating to gourds and similar plants.[117] The importance of the genus in folk taxonomies explains why Theophrastos contented himself with discussions of *genê* of wheat and of barley and did not attempt to break them down further into 'species'. Equating this latter word with Aristotle's *eidê* would be wholly anachronistic. It is certain that the 'three-month barley' was not a distinct species because all forms of barley, both wild and cultivated, are interfertile and so constitute one species in the sense in which geneticists (not taxonomists) employ that word. Columella regarded two-row barley as particularly suitable for spring sowing. It was the oldest cultivated form and was native to mountainous environments in the Middle East, explaining its adaptation to spring sowing. Columella rightly recognised two-row and six-row barley as the principal forms that exist, while Theophrastos also asserted that three-row, four-row and five-row barley existed.[118]

Nevertheless, recent archaeological research in south Russia, of which more below, proves that Theophrastos' contrast between soft autumn-sown and hard spring-sown wheat in the Pontos, i.e. the regions bordering the northern coast of the Black Sea, which has a different climate from the Mediterranean, is indeed a contrast between hexaploid and tetraploid naked wheats. This means that the translation of *puros* as Triticum vulgare (i.e. *T. aestivum*, bread wheat, in more recent literature) in Sir Arthur Hort's fine edition of Theophrastos *HP* must be emended to make it into a generic term covering all naked wheats. The word *genos* in the citation from Theophrastos in the last but one paragraph cannot be translated by any single English scientific word because the *genê* of barley in question were interfertile, but the *genê* of wheat in question were not.

His descriptions of different kinds of *puroi* in Greece itself probably also cover different species. The contrast between the heavy wheat of Boiotia and the very light wheat of Attica, made in a passage which modern scholars have often regarded as corrupt, could be a contrast between tetraploid and hexaploid naked wheats, but this is quite uncertain. The 5:3 ratio between the Athenian and the Boiotian wheats is in fact roughly the ratio of the densities of naked wheats in general to unprocessed hulled wheats in general. This may be the clue to the sense that Theophrastos intended to convey. It is also the price ratio between naked wheats in general and barley meal. In recent times a single variety of durum wheat called *monologhi* has predominated in both Attica and Boiotia.[119]

Theophrastos was satisfied with lumping together all naked wheats into a single *genos*, but his allusions to *polla genê* suggest that he could have gone into more detail if he had wanted to. Naked tetraploid wheats were first unequivocally described in the sixteenth century AD by botanists such as Dodoens. Over the last twenty years some scientists have tended to downplay the difference between the tetraploid (28 chromosomes) and hexaploid (42 chromosomes) levels because it has been realised that morphologically similar forms may occur in both levels.[120]

The ancients had a different reason for not pursuing classification too far, namely their observations on the mutability of cereals. This was thought to happen especially to cereals transplanted from one region to another. Their observations may be explained as a product of natural selection working on both interspecific and infraspecific variation in circumstances where the seeds of different species or varieties, as the case may be, had become mixed, either deliberately or unconsciously. Such crop mixtures are still deliberately used in isolated areas of modern Greece, and are advantageous in terms of productivity under traditional farming conditions (see section 3 above). The prohibition of the sowing of plant mixtures in ancient Israel furnishes a good example of the way in which religious beliefs may have impeded action motivated by purely economic considerations in the past, although Talmudic sources show that the prohibition was not always respected. Plant mixtures may also occur without the farmer's knowledge as a result of natural selection causing the seeds of one species to improve its fitness by mimicry of the seeds of another species (see section 9 below). Natural selection may also pick out certain individuals suited to the new conditions from a transplanted population of a single variety (i.e. a group of pure lines not exhibiting differences readily perceptible to the naked eye). Darwin observed that 'if several varieties of wheat be sown together, and the mixed seed be resown, some of the varieties which best suit the soil or climate, or are naturally the most fertile, will beat the others and so yield more seed, and will consequently in a few years quite supplant the other varieties'. He also noted that autumn and summer varieties of wheat sown in the spring and the autumn respectively in a cold region achieved extremely high mortality rates in the first year of sowing, but the offspring of the few individuals that survived had become acclimatised to the new season of sowing in the third year, i.e. the third generation. Such rapid selection of genotypes with a higher fitness under the new circumstances is frequently observed in evolutionary biology and demonstrates the power of natural selection.[121]

Jasny argued that *semidalités puros* also referred to autumn-sown wheat, besides meaning durum wheat, while bread wheat was always sown in the spring and harvested in the same year, *sitanios puros*. It is easy to see how such a distinction arose, since soft varieties of bread wheat are the only type of naked wheat likely to have any chance of succeeding in practice if sown at the start of spring, in areas with a true Mediterranean climate. Most varieties of durum wheat require vernalisation and need more moisture in the initial stages of growth (it is drought-resistant later on in its lifecycle) than is usually forthcoming from spring rainfall in the Mediterranean. Wild emmer was originally a species exhibiting the winter growth habit. The early domesticated tetraploid wheats which evolved from it tended to follow it in this respect, although spring forms of wild emmer do also occur.[122]

The ancient sources furnish some evidence for spring sowing of wheat. Some spring-sown wheat was also grown in early modern Greece. Theophrastos went part of the way towards realising that spring-sown wheat gives a lower yield per unit area than autumn-sown wheat, because of the shorter period of time available for photosynthesis, but characteristically thought in terms of the density of the wheat and of the seed:yield ratio rather than in terms of its yield per unit area (see section 9 below for the implications of this).[123] However, Jasny was wrong to draw the inference that bread wheat was normally sown in the spring in antiquity rather than in the autumn as it is today. Although Theophrastos speaks of the beginning of spring as one of the set seasons for sowing cereals, Hesiod, Columella and Pliny make it clear that this was an emergency and risky practice, undertaken only if something had gone seriously wrong with the autumn sowing, except in northerly and mountainous areas where it was too cold for cereals to survive the winter. Their testimony should be accepted. The time of sowing within the autumn season depended both on the weather and on the type of wheat in question. Emmer, which is protected from predators such as birds and ants by its husks, may be sown very early to await the arrival of the first autumn rains. The time of sowing of the various naked wheats is more critical. Xenophon advocated a safety first policy of spreading the sowing in Attica over a considerable period of time so that at least some of the seed encountered some rainfall. Staggered sowing is an adaptation to a particular temporal distribution pattern of rainfall.[124]

Wheat is not sown in the spring in modern Greece, although it must be remembered that only durum wheat is grown in modern Attica. Given the widely accepted similarity between the classical and modern Greek climates, it is unlikely that spring-sown wheat or barley ever has been a significant crop over most of Greece. As Attica has a very mild winter climate, it is improbable that any spring varieties of wheat or barley, i.e. varieties which do not require vernalisation in order to initiate flowering subsequently, need have been restricted to spring sowing in that particular environment. Since bread wheat grows successfully as a winter-sown crop in the Mediterranean today, we cannot draw any conclusions as to what type of wheat was grown in antiquity from the attested tendency to adhere to the winter sowing season, even though the Mediterranean heat does reduce bread wheat yields, especially by reducing the number of grains per spikelet.[125]

Galen helpfully explained that the term *sitanios*, which is rare in classical and Hellenistic sources, was seldom used by earlier writers because they included such wheat under the general heading of *puros*. This suggests that the Greek writers he had in mind did not feel any need to differentiate between types of naked wheats according to their season of sowing. In another passage he suggested that the adjective *sitanios* had developed from its original meaning to designate any wheat that yielded flour of a particular kind. In the Roman period there was probably more awareness of the spring sowing season simply because the Roman world reached higher latitudes than the Greek world.[126]

Even so, the Roman agronomists still suggest that no particular type of wheat was confined to the spring sowing season. Columella stated that wheat sown in the spring did not constitute a distinct type. Pliny flatly contradicted Columella, asserting that spring-sown wheat was a distinct *genus* of wheat.[127] However, the reason that Columella gives for his opinion, namely that any type of wheat which could be sown either in the autumn or in the *spring* (sc. in an area with a mild climate, permitting autumn sowing of spring varieties of wheat and barley) would produce a higher yield if sown in the autumn (the consequence of a longer period of photosynthesis in a plant whose time of ripening is fixed as a response to day-lengthening), is absolutely correct. On the other hand, Pliny's line of 'argument', consisting in an appeal to traditional belief without any rational argument, is worthless. Columella knew what he was talking about, while Pliny, whose method rarely rises above plagiarising Theophrastos, did not, and it should be accepted that bread wheat too was essentially an autumn-sown crop in antiquity. That Jasny had to misinterpret Columella in order to cobble together his argument is a clear sign that it is unsatisfactory. These polemics among Roman writers are very relevant to the Greek world, because Pliny expressly identifies the spring-sown wheat that was the topic of debate with Greek *sitanios* wheat.[128]

The three-field rotation system (first year winter wheat, second year spring barley or oats, third year fallow) of mediaeval northern Europe, which would have been required to facilitate the incorporation of spring-sown crops into the agricultural cycle on a regular basis, was absent from the ancient Greek world. It has not been important or profitable in the Mediterranean in more recent times either, for the summer drought makes it impossible there. An alternative three-course rotation system (first year winter wheat, second year winter legumes or summer crops, third year fallow), which is more suitable to the Mediterranean because it excludes spring-sown cereals, may have been widely utilised in antiquity. By cultivating the legumes after the cereals, it also averts the danger of legumes reducing the yield of a following winter wheat crop.[129]

Jasny's arguments concerning the geographical distribution of bread wheat also require criticism. He saw it as largely restricted to central and, especially, northern Italy. Recently Harlan has also given an interpretation of the history of bread wheat in classical antiquity which is tied inextricably to the insatiable desire of the Romans for the best of everything, although Harlan allows a much wider geographical distribution for bread wheat than Jasny did.[130] In my opinion the archaeological and literary evidence combine to suggest that hexaploid wheats had achieved a very wide geographical distribution by the classical Greek period. This is not to deny that emmer and barley were everywhere the most important crops before the classical period.[131]

Theophrastos mentions the cultivation of *sitanios* wheat in various parts of Greece, including the Athenian cleruchy of Lemnos, which is of particular interest for Athenian consumption patterns. He regarded the spring-sown wheat of that island as exceptionally heavy, perhaps owing to the exceptional fertility of the volcanic soils, or alternatively because of the use of a rare spring-sown variety of durum wheat.[132] Much more importantly, he also states that a very light and soft wheat, unquestionably consisting of bread wheat and the very closely related naked hexaploid club wheat (*Triticum compactum*), was the main autumn-sown crop in the Pontos, i.e. in the Crimea and the adjacent regions of south Russia. This information has been confirmed by archaeological excavations in south Russia, which have demonstrated that bread wheat was an important crop in these areas by the ninth century BC and became the dominant crop *c.* 600 BC. It was cultivated with the assistance of artificial irrigation in a low-rainfall area, while emmer ceased to be grown in lowland areas and was subsequently restricted to mountainous districts in south Russia. The same excavations also show that some naked tetraploid wheat, the hard, heavy spring wheat mentioned by Theophrastos as produced in the Pontos, was also grown in classical and earlier times in south Russia. However, finds of it were rare, confirming the arguments put forward above on the quantitative insignificance of spring-sown cereals in the ancient Greek world.[133]

It is now possible to explain why the Athenians were so interested in acquiring wheat from south Russia and were not so interested in obtaining wheat from other regions, Sicily or Egypt for example. South Russia was the first major wheat-exporting region of the ancient world in which bread wheat, the species of wheat which is incomparably best suited for breadmaking, acquired the status of being the single most important cultivated cereal, at a time when barley and tetraploid wheats poorly suited for breadmaking still predominated elsewhere in the Mediterranean world. Gernet was quite wrong to argue that Athenian interest in obtaining wheat from south Russia was a transitory phenomenon of the third quarter of the fourth century BC, motivated solely by the whims of Demosthenes, because there was a very good reason why the wheat of south Russia was especially desirable.[134]

Bread wheat owed its early triumph in south Russia, *inter alia*, to three factors which may conveniently be spotlighted here (other factors are discussed in section 9 below):

(1) the more northerly climate was more favourable to it than the climate of most parts of the Mediterranean and Fertile Crescent;

(2) the large area of land in south Russia, manifested by the size of the farms (see section 9 below) and the fairly low man/land ratio meant that low yields, as were undoubtedly obtained from the varieties of naked wheats available at the time (see section 12 below), did not matter so much;

(3) the proximity of south Russia to the Caucasus region and Soviet Transcaucasia where the biological evolution and initial diversification into varieties of bread wheat took place. It is possible that bread wheat, spelt wheat and rye were carried to the Crimea and adjoining regions across the Black Sea from Transcaucasia, rather than coming by land via Anatolia and the Balkans.

Finally, in favour of a wide geographical range, but not necessarily extensive cultivation, of bread wheat in the Mediterranean in classical antiquity it may be noted that Pliny regarded *siligo* as common to most countries. That statement could not have been made in the early modern period when durum wheat utterly dominated the scene in semi-arid lands in the Mediterranean and Middle East.[135]

9. Explanation of shifts in balance between different cereals

It was observed in section 7 above that ancient descriptions of *semidalitês puros* have points of similarity to modern durum wheat but are not necessarily identical to it in all respects. Recent scientific work makes it possible to propose another identification for at least some of the *semidalitai puroi*. The palaeobotanist Kislev has suggested that many of the finds of naked wheat dug up on archaeological sites of the pre-Christian era in south-eastern Europe and the Middle East should be attributed to a newly identified archaeobotanical species of tetraploid naked wheat, named *Triticum parvicoccum*. This plant may be similar to the synthetic tetraploid cultivar TetraCanthatch, which has been created in modern experiments by backcrossing and may be an ancestor of both bread and durum wheat.[136]

This archaeobotanical wheat is described as a naked wheat possessing short, dense, laterally compressed ears with very short internodes. Its oval or elliptical grains are very small compared to those of modern tetraploid naked wheats (less than 5 mm in length). The spikelets are two-grained, with a third vestigial floret. In this respect *T. parvicoccum* resembles the wild emmer of the Levant (*Triticum dicoccoides*), its presumed ancestor, as well as the endemic tetraploids of Transcaucasia, *T. araraticum* (wild) and *T. timopheevi* (cultivated). A comparison of these species with modern durum wheat and poulard wheat indicates that at the tetraploid level mutation to the free-threshing state preceded other genetic changes which increased the number of florets and of grains per spikelet. These latter changes probably occurred in the Levant, producing in durum and poulard wheats more attractive plants to farmers which eventually drove *T. parvicoccum* out of existence after it had come to depend on man for its propagation, like all domesticated wheats.[137]

Tracing the 'family tree' of tetraploid and hexaploid wheats involves a set of very complicated scientific problems, which may never be entirely resolved. Lewontin & Birch maintained that 'it is a fundamental difficulty of an historical science like evolution that we can never establish the cause of a past event. It is only possible to show that certain causes are plausible or at most likely, but because each species is a unique historical event we cannot say for certain what its genetic history was.'[138] However, Kislev's theory contains one nugget that must be emphasised here, supported by archaeological evidence, namely that much of the wheat found on early archaeological sites had smaller grains on average than modern varieties of wheat. This applies equally to south Russia and to Israel, Kislev's own special area, where climatic considerations should induce the expectation of the predominance of tetraploid wheats. Grains of wheat comparable to those of *T. parvicoccum* have been reported from elsewhere in the Mediterranean and from as far away as China in the first millennium BC. Grain size is a very promising field of research, first because palaeobotanical remains provide empirical evidence for it, secondly because classical sources indicate that great importance was attached to selection for increased seed size, thirdly because it has been neglected, and fourthly because the consequences of body size are an important topic in ecology.[139] 'It is, however, surprising how relatively slight is the literature on seed size and its genetic control in view of its manifest importance in agriculture and ecology and in understanding genetic control of early development.'[140]

The most remarkable manifestation of seed size evolution comes in the finds from the prehistoric lake dwellings in Switzerland, studied by Heer well over a century ago. The significance of these finds was realised by Darwin shortly afterwards.[141] A recent study of the wheat from the lake dwellings, remarkably well preserved in the unusual conditions of preservation at these archaeological sites, has demonstrated that it had similarities to modern durum wheat. However, it differed from modern durum wheat in having more but smaller grains per spikelet, as many as seven in some cases. This proves that the reproductive parts of the plant, in which farmers are interested, were subject to evolution in antiquity, and that the process of evolution affected at least one of the components of economic yield. The authors of this study insisted on a comparison with durum wheat, but it is possible that at least some of the Lake Dwellers' wheat was ancestral to something like modern poulard wheat instead, an archaeobotanical variety in which selection for an increased number of florets and grains per spikelet had occurred before selection for increases in seed size to the level characteristic of modern naked tetraploid wheats. The history of poulard or rivet wheat (*Triticum turgidum* s.s.) is very obscure. It is not mentioned in the report of any recent archaeological excavation in Europe, to my knowledge, and is ignored by Barker (1985), alongside durum wheat. However, Heer claimed to have identified it among the plant remains from the prehistoric Swiss lake dwellings, and Percival (1927) recognised it on the Mesopotamian site of Jemdet Nasr in the fourth millennium BC. This shortage of positive identifications of poulard wheat is probably testimony to the inadequacy of the currently available palaeobotanical techniques for identifying cereals, as classical sources mention two types of wheat with branching ears, which can only be poulard wheat.[142]

Varieties of durum wheat with very dense ears, analogous to those of the hexaploid club wheat, have been found in recent times in Ethiopia (with short grains) and in North Africa (with longer grains), *Triticum durum var. duro-compactum*. Such varieties may well have had a wider geographical distribution in the past and help to resolve the controversy over the Lake Dwellers' wheat, identified as a tetraploid and as a hexaploid wheat by different scholars in the past. The lax ear character is dominant over the dense ear character in *T. durum*, and the fact that the earliest tetraploid naked wheats had very dense ears leads to the inference that later on a mutation to a dominant gene for this character occurred.

The evidence increasingly suggests that the predominant type of naked wheat cultivated in the Mediterranean and the Middle East in the Neolithic was a type of tetraploid wheat which no longer exists today but which evolved into modern durum and poulard wheats later on. Plants with certain apparent similarities to these prehistoric cereals have been produced artificially from emmer by radiation. Kuckuck & Peters (1964) suggested that *T. vulgare antiquorum* was a dense-eared variety of *Triticum carthlicum* (= *T. persicum*), a rare tetraploid wheat now only sporadically cultivated in Anatolia, but which might conceivably have had a wider distribution in the past because of its resistance to drought and to various plant diseases. According to Udachin (1986) a type of wheat with grain morphology and size similar to those of *T. vulgare antiquorum* has been discovered recently in Soviet Tadzhikstan and assigned to *T. compactum vars. vavilovianum* and *griseovavilovianum*. This plant is probably a very recent evolutionary development at the hexaploid level in accordance with Vavilov's law of homologous variation, paralleling in certain respects the prehistoric tetraploid wheats in question.[143]

Experiments with modern varieties and species of wheat demonstrate that the evolution from the diploid (einkorn) to the tetraploid (emmer, durum wheat, poulard wheat) to the hexaploid (bread wheat, club wheat, spelt) level, and from wild to cultivated forms at the diploid and tetraploid levels, was accompanied by an increase in the productivity of the individual plant. An increase in grain size and weight was an important component of this trend towards higher potential individual plant productivity. This agrees with Darwin's opinion that a trend towards higher productivity is the main direction taken by the evolution of domesticated plants and animals under the pressure of selection by man. 'Domestication, as a general rule, increases the prolificness of animals and plants.' These experiments compared the productivity of different species.[144] Archaeological evidence for increases in seed size permits the suggestion that in the past evolution towards higher productivity also took place within certain individual species, e.g. from the prehistoric naked tetraploid wheats discussed above to the varieties available in classical times to the modern varieties. It is well known that the process of carbonisation, by means of which seeds have usually been preserved, may distort the size and shape of seeds, but Neolithic and Roman wheats are still different, after undergoing the same process of carbonisation.[145]

This increase in mean grain size creates the possibility that selective forces have also acted on other components of economic yield (number of tillers per plant, number of spikelets per ear, number of grains per spikelet, and leaf configuration to maximise energy intake during photosynthesis) in such a way as to maximise economic yield as a whole, favouring an attribute which is of the most extreme importance to farmers. Increase in seed size is being used here as a surrogate for increase in seed weight. Pliny's information on the density of Roman naked wheats is similar to that of modern varieties. However, archaeological evidence shows that average seed size was smaller in antiquity, suggesting that increase in seed weight was roughly proportional to increase in seed size. Increase in seed size is accomplished mainly by the production and storage of more carbohydrates in the endosperm, lowering the proportion of protein in the grain, but not its quantity in absolute terms. Theophrastos and Pliny were impressed by the size of cereal grains, the fruit of large-seeded grasses, relative to the seeds of some much larger members of the plant kingdom. This state of affairs is comprehensible in the context of r and K selection. Cereals put a large proportion of their resources into the reproductive effort, so achieving potentially high intrinsic rates of natural increase. Conversely trees concentrate on strengthening their ability to compete for light for photosynthesis via massive vegetative structures. Such structures are slow to build up, but enable K species like trees to overpower r species like cereals and other grasses in the long run, in accordance with the ecological phenomenon of plant succession.[146]

Some of these yield components (economic yield itself is not an inherited characteristic) are negatively correlated with each other, but the net outcome of the process has been an increase in the productivity of the naked tetraploid wheats characteristic of the Mediterranean, as will be argued below. Selection for larger seeds is a phenomenon attested for many plants cultivated by man. However, most historians interested in early agriculture have failed to follow Darwin and consider the evolution of wheat in these terms, even though the importance of selection for other attributes attractive to farmers, such as a more uniform height of the plant, a more uniform time of maturation and a non-shattering rachis, with their implications for harvesting, has been fully recognised.[147]

At this point it is necessary to consider the various objections that could be made to the line of argument followed here. These have been marshalled well by Donald & Hamblin (1983). Their approach to the problem concentrates on the conflicting demands between the reproductive parts of cereals to maximise the individual plant's contribution to the next generation and the vegetative parts of cereals to enable the individual plant to compete successfully with other members of the same species for environmental resources, especially sunlight for photosynthesis. In short, their hypothesis is that natural selection for plant height is of paramount importance and tends to prevent redeployment of the individual plant's biomass from its vegetative to its reproductive parts.

The arguments put forward by Donald & Hamblin are valid for wild plants. In other words they explain the balance of selective forces which prevents wild plants increasing their seed sizes indefinitely. However, they are unsatisfactory when it comes to accounting for the modified situation that arises under the pressure of the powerful forces of directional selection set up by farmers. Donald & Hamblin made the a priori assumption that increases in seed size do not take place, overlooking the archaeological evidence for such changes in the distant past, the well documented increases in seed size (weight) which have taken place under systematic plant breeding in recent times, and the contrast between modern wild and domesticated forms which are closely related to each other, e.g. wild einkorn (*T. boeoticum*) and domesticated einkorn (*T. monococcum*). The way forward must lie in accounting for the empirical data and then assessing what consequences, if any, changes in this particular component of economic yield had for economic yield as a whole.[148]

It must be stressed that large seeds did confer evolutionary fitness on plants in the past because they attracted the attention of men, both gatherers and farmers. This explains why wild einkorn and wild emmer (and also wild barley), grasses with very large seeds, were the first cereals to be domesticated, rather than any of the closely related but small-seeded species of the genus Aegilops. Large seeds facilitated rapid seedling establishment before the onset of winter, thus enabling wild cereals to acquire a head start over other types of grasses which do not commence their growth cycle until the spring. On points of detail the assumption of Donald & Hamblin (p. 99) that ancient farmers were interested in yield per unit area, rather than yield per plant, is contradicted by the historical evidence to be presented below. Their explanation (p. 103) of the historical shift from tetraploid to hexaploid wheats does not explain why the tetraploid wheats co-existed with and indeed prevailed over the hexaploid wheats for several thousand years until the first millennium BC. Nor did they consider the consequences of the operation of directional human selection upon the additional Mendelian variation generated even in pure lines by spontaneous mutations. This process is far too slow to interest modern plant breeders, but there has been plenty of time in the course of history and prehistory for it to have had substantial effects. Their conception of evolutionary fitness, which does not consider the presence of man in a domesticated cereal's natural environment, may also be criticised. These points will be developed further below.[149]

There is archaeological evidence that in the distant past domesticated plants tended to increase both their height and their mean seed size, i.e. the two parameters may have been positively rather than negatively correlated, at least in certain cases.[150] Ancient authors also occasionally thought about the balance between the reproductive and the vegetative parts of the plants. For example, Aristotle shrewdly observed that it is not the largest plants which produce the most fruit, the principle behind the breeding of the highly productive dwarf varieties of wheat in the 1960s. Pliny noticed a variety of emmer from North Africa bearing large ears on a short stalk, although by modern standards it would probably have to be classified as a tall variety, while Columella argued that a vine with abundant foliage does not flower well. However, within the class of traditional tall varieties and within the class of modern dwarf varieties of wheat it is in both cases slightly taller rather than slightly shorter varieties which give the highest yield. This explains the pre-eminent position of the very tall poulard wheat among traditional varieties of the diverse species of wheat with regard to economic yield. Simmonds expressed the problem concisely: 'in the inbred cereals, it has often been observed that plant stature and yield are positively (though not strongly) correlated yet ... reduction of stature and improved partition of assimilate towards grain yield has been a general feature of the recent breeding history of wheat, barley, rice and sorghum ... This is an example of a genetic-developmental correlation that has been effectively broken by prolonged selection ... '[151]

Theophrastos, Pliny and Dioskorides all made many comments on what are now regarded as consequences of plant evolution under domestication. They frequently noted that wild plants were smaller and less productive than the corresponding cultivated varieties and had a bitter taste, the chemical defences mentioned in Chapter I above which made products of wild varieties more useful for medicinal purposes than the products of the generally sweet-tasting cultivated varieties. The loss of chemical defence systems and the increases in seed size both made bearers of the respective genotypes more attractive to man, even though both developments would have reduced the fitness of wild plants. The prevalence of such developments in the history of crop plants only makes sense in the context of ecological mutualisms with man which increased their evolutionary fitness.[152] However, the ancients did not understand these developments as a constant ongoing process, lacking as they did the modern concept of evolution. There are three possible mechanisms for such developments in the case of cereals: (1) increase in total plant biomass; (2) redistribution of biomass from fertile to infertile tillers without any change in total biomass and with a reduction in tillering capacity; (3) redistribution of biomass within the individual tiller, e.g. from the glumes to the seeds. These three possibilities are not mutually exclusive.[153]

There is one wild plant whose history proves incontrovertibly that there were circumstances in the past in which increases in seed size conferred evolutionary fitness on the individual plant. It is very important to establish this point because merely reasoning in terms of yield per unit area, containing a large number of plants, would imply some kind of group selection, an illegitimate line of reasoning in evolutionary biology. The plant is darnel (*Lolium temulentum*), a weed whose seed is poisonous because of its own alkaloids or because it carries a poisonous fungus. Darnel is widespread in Attica and elsewhere in modern Greece. Examination of the archaeological record suggests that darnel evolved a whole series of characteristics, including increased seed size, which made it more similar to emmer and then to naked wheats as these displaced emmer, and thus enabled it to exploit the large new environment provided by farmers' arable land. The evolution of darnel gave it seeds which were so similar to those of wheat that they could pass through threshing and seed selection mixed with the wheat and then be sown by farmers at the next sowing. This is the clue to understanding Theophrastos' statement that many farmers who sowed, or rather thought they were sowing, wheat or barley reaped darnel. The methods of seed selection required to separate darnel seeds from wheat seeds were so laborious that they could only be applied on small farms. In the process darnel became semi-domesticated. As darnel was a serious pest, there is no doubt that no farmer desired to propagate it. This point is not invalidated by Columella's recommendation that boiled darnel could be fed to chickens and pigeons. The semi-domestication of darnel was a process which, though possessing a logic of its own, took place entirely outside the range of human consciousness at the time.

Observations of darnel's behaviour gave rise to fascinating discussions in Theophrastos as to whether it was possible for one 'species' (*genos*) to be transformed into another 'species'. In the Jewish Mishna wheat and darnel were classified as one species and exempted from the prohibition on sowing plant mixtures because of the similarity of their grains. But St Basil, in an interesting early Christian treatise on botany, correctly maintained that wheat and darnel were different species. The mystery of darnel's generation also gave rise to a Biblical parable, which became the standard Biblical text concerning religious freedom, arising from the question whether heretics should be destroyed in the same way that darnel may be uprooted before the harvest. It also led Galen's father to carry out experiments to try to determine if plants such as darnel and *aigilops* really were generated spontaneously. This is one of the infrequent texts which shows an ancient scientist actually carrying out an experiment to test an a priori idea, although the failure to purify the seed used vitiated the experiment.

Theophrastos viewed darnel's behaviour in an entirely static perspective. He did not realise that its characteristics at the end of the fourth century BC were merely a particular stage in a historical process of continuous evolutionary change. Today the advent of chemical weedkillers means that leading a sympatric way of life alongside wheat has ceased to be a strategy conferring increased evolutionary fitness on darnel. The final noteworthy point about darnel is that the increase in seed size took place within a single species, a simple diploid. No evolution of a quantum leap kind, such as polyploidy, was required. This should be kept in mind in considering changes in seed size within individual species of cereals, such as durum wheat. Darnel, an obligate weed, also had its own parasites, in particular the fungus *Endoconidium temulentum* which has been recovered from darnel remains from ancient Egypt. Turrill suggested that the grain trade led to weed dispersal in antiquity.[154]

Natural selection also induced other plants to change their seed size/shape in order to secure their propagation by being harvested and sown again by farmers alongside the seeds of crop plants. Several species are known which parasitise flax, one of the oldest cultivated plants, in this way, especially gold of pleasure, *Camelina sativa var. linicola*. Indeed as an oil-bearing plant gold of pleasure was of utility to farmers before the spread of olive cultivation in the Late Bronze Age in Greece. Ancient sources make it clear that these flax mimics already existed in antiquity, but their descriptions are too indefinite to enable us to identify the species in question. Flax was cultivated for linen production in Elis in classical Greece, on the wet western side of the Peloponnese. The Linear B tablets suggest that this was already taking place in the Mycenaean period. However, the varieties of flax characteristic of the Mediterranean, especially on its southern and eastern sides, have low, branched stems bearing large capsules with large seeds and are more suited to seed and oil production than to the production of long fibres for textiles. This is one reason for the importance of wool for making garments in the Mediterranean in antiquity from *c.* 3000 BC onwards, following the initial stages of the evolution of the woolly coat of sheep (see Chapter IV below). Indeed it has been argued that the *bussos* mentioned by Pausanias in Elis was not the common species of flax, *Linum usitatissimum*, but its wild ancestor *Linum angustifolium*, still frequently found in modern Greece, in which case its cultivation in classical times would indeed have been a relic of primitive farming practices from prehistoric times. The word *bussos* itself was derived from the pre-Hellenic vocabulary of Greece (Chapter I above).

Flax was important to the Athenian empire as it was used for making sails for triremes, but it is not known where the Athenians obtained it. Not much flax could have been grown in a dry region like Attica. There is evidence that linseed was eaten by humans in classical times in the Peloponnese and northern Italy, and Galen states that it was sometimes incorporated into bread. In other words flax was originally cultivated as a cereal. Linseed was also widely used for medicinal purposes in classical antiquity. Vavilov used the fact that flax is still cultivated as a cereal in Ethiopia as evidence of that country's importance as a centre of origin of cultivated plants. The ancient literary sources show that this is a wholly misguided argument. Oil production was probably a very important use of linseed in prehistoric Greece before the spread of olive cultivation in the Late Bronze Age on the mainland. Thereafter flax cultivation could concentrate on production of fibres for textiles. Columella shows how this was done in his statement that some people recommended sowing linseed very thickly so as to produce flax plants with slender stems and long thin fibres. This is a beautiful example of primitive farmers in the past switching from r selection to K selection during the history of the evolution of a domesticated crop plant in order to alter its demographic characteristics, by increasing plant population density and so inter-plant competition, when the interest of the farmers switched from the reproductive parts of flax (for linseed) to its vegetative parts (for fibres). As flax commenced its career as a domesticated plant as a cereal, this digression has not led us far from our main theme of cereals. The flax mimics and darnel prove that increasing seed size was advantageous in increasing individual evolutionary fitness in certain circumstances and that this was brought about by natural selection.[155]

Cereal productivity may be defined in two fundamentally different ways: yield per plant and yield per unit area (other ways of defining it are theoretically possible but not of practical importance). The former relates to the reproductive capacity of the individual plant, in the absence of competition and given an unrestricted supply of nutrients and moisture, in other words the intrinsic rate of natural increase. The latter depends not only on the reproductive capacity of the individual plant but also on considerations of plant population density and competition between plants for resources. Aristotle argued that animals wage war with each other for food and believed that if food were abundant most wild animals would live happily together, but did not consider the possibility that plants also have to compete for resources with each other. Plant demography differs from human demography, discussed in the previous chapter, in that plants, unlike animals, may respond to situations of resource abundance or scarcity by varying their number of parts, i.e. tillers or genets. In other words they exhibit indeterminate growth. Variation in the number of tillers per plant largely depends on plant population density and environmental factors. Economic yield depends not only on the number of fertile tillers per unit area but also on the proportion of the individual tiller that is devoted to the reproductive segments of the plant, i.e. the seeds. The conclusion of modern experiments is that seed size does not vary significantly phenotypically. Fischer & Turner (1978) suggested that under conditions of water deficit stress grain size is maintained at the expense of grain number so as to ensure satisfactory subsequent seedling establishment. Nevertheless the archaeological evidence discussed above shows that seed size of many crops has increased significantly in the course of history and prehistory, the result of a powerful selective force, namely man, not of interannual climatic fluctuations.[156]

The ancient Greeks and Romans generally thought in terms of the yield per plant, because it was much easier to measure than the yield per unit area. In the prehistoric period the Mycenaeans measured land in terms of the volume of seed sown, assuming a standard seeding rate and extending units of volume to measure land. They did not measure 'area' itself directly. Kula (1984) has argued that such a method of measuring land is appropriate to conditions of a low human population density. It gave way to measurement of land in terms of labour inputs into ploughing in the classical period, when both Greece and Italy supported a larger human population, although this change did not affect thinking in terms of the seed:yield ratio. Kula gave a fascinating account of why measuring land in terms of labour inputs or in terms of volume of seed sown, rather than in terms of its actual area, was generally more suited to the conditions of pre-industrial societies. However, evidently not being familiar with the sources for ancient history, he was quite wrong to suppose that measuring land by volume of seed sown, a technique which obviously ties in with the seed:yield ratio, was an innovation of late mediaeval Europe.[157]

Ancient Greek words such as *pentêkontachous, oligochous*, etc. refer to the seed:yield ratio or the yield per plant. Theophrastos regarded small-seeded cereals such as *kengchros*, a type of millet (section 10 below), as the most fertile. The millets do indeed produce large numbers of very small seeds, but have a minuscule 100 seed-weight of 1 g or less, depending on the species, and give a lower yield per unit area than any other cereal.[158] Yield per unit area was much harder to measure in practice. The Roman *iugerum* was originally the variable area of land which a yoke of oxen could plough in a day. Similarly the classical Greek unit of area, the *plethron*, appears to be derived from the verb *pelomai* and to mean 'a turning of the plough'. The word *guês*, used by Hesiod to designate a part of a plough, was also used as a unit of land measurement. The *zeugarion* of early modern Greece was the variable area of land which a yoke of oxen could plough in a season. Paul Cartledge pointed out to the author that the modern Greek unit of area, the *stremma*, now formally defined as one tenth of a hectare, is derived from *strephô*, 'to turn', as in *boustrophêdon*. Area is still measured in this way on Methana in modern Greece. Finally worth noting as another example of the ancient Greek reluctance to think in terms of units of area is the statement of Polybios that most people judged the size of a city by its circumference. The ancient Greek reluctance to get involved in measurement of land resulted in both Athens and Sparta in assessments for political and financial purposes of total agricultural production without any attempt to relate it to total area of land owned, most notably the classification of Athenian citizens into four *telê* ('classes') that existed after Solon's reforms.[159]

However, modern capitalist farmers think in terms of the yield per unit area not only because the advent of the metric system aided standardisation of measures of area, as Kula argued, but also because a strategy intended to maximise yield per plant tends in practice to reduce yield per unit area. Differences between ancient and modern ways of conceptualising cereal productivity meant that the operative selective forces in the past were not necessarily identical to those operating today. For example Roman writers on agriculture preferred *triticum* because it was the heaviest wheat, and tried to maximise average seed weight through seed selection. Modern durum wheat is indeed heavier than modern bread wheat, on average, but nevertheless it gives a lower yield per unit area than bread wheat, in terms of both weight and volume, because of a smaller number of grains per spikelet and of ears per plant. The balance between durum wheat and bread wheat in respect of the modern concept of economic productivity may have been different in antiquity from what it is today (see below for bread wheat), but that does not alter the fact that Columella did not think in terms of the modern concept of cereal productivity. A modern farmer would accept Columella's statement that *triticum* was heavier than *siligo* as factually correct, but would not accept the inference that Columella drew from this fact, namely that it is more profitable to grow *triticum* instead of *siligo*.[160]

Nevertheless the seed selection advocated by Columella could have played an important role in improving *triticum* because some modern experiments suggest that average grain weight and yield per unit area are significantly correlated in the case of durum wheat. The correlation is lower in the case of bread wheat in which tillering plays a more important role as a determinant of yield per unit area. It is now possible to explain such changes in seed size (weight) in terms of plant genetics. Genetic loci governing seed size are concentrated on the A genome of einkorn, the original large-seeded wild wheat. This explains the large difference in seed size between wild and domesticated einkorn observed by Evans & Dunstone (1970) and Dunstone & Evans (1974). The earliest naked tetraploid wheats (*T. parvicoccum*) had small seeds, as they evolved from small-seeded forms of wild emmer before conscious seed selection had started. The large-seeded forms of wild emmer which also exist today are probably the products of hybridisation between small-seeded forms of wild emmer and naked tetraploid wheats and cultivated emmer evolving under domestication, as Percival hinted. Nevertheless in the naked tetraploid wheats the combination of the A genome (the A genome of the tetraploid wild emmer may come from *T. urartu* rather than einkorn) and the B genome, derived from the small-seeded *Aegilops searsii* or *A. sharonensis* (?), did leave the way open for substantial increases in seed size. The archaeological record indicates that such increases did take place, and modern research suggests that in the naked tetraploid wheats grain size (weight) may be a significant component of economic yield.[161]

It is necessary at this point to dispose of one possible objection to the idea of selection. Jardé observed that there is no evidence for deliberate seed selection with respect to cereals in Theophrastos or other classical

Greek literature and that the earliest evidence for this in classical literature occurs in Roman authors such as Columella. Theophrastos' silence may or may not be significant, since he was not writing a manual of instruction for farmers as Columella was but a work of pure botany, albeit containing elements of economic botany. Moreover none of the Greek manuals of agronomy which certainly existed, such as the *Geôrgika* of Androtion and Demokritos, has survived.[162]

Columella, following Celsus, recommended that after an ordinary harvest the best ears should be selected to provide seed grain, but after a good harvest the largest and heaviest grains should be kept after threshing as seed grain. The latter method is much less effective. Pliny added the important point that ears with defects should be discarded. Varro suggested that the best part of the standing crop should be used for seed grain, a method approved by some agronomists in more recent times. Virgil observed that selected seed tends to run back, a phenomenon explained in detail by Kauffmann & McFadden (1963), taking Virgil as their starting point. The Roman methods of seed selection were mass selection techniques, which may improve yields in the short run by selecting the best pure lines, and also bring about some improvement in the long run by means of selection working on the additional variation generated by spontaneous mutations and genetic recombinations (rare in predominantly self-fertilised plants). However, the ancients do not appear to have practised the method of taking single ears or plants and propagating outstanding individuals, a method responsible for many successful wheat varieties in the nineteenth century AD.

Galen illustrates the tactics that could be used to fool the unwary with regard to the characteristics of grain. He recorded that farmers in Roman Asia Minor bringing wheat to the towns to pay taxes were in the habit of placing it in close proximity to jars of water so that the grains absorbed water, increasing their weight and volume and so decreasing the number of grains that the farmers actually had to hand over. Such a custom could seriously affect the dimensions of cereal grains as preserved after carbonisation on archaeological sites. There are also some hints of seed selection in Greek, as well as Roman, sources. For example, there is evidence for the *spermatopôlês*, a merchant specialising in trade in seeds, in classical Athens. Plutarch mentions the custom of merchants of offering a few grains of wheat, doubtless carefully chosen, to potential buyers in the Piraeus as a sample of the cargoes on board their ships. Aristotle records that retail grain merchants (*sitopôlai*) in the market at Athens displayed samples of their stock on boards (*têlia*).[163]

It has been argued that the history of the evolution of maize in the New World suggests that the Amerindians did not initially practise seed selection but eventually began to do so. Even today there are still some groups of primitive farmers in the world who do not practise any form of seed selection at all. This was probably generally the case at the start of the Neolithic period, when plant evolution under domestication was an entirely unconscious process.[164] However, it is important to realise that selection for size of seed eaten as a special case of selection for prey size by a predator does not require any *conscious* thought and may arise in any species of animal as a consequence of natural selection. There is a shortage of palaeobotanical evidence from classical Greek sites, because classical archaeologists do not usually take any interest in this type of material evidence. But the fact that large-seeded naked tetraploid wheats had already appeared in Egypt, for example, by the first century BC makes it likely that seed selection had begun to be practised on a significant scale some time before then. Furthermore Aristotle's books on animals show clearly that animal breeding was being practised in the fourth century BC (see Chapter IV below). This makes it likely that plant breeding was taking place as well by then.

Not only should Jardé's opinion on this point be rejected, but it is necessary to go to the other extreme. A consideration of both archaeological evidence and the distribution in recent times of the varieties of many types of cultivated plants suggests that farmers in the Mediterranean in the past may have been exceptional among primitive farmers for the extent to which they practised seed selection. 'It was established that while in the Mediterranean arose chiefly large-fruited, large-seeded and large-flowered forms, south-western Asia, Afghanistan, Turkestan, Bokhara, the districts adjoining India are characterised by small-seeded, small-fruited and small-flowered forms.' Vavilov commented on this situation as follows: 'To explain these differences by a greater antiquity of agriculture in the Mediterranean, or by primitive methods of cultivation in south-western Asia, would be a mistake as these differences refer not only to cultivated races but also to closely related wild species, as it may be seen for instance in wild peas, wild barley, wild wheat.' This comment is certainly erroneous in the cases of many of the plants in question because, as was shown above in the case of darnel, the effect of evolutionary processes on wild plants living as weeds among crops is to make the unwanted plants more and more similar to the crops that the farmer is trying to grow. Furthermore palaeobotanical evidence shows that large-seeded forms are generally of recent evolutionary origin.[165]

It is also important to note that a recommendation such as that made by Columella falls into Darwin's category of *unconscious selection* (not *methodical selection*) because it involves solely the preservation of the best existing individuals, not deliberate breeding with the aim of generating quite new characteristics. For example, modern plant breeders have hybridised wheat and rye to create a new genus of cereals, triticale, seeking in this way to combine desirable characteristics such as the superior bread-making quality of wheat and the superior winter hardiness of rye into a single plant for use in a particular type of environment. The ancients had to settle for obtaining future generations from the best individuals that already existed (e.g. those with the largest/heaviest seeds). Such seed selection does not require any knowledge or understanding whatsoever of the possibility of 'progress', i.e. of desirable evolutionary change in one's crop plants. There is no reason to suppose that Roman farmers actually knew that their durum wheat had larger grains than its Neolithic ancestors. In that sense selection was an unconscious process. However, real changes occurred because by seeking to reproduce the best individuals that already existed via mass selection of seed farmers in antiquity unconsciously exerted a powerful force of directional selection that could alter the average values of quantitative parameters such as seed size down the centuries and millennia without anyone noticing it. Regardless of the importance of human intentionality, the trend towards an increase in one of the components of economic yield permits us to hypothesise that the 'productivity' of naked tetraploid wheats was increasing, and then, working backwards, to explain the importance of hulled wheats during the early development of agriculture.[166]

It has already been argued that varieties of both hexaploid and tetraploid naked wheats evolved long before the classical period and that the centre of origin of bread wheat lay to the north of the centre of origin of durum wheat. However, the naked wheats did not occupy a dominant position among cereals in the earliest agricultural societies. Certain prehistoric archaeologists have suggested that naked wheats may be under-represented among palaeobotanical remains from archaeological sites simply because they are less likely than the hulled wheats to leave remains behind for the archaeologist to find. But classical literary sources corroborate the archaeological evidence, for example by stating that emmer was the main type of wheat grown in Latium in Italy until at least *c*. 500 BC. Similarly finds of cereals from classical archaeological sites are usually in agreement with the statements of literary sources as to what was cultivated in each region.[167] Before the first millennium BC emmer and barley were important crops everywhere. Barley doubtless prevailed in semi-arid zones, such as south-eastern Greece and Cyrenaica.[168]

Classical antiquity witnessed the climax of the process of the displacement of hulled by naked wheats, and also a substantial decrease in the importance of barley as a crop. This process, to be sure, was gradual, like most evolutionary processes, and indeed started in prehistory long before classical times. Hubbard (1980) applied statistical techniques to palaeobotanical remains to document the gradual decline of emmer as a crop in prehistoric European agriculture. However, it is demonstrable that it only reached its climax in the classical period. The final displacement of emmer by naked wheats may well have commenced in the Levant in the second millennium BC. It would not be surprising if the process started in that region, an important centre of origin of naked tetraploid wheats, but the Gezer agricultural calendar from Early Iron Age Israel does not make specific reference to any cereal except barley, and sources dating to the Roman period suggest that barley was still frequently eaten in Palestine then. Josephos noted that the rich ate wheat and the poor barley in Roman Palestine in the first century AD.[169]

In south Russia naked hexaploid wheats displaced emmer in the first half of the first millennium BC (see section 8 above). In Mesopotamia emmer was still an important crop in the time of the Assyrian empire, as revealed by the palace archives (see section 6 above), but durum wheat was the main crop grown by the Arabs in the mediaeval period. Bronze and Early Iron Age agriculture in Italy was similarly dominated by emmer and barley, and naked wheats only became important in the second half of the first millennium BC.[170] It has already been shown that a type of food now made from durum wheat in North Africa was characteristically made there from emmer as late as the first century AD (section 6 above). Even in faraway Poland and Britain the pattern is exactly the same. Emmer and barley were the main crops from the Neolithic period onwards, while bread wheat (with spelt wheat, oats and rye) only became an important crop in the first millennium BC.[171]

It may be inferred from the evidence which suggests that barley was still a very important crop in classical Greece that the crop balance of classical Greece was still in some respects closer to that of the prehistoric period than to that of, say, the mediaeval period. Emmer, barley and early tetraploid naked wheats were undoubtedly competitors, with early forms of bread wheat sitting on the sidelines as a luxury item in semi-arid areas, to which it is not so well adapted. It may be inferred that whenever classical sources indicate that emmer was still an important crop durum wheat had not yet achieved the dominant position that it occupied in the mediaeval period. Even under the Roman empire Columella bracketed emmer with *triticum* as the most useful cereals for the farmer and Pliny too gives the qualitative impression that emmer was still widely cultivated in the Mediterranean in Roman times.[172] It should also be recalled that the Roman army eventually ceased to use barley, preferring wheat instead, as an elite group of consumers.[173]

Important shifts in Greek and Latin terminology agree with the other evidence. The replacement of *triticum* by *frumentum* as the Latin word for naked wheat that is found in Diocletian's Price Edict reflects the fact that wheat had ceased to be just one among many cereals, and had become the cereal consumed by humans par excellence, 'grain in general', by the end of the third century AD.[174] The Greek word *sitos* went through an analogous change of meaning. The Suda s.v. *sitos*, drawing on lexicographers who commented on classical Greek literature, emphasised that *sitos* did not only mean *puros*, naked wheat, but included all cereals. Similarly the *sitophulakes* in fourth-century BC Athens oversaw the sale of food made from both wheat and barley, *artoi* and *alphita*. Originally the word *sitos* referred to legumes, which could be incorporated into bread, as well as to cereals.[175] In the Hellenistic period *sitos* tended to take on the more restricted meaning of naked wheat, which is what it signified for Galen, who contrasts *sitos* and *alphita* on Cyprus, incidentally showing that a lot of wheat was grown on Cyprus in his time. *Puros* and *triticum* have dropped out of modern Greek and Italian. Thus there is no doubting the reality of the change in the balance between different cereals.[176]

Jasny attempted to explain the increased cultivation of naked wheats in the classical period as a consequence of improvements in farming techniques. He did not specify what these improvements were nor has anyone else since. A few words need to be said about the possible significance of the spread of iron technology in the first millennium BC. It has often been suggested that iron ploughs made possible deeper furrows than their wooden predecessors. Modern experiments at the Butser Iron Age Farm cast doubt on this theory not only as regards light sandy soils but even with respect to heavy clay soils in Britain. In any case in semi-arid areas such as south-eastern Greece farmers prefer shallow ploughing and strive to avoid completely overturning the topsoil in order to conserve moisture in the soil. It is not obvious why making a furrow with a metal rather than a wooden plough should make any difference to the productivity of the actual cereals. The main benefit derived from the use of metal is a considerable increase in the lifetime of the ploughshare, before it becomes so worn that it needs replacing. In any case it is easy to overestimate the extent to which peasants in the past had access to iron tools. According to Michael Choniates there were no iron smithies at all in Athens in the late twelfth century AD, and most agricultural tools in Greece were made from wood as recently as the time of the Napoleonic Wars. This shortage of specialist craft products is linked to the poorly developed division of labour at a time of low population density (see Chapter II.2 above). Scholars who attach significance to the use of metal tools in ancient agriculture seriously underestimate what may be achieved with wooden tools, stone tools, fire, ingenuity and determination. Steensberg (1980) explained how dense forests and tough grassland were tackled in Stone Age conditions in New Guinea until a generation ago, drawing parallels with prehistoric agriculture in Europe.[177]

The parallel that Jasny drew with the displacement of spelt wheat by bread wheat in Germany in the last century as a result of the introduction of chemical fertilisers is not a useful analogy, because there is no evidence for any technological progress of that kind in antiquity nor any evidence for the conscious human endeavour that such developments require. Moreover archaeological evidence proves that the plants themselves were evolving, with the consequence that the course of progress cannot be reduced entirely to developments in technology.

However, Jasny's analogy does show that what mattered to farmers in Germany was the relative productivity of the two crops.[178]

At this point it is convenient to digress to discuss the evolution of spelt wheat (*T. spelta*). Jasny believed that spelt wheat did not appear until the time of the late Roman Empire, which would make it a late evolutionary offshoot, but this view now requires considerable modification. Recent archaeological research has shown that spelt certainly existed as early as the Neolithic period in northern Europe, but it did not become a major crop in its own right until the Iron Age. It is the most winter-hardy species of wheat. Spikelet fragments have provided recently conclusive evidence for its existence in Macedonia, Thessaly and as far south as the Argolid in the second and early first millennia BC.

These discoveries enable us to connect the two main areas of spelt cultivation in recent times, namely Germany and Iran. There is an important genetic difference between the German and Iranian types of spelt regarding the mechanism for determining the hulled character of the grain. The Iranian type of spelt is ancestral to bread wheat (*T. aestivum* s.s.), formed from it by mutation of the Tg gene on the D genome to tg, while the German type is apparently a descendant of the very same bread wheat, having evolved from it by a reversal of the Q to q mutation at the tetraploid level which created *T. parvicoccum* from emmer (*T. dicoccum*). Bread wheat itself did not become an important crop until the Iron Age either, for reasons to be examined later. The status of the prehistoric spelt wheat of the south Balkans is uncertain. It is not known whether it belonged to the Iranian type of spelt and represented a variety which never succeeded in establishing itself in Europe, or whether it represented a southern outpost of the German spelt which could not establish itself as a crop in a hot Mediterranean climate. This is relevant to the question of whether the German type of spelt actually evolved in northern Europe or was transported there from the Near East by man.

The traces of spelt in palaeobotanical samples from archaeological excavations in Greece represent an impurity in emmer crops, yet another crop mixture. In the nineteenth century AD, before the discovery of chromosomes and the acquisition of the knowledge that emmer and spelt have different numbers of chromosomes, spelt was sometimes regarded as a variety of emmer, since they are both hulled wheats. This is an important characteristic for anyone engaged in the practicalities of food production but is not so important from a modern taxonomic or phylogenetic viewpoint. St Jerome made an equation between Latin *spelta* and Greek *olura* in this way. Thus it is likely that spelt pursued its early career in Europe until the first millennium BC without being differentiated as a crop from emmer. This explains why it is not easy to identify spelt in classical literary sources, but none the less palaeobotanical evidence proves that it was present in the classical period. Not all aspects of the history of spelt wheat have been clarified yet, but the fact that it only became a major crop in the first millennium BC, hard on the heels of bread wheat, may indicate that the genetic mutation by means of which the modern German type of spelt evolved from bread wheat may not have occurred long before the Iron Age. All this means that the balance between bread wheat and spelt wheat in northern Europe in the first millennium BC, a product of crop evolution, had no connection with the balance between them in Germany in the nineteenth century AD, a product of the technology of the Industrial Revolution, and so Jasny's analogy falls to the ground.[179]

Helbaek, whose opinions were long influential in palaeobotany, tied together the decline of emmer and the rise of durum wheat as cause and effect in the sense that he argued that durum wheat did not actually *evolve* until the Hellenistic period. However, it was shown in section 6 above that palaeobotanical evidence is accumulating that tetraploid naked wheats existed long before the classical period. Moreover the Greek word *semidalitês* (*puros*) can be traced back to Mesopotamia in the third millennium BC.[180]

The shift in the crop balance has been ascribed on a regional basis to climatic change. It has been suggested that the transition from emmer and barley to spelt, bread wheat and oats in Britain in the first millennium BC was a move towards reliance on crops suited to a colder climate, connected with the change from the sub-Boreal to the sub-Atlantic climatic phase.[181] This is a possible explanation of what happened in cold Britain, although it will be seen in the course of this chapter that the development of all the crops in question may be explained satisfactorily in terms of crop evolution. However, it is an improbable explanation of the roughly contemporaneous displacement of emmer by naked wheats in warm Mediterranean regions such as Italy and Egypt. Moreover it is not clear what consequences the cycle of climatic phases following the end of the last glaciation that has been established for northern Europe by prehistorians would have had for southern Europe. The distinctiveness of the modern Balkan flora relative to the rest of Europe owes much to the fact that the Balkans were not as much affected as the rest of Europe by the Quaternary Ice Ages. The idea that the evolution of the hexaploid level was necessary to increase the adaptability of wheat and allow it to expand its geographical range is probably an exaggeration. Emmer grows perfectly well in Britain today at the Butser Iron Age Farm in Hampshire, just as archaeological evidence suggests it did in prehistoric Britain, while poulard wheat has been an important crop in England in historical times. Even durum wheat has now been introduced into southern England, to remedy the EEC's net deficit in wheat suitable for making macaroni.[182]

Jasny himself rightly criticised theories which put the accent on consumer preferences as a determinant of production, but such theories have enjoyed a renaissance since his time. Recently Rathbone (1983a) has tried to explain the spread of durum wheat cultivation in Egypt anachronistically as the production of a commodity desired by Greek consumers in the Aegean in order to raise money for the Ptolemies. In a similar fashion Harlan (1981) attempted to explain the spread of bread wheat cultivation in the Mediterranean as an expression of the growing influence of the consumer preferences of the Romans on the rest of the Mediterranean. His discussion does not explain why the consumer preference for bread wheat should have ceased to be of paramount importance in the mediaeval and early modern periods, when durum wheat dominated the Mediterranean, if it had been important enough to be a determining factor in the choice of crops in the classical period. Moreover, after arguing correctly that naked tetraploid wheats achieved a wide geographical distribution in the Neolithic period, he argues again correctly that emmer and barley were the most important crops for several thousand years until the first millennium BC, but does not offer any explanation why farmers preferred emmer if, as he himself states, durum wheat was also available as an option.

All attempts to invoke consumer preferences as an explanation fail to explain why tetraploid and hexaploid naked wheats did not become dominant crops long before the classical period, even though they had both evolved long beforehand. In the terms of Aristotelian logic, consumer preference explanations fail to take account of all the attested cases of the relative distribution of the two components of the equation, i.e. they might explain cases where naked wheats were preferred to emmer (in most regions from classical antiquity onwards), but do not and cannot explain cases in which emmer was preferred to naked wheats (in most areas before the first millennium BC).

Consumer preference explanations are also anachronistic because they fail to pay sufficient attention to the behaviour patterns of peasant farmers. The grain of the durum wheat grown in Greece in the early modern period was a nutritious food, but nevertheless unsuitable for making both top quality flour and top quality pasta, best only for porridge. Farmers in Attica continued to cultivate a relatively unattractive cereal even after modernisation because in a difficult environment the probability of crop failure, with its implications for the average yield, is a decisive consideration, particularly for peasant farmers aiming to satisfy the consumption requirements of their households (the EEC now encourages it). In the classical period the high population density forced many farmers to choose barley rather than wheat, but in mediaeval Attica with a low population density the choice was between two types of wheat. Durum wheat was preferred to bread wheat because it had a lower water requirement and a lower coefficient of variation of yields, more important considerations in a semi-arid climate than their respective merits as potential foods or marketable commodities. Even though cereal production in many rural communities in modern Greece is still not oriented towards the market, attempts to explain producer behaviour in ancient Attica and more generally in the ancient world as a whole anachronistically in terms of market forces are still encountered.[183]

Furthermore the ancient sources either show no awareness at all of the changes in the cereal crop pattern, or when they do, as Dionysios of Halikarnassos and Pliny did, they do not offer any explanation whatsoever as to why it had occurred, which makes the presumption of intentionality inherent in a consumer preference explanation a dangerous assumption. There is little evidence for the widespread, successful and purposeful diffusion of new varieties of cereals from one geographical region to another. The shift from emmer to bread wheat began in south Russia *c.* 1000 BC on the archaeological evidence, before any Greek colonisation in the Pontos had taken place. Pliny was probably right to say that wheat from the Crimea did not reach Italy in the classical Greek period, although it did reach Rome in the time of the Roman empire. As was noted in Chapter I above, the first millennium BC was an important phase of plant migration engineered by human agency, but acclimatisation of plants to a new environment may be a slow process, if carried out without methodical plant breeding. One of the authors of the Hippokratic corpus records that many unsuccessful attempts were made to transplant the *silphion*, laserwort (?), of Libya to the Peloponnese and to Ionia.[184]

A good example of the way in which evolutionary adaptation to a particular environment prevented a variety being transplanted success-fully to other geographical regions in antiquity is furnished by the thyme from whose nectar bees made the most famous honey of antiquity. It was said to require the sea breezes of Attica to flourish. However, Pliny adds that by his time some kind of thyme had been acclimatised as far west as the south of France. In the case of cereals the opinion held by ancient authors that seed transplanted to another land tended to be transformed into the native type in three years suggests that many attempts at transplanting cereal varieties in antiquity were unsuccessful. The evidence suggests a process of evolution that was taking place roughly simultaneously but yet independently in far-flung regions.[185]

As a final comment on Harlan, in northern Europe in the mediaeval period the adoption of the three-field rotation system reduced the area of land sown with wheat at the same time as increasing the level of production of other cereals (oats, rye, barley) and increasing the total volume of production of all cereals put together, by leaving arable land fallow only once every three years instead of once every two years. Harlan did not take account of the productivity dimension of this new crop rotation system in his discussion of why oats and rye are more prominent in the literature of mediaeval and early modern Europe than in Graeco-Roman literature. This shows that his influential and widely cited opinion that early farmers were just interested in achieving stability of yields and not in maximising productivity, at least as they conceptualised it, is unsatisfactory.

Harlan's approach illustrates the problems which arise if one merely studies individual crop plants in isolation without attempting to reconstruct the entire agricultural (ecological) system. In a highly seasonal environment such as the Mediterranean with a high degree of interannual harvest variability, peasant farmers have to seek to produce a surplus to immediate consumption requirements in good years to tide them over bad years, which occur every so often. This is the spur to increase agricultural production and it operates regardless of whether peasants are integrated into a market economy or have to raise money to pay taxes. In fact it is a very powerful motive for increasing agricultural production which would apply even to a peasant family in a Robinson Crusoe-like situation. Ethnographic studies of modern Greek peasants, e.g. on Methana by H. Forbes (1985), show that they attempt to keep several years' supply of grain in store, if possible, even though the farmers cultivate cereals solely to feed themselves and their families, not for sale on the market. This spur was equally powerful in antiquity, but much lower cereal yields made it inevitable that the surpluses of years of good harvests were much smaller than they are today. Hesiod advised that a man who had not laid in a year's supply of grain should not be wasting his time on lawsuits, while Galen tells us that it was customary for the cities of Roman Asia Minor to store a year's supply of grain after each harvest.

The emphasis on productivity here does not involve making any anachronistic modernising assumptions about the nature of the ancient economy. It is simply an extension to *Homo sapiens* of the fact that natural selection leads all animals to maximise net productivity (maximising net rate of energy gain while foraging for food), the topic called *optimal foraging theory* in ecology. In this context it is obvious that human hunter-gatherers preferred the large-seeded barley, einkorn and emmer to other grasses with smaller seeds during the evolution of agriculture because of the greater return in energy terms yielded by these particular wild grasses. These grasses could only be harvested during a very short period each year during which it was essential to gather as much as possible. Some recent research suggests that humans may have been gathering wild cereals regularly in the final stages of the Palaeolithic period, before any of the distinctive characteristics of domesticated crop plants had yet appeared. The interest of the Roman agronomists in selection with respect to seed size was not an innovation of Roman times. The pattern of behaviour in question evolved thousands (indeed, in all likelihood, literally millions) of years in the distant past (before the evolution of *Homo sapiens* – see Chapter IV below). It is a serious error to credit the Roman agronomists with any originality in this respect, as Jardé did.[186]

The most economical hypothesis that can be proposed to explain the gradual displacement of hulled wheats by naked wheats is that the 'productivity' of tetraploid naked wheats gradually evolved to attain a level sufficiently high to become superior to emmer in the eyes of farmers who assessed cereal productivity on the basis of seed size and weight of different varieties and species. In the earliest stages of agriculture farmers did not grow tetraploid naked wheats on a large scale because the earliest varieties were less 'productive' than barley or emmer. But over a long period of time selection took place resulting in an increase in the 'productivity' of naked wheats, especially as regards the weight of grain in the individual tiller, until it became worthwhile for farmers to abandon emmer in favour of naked wheats.

The increase in seed size discussed earlier provides direct evidence that at least one component of economic yield, the one of concern to ancient farmers, was subject to selection. Such a process could take place independently and simultaneously in different regions without there necessarily being any contact between them, because the modern view of a species is that its unity is a historical phenomenon based on common inheritance and does not require interbreeding between all segments of its population in each generation, and wheat is in any case a predominantly self-fertilised plant. The key to the puzzle was the simultaneous but yet independent action of similar selective forces on populations of a self-fertilised plant. It is hard to attach any credence to Pliny's claim that nothing is more fertile than wheat, *'tritico nihil est fertilius'*, since wheat in general was a less productive plant than barley, given similar environmental conditions, until the advent of scientific selective breeding in the twentieth century AD. However, the ability of naked wheats to compete with emmer and barley in many parts of the Mediterranean by Pliny's time was a fairly recent development.[187]

As was noted earlier, in the case of hexaploid bread wheat tillering capacity is an important determinant of economic yield, and seed size (weight) no longer appears to play a significant role with regard to economic productivity, although it has certainly increased in modern plant breeding. The addition to the tetraploid complex of another set of genes for small seeds derived from the addition of the D genome of *Aegilops squarrosa* reduced the average seed size of hexaploid relative to tetraploid wheats and also altered the relative importance of the various yield components, but in the case of *Triticum aestivum* it is possible to draw attention to other features in respect of which it was evolving in classical times. Pliny provides one vital piece of evidence that bread wheat was still evolving characteristics desired by farmers as late as the time of the Roman empire. He observed that *siligo* never ripened simultaneously. Moreover its ears when ripe tended to shatter very rapidly, depositing the grains on the ground and so impeding harvesting. This characteristic of *T. aestivum* s.s. explains why archaeological evidence indicates that farmers in northern Europe in the Early Iron Age preferred to grow club wheat (*T. compactum*) which today is notable for holding its grains very tightly, although it gives a lower yield and produces a flour less suitable for breadmaking than *T. aestivum*. Club wheat also played a significant role alongside bread wheat in arable farming in south Russia in the first millennium BC (see section 8 above).[188]

The rapid shattering of the ears of bread wheat provides the key to understanding the *vallus*, the reaping machine used in Gaul. Gaul (minus the Mediterranean coast) was by far the most important region of the Roman Empire in which *siligo* was a major crop, the others being Britain, northern Italy only and the Crimea. It is clear that the genotype of *siligo* set farmers problems at harvest-time which they did not have in harvesting *triticum*. The *vallus* was invented to cope with those problems, which made it essential to harvest the ears of *siligo* with the utmost rapidity, indeed before they were fully ripe. Furthermore even in modern times the hollow culms of bread wheat have tended to be weaker than the solid straw of durum wheat. The explanation in terms of evolutionary biology specifies why the reaping machine was characteristic of Gaul and was not used anywhere in the Mediterranean heartland of the Roman Empire. This is something which previous scholarly discussions, concentrating on an imaginary shortage of labour in Roman Gaul, have failed to do. Kolendo (1960) epitomises the efforts of modern scholars. The rainy climate of Gaul to which he drew attention is not pertinent, as bread wheat prefers a wetter climate than durum wheat anyway, while there is no evidence for the supposed labour shortage.

Palladius emphasises that the *vallus* made possible harvesting in hours rather than days and mentions rapid shattering of cereal ears as a problem. As bread wheat gradually evolved and began to correct some of its deficiencies farmers found that they could grow it successfully in place of club wheat, explaining the change in the balance revealed by the archaeological record. They also found that they could dispense with the expense of the *vallus*, which had gone out of use by the mediaeval period. By dispensing with it large landowners cut down on their monetary expenses, in line with the injunction of the Roman agronomists that the *paterfamilias* should be a seller, not a buyer. Neither the mentality of large landowners nor the state of the labour market differed significantly in Gaul from the pattern of the Mediterranean provinces of the Roman Empire. What did differ significantly was the genotypes of the two types of wheat, *siligo* and *triticum*. As a modern example of the effect on the harvestable economic yield of a crop that may be caused by rapid shattering of the ears, the domestication of American wild rice (*Zizania aquatica*), a plant collected by North American Indians, over the last thirty years or so by means of the selection of non-shattering mutants has raised its yield from about 100 kg/ha to about 700 kg/ha, turning it into a useful crop for a subsistence farmer. Columella mentions six-row barley as another crop plant which exhibited rapid shattering upon ripening and had to be harvested rapidly. He also noted the problem of shattering tendencies in connection with harvesting the panicles of the millets.[189]

Simultaneous ripening of grain to ease harvesting is a characteristic which some scholars have suggested would have evolved in the earliest stages of domestication in the Neolithic through a process of unconscious selection. However Pliny suggests that the process had not taken place as recently as two thousand years ago, as far as bread wheat was concerned.[190] No entirely wild hexaploid wheats are known, and it is generally assumed that they evolved in farmers' fields, but that does not mean that early hexaploid wheats were as highly domesticated as they are today. Domestication is a continuous process, not a sudden event. Pliny never dreamt of the concept of the theory of evolution even in his wildest dreams. His evidence shows that a methodical development was going on outside the level of human consciousness.[191]

Bread wheat in antiquity probably also exhibited deficiencies in other features of concern to farmers, for which unfortunately no direct evidence is available. Modern synthetic polyploids such as triticale have exhibited low fertility in early generations. It is probable that bread wheat too did not function very well early in its history, until a number of genetic loci made redundant by the accession of the D genome had been inactivated. In another passage Pliny states of a spring-sown wheat characteristic of cold northerly regions that it only had a single stem, probably because of the establishment of tillers being impeded by late sowing, and did not hold much grain. It is possible that in early hexaploids the flag leaf did not make a significant contribution to photosynthesis for grain production in the ear after anthesis as it does now. This could have cancelled out the advantages of increased stability for spikelet number, according to the experiments of Kushnir & Halloran (1982), and higher potential fertile floret number per spikelet possessed by hexaploids relative to tetraploids. Bread wheat does not have the large awns of durum wheat which act as organs for photosynthesis during grain production in the ear. Consequently its evolution into a useful crop plant required changes in the organs of photosynthesis. Flavell et al. (1981) showed that sequence translocation in the D genome of bread wheat subsequent to its incorporation in *T. aestivum* from *Aegilops squarrosa* provides evidence for evolution in bread wheat after the addition of the D genome to the A and B genomes of the tetraploid wheats.[192]

The knowledge of the differential ripening of bread wheat makes it likely that it also displayed variability in other ways, e.g. by fruiting at different heights, impeding harvesting. Pliny observed that scythes used to cut hay on large farms in Gaul were handled in such a way as to miss the shorter stalks. Even today species of wheat such as emmer and spelt which have not been subjected to intensive scientific breeding programmes are very variable in respect of fruiting heights. This variability means that it may have been easier to harvest them individually by uprooting them or by plucking them by hand rather than by using a sickle. Diodoros Siculus mentions the individual cutting of ears in Britain, an area of bread wheat cultivation, in the second half of the first millennium BC. For comparative purposes it is noteworthy that the retention of similar harvesting techniques in eastern Anatolia into modern times has assisted the primitive Transcaucasian tetraploid wheat (*T. timopheevi*) to retain its fragile rachis. Such harvesting techniques help to explain why the achievement of crop uniformity was an extremely slow process. They would also have enabled farmers in antiquity to end up with fairly pure stocks of harvested grain, which could easily mislead archaeologists with regard to the heterogeneity of standing crops in the field. For example, some prehistoric archaeologists have concluded that systematic crop rotation was being practised merely on the basis of finds of cereals and legumes on various archaeological sites in Greece and elsewhere. This is an illegitimate conclusion, as the different crops could easily have been sown together in the same field at the same time as a crop mixture and separated during harvesting. The phenomenon of fruiting at different heights enabled Periander to give his notorious advice to Thrasyboulos in the way in which he did.[193]

The interaction of plants within crop mixtures furnishes another very important reason why bread wheat did not establish itself early on as a major crop. Bread wheat evolved from spelt wheat, which was itself an impurity in emmer crops. In other words it had to compete directly against tetraploid wheats. Even if separated off from crops of hulled wheats, it would still probably have found itself competing against durum wheat in the Mediterranean, because primitive farmers even in recent times in regions such as Greece, North Africa and Ethiopia often sow all the naked wheats together. This is unavoidable because their seed sizes and weights overlap, making it impossible to separate them entirely by mass selection techniques alone. Columella said that the farmer should not use one type of wheat seed alone anyway because environmental conditions would not be uniform on any farm. He also recommended the use of four or five different varieties of vine as diversification to reduce risk in viticulture. In cereal mixtures bread wheat, although not eliminated entirely, tends to be reduced to a small percentage of the crop by durum wheat, a stronger competitor. Thus bread wheat in the Mediterranean would have found it difficult to emerge from durum wheat as a crop in its own right for as long as farmers were satisfied with the primaeval crop mixtures which had existed since the start of the Neolithic period, crop mixtures whose productivity was higher and more stable than that of primitive monocultures.[194]

Columella advised farmers not to grow *siligo* on the ground that it was inferior in weight, *pondere tamen vincitur*, although he acknowledged that *siligo* produced the most attractive bread. He did not consider the possibility that *siligo* could have given a higher yield per unit area in spite of being lighter than *triticum*.[195] Scythian and Greek farmers in south Russia in the fifth century BC could have ignored his advice, if they had been able to read the *De re rustica*, because they had a large area of land to exploit with a low population density. They could afford to specialise in a desirable crop with a low yield and still produce a sizeable surplus, in years in which rain came at the right time, to feed Athens in the fifth century BC and make possible Perikles' strategy of not opposing the Peloponnesian army on land in the Peloponnesian War. Archaeological research in the Crimea has shown that the farms there fell into several different sizes for the purpose of land allotments, but even the smallest of these farms was considerably larger than the estimates that have been made of the size of the average 'family farm' in mainland Greece in the same period. A considerable proportion of these farms was devoted to vineyards but even so they would have had more land devoted to cereals than the average hoplite farm in classical Greece, which Andrejev (1974) and Burford Cooper (1977/8) suggested was 40-60 *plethra* (3.6-5.3 ha) in area. The man/land ratio goes a considerable way towards explaining the importance of bread wheat in south Russia and the importance of barley in Greece during the same period, the fifth and fourth centuries BC. Furthermore in the Crimea there were large areas inland entirely devoted to cereal cultivation beyond the coastal region which specialised in the nascent art of viticulture.[196]

The fact that evolution of seed size did not play a significant role in the evolution of bread wheat is confirmed by what is known about the history of another hexaploid naked wheat, namely *Triticum sphaerococcum*. This species of wheat, which possesses small grains of a distinctive shape, was until recently a major crop in northern India. It was favoured by farmers because of its great resistance to drought. Archaeological finds show that it was a major crop already in the time of the Indus Valley civilisation in the third and second millennia BC, but it did not spread beyond the immediate vicinity of India. It has not significantly increased its seed size since antiquity, providing further evidence for the unimportance of this phenomenon at the hexaploid level.[197]

Another important topic concerning evolution of seed size is its phylogenetic significance, i.e. whether it is sufficient by itself to justify our speaking of a new species being created in this fashion. Kislev cited the small size of the grains of the prehistoric naked wheat in the Levant as the main reason for classifying it as a new species, T. *parvicoccum*. This procedure does not seem to be justifiable. If one compares, for example, wild and domesticated einkorn, there is no doubt that they are very closely related in spite of the difference in seed size between them. This is also true of the field bean and the broad bean, mentioned earlier. Similarly maize and its wild relative, teosinte, appear to be entirely interfertile and reducible to a single species in spite of the huge difference in cob size between them. *T. parvicoccum* was probably largely interfertile with durum and poulard wheats, being the earliest member of the complex of naked tetraploid wheats based on the AB genomes. It is perhaps best classified as *T. turgidum L. var. parvicoccum*.[198]

It is interesting to consider why emmer cultivation has survived in those few areas in which it has still been practised recently. Vavilov observed that the varieties of durum wheat that occur in the highlands of Ethiopia give low yields. This makes it still worthwhile growing emmer. In the mountainous areas of south Russia farmers still cultivated emmer until very recently on the grounds that it produces a crop in years when adverse climatic conditions lead other types of wheat to failure. The naked wheats had to come reasonably close to matching emmer in these two respects, 'yield' and probability of crop failure, before peasant farmers in the past would have considered growing them on a large scale. The evolution of 'yield' or 'productivity' was a gradual process. Farmers in antiquity defined cereal productivity in a different way from modern farmers, but it is possible that their emphasis on seed size and weight also had implications for the modern concept of cereal productivity in the case of the tetraploid wheats characteristic of the Mediterranean.[199]

It is possible to offer the conclusion that the changes in the crop balance that took place in the first millennium BC had their mainspring in the natural processes of biology, assisted by man. Charles Darwin observed that 'the key is man's power of accumulative selection: nature gives successive variations: man adds them up in certain directions useful to him'.[200]

In so far as the displacement of emmer by naked wheats was a rapid process in any particular region, this rapidity should be explained in terms of stimulus diffusion causing new agricultural practices to spread quickly among the farmers of the region. Peasant farmers are generally quick to adopt suggested modifications to their ways if they are convinced of the short-term benefits of the innovation. Such changes as the increase in seed size discussed above were dependent on selection among mutations in a number of genes influencing yield components whose values insofar as they are heritable depend on additive genetic variance, especially of dominant genes, a very slow process.[201] It is preferable to view evolution in general as very slow. However, certain other features in respect of which the earliest naked wheats may have been unsatisfactory crops for farmers, such as the shattering of the ears of bread wheat discussed above, may have required mutations in only one or two genes, and so were liable to more rapid alteration if a favourable mutation occurred and was picked up. More far-reaching evolution, of the kind necessary to split a species into two, probably only occurs rapidly during allopatric speciation, when part of a population moves into a new environment, and in the case of phenomena such as polyploidy in plants.

A process akin to allopatric speciation, with the assistance of random sampling and genetic drift, helps to explain the phenomenon noted earlier of why it is that mountainous areas such as Ethiopia and Afghanistan have yielded in recent times and doubtless also in the past more naturally occurring varieties of the various species of wheat and other cultivated plants than the lowland regions of the world which contribute the bulk of the world's production of cereals. Such mountainous areas offer a diversity of micro-environments within a small territorial compass in which small populations can become isolated and then evolve separately to yield new varieties.[202]

Conversely, lowland areas often offered a relatively homogeneous environment in which forces of selection arising from the environment were relatively invariant over large geographical areas. Evolution of wheat that could have been of advantage to early farmers may have been slow for the simple reason that the regions in which the great ancient civilisations developed (Egypt, Mesopotamia and Indus Valley) provided an environment that could support a large human population but was nevertheless unfavourable to the rapid evolution of cereals and the maintenance of a large number of different varieties within restricted geographical areas. However, the more rapid formation of new varieties in mountainous areas did not lead to more productive plants, although it represents a potentially valuable source of genetic variation for modern plant breeders, because the problem for wheat and barley was that self-fertilisation made it impossible to combine desirable traits in different varieties into a *single line*, a problem solved today by artificial hybridisation.

As another instance of the limitations of the methods of crop improvement available in antiquity and as the exception which proves the rule regarding the importance of selection for increased fruit size for Greek and Roman farmers, the lupin (Greek *thermos*, *Lupinus alba*) should be mentioned. The lupin contains the alkaloid lupinine which is poisonous to both men and animals, thus increasing its evolutionary fitness in the way mentioned in Chapter I above. The technique of mass selection did not make it easy for ancient farmers to spot individual plants with alleles for a reduced alkaloid content. Furthermore some large seeded varieties of lupins actually contain a higher proportion of the unwanted alkaloids than small seeded varieties. This then was a case in which selection for increased seed size could make a crop plant more undesirable in another respect, namely by making it more poisonous. A method of detoxifying the lupin was known in antiquity, but inevitably its potential as a crop was strictly limited. Indeed for Theophrastos the lupin was more a wild plant than a crop. It refused to grow on arable land prepared by farmers and was wild by nature, incapable of domestication, another instance of the static quality of his thought. The lupin still had dehiscent pods. It was only in classical times that it took the first steps along the path of domestication, although small-seeded lupins have been found on Bronze Age archaeological sites in Greece and Cyprus. Athenaios indicates that it was a food for the poor in classical Greece. The wild ancestor of the lupin is indigenous to the lands around the Aegean and the south Balkans. It is only in modern times that large-seeded lupins with a very low alkaloid content have been bred, and the lupin may now be on the verge of becoming an important crop plant for the first time. Lupins were brought from the Aegean to Mesopotamia, furnishing a contrary instance to the general rule of east to west migration.[203]

The contrast between a large human population growing large quantities of barley in classical Greece and a small human population in mediaeval Greece, hard pressed by plague, and growing durum wheat as the main cereal was the result of a complicated process in which plants and other living organisms were changing alongside human societies. David Hume's famous comments on the classical world – 'I do not remember a passage in any ancient author, where the growth of a city is ascribed to the establishment of a manufacture. The commerce, which is said to flourish, is chiefly the exchange of those commodities, for which different soils and climates were suited' – still stand up to critical scrutiny quite well, except for the important point that, writing before Darwin, he assumed nature to be static, which she is not.[204]

The approach advocated here has sought to improve upon Jasny's standard works on cereals in classical antiquity in two main ways:

(1) by emphasising the effects of changes in human population density on the crop mix;
(2) by emphasising the biological evolution of cereals, especially as regards their productivity.

Jasny knew that emmer is less productive than modern varieties of naked wheats grown under favourable conditions, although it is hardier, and inferred that this could not have been true in prehistoric and early historic periods, in order to explain the preference for emmer of early farmers. However, he then went on to attribute the abandonment of emmer to improvements in farming techniques, for which there is no evidence. This section has attempted to explain how the change took place through the process of evolution.

10. Cereals other than naked wheats in Attica

The alternatives to naked wheats must be considered. Oats, good for porridge and a good fodder crop for horses and mules generally associated with colder countries than Greece, is cultivated to a perhaps surprising extent in modern Attica, since it is suitable for poor soils (see section 2 above). However, Theophrastos described it as a weed. The lexicographer

Pollux significantly did not mention oats in a list of items of food for horses collected from his sources. Oats provides another example of crop evolution in the first and second millennia BC, as it is only then that it appears in the archaeological record in central Europe. It was originally a weed in fields of other cereals and became a secondary crop up mountain slopes in Anatolia and in northerly areas of Europe where the climate favoured it at the expense of wheat and barley. The modern cultivated hexaploid varieties of oats evolved in the later stages of the pre-Christian era. Oats does not appear to have been deliberately cultivated in classical Attica, although wild oats was doubtless ubiquitous as a weed. Galen mentions the cultivation of oats in Mysia in Asia Minor in the second century AD, while Servius, writing in the late Roman Empire, speaks of oats as cultivated in Thrace by then.

The evolution of oats is complicated and poorly understood, but it is possible to discern some of its features. Theophrastos regarded oats as a weed of emmer crops. This is undoubtedly how it spread, probably alongside spelt wheat, before being differentiated as a crop in its own right from early plant mixtures. Separating out the components of a crop mixture into pure crops was probably a very slow process because it was not necessarily economically rational for an early farmer to do it, given that crop mixtures are often more productive than monocultures under primitive conditions. Ladizinsky (1975b) noted that wild oats is harvested more slowly and gives a lower yield than wild wheat and wild barley, furnishing two good reasons for explaining the late domestication of oats relative to wheat and barley in terms of its economic productivity and of optimal foraging theory. Nevertheless it eventually came into its own in certain types of environment not suited to other cereals. In Ethiopia a tetraploid species of wild oats (*Avena abyssinica*), which was known to Pliny in antiquity, has become semi-domesticated in crop mixtures with barley and emmer through unconscious selection. This is another example of a crop mixture which gives a higher yield than monocultures of either crop under conditions of a low input of fertilisers. Columella and Pliny also mention the deliberate sowing of autumn-sown oats with six-row barley as part of *farrago*, a crop mixture for animals.

Pliny noted that *avena Graeca*, presumably characteristic of some part of the ancient Greek world, did not let its seed fall to the ground, i.e. it was a non-shattering variety. Now the species of oats most characteristic of modern Greece is not the *Avena sativa* of Scotland, but another hexaploid, *Avena byzantina*, whose phylogenetic relationship to *Avena sativa* is uncertain. Pliny's information suggests that *A. byzantina* had already developed non-shattering varieties, but other types of oats not associated with Greece (possibly *A. sativa*, although he could also have had some kind of wild oats in mind) had not yet done so, in which case harvesting was more difficult. *A. byzantina* and *A. sativa* are interfertile hexaploid varieties differentiated by such features as the way in which the rachilla fractures. Today *A. byzantina* possesses a more primitive method of kernel base attachment than *A. sativa* and tends to shatter more easily. This pattern of behaviour together with other characteristics such as *A. byzantina's* greater genetic resistance to various plant diseases and its red kernel colour as opposed to the white *A. sativa* suggests that it is a more ancient crop than *A. sativa*. The development of non-shattering tendencies was a very important aspect of the evolution of a new crop in the case of oats just as it was in the cases of bread wheat and lupins, discussed in section 9 above, because it increased the proportion of the crop that the farmer was likely to be able to harvest.[205]

The cereals that Theophrastos described as summer cereals require some irrigation in a semi-arid climate, or at least an abundant supply of moisture already in the ground before sowing. They are not cultivated in modern Attica. However, they were probably cultivated on a small scale in classical Attica, close to some of the many wells in the Mesogaia, because two species of millets, *Panicum miliaceum* and *Setaria italica*, are mentioned on the stelai of the *Hermokopidai*. Nevertheless the insignificance in modern Attica of maize, which occupies an ecological niche similar to that of millets in European agriculture, suggests that the millets were not an important element of production in classical Attica. The millets are the least productive of all cereals in terms of yield per unit area. They are indeed frequently mentioned by classical authors, but they were only cultivated because they had an ecological niche all to themselves, as there were no other cereals in Europe adapted to European summer daylengths until maize was brought from the western hemisphere after Columbus. A third species of millet, namely cockspur grass (*Echinochloa crus-galli*), is attested on prehistoric sites in Greece such as Kastanas. A variety of it (*var. frumentacea*) is cultivated in the Far East, and S. Barrett (1983) discussed its evolution into a mimic of rice in the Orient. However it never has been more than a weed in Europe. It is not mentioned in surviving classical literature, except doubtfully for the *galli-crus* of Apuleius, which seems to be the wrong plant. A fine philosophical point in a probably fictional debate between Zenon and Protagoras about sensory perception turned on the claim that the noise made by the fall of a single grain of proso millet (*kengchros*) was not audible, even though the fall of a whole *medimnos* of it made quite a noise.[206]

All the signs are that summer crops in classical Greece were of as little importance as they are there today. Some sesame was grown, but the competition of the olive tree in Greece prevented it from playing the role of providing oil that it filled in Babylonia, India and Egypt, even though it is a good preceding crop for wheat in a crop rotation system. Sesame is mentioned on a Linear A tablet from Haghia Triada in Crete and on Linear B tablets from Mycenae. This vindicates the arguments of Bedigian & Harlan (1986) that it is mentioned on Mesopotamian cuneiform texts and was cultivated in the Near East and Mediterranean by the second millennium BC, in spite of the current shortage of archaeological evidence for its cultivation there so early. Sesame occurs in the food deposits from Tutankhamun's tomb in Egypt, dating to the fourteenth century BC. Such finds render it more likely that the Akkadian word ancestral to Greek *sasama* indeed did refer specifically to sesame, as it was common in the Near East, and was not a word for oil-bearing plants in general, as some scholars have suggested.[207]

The Attic climate is too warm and dry for rye to be significant, except as a weed, and Attic Greek had no word corresponding to *sikalê*, the modern Greek word for rye. Nevertheless Galen suggests that rye was an important crop in Thrace and Macedonia and more northerly regions in the second century AD. This was a development of the first millennium BC, because rye was not a significant crop at important archaeological sites of the Late Bronze Age and Early Iron Age in northern Greece such as Assiros Toumba and Kastanas. Rye became a domesticated weed in Anatolia in the Neolithic period, but did not become a crop in its own right until much later. Rye cultivation also spread to western Europe in classical times, but it did not have the importance which it had in the early modern period, when more rye than wheat was grown in France.

Consonant with this conclusion is the absence of references in classical literary sources to ergotism, a disease which is well documented in European documentary sources from the *Annales Xantenses* of 857 AD onwards. Ergotism is caused by a poisonous fungus (*Claviceps purpurea*), which parasitises the flowers of rye when the glumes are open to receive pollen. Rye, unlike wheat and barley, is a predominantly cross-fertilised plant. However, the existence of ergotism in antiquity is confirmed by the finds of sclerotia of the fungus in the contents of the stomach of the Danish Iron Age Tollund man. The line of argument of Wasson et al. (1978) that ergot of barley, consumed in the potion called *kukeôn*, played an important role as a hallucinogen in the initiation rites of the Eleusinian Mysteries, is not convincing, although opium may have been used, since the poppy was a symbol of the goddess Demeter in works of art. Ergot does not commonly afflict wheat or barley, except for sterile hybrid plants which keep their glumes open, permitting it to enter. Moreover the translation of the word *erusibê* as 'ergot' by Wasson and his colleagues is not supported by any evidence. It is preferable to retain the equation of *erusibê* with cereal rust (see Chapter II.7 above), which is by no means synonymous with ergot.

The word *sikalê*, which was confused with *siligo* in the mediaeval period, belonged originally to certain languages of the Caucasus region. This is the centre of origin and of diversity of both wild and domesticated rye. Both the word itself and the plant as an impurity in wheat cargoes were probably brought to southern Greece by merchants by sea in the first millennium BC. Pliny thought that rye benefited from neglect, probably testimony to its semi-wild character then. The increase in the incidence of cereal pollen on isopoll maps for Europe over the last two thousand years mainly records the spread of the cultivation of rye, the most prolific producer of pollen among traditional European cereals.[208]

Domesticated einkorn (*tiphê*) gives low yields but was probably sown in Attica on very poor soils, where no other cereal would grow, to provide animal fodder. It was an important crop in northern Greece throughout the prehistoric period. Einkorn (*T. monococcum*), a diploid, is the most primitive species of wheat. Galen described it as a small wheat, *mikros puros*, recalling the fact that the evolution of the various species of wheat entailed an increase in average plant height and seed size as part of a general trend towards gigantism. In spite of its ability to grow on very poor soils and its resistance to frost and to various plant diseases einkorn was not cultivated as widely as emmer in the past. This must be attributed to its lower 'productivity'. Einkorn exists in two forms, with one-grained and two-grained spikelets respectively. Both have been recorded from prehistoric archaeological sites in Greece.[209]

Fixing a chronology on the disappearance of emmer as a major crop in Greece is one of the great mysteries of Greek agrarian history. G.E.M. Jones (1981) and Kroll (1981) found archaeological evidence for the importance of emmer in northern Greece in the Early Iron Age. However, virtually no palaeobotanical research has been carried out on classical sites in Greece. Varro interpreted the adjective *polupuros*, 'rich in wheat', which Homer applied to Argos, as referring to *triticum*. This may be right if the period in question was the eighth century BC, i.e. the period during which the Homeric epics came to approximate to their final shape. However, it is wrong if it is taken to refer to the actual Mycenaean period, when palaeobotanical evidence suggests that emmer was the main type of wheat cultivated in the Argolid.[210]

Classical literary sources denigrate emmer as a food for humans, and Pliny in particular indicates that it was not important in classical Greece. Artemidoros regarded the appearance of *zeia* (and of millet) in a dream as a sign of poverty. However Theophrastos mentions the use of *olura* and *zeia* ('land-races' of emmer) as animal fodder in Greece. Vavilov noted that the emmer of Europe comprises two main varieties (*var. farrum* and *var. rufum*), which are probably the identities of *olura* and *zeia* in ancient Greece. Hesykhios s.v. *Zea* thought that the harbour of that name in the Piraeus was named after the cereal, which may have some consequence for the nature of early Athenian grain imports. It is possible that ancient historians have underestimated the extent to which it was still cultivated in classical Greece, as Jasny suggested, and there is no way of telling what proportion of the wheat mentioned on the inscription IG II^2 1672 might have been emmer with the glumes removed. However, it is more likely that emmer was indeed on the way out in classical Greece, an opinion that will be justified below.[211]

The Linear B tablets show that the Mycenaean world had a hierarchy of evaluations of cereals, very similar to that of classical Greece, in which 2 units of 'wheat' (by volume) were regarded as equivalent to 3.75 units of barley at issues of grain rations in the palaces. This foreshadows the price ratio of roughly 3:5 or 1:2 that existed between barley meal and wheat in the classical Greek world and thereafter in the mediaeval period in the eastern Mediterranean. The recipients received rations that were intended to be of equal monetary (in terms of a standard of value) rather than nutritional value. It would be more accurate to regard the Mycenaean grain issues as wages in kind rather than rations. The expression of these values in monetary terms in the classical period was simply the reduction to a new and universally applicable standard of value of an equivalency which had its roots in an older agrarian economy which did not employ coinage as a medium of exchange at all. That this equivalency was not altered at all by the invention of coinage shows that the invention of coinage, which was undoubtedly not undertaken for 'economic' motives, did not herald any significant change whatsoever in the underlying basic structures of the economy.[212]

However, it is uncertain whether the wheat of the Linear B tablets was emmer or one or more species of naked wheat. Chadwick argued that it was a 'free-threshing' wheat, which would rule out emmer, on the grounds that the ration ratio indicates that the wheat in question was nearly twice as nutritious as barley and yielded more flour for a given volume of grain than barley. Although classical literary sources unanimously expressed the opinion that wheat was more nutritious, more easily digestible and in every way superior to barley, the difference in nutritional value is a long way short of 2:3.75. It is more plausible to explain the difference in terms of characteristics of the production of these cereals, such as the labour inputs required for their cultivation. No conclusions can be drawn from Chadwick's observation that wheat and barley are mentioned in roughly equal quantities on the Pylos tablets because it is possible that the palace took most of the 'wheat' produced as tribute/tax and left the actual producers (invisible on the tablets) to eat mainly barley.[213]

The Mycenaean ideogram for flour shows a person pounding grain in a mortar with a pestle, an operation required for emmer but not for free-threshing wheats.[214] Moreover emmer occurs much more frequently than free-threshing wheats on Late Bronze Age and Early Iron Age sites in Greece. This makes it likely that emmer was indeed an important item of consumption. The simplest solution to the problem is to assume that the Mycenaean wheat rations included both emmer with the glumes already removed and naked wheat. Jasny argued that in the Roman imperial period emmer with the glumes removed was similar in value to naked wheats, while the value of hulled emmer was much closer to that of barley.[215]

The archaeological evidence from south Russia shows that emmer ceased to be cultivated in lowland areas there in the course of the first half of the first millennium BC. The scanty available evidence suggests that a similar chronology fits Greece itself. Taking account of the environment, naked wheats probably displaced emmer in the lowland and coastal parts of the Aegean basin before they displaced it in a harsher environment such as central Anatolia. In this connection it is interesting to note the difference between the opinion of Herodotos, a native of Halikarnassos on the Aegean coast of Turkey, who described Egyptian consumption of emmer in such a way as to suggest that it was contrary to Greek customs, and that of Galen, who regarded emmer and einkorn as still very important crops and items of human consumption several centuries later in the territory of Pergamum.[216]

This comparison, which suggests that the varieties of naked wheats available in antiquity found life easier on the coast of Anatolia than in the interior, is paralleled by the experience of farmers there during the last twenty years. The new High-Yielding Varieties of wheat developed in Mexico, the backbone of the 'Green Revolution' of the 1960s and 1970s, performed very well on the western and southern coasts of Turkey, but badly on the central Anatolian plateau in comparison to the local varieties of durum wheat, which had acclimatised to the rigorous climate and largely displaced emmer and einkorn during the centuries since Galen. The rise in agricultural productivity on the coast boosted the income of farmers there, but this did not happen in the interior of Turkey. Changes in agricultural productivity are an important component of economic development.[217]

This brief digression into the agrarian history of Turkey helps to illustrate one of our main themes, namely that the adoption of naked wheats by farmers in the past was the culmination of a process of selection in response to local conditions of plants evolving in competition with each other. We may then accept Pliny's statement on the insignificance of emmer in classical Greece and tentatively advance the hypothesis that naked wheats were sufficiently far advanced as regards 'productivity' to have been able largely to oust emmer in lands bordering on the Aegean, but had not yet evolved to the point where they could do this in the more testing environment of the Anatolian plateau.[218]

So much for the cereals insignificant in classical Attica. Before closing this section, it is necessary to emphasise the factors that favoured the most significant cereal, namely barley. There is no need to invoke any irrational factors to explain the importance of barley in classical Attica. It was simply a strategy which required choosing the cereal that would maximise the chances of actually achieving a certain level of production each year rather than the cereal which provided the most attractive food for humans or was most in demand in the market, in a difficult environment on a land with a high population density.

However even the most intelligent of the ancient Greeks conceived the problem of maximising *ploutos*, 'wealth', in much simpler terms. For both Theophrastos and Xenophon agriculture was a matter above all else of accommodating man to the environment, rather than modifying the environment to suit man's preconceived interests, reflecting the fundamental divide between technology in pre-modern societies as the traditional means or method of getting something done, as defined by Marcel Mauss, and technology in the industrial era. Theophrastos emphasises over and over again that the most important thing in agriculture was to find the best location for each crop, taking account of the land, soil and climate.[219]

As these factors were actually the given starting point, it was a question of choosing the right crop. Attica was the ideal location for barley. It is not as winter-hardy as bread wheat and appreciates the mild winter of Attica, needs less water in its growth period than wheats in general and is thus better adapted to semi-aridity, matures more rapidly than wheats in general and so avoids the worst of the summer heat in Attica, and finally is better adapted to the slightly alkaline soils of Attica than wheat. The ancient Greeks grew autumn-sown dense-eared varieties of six-row hulled barley. Much more has been said about wheat than about barley in this chapter, first because the naked wheats were becoming more important in the first millennium BC and secondly because the evolution of wheat is much more complicated and interesting than the evolution of barley, whose weakly buffered complement of chromosomes does not permit it to hybridise with other species. However, this should not be allowed to obscure the very important role of barley as an item of human food consumption in classical Greece. It was also used as animal fodder. Wild barley (*Hordeum spontaneum*) has turned up in Mesolithic levels at Franchthi cave in the Argolid. Naked barley is found frequently on Neolithic archaeological sites in the Middle East. However, it then largely disappears from the archaeological record. Little attention is paid to it in literary sources for early civilisations, including Greek and Roman and Mesopotamian literature, and there is no doubt that the barley of classical Greece was characteristically hulled. Naked barley has also been an insignificant crop in Europe in modern times. The decline of naked barley as a crop runs parallel to the increasing cultivation of naked wheats in antiquity.[220]

11. Greece and Egypt

Relations and differences between Greece and Egypt have a certain bearing on some of the problems discussed above. It has already been noted (section 6 above) that recent literature on agriculture in Hellenistic Egypt has been influenced by Helbaek's view that durum wheat did not exist before the Hellenistic period, with the consequence that its introduction to Egypt has been interpreted as a by-product of the Macedonian and Greek takeover, intended to produce a commodity for export desired by Greek consumers in the Aegean in order to raise money for the Ptolemies to pay for essential imports. In fact the Egyptians had long been exporting grain, at least on an occasional basis. This is shown by Bronze Age documentary sources, Biblical texts and Bakkhylides for the fifth century BC. It will be obvious from what has already been said in this chapter that the complex of problems discussed in this literature needs to be viewed in a rather different perspective.[221]

The most problematic assumption made by recent writers on this topic is that the desire for 'top quality flour' on the part of Greeks, both in the Aegean and in Hellenistic Egypt itself, signifies a desire for durum wheat. Wherever durum wheat has been cultivated in more recent times, the reason for it is that it is better adapted than bread wheat to a semi-arid environment, as in Attica or in North Dakota in the United States, or that there is a strong demand for pasta-type foods, as in Italy, not because it produces the finest flour, which it does not. Production of durum wheat in Egypt in any case would not have enabled Egypt to compete with the well attested production of bread wheat in south Russia in meeting consumer preferences, except during times of serious food shortage when hungry people will eat anything. Rostovtzeff thought that the demand for imported grain in Hellenistic Greece was so great anyway that there was plenty of room for imports from both the Pontos and Egypt in market-places in Greece. Jasny argued that *siligo*, bread wheat, was more expensive than *triticum*, durum wheat, in antiquity. EEC farm support policies, designed to assure the Common Market's supply of macaroni, have reversed this situation nowadays. If they were left to their own devices, farmers in the Mediterranean today would generally grow bread wheat because it gives a higher yield per unit area than durum wheat.[222]

The facts, as interpreted by Jasny and accepted by Rathbone, disprove the latter's assumption that the categories of analysis appropriate to a modern economy with a fully integrated system of price-making markets are also applicable to antiquity, because according to Jasny most producers in the Mediterranean in the classical period did not respond to the consumer preference for bread wheat, which he accepted existed, but grew durum wheat instead. The proper logical conclusion to be drawn is that consumer preferences were not an important factor governing production decisions in classical antiquity. Columella preferred *triticum* to *siligo* even though he admitted that *siligo* produced the most attractive bread. There is a shortage of the type of evidence required to evaluate the relative importance of tetraploid and hexaploid naked wheats in most regions of the classical world. Harlan (1981) suggested that the Mediterranean produced mainly bread wheat in the Roman period, having no further evidence beyond that which led Jasny to assert the predominance of durum wheat. This problem already has received adequate attention above.

The cultivation of naked wheats undoubtedly increased at the expense of emmer in Hellenistic Egypt, as the Greek colonists attempted to reproduce the ecosystem of Greece in the new environment. Cereal rations in the papyri of the Zenon 'archive' in the third century BC usually refer to *artoi semidalitai*, although it may not be safe to generalise from evidence for the diet of a small elite group and their servants to that of the mass of the population of Hellenistic Egypt. However, the interesting problem of why the Egyptians themselves preferred emmer remains to be solved. This problem will be the focus of attention in this section. Biological evolution accounts for the Egyptian preference for emmer as well as it does for the evidence from other regions.[223]

Dorothy Thompson wrote that 'the only cause for surprise is the silence of the sources. The change is well documented but no comment on it has survived anywhere in the papyri or the agricultural writers.' Sir Moses Finley showed no surprise in his observations on the Zenon 'archive': 'presumably he and his associates could with considerable effort have produced more synthetic accounts, perhaps of the annual grain yield over the whole period of his management, of price fluctuations, of changes in the crop mix, and so on. However all the evidence satisfies me that such notions were alien to him and his society ... the mass of paper gives the illusion of an all-embracing retrospective accounting and forward planning, but it is only an illusion.' This is true as far as it goes, but the changes in the crop mix are well documented from archaeological evidence. Finley here failed to go beyond ancient literary and epigraphic sources in a book paradoxically devoted to arguing, rightly, that ancient historians should not devote themselves to asking questions drawn directly from the available written sources.[224]

Observations such as those of Thompson and Finley ought to lead us to seek a type of explanation which does not make the presumption of human intentionality, or at least of human comprehension of what was going on. Such an explanation is furnished by the theory of evolution. Before coming to this, it should be noted that the absence of finds of naked wheats on archaeological sites of the Dynastic period in Egypt may simply be fortuitous. There is no doubt that naked wheats had existed for millennia in neighbouring Palestine, with which the Egyptians had long had contact, and to which they may have introduced the papyrus plant as early as the third millennium BC. The word *s-w-t* in Egyptian papyri probably refers to naked wheat of some kind or other.[225]

Be that as it may, the ancient sources provide us with the material required to explain the Egyptian preference for emmer in purely rational terms. Pliny provides the vital information that the *olura* of Egypt gave a good yield and was easy to thresh, differing in these characteristics from the emmer cultivated in Greece itself. We should also note Theophrastos' statement that *olura* was a more delicate plant than *zeia*, suggesting that it was less well adapted to compete with weeds and so more highly domesticated. Also relevant is Galen's testimony that *olura* (presumably around Pergamum in Asia Minor) had a thicker covering of glumes than *zeia*, which supports Pliny's evidence that the *olura* of Greece was difficult to thresh. The words *olura* and *zeia* were sometimes confused. Herodotos states that some people used the word *zeia* to designate what he called *olura* in Egypt.[226] However, it is clear that there were significant regional differences between types of emmer, such as *far, semen, arinca, zeia* and *olura*, in areas such as Italy, North Africa, Gaul, Greece and Egypt. These 'types' are best classified as 'land-races' in botanical terminology, not varieties or species.[227]

Pliny's contrast between emmer in Greece and in Egypt enables us to infer that a long period of intensive cultivation in ancient Egypt, under the conditions of a high supply of nutrients caused by the fertilising effect of the silt brought down by the Nile flood each year, had turned the local emmer into a more highly domesticated crop plant than the emmer of Greece, i.e. a plant which had travelled further along the path of evolving characteristics desired by farmers. Scientists have long hypothesised that durum wheat evolved from emmer by a series of mutations. In fact even today there are varieties of emmer in which the glumes do not hold the grain tightly. This suggests that the differences between emmer and durum wheat in Egypt in the first millennium BC may not have been quite as great as is usually supposed.[228]

Pliny's details (*olyra in Aegypto facilis* (sc. *exteritur*) *fertilisque*) explain the ancient Egyptian preference for emmer in purely rational terms. Jasny as usual inserted these details into a totally static perspective, but no character is likely to be immune to selection for very long. He attributed the difficulty of separating the kernels of emmer from the glumes in Greece to 'small production and insufficient experience in the hulling of the emmer'. Suffice it to say that by the time of Perikles the inhabitants of Greece had had more than 5,500 years of experience in dealing with cultivated emmer, according to the archaeological evidence. This shows how unsatisfactory Jasny's approach is. The twin characteristics of easy threshing and fertility displayed by the Egyptian emmer according to Pliny are not unrelated to each other. It has been observed that 'dicoccum types with a loose investment (sc. of the kernels by the glumes) have a high 1,000 seed weight, whereas those with a very tight investment have a very low 1,000 seed weight'. In emmer redistribution of biomass from the glumes to the seeds makes it easier to thresh the grains out of the glumes, and high seed weight was a criterion of importance for farmers in the Mediterranean in antiquity. The perspective from evolutionary biology enables us to discard Herodotos' assumption of irrational behaviour on the part of the Egyptians, whose customs were diametrically opposed to those of other people (sc. the Greeks).[229]

The changes in the crop balance that took place in ancient Egypt in the last three millennia BC can be explained in terms of gradual selection for higher 'productivity' making feasible reliance on plants that furnished more attractive food for human consumption. This is the way to interpret the displacement of barley, the main crop of Old and Middle Kingdom Egypt, by emmer, the main crop of New Kingdom Egypt, which in its turn was largely displaced by naked wheats of one kind or another in the first millennium BC. If emmer in Egypt was able to resist the competition from naked wheats longer than it did in the Aegean region, this was for the perfectly rational reason that the Egyptian 'land-race' of emmer had evolved into a plant that was more attractive to farmers than the emmer of Greece. The botanical basis for the distinction is that the emmer of ancient Egypt belonged to a family of varieties today found in Ethiopia and India, while the emmer of ancient Greece belonged to a different family of varieties with a more northerly geographical distribution.

12. Cereal yields

It has been argued that naked tetraploid wheats gradually displaced einkorn, emmer and barley in the Mediterranean as improvements in their 'productivity' made them into a viable proposition for farmers, as a result of natural selection and evolution, while the hexaploid wheats achieved their success in northern Europe as a consequence of evolutionary developments affecting other features of the species in question. This purely qualitative statement is valuable by itself as an indication of a trend. However it is worth taking the analysis a little further and attempting to express this trend in quantitative terms.

Guiraud, in his pioneering study of the agrarian world of ancient Greece, argued that yields were considerably higher in classical Greece than in Greece in the nineteenth century AD, partly on the grounds that erosion had reduced the fertility of the soil since the classical period. His evidence for high yields, derived from sources such as Theophrastos, was severely criticised shortly afterwards and will be subjected to further criticism below. The possibility of erosion raises a set of complicated issues concerning the history of the Greek landscape which can only be treated in a very summary fashion here.[230] Degradation of the landscape has undoubtedly taken place in some areas since antiquity (see section 4 above). On the other hand, it is arguable that the very same process of erosion of upland areas has led to the deposition of new soils, the so-called Younger Fill.[231]

It is uncertain whether this phase in the development of the landscape should be attributed to natural factors, such as climatic change, or to the small size of the human population of Roman and mediaeval Greece with its effect on the size of the labour force and the maintenance of terrace walls on hillsides, or to purely man-made factors such as political instability, or more probably to a combination of all of these factors. The dating of the deposition of the Younger Fill and indeed its very unity, as a process, are also matters of controversy. The most recent research, namely van Andel & Runnels (1987), indicates that the Younger Fill must be subdivided into several separate phases of deposition. Bousquet et al. (1983) claimed that landscape stability in Roman Greece was a benefit of the *pax Romana*. However, this had nothing whatsoever to do with Roman policy. It was a direct consequence of the decrease in the human population in the late Hellenistic period, which reduced pressure on the land. Pausanias displayed a good understanding of some of the environmental consequences of the incorporation of Greece into the Roman empire. He stated that the river Achelous did not bring down as much sediment in his own time as it had formerly done because Aitolia was desolate and uncultivated as a result of the population decrease of the early Roman period. The Romans and the Aitolians had not always been the best of friends, but there is much more to understanding the collapse of the population of the classical period than this, as we have seen. Even if the rich lowland alluvial soils existed then, it would not have been as easy to exploit them as it is today. For example, the modern prosperity of the Troizen plain depends on recent innovations such as chemical fertilisers, much greater effective demand for cash crops, pumping technology to facilitate the cultivation of cash crops in wetlands, the eradication of malaria, etc.[232]

Regardless of how much erosion took place, the proportion of modern Greece that is cultivated is still very substantial and has indeed increased considerably since the mid-nineteenth century AD. No one has demonstrated that the area of potential arable land today is radically different from what it was in the classical period. Probably many of the steep Greek hillsides which are covered by maquis today could never have supported a fully developed climax forest vegetation under present climatic conditions. In any case cereal yields in antiquity would have depended on the level of artificial inputs of fertilisers just as much as they do today. The red-brown soils of the Mesogaia, for example, one of Attica's best farming areas, the product of the Mediterranean climate with its alternating wet and dry seasons which induce mechanical rather than chemical weathering of rocks, may well have originally contained a plentiful supply of nitrogen, phosphorus and other chemical elements required by cereals. However, a very few years of continuous cropping of wheat or barley would have exhausted the soil's supply of these elements. If biennial fallow had been practised from the inception of farming in a semi-arid area, with low seeding rates, the soil might have retained its natural fertility for fifty or even a hundred years, because the inadequate supply of moisture would have inhibited plants' capacity to take up chemicals from the soil.[233]

Modern experience shows that beyond that span of time a decline in soil fertility and crop yields is inevitable. After the Neolithic period, when pollen cores show that man was already having a significant impact on the landscape of southern Greece by reducing the extent of the climax forest vegetation, crop yields depended on artificial inputs and, equally importantly, on the reaction of plants to those inputs, not on the soil itself, insofar as any yields were obtained above a very low level. Arnon emphasised that thousands of years of cultivation in the Middle East have drained the soil of the chemical elements required by cereals, ensuring extremely low yields, 500 to 800 kg per ha. Ancient Greek sources do not provide the evidence that would be needed to affirm straight away that this was already the state of affairs in the classical period. We can only approach cereal yields in ancient Attica by two complementary and roundabout routes. The first of these lies in the examination of empirical, comparative evidence.[234]

The Roman evidence, which is often misunderstood, is worth examining. Columella stated that the yield:seed ratio in Italy rarely reached 4:1. He also gives information on sowing rates which may be used by modern scholars to calculate that this was equivalent to a gross yield per unit area of 500 kg/ha at the most. This is a more revealing statistic than the seed:yield ratio. However, it is very important to note that Columella did not think in terms of the yield per unit area himself, as modern farmers do, and did not perform this calculation himself. This yield per unit area derived from Columella may be analysed as follows: his sowing rate (126 kg/ha) is higher than the 100 kg/ha recommended today for wheat cultivation under dry-farming conditions in semi-arid areas, but seed quality was lower in the past, resulting in a smaller proportion of the seeds sown producing fertile plants; consequently tillering might have been more important as a way of filling the field, but the naked tetraploid wheats do not tiller much, the proportion of tillers that eventually produced fertile ears of grain was probably lower than it is today, and the weight of grain per tiller was lower than it is nowadays. Moreover the practice of sowing seed broadcast by hand inevitably led to an inefficient utilisation of seed grain, and it has been suggested that threshing durum wheat may destroy or damage the embryo in a considerable proportion of the grains.[235]

Columella was absolutely right. He was a sharp observer and the message of the *De re rustica* that viticulture is the way to make money from farming is indeed the experience of farmers in modern Attica. The low evaluation of cereals as a way of securing a financial profit from farming found in the Roman agronomists differs in no way from the judgment of farmers in the Mediterranean today, where cereals are regarded as a crop that produces a low monetary income, a consequence of the small labour inputs required for their cultivation. The utterly misguided idea that Cato's ranking of cereal cultivation in sixth place (out of nine) on a scale of decreasing profitability of types of land use constitutes evidence for long-lasting effects of the devastation of Italy by

Hannibal in the Second Punic War has received far more credence than it deserves from historians. Insofar as the theory of increasing large-scale transhumance in Roman Italy during the late Republic has any validity at all, it may still confuse cause and effect, because a dense human population need not make for a stable ecosystem (as Pausanias realised in the case of early Hellenistic Aitolia). It is possible that any shift to animal husbandry which did occur in late Republican Italy (as in late Hellenistic Greece) exploited a decrease in the human population which was happening for quite different reasons, e.g. a phase of decrease in a crudely cyclical pattern of human population fluctuations caused by deterministic chaos.[236]

In the case of wine Columella did think in terms of the yield per unit area, as it is not possible to employ the seed:yield ratio to calculate wine yields, but even here he also thought in terms of the number and size of bunches of grapes per vine. The Romans noted that the famous Greek varieties of vine from Thasos and Chios produced a high quality wine, but bunches of grapes so small that it was not worth growing them except on very fertile soil. Vines and olive trees cannot be propagated by seed because their long lifespan means that they have only passed through a small number of generations since domestication commenced. Presumably the appearance of the technique of grafting in the Mediterranean in the first millennium BC was important for the development of high quality vintages. The characteristics of domestication have not yet become sufficiently differentiated from the characteristics of wild plants for the relevant genotypic elements to be reliably transmitted to progeny by the normal means of sexual reproduction by means of which wild vines and wild olive trees are propagated.[237]

Columella's yield:seed ratio and the yield per unit area, both maxima, derived from it are somewhat below many of the yields attested in mediaeval and early modern Europe.[238] This is compatible with the hypothesis that cereal yields were lower in the distant past than they have been in recent periods of history. The scanty evidence from mediaeval and early modern Greece indicates yield:seed ratios of 3:1 to 5:1, the latter being the level attained across the country as a whole on the eve of the introduction of chemical fertilisers, but the yield per unit area was rather higher than that derived from Columella, with a higher seeding rate.[239] This yield was achieved at a time when biennial fallow was still a regular feature of Greek agriculture, an important point since continuous cropping would have led to much lower yields. It is clear both in mediaeval Greece and in mediaeval Europe as a whole that any cereal yields that were substantially higher than that were due to exceptional circumstances, such as an unusually large supply of animal manure, or were simply exaggerated, or refer to tillering. The totality of the later evidence suggests that Columella's estimate was correct, if interpreted as a mean value.[240]

The very existence of a mean implies deviations and a range of variation around the mean, a natural phenomenon which is only to be expected in relation to any quantitative characteristic of a population of living organisms, such as the yield of cereals, which is subject to control by many genes, as well as by environmental factors. The other Roman literary sources direct us to the two main classes of deviations. It is not helpful to assume, in discussing the Roman sources, as many scholars have done, that one of them must be right and the others wrong, and then discuss which of them was right. The fact of a range of variation in all populations is the most elementary and the most important fact in biology, the starting point of Darwin's *Origin of Species*.[241]

Some regions simply have more fertile soil than others. The archetype on a small scale is the volcanic soil of the area around Mt Vesuvius, on a large scale the loess soil of the plains of north China, the foundation for the earliest Chinese civilisation. The Athenian cleruchy of Lemnos, the island of Melos and the peninsula of Methana also fall into this category, as they all have fertile volcanic soils.[242] Parts of Sicily may be very fertile, especially the volcanic soils around Mt Etna, but Cicero's statements do not indicate yields any higher than those achieved in various regions of Italy in the early modern period.[243] No author, ancient, mediaeval or modern, has ever regarded Attica as being of exceptional natural fertility and so there is no reason to include Attica in this category. A source such as Xenophon's *Poroi* obviously has an axe to grind and, in the absence of both a comparative perspective and a quantitative dimension, tells us nothing whatsoever.[244]

Attica does not fall into the second category of deviation either, namely the exceedingly high 'yields' recorded by sources such as Pliny and Varro for areas like Byzacium in North Africa and the territory of Sybaris in Italy. Nevertheless it is worth discussing these sources at some length because of the light that they shed on the mechanics of large-scale grain production in the ancient world. They have been persistently misunderstood, all the way from Guiraud, who incorrectly attributed them to the application of fertilisers on a large scale, to a recent writer such as J.K. Evans, who quite wrongly dismissed them altogether.[245]

This phenomenon, as described by Pliny, clearly refers to tillering. This means that the plant took advantage of favourable environmental conditions during the initial stages of growth to put out many additional stems from its base. This creates the possibility of many grains on a single wheat plant, although the number of tillers and their survival rate are inversely proportional to each other. Plant breeders and farmers today do not find tillering advantageous. Modern varieties of wheat are usually bred in such a way as to reduce the propensity to tiller. Moreover a comparison of wheat species and related plants such as the genus Aegilops shows that the evolution of wheat has been accompanied by a gradual decrease in tillering capacity. In the course of its evolution wheat has reduced its dependence on a variable number of crown roots serving tillers in favour of greater dependence on an increasing (but fixed at seed development) number of seminal roots serving the main culm. This shift helped to make possible a larger number of bigger grains on the main stem at the same time as the number of unproductive side shoots was reduced.[246]

Plants compete with each other for nutrients and moisture. Tillering on a large scale implies a very low seeding rate, with very few plants per unit area. Consequently the yield of grain per unit area, when tillering occurs on a very substantial scale, is nowhere near as impressive as the number of grains on an individual plant may suggest at first sight. In practice the seed:yield ratio tends to follow the pattern of the logistic curve, and the highest net return is obtained at intermediate seeding rates or plant population densities. In fact there is nothing exceptional at all about the single plant of *triticum* with 400 grains mentioned by Pliny, but it amounts to a very low yield per unit area, because at very low seeding rates the tillering capacity of the plant does not compensate for the very low plant population density. Percival describes an experiment in which a single wheat plant, grown in a plot of four square feet, produced 354 grains, i.e. a yield of only about 395 kg/ha. The tillering capacity of durum wheat is lower than that of any other species of wheat. Pliny's information on the density of Roman wheats supports the idea that bread wheat was cultivated in Gaul and south Russia and naked tetraploid wheats in more southerly and hotter regions, including North Africa.

The connection between extensive tillering and a low plant population density is made especially clear in a passage of Strabo on Susiana, where the furrows were unusually widely spaced, resulting in a low plant population density and high seed:yield ratios. It has been argued that farmers in the Near East in certain periods in antiquity did not leave entire fields fallow for a year, but instead left alternate furrows fallow each year, a method of farming which has drastic effects on calculations of yield per unit area and has also been practised in North Africa in recent times. A low seeding rate is an adaptation to very low and variable rainfall in semi-arid areas, which include the great wheat-producing regions of the globe. It is an acknowledgment of the possibility that the available moisture may only be sufficient to produce a poor crop, or sometimes no crop at all. Strabo gives us a description of a wheat plant in Numidia. It was clearly a very impressive individual plant, with a height in the height range for modern poulard wheat (*T. turgidum*), the tallest species of wheat, even after adopting the lowest known value of the ancient Greek unit *pêchus*, 'cubit', used by Strabo. It also had a stem as thick as a little finger, and a large number of grains, judging by the seed:yield ratio. Such outstanding individual specimens could only have been few and far between in a semi-arid region on the edge of the Sahara desert.[247]

Occasionally a very favourable conjunction of all the environmental parameters occurs in such an environment, in which case a very high seed:yield ratio may be obtained. This phenomenon occurs every now and again in modern Tunisia (ancient Byzacium), for example. However, a glance at recent production statistics for that same country makes it clear that it does not happen sufficiently frequently over a sufficiently large area to raise the mean value of seed:yield ratios across the whole country above an extremely low level, often no more than 2:5.1.[248] Pliny and Varro do not contradict Columella any more than Cicero does. The difference between them is that the eyes of Pliny and Varro were drawn to the rare phenomenon, while Columella concentrated on the norm. In Greece, which is rather wetter than the parts of Tunisia in question, it is more advantageous to sow a larger quantity of seed to exploit the higher rainfall, i.e. to have more plants and fewer tillers per plant. This also helps the cereals to compete against weeds, an important point before the invention of modern herbicides.[249] The wider significance of all this for the nature of the ancient economy is that it suggests that low seeding rates and consequently an extensive pattern of land use were employed in areas with a great reputation in antiquity as grain-producing regions, such as North Africa, Sybaris and Cyrene, as an adaptation to rainfall which was as low and variable then as it is today.[250]

The very high seed:yield ratios recorded by ancient sources for North Africa were undoubtedly produced under dry-farming conditions, not under 'arid zone irrigation', in spite of Brent Shaw's arguments to the contrary. 'Arid zone irrigation', which is simply the collection of rainwater from an area larger than the cultivated area and does not permit keeping fields under water permanently (excluding rice cultivation in the Mediterranean in antiquity), would be expected to raise yields to a certain extent and to reduce interannual harvest variability insofar as it stabilised the water supply. The alternative term 'runoff farming', employed by geographers, gives a more accurate and less grandiose view of what it entails than the term employed by Shaw. However there remains a colossal difference between the 8:1 or so average yield:seed ratios recorded in, for example, the Byzantine Nessana papyri, which were obtained by means of runoff farming, and the seed:yield ratios of Pliny and Herodotos, for example. Shaw's explanation of the ancient sources is incorrect, although his observation of the low human population density of Roman North Africa is noteworthy. Even in modern times indigenous farmers in Tunisia have continued to use the seed:yield ratio, not the yield per unit area which was introduced by the French colonists in the nineteenth century AD.

The essential point is that any given seed:yield ratio may be obtained from any area of land, within certain very wide limits. If a high seed:yield ratio from a given quantity of seed is obtained from a small area of land, then it is equivalent to a high yield per unit area. However, if the same

seed:yield ratio from the same absolute quantity of seed is obtained from
a large area of land, then it may be equivalent to a very low yield per unit
area. Combinations of seed:yield ratios of the magnitude of those
recorded by Pliny and Herodotos with very high yields per unit area do
not occur even in the most productive farming systems using the most
sophisticated technology available in the world today for wheat and
barley cultivation. Thus it is the only logical alternative, the combination
of a high seed:yield ratio with a low yield per unit area, which provides
the key to understanding the ancient sources on cereals in North Africa.
Exactly the same type of analysis is valid for olive cultivation as well in
North Africa, where highly productive individual trees existed under
conditions of a low tree population density. This information comes from
the Carthaginian writer Mago cited by Pliny, who mentions extraordinarily productive individual trees and then in the same breath states
that olive trees had to be planted considerably further apart in North
Africa than in Italy. The account of tillering given here differs from that
given by Powell (1985) for ancient Sumeria because the two situations are
not identical. For example different species of wheat with different
tillering capacities are in question, as well as different agricultural
systems (Mediterranean dry-farming v. Mesopotamian irrigation
agriculture).[251]

It is a quite straightforward conclusion that cereal yields in these
regions were as low and as variable in antiquity as they have been up to
very recent times. However, it would be quite wrong to draw immediately
the conclusion that a surplus could not have been produced in these areas
in antiquity, in years in which rainfall came at the right time. It all
depended on the human population density, on the man:land ratio. The
reader will recall that a similar conclusion was reached in sections 8 & 9
above, by a different route, in relation to large-scale grain production in
south Russia in antiquity. Exactly the same principle applied in antiquity
as applies in the modern world, namely that production of a significant
grain surplus in absolute terms was correlated with relatively low yields
in large semi-arid areas which had a low human population density, as in
the USA, Argentina, Canada and Australia today.

The Romans saw in Byzacium a very fertile country where modern
scholars see a barren land, on the edge of the Sahara desert, because their
conception of cereal productivity differed from that employed by modern
scientists. In fact the Sahara was as dry in Roman times as it is today (see
Chapter I above). Colinvaux described the Roman demand before the
Third Punic War that the Carthaginians should move to a new city at
least ten miles from the coast as an 'ecological sentence of death'. The
Greek and Roman conception measured the maximum reproductive
capacity of the plant under conditions of an extremely low population
density with little competition for nutrients and moisture, and modern
experiments show that a very high yield per plant and a very low yield

per unit area are one and the same thing, i.e. seed:yield ratio and yield per unit area may be inversely correlated in certain circumstances. In theoretical terms the intrinsic rate of natural increase, r, which is achieved under uncompetitive conditions, is an unreliable guide to evolutionary fitness under competitive conditions (at K). Modern plant breeders have found that this general principle is applicable to cereals. This is why data on seed:yield ratios or yields per plant in historical records cannot be translated accurately into the yield per unit area terms which are generally employed today. MacArthur & Wilson (1967) reached the conclusion that in general evolutionary fitness should be defined in terms of K, rather than r.

The irony of the Roman 'system of thought', to use Foucault's concept, is that in all probability cereal yields per unit area in Roman Italy, with its more favourable rainfall regime, were higher than in North Africa (excluding Egypt) throughout antiquity just as they have been in recent times. That was the resource base which enabled Rome to feed the apparently inexhaustible manpower that allowed her to overcome Carthage in the Second Punic War. Even as recently as after the First World War the average yield per unit area of the durum wheat cultivated by indigenous farmers in the arid central and southern regions of Tunisia was only 150 kg/ha. There is no reason whatsoever for supposing that it was any higher in antiquity. In this context it should be noted that the information that over half of the land of the late Roman province of Byzacena was not occupied in AD 422 simply reflects its marginal location on the periphery of the desert and does not necessarily imply that there was any great increase in abandoned agricultural land, *agri deserti*, in this region as part of the decline and fall of the Roman empire. The seed:yield ratio has certain uses but also severe limitations, usually not appreciated by historians who generally use it because most historical records relating to cereal yields employ it, rather than the yield per unit area. Campbell (1983), a rare example of a historian aware of some of these phenomena, used evidence from mediaeval England to demonstrate the unreliability of seed:yield ratios as a guide to yields per unit area.[252]

So far our argument for low yields in ancient Greece has rested mainly on citing empirical evidence of a comparative nature. It is time now to explain in terms of the concepts of evolutionary biology why high yields could not have been obtained from varieties of naked wheats in semi-arid areas in antiquity. Darwin made the following observation: 'at each successive period the state of agriculture will have determined the maximum degree of productiveness; for it would be impossible to cultivate a highly productive variety unless the land contained a sufficient supply of the necessary chemical elements.' The logical corollary of this is that in the absence of the necessary chemical elements highly productive varieties could not only not have been cultivated, they could not have evolved and existed in the first place.[253]

When chemical fertilisers were first introduced into semi-arid zones of the Mediterranean and Middle East, it was found that the existing varieties of wheat either did not respond to them or tended to respond in a manner undesirable for the farmer, with excessive growth of the vegetative parts of the plant leading to 'lodging', i.e. the unnaturally extended stalks of the plants become unable to support the ears of grain on top. Pliny knew that large doses of fertiliser led to lodging.[254]

Over thousands of years varieties of naked wheats in these areas had evolved in the context of a very low supply of nutrients and often inadequate moisture. This meant that their genetic constitution was simply incapable of responding to the sudden arrival of the unexpected supply of nutrients represented by the innovation of chemical fertilisers. Productive use of chemical fertilisers in these regions has therefore depended on scientific selective breeding of cereals, which was not practised in antiquity. The achievement of the 'Green Revolution' of the 1960s was the breeding in Mexico of new dwarf and semi-dwarf varieties of wheat whose novel characteristic is their ability to respond to very large doses of chemical fertilisers by dramatically increasing seed production at the expense of the growth of the vegetative parts of the plant. This feature immediately led to a very sharp increase in agricultural productivity upon their introduction to Greece in the mid-1960s.

If we turn back to the classical period now, the logical inference is that Guiraud's claim that high yields (per unit area) were obtained in antiquity implies two further claims. First it requires that varieties of wheat existed in antiquity whose genotype enabled them to respond to substantial applications of fertilisers, varieties that had subsequently disappeared by modern times in semi-arid Mediterranean and Middle Eastern lands. Secondly, it demands that substantial quantities of fertilisers were in fact available. There is of course no evidence whatsoever for evolution going backwards in such a way, for the existence of high yielding varieties in the past which have become extinct since then. On the contrary, all the evidence indicates that naked wheats struggled to compete with barley and emmer for thousands of years in prehistory. Nor is there any evidence for the regular availability of the large quantities of fertilisers which could have permitted cereals to evolve in such a way that they could respond to human inputs of this kind.

It is necessary at this point to discuss the availability of fertilisers in classical Attica. Cicero's observation that Hesiod did not mention fertilisers or manure in the *Works & Days* forms a suitable preface to this digression.[255] The most important chemical elements in question are nitrogen and phosphorus. A shortage of either one of them will restrict yields regardless of how much of the other is available. It is widely agreed that Mediterranean soils were short of phosphates in the past. The one scholar who strongly argued for the use of phosphatic fertilisers in antiquity had to concede that they were only employed in certain very restricted geographical areas in which prominent deposits of phosphate minerals occurred. Bones are not a reliable source of phosphates unless treated with acid. Manure, if available, does supply these elements, but may not enable a farmer to correct imbalances between different elements in the soil or make up for deficiencies in trace elements.[256]

The availability of nitrogen in the soils of Attica is a more complicated question. Even in the absence of artificial chemical fertilisers, nitrogen could theoretically have been provided by a wide variety of sources, including green manure, human manure, bacteria living in symbiosis with leguminous plants, animal manure, and bacteria and algae living in the soil. Modern literature on agriculture shows that the use of green manure (ploughing a leguminous crop into the soil) does raise yields significantly but is beset in semi-arid areas by difficult practical problems.[257] Human manure was undoubtedly employed in classical Attica, especially in gardens in and around Athens itself, but its availability was restricted to the immediate vicinity. of human settlements. The concentrations of potsherds around ancient sites seems to indicate the application of manure from compost heaps in which rubbish was deposited. In Athens the town magistrates (*astunomoi*) had to ensure that the refuse collectors (*koprologoi*) deposited the products of their labours well outside the walls of Athens.[258]

It was noted in section 2 above that a leguminous fodder plant such as lucerne, which certainly has the potential to rejuvenate the soil's supply of nitrogen, was not an important crop in Greece until very recently and indeed does not give high yields without irrigation in a semi-arid environment. This is very significant because the simplest way in which a cereal:bare fallow rotation may be improved is by replacing the fallow with a leguminous fodder crop. Edible pulses are also legumes, but they remove nitrogen from the soil, besides fixing it themselves. They are not a suitable component of a rotation system whose main aim is maximising cereal production unless substantial quantities of chemical fertilisers and pesticides are applied as in technologically advanced farming systems, in which case the pulses become largely dispensable anyway, except as a disease break. The best way of rotating cereals and pulses in Mediterranean semi-arid rainfed farming conditions is to use a three-year crop rotation, with autumn-sown cereals in the first year, autumn-sown pulses (or a summer crop) in the second year, and the third year fallow.[259]

The shortage of meadowland and fodder crops led in the past to a considerable division between arable farming and animal husbandry, as sheep and goats had to spend a considerable part of the year grazing away from the arable fields, during which time their dung would be lost to the farmer. Moreover manure rapidly deteriorates and loses its value in a hot, dry climate. In any case it is frequently burnt as fuel in

Mediterranean regions where wood is in short supply. Some recent scholarly literature has attempted to revise this traditional view, arguing that animal husbandry was integrated more closely with cereal cultivation in antiquity than has generally been supposed. It is a question of where the emphasis should be placed. There is no doubt that animal husbandry was not as important in the ecosystem of classical Greece as it traditionally has been in the agricultural system of the British Isles, for example, with its large areas of well watered meadowland. It is right to emphasise the lower degree of integration of arable farming and animal husbandry in ancient Greece, because it helps us to understand what differentiates the agricultural system of classical Greece from those of other parts of the world and other periods of history.[260]

Animal population density in Greek history has been inversely correlated with human population density because of the competition between men and animals to eat the plants on the land. In the early nineteenth century AD transhumant shepherds brought large numbers of sheep and goats each winter from Thessaly to pasture on land they rented in Attica.[261] The small human population of Attica, a tiny fraction of the classical population, had land to spare. McGrew (1985) argued that a larger proportion of the small human population lived off animal products than lived off cereals in early modern Greece before the War of Independence, since the lowlands were abandoned to the Turks. In contrast, the population of classical Attica was struggling to feed itself. There was no room for large numbers of animals in classical Greece. Indeed it would have been much harder to bring flocks across the multitude of political boundaries between Thessaly and Attica in the classical period than it was to move them around under the political unity imposed by the *Tourkokratia*.

Animal husbandry was probably also very important in Dark Age Greece in another period of low human population density, as argued by Foraboschi (1984) and Snodgrass (1987). The fact that Hesiod says nothing about it in the *Works & Days* is simply a reflection of its lack of integration with arable farming. It is worth noting at this point that the model of ancient Greek society set up in Chapter II.5-6 above may be reconciled with both Snodgrass's emphasis on pastoralism divorced from arable farming and Halstead's emphasis on the integration of animal husbandry into horticultural farming systems, because age class systems exist today in the context of true nomadic pastoralism in East Africa and in the context of subsistence horticulture in New Guinea. It is dangerous to assume that there were necessarily any rigid deterministic links between society and economy in antiquity. Hallpike (1986) argued that in general under primitive conditions a very wide range of ascriptive institutional arrangements may all work perfectly well because demands on functional and adaptive efficiency are low. He also cautioned against simplistic models of environmental determinism, arguing that similar social structures may be found in quite different environments.

Meadowland and good quality land for pasturage have always been in very short supply in Attica. However even in other parts of the ancient world endowed with higher average annual rainfall the most advantageous way of combining animal husbandry with the production of cereals for human consumption was not practised in classical antiquity. The great innovation of the Agricultural Revolution in early modern England was the spread of ley-arable systems. In these systems of land use grass is sown for a few years to provide pasturage for animals. It has the incidental effect of sharply increasing the organic matter content of the soil, which bears a fairly constant relationship to the nitrogen content of the soil. In short, it considerably increases soil fertility. After a few years the grass is ploughed up, and cereals are then sown for a few years, producing high yields. After a few more years grass is sown again to repeat the cycle. Ley-arable systems both produce high cereal yields and sustain animals to produce meat and dairy products that give a high monetary income, and the animals in turn contribute manure which pushes the cereal yields still higher. The widespread adoption of ley-arable systems doubled food production in England. There is no evidence that they were employed on a significant scale anywhere in Europe before the early modern period. The ideas of Chatterton (1985) on antiquity, although ingenious, rest on no evidence whatsoever.[262]

In a ley-arable system there is no distinction whatsoever between arable land and pasture land. In contrast some of the Roman agronomists, debating the question of whether animal husbandry was part of *agri cultura*, decided that it was not. They all regarded meadows, especially water meadows, as a very profitable way of using land, sharing in this respect the judgment of modern farmers, and did realise that grassland, ploughed up and sown with cereals, increased cereal yields. However, they only recommended doing this for one year every so often as part of a scheme for rejuvenating old pasture land. The Roman agronomists thought that, as meadowland was the most financially profitable method of land-use, they should strive to maintain *permanent* meadows. Thus it is correct to maintain that animal husbandry and cultivation of arable land were not properly integrated in antiquity. A very good example of the ancient mentality is Pliny's last comment on meadows. He regarded breeding horses for chariot-racing as a profitable way of using meadows, a very different pattern of thought from that which inspired the Agricultural Revolution in early modern England.[263]

Pliny, drawing on Amphilochos, an Athenian author of unknown date, mentions one innovation in classical Greece which serves to stress this point. In describing *kutisos*, shrub-trefoil (*Medicago arborea*), which had spread from Kythnos in the Cyclades and then to mainland Greece, he states that its cultivation had considerably increased the supply of cheese, an important source of protein, to Greek cities. It may be inferred that maintaining animals near major settlements, which were generally situated in or next to areas of good arable land, was a severe problem. The solution to the problem which he mentions did not depend on integrating animal husbandry with arable farming, since shrub-trefoil is a perennial plant. Aiskhylides, a Greek writer on agriculture, states that sheep were fed on *kutisos*, inter alia, on Keos because of the shortage of pasture there, and Kythnian cheese was made from the milk obtained in that way. The Roman agronomists stressed that *kutisos*, a leguminous plant, was adapted to very poor soils, and its importance as a crop on Keos should not be interpreted as a sign that agriculture on Keos was highly productive. Indeed the high price of the cheese suggests that it was a scarce commodity. Shrub-trefoil prefers limestone soils and occurs frequently in modern Attica. It is an example of a plant that was cultivated in the past but has been abandoned by modern farmers who do not find it useful, precisely because it does not fit into modern crop rotation systems. It is now only used for ornamental purposes. Finds at Kastanas suggest that cultivation of *kutisos* may have started during the Mycenaean period, been abandoned during the Dark Ages, and rediscovered later. The word is attested on a Linear B tablet, but refers there to the wood of a tree, the laburnum, which also bore this name in classical Greek. Pliny recommended the sowing of onions and garlic in between the rows of *kutisos*, another crop mixture.[264]

Animal manure was not available in classical Attica in sufficient quantities to make a big difference to cereal yields. Even in modern Greece there is little integration between arable farming and animal husbandry, since only 10 per cent of the sheep and 20 per cent of the goats are based on farms, the rest being free-ranging flocks, according to government statistics.[265] The cereal yields of early modern Greece in a good year, on the eve of the introduction of chemical fertilisers, were above all the result of the practice of biennial fallow.[266] The spread of the use of chemical fertilisers over the last sixty years and the steep decrease in the proportion of arable land left fallow during the same period of time are cause and effect. Experiments have demonstrated that in areas with a level of precipitation comparable to that of Attica, fallow is not necessary so long as suitable doses of chemical fertilisers are applied by farmers.[267] The role of fallow in agriculture in the past is often misunderstood.[268] It does serve to retain about 20 per cent of the rainfall of the fallow year in the soil.[269] This extra water may be critical for the success of crops in areas that shade into the desert, with, say, 250 mm of rainfall a year. However in areas with 400 mm or more of precipitation on average per year, the main function of fallow in the past was to permit natural processes to fix nitrogen in the soil for a year and so maintain soil fertility above rock bottom (see also Chapter II.2 above). Virtually all of Greece falls into this category. Chemical fertilisers were not available in classical antiquity. This is the reason why we should accept the statements of classical authors that fallow was a regular practice in antiquity. Hesiod described fallow as the averter of Hades ('death'). As far as Attica itself is concerned, it is possible now to estimate that out of the circa 30 per cent of Attica that could have been used as arable land for cereals, about 15 per cent was sown each year with wheat or barley, increasing Jardé's estimate of 10 per cent by about half.[270]

For the sake of completeness it is necessary to mention briefly two regions of the ancient world for which much higher cereal yields have been claimed than are postulated here and indicate how these two situations fit into this framework. Research at the Butser Ancient Farm Research Project in Hampshire claims that farmers in Iron Age Britain were able to obtain cereal yields which, in a comparative perspective, are roughly equivalent to those obtained by farmers in the USA today. These experiments were conducted with emmer, einkorn and spelt wheat. The results show that these cereals are more productive plants than has often been thought in the past. This means that they provided stiff competition for naked wheats in the past and indeed explains why early farmers preferred crops whose conversion into food is a considerably more complicated process than in the case of the naked wheats. Thus the results of the Butser experiments do not conflict with the theoretical framework adopted here and the arguments here for low yields of naked wheats in antiquity.[271]

However there are various technical problems. Entirely virgin grassland was used for the experiments, making the results of doubtful relevance to areas in which the land has long been cultivated, because of the extremely high organic matter content of the soil. Emmer is better adapted than durum wheat to take advantage of such conditions because of its higher tillering capacity. The data provided show that the seven years of the experiment had consumed a quantity of organic matter equal to at least the entire average organic matter content of soils on old arable land. Once the soil at the Butser farm is almost exhausted of organic matter, the cereal yields would be expected to stabilise at a lower level. What is needed are similar experiments to investigate the yields of the primitive wheats on old arable land which is short of both organic matter and of chemical elements such as phosphorus and potassium. One other recent experiment in England, admittedly on a very small scale, produced emmer yields much lower than those from the Butser Farm and in conformity with the yield per unit area derived from Columella. Some of the results of the Butser experiments, such as the success of einkorn and the failure of modern naked wheat varieties, were the product of the choice of site, with the associated environment, and could have been foreseen. The modern varieties do outyield the primitive wheats if cultivated under favourable conditions.[272]

In experiments such as those performed at the Butser Farm anachronism is always a grave danger. For example Reynolds observed that broadcasting seed by hand without using a seed-drill and without subsequent use of a harrow is merely an extravagant way of feeding the birds. However, neither of those instruments was employed in classical Greece. Darwin's observation on birds and cereal seed suggests that the plots at the Butser Farm are simply too small to give an accurate impression of large-scale farming. Broadcasting seed by hand was the only method of sowing known in classical antiquity, with a labourer following up to rake soil over the seeds. Columella thought that harrowing was not necessary if the seed-bed had been prepared properly beforehand. This illustrates the fundamental point that where a modern mind like that of Reynolds, living in a world in which the idea of constant technological progress is taken for granted, inevitably looks for a new gadget or a new piece of machinery to solve a problem, ancient Greek and Roman farmers only considered the application of additional human labour, ideally the labour of slaves. Buckland (1981) criticised the Butser experiments for not taking account of storage losses caused by the grain fauna introduced to Britain in Roman times (see Chapter I above). In addition it is impossible for such experiments to reproduce the disease environment encountered by cereals in ancient Britain (see Chapter II.7 above). The primitive wheat species are now exotic species in Britain.[273]

Irrespective of their validity for prehistoric Britain, it is better not to take too much account of the Butser experiments in considering agriculture in semi-arid regions of the Mediterranean in antiquity because of the vast differences in the respective environments. In Britain the much larger proportion of land that provides meadowland and good pasturage for animals made it possible to obtain a much larger supply of manure in the past than was possible in an area like Attica. Rainfall in Britain is such that shortage of moisture is a limiting factor on plant growth and uptake of nutrients from the soil less frequently than in the Mediterranean. Moreover the soil contains a higher proportion of organic matter. It is quite possible that cereals in Iron Age Britain responded to these more favourable environmental conditions by giving higher yields than they did in semi-arid zones of the Mediterranean and Middle East in antiquity. Britain was a grain exporting area in the fourth century AD. Indeed this divergence has been observed in more recent periods. In early modern France seed:yield ratios were only 4-5:1 on the Mediterranean coast, but 8-9:1 in the wetter north. Jasny commented on the tendency of all cereals to produce taller plants with larger ears of grain in moist climates, with reference to the 'land-race' of emmer called *arinca* in Gaul. The biomass productivity of natural vegetation communities in the Mediterranean is lower than that of both temperate regions to the north and tropical regions to the south because of the summer drought.[274] The more favourable environment of Britain facilitated advances in agricultural productivity which helped to create the labour force to man the new factories during the Industrial Revolution.[275]

The second area to be mentioned is the irrigation agriculture of Egypt and Mesopotamia.[276] In Egypt the Nile acted as farmer, as Pliny quaintly put it, bringing down silt eroded from the highlands of Ethiopia to refertilise the land each year. The Nile sediment replenishes the phosphate content of Egyptian soils. Observations of the Nile led the ancient Greeks to think that water by itself created fertility.[277] As in Britain, we have here a situation in which the availability of water is not a limiting factor, provided that the Nile flood is not too low, and a relatively abundant supply of nutrients is available. Under such circumstances it was possible for local varieties of cereals to give higher yields. Moreover the documentary evidence for high yields in Dynastic Egypt and ancient Mesopotamia refers mainly to yields of emmer and barley, while the documentary evidence often quoted for low yields in mediaeval Egypt (e.g. in al-Maqrizi) refers to naked wheats. The evidence from Egypt and Mesopotamia is easily accommodated within the framework proposed here, as is the evidence from the Butser Farm.

The Butser and Reading experiments suggest that the productivity of modern naked wheat varieties compares unfavourably with that of the hulled wheats einkorn, emmer and spelt under conditions of very low levels of artificial inputs by farmers in the way of fertilisers, pesticides etc. The preference of early farmers for these hulled wheats was motivated by considerations of economic productivity. Harlan showed that stands of wild einkorn (*Triticum boeoticum*) and wild emmer (*Triticum dicoccoides*) in the Middle East may produce yields of up to 500-800 kg/ha in years with high rainfall, in areas of very fertile volcanic soils but also very high interannual climatic variability. How could yields of *triticum* in Roman Italy, obtained by farmers who were part of a sophisticated civilisation, have been lower than the yields of wild cereals in the Middle East today, as the information provided by Columella suggests they were?[278]

A cultivated cereal would be like a child with spina bifida, if it were not tended by man. It could not propagate itself and would exhibit an abysmally low degree of reproductive fitness. The low yield of early varieties of naked wheats was part of a complex of characteristics which made them very unfit in unaided competition with wild plants and wheats that were more 'primitive' (i.e. better equipped to survive with a minimum of interference from man). Nevertheless they possessed certain characteristics which made them attractive to a potential propagating agent, *Homo sapiens*. Once man became involved in ecological mutualisms with them and started to tend them, improvement was possible in antiquity through elementary forms of seed selection, and is now also possible through recombinations of the diversity of genetic material to be found in the tetraploid and hexaploid naked wheats as a result of their hybrid origins.[279]

Darwin observed that 'wheat might have been improved long ago up to that standard of excellence which was possible under the then existing state of agriculture'. However, he did not attempt to date the point at which a plateau was reached. One of the conclusions of this chapter must be that naked wheats were able to improve significantly until the first millennium BC, but did not manage any further very significant improvement before the start of the modern period. There were two main reasons for this. One was the shortage of fertilisers in the Mediterranean. The second is that there is a limit to what may be achieved with the methods of seed selection employed in antiquity. Seed size has continued to increase to the present day. However the average seed size of naked tetraploid wheats in the Mediterranean increased more from Neolithic to Roman times than it has subsequently increased from Roman times to the present day. Modern plant breeders have adopted more sophisticated techniques which may themselves have limits too. It is likely that the breeding of dwarf varieties of cereals, with the consequent redistribution of biomass from the vegetative to the reproductive parts of the plants, can only be carried so far, and eventually it will be necessary to concentrate on selecting for increases in total biomass again.[280]

This chapter closes by subscribing to Grigg's opinion that cereal yields in the Mediterranean in the past could have exceeded 650 kg/ha only rarely, except on very good soils.[281] The nineteenth-century English historian of Greece, Finlay, who had personal experience of running a farm in Attica, affirmed that tithed land yielded 'the smallest return for the labour and seed annually bestowed on it that is compatible with the existence of the agricultural population'.[282] The agricultural population certainly found life even tougher in classical Attica in respect of agricultural productivity, accounting for the importance of barley in classical Attica in contrast to the wheat of the nineteenth century AD. However, the absence of regular taxation on the land in classical times meant that one burden of peasants in Finlay's Attica was absent in the fifth and fourth centuries BC during the existence of the classical democracy.

IV

Conclusions

This chapter aims to tie a few loose ends together, return to some of the philosophical and methodological questions raised in the first chapter, and draw some conclusions. The discussion of the effects of climatic change in that chapter referred to long-term climatic variations, on a millennial timescale. The possibility of variations over shorter periods of time, such as periods of centuries, needs to be considered now, as well as interannual climatic variability. Aschmann (1984) gave a restrictive definition of the Mediterranean climate in terms of the following three parameters: (1) enough rainfall for successful dry-farming in most years, but not enough to support either a dense coniferous or a broadleaf deciduous forest; (2) mild winters without intense, prolonged cold weather; (3) at least 65 per cent of total precipitation falls within the winter half of the year, with a marked dry season in summer. Although this definition excludes certain regions usually regarded as possessing a Mediterranean climate, it outlines the main features of the Mediterranean climate. It is better to define the Mediterranean climate in terms of purely climatic variables, rather than using bioclimatic factors such as the distribution of the olive tree, because living organisms usually are not perfectly adapted to their environment.

Regions with a Mediterranean climate tend to have a fairly low average annual rainfall. The lower it is the greater the variability in precipitation. This has very important implications for agriculture in the Mediterranean countries, which were discussed in detail by Garnsey (1988). Consequently little need be said here about the effects of interannual rainfall variability. There is a statistical correlation between cereal yields and total annual precipitation. This correlation decreases as average annual rainfall increases. However, there is an even stronger correlation between cereal yields and the monthly distribution pattern of rainfall during the year. Ideally, it would be preferable to investigate the variability of data for actual cereal production rather than working on rainfall variability as Garnsey did, a type of proxy data by no means synonymous with yield variation, but there are no surviving time series data for agricultural production from antiquity, and indeed none ever existed.

The pattern of interannual climatic variability in classical Greece, illustrated by variations in tree-ring widths in wood from the Parthenon in Athens dating to the fifth century BC, was very similar to the modern pattern. The research of Kuniholm & Striker (1983) & (1987) on dendrochronology in Greece and Turkey raises the possibility of writing a history of interannual rainfall variations in semi-arid regions in antiquity, if the absolute dating of the tree-ring chronologies, which currently stretches into the mediaeval period, can be extended back to antiquity. Further research in this field is our best hope for extending knowledge of climatic variability in the classical period. It is possible to correlate tree-ring patterns from all over Greece and Turkey, suggesting that the macroclimate of that entire geographical region behaved as a unit in the past.[1]

The possibility of variations in the climate in classical antiquity over periods of centuries has attracted less attention in recent literature than interannual variability. Fairly small variations may have quite considerable consequences. For example, the 'Little Ice Age' in early modern Europe was caused by a reduction in temperature of only 1-2°C. The shortage of evidence makes it almost impossible to investigate the possibility of such variations in Greece in classical antiquity. There is nothing comparable to the phenological data, such as vine harvest dates, used by Le Roy Ladurie (1971), or the evidence for glaciers exploited by Grove (1988) in research on the 'Little Ice Age'. Similarly little research has been carried out in Greece in palynology, the main tool used by Quaternary palaeoecologists to explore climatic variation in the Holocene. A consensus has developed among ancient historians that the climate of Greece in the fifth and fourth centuries BC was virtually identical to the present-day climate. This conclusion depends principally on the distribution and behaviour of various species of plants described by Theophrastos. Eginitis concluded that the mean temperature *c.* 300 BC, at the time of Theophrastos, was within a degree of the modern value.[2]

However, there may have been significant climatic variations in other periods of ancient history. Carpenter (1966) suggested that a period of excessive aridity at the end of the Bronze Age explained the collapse of the Mycenaean civilisation, but there is no more evidence for this than there is for the equally far-fetched hypothesis of E. Williams (1962) that a pandemic of bubonic plague caused the collapse of Bronze Age civilisations in the eastern Mediterranean. In antiquity Aristotle explained the shift of power in the Argolid from Mycenae to Argos in terms of changes in the hydrology of the areas around those towns, with Argos becoming less marshy and Mycenae becoming too dry for agriculture. Apparently he thought that the epithets attached to Mycenae and Argos in the Homeric poems were rather inappropriate in his own time, and inferred that their respective water supplies altered during what are now called the Dark Ages and Archaic period. Kraft et al. (1977) argued that his theory does have a factual foundation, in marine retrogression. It remains a fascinating idea, stressing environmental changes affecting the agricultural potential of the regions under consideration and so their environmental carrying capacity. It is a very different kind of theory from the types of explanation advanced by most modern historians, and serves once again to illustrate Aristotle's powers of abstract thought.[3]

Huntington, who pioneered research into the effects of climatic change on human society and proposed the theory of cyclical fluctuations in the climate of the Eurasian steppes, suggested that the deposition of the sediments now called the Younger Fill at Olympia was caused by climatic change. However, the difficult problems of verifying such ideas, given the shortage of evidence, became apparent immediately and have intensified in more recent research on the Younger Fill (see Chapter III.12 above). Geomorphological evidence is only a type of proxy data for climatic change, and all types of proxy data must be treated with caution.

Other scholars have suggested that the climate of Greece shifted in the direction of increased aridity in the late fourth and early third century BC. Myres argued that the prosperity of the Aitolians in north-west Greece and the decline of states such as Athens in south-east Greece occurred because of a decrease in precipitation, which fell from extremely high levels in mountainous north-west Greece to more reasonable levels, while in south-east Greece it declined to levels that were dangerously low for agriculture. Unfortunately this interesting theory, which recalls Aristotle on Mycenae and Argos, does not explain the success of Crete, still further to the south-east, in the Hellenistic period. Camp (1982) proposed the hypothesis that there was a drought lasting for more than a generation in the second half of the fourth century BC in Greece. It is worth subjecting his arguments to careful scrutiny to show how careful it is necessary to be to advocate such theories successfully.[4]

Camp showed that many wells in the Agora in Athens were abandoned in the third quarter of the fourth century BC, while there was a considerable increase in the use of cisterns in private houses to collect rainwater. He exploited this evidence to try to connect the two major periods of food supply problems *c.* 360 BC and *c.* 330 BC, which stand out in the sources for the fourth century, into a single prolonged period of drought. However, this kind of evidence is ambiguous because it is susceptible to alternative interpretations. Aristotle states that a new method of waterproofing cisterns had recently been discovered. He mentions it in the context of considering ways in which cities could be strengthened to make them better able to resist a siege, a topical subject in the light of the prowess of the Macedonians in siege-warfare at the time. The fact that for Aristotle cisterns were a device for securing one's water supply in time of war, and not a response to climatic change, is all the more striking when we remember that he did consider the role of climatic change in historical explanation.

Camp also pointed out that several major waterworks were constructed in Athens in the period in question, including for example an aqueduct bringing water from Mt Parnes to Athens. However, these waterworks, like all the other buildings which were erected while Lykourgos was in charge of the public finances of Athens, probably simply reflect the fact that there was a quite a lot of money to spend at the time, because of the success of Lykourgos and earlier Euboulos at raising money on behalf of the *polis*. Camp acknowledges that there was a tradition of investments in waterworks by leading politicians going back to Themistokles, and Solon was also concerned about the problems of water supply. The waterworks of the Lykourgan age might not have been any more 'necessary' than the Parthenon was, i.e. they might just have been monumental constructions to boost the prestige of the *polis* of Athens.

In fact there is other evidence which permits us to dismiss the hypothesis of a continuous forty-year drought. There are sources which show that there were episodes of heavy rainfall in the period in question. Theophrastos speaks of heavy rainfall which led to Lake Kopais in Boiotia being raised to an exceptionally high level in the years preceding the battle of Khaironeia in 338 BC. In Attica Demosthenes mentions torrential rains which caused problems for farmers around Eleusis, recalling the winters with heavy rain at the beginning of the Peloponnesian War. Rather than thinking in terms of a continuous drought for over forty years, it is better to regard the age of Demosthenes as a period marked by alternating wet and dry phases. Both could be bad for crops. Theophrastos thought that on the whole too little rain was better for cereals than too much, and Aristotle regarded the marshiness of Argos as an impediment in the early stages of its history.[5]

Nevertheless there is plenty of evidence for food supply problems in the periods *c.* 360 BC and *c.* 330 BC onwards. In 361/360 BC there was a drought in which there was said to be no water at the bottom of wells and not enough to grow vegetables in gardens. There was a food shortage among all nations in 357 BC. A drought extending over a very large geographical area is the most likely cause of such an event. This applies too to the years following 330 BC. No source explicitly attributes the food supply problems of that time to drought. Consequently several scholars have attempted to explain the large donations of grain given by Cyrene to about forty states in the lands around the Aegean in purely political terms, as part of the machinations and intrigues between the Macedonians and their allies and enemies in the Greek world. However, the details of such a hypothesis inevitably remain hazy, first because the Cyrene inscription cannot be dated accurately, and secondly because no ancient source explicitly states that the recipients of the grain were chosen for political reasons.

Peter Garnsey has shown that the geographical distribution of those states in Greece which received grain from Cyrene corresponds to those regions of Greece with the lowest average annual rainfall today. This makes it likely that a drought was the principal causal factor, although conflicts such as the naval war between the Persians and the Macedonians in the Aegean in the late 330s, or the war between Sparta and Macedon, may well have helped to disrupt relief efforts.[6]

In the case of Athens, we have one inscription recording the first fruits offered at Eleusis in 329/8 BC, from which the total cereal production of Attica and the Athenian cleruchies may be calculated for one year, providing that the ratio between first fruits and total production had not changed from the ratio mentioned in a fifth-century inscription. We must also assume that farmers were reasonably honest in dedicating the appropriate proportion of their produce. Even if the calculation is correct, the information derived from it is of limited value because we do not know whether it represents a good, bad or average year. A continuous run of data for twenty or thirty years would be needed to obtain statistically significant results for total production. However, if the information from the inscription is related to the proportion of Attica that is devoted to agriculture today, about a third according to official statistics (see Chapter III.2 above), productivity per unit area would be so low, even assuming that yields were low on average anyway (Chapter III.12 above), that it is an inevitable conclusion that the harvest recorded on the inscription was that of a below average year (Chapter II.2 above). Attica lies in a rain shadow on the eastern side of Greece. It was noted in antiquity that rain, when it came, was brought by the north-east wind (*Hellêspontias*).

Prices are another form of proxy data which do not provide reliable testimony to variations in agricultural production and to climatic variability. For example, the speaker of speech XLII in the Demosthenic corpus alleges that his opponent Phainippos had been making big profits by selling barley and wine at three times their normal prices, apparently during the period of food shortages in the 320s. Even if we assume that the speaker was telling the truth, which is very far from certain, it is impossible to make any reliable inferences from his remarks as to what was happening to production at the time, rather than to prices. In early modern England and France there were runs of years of high and of low prices, but these are not statistically correlated with similar trends in variations in agricultural production, which were apparently random. High cereal prices in one year do not necessarily reflect a bad harvest in the same year, but may be caused by a low level of carryover of stocks from the previous year. Le Roy Ladurie suggested that in Mediterranean countries bad harvests generally resulted in increased prices in the year after the bad harvest.

There is also little to be gained from the scale of the price rises claimed in the Demosthenic speech, because cereal prices tend to rise in a steadily increasing ratio to decreases in production. It may seem plausible that farmers with some grain to spare should be able to make large profits in a situation of scarcity caused by bad harvests. However, experience in more recent periods of history has shown that in such situations the price rises often do not compensate the farmers for the fall in the volume of grain available for sale, after meeting the requirements of their own households which aimed at self-sufficiency, unless their estates are very large. The speaker's claims that farmers such as Phainippos were making big profits, while mine lessees such as himself were faring badly, are probably entirely spurious.[7]

Moreover our sources are very far from complete. There is no doubt that there were fluctuations in agricultural production in the classical period caused by climatic variability which have not been recorded. The evidence for olive harvests in antiquity serves to emphasise this point. Olive harvests are extremely variable because of the biennial rhythm of production under dry-farming conditions, even without taking any account of the effects of pests, diseases and climatic variability. In fact the ordinary run of interannual harvest variability is simply taken for granted by our sources. Only really disastrous years stood a chance of being recorded. An inscription mentions a failure of the olive harvest in Attica in the early second century BC. Theophrastos states that a sudden improvement in climatic conditions resulted in the yield of olive oil in 314 BC in Attica being much better than anyone had anticipated. He adds that such events had happened many times before, but no earlier source mentions any of them. Elsewhere he states that a dry wind in winter badly damaged olive trees at Khalkis in Euboia in 321/320 BC. The fact that no variations in the olive harvest in Attica are recorded in our sources during the period *c*. 360-330 BC, even though they undoubtedly occurred, is entirely fortuitous.[8]

In south-eastern Greece runs of several years with significantly below average rainfall tend to occur two or three times a century on average. In that sense crises of food supply such as those *c*. 360 and *c*. 330 BC were 'normal', in the sense that such events tend to recur statistically every so often. Consequently it has not been demonstrated that the events of the 320s BC heralded a major climatic shift towards increased aridity, instead of exhibiting the typical Mediterranean pattern of extreme interannual climatic variability. This is not to rule out the possibility that there were significant alterations in the climate on a secular basis in antiquity, but simply to declare that advocates of such theories will have to come up with better evidence than they have done so far.

The question of secular changes in the climate in classical antiquity and their possible causes and effects remains an interesting field for future research. It has been suggested, for example, that the fact that the vine was cultivated in Roman Britain indicates that the climate in the early Roman period was significantly warmer than it is today.[9] However, the evidence is as scanty in the case of Britain as it is in the case of Greece. Le Roy Ladurie (1971) argued that minor climatic variations may have no significant effects on humans, but if they do have any such effects, these should be most visible in a region like southeastern Greece, one of the driest parts of Europe.

So far the effects of climatic variations and variability have been discussed in relation to plants, but they also affect animals, both herbivores and carnivores. Before coming on to this, a few observations on the ecological relations between humans and other animals in antiquity will be of interest. Domestications of animals created new ecological mutualisms analogous to those created by plant domestication in the sense that co-evolution was not balanced (see Chapter I above). However, the mechanisms of animal domestication were quite different from the mechanisms of plant domestication in certain respects. Nothing like polyploidy occurs in mammals, at least in a stable form. Human polyploids end up as spontaneous abortions. The early stages of animal domestication were generally marked by notable decreases in body size, in contrast to the trend towards gigantism usually found in domesticated plants in the early stages of agriculture. The productivity of the individual animal was unimportant in the early phases of animal domestication because first of all behavioural changes had to evolve to make the animals malleable to human control.

This was accomplished by means of neoteny, in which characteristics of the behaviour of juveniles were transferred to the adult form, as individuals which ceased their development at an earlier age than is normal among wild animals increased their evolutionary fitness by altering their behavioural patterns in ways which made them more attractive to humans, who took care of them. The difference between the dog and the wolf is the prime example of the behavioural consequences of animal domestication. The freezing of development at an abnormally early age explains the reduced body size. Dog, cat, pig, goat, sheep and cattle all decreased in size upon domestication. On theoretical grounds the shift to smaller animal size should have made possible an increase in total animal biomass, if an increase in primary production to support the enlarged population was possible. This happened as a result of the provision of fodder and forage crops by humans to domesticated animals. Palaeozoological remains suggest that neoteny, like most other evolutionary processes, was a gradual process which developed over several thousand years from the Neolithic to the Iron Age.[10]

Aristotle, who took a great interest in the differences between wild and domesticated animals, observed other aspects of the increased productivity of domesticated animals. He noted that wild animals tend to breed once a year in spring, choosing the season best suited to raising the young, while many domesticated animals, like humans, breed all the year round. (However, even humans still have seasonal fluctuations in sperm production and conception rates, recalling the fact that hominids too were once, so to speak, wild animals.) The achievement of higher rates of reproduction was a gradual process. Aristotle stated that all domesticated animals have a corresponding wild form. He took a particular interest in the ages at which various species of animal first reproduce and in their longevity. He also concluded that animals are less fertile the larger they are. The existence of allometrically scaled relationships of this kind has been confirmed by modern research.

Aristotle commented on the stupidity of sheep. This is an interesting observation which may be correlated with the archaeological evidence that brain size was reduced during animal domestication, since domestic animals no longer needed to expend so much energy on maintaining a large brain to be able to take care of themselves when humans began to assure their food supply and protect them (cf. Chapter I above on plant chemical defences). The reduction in brain size was also related to the decrease in body size. The high intelligence characteristic of *Homo sapiens sapiens* is very rare in the animal kingdom because it is advantageous in terms of evolutionary fitness for animals to reduce energy expenditure on their central nervous systems, and on all their other organs, whenever possible (cf. the evolution of flightless birds like the dodo on islands where carnivores were absent). Aristotle also took an interest in honeybees, which were of considerable economic importance. He observed that domesticated honeybees are less hairy, less active and less difficult to handle than wild bees. They also produce more honey. Finally Aristotle drew attention to unconscious associations between man and arthropods, for example the clothes moth and bookworms.[11]

Although animal domestication, like plant domestication, commenced outside the range of human consciousness, eventually conscious artificial breeding by humans developed as well. It first occurred in Mesopotamia *c.* 3000 BC or perhaps a little earlier. In the 'secondary products revolution' of Sherratt (1981) animals like sheep, which were originally only exploited as a source of meat, began to be exploited for secondary products such as wool as well. In the case of sheep this required fleece evolution, which is manifest from the Early Bronze Age onwards. In the Iron Age sheep started to evolve a wider range of natural colours and then began to lose their innate tendency to moult annually. This was assisted by the invention of shears and of the process of dyeing *c.* 1000 BC, according to the *magnum opus* of Ryder (1983).

The modern types of fleece began to spread during the Roman period, although primitive fleece types were still widespread throughout classical antiquity. A Scythian tomb near Nymphaion in the Crimea, a Milesian colony which became an Athenian cleruchy, dating to the fifth century BC provides the earliest evidence for true fine wool. It was probably imported from Athens or Miletus, both of which had a reputation for fine wool.

However, Athens could not have exported large quantities of wool (see Chapter III.4 above). The distinction which exists in modern Attica between sheep with fine wool kept in small stationary flocks in the lowland plains and larger flocks of hairy transhumant sheep allowed to roam the hills already existed by the fifth century BC, as ancient authors mention 'jacketed' or 'coated' sheep with fine wool which received special treatment.[12]

Interest in increasing the physical strength of animals for the purposes of traction and carriage and in increasing the meat supply eventually led in classical times to artificial selection for increased animal size, parallel to selection for seed size in the case of domesticated plants (see Chapter III.9 above). According to Cope's Rule larger species tend to appear late in the phylogeny of taxa of animals, for example the horse family, probably because evolution is easier in small animals via neoteny. S. Stanley (1973) suggested that for broader taxa the maximum size tends to increase with evolution, but the median and minimum sizes are hardly affected. The distinctive feature of artificial selection for increased animal size by humans is that it increases average size. The Romans introduced new breeds of domestic animals from Italy to Pannonia in the north Balkans, for example, and interbred them with the more primitive local varieties. The average body size of most species of domesticated animals, but especially cattle, sheep and hens, increased by about 20 per cent compared to the breeds of the La Tène period which preceded the Roman occupation. For example the pre-Roman hens in Pannonia weighed about 1.0-1.5 kg, while Roman hens weighed over 2 kg on average. This is another important aspect of the increases in agricultural productivity in classical times which increased K and facilitated human population growth.[13]

The consequences of selective breeding for larger body size are most interesting in the case of the horse (see also Chapters I & III.4 above). Horse riding was undoubtedly practised from the beginning of domestication in south Russia in the fourth millennium BC, if not earlier, because horses could not have been controlled on the steppes without it. The horse, like the sheep, was originally another source of meat. Use of early domesticated horses for traction and carrying humans was limited because of their physical weakness, which is directly correlated to their short stature. Consequently fully fledged pastoral nomadism took two or three millennia to develop after horse domestication commenced.

The earliest domesticated horses stood no more than 1.50 metres tall at the withers and were no bigger than modern ponies. They were strong enough to transport a man on their backs, but were not powerful enough to carry heavy armour as well, like the suit of Mycenaean armour found at Dendra. Armour to protect both rider and horse was essential to make cavalry effective in pitched battle. Xenophon recommended that both rider and horse should carry as much armour as possible. After the horse spread throughout the Middle East, Mediterranean and Europe from the late third millennium BC onwards it was not used to transport soldiers with heavy armour on its back, because of its physical weakness, but to draw light chariots carrying the soldiers, who either relied on throwing missiles from the chariot or disembarked when they came into contact with the enemy and fought on foot. This is the type of warfare described in the Homeric epics, which are in this respect perfectly realistic.

During the first millennium BC horse breeding for increased height developed in the Middle East, especially in Iran and adjoining regions. Assyria was the first state to deploy true cavalry. During the Persian Wars in the fifth century BC and the invasion of the Persian empire by Alexander the Great in the fourth century BC the Greeks and Macedonians found themselves up against Iranian cavalry which were more powerful and more heavily armoured than their own cavalry. This situation continued to develop until the battle of Adrianople in AD 378, when a mounted barbarian army routed the Roman legions. The small size and physical weakness of early domesticated horses also explains why farmers in antiquity preferred the ox as a draught animal for ploughing. Consequently what mattered in the course of the development of the ecological mutualism between man and horse was not alleged innovations in harness technology, but biological evolution of the horse. Roman cavalrymen used pommels to achieve stability on horseback. Spruytte (1983) demolished the ideas of Lefebvre des Noëttes about harness technology.[14]

The types of biological models outlined here are essential to explanation and comprehension of later periods of history as well. For example, let us consider L. White (1962), a well-known book which correctly drew attention to certain important aspects of the transformation of the ancient world into the mediaeval world. Unfortunately it is riddled with anachronism from the second word of the title 'Mediaeval *technology* and social change' onwards. Attempting to modify the false hypotheses of Lefebvre des Noëttes, White claimed that innovations in technology made possible the development of the mounted knights of mediaeval Europe, when in fact it was horse evolution which played the fundamental role. Again he interpreted the development of the three-field crop rotation system of mediaeval northern Europe, which boosted agricultural productivity, as an innovation in 'technology', when what actually happened was the biological evolution under domestication of oats and rye as new crops (see Chapter III.10 above), followed by their integration into new ecological mutualisms with man and horse, providing more food for the former and a new and better source of food for the latter. The spread of the custom of sowing spring crops such as oats and barley if the winter wheat crop had failed eliminated subsistence crises in early modern western Europe.[15]

The feudal societies of mediaeval Europe, which were dominated by a rural aristocracy using heavy cavalry to control and exploit the bulk of the population, were not possible until a certain stage in horse evolution had been reached. They could not have existed in the Bronze Age, for example, for that reason alone, irrespective of any other considerations. Horse evolution was a necessary but not sufficient condition for feudalism. In the classical era the Greeks and Romans only had light cavalry available, which could not be used to launch a frontal attack on well prepared heavy infantry. They could only be used to outflank infantry armies and attack them from the rear, if possible, as happened in the major battles of the Second Punic War. Achieving that depended not on how heavily armoured they were but on the talent of their commander. As great generals were few and far between, the Romans continued to rely on infantry armies in spite of the successful use of light cavalry made by Hannibal and Scipio Africanus in the Second Punic War. In Greece Aristotle thought that a cavalry era in the archaic period, most notably on Euboia during the Lelantine War, preceded the hoplite era in the classical period. This is an anachronistic reconstruction if the 'cavalry' are thought of in terms of the knights of mediaeval Europe, and there is no certain evidence for the existence of a regular cavalry force within the Athenian army before the fifth century BC. Nevertheless horse riding was practised in Greece long before the fifth century BC.[16]

Although *Homo sapiens* entered mutualisms with some other animals in antiquity, he had an antagonistic relationship with other animals. Human hunting helped to constrain the distribution and abundance of some species of animal in classical times. For example, Ammianus Marcellinus records that the hippopotamus had been restricted to the territory of the Blemmyae in the extreme south of Egypt by hunting. Earlier, in the first millennium BC, skeletal remains show that it had existed as far north as the wetlands along the coast of Israel. The Athenians waged a constant struggle against the wolf, according to Plutarch. The Spartans probably did so as well in the Dark Ages, judging by the meaning of the name 'Lykourgos' (Chapter II.5 above). By the classical period, a time of high human population density, wild animals like the wolf were relatively rare in Greece. The comic poet Nausikrates comments on the difficulty of finding so much as a hare in Attica, although Pausanias states that bears and boars were hunted in the forests on Mt Parnes. Wild animals became commoner in Greece in later periods of low human population density, such as the early modern period. In the early nineteenth century AD the rich wild life of Mt Parnassos included lynx, wild cat, wild boar, wild goat, stag, roebuck, badger, marten and squirrel. There was otter in Boiotia, wolf, fox, jackal, weasel and hare in Marathon, and bats in Athens. At the time the human inhabitants of Attica, including women and children, only numbered about 12,000, at the most about 10 per cent of the 'citizen' population of Athens in the fourth century BC. The population density of domesticated animals also varied in relation to variations in human population density (see Chapter III.12 above).[17]

In antiquity man also encountered more formidable predators than the wolf, especially the lion. According to Herodotos, followed by Aristotle, lions only existed in Europe in the fifth century BC in northern Greece, in between the rivers Nessos and Achelous. All words in Indo-European languages for 'lion' are derived from Greek via Latin. Herodotos may well be right on this point. The recently discovered tomb of Philip II of Macedon at Vergina contained a fresco depicting a lion hunt. Evidence from the Bronze Age such as the monumental Lion Gate at Mycenae and the Lion Hunt Dagger from the Mycenae Shaft Graves may also indicate that the lion was known in Greece at that time. However the most interesting piece of evidence for the presence of the lion in Greece in antiquity is the discovery of two bones of a lion in an LHIIIB level at Tiryns. The lion similes in the Homeric poems do not furnish any evidence whatsoever for either the survival of Bronze Age traditions or Oriental influence on Homer. The lion was undoubtedly on the verge of extinction in the fourth century BC in Greece. Dio Chrysostom states that it had become extinct in Macedonia by the second century AD. It is interesting to consider why the lion and other large carnivores have been rare in Europe in recent times. Hunting by man is certainly one reason, but is not the only reason nor in all probability the most important reason. Ammianus Marcellinus states that lions were still common in the fourth century AD in Mesopotamia, the home of the world's first urban civilisation over three thousand years earlier. However, the lion had disappeared long before that from most of Europe, which did not develop large human population centres until much later than Mesopotamia. This does not support the idea that human activity was the key factor.[18]

The lion is restricted today to sub-Saharan Africa and India, but it would be quite wrong to suppose that it requires a tropical climate. Fossil evidence shows that the lion, a warm-blooded mammal which can control its own body temperature, was widespread in Europe during the Pleistocene, not only the modern lion of modest dimensions but also prehistoric giant lions. This suggests that the distribution of lion depends not on the climate but on the distribution and abundance of potential prey. During the Pleistocene Eurasia was occupied by large numbers of large herbivores, for example woolly mammoths and rhinoceroses. In Greece itself, elephant, hippopotamus and lion have been discovered at Megalopolis, for example. Some cases of finds of giant bones by the ancient Greeks, for instance the bones of Orestes, undoubtedly belonged to Pleistocene megafauna. Most of the megafauna became extinct in Eurasia suddenly at the end of the last glaciation. This also applies to other parts of the world such as the Americas. Two main theories have been proposed to account for the extinctions of megafauna at the beginning of the Holocene: (1) human hunting – the 'overkill' hypothesis;

(2) climatic change. The second explanation is preferable because the correlation between climatic change and the extinctions is close, while the correlation between the spread of *Homo sapiens sapiens* and the extinctions is much weaker.

Human hunting may have played a subsidiary role in Europe. However, it is hard to believe that it played any significant role in the contemporaneous extinction of the mammoth in northern Siberia, where there are few humans today and surely were not many during the Ice Ages, following the line of argument of Sutcliffe (1985). The key factor in the extinction of the megafauna of Eurasia was the extinction of the food supply of the large herbivores, in Siberia the very rich grassland vegetation called 'Artemisia steppe' by palaeoecologists, which lay in between the tundra and the taiga. It also dominated northern Greece during the last Würm glaciation. During the Ice Ages the proportion of the earth occupied by grasslands was much larger than it is today because the climate was drier and cooler, favouring annual vegetation against perennial vegetation. Grasslands, not dense forests, are the favoured habitat of most large herbivorous animals. The extension of grasslands during the glaciations and the preceding geological epochs favoured the evolution of megafauna. As the climate changed very rapidly at the end of the last glaciation the vegetation in question contracted sharply, the populations of large herbivores which depended on the vegetation collapsed almost immediately, and the populations of large carnivores, which depended on the herbivores, collapsed in turn.

Megafauna generally require very large geographical areas with a suitable habitat to support them. Some recent research in conservation in the United States suggests that even the huge national parks of that country may not be big enough to sustain viable populations of large animals, and the large animals of today are much smaller than the megafauna of the Pleistocene. The Mediterranean islands present interesting data for the study of the effects of small habitat size. During the Pleistocene some herbivorous animals developed dwarf forms on the Mediterranean islands, because the resource base was too small to support animals above a certain size. At times of lower sea level good swimmers like the hippopotamus could swim out to many of the Aegean islands. The K of carnivores is always much smaller than the K of their prey because of the higher position of carnivores on food chains. Consequently it is difficult for carnivores to survive on islands, where the prey populations are smaller than on continental mainlands. Pliny noted that there were no large predatory animals or harmful creatures on Crete, except a poisonous spider. This was not just a consequence of human activity. After the end of the last glaciation, as deciduous and coniferous forests expanded, it was difficult for megafauna to survive anywhere in Europe. This explains why the wild horse, which existed all over Europe during the Pleistocene, virtually disappeared from Europe at the end of the last glaciation and was confined to the steppes of south Russia, until humans began to cut down the forests and re-introduced the horse to the areas where it had become extinct.[19]

Man was as much affected by the end of the last glaciation as other large animals were. Hominids evolved and spread across the whole world during the Ice Ages. This is not accident or coincidence. Early hominids occupied a particular ecological niche. According to E.O. Wilson, the pioneer in sociobiology, they were 'the carnivorous primates of the African plains', omnivores exploiting both the animal and plant resources of the grasslands. Jolly (1970) suggested that the distinctive features, such as the enlarged posterior dentition and improved hand-eye co-ordination, of hominids, in particular the robust australopithecines, evolved to facilitate exploitation of grass seeds on the plains. R. Foley (1987) concluded that in contrast to Australopithecus early members of the genus Homo show dental and jaw morphology that is not so highly specialised for grinding seeds, nuts and hard fruits. Consequently Homo seems to have adopted initially a generalist strategy for meeting nutritional requirements, in contrast to the early specialisation of Australopithecus which turned out to be an evolutionary blind alley. However, Homo too eventually did evolve dependence on the grasses that were the main component of the flora of the natural habitat of hominids. Because that dependence, the evolution of agriculture, involved ecological mutualisms which increased abundance of prey as well as predator, it facilitated massive population growth and so turned out to be a much more successful evolutionary adaptation than the specialisation of Australopithecus in predation on grass seeds and other hard parts of plants.[20]

As far as the animal resources of the grasslands are concerned, attempts have been made in recent years to reassess the importance of hunting among prehistoric hunter-gatherers, with a shift in emphasis from 'Man the hunter' to 'Woman the gatherer'. However, it should not be forgotten that modern hunter-gatherers, like the !Kung Bushmen in southern Africa, do not have the same range of options as prehistoric hunter-gatherers, because most of the Pleistocene megafauna is now extinct. Similarly most of the animals found at some of the major prehistoric sites which were originally used as evidence for the 'overkill' hypothesis may in fact have died from natural causes, rather than as a result of human predation. Nevertheless it remains true that the extent of meat consumption by man is unparalleled among other primates. Foley (1987) argued that meat consumption evolved among hominids as a strategy for coping with the seasonal shortage of plant foods during the dry season in semi-arid environments.[21]

The enlarged grasslands of the Ice Ages increased the area of very favourable terrain for man as a hunter-gatherer. They go a long way towards explaining the successful spread of man during the glacial periods. The lion spread widely at the same time for the same reason. When the grasslands contracted suddenly at the end of the last glaciation, in both the tropics and in regions closer to the poles, man was severely affected by the contraction of potential prey populations of both flora and fauna in his favoured habitat. Consequently man was forced to diversify his food supply by adopting the broad-spectrum diet characteristic of Mesolithic hunter-gatherers. Then some groups of men became farmers by evolving ecological mutualisms with various plants. These changes were probably forced upon them, rather than being undertaken willingly, because early horticulture required high labour inputs and hard work (see Chapter II.2 above) and the nutritional status and health of early farmers were bad (Chapter II.7 above).

It is only by invoking a global ecological process, which affected all parts of the world equally and simultaneously, that it is possible to explain why agriculture developed at virtually the same time, tens of thousands of years after the evolution of *Homo sapiens sapiens*, in different parts of the world. Remains of modern man have been found on Mt Carmel in the Levant dating to at least 90,000 years ago. This means that the evolution of agriculture cannot be explained by the arrival of *H. sapiens* alone. The key fact in explaining the exact timing of the evolution of agriculture is that the total biomass of life on earth, in respect of both large animals and the types of plant food required to sustain large animals, decreased very sharply and suddenly at the end of the last Ice Age. That was the reason why human hunter-gatherers suddenly needed to find new ways of procuring food. In contrast the lion, for example, failed to discover any new way of obtaining food and so its geographical range contracted very sharply. This is the ecological explanation of why man alone among large animals experienced population growth after the end of the last glaciation.

The sequel to this process, namely the gradual filling of the vacuum created in Europe during the last glaciation by living organisms capable of living in temperate and Mediterranean climates, has already been described. It is necessary now to explain how this increase in ecosystem complexity influenced the development of human societies in ancient Greece. Age class systems in East Africa and New Guinea have a history extending at least as far back into antiquity as those in ancient Greece. Although there are no documentary sources for East Africa and New Guinea dating to the pre-Christian era, philological research into the history of the languages spoken in these regions, relying on assumptions about the rate at which languages change (glottochronology), indicates that words signifying elements of age class organisation already existed in both these regions in the first millennium BC. Age class systems have continued to exist in East Africa and New Guinea until the present day, but they broke down in Greece in the first millennium BC.[22]

A very important difference between Greece and the other two regions, which is intimately related to their different courses of historical development, is that the ancient Greeks were the only one of the three groups of peoples in question to engage in monumental building, from the eighth century BC onwards. This is marked by stone instead of wooden temples, large cities with monumental public buildings, and a large volume of production of craft products made out of metal, wood and stone, exemplified for example by the massive increase in votive offerings in the eighth century, and the output of armour and weapons. This suggests that the ancient Greeks experienced a phase of economic growth unparalleled in East Africa and New Guinea even much later.

It is instructive to consider the systematic contrasts drawn by Feil (1987) between societies in the western and eastern halves of the highlands of Papua New Guinea. The introduction of the sweet potato (*Ipomoea batatas*) as a new crop to supplement the native taro increased agricultural productivity, permitting an increase in population density, increasing accumulation of wealth and so the possibility of using wealth as an alternative principle of social organisation to age class organisation. The spread of sweet potato cultivation was gradual. Some parts of the island felt its effects before other areas did. Feil concluded that in those societies in New Guinea in which agricultural intensification had commenced earliest, age class institutions had been displaced by exchange institutions. In this radical new basis of social organisation competitive gift exchange of the new wealth between individual 'big-men' replaced the collective activities of age groups in age class systems. This process had the same demographic implications as in ancient Greece, as the demographic checks built into age class systems ceased to operate, facilitating massive population growth in New Guinea in recent times. Finally Feil reached the following important conclusion: 'nascently intensifying agricultural societies in the highlands are those in which male initiation and intersexual hostility coalesce.'[23]

Similarly in East Africa Ethiopia is of particular interest because it was the only part of sub-Saharan Africa to acquire and use the plough before European colonisation in modern times (see Chapter II.2 above). Again this permitted a form of agricultural intensification, albeit different in its details from the horticulture of New Guinea which exploited a new crop. Nevertheless the end product was in some respects similar, as social class divisions based on wealth developed and were superimposed on older age class systems. In other parts of East Africa where the plough could not be used profitably age class systems continued to exist in full vigour until recently in the context of poorly developed economies with low levels of productivity in which wealth accumulation and transmission across the generations were difficult, preserving the tendencies toward egalitarianism inherent in age class systems.[24]

Geoffrey Lloyd once made the following remark to the present author:

'Equality is as common as dirt in Africa. The real problem is to explain how only the Greeks were able to develop an *ideology* of equality.' The fact that the Greek age class societies in the Dark Ages, which were originally egalitarian in character, experienced an increase in ecosystem complexity and consequently economic growth and social class differentiation explains how in the classical period an ideology of equality, which we call democracy, was able to exist (uneasily) within a society characterised in practice by a high level of social inequality in respect of wealth even within the citizen body, without taking any account of inferior status groups such as slaves and metics. This is the solution offered here, in respect of ancient Greece, to the fundamental sociological problem of explaining how social inequality developed out of the primaeval state of equality.

As evidence of the egalitarian character of Dark Age Greece, beside the shortage of material wealth emphasised by Snodgrass, the absence of the rhetoric of class struggle in both Homer and Hesiod should be noted. The Homeric epics appear to be enormously exaggerated accounts of the causes and consequences of a conflict between two confederations of small tribes over an abducted woman, Helen, a common enough situation among 'primitive' tribes studied by anthropologists, such as the Yanomamo in South America. Quiller (1981) gave a convincing interpretation of the *basileis*, the political leaders of the societies described in Homer and Hesiod, as 'big-men'. 'Big-men' are fairly wealthy, but have to construct their power over others personally, instead of coming to power by hereditary succession. The prime examples in Greece were Odysseus and his father Laertes, whose position depended entirely on their own efforts and could not be passed on easily to the next generation in the absence of state institutions legitimating hereditary rule. Thucydides noted that in early Greece all free men customarily carried weapons because there was no police force to defend them or their homes. This led to the situation in the classical period in which hoplite soldiers had to provide and pay for their own weapons. In other words there was no 'government' monopolising the legitimate use of force. The main criterion of the 'state' used by Max Weber is consequently not applicable to the ancient Greek world, or to other age class societies.[25]

Quiller, building on Finley (1978), argued that the *basileis* in Homer were engaged in competitive gift exchange. Finley's gift exchange, ultimately inspired by Marcel Mauss, was only part of a very complicated process in Dark Age Greece. Gift exchange occurs in many parts of the world in societies which are otherwise very different. Similarly ritualised friendship, recalling ancient Greek *xenia*, still exists in modern Mediterranean societies which are very different from the ancient *polis*. Gift exchange and ritualised friendship are modes of personal relations which do not by themselves suffice to create a political structure. The political structures of classical Greece were derived from age class organisation, not from gift exchange. Nevertheless the competitive exchange of wealth described by Finley and Quiller does fit into the context of increasing social class differentiation which competed with age class organisation as a principle of social organisation as ecosystem complexity and productivity increased. Consequently Quiller was right to date the society described in the Homeric epics to the eighth century BC, at the end of the Dark Ages when most of the Dark Age age class systems were breaking down, rather than putting it in the middle of the Dark Ages as Finley did. The parallels with New Guinea, as described by Feil, are very striking in all respects. In Greece Sparta and Crete maintained their age class systems for longer than anywhere else because those systems were reinstitutionalised for military purposes to maintain control over subject serf populations.

By the classical period elements of political organisation based on wealth were widespread in the Greek world. However there was one backward part of classical Greece in which there is evidence for the destructive effects of an increasing accumulation of wealth on an age class system in the fourth century BC. Timaios tells us how the acquisition of large numbers of slaves in warfare by the leaders of Phokis, using the treasures of the temple of Delphi to purchase the services of mercenaries, led to the disruption of the traditional social structure as slaves took over the duty previously fulfilled by young citizens of serving their elders (cf. Chapter II.5 above). The same tension between these two principles of social organisation is found in Aristotle's *Politics*. Aristotle regarded age class organisation as the essence of the *polis* in its pristine form. However, he knew full well that class conflicts were frequent in the Greek cities in his own time, and indeed *stasis* based on class struggle dominates the *Politics*. Hallpike (1986) discussed the idea that different societies are characterised by different *principles of social organisation*, which are often spread historically by the speakers of particular groups of languages. This type of analysis is very appropriate for the three main areas of age class systems, namely Greece, East Africa and New Guinea.[26]

The population growth which occurred as one aspect of the ecological changes described here played a role in the disruption of the social structure of the *polis*. It also provided the manpower for military purposes which increased the political power of the major Greek *poleis*. However, that process of population growth was not irrevocable, as we have seen. It was merely a phase in a cycle of chaotic population fluctuations. The ensuing population collapse in the Hellenistic period removed the demographic foundations of Greek political power, but the old social structure of an age class system had vanished for ever.

This interaction of biological and sociological phenomena brings us back to the philosophical problems raised in Chapter I above of the intrinsic unity of all branches of knowledge and the central place of biology in Aristotle's thought. Judging by the extant works in his corpus Aristotle spent more time thinking and writing about the world of nature than he did about anything else, even though Sokrates had previously tried to turn philosophy away from nature to focus on man instead. However most modern philosophers tend to concentrate on his works on ethics, logic and politics.

Aristotle's 'biology' (a concept which did not exist until quite recently) is neglected partly because it is regarded as backward in relation to modern science. However, specialists in classical philosophy usually know little about the methods and problems of modern biology. For a fascinating alternative view of Aristotle's biology it is useful to draw attention to the opinions expressed by E. Mayr, a leading specialist in evolutionary biology. Summarising the views of some earlier scholarship in the field of the history of science, Mayr rightly observes that translations of Aristotle's biological works employ obsolete language. There is no reason why we should continue to privilege interpretations of Aristotle made several centuries ago, when his works were rediscovered in western Europe, by scholars whose world-view corresponded neither to Aristotle's in the fourth century BC nor to ours in the late twentieth century AD.[27]

On the vexed question of teleology, Mayr argues that teleological explanations are valid in certain areas of modern biology because every living organism possesses a genetic programme at the beginning of its life which governs its subsequent development. Aristotle's mistake was not that he employed teleological explanations, but that he extended the concept of teleology to the inanimate world, for which it is inappropriate. He correctly assumed that living organisms must have a governing principle that gave them their form. In this particular respect his thought was far superior to Darwin's ideas, and anticipated the modern conclusion that life is self-organisation of matter (in a reproducible form), or, as E. Schrödinger put it, negative entropy. However Aristotle did not possess the instruments necessary to see the form-giving principle (DNA) and so assumed that it must be non-material in nature, a reasonable hypothesis under the circumstances. Mayr concludes that in order to elucidate Aristotle's thought it is legitimate to translate the word *eidos* in certain contexts in his texts as the 'genetic programme', leading to the final shape (*telos*) of an organism. This translation makes Aristotle's biology look very much more modern than it is generally portrayed by modern philosophers. It will probably horrify classicists. However Mayr's argument shows that some of Aristotle's ideas can be developed in the general direction of modern theories.

There was a very direct link between biology and politics in ancient Greece both in reality and in Aristotle's intellectual enterprise, and it was not simply a matter of applying biological 'metaphors' to human social organisation, in the wholly misguided terms sometimes used by modern scholars. We can now summarise the results of the investigation of ancient Greek socio-political organisation in Chapter II.5-6 above with the statement that the distinguishing characteristic of the *polis* was that it took the human body and its various stages of development as the basis for subdividing its citizens into categories and assigning rights and duties to those categories in a hierarchical manner. This definition applies to the concept of *polis* as a distinctive kind of socio-political organisation found in Greece, as in Aristotle's *Politics* for example. Of course the word also had the more elementary meaning of 'fortified place', as in Homer. This meaning was not unique to the Greeks, since the same root with the same sense occurs in various other Indo-European languages.

So far in applying the concept of an age class system to ancient Greece we have been transferring ideas from social anthropology to ancient history. However, it would be quite wrong to assume that this is a one-way process and that ancient history has nothing to contribute to anthropology. There is, as is only to be expected, a plurality of views among anthropologists as to the significance of age as a principle of social organisation. This is typified by the contrast between Bernardi (1985), who emphasised the political aspects of age class organisation, and Baxter & Almagor (1978), who concluded that age class organisation only operated in relation to organising ritual activities in the particular societies which they happened to study and did not have notable political functions.

This raises the question of whether those particular societies had always been like that, or whether alternatively their age class systems also once had political functions which have been lost in the course of history. Of course this leads on to the fundamental question of whether it is possible any longer for anthropologists to find genuinely 'primitive' societies to study, or whether all that remain for them to study are deracinated societies whose traditional social structures have been disrupted by contact with colonists of European origin in modern times. The evidence from ancient Greece permits us to adjudicate decisively between Bernardi and Baxter & Almagor. The fact that western political theory developed out of reflections, recorded in the pages of Plato and Aristotle, on the nature of age class systems in ancient Greece proves that age class systems indeed had political functions in the distant past. That is why the analysis of Bernardi (1985) is judged here to be far more illuminating and powerful than that of Baxter & Almagor (1978).

The first well documented event in Athenian history was an unsuccessful challenge to the older generation by the younger generation during the conspiracy of Kylon (see Chapter II.5 above). It was a fitting conclusion to the history of classical Athens as a society founded on an age class system that the last events leading up to Athens's demise as a major power were marked by the alleged failure of the older generation to deliver the goods. In the aftermath of the corruption revealed by the Harpalos affair which preceded the Lamian War in 323 BC the orator

Hypereides observed that the old orators should be training the young, their eventual successors, but as a result of the Harpalos affair the young were being forced to attack the old who had failed in their duties.[28]

The episode of the trial and execution of Sokrates illustrates why the age class systems of the *poleis* had difficulty adapting to meet changing circumstances. Sokrates was convicted on the charges of impiety (not duly acknowledging the traditional deities accepted by the *polis* and introducing strange new deities) and of teaching young men to question the laws. Sokrates was regarded as a threat by both the democrats, who had him executed, and by the oligarchic Thirty Tyrants, who banned him from conversing with those aged under thirty. Nor was he the only philosopher accused of corrupting the young. The comic poet Alexis puts words into the mouth of a father who made this very same charge against Xenokrates in the fourth century BC. By teaching young men to question the laws philosophers like Sokrates and Xenokrates were threatening to undermine the foundations of the *polis* in a manner which it is appropriate to describe as having a social revolutionary effect, if not intention. The ideology of the *polis* was like that of an idealised communist society, which never has and never will exist, in the sense that men were equal, but not free to lead their lives in whatever way they wished. Plato's emphasis on 'ruling and being ruled' in the formation of the citizen did not leave any room for freedom of choice. In this respect Plato accurately reproduced the mentality of most of his compatriots.[29]

The *polis* depended for its social reproduction on indoctrinating its members from childhood onwards with its ideology and teaching them to accept without question the regulations of the age class system for the rest of their lives. Modern historians generally have regarded the execution of Sokrates as a crime and a blot on the record of the Athenian democracy. This can only be described as appallingly bad historiography. If our aim is to understand the behaviour of Athenians in the classical period, it is inane to judge them by modern values and standards which were entirely alien to the world of classical Greece. The education provided by Sokrates did threaten the traditional system of socialisation of the *polis*, the glue that held it together. If young men were taught to question the laws, there was nothing else to hold the *polis* together, and anarchy would have been inevitable. Consequently Sokrates was a threat to the foundations of the *polis*, regardless of whether it was democratic or oligarchic. If the Athenians wished to maintain their traditional system as they did (although interpretations of 'the ancestral constitution' differed), they were fully justified in getting rid of Sokrates.

Apart from the discovery of new sources, progress in historiography can only be made by asking new questions about a historical situation that were not asked by anyone alive at the time. In doing so, however, there is always the grave danger of imputing attitudes, motives and values to the people under study which they had never heard or dreamed of.

Anachronism is a constant danger for historians. To minimise this risk this book has concentrated on processes that were outside the range of human consciousness at the time, instead of concentrating on the 'mentalité' of the ancient Greeks as the overwhelming vast majority of classical scholars are in the habit of doing. It is inevitable that each age will attempt to reinterpret the past in ways that are relevant to its own concerns and preoccupations, a procedure which is very likely to introduce anachronism into historical explanation if historians are not consciously aware that they are attempting to interpret the past in the light of the concerns of their own time. Ancient historians have exhibited a remarkable propensity for falling into this trap. It is instructive to consider briefly the interpretations of the classical world proposed by the major German historians of the last century, and also by an English historian like George Grote. They offered interpretations of ancient history that were heavily influenced by the experiences of the societies in which they lived, and in many ways tell us more about nineteenth-century Europe than they do about ancient Greece or Rome.

For example, they believed that classical Athens was a great trading and manufacturing nation, when there is hardly any evidence that the Athenians exported anything, if the ancient sources are considered 'objectively', with an open mind. There is almost no evidence for exports of manufactured goods of any type, except pottery whose importance can easily be overemphasised, while the evidence for the export of raw materials such as olive oil and silver is scanty. The historians of the last century were extrapolating back to antiquity the conditions of countries like England during the Industrial Revolution, whose prosperity depended on exporting manufactured goods to colonies or less developed countries in return for raw materials. As the proportion of the working population employed in manufacturing industries has decreased in developed countries in the course of the twentieth century, while the tertiary sector of service industries has increased, it is easy to see now that the interpretation of the classical Athenian economy offered by the major historians of the last century could not have been conceived at any time in history other than the nineteenth century AD. The idea that a large proportion of the working population should be employed in producing manufactured goods for export may well seem as alien to historians in the future as it undoubtedly would have seemed to Aristotle and all other Greeks in the classical period, if they had ever heard of it. Instead it is preferable to take the ancient sources seriously and construct our interpretation of ancient history upon the idea of self-sufficiency, *autarkeia*, which is unambiguously attested in the ancient sources.[30]

To take another example, in their research on politics in classical Athens the major historians of the last century *invented* (not too strong a word) political parties in classical Athens, which were of course carbon copies of the political parties which existed in western European countries in their own time. More recent research has discredited such hypotheses and shown that there were only individual politicians, supported by very loose factions of supporters who did not have any party organisation independent of the politician who happened to lead the faction. There was nothing in classical Athens comparable to a modern 'government', which a political party could have aspired to become.[31]

The modern revival of the Olympic Games provides a third example of anachronistic interpretations of this kind. The refounders of the Olympic Games, with their emphasis on amateurism in athletics, claimed to be reviving the spirit of athletic contests in antiquity. In fact the ancient sources make it abundantly clear that there were professional athletes in ancient Greece and that professionalism was fully accepted and taken for granted. The modern refounders of the Olympic Games, in the guise of reproducing the social conditions of ancient Greece, were in fact reproducing some aspects of the ethics and customs of politically dispossessed European aristocracies during the nineteenth century AD which were entirely alien to ancient Greece. This point deserves generalisation beyond the context of the Olympic Games. The application of the concept of 'aristocracy' to ancient Greece made by classicists was rejected in Chapter II.6 above because it is an anachronistic retrojection back to antiquity of the image of upper-class European élites, from whose ranks most scholars of the time were (and to a substantial extent still are) drawn, in the last century. It had no parallel in ancient Greece.[32]

The fourth and most provocative example of the way in which the historical interpretations of the major historians of the last century were moulded by the conditions of the societies in which they were educated and lived is derived from Bernal (1987), whose historiography is brilliant even if his own interpretation of ancient history is unsatisfactory. (There is no space to discuss it here.) He shows how the historians of the last century rejected out of hand the possibility that the ancient Greeks were deeply influenced by contacts with the peoples of the ancient Near East for essentially racialist reasons, i.e. during an age when peoples of European origin were conquering most of the rest of the world, it was simply inconceivable that the ancient Greeks, who were regarded as the forbears of modern European civilisation, could have been influenced by any of the peoples in underdeveloped countries which had fallen under European domination.

Of course it is unfair to criticise the historians of the last century for proceeding in a way that is virtually unavoidable in practice, namely attempting to interpret the past in relation to their own experiences. I am as guilty of this charge as they were, and all other historians are equally guilty of it, whether or not they admit it. However it is quite justifiable to criticise the historians of the last century for refusing to acknowledge that they were proceeding in that manner, and claiming that they were collecting the 'facts' and studying the ancient sources with 'an open mind'. If the historian openly admits that he or she is reinterpreting the past in relation to current preoccupations, it is much easier to exercise control over one's own assumptions and be aware of what one is doing. The presentation of an ecological perspective on ancient history in this book is the product of reflections on new areas of concern which are assuming an increasing importance in world affairs as the twentieth century draws to a close.

The question then arises of what general inferences may be drawn from the past that are of relevance to understanding current problems, and the issue of what will happen to humanity in the future. The precise details of the epidemic that struck Athens in 430 BC, for example, are only of academic interest, since smallpox is now confined to the laboratory and condemned to extinction. However, an understanding of the general principles of ecology is of fundamental importance for considering the future of humanity. All biological processes have a temporal dimension. Since the stochastic and chaotic nature of many biological processes makes it difficult to predict the future, we can only conjecture what may happen in the future on the basis of what has happened in the past.

For example, let us consider the greenhouse effect. It has recently been discovered that the proportion of carbon dioxide in the atmosphere has varied significantly in the past. The Ice Ages were probably caused by a reversal of the greenhouse effect, as the atmospheric content of carbon dioxide dropped sharply below the level that existed just before the Industrial Revolution. It probably involved positive feedback, along the lines suggested by the Gaia hypothesis of Lovelock (1988). The most important factor was the ability, which varies with temperature, of plankton in the sea to absorb carbon dioxide. In addition the enlarged grasslands of the glaciations, spread over a larger area of dry land during periods of lower sea level, may have supported a larger biomass than exists today, indicated by the size of the Pleistocene megafauna at the summits of the food chains of the time, which implies that the bases of Pleistocene food chains were broader than today. The increased biomass was able to extract more carbon dioxide from the atmosphere than it does today. The effects predicted by Milankovitch of variations in the relative positions of the earth and the sun also played an important role as an initial trigger, alongside changes in ocean currents. The Ice Ages and their aftermath shaped the whole of human evolution and history, not only during the glacial periods but even later, as late as the classical period as far as Greece and the origins of European civilisation are concerned. In other words the unconscious forces in ancient history were many times more powerful than even the greatest individuals. All that is happening now in the late twentieth century AD is that we are becoming conscious of the existence of these forces, which have long dominated human history without our being aware of it.[33]

The quasi-personification of *phusis*, nature, found in Aristotle and the central role of biology in his thought is very pertinent here. He was able to perceive the importance of biological processes in antiquity, in contrast to modern scholars who search the sources for evidence for innovations in technology instead, because he did not share the experiences of scholars in the modern world during and following the Industrial Revolution, which caused a drastic break with the past. In this book we have sharply criticised the technological perspective on prehistory and ancient history, exemplified above all else by the threefold division into Stone, Bronze and Iron Ages made by archaeologists who lived during the Industrial Revolution.

It is only by considering the past that we can obtain empirical evidence pertaining to the possible consequences of massive fluctuations in the carbon dioxide content of the earth's atmosphere in the future. Those academic ecologists who lay stress on equilibrium in ecosystems tend to dislike history and deliberately neglect it. This is inevitable because history is an embarrassment for them. It is only by adopting a historical approach that it is possible to offer a conclusive answer to the problem of the stability or instability of natural ecosystems. It has been argued here that the ecosystem of ancient Greece was marked by constant instability, at a time when man's ability to influence the environment, although certainly not negligible, was very much weaker than it is today. We cannot assume that if we do nothing, then the climate will stay the same. The implications of this stretch to the entire conservationist movement. It is a vain overestimation of man's ability to control the environment at the present time to assume that it lies within man's power to preserve the environment in its present state, even if there were general agreement that this is desirable. The greenhouse effect, or its reverse, could happen in the complete absence of human activity.

The attempt to run together the biological and social sciences presented in this book inevitably leaves the present author open to the charge of reductionism. However it is only by attempting to devise theories that make large bodies of data explicable in terms of general principles that are equally applicable to a large number of individual items of data, and then by attempting to devise theories of ever increasing range of applicability, that research can rise above the level of the collection of data, without explaining anything, as in antiquarianism in relation to history, or its counterpart in relation to the biological sciences, the old natural history. I am happy to be called a reductionist, at least in relation to methodological problems. This book has tried to show what may be achieved if we forsake the principle of 'knowing more and more about less and less' which dominates academic research in British universities today.

It is worth recalling Darwin's criticism of the views of Galton on the ancient Greeks. Galton, a researcher into eugenics, had compared the number of outstanding individuals to the size of the population and concluded that the classical Athenian population was on average more intelligent than modern populations.

> It has been argued by several writers that as high intellectual powers are advantageous to a nation, the old Greeks, who stood some grades higher in intellect than any race that has ever existed, ought, if the power of natural selection were real, to have risen still higher in the scale, increased in number, and stocked the whole of Europe. Here we have the tacit assumption, so often made with respect to corporeal structures, that there is some innate tendency towards continued development in mind and body. But development of all kinds depends on many concurrent favourable circumstances. Natural selection acts only tentatively. Individuals and races may have acquired certain indisputable advantages, and yet have perished from failing in other characters. The Greeks may have retrograded from a want of coherence between the many small states, from the small size of their whole country, or from extreme sensuality; for they did not succumb until 'they were enervated and rotten to the core'.[34]

Presumably no one today would wish to subscribe to Galton's hypothesis that the ancient Greeks as a population were more intelligent than modern humans, although one outstanding individual, Aristotle, the very summit of the range of variation with regard to intelligence within that population, wrote the most brilliant books ever written, in relation to what had been written before. Darwin explained elsewhere in his works why Galton's assumption of an 'innate tendency towards continued development in mind and body' is not in fact inevitable. Nevertheless it has been necessary to go a long way beyond the level of analysis in the last sentence of the passage cited above and consider a wider range of material to produce a book on the ecology of the ancient Greek world that is satisfactory in the light of the knowledge now available. The importance of holism in intellectual explanation requires the utmost stress. S. James (1984) provided a philosophical defence of holism. It is impossible to understand factors as diverse as political organisation, human demographic patterns, social structure, the proportion of carbon dioxide in the atmosphere, kinship, the distribution and abundance of other living organisms, and the rise and fall of civilisations if they are considered in isolation from each other.

Attention should be drawn to some of the differences between the models which have been used here for population history and the other types of models used by other historians mentioned earlier. The models used in this book are dynamic models which enable us to explain changes in the behaviour of a population over time, and change over time is the essence of history. In contrast, other ancient historians who have taken an interest in the demography of the Graeco-Roman world have employed static models. It is only by concentrating on reproduction that it is possible to explain dynamic change from generation to generation. The focus on mortality derived from the use of model 'life' tables (a euphemism), which represent stable populations by definition, can only generate static models and linear dynamics. However, in the real world of nature nonlinear dynamics prevail in practice.

Similarly many of the models used by other scholars to interpret ancient society, such as Finley's 'consumer city' and his 'gift exchange' in Homeric Greece, are also static models. Consequently they also suffer from the grave weakness of not being able to explain change over time, although they remain of interest. Marx attempted to conjure up models for historical interpretation which were dynamic in character, employing the idea of 'internal contradictions' to account for the shift from each mode of production to the next. However, Marx's models suffered from the fatal weakness that they were deterministic models. He assumed that the course of history had to follow a pre-determined path, from primitive communism, through the slave mode of production in antiquity, feudalism and capitalism to communism. This theory has been refuted by the subsequent course of history. Quite apart from the fact that the first communist revolution occurred in the wrong country, and the annoying failure of societies with the Asiatic or tributary mode of production to fit into the general developmental framework, Marx failed to consider what would come after communism, a question of current interest as it shows signs of crumbling behind the Iron Curtain at the time of writing.

In considering population history in this book, the idea of deterministic chaos has been employed to help to explain the great fluctuations and irregularities in the demography of the ancient Greek world. In this particular context the word 'deterministic' simply signifies the absence of any extrinsic factors in causation of the fluctuations. All demographic processes are ultimately stochastic in character, because natural selection is blind and does not have any teleological objectives, even though each individual living organism has a genetic programme governing its own development in a teleological manner. If history as an academic subject is to rise above the level of antiquarianism, the great methodological challenge for historians is to devise models that are both dynamic and stochastic in character. The impending fate of Marxism shows that this applies to all branches of history, not just to population history.

To conclude this book it is necessary to say a few words about the significance of the history of ancient Greece in the context of the history of humanity as a whole. The vast majority of classicists, if asked why the civilisation of ancient Greece is worth studying, will reply that its value lies in appreciating the great works of literature, the Homeric epics, the tragedies of Aiskhylos, Sophokles and Euripides, etc. There is no particular reason why we should disagree with the assessment of these works as great works of literature, although literary criticism is notoriously subjective in character. (For example, in later periods of antiquity Menander was judged to be the greatest poet of classical Athens, an evaluation shared by no critic in the twentieth century.)

However, no genuine historian can possibly find this answer satisfying, because it depends on criteria of evaluation of artistic merit which are entirely alien to the methods employed by historians. Ancient history requires methods different from those employed by literary critics. It has, or should have, far more in common with prehistory, mediaeval and modern history than it has with literary criticism. Nevertheless it must be acknowledged that ancient history as an academic subject as it is generally practised in universities around the world today does have a peculiar character. This has nothing whatsoever to do with the sources or the character of the evidence for the ancient world. It is solely a consequence of the way that universities happen to be organised. The study of Shakespeare and the study of the history of Tudor England, for example, are carried out in different university faculties and are divorced from each other. It is only in relation to the ancient world that history and literary criticism are jumbled together. In practice, as a result of the historical development of classics as an academic subject over the last two hundred years, literary criticism generally predominates in classics faculties, and prospective ancient historians are exposed to large doses of it in the formative stages of their careers, moulding their assumptions in undesirable ways, before they can concentrate on ancient history. I believe that ancient history should stand as a subject on its own, separate from classics as literary criticism, in the same way that Snodgrass has argued recently that classical archaeology can exist as a subject in its own right independently of classics. The line of argument that follows applies to ancient history, not to the rest of the conglomerate of subjects which shelter under the wings of classics.[35]

It has been argued that the Greek *polis* shared a single principle of social organisation, age, with various societies in East Africa and New Guinea. Insofar as social anthropologists have engaged in comparative research in recent years, and it is to be regretted that few do so, the conclusion has been reached that societies in developing countries in Africa, for example, are fundamentally different from societies in Eurasia in modern times. Of particular interest here is Goody (1976), who statistically correlated differences between African and Eurasian societies in respect of a whole range of domestic social institutions with differences in their respective mode of production, in particular the contrast between hoe agriculture in Africa, predominantly work for women, and plough agriculture in Eurasia, which mainly provides work for men (see also Chapter II.2 above). Goody emphasised the role of the plough in agricultural intensification in Eurasia, creating the increased productivity necessary for social class differentiation to occur. In my opinion the introduction of the plough is just one possible form of agricultural intensification, and there certainly are other possibilities such as the introduction of new crops. However, this is a minor detail in the present context.

The important point is that the patterns of correlations and so the contrast between African and Eurasian societies traced by Goody have a history. The evidence from antiquity shows that elements of social organisation characteristic of various African societies in recent times, such as age class organisation at the political level and bridewealth as an example of domestic institutions (see Chapter II.6 above) also existed in ancient Greece but have since disappeared. Until the first millennium BC Europe was part of the Third World in the sense that as late as the Early Iron Age societies in Greece, and probably elsewhere in Europe too, possessed social institutions and forms of political organisation which were similar to those possessed by primitive tribes in Africa and New Guinea in modern times. As far as I am concerned, the significance of the history of ancient Greece is that the breakdown of age class systems in Greece in the course of the first millennium BC marked the point at which the history of Europe began to diverge from the history of the rest of the world and follow the unique path which culminated in the Industrial Revolution. This is the kind of answer to the question of the significance of ancient Greek history and why it is worth studying which ought to be given by anyone who regards himself or herself as a proper historian, rather than a literary critic.

The question of the origins of age class organisation in Greece deserves some brief discussion. Brelich (1969) raised the possibility of diffusion of social institutions from Africa to Greece. However the three main areas of age class organisation are all quite different from each other in respect of the details of socio-political organisation, even though they all share the same basic principle of social organisation. For example in the domain of sexual customs, institutionalised paederasty, prevalent in Greece, was entirely absent from East Africa. It existed in New Guinea, but the main form it took there was quite different from the form it took in ancient Greece. The final word on this question belongs to Aristotle. He maintained that the *sussitia*, common messes of an age class system, had been invented several times independently, like all other political institutions. He was undoubtedly right about this and his thesis of independent origins, if applied to ancient Greece as a whole in relation to the rest of the world, does not require any modification today.[36]

History, like evolution, does not repeat itself. Although developing countries in the Third World today, in attempting to modernise themselves, are starting from the same kind of social institutions which existed in Europe three thousand years ago, the context in which they have to try to modernise themselves has changed. Consequently it is impossible for developing countries today to move along the same path that Europe followed, beginning in the first millennium BC, explaining the difficulty which so many of them have encountered in trying to imitate European models. This exemplifies the fact that it is impossible to comprehend the present, or contemplate the future, without understanding the past.

Notes

Chapter I

1. Finley (1985a) 17-22 on *oikonomia*, 'household management'. In this chapter documentation is only given in the notes for matters which will not be raised again in subsequent chapters. The names of authors of species are omitted in this book.

2. Glacken (1967), esp. 3-149 on antiquity, and Worster (1985) for popular accounts of the history of ecology; R.P. McIntosh (1985) for more technical details of recent trends; Shepard & McKinley (1969); G. Young (1974) and Hawley (1986); Boyden (1987) for the concept of *biohistory*; Hughes (1975a), (1975b) & (1980) on the attitudes of the ancient Greeks and Romans towards nature; Andrewartha & Birch (1984), Begon et al. (1986), Colinvaux (1986) and Pianka (1988) for modern standard textbooks on ecology; Birks & Birks (1980) 1-8 on the philosophy of palaeoecology; Welinder (1979) & (1983) is an example of an archaeological approach to the ecological and demographic history of part of Iron Age Europe.

3. P.B. Sears, cited by R.P. McIntosh (1985) 1; Lovelock (1988) offers unconventional views on such issues as the ozone layer and nuclear pollution.

4. Andrewartha & Birch (1984) 3; Aristotle *HA* 589a3-5; it should be noted that Lovelock (1988) criticised mainstream ecologists for not paying attention to the physical environment and argued that the divide between the earth sciences and life sciences is a barrier to understanding, but this book conforms to the mainstream because our interest here is in population studies.

5. Rickert (1986); Aristotle *PA* 644b28-645a30.

6. Coleman & Schofield (1986) 4.

7. Seager (1986) 141.

8. N. Weber (1972) and Beattie (1985) on ant mutualisms with fungi and higher plants, cf. May (1989b); Hagen (1966) and Theophrastos *HP* IV.14.3 & 9-10 on pests of olives; the Stoic philosopher Kleanthes F515 ed. von Arnim vol. 1 reckoned that ants had powers of reasoning, while Aristotle *HA* 488a7-10 classed ants as one of the 'social' (*politika*) animals; Georgi (1982) and Theophrastos *HP* II.8.1-4 & *CP* III.18.1 for the fig and the date palm, the main exceptions to the pollination rule; Boucher et al. (1982) and Begon et al. (1986) 461-496 on the prevalence of mutualisms in nature, whose most important manifestation, according to L. Margulis, is the combination of organs like mitochondria that were once independent organisms to form the cells of all higher forms of life.

9. Levin (1976) on plant chemical defences; references in ancient sources will be given in Chapter III.9; Dioskorides *MM* (*peri hulês iatrikês*) I.104 ed. Wellmann describes the extraction and use of salicin from the willow tree (Greek *itea*); Theophrastos *HP* IX.20.3 mentions a plant called *thapsia* (*Thapsia garganica*) in Attica which was not eaten by indigenous cattle, but imported cattle which ate it died from diarrhoea; Dioskorides *MM* IV.153 for its use in medicine; Tammaro & Xepapadakis (1986) for medicinal use of plants in modern Greece; Cook et al. (1989) found that human bones from late Roman Egypt contained the antibiotic tetracycline, probably derived from consumption of contaminated grain.

420

10. Aretaios *peri aitiôn kai sêmeiôn oxeôn kai chroniôn pathôn* IV.7 ed. Hude; Cooke & Holmes (1984).

11. Aristotle *Politics* 1264a3-4.

12. Theophrastos *HP* IV.4.11 and Pliny *NH* XII.xiv.26 on the olive tree of India (all references to 'Pliny' in this book are to Pliny the Elder); M. Davis (1986) on ecological instability caused by climatic change.

13. Pliny *NH* XIX.vii-viii.26-30 on esparto grass; Livy XXII.20.6; Laumont & Berbigier (1953) for details of its cultivation in recent times; Darwin (1968) 151 & 232-233.

14. Homer *Iliad* VIII.306-307, Hippokrates *Gunaikeiôn* II.201 ed. Littré vol. 8, pp. 386-387, Theophrastos *HP* IX.12.3-5, Dioskorides *MM* IV.64 and Pliny *NH* XIX.liii.167-169 & XX.lxxvi-lxxx.198-209 on the opium poppy and other species of poppies (Greek *mêkôn*); Thucydides IV.26.8 mentions consumption of poppy seeds, which do not contain any drugs, by the Spartans, cf. Galen *peri trophôn dunameôn* I.31 ed. Kühn vol. 6, p. 548 and Andrews (1952); Kritikos & Papadaki (1967) list all the evidence for the opium poppy in prehistoric and classical Greece; Bakels (1982) and Merlin (1984) opted for the western Mediterranean as the place of origin of the domesticated opium poppy, in accordance with the *Flora Europaea*; Livy I.54.6 for the opium poppy in early Roman traditions; D. Crawford (1973b) for the unsuccessful attempt in the third century BC by the Greeks to persuade Egyptian peasants to cultivate the opium poppy on a large scale as a cash crop and an oil crop.

15. Herodotos IV.74; Columella *RR* II.10.21; Pliny *NH* XIX.lvi.173-174; Godwin (1967); Brunner (1973).

16. See Chapters III.4 & IV on the horse; Aristotle *HA* 580b17-20, Pliny *NH* VIII.lxxxii.220-223, Strabo III.4.18.165c and Aelian *peri zôiôn idiotêtos* VI.41 & XVII.41 on field mice as a pest of cereal fields.

17. J. Allan (1981) on the Sahara.

18. Clark & Stemmler (1975); Watson (1983) 9-14 for the mediaeval spread of sorghum; Cleuziou & Costantini (1980) on Oman, also Gwynne (1975) on links between E. Africa and the Orient; see also Chapter III.

19. Te-Tzu Chang (1983) on early rice cultivation in China; K. Thomas (1983) on the Indus Valley; R. Thompson (1949) 106-107 on Assyria; P.H. Davis (1985) 199 on Anatolia; Strabo XV.1.13.690c & XV.1.18.692c on India and on Palestine; Feliks (1963) on Jewish sources; Theophrastos *HP* IV.4.10 and Diodoros Siculus XIX.13.6 on rice in India; Sophokles F552 ed. Nauck²; Kroll (1982) 469 on Tiryns; Knorzer (1966) on Germany; Dioskorides *MM* II.95; Galen *peri trophôn dunameôn* I.17 ed. Kühn vol. VI, p. 525; Chevalier (1939) 653; Strabo XVII.3.23.838c on Cyrene; S.K. McIntosh & R.J. McIntosh (1983) on Jenne-jeno; Chevalier (1938) 315-316 on *O. glaberrima*; Nayar (1973) 178-184 & 193-194 argued for the late evolution of *O. glaberrima* from *O. sativa*; Te-Tzu Chang (1976) proposed the alternative theory of continental drift, cf. Sécond (1986) and Oka (1988) 12 & 18-22 for evidence for the independent evolution of *O. glaberrima*; the *Periplous tês Eruthras Thalassês* XIV, XXXVII & XLI ed. Müller *Geographici Graeci minores* vol. 1 mentions the export of rice and sugar cane from Barugaza and Ariake in India to Somalia, also rice cultivation in Gedrosia in southern Iran; as an illustration of the difficulties that might be encountered by farmers moving from one region to another even within rainfed-farming areas of the Mediterranean note Theophrastos *HP* VIII.6.3 & *CP* III.20.5 on the experiences of the Greeks who left Greece, especially Corinth, for Syracuse in the 340s BC answering Timoleon's call for colonists to repopulate Sicily.

20. Nayar & Mehra (1970) and Bedigian & Harlan (1986) on sesame.

21. Richardson (1972) on bottle gourd.

22. Theophrastos *HP* VIII.3.2 & VIII.11.1 and Galen *peri trophôn dunameôn* I.28 ed. Kühn vol. VI, pp. 541-546 on cowpea (Greek *dolichos*); Zhukovskij (1962) 25; Chevalier (1944); Steele, Allen & Summerfield (1985).

23. Herodotos III.106 & VII.65; Theophrastos *HP* IV.4.8 & IV.7.7-8; Pliny *NH* XIII.xxviii.90 & XIX.ii.14 differentiating the African and Indian varieties; Arrian *Indika* VII.3 & XVI.1-2; Chowdhury & Buth (1971); Phillips in Simmonds (1976) 194-200; R.C. Thompson (1949) 113 on Assyria; besides the seven discussed in the text, there are other crop plants common to sub-Saharan Africa and India, e.g. finger millet (*Eleusine coracana*) and pearl millet (*Pennisetum typhoides*) but these are not considered here because they are not cultivated in the Mediterranean.

24. Aristotle F246 Rose, Seneca *QN* VI.8.3-5, *Anonymus Florentinus* et al. FGH647 F1-3 Jacoby, Strabo XVII.1.5.789c and Arrian *Indika* VI.6-8 on the origin of the Nile, cf. Herodotos II.28-34; Nesteroff et al. (1982); Desanges (1978).

25. See Chapter III.11 on papyrus, also Warren (1976) and Betts (1978) on the Bronze Age paintings, but their identification of papyrus is rejected by Negbi (1989) 32-34 who prefers *Cyperus longus* instead; Muthuri & Kinyamario (1989) on the nutritional value of papyrus, a plant with a very high rate of biomass production; Theophrastos *HP* IV.8.2, 6 & 12, Zhukovskij (1962) 21 and Negbi (1989) 34-35 on chufa (Greek *mnasion*); P.F. Mattingly (1983) and Chapter II.7 on malaria; R.C. Gallo & Montagnier (1988) on AIDS, Essex & Kanki (1988) and Mulder (1988) on its origin, contra Sharp & Wen-Hsiung Li (1988).

26. Hanno *Periplous* ed. Oikonomides; Herodotos IV.42.2-4 on the Phoenicians; Herodotos I.80.2-5 for the surprise use of camels in battle made by Cyrus of Persia against Croesus of Lydia; Aristotle *HA* 499a13-30 knew the Arabian and Bactrian camels; Josephos *Ioudaikos Polemos* IV.436 ed. Naber for camels as common in Palestine in the first century AD; Pliny *NH* VIII.xxvi.67-68; Zeuner (1963) 338-366, Planhol (1968), B. Shaw (1979), Gauthier-Pilters & Dagg (1981) 115-122, Ripinsky (1983) and Mason (1984) 106-115 on the Arabian camel, the one-humped dromedary (*Camellus dromedarius*); Aelian *peri zôiôn idiotêtos* III.2 & XIV.11 on Libyan horses and wild Libyan cattle; Herodotos IV.183.4 on the Garamantes, cf. Diodoros Siculus XX.64.3 on chariots; Polybios I.19.2-4 and Livy XXIII.48.5 & XXXV.11 on Numidian cavalry; D. Livingstone (1975), J. Allan (1981), Street (1981), Hamilton (1982) and Gasse et al. (1989) on African climatic history.

27. Livy *Periochae* 60, Julius Obsequens 30 and Orosius V.11.1-2 ed. Meister on 125 BC; Livy XXX.2.10, XLII.2.5 & 10.7-8 records epidemics of locusts in Campania, the Pomptine marsh region and Apulia in 203 and 173 BC, with the Roman army intervening in the last case; Plutarch *Moralia* 637b on Sicily; Pliny *NH* XI.xxxv.101-107 on Cyrene and Lemnos; Plutarch *Moralia* 380f and Aelian *peri zôiôn idiotêtos* III.12 on Lemnos, and XVII.19 on Asia Minor; Theophrastos *HP* II.3.3 on locusts in Boiotia; Pausanias I.24.8; Aristotle *HA* 556a8-13 & 556b1-2; Diodoros Siculus III.29.1-4 and Agatharkides *peri tês Eruthras Thalassês* cited by Photios 453a2-453b17 ed. Henry for the *Akridophagoi*, 'locust eaters', in North Africa, also Herodotos IV.172.1 on the Nasamones; Alexis F162 Kock for consumption in Greece of *tettix*, a cicada, grasshopper, cricket or locust – on the exact meaning of the various Greek words for these insects see Davies & Kathirithamby (1986) 134-149; Poseidonios F223 eds. Edelstein & Kidd on Libya; Columella *RR* VIII.11.15 on peacocks; Walsh (1986); the hypothesis of Chevalier (1938), namely that the Sahara was an important centre of origin of domesticated plants, is unsound.

28. Fowler (1986); Louw & Seely (1982).

29. Ford-Lloyd & Williams (1975) on beets; Theophrastos *HP* VII.4.4 for the two main types of leaf-beets (Greek *teutlon*), distinguished by the colour of their leaves, known to the Greeks, cf. Pliny *NH* XIX.xl.132-135. Pliny *NH* XII.xvii.32 knew sugar-cane (Latin *saccharum*) in Arabia. Columella *RR* IX.14.19 mentions beehives being moved from other parts of Greece to take advantage of flowering plants in bloom in Attica.

30. E.M. Davis (1981) on bitter vetch at Stobi; Kislev (1989) on grass pea; Columella *RR* III.8.4-5 and Pliny *NH* XXVII.i.2-3 on plant movements to Italy; Pliny *NH* XII.vii.14 on the Greek origin of Latin names of many trees (cf. Varro *De lingua latina* V.102-106 & 108 and Friedrich (1970) 172), XII.liv.111 on triumphs, XV.xi.39-40 & xiii.44-45 on peach, XV.xv.49-52 on varieties of apple (many introduced from abroad), XV.xii.41-42 on plum, XV.xvi.53-56 & xvii.58 on pear, XV.xix.68-xxi.83 on fig, XV.xxiv.86-88 on walnut, XV.xxiv.88-89 on hazel (from north Anatolia), XV.xxiv.89-90 on almond (*nux Graeca*), XIII.x.51 & XV.xxiv.91 on pistachio (from Syria), XV.xxv.92-94 on chestnut (from Sardis in Asia Minor), XV.xxx.102-104 on cherry, cf. XVI.lix.138, XV.xxxvi-xxxviii.119-126 on myrtle, XVI.lx.139-142 on cypress (*Cypressus sempervivens*, from Crete), with Theophrastos *HP* IV.5.2, Cato *de agricultura* XLVIII & CLI and Liphschitz & Biger (1989); Pliny *NH* XVII.xxii-xxvi.99-122, XVII.xxx.129 & XVII.xxx.137-138 on the technique of grafting, XV.xvii.57 for its religious aspects, e.g. grafting onto thorns was prohibited, cf. XVII.xxiv.108 for the rule that the graft must be inserted when the moon is waxing; Huntley & Birks (1983) 161-166 & 238-242 on chestnut and walnut pollen; Theophrastos *HP* IV.2.4, Pliny *NH* XIII.xvi.59 & XV.xxvi.95 and Liphschitz (1987) on the carob tree (Greek *kerônia*); Zohary & Hopf (1988) 128-166 on fruit trees; Columella *RR* V.11.1-15 on grafting, cf. *De arboribus* XX.2 in which he expressed the opinion that engrafted trees were more productive than trees propagated any other way; Theophrastos *HP* II.5.3-6 on grafting in Greece.

31. Helbaek (1964); many references to the lentil (ancient Greek *phakos*) in Theophrastos *HP* VIII; Willcox (1977) lists remains of other exotic plants found on Roman sites in Britain, e.g. the peach (*Prunus persica*), although it is difficult to tell whether they were actually cultivated in Britain or merely imported; Buckland (1981) on stored products insects, also Theophrastos *HP* VIII.11.2-4, Columella *RR* I.6.16-17, II.10.11-12 & 16 and Pliny *NH* XVIII.lxxiii.301-308.

32. van Zeist (1987) on the weeds.

33. Alessio (1946); Battisti (1960); Szemerényi (1974) 152; the *hyakinthos* was considered to have the property of retarding puberty (Pliny *NH* XXI.clxx.97 and Dioskorides *MM* IV.62) – an idea to be kept in mind in connection with such festivals as the *Hyakinthia* in Sparta and the initiation rites whose significance for human demography will be considered in Chapter II.5; G. Huxley (1971) conjured up some interesting arguments in defence of Aristotle's belief that on Crete at least the invading Dorians assimilated the indigenous inhabitants and adopted their political institutions.

34. E. Masson (1967) 46-60 and M. Masson (1988) on Semitic loan words; J. Brown (1969) and Zohary & Hopf (1988) 136-142 on vines.

35. Corvisier (1985) 33.

36. André (1985) xiii-xiv for data on the proportion of Latin phytonyms of Greek derivation. As an example of the difficulties that rapidly arise if the importance of Greek influence on Rome is denied, Carandini's ideas (in Kolendo (1980) xix) should be considered. He attempted to use Vitruvius II.8 as evidence for west central Roman Italy as the 'dominant exception' in respect of the importance of slavery in the ancient economy, overlooking the Greek antecedent of Vitruvius in Demokritos 68 B28 eds. Diels-Kranz (in Columella *RR* XI.3.2), one of the very few surviving fragments of Demokritos' *Geôrgika*. (It might be argued that this fragment of 'Demokritos' should be attributed to the second-century BC Egyptian writer Bolos Mendesios, who also wrote works on farming which were falsely ascribed to Demokritos. Even if this were the case, it would still show that the idea behind the construction technique in question was current in the Greek world before Roman technical literature began to develop. However, there is no doubt whatsoever that the philosopher Demokritos did write about plants and agriculture, because Theophrastos quotes his opinions several times, e.g. *CP* II.11.7-9.) The observations of van Andel & Runnels (1987) 145 suggest that Greek farmers down the ages have followed Demokritos' precept in regard to the construction of agricultural terrace walls. Carandini also did not realise that the Greek and Roman idea in question simply took account of the *physical life* of the product, ignoring what a modern economist would call its *economic life* (see Kuznets (1974) 154-156 for this important conceptual distinction). This puts the proper interpretation of Vitruvius in agreement with Finley's view that the Romans did not possess the concept of the 'economy'.

37. Powell (1987) on the apricot (*Prunus armeniaca*), opting for a late date of arrival in the west from China, but note Chevalier (1932) 761 who suggested that it may have been domesticated further west, in Turkestan or even in Anatolia, as well as in China, because of the existence of semi-wild forms in these regions; references for melon, citron and lucerne in Chapter III; on the taro or yam (*Colocasia esculenta*), a tropical root crop which had reached Egypt from India perhaps by the time of Theophrastos and then Italy in the first century AD, see Thiselton-Dyer (1918) 299-304 and Burkill (1937/38).

38. Stoianovitch (1966), Crosby (1972), Hémardinquer (1973) and Langer (1975) on New World crops in the Old World; C. Russell & Felker (1987) on the cactus (*Opuntia ficus-indica*) and McGrew (1985) 12 for human consumption of it in early modern Greece.

39. Negbi (1989) 38-39 mentions incipient cultivation in antiquity of several other species of plant that are now only wild; Hinman (1986) on crambe.

40. Columella *RR* I.1.4-5; Theophrastos *HP* VI.2.4; Pliny *NH* XV.i.1 & XXI.xxxi.57; in Columella *RR* V.8.5 the manuscript reading for the maximum distance from the coast at which olive cultivation was generally thought to be possible is uncertain; Gras (1985) 212-215 updated Vallet on olives in central Italy; Pliny *NH* XIV.xiii-xiv.87-91 & XVIII.v.24 on late development of Roman viticulture, cf. Gras (1985) 367-390 on the introduction of the vine to early Republican Rome; Diodoros Siculus XIII.81.4-5 & XX.8.4, cf. Strabo XVII.3.20.836c mentioning export of wine to Cyrene in exchange for *silphion* at a later stage of Carthaginian history; Skylax *Periplous* CX ed. Peretti mentions use of oil of oleaster on the island of Djerba off the N. African coast; Justin XLIII.4.1-2 ed. Seel, with Brun (1984), cf. Crumley (1987), on archaeological evidence from south France (nothing currently earlier than fourth century BC); Demosthenes XXXV.35; Janushevitch, Nikolaenko & Kuzminova (1985); (Aristotle) *peri thaumasiôn akousmatôn* 844a17-24 states that the Phoenicians exported olive oil to Tartessos in Spain, today by far the world's largest producer of olive oil, in exchange for silver; Shipley (1987) 61 on export of olive oil from Samos to Etruria *c.* 600 BC.

41. G. Barker in *The Times*, Tuesday 11 August 1987 on the British School's work, also Barker (1988); Huntley & Birks (1983) 36 & 264-268 on olive pollen; Maggiani (1972) for the earliest written evidence for the olive in Etruria; Moody (1987) 127-128 claims that olive cultivation was already taking place in the Early Neolithic period in the south-west Peloponnese solely on the basis of the occurrence of olive pollen in pollen cores, but this is a non sequitur, as the olive pollen simply shows the natural spread of the oleaster, a good producer of pollen, as the climate became warmer, a process favoured by the occurrence in the Neolithic period of higher summer rainfall than today (see Chapter III.3); L. Costantini in Harris & Hillman (1989) 199 found evidence for the oleaster at the Mesolithic/Neolithic transition at Grotta dell'Uzzo in Sicily.

42. Aristotle *GA* 741a9-10, *HA* 588b28 & *peri makrobiotêtos* ... 467a24 argued that animals possess sensory perception but plants don't; Dombrowski (1985) on vegetarianism; contrast Burkert (1983) on the importance of animal sacrifice in ancient Greek religion (two points of view on every issue!).

43. Nriagu (1983) 309-424 compiled evidence for the reproductive consequences of lead intake in antiquity in an exhaustive but uncritical manner; bones from ancient Greek cemeteries could be analysed to determine their lead content, but no research of this kind has yet been carried out to my knowledge; Xenophon *Memorabilia* III.6.12 on Laurion; Vitruvius *De architectura* VIII.6.10-11 on the danger to health posed by water from lead pipes.

44. Thirgood (1981), Hughes & Thirgood (1982) and Hughes (1983b) advocate the thesis of large-scale deforestation, but it has been refuted by O. Rackham (1982) & (1983) and van Andel & Runnels (1987), among others; see also ch. III.12 below on deforestation; Hutchinson et al. (1970) on Monterosi; Huntley & Birks (1983) 309 on pine pollen; Vokou et al. (1988) and Andrews (1961b), with Theophrastos *HP* I.9.4, VI.2.3 & IX.7.3 on various kinds of oregano (Greek *amarakon* and *origanon*); Arianoutsou-Faraggitaki & Margaris in Margaris & Mooney (1981) 181-190 and the series of articles in EM XIII.4 (1987) entitled 'Influence of fire on the stability of Mediterranean forest ecosystems'; Moody (1987) 46 and Lange (1988) for other adaptations of Mediterranean plants to drought.

45. Empedokles 21 B61 eds. Diels-Kranz and Aristotle *Physics* 198b28-32, discussed by Blundell (1986) 73-99; Darwin (1968) 53-54; Dikaiarchos F48 & 51 ed. Wehrli, with Khazanov (1984) 85-118; Khrysippos F1152-1167 ed. von Arnim vol. 2; Xenophon *Memorabilia* IV.3.10 and Aristotle *Politics* 1256b15-22 for the utilitarian interpretation in fourth-century literature.

46. Lucretius *de rerum natura* V.918-924.

47. Hippokrates *peri aërôn, hudatôn, topôn* XIV ed. Littré vol. 2, pp. 58-61 and Aristotle *GA* 721b29-34 on inheritance of acquired characteristics in man; Aristotle *GA* 716a6-7, 738b20-21 & 765b10-19 for his belief that the female supplied the raw material (*hulê*) which had to be shaped by the male moving principle; Aristotle *GA* 746a30-b16 on fertility of some mammalian hybrids, 747a23-749a6 on mules, 762a8-763b16 and *HA* 539a21-25 on spontaneous generation of certain animals, wholeheartedly accepting it, cf. Byl (1980) 269-277; Theophrastos *CP* I.5.1-5 on spontaneous generation of some plants, expressing doubts but nevertheless ultimately accepting it; Aristotle *GA* 721b21-35 & 767a36-769b10 and *HA* 585b28-586a14 and Hippokrates *peri gonês* VIII ed. Littré vol. 7, pp. 480-483 on the resemblances of children to their parents, represent two attempts in antiquity to approach the fundamental problem of heredity, an essential foundation for population biology, which also stumped Darwin but not Mendel; Lloyd (1983) 86-94; Egerton (1968) & (1975).

48. Foucault (1979) 16-18; Aristotle *Physics* 195b30-198a14 on chance; Sambursky (1956); Plutarch *Agesilaos* II.6; cf. Xenophon *Cyropaedia* VIII.4.20. Aristotle *NE* 1094b25-27 exemplifies the exclusion of probability from the domain of mathematics in antiquity.

49. Ammianus Marcellinus XXIII.6.24, Dio Cassius LXXI.2.4 and SHA *Verus* VIII.1-2 and Chapter II.7 on the epidemic; Cartledge (forthcoming) on the peacock

(Greek *tahôs*), with Aristotle *HA* 564a25-b5, Aelian *peri zôiôn idiotêtos* V.21 and Columella *RR* VIII.11.

50. Elton (1942) 2-6 on animal population fluctuations in antiquity.

51. Hegesandros F42 ed. Müller *FHG* vol. IV, p. 421; Aelian *peri zôiôn idiotêtos* XIII.14 and Xenophon *Cyropaedia* I.6.40 & *Memorabilia* III.11.7-8 describe the use of dogs to hunt hares (*dasupous* and *lagôs* in Greek; *tachinas* in the Spartan dialect, according to Aelian *peri zôiôn idiotêtos* VII.47). The ancient Greek partridge of Astypalaia (*perdix*) was probably either the rock partridge (*Alectoris graeca*), or the chukar (*Alectoris chukar*), the latter reported recently from Naxos in the list of birds of the Cyclades in Magioris (1987), rather than the more familiar common or grey partridge (*Perdix perdix*) whose modern range does not quite extend into southern Greece. On partridges note also Athenaios IX.388f-390c, observing that the Boiotian and Attic partridges were not identical; Aristotle *HA* 541a26-31, 564a20-24 & 613a6-614a32, and *GA* 785b35; in the last passage he mentions a white *perdix*, an albino, an interesting genetic mutation or recessive homozygote; Aelian *peri zôiôn idiotêtos* III.5 & 16, IV.1, 12-13 & 16; Aristotle F366 ed. Rose mentions a peculiarity of the ecology of Astypalaia, namely that it did not support snakes, and Pliny *NH* VIII.lix.140 says that it produced the best snails; the summary of Theophrastos' work *peri tôn athroôs phainomenôn zôiôn* ('On animals which appear all at once in large numbers') is in Photios 527b11-528a39; Diogenes Laertios V.43 also records this book title; Pliny *NH* VIII.xliii.104 states that a population explosion of mice drove the inhabitants of the island of Gyara in the Cyclades from their home, cf. X.lxxxv.185-186 on their fertility.

52. Strabo III.2.6.144c & III.5.2.168c states that the rabbit existed in Spain, southern France as far as Massilia and the western Mediterranean islands; Pliny *NH* VIII.lxxxi.217-218; Galen *peri trophôn dunameôn* III.2 ed. Kühn vol. VI, p. 666 still regarded the rabbit (*kounikoulos* in Galen, a loan word from Latin, but *lebêris* in the Massalian dialect of Greek according to Polemarchos) as characteristic of the Iberian peninsula in the second century AD; Aelian *peri zôiôn idiotêtos* XIII.15; Poseidonios F52 eds. Edelstein & Kidd mentions rabbits on an island off the coast of Campania in Italy; Polybios XII.3.10 for rabbits on Corsica; Pliny *NH* VIII.xliii.43 & lxxxi.217-220; R. Robinson in Mason (1984) 239-246; Fenner & Ratcliffe (1965) and Fenner (1983) on myxomatosis; Andrewartha & Birch (1984) 313-371 on the rabbit's ecology; Bodson (1978).

53. Williamson (1981) 167 on evolution and immigration on islands; Polunin (1980) 60 on the Cretan and Cypriot flora, also Greuter (1979) who classed 20 per cent of the plant species on Crete as endemic, nearly 50 per cent as belonging to the relict element and about a third as introduced by man; Hemmer et al. (1981) and Groves (1989) discuss some of the problems of island zoogeography in the Mediterranean.

54. Aristotle *HA* 580b10-29; Egerton (1973) discussed the history of the 'balance of nature' idea rejected by Elton, esp. 325-330 on antiquity, starting with Herodotos III.108-109.

Chapter II

1. M. Hansen (1985) 10-11.

2. Finley (1981a) 157.

3. R. Finlay (1981) 16 on London; Aristotle *HA* 605b22-606b8 on the existence of different varieties of animals in different environments, sometimes in very close geographical areas.

4. Elton (1942) 158-159.

5. Aristotle *Politics* 1270a29-b6; Strabo IX.1.22.399c on Oropos as a paradigm of border conflicts; Herodotos VIII.125.2 and Plutarch *Themistokles* XVIII on Seriphos; Delbrück (1913) 25ff., cf. Thucydides VI.33.5-6, Pausanias IV.25.5 and Ammianus Marcellinus XXXI.4.7-8; Diodoros Siculus XIX.21.3, cf. Herodotus I.136.1 and Xenophon *Cyropaedia* I.2.15 & VII.5.34 on Persia.

6. G. Simmel in Wolff (1950) 87-177 (scattered, interesting observations on ancient Greece) discussed properties of social relationships that stem directly from the number of people involved; Beloch (1886) 55-108 on Attica.

7. Plato *Laws* 740b1-741a5 & 708b4; Veyne (1982); Meiggs & Lewis *GHI* no. 13, lines 7-9, Hypereides F27 ed. Jensen, and M. Osborne (1983) vol. 3, pp. 33-37 for enfranchisement to replenish military manpower; modern historians have tended to follow Plato in neglecting the possible advantages of a low population density, e.g. Glotz (1968) 303-309 regarded *oliganthrôpia* as an impediment to the *polis*'s ability to carry out an active *bios politikos*, cf. Aristotle *Politics* 1265a20-28; L. Gallo (1980b) discussed *oliganthrôpia* and *poluanthrôpia* as literary *topoi*, but they were very real problems as well, as will be stressed here.

8. Plato *Laws* 740d3-9, also 707e on the rest of Crete as densely populated; Malthus (1970); Boserup (1965) & (1981); Dupâquier et al. (1983) on Malthus; Hume (1875) vol. 1, p. 383.

9. Vries (1984) 17; while disparaging the ancient sources it would be wrong to forget Morgenstern (1963) on the large margins of error carried by sets of numerical data in the modern world which might seem reliable at first sight.

10. See, for example, Mols (1972) 22 on how the census at Venice in 1509 AD, whose official records have partially survived, was 'reported' by contemporary literary sources – a good analogy for the 400,000 slaves of Athenaios, discussed below in the text.

11. Justin IX.5.6.

12. Finley (1981b) 20.

13. Ktesikles in Athenaios VI.272c; Jacoby's commentary on Stesikleides FGH245 F1 and Philochoros FGH328 F119; Ferguson (1973) 54-55; Gomme (1933) 18-19 & (1959); Mossé (1962) 137-147, 171-174 & 181-185; Reinmuth (1971) 108-115; Isager & Hansen (1975) 11-17; Gehrke (1978) 178-181; M. Hansen (1985) 28-36; Whitehead (1986) 81-85 on the distribution of metics in Attica; (Demosthenes) L.6-7 and Ste. Croix (1981) 207 for other references to thetes in the *katalogoi*.

14. Herodotos V.97.2, Plato *Symposion* 175e, Menander *Epitrepontes* 1087-1089 ed. Sandbach and Aristophanes *Ekklêsiazousai* 1132-1133 mention the stock number as 30,000, cf. L. Gallo (1979a); (Demosthenes) XXV.51, Plato *Kritias* 112d, Philochoros FGH328 F95 Jacoby and (Plato) *Axiochos* 368e speak of 20,000 citizens. Julius Caesar *BG* I.29 and Dionysios Hal. *AR* IX.25.2 used a multiplier of four to calculate total population size from the number of adult males.

15. Diodoros Siculus XVIII.70.1 & XX.84 on Megalopolis and Rhodes; Olbia, under siege in 331 BC, awarded citizenship to free resident aliens and freedom to slaves to boost its military strength (Makrobios *Saturnalia* I.11.33), in contrast to Demetrios' reductions in the size of the Athenian citizen body, if his census was indeed for military purposes; the Athenian democracy considered similar measures after the battle of Chaironeia in 338 BC but eventually rejected them (Hypereides F27-29 ed. Jensen and Plutarch *Moralia* 848f); Finley (1985a) 133; M. Hansen (1988) 7-13.

16. Hume (1875) vol. 1, pp. 419-421.

17. E.g. Martin (1913) 243, Stirling (1965) 47-48, K. White (1970a) 345, J. Davis (1973) 96 & Appendix VI, and Peristiany (1976) 153 on the low labour inputs of

Mediterranean agriculture, an important reason why the Athenians, for example, were able to devote so much time to politics – also Webb & Hawtin (1981) 131 for 60 per cent of the total production costs of lentils in Syria being harvesting expenses, nearly all labour; Hesiod *WD* 493-495 & 663-677 in his recommendations on use of slack periods of the year said nothing about weeding, cf. Sophokles *Trachiniai* 32-33 for a farmer only visiting a distant field for sowing and harvesting, with Thiersch (1833) vol. 1, p. 284 for this practice in early modern Greece. Columella permitted his slaves a thirty-day period of rest after the autumn sowing period was over and allowed forty-five days to be lost annually through rain as far as fieldwork was concerned. He also states that after making these allowances and completing all the necessary tasks for crop production there were still four whole months left. Kolendo (1980) makes an unnecessary fuss over the data on labour inputs for agricultural operations in the Roman agronomists (Columella *RR* II.12). The ratio of the prices of different crops is determined by the labour inputs required for their cultivation. The ratio of wheat-barley prices, for example, was the same in Mycenaean Greece and Mesopotamia in the second and third millennia BC as it was in Roman times, proving that the fact that wheat requires more labour than barley was known thousands of years before Columella. The Roman agronomists do not show that the Romans had developed an interest, not shared by their predecessors, in labour productivity (see Chapter III). Xenophon *Poroi* IV.5 makes the commonsense observation that every farmer knew how many labourers and how many oxen his farm needed. This statement makes Columella, writing centuries later, look uninspiring and devoid of originality. See Demosthenes XVIII.51 on harvesters (*theristai*) as characteristically hired labourers, also Varro *RR* I.17.3.

18. Philodemos *peri oikonomias* col. IX ed. Jensen; in *Oikonomikos* V.14 Xenophon is drawing an analogy between two hierarchical relationships: (i) the general who gives orders to ordinary private soldiers; (ii) the gentleman farmer who gives orders to his slaves; Xenophon *Hellênika* III.3.4-11 on Kinadon.

19. Hesiod *WD* 405; Aristotle *Politics* 1252b12. In the *Politics* Aristotle said that the *euporoi*, the 'well-off', were hoplites, while the *aporoi* were not (1289b29-32 & 1321a12-13) and did not have slaves (1323a5-6), even though they were not necessarily entirely without property (1279b18-19). The critique of Jameson by E.M. Wood (1983) & (1988) 51-80 is interesting, but it is insufficient to discuss 'labour' as an indivisible abstract category as she does. In an exhaustive treatment of the subject it would be essential to break it down and consider individually the labour requirements on a seasonal basis of each crop cultivated in ancient Greece.

20. Walpole (1817) 144; on p. 151 he noted that in early modern Greece labourers exploited differences in the time of ripening of crops – for example, the fact that the harvest took place later around Thebes than in Attica – to increase their income, but the multitude of political boundaries probably restricted such labour migrations in ancient Greece.

21. Slicher van Bath (1963) 183 on England; Isaios IX.28; Finley (1952) 73 concluded that slavery was insignificant in agriculture in Attica because of the shortage of references to slaves in connection with agricultural land on the *horoi* inscriptions.

22. Conophagos (1980) 348 on the labour force; Xenophon *Poroi* IV.6; Giovannini (1978) 61-62; Schönert-Geiss (1974) on fourth-century coinage; Conophagos' observations on the importance of skilled craftsmen in mining are very relevant to the interpretation of the word *cheirotechnai* in Thucydides VII.27.5, as Ste. Croix (1981) 506, for example, assumes that most of the slaves in

the mines were unskilled, a patently unsatisfactory assumption, cf. Fogel & Engerman (1974) 38-39 on the importance of skilled slave labour in the southern USA; the elevated calculations of silver production in Isager & Hansen (1975) 44-45 rest on the unsatisfactory assumption (*inter alia*) that everyone who tried to exploit the silver mines succeeded in making a profit all the time; Xenophon *Poroi* IV.24-25; Hypereides F29 Jensen.

23. J. Davies (1971) 126-138 on Demosthenes; Plato *Republic* 578e regarded fifty slaves as a large slaveholding, cf. Fogel & Engerman (1974) 134 expressing the same opinion for the USA; A.H.M. Jones (1957) 78-79 (cf. Gomme (1946)) for the estimate of 20,000, which could be correct although no confidence should be placed in his argument from grain consumption, on which see Garnsey (1988); Mossé (1962) 184 n. 3 lists guesses of the size of the Athenian slave population made by other scholars, to which Isager & Hansen (1975) 17 and Garlan (1982) 68ff. may be added.

24. Aristotle *Politics* 1326a5-25; cf. Thucydides V.68.2 & VI.17.5; Diodoros Siculus XV.23.4, not distinguishing the few Spartiates from the much more numerous Helot and perioikic populations, illustrates the popular attitude criticised by Aristotle.

25. Veblen (1970) 54-58; Olympiodoros F44 ed. Müller *FGH* vol. 4, pp. 67-68, an author prone to exaggeration; Herodotos VII.60; Gottwald (1979) 270-275 on Biblical censuses; Lacoste (1969) 192 on Ibn Khaldoun.

26. Strabo VIII.339c & 350-353c; J. Chadwick (1976) 185-186.

27. Compare Bintliff & Snodgrass (1985) on Boiotia with van Andel et al. (1986) on the southern Argolid; Feyel (1942) 209-217 thought that depopulation in Boiotia only set in at the end of the third century BC; Snodgrass (1983b) 90 cites the unpublished survey of Megalopolis in Arkadia, and his other works (1971), (1977), (1980), (1983a) & (1987) 170-210 are all fundamental on the Early Iron Age; Whitley (1987), important on Dark Age Attica; Fossey (1986) 85-113 on Phokis; Cartledge (1979) 67-71 for the population collapse at the end of LHIIIC in Lakonia and Messenia; Morgan (1986) esp. 55, 96 & 99 on the lack of Early Iron Age activity in the lands bordering the Corinthian Gulf; Alcock (1989) 45-76 gives a cautious but comprehensive survey of the so far mostly unpublished evidence from surveys for population fluctuations in Hellenistic Greece; A. Foley (1988) on the Argolid; Keller & Rupp (1983) on survey in the Mediterranean.

28. Francis & Vickers (1985) have not found favour in the archaeological establishment, e.g. Snodgrass (1987) 62-64.

29. Snodgrass (1987) 179-180.

30. On animal population fluctuations see Elton (1942), Lack (1954) esp. 204-226 whose views, emphasising stability of bird populations in Britain, differ from Elton's because he was *not* concentrating on populations in very highly seasonal environments, Andrewartha & Birch (1954) & (1984) who also emphasised fluctuations in seasonal environments, and the shorter surveys in Begon et al. (1986) esp. 350-358 & 559-571 and Colinvaux (1986) esp. 300-318. More detailed and specialised recent books of considerable interest on the subject are Finerty (1980) and Cockburn (1988).

31. Livy V.32-49 on the Gauls in 390; Pausanias I.3.5-4.6 & X.19.4-23.9 on the Celts in 280-279, also Memnon FGH434 F8.8 Jacoby stressing famine as the cause of their migration; Hippokrates *peri aërôn, hudatôn, topôn* XVIII ed. Littré vol. 2, pp. 68-69 on the Scythian custom of living in ox-drawn wheeled wagons, cf. Herodotos IV.46.3.

32. Colinvaux (1980), cf. Martinet (1986) 25-31 for the views of a philologist on the causes of the P-I-E migrations; Friedrich (1970) showed that P-I-E tree names

are characteristic of a temperate wooded area such as parts of eastern Europe and south Russia; Synesios of Cyrene *peri basileias* ed. Migne *Patrologiae cursus completus* vol. 66, cols. 1081-1082; Rendine et al. (1986) extended to the Indo-European migrations from south Russia the 'wave-of-advance' demographic model used by Ammermann & Cavalli-Sforza (1984) to explain the spread of Neolithic farmers into Greece and up through the Balkans into central Europe, following the favourable climatic conditions of the period when central Europe was about 2°C warmer than it is today, according to Huntley & Prentice (1988) – there are two major problems with the 'wave-of-advance' model: first, in the case of the Indo-Europeans, Rendine et al. did not consider the cyclical nature of human demography in Eurasia; secondly, in the case of Neolithic farming, the rate of advance of the wave may not be a factor of human demography at all, but may rather represent the rate of evolution of adaptation of crop plants to new environments, e.g. with summer rainfall in central Europe compared to summer droughts in lower latitudes in the Middle East – Kushnir & Halloran (1982) showed that in wild emmer decreases in yield owing to a reduction in spikelet number per plant occur when the plant's normal temperature and photoperiodic requirements are not satisfied, and this may well have been true of early domesticated emmer as well.

33. Khazanov (1984) 73 on nomad demography; Fretwell (1972) on animal populations in seasonal environments; Boyce (1984) and Colinvaux (1986) 243-265 on r- and K-selection; Kot & Schaffer (1984) on seasonality in relation to population cycles.

34. Testart (1982) is relevant here.

35. Aron & Anderson (1982) 17; Hippokrates *Epidemics* III Constitution III Case XV and *Epidemics* II section I.5 ed. Littré vol. 3, pp. 98-101 & vol. 5, pp. 74-75 respectively on seasonal variations in disease patterns, also the whole treatise *peri aërôn, hudatôn, topôn* ed. Littré vol. 2; Poinsot-Balaguer (1984) described how the Mediterranean climate creates seasonal population cycles among soil microfauna such as mites and collembola.

36. O. Rackham (1980) 257-266, Huntley & Birks (1983) 411-415 and Girling & Greig (1985) on elm disease.

37. Utida (1957) and Deevey (1958) on gradual damping down of oscillations in deterministic models of fluctuating populations; May (1981) showed that it is theoretically possible for a stable limit cycle to occur in a population without damping down of oscillations; May (1976) and Pool (1989b) on deterministic chaos, also Gleick (1988) 57-80 for a popular account.

38. Le Roy Ladurie (1981) 1-27; Polybios VI.51; Vries (1984) 122 cited Herodotos I.5.4 to contrast the classical world with early modern Europe in respect of urban stability; Hippokrates *peri diaitês* I.25 ed. Littré vol. 6, pp. 498-499.

39. Beloch (1886) 55-57 on the area of Attica; Corvisier (1980) 169 stated that some of Beloch's estimates of the areas of ancient *poleis* are inaccurate – Corvisier's stress on the need for modern scholars to use estimates of ancient population sizes instead of relying on the figures to be found in ancient sources is important; Jardé (1925) 142-144.

40. Bates & Lees (1979) and Dewar (1984) on K and Cc; Pianka (1988) 125-181; Colinvaux (1986) 134-149 & 172-191.

41. Alkman F12 ed. Calame; Pearl (1924) & (1925), Lotka (1939) 48-63, D. Leach (1981), Rose (1987) and Biswas (1988) 199-234 on the logistic equation; Aristotle *HA* 608b19-35.

42. Lampe & Jackson (1982) 168; Stoianovitch (1967) 165 regarded 20-30

people/km² as a saturation point in the Balkans.

43. Jackson (1985) on the nineteenth-century Greek population; H. Forbes (1985) 61 noted that the population of Methana in 1907 AD had reached a saturation point creating land shortage and emigration; Valaoras (1960).

44. Freris (1986) 21-23 on the currant vine; Ordish (1972) on Phylloxera, esp. 177-178 on Greece; Theophrastos *HP* III.17.6; Thiselton-Dyer (1918) 294-297; Weaver (1960).

45. Vandier (1936) on Egypt; Xenophon *Anabasis* III.2.26 for the option of emigration; Herodotos IV.151 on Thera and Cyrene, a colony founded because of a subsistence crisis brought on by drought, also Strabo VI.1.6.257c on Khalkis and Rhegion; Newsome (1969), Lidicker (1975), Tamarin (1977), Abramsky & Tracy (1979), Gaines et al. (1979) and Stickel (1979) on field mice; Berry (1981) on house mouse demography; Menander *Hêrôs* 27-32 ed. Sandbach, a rare example of starvation as a possible direct cause of death in Greek literature; Jutikkala & Kauppinen (1971) on the prevalence of death from disease even during famine, so there is nothing surprising about Jameson's (1983) 6 conclusion on the lack of effect of famine on mortality in antiquity, which does not rule out the importance of population pressure.

46. Valaoras et al. (1965) & (1969) on voluntary family limitation in modern Greece.

47. L. Gallo (1984b) esp. 67-69; Garnsey (1988) 89-106; Fussell (1976) 8-16.

48. Boserup (1965) & (1981), influencing Grigg (1980) & (1982).

49. Halstead (1981), (1984) & (1987); Sherratt (1981); Rowley-Conwy in Mercer (1981) 85-96 demolished the use of palynology made by Boserup (1981) 47; McGrath (1987) on tropical shifting cultivation.

50. Hesiod *WD* 405-410 & 453-454 on the need to possess oxen for ploughing; Pliny *NH* XIX.xix.51, also 57 on gardening as work suitable for women; Hesiod *WD* 405-406 mentions a woman, *gunê ktêtê* (see section 6 of this chapter), to assist the ploughman, but in 441-447 lays down stringent requirements for the ploughman himself; otherwise little is heard about women in agriculture in ancient Greece – (Demosthenes) LVII.45 mentions *trugêtriai*, women engaged in work in vineyards gathering in the grapes, clearly not regarded as a desirable state of affairs; Pollux *Onomasticon* VII.141 & 150 for seasonal wage-labour in harvesting by women; on food preparation Thucydides II.78.3 on the 110 *sitopoioi* who stayed with the 480 men garrisoning Plataia; Aristotle *Politics* 1300a4-7 & 1323a3-6; Isaios III.14 and Lysias III.6-7 on the seclusion of Athenian women, connected with the sexual division of labour.

51. Boserup's ideas on rising labour inputs may be applicable to a country like China, where steadily increasing labour inputs raise wet-rice yields – Rawski (1972) 11ff. & 32ff., also Cho-yun Hsu (1981); Boserup (1981) 43-62 on antiquity, 9 & 58 on the population densities associated with short-fallow farming – classical Greece falls into her density group 7; Kayser & Thompson (1964) 202 on modern Attica; Mols (1972) 38-39 estimated population densities AD 1500-1700 ranging from 30/mile² in Poland to 90-120/mile² in parts of Italy (1 mile² = 2.6 km²), cf. Braudel (1972) vol. 1, pp. 394-418.

52. Snodgrass (1977).

53. Thucydides I.2.2 (*oude gên phuteuontes*).

54. Patterson (1981) 40-81, M. Hansen (1985) 9-11 & (1988) 8-9, and I. Morris (1987) 23 & 57 reject the possibility of rapid population growth in the past on a priori grounds; contra Darwin (1968) 114-129, esp. 117, & (1901) 66-70; Colinvaux (1986) 302, reiterating Darwin, is a summary statement of the modern scientific position; McClelland & Zeckhauser (1982) 72 & 100 and Franklin (1751) on the USA; McKeown (1976) on medicine; Birdsell (1957) on the small islands, e.g. Tristan da Cunha; Rendine et al. (1986) suggested that the rate of population growth during the initial stages of the expansion of Neolithic farming across Europe was about 2.7 per cent per annum; Braudel (1972) vol. 1, pp. 402-403 argued that the population of the Mediterranean as a whole doubled in the century AD 1450-1550, when it was filling the gaps left by the ravages of plague, which facilitated rapid population growth all over Europe.

55. Crosby (1972) 113 on the Americas; Columella *RR* VI.24.4 observed that where there is a great abundance of food a calf may be reared from a cow every year, but where food is scarce only in alternate years, cf. Aristotle *HA* 575b31-33 noting that horses may start breeding earlier than the usual age if they have plenty of good pasture, also *HA* 573b20-22 and Theophrastos *CP* I.14.1 for sheep reproducing twice a year in favourable conditions; Graunt (1939) 70, one of the founders of mathematical demography in the seventeenth century, calculated that it was possible for the population of London to double in 64 years, but, writing before Darwin, he concluded that the fact that human populations were capable of increasing so rapidly proved that the world could not be any older than the Bible said it was (!), reckoned to be 4004 BC – the moral of this tale is that populations are capable of phases of rapid growth, but such phases are of short duration in practice, because the carrying capacity is always reached rapidly.

56. Snodgrass (1977); Whitehead (1986) 5-9; Whitley (1987) 96-104 on the internal colonisation of Attica; R. Finlay (1981) 3 & 8-10 on London, see also section 7 below; Darwin (1901) 213 knew that mortality is generally higher in towns than in rural areas; Matessi & Menozzi (1979); Scobie (1986) on Rome.

57. Finley (1985b) 63-64; *Letter of Aristeas to Philokrates* 108-111 ed. Pelletier; A.S. Hunt & C.G. Edgar (eds) *Select papyri* vol. 2 (1963) no. 215; Brunt (1971) 143-146 & 383-388 on Rome; Ammianus Marcellinus XXVII.4.14 contrasted the healthiness of the inhabitants of the mountainous regions of Thrace with the unhealthiness of the Romans; although a moralising passage not based on numerical data, it is still probably quite accurate.

58. Pulliam (1988) on population sinks; Coale (1972) 7 & 58, with Eaton & Mayer (1953) and T.E. Smith (1960); Keyfitz (1971a); according to statistics cited by Krzywicki (1934) 273 n. 2 the crude birth rate never dropped below 50/1,000 around Moscow in the period AD 1885-1904, reaching a peak of 56.2/1,000 in 1902, similarly Lorimer (1954) 31-32 cites data for Soviet Armenia showing that the population had a crude birth rate of about 55/1,000 and an average completed family size of 7.9 in 1926, averaging a rate of natural increase of 31/1,000 per annum in the period 1926-1939, a close parallel for our hypothesis about Late Geometric Attica; Schacht (1980) on a phase of rapid population growth in Mesopotamia during the Uruk period in the fourth millennium BC, at the birth of the world's first urban civilisation, cf. Adams (1981) for population fluctuations in Mesopotamia; D.E. Davis (1986) applied the logistic model to the period of growth in mediaeval Europe which ended before the Black Death (see section 7 of this chapter).

59. Thucydides I.2.6 on the 'Ionian migration', cf. Diodoros Siculus XV.49.1.

60. Herodotos IV.156.2 on the Cyrene expedition, consisting of two fifty-oared boats, & IV.144 on Khalkedon and Byzantion; Boardman (1980) on Greek colonisation; McNeill (1984) and K. Weiss (1988).

61. Myres (1915/16), criticised by Carr-Saunders (1922) 297-299, in turn rightly criticised by Caldwell (1987).

62. Plutarch *Solon* XIII.4-5.

63. (Aristotle) *Athênaiôn Politeia* XIII.4-5 & XVI.2-6 and Herodotos I.59.3 for

Peisistratos' activities, including his assistance to farmers; Plutarch *Solon* VIII-X on Salamis and Herodotos V.94 on Sigeion, VI.136-140 on Lemnos, VI.41.2 & 104 on Imbros relate the stories of the first Athenian ventures abroad, while Skyros was acquired shortly after the Persian Wars (Thucydides I.98.2), and the early history of Eleutherai and Oropos is obscure.

64. Herodotos V.97.2; Garnsey (1988) 107-119.

65. Patterson (1981) 69-71 put forward the mass enfranchisement theory; M. Osborne (1981-1983) and Prandi (1982) cite the evidence for block grants; D. Whitehead in *LCM* 9.1 (1984).

66. Brunt (1966); Ph. Gauthier (1973); 'Aristoteles decree' (IG II^2 43) ed. Cargill (1981) lines 35-46, cf. Thucydides I.143.4, (Xenophon) *Athênaiôn Politeia* I.19 and Diodoros Siculus XV.23.4; Thucydides II.58.3 & VI.26.2.

67. Xenophon *Memorabilia* II.8 on Eutheros; Finley (1981b) 41-61 on the economic benefits of empire; Garnsey (1988) 120-133, esp. 127; M. Hansen (1988) 7-13; Thucydides V.14.3 & VII.28.3; (Xenophon) *Athênaiôn Politeia* II.3-6 & 11-16.

68. Diodoros Siculus XII.58.2-4; Thucydides III.87.3 & II.14-16; Dionysios Hal. *Lysias* XXXII; Ober (1985) 27 argued that feeding the rural population of Attica for even a single year in the fourth century BC, if all the home production was lost, would have bankrupted the public treasury.

69. Aristotle F93 Rose, Diogenes Laertios II.26, Plutarch *Aristeides* XXVII, Pépin '*peri eugeneias* fr. 3' in Schuhl (1968) 116-133 and A. Harrison (1968) 16-17 on the decree; Aulus Gellius *NA* XV.20.6 claims that Euripides also had two wives under the same decree, cf. Athenaios 555d-556b; Sealey (1984); Hajnal (1965) 126 n. 1 noted the demographic interest of such measures; Plutarch *Moralia* 302e-f (cf. Diodoros Siculus XIX.60.3 for the context) for citizen women being obliged to have sexual relations with freedmen and metics at Khalkedon *c.* 315 BC as a result of *oliganthrôpia* after a military disaster; M. Hansen (1988) 14-20 and Strauss (1987) 70-86 & 179-182 on mortalities in the Peloponnesian War, cf. (Aristotle) *Athênaiôn Politeia* XXVI.1 on the *Pentêkontaëtia*; Aristarchos, left to take care of fourteen female relatives, is an exaggerated example of the unbalanced sex ratio (Xenophon *Memorabilia* II.7).

70. Aristotle *Politics* 1286b9-10 & 20-21, 1293a1-2, 1297b26-27 & 1305a18-19 on population growth, whose role in Aristotle's thought was examined by Contogiorgis (1978); Thucydides I.11.1 underestimated *oliganthrôpia* in early Greek history, as the migratory way of life of I.2.1 implies a very low population density; Demosthenes IX.40; Thucydides I.5.3-6.3 on the archaic Greek habit of always carrying arms, which the Athenians were among the first to abandon; Aristotle *Politics* 1320a17 noted that democracies tended to have larger populations than oligarchies, and that (1321a14-21) under such conditions the *aporoi*, even though poorly equipped, might overcome hoplites, cf. 1274a5-15 on the Athenian democracy as the product of chance; Carneiro (1967) & (1970) for the modern political thought in question; Brulé (1978) 145-150 & 170-184 on consequences of population growth in early Hellenistic Crete.

71. Aristotle *Politics* 1265a40-b1 (see also section 6 of this chapter).

72. M. Hansen (1985) 70-72; scholiast to Aiskhines I.53, Philochoros FGH328 F154 Jacoby, Strabo XIV.1.18.638c and Aristotle F611.35 Rose on Samos; Isokrates XV.112-113 and Tod *GHI* no. 146 on Potidaia; Isokrates op. cit. and Demosthenes VIII.6 & *hypothesis* 1 on the Thracian Chersonese; Diodoros Siculus XVI.34.3-4 on Sestos; Braccesi (1977) on the projected Athenian colony to somewhere in the Adriatic in the mid-320s BC, whose fate is unknown; Diodoros Siculus XVIII.18.4 on the colony in Thrace offered by Antipater to poor Athenians

deprived of citizenship after the Lamian War.

73. Parke (1933) collected the sources for Greek mercenaries, especially Demosthenes XIV.31 for the Persia-Egypt conflicts, Arrian I.29.5 & III.6.2 and Q. Curtius Rufus III.1.9 for Athenians fighting for Persia against Macedon; Aiskhines II.147 attributed the departure of one Athenian to poverty and the desire to escape from the Thirty at Athens; scepticism is in order as regards Xenophon's indignant denial that the Ten Thousand had been driven to mercenary service by poverty – *Anabasis* VI.4.8, contra Isokrates IV (*Panegyr.*) 146; Brulé (1978) 163ff. argued for the *permanent* emigration of mercenaries from Hellenistic Crete; Langer (1972) on the Swiss; Meiggs & Lewis *GHI* no. 7 for Greek mercenaries in the archaic period; Plutarch *Timoleon* XXIII.6 and Diodoros Siculus XVI.82.5, who underestimated the number of colonists who responded to Timoleon's call, according to Talbert (1974) 146-160, using archaeological evidence (see also Chapter I n. 19 above).

74. On the Seleucid colonies see Appian *Syr.* 57 and Plutarch *Moralia* 328e, with G. Cohen (1978); Diodoros Siculus XX.40.6-7 & XX.41.1 on Ophellas, whose assault on Carthage was interpreted by Applebaum (1979) 82 & 99-109 as a response to land shortage in Cyrene, of interest because Cyrenaica had a great reputation for fertility in antiquity (Chapter III.12); another group of Athenians emigrated to Antigoneia, the short-lived capital of Antigonos I Monophthalmos, and were transferred to the new towns of Seleucia Pieria and Antioch set up by Seleukos I in 300 BC after the battle of Ipsos (Diodoros Siculus XX.47.5-6, Pausanias (not the *periêgêtês*) F4 ed. Müller *FGH* vol. IV, p. 469 and Downey (1961) 76-81); M.N. Tod in *JHS* 63 (1943) 112-113 for an Athenian on Failaka; L. Robert (1969) 328ff. on Laodicea on the Lykos, where a tribal name Athenais indicates Athenian colonists *c.* 260 BC.

75. Deevey (1958); May (1981); Keyfitz (1971b).

76. Valverde et al. (1977) on malnutrition and size of landholding; Mosley (1979) 95-97 and Bongaarts & Potter (1983) 14 for moderate chronic malnutrition as having a minor effect on fertility, by delaying menarche and perhaps also by earlier onset of menopause; Pearl (1925) 131-157, W.M.S. & C. Russell (1968) and Galle & Gove (1978) reviewed the possibility of stress syndromes affecting reproduction in relation to man.

77. Aristotle *Meteôrologika* 351b13-22; Dikaiarkhos *peri anthrôpôn phthoras* F24 ed. Wehrli; a fragment of the lost epic poem, the *Cypria* F1 ed. Allen, puts forward the idea that Zeus initiated the legendary expedition against Thebes and the Trojan War in order to relieve the burden of mankind on the earth; Aristotle *Politics* 1321b14-18 regarded self-sufficiency as the aim of existing *poleis*.

78. Butzer (1976) 83 on Egyptian population densities; Préaux (1939) 387 on Hellenistic Egypt as densely populated; classical Greece should also be compared to prehistoric Greece, for which C. Renfrew (1972a) 394 estimated population densities ranging from 4.3 to $31.3/km^2$, with only Messenia (63.3) – a region with a much larger proportion of cultivatable land than Attica – being above that range; Carothers & McDonald (1979) criticised his method of working; D.J. Crawford (1973a), (1973b) & (1979) on Greek agriculture in Egypt.

79. Pope & van Andel (1984); Runnels & van Andel (1987); van Andel & Runnels (1987); H. Forbes (1985) 187; Aristotle *Politics* 1306b11-16.

80. Isokrates XIX (*Aiginêtikos*) 22; Theophrastos *HP* IX.18.11 ed. Wimmer (not included in the Hort edition), repeated by Pliny *NH* XIV.xxii.117 and Athenaios I.31f.; Aristotle F596 Rose names varieties of vine at Troizen, suggesting that the ultimate source for all this information on Troizen was his *Constitution of the Troizenians*; Riddle (1985) 58-64 concluded that contraceptive drugs in antiquity

may have had a limited effect, cf. R. Weiss (1988) 317-321 and Ripley (1980) 356-357; Aristotle *Politics* 1335a15-22, cf. *HA* 582a20-21; L. Henry in Leridon & Menken (1979) 26, Leridon (1984) 95, McFalls (1984) 45, and Tabutin (1981) 110 for reduced fertility, and Darwin (1901) 213 for higher mortality, among women marrying before the age of seventeen; difficult labour in Troizen complemented the other explanation for low fertility in the context of early marriage, floated by Leridon, namely that very early marriage may lead to a lowering of the frequency of coitus, reducing the chances of conception, while the woman is still in her reproductive years, since coital frequency is inversely proportional to length of marriage; Edelstein (1945) vol. 2, pp. 158-159 & n. 3 on the unhealthy locations of *Asklêpieia*, cf. Plutarch *Moralia* 286d, who thought they were put in high and clean places, and Vitruvius *De architectura* I.2.7; Edelstein (1945) vol. 1, T423 II.34 records a woman of Troizen who visited Epidauros to seek help for infertility, and II.33 a man from Halieis who had tuberculosis.

81. Columella *RR* I.1.1-7; Littlejohn (1946); Loizides (1958); Halstead (1987); Wrigley (1987) 116 speculates on ways in which a falling population might be associated with falling net agricultural productivity, preventing a subsequent recovery.

82. Strabo VIII.8.1.388c on Arkadia, cf. VIII.4.11.362c on Lakonia; S. & H. Hodkinson (1981) 271-279 on Mantinea; Bintliff & Snodgrass (1988) on urban surveys; Symeonoglu (1985) 203-208 & Pausanias IX.7.6 on Thebes; as signs of population pressure in Boiotia in the fourth century BC, the site of Thebes was ploughed and sown by the other Boiotians after its destruction by Alexander in 335 BC (Deinarchos I (*Ag. Demosthenes*) 24), also note the attempt (unsuccessful because of *stasis* among the Boiotians) by Alexander's engineer Krates to drain Lake Kopais (Strabo IX.2.18.407c); Athanasiadis (1975) on Thessaly; J. Salmon (1984) 131 on the scale of classical Corinthian grain imports, is also of interest; Plutarch *Moralia* 413f-414a on Megara.

83. Pausanias I.4.4 & VII.7.1; Thucydides I.5.1-2 on piracy; Bommeljé & Doorn (1987) for the Dutch Aitolia survey; Briant (1982b) 271 on the monarchs' policy.

84. Setton (1975a) 228 & 243-244 and J. Russell (1960) on mediaeval and early modern Athens; Patlagean (1977) 307 on the Balkans in late antiquity, also Finley (1977) 146-153; Boyden (1987) 104.

85. M. Hansen (1985) 11-12 and R. Osborne (1985) 43-45 & 196 adopted life tables on a priori grounds; Lenski & Service (1982) on the calculation of rates of increase from survivorship and fertility data.

86. (Demosthenes) XLIII.57-58; Aelian *Poikilê historia* V.14 ed. Dilts; Pausanias I.32.5; Whitehead (1986) 137; Diodoros Siculus XIII.100-101 and Xenophon *Hellênika* I.7.4-35.

87. See all articles by Angel in the bibliography, esp. (1969a) 429 estimating the average age of death for adults (those who reached age 15) as 44 for men and 36 for women in the period c. 650-350 BC (42.5 and 36 respectively in the following period, c. 350-200 BC) — he revised these figures slightly in (1984) 55-56, but only the earlier article provides the age-specific mortality essential for life table construction; Grmek (1983) 151-159 reviewed Angel's research; K. Weiss (1973) chs. 3 & 7 for life table construction; Vallois (1960) is derived from Angel; Bisel (1980) 42 gave the average age at death of adults in classical Akanthos as 39.6 for males (N = 43) and 38.3 for females (N = 30) but provided no age-specific mortality data; the skeletal remains from Dark Age Lefkandi studied by Musgrave (1980) were too poorly preserved to be useful for demographic purposes; McGeorge (1988) gave average age of death of 31-35 for men and 28 for women in Minoan Crete; Hombert & Préaux (1945) calculated an average age of death of 34 for men and 29

for women in Egypt relying on documentary evidence; Angel's breakdown of female mortality by age for the period *c*. 650-350 BC is as follows:

0–1	1–4	5–9	10–14	15–19	20–24	25–29	30–34	35–39	40–44
17	6	4	1	3	6	2	5	8	2

45–49	50–54	55–59	60–64	65+
3	4	0	1	0

88. Reyment (1971) on quantitative palaeoecology; for the period 650-350 BC Angel's skeletons yielded a sex ratio of 129 for adults and 135 for children; K. Weiss (1973) 58 expressed suspicion of such high sex ratios; contrast K. Weiss (1972) and Meindl et al. (1983) & (1985) on the question of sexing skeletons; Aristotle *GA* 745a16-17 on bones' wasting away with old age, and *PA* 655a12-13 asserting that the bones of males are harder than those of females; Acsádi & Nemeskéri (1970) 73-137 and Zimmermann & Angel (1986) 179-220 on determination of age and sex of skeletons; osteoporosis is usually a post-menopausal problem for women in developed countries today, but pre-menopausal osteoporosis occurs among female athletes on special diets, and may have been commoner in historical populations – Zimmermann & Angel (1986) 217.

89. K. Weiss (1973) 47; Acsádi & Nemeskéri (1970) 190 criticised Angel's methods; Whitley (1987) 111-118.

90. The most important sets of life tables are Coale & Demeny (1983) and *United Nations Population Studies* 22 (1955) & 77 (1982), using data from modern populations; Acsádi & Nemeskéri (1970) and K. Weiss (1973) rely on palaeo-demography; Howell (1979) 77-79 & (1986) 225 criticised Weiss; Bocquet-Appel & Mosset (1982) and Mosset & Parzysz (1985) expressed scepticism about palaeo-demography, contra van Gerven & Armelagos (1983) and Buikstra & Konigsberg (1985); Weiss (1973) 44 and Howell (1979) 77-78 compared different sets of life tables; Grmek (1983) 162, using the (1955) UN tables, independently obtained a value for life expectancy at birth from the ephebe-arbitrator ratio in Athens similar to that obtained by me from the Weiss tables.

91. From the table of the distribution of chi-square values in Reyment (1971) 194-195 80 per cent = 6.179, 90 per cent = 4.865, 95 per cent = 3.940, 98 per cent = 3.059, 99 per cent = 2.558; Frier (1983), performing a similar exercise on skeletons from Roman Pannonia, obtained a chi-square value significant at the 68 per cent level.

92. Wrigley & Schofield (1981) 235-236 (e^0 range of 32-41); Etienne (1988) 94-99 on Ausonius; Biraben (1988) discussed the arguments of Cl. Mosset that age at death has generally been underestimated by physical anthropologists.

93. Livi-Bacci (1977) 293 on Italy; K. Weiss (1975b) on effects of a sudden increase in fertility; Coale (1957) & (1972) 40.

94. Angel (1984) 55 on estimates of fertility from pelvic remains, also Ullrich (1975) and Zimmermann & Angel (1986) 213, criticised by Herrmann & Bergfelder (1978) and Suchey et al. (1979); for the misguided older approach emphasising changes in mortality see Acsádi & Nemeskéri (1970) 188; for the more satisfactory newer approach see Sattenspiel & Harpending (1983), esp. 494-495 on Angel, and Johannson & Horowitz (1986), cf. Carrier (1958); Angel (1984) on the Neolithic, and other papers in the same volume; Lee (1972) & (1980) on the demographic consequences of sedentarisation.

95. Schneider & Reed (1985) for modern research, unfruitful so far, on the possibility of extending the maximum lifespan; the osteological evidence from

Pompeii indicates that there were quite a lot of elderly people there at the time of the eruption of Vesuvius in AD 79 (E. Lazer – Cambridge seminar paper), although it is possible that the sample is biased because it was old people who found it most difficult to attempt to flee before the impending catastrophe; Solon F27 ed. West, Aristotle *Politics* 1335a34-35 and Herodotos I.32.2 for a seventy-year lifespan, although in III.22.4 he thought in terms of eighty years; Laslett (1983) 110 (expressed more clearly in the (1971) edition of his book on p. 103) on Tudor England; Bible Psalms 90:10; Aristotle *Politics* 1334b39-1335a1 on support from children; Aristotle *peri makrobiotêtos kai brachubiotêtos* 466a13-14 and *GA* 777b3-4 bracketed man with the elephant as the longest-lived animals, although he realised that the greatest longevity is found among trees in the plant kingdom (467a6-8); Ulpian's 'life table', discussed by Dupâquier (1973) and Frier (1982), is not considered here because it falls outside the main geographical and chronological limits of this book.

96. Jerphagon (1981); Boyaval (1977a), Frier (1983) and J.C. Russell (1985) on Roman funerary inscriptions; Grmek (1983) 159-162 dealt admirably with the scanty Greek evidence on this topic, on which Valaoras (1938) had relied; Pliny *NH* VII.xlix.164, cf. Diodoros Siculus I.26.4; Phlegon of Tralles FGH257 F37 Jacoby lists Italians who reached the age of 100; Preston (1982) 229-231 on Georgia; Isaios VI.18 and Aiskhines II.147 & III.191; Humphreys (1983) 107 for epigraphic evidence for maximum longevity in Athens.

97. Snodgrass (1983a) on infant & juvenile mortality at Lefkandi; D. Robinson (1942) 166 reported that about 30 per cent of burials at Olynthos in the fourth century BC were of infants and small children, the kind of proportion to be expected in relation to the levels of life expectancy at birth suggested here; Breitinger (1939) and subsequent accounts by Kübler in the series of excavation reports on the Kerameikos cemetery in Athens; Myres (1915/16) 37 on Gela in Sicily; Aristotle *HA* 588a8-10 (referring to Assos, perhaps, where the *HA* may have been written?), Hesykhios s.v. *hebdomai* and Harpokration s.v. *hebdomeuomenou*, cf. Howell (1979) 120 on the Dobe !Kung for an analogy; Isaios III.30, Demosthenes XXXIX.22 and XL.28 & 59, and Aristophanes *Ornithes* 494 & 922 on the *dekatê*; Boulanger & Tabutin (1980); Preston (1978) and Coale & Watkins (1986) on mortality and the demographic transition.

98. Pliny *NH* VII.l.170; Xenophon *Oikonomikos* IX.5 and (Aristotle) *Oikonomika* I.1344b17-18 ed. Victor on slave breeding in Greece; Demosthenes XXI.48 on slaves as *barbaroi*; (Xenophon) *Athênaiôn Politeia* I.10-12.

99. The position of Ste. Croix (1981) 229-237 is preferable to that of Finley (1980) 130 & (1981) 103-104 regarding the demography of ancient slavery; some ancient authors, e.g. Varro *RR* II.1.26 & II.10.6, cf. I.17.5, even looked forward to an increase in the numbers of slave shepherds and herdsmen through natural breeding, but such environments were healthier than cities in any case; Fogel & Engerman (1974) on the USA, with Laslett (1977) 233-260; Kiple (1984) 104-119 on the demography of slaves in the West Indies, who did not reproduce themselves.

100. A.H.M. Jones (1957) 82-83; Gomme (1933) 10; (Aristotle) *Athênaiôn Politeia* XLII & LIII; Aiskhines I.49 & II.167 for the antecedents to the *ephêbeia*.

101. Demosthenes IV.21, in consideration of which we may set aside the introduction of peltasts into the debate by M. Hansen (1985) 48-49 & 100 n. 1, as there is no evidence that classical Athens ever had a regular force of *citizen* peltasts distinct from the ten tribal hoplite regiments (cf. Thucydides IV.94.1), and (Aristotle) *Athênaiôn Politeia* XLII.3 does not bear the weight which Hansen put on it; L. Gallo (1980a) suggested an average of 460 ephebes per annum, while Reinmuth (1971) suggested 480; Pélékides (1962) 283-294 suggested 600-700; M.

Hansen (1985) 47-50 & (1988) 3-6; Rhodes (1980); the ephebic catalogues of the Boiotian Confederacy in the third century BC, which also indicate groups of about 500 ephebes, may be connected with other sources for Boiotian armies of 10,000 and larger – Feyel (1942) 208; Ruschenbusch (1979) & (1981).

102. (Aristotle) *Athênaiôn Politeia* XLII.1 and Lykourgos *Ag. Leokrates* 76 suggest that all citizens were eligible for ephebic service, while Aristotle F454 Rose suggests that all surviving citizens became arbitrators; Ste. Croix cited by Rhodes (1981) 143 & 145. As regards the Solonian classes, the gap between top and bottom is far too narrow (a ratio of 2.5:1). Compare the 42:1 ratio between the 14 talent wealth of Demosthenes' father as estimated by the orator and the 2000 *drachmai* property qualification for citizenship imposed after the Lamian War. Secondly, the supposed upper limit for the thetic class of 199 *medimnoi* of agricultural produce (enough to keep a man alive for up to *forty* years) seems far too high for people depicted in our sources as extremely poor, happy to row triremes for a few obols a day to make ends meet. A Spartiate and his wife were supposed to live as rentiers from 82 Spartan-Aiginetan (123 Attic) *medimnoi* – a long way within the bounds of possibility even if it only represents third-century propaganda (Cartledge (1979) 170-171). There was once a qualification for citizenship of 45 *medimnoi* in the oligarchy of Orchomenos in Boiotia, a reasonable level of production for a middling peasant, providing a small surplus beyond the consumption requirements of an ordinary family (Aristotle F566 Rose).

103. IG II^2 1926 and the fragments joined by D. Lewis (1955); Ruschenbusch (1982) & (1984a).

104. Patlagean (1977) 97-99; Talbot (1984) on Byzantium, reporting that P. Burns has calculated a mean age of death of 34.8 years from skeletal data for Corinth *c.* AD 1050-1300 (N = 184); Panayotopoulos in Piault (1985) 29-44 on early modern Greece; Dupâquier et al. (1988); Wrigley & Schofield (1981).

105. Leridon (1977) 147 for the estimates of possible family size.

106. Cartledge (1975), (1976) and personal communication on Spartan tomb archaeology, with Plutarch *Lykourgos* XXVII.1-3 ed. Ziegler, reading *lechous apothanontôn* after IG V.1.713-714; Aristotle F611.13 Rose said that Spartan tombs were cheap and all the same; Herodotos VI.58-59 and Cartledge (1987) 331-343 on the kings; I. Morris (1987) 50 & 154 on Sparta; his division of the age structure of skeletal populations at age 10 is not helpful, as physical anthropologists place adulthood at a later age (e.g. Angel at 15), while demographers prefer a division at age 5 if only a single division is permitted, as attempts have been made to estimate life expectancy at birth from mortality in the 0-5 age group.

107. Thucydides I.10.1-2.

108. Henry (1976) 143 on modal age at death; Carr (1971) 76 on the sex ratio of spontaneous abortions, many of which are caused by chromosomal abnormalities; Aristotle *GA* 770a33-35 reckoned that deformed infants are produced less frequently in humans than in other animals, because the offspring is perfected by the time of birth, but ignored the frequent spontaneous abortions early in pregnancy which may leave little trace, cf. Hippokrates *aphorismoi* V.45 ed. Littré vol. 4, pp. 548-549, and Wilcox et al. (1988) on the 31 per cent rate of pregnancy loss after implantation; Aristotle *GA* 775a4-12 expressed the opinion that more males are born deformed than females in humans, which is linked nowadays with deleterious genes carried on the X chromosome of which males only have one, but females two, providing cover; Boué et al. (1985).

109. Tabutin (1978), Preston (1982) 28 and Heligman (1983) on sex-differential life expectancy, also Agyei (1988) 77 on the situation in Papua New Guinea; Rosenberg (1980) on sex-differential nutrition; Aristotle *HA* 608b7-15, on the differences between male and female in humans, said that females need less food, cf. Xenophon *Lakedaimoniôn Politeia* I.3 on Sparta and *Oikonomikos* VII. 6; at Persepolis in Persia mothers of boys received double the extra rations given to the mothers of girls (Hallock (1969) 37-38 & 344-353); Simoons (1961); Finkel (1982) on sexual dimorphism in Angel's skeletal populations from Athens.

110. For maternal mortality in pregnancy or soon after delivery in the Hippokratic corpus see *Epidemics* I 2nd Constitution Cases IV, V (a case of recovery from puerperal fever) & XI ed. Littré vol. 2, pp. 691-699 & 708-711, *Epidemics* III Cases X, XI & XII ed. Littré vol. 3, pp. 60-67 (the latter a case of a seventeen-year-old woman dying after a painful delivery of a first male child, fitting into the pattern discussed in section 2 above in relation to Troizen), *Epidemics* III Constitution III chs. XV & XVII.14 ed. Littré vol. 3, pp. 108-113 & 140-143 (death following birth of twins in the latter case), *Epidemics* VII.41 ed. Littré vol. 5, pp. 408-409; *Gunaikeiôn* I.33 ed. Littré vol. 8, pp. 78-79 on maternal mortality in the case of the foetus not presenting itself head first; Aristotle *GA* 775a32-37 on hard work; Euripides *Iphigeneia in Tauris* 1464-1467 on Brauron; Plutarch *Lykourgos* XXVII on Sparta; Howell (1979) 58 on the Bushmen; Schofield (1986) and Loudon (1986) on early modern England; Högberg et al. (1987) on excess female mortality in the reproductive age groups in mediaeval Sweden, detected via life table analysis but not directly by means of osteological studies; Scholten (1985) 22 for low rates of maternal mortality in the early modern USA; Wells (1975b) argued for insignificance of maternal mortality in prehistoric populations, cf. Acsádi & Nemeskéri (1970) 182-186; Preuss (1978) 427-428 on frequency of maternal mortality in the Jewish Talmud.

111. Eaton & Mayer (1953) 217; T.E. Smith (1960) 124; Weinberg (1984) for the medical research; Procopius *huper tôn polemôn* II.23.35, with Biraben (1975) vol. 2, p. 29; note also Dionysios Hal. *AR* IV.69.2 & IX.40.2, cf. Orosius IV.2; Hippokrates *Aphorismoi* V.30 ed. Littré vol. 4, pp. 542-543.

112. Aristotle *HA* 582a21-24 & 583b26-28, *GA* 775a13-16 and *peri makrobiotêtos kai brachubiotêtos* 466b15-16 & 467a31-32 on higher mortality of women, cf. Soranos *Gunaikologia* I.42.5 ed. Ilberg; Thiersch (1833) vol. 1, pp. 289-290 and Wrightson & Levine (1979) 58-59 on early modern Greece and England; Horowitz (1976) and Morsink (1979) for the debate; Aristotle *GA* 727a18 on the female as an infertile male, cf. *PA* 648a12; Byl (1980) 210-222 & 335-337 on Aristotle's bias against the female sex, cf. Lloyd (1983) 94-105.

113. Hippokrates *Aphorismoi* V.55 ed. Littré vol. 4, pp. 552-553, *Epidemics* I 2nd Constitution VIII, ed. Littré vol. 2, pp. 648-649, *Epidemics* VII.41 ed. Littré vol. 5, pp. 408-409, and *Gunaikeiôn* I.25 ed. Littré vol. 8, pp. 65-69, cf. *Epidemics* V.53 ed. Littré vol. 5, pp. 238-239, for abortion / miscarriage / painful delivery following illness during pregnancy.

114. Aristotle *Politics* 1260b18-19 & 1269b14-19 and *Rhetoric* 1361a9-11; Plato *Laws* 806c; Pausanias VII.21.14; the human remains from Pompeii reveal a roughly equal sex ratio in 79 AD (E. Lazer – Cambridge seminar paper); Holden (1987); R.A. Fisher (1958) 146-160; Darwin (1901) 331-334 & 374-379 on the sex ratio; R.F. Shaw (1961); W.H. James (1987) on determinants of the sex ratio at conception in *Homo sapiens*.

115. Pearl (1939) 28 & 36 on the two American ladies, also cites another woman alleged to have had 43 children, but this particular case does not seem to be well-documented; Klapisch-Zuber (1983) 36 n. 10 claims that a woman in Florence in the fifteenth century AD had 36 children – again it is not clear if this is

reliable; Pliny *NH* VII.iii.34; *Greek Anthology* ed. Stadtmüller VII.743, by Antipater of Sidon, for Hermokrateia, and VII.224, by an unknown author, for Kallikrateia; Eaton & Mayer (1953) and Lang & Göhlen (1985) on Hutterite family size; Darwin (1901) 66.

116. L. Henry (1961) & (1976); Leridon (1977); Bongaarts & Potter (1983) 21-51; *Pap. Oxy.* 744, lines 9-10, with Apuleius *Asinus Aureus* X.23 as the fictional text; Eyben (1980/1) exemplifies the approach criticised in the text; Germain (1969) & (1975) on tragedy; Laslett (1983) 81-90 on Shakespeare.

117. Banks (1954) on England; van de Walle (1980) on France; Livi-Bacci (1977) on Italy; Colinvaux (1982) 396; Aristotle *Politics* 1290b14-17, cf. 1280a1-2, considered the possibility that rich citizens could outnumber poor citizens, as at Kolophon.

118. Isaios II.3, V.5, VI.10, VIII.40, XI.37; Lysias XVI.10; (Demosthenes) XL.6-7, XLIII.74, XLIV.9, LVII.37, also XLIII with Isaios XI on the family of Bouselos, who had five sons; in Demosthenes LVII.28 the speaker claimed to have had four brothers who died as *paides*, although this may not be reliable.

119. Engels (1984); Aristotle *Politics* 1335b19-26 acknowledged hostility to infanticide, and *Rhetoric* 1360b20 & 1361a4-5 on *poluteknia*, with G.E.R. Lloyd (personal communication); Raepsaet (1971a) & (1971b).

120. Howell (1979) on the Dobe !Kung, the best documented 'primitive' society in the world today, as far as demography is concerned; Wood, Johnson & Campbell (1985) on the Gainj; Scholten (1985) 9-10 on the USA; Livi-Bacci (1977) 16 recorded average completed family size of between five and six in Italy in the last century, typical of many European countries; Corvisier (1985) 161-166; Theophrastos *HP* IX.18.10-11 ed. Wimmer.

121. Lysias I.9-10, cf. Agyei (1984) and (1988) 44-46 & 49 on Papua New Guinea; K. Bradley (1980) 322 n. 5 lists the evidence for duration of wet-nursing contracts in Roman Egypt, which varied from six months to three years, but was most commonly two years; Fildes (1986) 17-25; Khrysippos F733 ed. von Arnim vol. 3 spoke of having a nurse for three years; Hippokrates *Epidemics* IV.24 & V.11 ed. Littré vol. 5, pp. 164-165 & 210-211 mentions two women, one of whom had amenorrhoea for two years after giving birth, while the other became pregnant after four years of amenorrhoea; Maccabees II, ch. VII.27 for breastfeeding for three years in the Bible, although two years was more normal in Talmudic times, according to Preuss (1978) 404-410; Galen *hugieinôn logos* I.9 ed. Kühn vol. VI, pp. 45-46 recommended breastfeeding to the third year and abstention from intercourse during lactation; Oribasios *pros Eustathion* V.5.3 recommended breastfeeding for two years; Aristotle *GA* 776b28-34, 777a13-14 & *HA* 587b30-31, cf. 582b13-14, on human lactation, and 522b2-523a12 on mammals; Diamond (1987) for recent research confirming Aristotle's theory that teat number is correlated with average litter size in all mammals, including man cf. Plutarch *Moralia* 3d; Hippokrates *Gunaikeiôn* I.73 ed. Littré vol. 8, pp. 152-155 tried to explain the absence of menstruation during lactation by the 'nourishment's' being taken to the breasts, instead of to the vagina.

122. Soranos *Gunaikologia* II.25.2, 28.4, 38, 39.1 & 43-44; Aulus Gellius *NA* XII.1.1-24 for moralising advice to upper-class women; Demosthenes LVII.35; V. Robinson (1938); Fildes (1988) 1-25; Plutarch *Lykourgos* XVI.2-3 on Sparta, with Ullman (1975) 183-184; Wilkes (1953) on animal milk, cf. J. Preuss (1978) 409; Galen *peri trophôn dunameôn* III.15 ed. Kühn vol. VI, p. 686 describes the problems of women, who depended on breast milk, struggling to feed their infants during a famine; Hippokrates *Epidemics* III Constitution III case XVII.14 ed. Littré vol. 3, pp. 140-143 describes the case of a man who became ill after drinking a lot of milk, a foolish act if by chance he was deficient in the ability to make lactase; Plato *Laws* 789e-790a on infant care, also mentioning rickets – Grmek (1983) 118-120 did not consider Plato and denied the existence of rickets in classical Greece because of its absence in skeletal remains – this is a question again of the skeletal populations being too small.

123. Hippokrates *peri diaitês hygieinês* VI ed. Littré vol. 6, pp. 80-81 on dilute wine and children, also Ullman (1975) 181 for Rufus, *contra* Aristotle *Politics* 1336a8 and the Hellenistic (Pythagorean) *Letter of Muia to Phyllis* ed. Hercher *Epistologr. Graeci* p. 608; S. Hodkinson (personal communication) for information on breastfeeding, also Masnick (1979), Harrell (1981), Short (1984) and Raphael (1984); Stini (1982) 404-406 on provision of immunological protection to infants by breast milk, cf. Gillen et al. (1983) showing that human milk kills the protozoa of amoebic dysentery (*Entamoeba histolytica*); Hippokrates *peri gunaikeiês phusios* XXIII, LIX, CVI & CIX ed. Littré vol. 7, pp. 342-343, 398-399 & 420-423 on ways of inducing the return of the menstrual cycle and making an infertile woman have children, also the whole treatise *peri aphorôn* ed. Littré vol. 8, pp. 408-463.

124. Agyei (1988) 99 on New Guinea; Isaios VII.30 on *oikoi erêmoi* and funerary rites.

125. Of importance here is Lysias XXIV by an invalid, esp. ch. 6, claiming support from the *polis* on the grounds (it does not matter whether or not he was telling the truth, and the speech is still of value as evidence for popular mentality even if it is a rhetorical exercise as has been suggested) that he had been supporting his own mother until her own death two years previously, and had no children to support himself now that he was unable to work; Hesiod *WD* 187-189 & 331-332, Isaios II.10-12, Lysias XIII.45, Demosthenes XXIV.107, Deinarchos II (*Ag. Aristogeiton*) 8-11, Aiskhines I.13 & 28, Xenophon *Memorabilia* II.2.13 and *Oikonomikos* VII.12 & 19, (Aristotle) *Oikonomikos* I.1343b20-23 ed. Victor, Alexis F304 ed. Kock and *Greek Anthology* VII.647 ed. Stadtmüller on children's duty to support their parents; Andokides I (*peri tôn mustêriôn*) 74 on Aigospotamoi; Aristotle *NE* 1149b6-13 records the case of a man who defended himself in court against the accusation that he had maltreated his father on the grounds that it ran in the family (!); Lerat (1943) for an Early Hellenistic law from Delphi that prescribed imprisonment for anyone who did not feed his father or mother; Cain (1982) on the Third World; Laslett (1977) 176-177, an interesting contrast, suggests that the obligations of children to their parents were not taken as seriously in early modern England as they were in Greece. Herodotus II.35.4 contrasts Greece with Egypt, where daughters had to support their parents by law; Plato *Menexenos* 248d suggests that parents of sons who died in war were supported at public expense in Athens, the only group of citizens to benefit in that way.

126. Stoianovitch (1976) and the papers in Laslett & Wall (1972) 335-427 on northern Balkan family structures.

127. Hesiod *WD* 376-380. West (1978) ad loc. interpreted the *heteron paida* of Hesiod as a *grandson* rather than a second son, in which case Hesiod recommends that one should survive to old age, presumably in order to receive recompense from the grandson. However, the second couplet refers to additional sons, and makes perfect sense in the context of Chayanov's theory of the peasant economy. See Aristotle *Politics* 1265b6-12, 1266b8-14 & 1270b4-6 on the fourth-century situation, and Thiersch (1833) vol. 1, p. 303 on Greece in the last century: 'Les domestiques n'entraînent ici à aucune dépense; c'est la coutume que chaque famille, avec ses enfans, prenne soin elle-même de ses affaires, dont l'étendue et le

gain augmentent en raison du nombre des enfans.'

128. Cochrane (1975) on economic models of children as investment goods, cf. Carr-Saunders (1922) 289-290, 308 & 319 on high fertility as economically advantageous for labourers in Britain before the Factory Acts, also as providing support in old age; Pliny *NH* XIII.xlvii.132 said that *kutisos*, tree-medick (see Chapter III.12), could be cut very cheaply even by boys or old women – the fact that he thought this worthy of mention suggests that the use of such labour in agricultural operations was unusual.

129. Diodoros Siculus I.80.6, Plutarch *Moralia* 143b; Heer & Smith (1968); Thucydides II.44.3; Daube (1977).

130. On puberty see Aristotle *GA* 727a5-8, 728b22-25 & 30-32, *HA* 544b25-27, 581a12-14 & 31-b1; Soranos *Gunaikologia* I.24.2; Amundsen & Diers (1969); Eyben (1972); Johnston (1974) for a summary of factors that control age of menarche; Aristotle *Physics* 230b1-2; Zimmermann & Angel (1986) 182 & 188 accepted the testimony of classical literary sources for puberty at ages 13-14 and neglected the possibility of class-specific differences in developmental rates, which may have consequences for their scheme for inferring chronological age from the biological age of bones; Hippokrates *peri aërôn, hudatôn, topôn* IV ed. Littré vol. 2, pp. 22-23 reckoned that unfavourable environmental conditions caused a late onset of puberty in certain regions; Solon F27 ed. West divided the human lifespan into ten periods each of seven years, cf. Hippokrates *peri hebdomadôn* V ed. Littré vol. 8, pp. 636-637 with Mansfeld (1970) – Aristotle *Metaphysics* 1093a1-20 criticised overenthusiasm for the number seven, cf. *Politics* 1335b32-34 & 1336b37-42; Howell (1979) 178 on late menarche among the Dobe !Kung; Laslett (1977) 214-232 on the fall in the average age of menarche in Europe since the Industrial Revolution, cf. Tanner (1981) 1-12; Durling (1986) on slaves; Thiersch (1833) vol. 1, p. 289 on early modern Greece.

131. Aristotle *HA* 545b26-31 & 585b2-8 and *Politics* 1335a6-10, Marx (1988) and Amundsen & Diers (1970) on menopause; Nag (1968) 107-113, Gray (1979) 221-227 and Aristotle *HA* 544b13-19, 582a16-17 & 585a34-b1 on adolescent sterility; Hippokrates *Epidemics* V.25 ed. Littré vol. 5, pp. 224-225 was surprised at an ill *amphipolos*, slave girl, who had been having sexual relations with her master but had not yet become pregnant at the age of sixteen.

132. Xenophon *Memorabilia* II.2.4; Malthus (1970).

133. Aristotle *Politics* 1272a23-26 – unfortunately he did not fulfil his promise to give the problem further consideration, at least in the surviving corpus; Brulé (1978) for population growth on Crete in that period; the Gortyn law code IV.10ff. eds. Solmsen & Fraenkel did permit child exposure, but in certain special circumstances, in the fifth century BC.

134. Lucretius *de rerum natura* IV.1264-1267; Dover (1978) 100-101; Aristotle *HA* 634b35-38; Artemidoros *Oneirocriticon* I.79 ed. Pack on coitus in various species of animals; Plutarch *Solon* XX and *Moralia* 769c; Pearl (1939) 66-79 (an average median value of 7.28 times a month for a number of series of different age groups), Kinsey et al. (1953) 348-352 (2.2 times a week for females at age 30) and Nag (1968) 72-77 on frequency of coitus in modern populations; Hippokrates *Gunaikeiôn* I.17 ed. Littré vol. 8, pp. 56-57, Aristotle *HA* 582b11-12 and Soranos *Gunaikologia* I.36.2 for conception before or after menstruation, although Soranos I.41 rejected restricting coitus for procreation to the time when the moon was waning, because successful conceptions take place in all seasons; Bongaarts & Potter (1983) 196 on the USA; Andelman (1987) suggested that concealed ovulation in *Cercopithecus aethiops* prevents the male monkey from knowing when conception has taken place and so which infants are his, discouraging him from attempting to kill infants sired by other males, as the males of some primate species do, cf. S. Hrdy (1979) and Daniels (1983) (in passing it is interesting to note that the promiscuity of this monkey is an important factor in the spread of the SIV virus, related to AIDS, which is endemic in populations of *C. aethiops*, see also section 7 of this chapter); Aristotle *HA* 584a35-b1 & *GA* 772b7-11; Pliny *NH* VII.v.38-40.

135. Leridon (1984) on biological aspects of fertility; Trussell & Wilson (1985) on age-specific patterns of sterility; McFalls (1984) 387-426 on demographic consequences of induced abortion, cf. Hippokrates *Gunaikeiôn* I.67 ed. Littré vol. 8, pp. 140-143, and Pantelakis et al. (1973) on modern Greece; Aristotle *GA* 746b16-747a24 on sterility in man, cf. 726a3-6 & *HA* 520b6-7 on fat animals as poor breeders, *GA* 767a23-28 & *HA* 585b8-10 on change of spouse often leading to fertility; Isaios II.6-8 for divorce on the grounds of childlessness; Dupâquier et al. (1981) on remarriage, with (Demosthenes) XL.6-7 and Hypereides I (*For Lykophron*) 5 as Athenian examples, and W.E. Thompson (1972) cites others; Edelstein (1945) T423 II.31, 34, 39 & 42 for cases of infertility at Epidauros; Corvisier (1985) 161-163 suggested that about 10 per cent of all women in classical Greece were sterile, cf. Livi-Bacci (1977) 93 for about 8-9 per cent of each cohort remaining childless throughout the reproductive period in early modern Italy; Ericksen et al. (1979) for sterility as a significant constraint on fertility among the Old Order Amish, another rapidly increasing North American religious sect.

136. On age of marriage for men see Solon F27 West, lines 9-10, Hesiod *WD* 695-697, Plato *Laws* 721b & 785b, Aristotle *Politics* 1335a6-35; Lysias XXXII.4 for a man marrying his brother's daughter, suggesting a substantial age gap between husband and wife; Aristotle *Rhetoric* 1390b9-11 states that the ages 30-35 were regarded as the peak (*akmê*) of life for men, doubtless why marriage then was recommended; Pauly-Wissowa *RE* s.v. Pythias; (Demosthenes) XL.4 & 12 is a case of an Athenian male marrying early, at eighteen, but in exceedingly dubious family circumstances.

137. Hesiod *WD* 698 is generally and probably rightly interpreted to mean marriage for women at eighteen, but some later sources in antiquity (Pollux *Onomasticon* I.58 and Porphyry on Homer *Iliad* X.252) did interpret Hesiod's text differently, cf. the discussion of West (1978) ad loc.; other evidence for age of marriage of women in Xenophon *Oikonomikos* VII.5, (Aristotle) *Athênaiôn Politeia* LVI.7, Plato *Laws* 785b, Aristotle *Politics* 1335a6-35; Hippokrates *peri parthenôn* ed. Littré vol. 8, pp. 468-471 advised girls to marry as early as possible, by the time of puberty; Isaios VI.14 states that a woman, if she was thirty years old, should have been married long ago; Demosthenes XXVI.5 & XXIX.43 indicates that Demosthenes' father expected in his will that his five-year-old daughter, betrothed to his nephew Demophon, would have reached puberty and married at the age of fifteen; Plutarch *Moralia* 249d on Keos; Cartledge (1981a) 94-95 on Sparta.

138. Pearl (1939) and Kinsey et al. (1953).

139. Aristotle *NE* 1158b11-13, also 1160b32-34 & 1161a22-25.

140. Henry (1976) 90-94, cf. Flinn (1981) 29-34 on effects of nuptiality on family size in Europe; Lesthaeghe (1971) showed that changes in nuptiality have important consequences in Islamic populations in North Africa and the Middle East, where women traditionally marry earlier, closer to the range of marriage ages found in ancient Greece, than in north European countries; Trussell et al. (1981); Thiersch (1833) vol. 1, p. 289 on Greece early in the last century.

141. Patterson (1985) 104 n. 3 for the quotation; Angel (1945) 311-312 found the remains of 175 newborn foetuses and 100 dogs deposited in a well in late Hellenistic Athens, but this was probably an exceptional response to the crisis of the siege of Athens by Sulla; Aelian *poikilê historia* II.7 states that poor men were allowed to sell children into slavery (as in the Athens of Solon) in Thebes, where infant exposure was banned.

142. Poseidippos F11 ed. Kock.

143. Colinvaux (1980) 25-26 & (1982) 395-397; Lack (1954) esp. 45-47, also 94-98 comparing age mortality patterns of humans and birds, and 176-178 on the regulation of human numbers; Hobcraft et al. (1985) and Thapa et al. (1988); Krzywicki (1934) passim, esp. 99, 124 & 129 on primitive societies; Howell (1979) 120 on the Bushmen; J. Preuss (1978) 406 for twins in Israel; M. Harris & Ross (1987), esp. 78-84 on ancient Greece & Rome, is vitiated, first, by lack of comprehension of the theory of evolution, and secondly, by failure to understand the concept of natural fertility; the cross-cultural survey of infanticide of Divale & Harris (1976) may be subjected to devastating criticism, as in e.g. Bates & Lees (1979) to whose conclusions the present author subscribes, the most notable point being that Divale & Harris failed to show that any of the societies they considered was actually in a state of equilibrium, in which case it is nonsense to argue that selective female infanticide was a device used to maintain population stability; Schrire & Steiger (1974), discussed by Acker & Townsend (1975), showed by computer simulation the likely disastrous consequences of large-scale selective female infanticide; on classical antiquity note the debate between Engels (1980) and W. Harris (1982), also Oldenziel (1987).

144. The account of the Miletos inscriptions given by Brulé (1978) 165-170 is preferable to that of Pomeroy (1983), who was rightly criticised by L. Gallo (1984a) and Patterson (1985); see Keyfitz (1977) 399-412 and Bocquet-Appel (1985) on the problem of stochastic fluctuations in small populations; Eyben (1980/1) 5 displayed a lack of demographic awareness in his statement that most families were small in antiquity (cf. section 6 of this chapter); Plutarch *Moralia* 612a shows that infants who died soon after birth, presumably before the *dekatê* ceremony, did not receive the usual burial rites, a consequence of high infant mortality, cf. Golden (1988).

145. Himes (1936) 101; Barclay et al. (1976) and Coale (1985) on natural fertility in China; Scholten (1985) 9 & 14 stated that shortage of voluntary family limitation in the early modern USA was not caused by a lack of knowledge about family limitation techniques; Dickeman (1975) 108; Germain (1969) & (1975); *Twelve Tables* IV.1 ed. Warmington and Dionysios Hal. *AR* II.15.2 for Rome; Sextus Empiricus *Pyrrhôneiôn Hypotypôseôn* III.211 eds. Mutschmann & Mau, a late source, states that Solon allowed parents to kill their own children, but Isokrates V (*Panathênaikos*) 121-122 states that the Athenians had never committed the crime of infanticide; for the horror felt in relation to abnormal infants note the story in Phlegon of Tralles FGH257 F36(II) Jacoby about the birth of an hermaphrodite to the Lokrian wife of an Aitolian man, interpreted as a prophecy of war between the two peoples.

146. Valaoras et al. (1965) & (1969) on modern Greece; Hippokrates *peri gunaikeiês phusios* XVI ed. Littré vol. 7, pp. 334-335, also *peri phusios paidiou* VII ed. Littré vol. 7, pp. 490-491 and *peri sarkôn* XIX ed. Littré vol. 8, pp. 610-611 on prostitutes; Aristotle *Politics* 1335b19-26; Khrysippos F806 ed. von Arnim vol. 2; Krenkel (1971); Nardi (1980) & (1971), esp. 33-41 on the laws of Solon and Lykourgos cited by Galen *ei zôion to kata gastros* V ed. Kühn vol. XIX pp. 179-180; Dickison (1973) reviewed Nardi; Plutarch *Lykourgos* III for a legend concerning Lykourgos and abortion; Devereux (1976) for cross-cultural research on abortion;

Lysias ed. Gernet-Bizos vol. 2, pp. 238-240 and Harrison (1968) 72-73; Cicero *pro Cluentio* XI.31-32; Diodoros Siculus I.77.9; Feen (1983); Hippokrates *Horkos* ed. Littré vol. 4, pp. 630-631, with L. Edelstein (1979).

147. Aristotle *HA* 583a21-24; A. Preuss (1975); Stopes (1931) 359 on olive oil; Riddle (1985) 58-64 on contraceptive drugs; Hippokrates *peri aphorôn* CCXVIII ed. Littré vol. 8, pp. 422-423 on hot baths, also Devine (1985).

148. Ebert & Luppe (1975) lines 13-16 edited the Archilochos papyrus; Herodotos I.61.1 on Peisistratos; J. Preuss (1978) 406 & 458-459; (Demosthenes) LIX.122.

149. I agree with the criticisms of Golden (1981) made by L. Gallo (1984a) and Patterson (1985); Schoen (1983); (Demosthenes) LIX.8 said that no one would want to marry a woman without a dowry, but XXX.34 said that a young woman from a rich family would expect to remarry rapidly after being widowed; Plutarch *Aristeides* XXVII.6 records that the Athenians gave a dowry to the grand-daughter of Aristogeiton, who was living on Lemnos unmarried because of poverty; (Demosthenes) XLIII.54 and Schaps (1979) 37-38 on the thetic *epiklêroi*; Dio Chrysostom XV.3 suggests that poor women could not find husbands in Roman Athens and poverty was not a bar to procreation; Lysias XII.21 for inability to get married as a serious injustice; Plutarch *Moralia* 227f attributes the motive of preventing girls from being left unmarried to the supposed Lykourgan ban on dowries in Sparta (cf. section 6 of this chapter); Darwin (1901) 43 n. 13 & 893 on Theognis.

150. Bongaarts & Potter (1983) 58-60.

151. Jackson (1985) 248 on the unreliability of Greek censuses; Schaps (1977) on the low profile of women in the orators; Plutarch *Alkibiades* I.3 illustrates the tendency of literary sources to avoid naming 'citizen' women; Raepsaet (1971).

152. Polybios XXXVI.17.7, partly confirmed by Herakleides Creticus I.25 ed. Pfister, as Feyel (1942) 175-176 observed; Bintliff & Snodgrass (1985) & (1988), also Alcock (1989) and Landry (1936); Menander F404 Kock for the folly of the poor man (*penês*) marrying and having children, cf. Demokritos 68 B275-278 eds. Diels-Kranz vol. 2, pp. 201-203 for the thoughts of a fifth-century philosopher on human childbearing (if the fragments are genuine); Wrigley (1987) on Colyton.

153. Keyfitz (1971a) and Preston (1986) on momentum of population growth; Patterson (1985) 104 n. 3.

154. Livi-Bacci (1977) 276-281 on Italy; Hammond & Walbank (1988) 458 n. 2 on Albania, also 431 & 515 on Livy XXXIII.3.1-5, XXXIX.24.3, also XLII.51 saying that the Macedonian manpower losses were made good in the twenty-six-year period from the battle of Kynoskephalai to the war between Perseus and Rome – this 'recovery' is explicable in a similar manner to the Athenian 'recovery' after the great epidemic by the time of the Syracusan expedition (see section 7 of this chapter); Swee-Hock (1980) for the population regulation policies of Singapore; Tien (1984) on China.

155. Weber (1968) vol. 2, esp. pp. 1282-1300, 1308-1317 & 1339-1372; Andreski (1968) expanded Weber's ideas on military organisation; Finley (1981b) 3-23 & (1985b) 67-88.

156. Aristotle *Politics* 1338b24-29; Thucydides I.141.3-5, II.39 & III.15.2; Plutarch *Agesilaos* XXVI; Demosthenes IX.47-50 noted the changes in methods of warfare introduced by Philip II of Macedon.

157. Xenophon *Lakedaimoniôn Politeia* XI.5-10; the anecdote about catapult-driven darts in Plutarch *Moralia* 191d & 219a, even if apocryphal, illustrates how alien the idea of innovation in war was to the Spartans, the only full-time citizen army in classical Greece.

158. Aristotle *Politics* 1329a13-17 & 1332b12-42; Plato *Laws* 690a-b; Dionysios

Hal. *AR* II.26.2 contrasts Greek and Roman practices in the field of relations between fathers and sons; Aristotle *Metaphysics* 1016b11-17 & 1041b11-19 on 'structures', also Braudel (1982) 458-466 & 514 on 'hierarchies'; the failure of the work of Aristophanes of Byzantium on the age grades (*peri onomasias hêlikiôn*) to survive the passage of time complete is a great loss for the present inquiry (Slater (1986) 28-39 gives the surviving fragments).

159. Jeanmaire (1913) & (1939); Eisenstadt (1956) esp. pp. 92, 141-148, 204-212 & 284-287 on Athens, Sparta and Rome.

160. Bernardi (1985) is the best recent book on age as a principle of social organisation, for reasons explained in Chapter IV. It is the fact that he makes no reference whatsoever to ancient Greek history and so does not have an axe to grind in that subject which makes it particularly interesting for the ancient historian, who can investigate for himself or herself how Bernardi's ideas on age class systems as a type of social organisation, constructed on evidence from Africa which is entirely independent of classical sources, fit the empirical evidence from ancient Greece. Note also the comments of M. Fortes on ancient Greece in Kertzer & Keith (1984) 113-114. Literature used as sources of information for New Guinea includes Nelson (1971), P. Brown (1978), Gressitt (1982), Herdt (1982) & (1984), and Feil (1987).

161. Plutarch *Lykourgos* XIII.3 ed. Ziegler; Aristotle *Politics* 1263b35-36 for *paideia* as a bond of the *polis*; Plato *Laws* 643e regarded bringing up the citizen to rule and be ruled as the objective of *paideia*; Brelich (1969) 113-207, Hodkinson (1983) 245-251 and Cartledge (1987) 20-33 on the *agôgê*; Jameson (1980) on Apollo Lykeios; Aelian *peri zôiôn idiotêtos* X.26 on the association of the wolf with Apollo.

162. Plutarch *Lykourgos* XIV.1; cf. Plato *Laws* 631d-e, 720e & 842d-e.

163. Plutarch *Lykourgos* XVI.1-2; Plutarch *Moralia* 242c mentions a Spartan girl who had become pregnant without her father's knowledge having an abortion; Cartledge (1987) 22 discussed the significance of the fact that Agesilaos, although congenitally lame, was not exposed.

164. Plutarch *Lykourgos* XVI.7.

165. Hesykhios s.v. *apagelos*.

166. Xenophon *Lak. Pol.* II.8; Plato *Laws* 633bc; Plutarch *Lykourgos* XVIII.2; Pausanias III.16.10-11 and Calame (1977) vol. 1, pp. 278-297 on Artemis Orthia; Marrou (1946), Meister (1963), Tazelaar (1967) and MacDowell (1986) 159-167 on the sequence of age grades in the Spartan *agelai*; Pausanias III.14.8-10 on Lykourgos' regulations for contests between *moirai* of boys.

167. Plutarch *Lykourgos* XVII.1; Sergent (1986) 74-95; Xenophon *Memorabilia* IV.4.20 indicates the existence in ancient Athens of paederasty in the modern sense of sexual abuse of very young children, cf. Aiskhines I.9-12 and Aelian *poikilê historia* III.12 ed. Dilts.

168. Plutarch *Agesilaos* I.4-II.1.

169. Dover (1978) 201. Sergent (1984) is better, although it is impossible to share his confidence that it is possible to write Mycenaean political history on the basis of classical Greek mythology. Paederasty was a way of relating two different age grades of 'citizens', not a way of differentiating citizens from outsiders such as slaves, as was claimed by Golden (1984).

170. Plutarch *Lykourgos* XVII.1; Sergent (1984) 53.

171. Aristotle *Politics* 1335a28-29; Plato *Laws* 721b-d, 772d-e, 774a & 785b (not all mutually consistent).

172. Xenophon *Lak. Pol.* II.13; Aelian *peri zôiôn idiotêtos* IV.1, Ephoros FGH70 F149, Konon FGH26 F1(XVI) Jacoby, Strabo X.4.12.478c and Aristotle *Eudemian*

Ethics 1229a23-24 ed. Susemihl on Crete; Sergent (1984) 133.

173. Rightly stressed by Cartledge (1981b); Aelian *poikilê historia* III.10; cf. Creed (1984) and Herdt (1984) on the Melanesian societies to which van Gennep (1960 E.T.; original 1909) drew attention. As Herdt (1984) 7 noted, 'typically groups often forbid heterosexual contacts during the same period when the boys are being inseminated by older males' (most commonly by fellatio, in New Guinea), illlustrated by Kelly (1976) 46-47; Leakey (1930) 190 for the banning of heterosexual relations during initiation among the Masai in Africa.

174. Sergent (1984) 73-74; Xenophon *Lak. Pol.* II.12 & *Symposion* VIII.34; Plutarch *Pelopidas* XIX for the Theban lawgivers, also *Moralia* 761b.

175. Plutarch *Solon* I.4-6 records his law banning slaves from paederastic relationships and the tradition that Solon was the *erastês* of Peisistratos; Solon F25 West; Aiskhines I.139; Sergent (1986) 96-136. Hermias Alexandrinus *in Plat. Phaidros* 231e ed. Couvreur p. 38 gives further details of Solon's laws, saying that those who did not go on military campaigns, deserted the ranks or did not feed their parents were also barred from paederastic relationships. Aiskhines III.175-176 mentions other civic activities from which the above-mentioned categories were banned. Combining these sources, it appears that playing the role of *erastês* in Solon's Athens was a prerogative of full citizen status, i.e. of membership of certain age grades, and failure to fulfil various duties incumbent on full citizen status entailed loss of this prerogative, among other penalties. Thucydides VI.54.2 for Aristogeiton and Harmodios.

176. Plutarch *Moralia* 712c.

177. Aiskhines I.135-136; Lysias III.4; Sergent (1984) 285-296 on Homer; Plato *Laws* 680c on Homer's Ionian character; Plato *Symposion* 182a-b on Ionia; Plutarch *Pelopidas* XVIII and Sergent (1986) 42-52 on Thebes; Soranos in Caelius Aurelianus *Chr.* IV.9 ed. Drabkin, cf. Rufus *peri aphrodisiôn* in Oribasios *Coll. Med.* VI.38 ed. Raeder; Xenophon of Ephesos *tôn kata Anthian kai Abrokomên Ephesiakôn* I.2.2-4 ed. Papanikolaou.

178. Plutarch *Solon* XXIII.2; contrast Hypereides I (*Ag. Lykophron*) 12-13 for the fourth-century situation; Hippomenes, the last Medontid archon of Athens (discussed by Carlier (1984) 365), killed his daughter Leimone, who had had coitus while still unmarried, in a notorious incident (Aiskhines I.182, Aristotle F611.1 Rose, Diodoros Siculus VIII.22 & Nikolaos of Damascus FGH90 F49 Jacoby); Philemon *Adelphoi* F4 Kock records that Solon provided public brothels for young men (because they were prohibited from marriage with 'citizen' women?).

179. E.g. Legesse (1973) on the Oromo or Galla of Ethiopia.

180. Leridon (1977) 9.

181. Varro *RR* II.10.9 on Illyricum; Herodotos V.6.1 on Thrace, also Aristotle F611.58 Rose on polygamy and bridewealth in Thrace (section 6 of this chapter); *Dissoi Logoi* II.12-14 eds. Diels-Kranz 90 on Macedon, also Marsyas FGH135/136 F24 Jacoby mentioning *korinaios*, a special term for the son of an unmarried girl in the Macedonian dialect of Greek; Herodotos I.196.1 on Illyricum.

182. Plutarch *Lykourgos* XV.9-13 & 17-18; Polybios XII.6b.8; Xenophon *Lak. Pol.* I.7-8; Baxter & Almagor (1978) 17; Plutarch *Solon* XX.2-3 on *epiklêroi*; Leakey (1930) 194, on the Masai of Kenya, in which men in the warrior age classes are permitted to have sexual relations with unmarried girls, but not with initiated girls and married women. The Hellenistic philosopher Hagnon in Athenaios XIII.602d suggests that Spartan *parthenoi* engaged in anal intercourse in the same way that adolescent boys did. This may be the correct interpretation of Hagnon's words, *pace* Calame (1977) vol. 1, p. 434. Herodotos II.80 and Aelian *peri zôiôn idiotêtos* VI.61 state that young adult Spartans had to give way to their elders and stand up in their presence, except if the older man was a bachelor. More generally, *hubris*, outrageous and typically violent behaviour, was characteristic of *neoi* – Aristotle *Rhetoric* 1378b26-29.

183. Legesse (1973) – the weakest point in his elaborate reconstruction is his assumption that the Galla age class system was instituted suddenly, an assumption like that made by many historians of ancient Sparta; Bernardi (1985) 149-151 & 170 (for the quotation); Kreager (1982) 254-256 on another African age class society, the Rendille, who invert the usual situation, as men have to marry at an early age, but certain age classes of women cannot marry until they are in their thirties, a scheme which has obvious demographic consequences, cf. Krzywicki (1934) 120 & n. 5 on tribes of Australian aborigines in which only infants born to mothers aged thirty or over were permitted to live; Feil (1987) 152 & 200 mentions compulsory marriage of age grades in New Guinea.

184. Aristotle *Politics* 1272b16-18 & 1272a23-26 on Crete (cf. Chapter I on isolated island ecosystems); Sergent (1984) 40.

185. Brelich (1969) 196-207 compared Spartan and Cretan institutions.

186. Cartledge (1979) 307-318 on Spartan manpower shortage; Diodoros Siculus XV.23.4 and Thucydides IV.80.3 on the rest of the population of Lakonia and Messenia; Figueira (1986) offered an alternative chronology for the development of Spartan *oliganthrôpia*.

187. See Chapter III n. 71 below.

188. Aristotle *Politics* 1271a28-32.

189. Aristotle *Politics* 1270a39-b4; Xenophon *Lak. Pol.* IX.5; Plutarch *Lykourgos* XIV.1-3 & XV.1.

190. Diodoros Siculus XI.63.1-2 and Plutarch *Kimon* XVI.4-5 on the earthquake; Baxter & Almagor (1978) 18; Plutarch *Lykourgos* XIII.1 and Isokrates XV (*Panathênaikos*) 209 ed. Blass on the absence of written laws in Sparta, cf. *Dissoi Logoi* II.10 eds. Diels-Kranz 90, and Aristotle F611.15 Rose on Crete; Cartledge (1978); Klearchos F73 ed. Wehrli for social pressure on Spartan bachelors to marry; Plato *Laws* 793a regarded the ancestral laws (*patrioi nomoi*) of the Greeks as no more than unwritten customs (*agrapha nomima*).

191. Plutarch *Lykourgos* XVIII.9; Calame (1977) vol. 1, pp. 433-436.

192. Bernardi (1985) 132-142.

193. Aristotle *Politics* 1265a8-9 & 1266a35-36; Plato *Laws* 806e.

194. Pausanias V.16.2-4; Pindar F112 ed. Snell spoke of an *agela parthenôn* in Sparta, but Brelich (1969) 157-166 was right to maintain that there was no female age class system parallel to the male one in classical Sparta.

195. Ephoros FGH70 F149 Jacoby; Sergent (1984) 15-53; Plutarch *Lykourgos* XXVIII.2; Plato *Laws* 633bc & scholiast; Aristotle F611.10 Rose; Jeanmaire (1913); Brelich (1969) 156-157 attempted to revise Jeanmaire's original thesis, but cases of large-scale headhunting are known (see Herdt (1984) 27); Aristotle *Politics* 1324b15-17 records that the Macedonians once had a law that a man who had never killed an enemy must wear a horse halter, a custom which probably had an origin similar to that of the Spartan *krupteia*, note also the story about Kassander in Hegesandros F33 ed. Müller *FHG* vol. 4, p. 419; Diodoros Siculus V.29.4-5, Herodotos IV.64-65, Livy XXIII.24.12, Polybios III.67.3 and Poseidonios F274 eds. Edelstein & Kidd on headhunting among the Scythians and Gauls (a primaeval Indo-European institution?).

196. Aristotle *Politics* 1324b6-9; Herodotos I.65; Plato *Laws* 625c-626b for Crete; Vidal-Naquet (1981) 151-174 symbolically contrasted two methods of warfare instead, but the *krupteia* did not give the Spartans any experience of

guerrilla warfare (Thucydides IV.41.3), because the *kruptos* was on his own.

197. Bernardi (1985) 30-31; Ferguson (1918) compared the Spartan and Zulu systems of *military* organisation, not their *social* organisations in a wider sense; Thucydides II.80.3.

198. See n. 158 above; Plutarch *Lykourgos* XXXI.2 on Plato.

199. Plutarch *Agesilaos* XXVI.5 & *Lykourgos* XIII.8-11; Legesse (1973) 8 – 'before assuming a position of leadership, the Gada class is required to wage war against a community that none of their ancestors had raided ... waged on schedule every eight years'; Brelich (1961a) on 'wars' between neighbours in archaic Greece, cf. Connor (1988); Plutarch *Moralia* 224b gives the rationalising explanation that the Spartans refrained from exterminating the Argives because they needed them to give experience of warfare to the younger generation.

200. Plutarch *Lykourgos* X & XII on Sparta; Hodkinson (1983) 253 suggested that a youth usually joined the *sussition* of his *erastês* in Sparta; Aristotle F611.15 Rose, Ephoros FGH70 F149 Jacoby and Nikolaos of Damascus FGH90 F103(aa) Jacoby on the Cretan messes.

201. Xenophon *Lak. Pol.* II.5-7 & V.3 and Plutarch *Lykourgos* XVI on Sparta; Dosiadas FGH458 F2 and Pyrgion FGH467 F1 Jacoby on Crete; Plato *Laws* 666a-b wished to restrict access to wine on the basis of age.

202. Xenophon *Lak. Pol.* V.5; Plutarch *Lykourgos* XII.

203. Aristotle *Politics* 1264a8.

204. Aristotle *Politics* 1271b30-32, 1329b5-7 & 1330a3-5.

205. Polybios IV.53.7-9; Plutarch *Agis* VI.1-2; Diodoros Siculus XI.50; Bloedow (1981); Aristotle *Politics* 1313a41 advised tyrants to abolish *sussitia* as a safety measure.

206. Plato *Laws* 636b & 682d, cf. Diodoros Siculus XVIII.46.3 on Termessos. Although classical Athens did not have *sussitia* embracing the entire citizen body, one should not forget the fifty members of the *boulê* who dined together (*sussitousi*) during their term of prytany – (Aristotle) *Athênaiôn Politeia* XLIII.3. The Solonic law on associations (Digest XLVII.xxii.4) mentions *sussitoi* as private associations. On Tarentum and the Spartan *Partheniai* see Aristotle F611.57 Rose & *Politics* 1306b29-31, Antiochos FGH555 F13, Ephoros FGH70 F216 and Theopompos FGH115 F171 Jacoby, Diodoros Siculus VIII.21.1-3, Dionysios Hal. *AR* XIX.1.1-4, Pausanias X.10.6-8 and Justin III.4-18; Vidal-Naquet (1981) 267-288.

207. Thucydides VI.13.1, 18.6 & 24.3.

208. Herodotos V.71.1; Thucydides I.126.3-12; Plutarch *Solon* XII; Aiskhines I.6-8; Lévy (1978), building on Lenschau (1936), is an important article on Kylon; it was the Athenian *neoi* who were eager to fight Megara for possession of Salamis (Plutarch *Solon* VIII); Chantraine (1956) 156-160 for the meaning of *hêlikia*; Hutter (1978) 26-34 for the types of groups of friends characteristic of age class societies; Neanthes of Kyzikos FGH84 F16 Jacoby, criticised by Polemon F53 Preller.

209. (Aristotle) *Athênaiôn Politeia* XXX.2, LXIII.3, XLII.2 & LIII.4 respectively. Develin (1985) argued that Athenian magistrates did not have to be above the age of thirty, but this is beside the point, even if correct, which is far from certain. The point is rather that there was a whole series of different ages at which new privileges and duties were acquired as one moved through the human lifespan. In any case Thucydides VI.38.5 suggests that there definitely was a minimum age for eligibility to office in democratic Syracuse.

210. Aiskhines I.23-25 & III.2-4 (cf. II.22 & 108 for an embassy to Philip); Stobaios V p. 1026 ed. Hense for a law of Solon banning a young man from holding office or expressing an opinion in the assembly; Plutarch *Demosthenes* XV.3, which contends that certain speeches written by Demosthenes at the ages of 27/28 could not have been delivered by Demosthenes himself in public at that age, suggests that it was not normal for an Athenian below the age of thirty to speak in public, cf. Thucydides V.43.2 for Athenian attitudes to the 'young' Alkibiades. Lysias XVI.20 also indicates that public speeches from young men were not welcomed, and the young speaker of Demosthenes LVIII.61 had to appeal to the jury to make it clear that a man of any age could hope to obtain justice from them, instead of the old being favoured. Note also Demosthenes XXIX.23 & LIII.4 on the importance of age in the formation of friendships, LIV.22 for criticism of a man over fifty years old for not keeping his sons under control, Antiphon *peri tou choreutou* XXII for young and old being placed alongside slave and free as a fundamental division of any heterogeneous group of people, and *Third Tetralogy* III.2 & IV.2 for manipulation of age stereotypes by the orators for their own purposes. (Demosthenes) XXV.29 states that if anyone proposed that speakers in the assembly should be restricted to the youngest (*neôtatoi*), he would be put to death for subverting the democracy. The reverse chain of thought, namely that discriminating in favour of old men could be undemocratic, never occurred to the author of this piece.

211. Plutarch *Lykourgos* XXV.1, where the *agora* is the market, but the exclusion of the *neoi* from the marketplace may not have had purely 'economic' objectives; Plato *Laws* 634d-e states that in Sparta and Crete *neoi* were prevented by law from discussing the laws or challenging the propriety of any of them; Xenophon *Lak. Pol.* VI.1 and Plutarch *Lykourgos* XVII.1 on the power of all adult males over all boys; the situation may have been similar on Crete, as Hesykhios s.v. *iettas* (an error for *tettas*) shows that 'elders' and 'fathers' were equated on Crete; according to Xenophon *Memorabilia* III.5.15, cf. II.3.16, the Athenians did not show as much respect for their fathers as the Spartans did; Cicero *De senectute* XVIII.63.

212. Bernardi (1985) 28.

213. Ephoros FGH70 F149 Jacoby.

214. Xenophon *Lak. Pol.* I.6.

215. Plutarch *Lykourgos* XV.6-9; Xenophon *Lak. Pol.* I.5-6; Hesykhios s.v. *agamoi*; MacDowell (1986) 72-77 on ages of marriage in Sparta; Sindiga (1987), on the Masai, showed how delaying of first marriage of men until a late age by traditional social controls, *inter alia*, reduces their population growth rate relative to that of sedentary farming populations in the same country; Kelly (1976) 43-45 on taboos against heterosexual intercourse among the Etoro, one of the New Guinea age class societies, covering between 205 and 260 days of the year, noting that they even attempt to make their domestic animals observe the same periods of abstinence! Flandrin (1984) investigated the demographic consequences of periods of abstinence from coitus in the Christian societies of early mediaeval Europe.

216. Pollux *Onomasticon* III.48; P. Roussel (1951) 212; according to Plutarch *Moralia* 493e, a corrupt text, the laws of Lykourgos and also of Solon covered failure to marry and late marriage.

217. (Aristotle) *Athênaiôn Politeia* XLII.3-4; Pélékides (1962); even in the Lamian War only men up to the age of forty were called up – Diodoros Siculus XVIII.10.2, cf. Plutarch *Phokion* XXIV.4-5 and Lykourgos *Ag. Leokrates* 39; Plutarch *Agesilaos* XXIV.3 for Sparta; Benveniste (1970) vol. 2, pp. 89-95 and Carlier (1984) 107 on the *laos* (also attested in Hittite and Phrygian); some of the longest surviving fragments of Tyrtaios (F10 & F12 West) are full of appeals to the *neoi* not to let their elders down.

218. (Aristotle) *Athênaiôn Politeia* LIII.4 & 7.

219. Aristotle *Politics* 1275a14-16 & 1275b22-23.

220. Hesiod F321 eds. Merkelbach-West.

221. Plutarch *Solon* XXII; for the control over tradition exercised by older men in Athens see Thucydides I.42.1 and Lysias XXIII.5.

222. Aristotle *Politics* 1270b35-1271a6, 1272a7-8, 1272a33-35 & 1306a12-19; Xenophon *Lak. Pol.* X.1-3; Plutarch *Lykourgos* V.10-14 & XXVI.1; Demosthenes XX.107 and Aiskhines I.180-181 for Athenian views of the Spartan *gerousia*; Hesykhios s.v. *geronia* or *gerontia* (as in Xenophon *Lak. Pol.* X.1) (= *geroia?*) for its actual name in the Spartan dialect of Greek (*gerôkhia* in the manuscripts of Aristophanes *Lysistrata* 980); Cartledge (1987) 121-125.

223. Homer *Odyssey* VII.189 for Phaiakia; more references in Carlier (1984) 150.

224. (Aristotle) *Athênaiôn Politeia* VIII.4; Aristotle *Politics* 1265b38; in Khalkis, for example, one could not hold a magistracy or go on an embassy until the age of fifty (Aristotle F611.63 Rose), note also Hesykhios s.v. *khalkidizein* and Athenaios XIII.601e for another aspect of the age class system of Khalkis.

225. Strabo X.5.6.486c citing Menander F613 Kock. Plato *Laws* 638b, with his usual idiosyncrasy, used Athens's conquest of Keos as an illustration of the principle that it is wrong to infer that the constitution of a large *polis* is superior to that of a small *polis* from the fact that the large one had been able to defeat the small one in war. This is a strange example in the light of the treatment of 'old age pensioners' on Keos. Theophrastos *HP* IX.16.9 describes the manufacture on Keos of the poison used, hemlock (*kôneion*), on which see also Dioskorides *MM* IV.78. Aristotle F611.29 Rose states that opium was also used. See also Valerius Maximus II.6.8. Isokrates XIX.13 states that the laws of Keos were also employed on Siphnos. Foner (1984) 106 suggested that killing of the elderly is quite common on a cross-cultural basis.

226. See Chapter III, n. 48 below for Aigina; Aiskhylides cited by Aelian *peri zôiôn idiotêtos* XVI.32 described the soil of Keos as very poor, although he also said it produced good pears, according to Athenaios XIV.650d; Plutarch *Moralia* 249d.

227. Aristotle *Politics* 1252b19-21 & 1259b10-17.

228. Aristotle *Politics* 1332b32-41; Carlier (1984) v. Xenophon *Agesilaos* II.16 regarded it as the duty of a Spartan king to rule and be ruled in accordance with the laws. This principle is the primary, and the kingship a secondary, phenomenon. 'Agesilaos … was a classic product of the Spartan system of education' – Cartledge (1987) 33.

229. Thucydides I.13.1; Aristotle *Politics* 1285b3-19.

230. Bernardi (1985) 112-119 on the Zulus; Aristotle *Politics* 1285a3-18, 1287a4-6 & 1310b31-39 on the Spartan kings, regarding their office as one which could be found in any constitution.

231. Bernardi (1985) xiv.

232. Carlier (1984) 176.

233. Aristotle *Politics* 1294b19-29.

234. (Aristotle) *Athênaiôn Politeia* XXV; Aristotle *Politics* 1274a8-9.

235. Herodotos II.147.

236. Plutarch *Agis* XI.4-5, Parke (1945) and Carlier (1984) 294-296 on the Spartan ritual, cf. Strabo IX.2.11.404c for the Athenians watching the sky for lightning to decide whether to dispatch a religious embassy, the *Pythais*, to Delphi; on Crete see Homer *Odyssey* XIX.178-179 (proving the antiquity of the institution), Aristotle F611.14 Rose, Plato *Laws* 624a-b & *Minos* 319b-c, Strabo X.4.8.476c, Diodoros Siculus V.78; on Theseus Homer *Iliad* I.265 & *Odyssey* XI.321-325, Bakkhylides XVII ed. Jebb, Thucydides II.15.2, Diodoros Siculus

IV.60-61, Plutarch *Theseus* XV.1-2, Plato *Laws* 706b and Pausanias I.17.3-6. By classical times the Theseus legend had undergone considerable modifications and divergent traditions existed. Aristotle F485 Rose thought that the *kouroi* and *korai* were not killed by the Minotaur in the original version of the legend. Dugas (1943) expanded our knowledge of the development of the stories concerning Theseus by considering the evidence of vase paintings. See also Ward (1970), and Sergent (1984) 229-231 for speculations on the earliest form of the legend, including the hypothesis that Theseus and Minos were not antagonists and had a relationship as novice-educator. Note also Pliny *NH* VIII.xxxiv.81 for the legend of Euanthes in Arkadia, another non-Dorian region of Greece, which may also be interpreted as an octennial rite of passage, cf. Pausanias VI.8.2 & VIII.2.3-6.

237. Censorinus *De die natali* XVIII ed. Sallmann, esp. 6. Note also Plutarch *Moralia* 293b-c, 418a & 421c, Pausanias II.7.7 and Brelich (1969) 387-438 on Delphi. As Brelich (1969) 102 n. 142 observed, 'le classi d'età hanno il loro suolo piu fecondo la dove le iniziazioni hanno luogo con una periodicità pluriennale'.

238. Jeanmaire (1939) & (1951). As Bernardi (1985) 36-37 noted, the periodicity of the age class system may be used as a basis for historical chronology. In this context it is worth remembering the habit of Greek chronographers such as Apollodoros of trying to date a person's 'peak', *akmê*.

239. G. Thomson (1943). There is no evidence, however, that the Olympic Games were ever an octennial festival, leaving no barrier to accepting the view that they were originally an annual festival (so Lévy (1978)). Their ultimate origins as a male initiation ceremony (Meuli & Burkert) explain why women were excluded. The traditional starting date for the Olympic Games of 776 BC is highly anomalous relative to the evidence for all the other major games, and there is no archaeological evidence for sporting activity at Olympia so early (Morgan (1986) 117-121 and Mallwitz (1988)). The short chronology espoused by Lenschau and Lévy is preferable because it would mean that all the four major sets of games, as well as the Panathenaia, assumed something like their classical shape during a single generation in the first half of the sixth century BC. In other words the very idea of a Panhellenic festival was an innovation of that period. This is not to deny that there were local festivals much earlier than the sixth century, and Phlegon of Tralles FGH257 F1 Jacoby states that there were 27 Olympiads before Koroibos, the first recorded victor. Plutarch *Numa* I.6 doubted that Hippias of Elis had any reliable evidence for the compilation of the Olympic victor list.

240. Hesiod *WD* 765-782 on the moon; Pliny *NH* XVIII.lxxv.321-322 on the performance of agricultural operations in accordance with the moon's phases, an idea also found in the Roman agronomists – Tavenner (1918); R. & E. Blum (1965) 31; Aristotle *GA* 738a17-18 & 767a2-8 and *HA* 582a34-b3 connected the lunar cycle with the female menstrual cycle, cf. Cutler et al. (1987) for modern research on this topic.

241. Jeanmaire (1951) 218-219.

242. Bernardi (1985) 122.

243. D. Roussel (1976); Finley (1985b) 90-91; Brelich (1969) 224-226.

244. Whitley (1987) 164, 248 & 304.

245. Uchitel (1984) reveals some of the possibilities. Hesykhios s.v. *balikiôtês*, attesting the original digamma, testifies to the antiquity of the word *hêlikiôtês* on Crete.

246. G.E. Mendenhall cited by Gottwald (1979) 326-327; Cartledge (1979) 94-95 & 114-116 on the Dorians as transhumant pastoralists and on population pressure as the motive for the attack on Messenia, cf. Snodgrass (1987) 193-207.

247. Plutarch *Lykourgos* XXI.3 for the three choirs at festivals, composed of *gerontes, akmazontes*, and *paides*; Brelich (1969) 141-148 and Calame (1977) vol. 1, pp. 305-323 on the more complicated organisation at the *Hyakinthia*, cf. Plato *Laws* 664b; Mikalson (1976) argued that the Spartan *Hyakinthia* and the Athenian *Panathênaia* were originally the same festival.

248. Bernardi (1985) 41 & 120-131; Calame (1977) vol. 1, pp. 108-115 on Theseus as a *chorêgos*; Polybios IV.20-21 described the integration of music into the whole social organisation of the Arkadians, to be understood in terms of the basic principles of age class systems, as argued by Brelich (1969) 209-214, cf. the recently discovered *sumpoliteia* inscription published by Riele (1987), line 17, which states that the citizens of Helisson, a small *polis* that was being incorporated into Mantinea, were to be registered by age (*kat'alikian*); evidence for age class organisation from Arkadia is interesting for two reasons: (1) it shows that *ethnê* shared the same basic principles of social organisation as the *poleis* (cf. Aristotle *Politics* 1261a27-29); (2) it is relevant to the question of continuity from the Mycenaean period, given the close relationship between the Arkadian and the Mycenaean dialects of Greek.

249. Jeanmaire (1939); Brelich (1969) 229-311; Cole (1984) and Sourvinou-Inwood (1988) for more recent views on these women's rituals; Burkert (1983) 248-297; Lincoln (1981) 71-90.

250. Polignac (1984) 51-54, 67-72 & 87-89 on the extra-urban sanctuaries. It is unclear why he is unwilling to regard Eleusis, say, or Brauron as extra-urban sanctuaries opposed to Athens. The agricultural interpretation of the Demeter-Kore myth put forward by the *Homeric Hymn to Demeter* 303-482 ed. Richardson in the archaic period held sway for the rest of antiquity and ended up in Augustine *de civitate Dei* VII.20, cf. Varro *RR* III.1.6 describing the sacred rites of Ceres as *initia*.

251. Szemerényi (1974) 157; J. Chadwick in *Cambridge Ancient History* vol. II, part 2B (1975) 807; Sergent (1986) 95 & 146 suggested that the existence of the word *aitas* as a synonym of *erômenos* in both the Spartan Doric and Thessalian dialects (as in Theokritos XII.14) of Greek indicates that institutionalised paederasty dates back to the time of the antecedent proto-Doric (or 'north Greek') dialect, in the second millennium BC.

252. Some of the African age class systems are classed in a different model, the 'generation model' in which the basic principle of class recruitment stresses the relationship formed between an individual and his parents at birth. Generational age class systems are not attested empirically in the sources for ancient Greece, although there are certainly many traces of informal generational thought in ancient Greek literature, on which see Nash (1978). Herodotos III.142.2 regarded a century as made up of three generations.

253. (Aristotle) *Athênaiôn Politeia* XLII.1-2; Plato *Laws* 925a; Aristophanes *Sphêkes* 578.

254. Plato *Laws* 785b; note also the description of admission to citizenship by the Attic orators as 'being judged to be a man' (*anêr*), e.g. Lysias XXVI.21 & XXXII.9.

255. Gottwald (1979) also concluded that ancient Jewish social organisation had nothing in common with Greek social organisation (note pp. 350-352 & 887-889 dismissing the analogy between the Delphic Amphictyony and the Twelve Tribes of Israel); Frick (1985) on Israel as a segmentary society; J. Preuss (1978) 490-493 on paederasty; Lane Fox (1986) 312 observed that Christianity did not spread among age mates.

256. Relevant here is the juggling of the calendar necessary to accommodate the initiation of the Macedonian Demetrios Poliorcetes into the Eleusinian

Mysteries at a time when Athens was no longer mistress of her own destiny –
Plutarch *Demetrios* XII; Xenophon *Lak. Pol.* III.3 and Plutarch *Moralia* 235b-c &
238e on Sparta.

257. Aristotle *Politics* 1275b22-34, also 1278a31-34 for the tendency to expel
subsequently, when the situation improved, aliens who had been awarded
citizenship to boost military manpower out of sheer necessity; Feil (1987) 85 for
similar habits among the New Guinea age class societies.

258. Xenophon *Cyropaedia* I.2.4-15. Cartledge (1987) 24 observed that
Agesilaos was the prototype for the fictional Cyrus the Great, experiencing the
same *paideia* as the *homotimoi*, as Agesilaos, exceptionally for a Spartan king,
did. Cf. Herodotos I.99.2 for the idea of equality between age mates, this time in
Median guise. For the contradictory and socially disruptive notion of a person
openly standing out amongst his age mates see Herodotos V.42 for Dorieus of
Sparta. Arguably the Median Deiokes was smarter than the would-be king
Dorieus.

259. F. Poland, cited by Jeanmaire (1939) 464. Censorinus *De die natali* XIV.2
cited Varro's classification of Roman age grades, but these did not have the
significance which age grades had in the Greek world. Early Roman history was
marked by social institutions unparalleled in Greece (the *gentes*, the patricians
and plebeians, the various *comitia*, the *patroni* and the *clientes* – a pair of
hierarchical statuses linking individuals which was impossible in Greece because
age class systems relate groups, not individuals – explaining for example why the
Helots as a group were subordinated to the *Spartiatai* as a group, possessing a
status which in this perspective can be seen to have nothing whatsoever to do
with serfdom in mediaeval Europe); Gaius *Inst.* I.9.2 for *patria potestas*, which
linked individuals, not groups, in the same way that *clientela* did.

260. Eisenstadt (1956).

261. Gauthier (1974) & (1981) rightly affirms that 'the ancient city' is an
illegitimate category of analysis, but did not penetrate to the bottom of the
differences in social structure between Greece and Rome which explain their
respective conceptions of citizenship; Benveniste (1970) for the linguistic
expressions of the phenomenon; Philip V of Macedon in Ditt. *Syll.*[3] 543, lines
31-34 and Claudius in Tacitus *Annales* XI.24 contrasted the Greek and Roman
conceptions of citizenship.

262. Livy XXVIII.34.9; Pausanias VII.8.5 & VIII.51.3; Plutarch *Philopoimen*
XVI.5.

263. Braudel (1981) 515-519.

264. Davies (1971) 77-89 on Bouselos; Vial (1984) 287-289 on Delos, cf.
Ferguson (1973) 374 who long ago (original edition in 1911) reached a similar
conclusion for Hellenistic Athens; Isager (1981/2) 93-94 listed the children of 34
dead men as 'reported' by Isaios, most of whom had less than the 4-5 children
necessary to reproduce such a population.

265. R.A. Fisher (1958) 207-228 on inherited variations in human fertility;
Sorensen et al. (1988) for the heritable component of premature death in adults;
Lotka (1939) 123-136 and Wrigley (1978) on the theory of patriline discontinuity,
with Laslett (1978) and Le Roy Ladurie (1966) vol. 1, pp. 161-162 for practical
historical examples.

266. Aristotle *Politics* 1265a39-b1, saying nothing whatsoever about a 'rising
birth rate' leading to revolutions, as Lane Fox (1985) 211 read him.

267. Laslett in Laslett & Wall (1972) 18ff. on the concept of 'patriline', a good
translation of *genos* in e.g. Plato *Theaitetos* 174e, cf. Isaios VIII.33 showing that it
only applied to direct lineal descendants of ego, excluding even ego's siblings;

(Plutarch) *Moralia* 842f-843e, with Davies (1971) 348-353, illustrates the problems of maintaining patriline continuity; Isokrates VIII (*Eirênê*) 88 observed that many patrilines became extinct during the Peloponnesian War, when the Athenian population as a whole was reduced in size; Schaps (1979) 32-33 & 39-43 on the epiklerate.

268. Plutarch *Solon* XXI.2 and A. Harrison (1968) 82-96 & 130-155; Hesiod *WD* 342-351 & 371; considering Hesiod's suggestion in line 341 that land might have to be sold off to pay debts, the destruction of the imaginary *genos* of Fustel de Coulanges has destroyed the hypothesis of Fine (1951) 180-181 that land was inalienable in Attica until the Peloponnesian War.

269. (Demosthenes) LIX.22 for a married man having his elderly mother living in the same house; Aristotle *Politics* 1265b1-6; (Demosthenes) XXV.88 on the three-generation family; Ruzicka & Hansluwka (1983) on three-generation families under high-mortality conditions.

270. Lysias XXXII.4 and (Demosthenes) XLIV.10 for brothers not dividing estates.

271. Aristotle *Politics* 1252a26-30 & 1253a18-29 and *NE* 1162a17-19; Le Roy Ladurie (1978) 24.

272. Lévi-Strauss (1985) 89-97; Vartigian (1983) 152 described the Athenians as monogamous, with no exogamous unilineal descent groups, endogamy is well documented, and the rule of marital residence is not so clear, but lies somewhere between patrilocal and neolocal (tending to the former).

273. Goody (1976) 66-85 on adoption; Aristotle *Metaphysics* 1053a23-25 distinguished the *genos* of the Herakleidai from a *genos* in nature, cf. Boylan (1983) 50-59 and Chapter III.9.

274. A.C. Murray (1983) on the Germans; the critique of Murray in Herlihy (1985) 45-47 is unconvincing, as he continues to attribute significance to the ancient German *Sippe*, even though he admits (p. 47) that the word rarely occurs in the sources (!), making the same mistake that many ancient historians have made in considering the Greek *genos*; Pausanias VII.7.8 noted the difference between Greek and Roman systems of nomenclature; Benveniste (1969) vol. 1, pp. 279-292, Sergent (1979) & (1980) and Briquel (1982) on I-E trifunctionality; Magrath (1975) attempted to interpret the Athenian king list in terms of the tripartite ideology; Bremmer (1980) and Sergent (1986) suggested on scanty evidence that institutionalised paederasty was characteristic of P-I-E society.

275. Franciosi (1978) esp. 123-129, where he may err in thinking that the Romans originally only had a *praenomen*, as the Praeneste fibula (now discredited as a fake) and Plutarch *Romulus* which he cites to support his view are hardly the best of sources; Pliny *NH* XXXV.ii.6 describes the preservation of Roman family trees in pictorial form.

276. Herakleides Pontikos F102 ed. Wehrli; Hornblower (1981) 140-141 & 248 lists other early Greek references to Rome; Aristotle *Politics* 1272b24-1273b26 espied such institutions as *sussitia* and a *gerousia* in the constitution of Carthage, which justified describing it as a *polis*.

277. *Kasignêtos* occurs in e.g. Homer *Iliad* VI.239 & XVI.456 and *Odyssey* XV.273, where it is closely associated with *etai* (from *hetairos*), and Herodotos I.171.6 & IV.104, and is attested also in the Cypriot, Lesbian and Thessalian dialects of Greek, cf. Chantraine (1968) 503, Benveniste (1969) vol. 1, pp. 220-222, and Szemerényi (1977) 23; Eustathios on *Iliad* XV.545; Hesykhios s.v. *kasis*, conventionally translated as 'brother', glosses it as *hêlikiôtês*, 'age-mate', while he interpreted *kasioi* in Sparta as a designation of brothers and cousins, i.e. kinsmen of the same generation, who belonged to the same *agela*, and states that the word also applied to females in Sparta; the related word *kasen*, referring to foster ties, appears frequently in Spartan inscriptions from Hellenistic times onwards, e.g. IG V.1.60 & 115; Hesykhios s.v. *eor*, with Szemerényi (1977) 33; Franciosi (1978) 239-272 on descriptive and classificatory elements in Roman kinship terminology.

278. Vartigian (1983) 140 & 149.

279. Vartigian (1983) 17-18, Isaios XI.1-3 and (Demosthenes) XLIII.51 on the *angchisteia*; Bourriot (1976) vol. 1, pp. 223-234 on the *genos* as a four-generation group.

280. Isaios VIII.32 considered the great-grandparents as part of the *genos if they were still alive* (if they were already dead their property would already have been inherited by others and they would no longer be relevant to the lawsuit in question); Bush (1971) on the Roman kinship system's embracing three ascending generations from ego, also Franciosi (1980) 126 who hit the nail on the head; D.R. Hopkins (1985) 202 on Israel; N. Chadwick (1978) 113-114 on the Celts, also the German *Sippe* in n. 273 above; Stirling (1965) 158-159 on Turkey, showing a somewhat more cohesive group; some anthropologists, e.g. Kuper (1982) & (1988), are now criticising the value of lineage theory altogether.

281. I. Morris (1987) 90-91.

282. Philon *peri tôn en merei diatagmatôn* III.22 ed. Cohen-Wendland; Demosthenes LVII.20 for an example of homopatric brother-half-sister marriage; W.E. Thompson (1967); Hammell et al. (1979) for demographic consequences of incest taboos.

283. Whitehead (1986) 18-21 on the number of demes in Attica.

284. Goody (1976) 86-98.

285. Hesiod *WD* 376-377, contrast Euripides *Ion* 472-480.

286. Donlan (1980) 148 for the quotation; Demosthenes XVIII.256-268.

287. R.A. Fisher (1958) 229-274, esp. 241 on antiquity; Laslett (1978).

288. Davies (1981) 73-87 on discontinuity within the liturgical class; Goody (1976) 134 for the data in the paragraph; Herodotos VI.86 and (Demosthenes) LII.9 for examples of patriline discontinuity in Sparta and Argos respectively.

289. Aristotle *Rhetoric* 1387a11-31 & 1391a14-19; possession of wealth and other desirable qualities such as noble birth was attributed to *eutuchia*, good fortune – Aristotle *Rhetoric* 1390b14-1391a30, cf. *NE* 1100b22ff. & 1153b21ff. and *Politics* 1332a29-31; Veblen (1970) 182-192 on the role of a belief in fortune in a society with a rentier mentality; Schuhl (1968) 81-133 on *eugeneia*, noble birth; Kratinos *Ploutoi* ed. Carrière (1979) 222ff.; Lysias XXV.30, XXVII.9-11 & XXX.27; Demosthenes VIII.66 & XVIII.131; Libanios' *hypothesis* to (Demosthenes) XVII used the word *neoploutoi* in XVII.23 to deny the speech's authenticity, saying that it was characteristic of Hypereides instead.

290. Aristotle *Rhetoric* 1387b25-28 & 1388a14-21.

291. Xenophon *Oikonomikos* XX.22-29 and Davies (1971) 265-268 on Ischomachos' father; V.D. Hanson (1981).

292. (Aristotle) *Athênaiôn Politeia* II, VI & XI-XII and Aristotle F389 Rose, preferable to Plutarch *Solon* XIII, as argued by Biscardi (1984); Finley (1981b) 150-166; Amouretti (1986) 210 suggested that the *hektêmoroi* were cultivating olive trees, but there is no reason why they should not have been cultivating cereals as well; Biraschi (1984) on Thucydides on archaic Attica; Cato *De agricultura* CXXXVI on sharecroppers receiving a fifth of the harvest in Roman Italy; Newman (1932) 54 on sharecroppers in the Talmud receiving from 25 per cent to 75 per cent of the crop, depending on circumstances; Thiersch (1833) vol. 1, p. 303 on early modern Greece; Bentley (1987) on partible inheritance, population growth and land fragmentation; Bourdieu (1980) 218-220 and Valensi (1985)

107-109 discussed the *khammes* in modern Algeria, a sharecropper tied by debt bondage into a patron-client relationship who has to turn over 80 per cent of the harvest to his patron, an interesting parallel to the *hektêmoros*; incidentally Bourdieu (1980) 194 also provides an analogy for another supposedly long-lost Athenian institution, namely the *prasis epi lusei* loans discussed by Finley (1952) (they have nothing to do with the *hektêmoroi*) – Finley was right that one had to be fairly well-to-do to take on such a loan in the first place, in the sense of having land to offer as security, but such a person might still be in trouble in the sense of being desperately short of cash – the alternative to taking on a loan of that kind would be to sell land to raise cash, cf. Catiline's problems in Rome, and the Agesilaos (uncle of Agis IV) in Plutarch *Agis* XIII.2 – all this is comprehensible in the context of an economy in which money in the form of coinage was in chronically short supply (see section 2 of this chapter).

293. Finley (1980) 86-89; Appian *BC* I.7; Hesiod *WD* 602-603 with the commentary of West (1978), although he also took slave labour for granted, as in e.g. *WD* 458-461; Solon F13, lines 47-48; Homer *Iliad* XXI.444-445; Martin (1913) 244 for modern Greece; for the equation of wage labour with slavery see Xenophon *Memorabilia* II.8 and Khrysippos F352 ed. von Arnim vol. 3; Varro *RR* I.16.4 for hiring of some types of labour on a yearly basis in Roman Italy.

294. Wrigley & Schofield (1981) and Laslett (1983) on England; Dupâquier (1972) & (1988) and Bideau (1984) on France.

295. Darwin (1968) 243-247 and E.O. Wilson (1971) 364-371 on slavery in ants; Aristotle *Politics* 1252a30-b9, 1253b23-1255b40 & 1260a33-b7; Kullmann (1984) argued that Aristotle's political thought was heavily influenced by his ethological observations, for example that some animal societies exhibit ranking, e.g. *HA* 488a10-13.

296. Aristotle *Politics* 1273b18-21 & 1320b4-7; Livy XXII.9.10-10.8, Strabo V.4.12.250c, Pliny *NH* III.xiii.110 and Dionysios Hal. *AR* I.16 on *ver sacrum*.

297. Aristotle *Rhetoric* 1366b9-11; Plato *Laws* 740-741; cf. Peristiany (1976) 149-150 on the problem of maintaining estates large enough for plough agriculture in modern Tunisia; Laiou-Thomadakis (1978) 193-197.

298. Plato *Laws* 773; Menander *Dyskolos* ed. Sandbach 784-819.

299. Aiskhines I.95 (with scholiast) and Demosthenes LVII.41 for cases of enrichment through marriage to an heiress.

300. E.g. J. Davis (1973) 111; Stirling (1965) 126 & 167; Bourdieu (1980) 249-270; (Aristotle) *Athênaiôn Politeia* IX on the obscurity of Athenian legislation.

301. Aristotle *Politics* 1270a23-29, cf. 1304a4-13 on *epiklêroi* in Sparta; Cartledge (1981a) on Spartan women; Hodkinson (1986) & (1989); Brulé (1978) 176-177, on the *apetairoi* of Crete, provides a good parallel for the Spartan *hupomeiones*; Henige (1974) 207-213, with the modifications of Cartledge (1979) 341-346, on the king-lists.

302. Friedl (1962) 48-74 and Saulnier-Thiercelin in Piault (1985) 47-93 on land fragmentation in modern Greece; H. Forbes (1985) 324ff. on its agricultural consequences; Schaps (1975) argued that the existence of a brother excluded a sister from inheriting land in most *poleis*; Aristotle *Politics* 1265b26 commented on the difficulty of managing two households simultaneously, with reference to Plato's idea of dividing farms into two separate portions in his ideal *polis*, while in 1266b13-14 he noted that *stasis* was likely to be caused by partible inheritance impoverishing sons of a rich family.

303. Aristotle *Politics* 1253b9-10; Benveniste (1969) vol. 1, pp. 239-244; (Demosthenes) LIX.122.

304. (Demosthenes) XLIV.49 & XLVI.18; Isaios III.39 on the *pallakai*.

305. Plutarch *Solon* XX; Hesiod *WD* 405-406 with West (1978) ad loc.; Homer *Iliad* XVIII.593 and *Homeric Hymn to Aphrodite* 119 speak of 'cattle-earning maidens', *parthenoi alphesiboiai*, cf. the pastoral component of African age class societies which practise bridewealth; Szemerényi (1977) 203-204 on *eedna*; Aristotle *Politics* 1268b41 on bridewealth; Goody & Tambiah (1973).

306. Aristotle *NE* 1142a11-19 on the need for *neoi* to acquire experience before holding political office, and *Rhetoric* 1389a3-b12 & 1390b3-6 on age and sexual behaviour.

307. Peristiany (1976) 71 & 236.

308. J. Preuss (1978) 451-452 on Israel.

309. Colinvaux (1982) 397-398; Darwin (1901) 283.

310. F. Black (1966) and in A. Evans (1984) 397-418 on measles; Schaffer & Kot (1985) and Pool (1989a) on chaos; Cliff et al. (1981) on population biology of diseases in island populations.

311. L. Bradley (1977) on Eyam; Biraben (1975) vol. 1, pp. 188-189 on rapid recovery after plague epidemics, and on plague accelerating population declines; Anderson & May (1988) and Anderson, May & McLean (1988) on AIDS.

312. Hippokrates *peri phusios anthrôpou* IX, *peri phusôn* VI and *peri diaitês oxeôn* II ed. Littré vol. 6, pp. 52-57 & 96-99 and vol. 2, pp. 232-235; *Anonymus Londinensis* ed. W.H.S. Jones (1947) V.35-VII.40 for Hippokrates' views on disease causation; (Aristotle) *Problems* I.7.859b15-20; Grmek (1983) 456; Pollux *Onomasticon* IV.184-207 and Galen *therapeutikês methodou* II ed. Kühn vol. X, pp. 81-85 listed Greek words referring to diseases and their symptoms; Plutarch *Moralia* 1128e, perhaps based on the comments of Herodotos I.197 on Babylonia.

313. Theophrastos *HP* IX.20.5; Pliny *NH* XXVII.cxx.145; Hippokrates *peri diaitês oxeôn (notha)* XVIII ed. Littré vol. 2, pp. 492-495 and Galen *peri trophôn dunameôn* III.2 ed. Kühn vol. VI, p. 661 for pork as the most nourishing meat, but Hippokrates *peri pathôn* LII ed. Littré vol. 6, pp. 262-263 said that pork is too strong for ill people; Thucydides III.94.5; the desire of members of low status groups in Lakonia to eat Spartiates raw (Xenophon *Hellênika* III.3.6) would gain an added point if it was normal to eat cooked meat in Lakonia; Simoons (1961) on pork; Hippokrates *peri archaikês iatrikês* III ed. Littré vol. 1, pp. 574-579 on proper food preparation reducing disease and mortality, cf. XIII, pp. 598-599 on cooked meat and processed cereal products as superior to raw meat and unrefined cereals, and *Epidemics* VII.102 ed. Littré vol. 5, pp. 454-455 for food poisoning attributed to consumption of a raw mushroom; Hoeppli (1959) 7-17 on parasitic worms in antiquity; Hubbert et al. (1975) 581-600 & 678-686 on diseases caused by worms; Aristotle *HA* 551a1-13 on spontaneous generation, also 603b16-26 for cysticercal larvae in pigs; Edelstein (1945) T422 (Aelian *peri zôiôn idiotêtos* IX.33) and T423 II.23; Hippokrates *peri nousôn* IV.54 ed. Littré vol. 7, pp. 595-601 on parasitic worms, also *Prognôstikon* XI ed. Littré vol. 2, pp. 136-137; Dioskorides *MM* I.110.3, 126.2 & II.152.2 on herbal remedies; Columella *RR* VI.25 & 30.9 noted worms in domesticated animals.

314. Lucretius *De rerum natura* VI.1110-1118, also mentioning leprosy in Egypt and trachoma in Achaia; Pliny *NH* XXVI.lxiv-lxv.100-102 regarded gout (*podagra*) as a disease alien to Italy because it did not have a Latin name, although it did exist in classical Greece judging by the Hippokratic corpus; Lucian wrote a mini-tragedy called *Podagra*; Pliny *NH* XXXI.viii.11, cf. xxii.36 stated that diseases of the feet were prevalent in Troizen, attributed to bad water; other possible identifications for diseases of the feet are: (1) the poorly understood 'burning feet syndrome', on which see Passmore & Eastwood (1986) 328,

associated with diets deficient in proteins and B vitamins in developing countries; (2) famine oedema (see n. 322 below); Byl (1988) considers gout.

315. Hippokrates *aphorismoi* VII.55 ed. Littré vol. 4, pp. 594-595 and Hubbert (1975) 690 on cystic hydatid disease; Hippokrates *peri diaitês* I.46 ed. Littré vol. 6, pp. 546-547 and Diokles F93 ed. Wellmann and Simoons (1961) on dogmeat; Hippokrates *peri tôn entos pathôn* XXXVII ed. Littré vol. 7, pp. 258-261 and R.W. McCollum in A. Evans (1984) 327-350 on hepatitis.

316. Grmek (1983) 16; Corvisier (1985) 116-127 on frequency of diseases in classical Greece; Goodall (1934); Siegel (1960); Patrick (1967); Zinsser (1935).

317. Grmek (1983) 140.

318. A.J. Nahmias & W.E. Josey in A. Evans (1984) 351-372 on herpes, also Grmek (1983) 221-222; Beswick (1962) cited Hippokrates *Epidemics* VI, section VIII.21 ed. Littré vol. 5, pp. 353-354 for herpes simplex on the lips; Scribonius Largus *Compositiones* LXIII, also CVI, ed. Sconocchia; Pliny *NH* XXVI.lxxiv.121; Hope-Simpson (1954) and T.H. Weller in A. Evans (1984) 569-595 on varicella; Grmek (1983) 477-478 cited Hippokrates *Kôakai prognôseis* VII.35.618 ed. Littré vol. 5, pp. 728-729 for shingles, and P. Potter's interpretation of Hippokrates *peri nousôn* III.7 ed. Littré vol. 7, pp. 124-126 for chickenpox.

319. Grmek (1983) 491-496 cited Hippokrates *Epidemics* VII.11 ed. Littré vol. 5, pp. 382-387 for typhoid fever; R.B. Hornick in Evans & Feldman (1982) 659-676.

320. Diogenes Laertios I.110 (= Epimenides 3 A1 & B1 eds. Diels-Kranz) with Lévy (1978), cf. Rhodes (1981) 79-83; Plutarch *Theseus* XV.1 for crop failure and epidemic during Minos' war on Attica; Dionysios Hal. *AR* I.23.2-3 for famine and epidemic among the Pelasgians; Herodotos VII.171.1-2 for epidemic and famine decimating the Cretans returning home from the Trojan War; Pausanias I.14.4 on Thales of Gortyn stopping a disease for the Spartans, I.43.7 on an epidemic in Megara, IV.9.1 on disease in Messenia during the wars with Sparta, V.4.6 for an epidemic in Greece in the time of Iphitos, who re-established the Olympic Games after a break, IX.8.2, 36.3 & 38.3 for other epidemics; C. Alldred in *Cambridge Ancient History* (3rd ed. 1975) vol. II part 2A, pp. 19 & 84 and Pritchard (1969) 394-396, cf. 347, on the Hittite prayers of Mursilis.

321. Hesiod *WD* 243 associates *limos* and *loimos*; Homer *Odyssey* XV.407-408 classes famine as a 'disease', but uses the word *peinê*, not *limos*; Thucydides II.54.2-3; Chantraine (1980) 641 on the etymology; Bourguet (1927) 17 n. 2 suggested that *loimos* meant 'famine' in the Lakonian dialect of Greek; Borza (1979) 120 n. 33 suggested that the *loimos* of Theophrastos *HP* IV.11.3, cf. Pliny *NH* XVI.lxvi.169, was epidemic malaria, but there is no other evidence for an epidemic at the time of the period of food shortages of *c.* 330 onwards, mentioned by Theophrastos *Charaktêres* XXIII (*alazôn*); Dupont (1984) on 'pestilence' as a literary theme (her criticism of Grmek is baseless), also Grimm (1965) and Gervais (1972).

322. Herodotos VIII.115.2-3 with Demont (1988), cf. Hippokrates *peri pathôn* XXIII-XXV ed. Littré vol. 6, pp. 234-237 on *dusenteria* and *diarrhoia*; Galen *peri euchumias kai kakochumias trophôn* I ed. Kühn vol. VI, pp. 749-753; Hesiod *WD* 243-244 and Le Roy Ladurie (1975) on famine amenorrhoea; Hesiod *WD* 41, Plutarch *eis ta Hêsiodou erga* F26 ed. Sandbach, Galen *peri trophôn dunameôn* II.65 ed. Kühn vol. VI, pp. 651-652, Theophrastos *HP* VII.12.1 & 13.1-4, Negbi (1989) 29-30 and Atchley (1938) on asphodel, also Porphyry *Life of Pythagoras* XXXIV ed. Nauck; Hesiod *WD* 496-499, Plutarch *eis ta Hêsiodou erga* F69 citing a law of Ephesos preventing a father from selling an infant unless the father was suffering from famine oedema (the Greek text is ambiguous, but famine oedema

is characteristic of old people, not infants), (Aristotle) *Problems* I.5.859b1-4, Josephos *Ioudaikos Polemos* V.549 ed. Naber, Schiller (1921) and Passmore & Eastwood (1986) 263-264 on famine oedema; Hesiod *WD* 299-302, 363, 404 & 646-647; legendary famines in e.g. Pausanias I.44.9, II.29.7-8, II.31.10 & IX.40.1; Valaoras (1946) on the famine in Athens during the Second World War; Henige (1982) 89-90 for the anthropological research.

323. Arrian *Anabasis* IV.4.9; Lucian *peri tês Peregrinou teleutês* XIX; Grmek (1983) 494 & 501-502 cited Hippokrates *Epidemics* I.10 & VII.55 ed. Littré vol. 2, pp. 704-709 & vol. 5, pp. 422-423 for salmonella and amoebic dysentery respectively; D.R. Snydman & S.L. Gorbach in Evans & Feldman (1982) 463-485 on nontyphoidal salmonellosis; G.T. Keutsch in Evans & Feldman (1982) 487-509 on shigellosis; Hippokrates *peri odontophuiês* XVI ed. Littré vol. 8, pp. 546-547 on weaning.

324. Corvisier (1985) 146-147; Aretaios *peri sêmeiôn kai aitiôn oxeiôn kai chroniôn pathôn* I.9 ed. Hude, Grmek (1983) 480-481, J. Preuss (1978) 157-160 and P.F. Wehrle in Evans & Feldman (1982) 207-218 on diphtheria; Grmek (1983) 467 and E.A. Mortimer in Evans & Feldman (1982) 393-402 on whooping cough; R.W. Quinn in Evans & Feldman (1982) 525-552 on streptococcal infections; Bradley (1971) on Bernoulli.

325. H.A. Feldman in A. Evans (1984) 419-440 on mumps (cf. W.D. Glezen et al. in A. Evans (1984) 441-454 on parainfluenza); Hippokrates *Epidemics* I 1st Constitution I ed. Littré vol. 2, pp. 600-605 on Thasos.

326. Zeuner (1963) 443-455 and R.D. Crawford in Mason (1984) 298-311; Porphyry *peri apochês empsuchôn* IV.16; Julius Caesar *de bello Gallico* V.12.6; Simoons (1961); Columella *RR* VIII.2.4-5; Diokles of Karystos F141 Wellmann; Aristotle *GA* 730a9-11 mentions breeders of domestic fowl; West & Ben-Xiong Zhou (1988) acknowledge that the main period of diffusion of the chicken through Europe was the first millennium BC, but claim a number of sporadic finds in contexts dating to the Late Neolithic-Early Bronze Age, in Greece from Kommos and the Trapeza cave, Lasithi in Crete, Lerna, Rhodes, and Ayios Stephanos in Lakonia – scepticism about these isolated early finds is justified until they have been investigated thoroughly because West & Ben-Xiong Zhou do not appear to have perused original excavation reports in compiling their catalogue of finds, e.g. they cite without qualification the chicken finds from EBA Lerna which were made in *mixed and surface strata only* according to the excavators (Gejvall (1969) 49) and so are obviously unreliable; Allan (1971) on Newcastle disease.

327. L. Morris (1972) 301-407; Underwood (1979) 117-125 & 172-194; Cazes (1980); F. Livingstone (1987); Cazes & Bonné-Tamir (1984) on the Samaritans; Navajas y Navarro & Britton-Davidian (1989) on multiple founding events followed by independent evolution as responsible for genetic differentiation among mouse populations on the Mediterranean islands.

328. Feigenbaum (1956) cited Hippokrates *Epidemics* III.7 ed. Littré vol. 3, pp. 84-85; Lehner & Barnes (1986).

329. Strabo X.5.9.487c and Plutarch *Moralia* 616b on Mykonos; Zenobios V.17 & *Appendix Proverbiorum* IV.52 eds. Leutsch & Schneidewin *Corpus Paroemiographorum Graecorum* vol. 1, pp. 122 & 445 offer two alternative explanations for the proverb *Mia Mykonos* which Strabo was grappling with; Aristotle *GA* 782a9-16, 783b8-784a22, *HA* 518a7-b28 and Rook & Dawber (1982) 97-98 on baldness; Aelian *peri zôiôn idiotêtos* V.42 states that there were no bees on Mykonos, a peculiarity of its ecology.

330. J. Black et al. (1963) and Roberts (1971) on Tristan da Cunha; Ericksen et al. (1979) on the Old Order Amish; Hodkinson (1989) 107-109 on

Sparta; Bittles & Makov (1988) 164 for the quotation in the text; Kolodny (1974) vol. 1, pp. 133-135 on Amorgos; Roberts et al. (1965) on genetic isolation in isolated endogamous villages on Tenos; Fix (1979).

331. Wiesenfeld (1967) and S.J. Edelstein (1986) 55-56 on sickle-cell anaemia; Grmek (1983) 382-383 envisaged difficulties explaining the early diffusion of the haemoglobin S allele from tropical Africa to India, but did not consider the evidence for Bronze Age contacts between E. Africa and India presented in Chapter I; Grmek (1983) 355-407 on thalassaemia; F. Livingstone (1967) esp. 17-21, 67-75 & 242-262, (1971) & (1985) 250; Hart (1980); F. Livingstone (1984) suggested that a pre-existing high frequency of the recessive Duffy negative allele prevented vivax malaria from ever *establishing* itself in tropical Africa, an idea which runs contrary to widely accepted views on natural selection as he recognised, but he did not consider the evidence for climatic change; P. Mattingly (1983) argued that vivax malaria evolved in Africa, while the vivax group malaria parasites of apes in south-east Asia are significantly different from human vivax malaria.

332. Meinecke (1927) collected ancient references to tuberculosis; Sharpe (1962); Hubbert et al. (1975) 303-360 on bovine TB, described by Aristotle *HA* 604a14 & 16-21 (Greek *krauros*) and Columella *RR* VI.14.1; Fiennes (1978) 27 & 96-101 suggested that human TB was unknown in antiquity and all the cases described in ancient sources were bovine TB, a misguided idea; Youmans (1979) 356-369 on epidemiology of TB; Grmek (1983) 261-290; Manchester (1984); Corvisier (1985) 13, 96-97 & 135; Coale & Demeny (1983) 3; Hippokrates *Epidemics* 1st Constitution II & III ed. Littré vol. 2, pp. 604-615 for TB causing great mortality at Thasos, while no other disease did so, *Epidemics* III 3rd Constitution XIII ed. Littré vol. 3, pp. 92-97 on TB as the most lethal disease, *peri arthrôn* XLI ed. Littré vol. 4, pp. 177-183 on bone lesions caused by TB, *Aphorismoi* V.9 & *Kôakai prognôseis* II.21.431 ed. Littré vol. 4, pp. 534-535 & vol. 5, pp. 680-681 respectively on ages 18-35 as most dangerous for TB, *Kôakai prognôseis* VI.31.513 ed. Littré vol. 5, pp. 702-703 and Youmans (1979) 203-204 on the danger of TB to pregnant women, *peri nousôn* I.3 ed. Littré vol. 6, pp. 144-145 on TB as invariably fatal, *prorrhêtikon* VII ed. Littré vol. 9, pp. 24-25 on susceptibility of unmarried girls and women to TB; Isokrates XIX (*Aiginêtikos*) was written for the heir of a man suffering from TB; Aretaios *peri aitiôn kai sêmeiôn oxeôn kai chroniôn pathôn* III.8 ed. Hude is the best ancient description of TB; Formicola et al. (1987) give evidence for the existence of TB in Neolithic Italy.

333. Moschion *peri tôn gunaikeiôn pathôn* (i.e. the *de mulierum passionibus liber* of Mustio, who originally wrote in Latin, a point not realised by the editor) CXLII ed. Dewez on TB as a cause of sterility in women; McFalls (1984) 75-98 on the demographic effects of genital TB (receiving a dismissive review on this point from R.H. Gray in *PS* 40 (1986) 327-328); Steinbock (1976) 170-212 and Zivanovich (1982) 225-232 on osteological evidence for TB and leprosy.

334. Simoons (1979), Passmore & Eastwood (1986) 441-442 and Flatz (1987) on lactose intolerance; Homer *Iliad* XIII.5-6, Hesiod F150.15 & 151 eds. Merkelbach-West, Hippokrates *peri aërôn, hudatôn, topôn* XVIII ed. Littré vol. 2, pp. 68-69, Herodotos IV.23.3 and Theopompos FGH115 F45 Jacoby for Scythian consumption of milk, cf. Columella *RR* VII.2.2; Briant (1982a) on Greek attitudes to nomads, cf. B. Shaw (1982/83).

335. Siegel (1960) 85-86 cited Hippokrates *Epidemics* II section III.1 ed. Littré vol. 5, pp. 100-103, contrast Grmek (1983) 465; Fiennes (1978) 56-57.

336. J. Preuss (1978) 323-339 identified Hebrew *tzaraath* as leprosy, while the *leprê* or *leukê* of Herodotos I.138.1-2 in Persia may well refer to leprosy; Fiennes (1978) 25-27; Grmek (1983) 227-260 & 291-306 and Manchester (1984) on the theory of its interaction with tuberculosis; Grmek states that leprosy is *not* highly contagious, but this is mistaken, as only its pathogenicity is low; Andersen (1969) 17-43, also 45 on Alexander (cf. Q. Curtius Rufus IX.10.1); S.G. Browne in Hastings (1985) 1-14; Blake (1987) and Reich et al. (1987) for the two competing hypotheses; Pliny *NH* XXVI.i-vi.9, Plutarch *Moralia* 731b and Oribasios *Coll. Med.* XLV.28 ed. Raeder citing Rufus *peri elephantiaseôs* on leprosy as a new disease, also the whole Plutarch passage 731a-734c for the general issue of new diseases; Dzierzykray-Rogalski (1980) on Dakleh; Aretaios *peri aitiôn kai sêmeiôn oxeôn kai chroniôn pathôn* IV.13.

337. Grmek (1983) 199-225 on syphilis; McFalls (1984) 309-349 for its rather limited effects on fertility.

338. Fiennes (1978) 37-45 and F.M. Davenport in A. Evans (1984) 373-396 on influenza; Grmek (1983) 474-475; Livy IV.52.3-11 & XXVII.23.6-7 for big epidemics with a low case mortality rate.

339. Corvisier (1985) 49-50 & 59; Hippokrates *peri diaitês hugieinês* III ed. Littré vol. 6, pp. 76-77 recommended frequent bathing in summer, not so frequent in winter.

340. Hippokrates *Epistolai* ed. Littré vol. 9, pp. 313-321, 400-403 & 418-421 and Pliny *NH* VII.xxxvii.123, with Pinault (1986); Herodotos VI.27.2; Thucydides V.41.2; Plutarch *Kimon* XIX.4 states that the people of Kition in Cyprus were advised to honour Kimon as a god during an epidemic and famine.

341. The possible readings *peri loimôn* or *peri loimikôn kakôn* of the work by Demokritos mentioned by Aulus Gellius *NA* IV.13.3 and Caelius Aurelianus were rejected in favour of *peri logikôn kanôn* by Diels-Kranz s.v. Demokritos 68 A33, following Sextus Empiricus *pros mathêmatikous* VII.138 & VIII.328; Mugler (1967) discussed Plutarch *Moralia* 733d on the extra-terrestrial theory; Aristotle *PA* 653a8-9; Diogenes Laertios V.44 on Theophrastos; Plato *Laws* 709a regarded epidemics as a possible cause of political strife and revolution.

342. Livy II.34.5 – a *pestilentia* among the Volsci during the secession of the plebs in 492 BC, cf. Dionysios Hal. *AR* VII.12.4-5 claiming 90 per cent mortality out of the entire population at Velitrae; Livy III.2.1 – an epidemic struck a Roman army camp in Latium in 466/5 BC; III.6.1-8.1 – a bad epidemic in 463 BC affecting most men of military age, fields not cultivated, cf. Orosios II.12.2-3; Livy III.32.2-4 and Diony. Hal. *AR* X.53 for epidemic followed by famine at Rome 453-452 BC, half the citizens and almost all slaves killed; Livy IV.20.9-21.7 – a period of epidemics 437-435 BC; IV.25.3-6 & 26.5 – an epidemic in 433 BC leading to fear of famine, many men of military age killed, cattle also affected; Livy IV.30.7-9 and Diony. Hal. *AR* XII.6 – an epidemic spread allegedly from cattle to men, producing dreadful skin pains, but no famine, in 428 BC; Livy IV.52.3-5 – an epidemic in 412 BC affected many but killed few, causing neglect of cultivation of land; V.14.4 – epidemic in 399 BC; V.31.5-8 and Diony. Hal. *AR* XIII.4 epidemic and food crisis brought on by heat and drought in 392 BC, small *exanthêmata* on skin developed into large *helkê*, accompanied by terrible skin pain; Livy V.48.1-3 – famine then disease struck the Gauls attacking Rome in 390 BC; VI.20.15 – epidemic with no obvious causes in 384 BC, then food shortage; VII.1.7-2.3 – an epidemic with high mortality in 365/4 BC, cf. Orosios III.4.1-5; Livy VII.27.1 – an epidemic in 347/6 BC; X.31.8a – a severe epidemic in 295 BC; X.47.6-7 – an epidemic in 292 BC; Polybios II.31.10 – an epidemic among Roman troops in the Po valley in 224 BC; Livy XXVII.23.6-7 an epidemic in 208 BC, a long but not fatal disease; XXVIII.46.15 & XXIX.10.1 – an epidemic in 205 BC affecting both Roman

and Carthaginian armies, the latter also weakened by hunger; XXXVIII.44.7 – an epidemic at Rome in 187 BC; XL.19.3-7 & 36.14 for epidemics 182-180 BC; the narrative of Livy is not completely preserved for the whole of the chronological period surveyed in this note.

343. Diodoros Siculus XIII.12.1 & 4 and Thucydides VII.47.1-2 on the epidemic striking the Athenian army at Syracuse in 413 BC, identified as falciparum malaria by Grmek (1979); Diodoros Siculus XIII.86.2 & 114.2, XIV.41.1-2, 45.3 & 70.4-71.4 (with Littman (1984) on this epidemic in 396 BC; Grmek (1979) 160 gives a different interpretation) and XV.24.2 for epidemics in N. Africa and in Carthaginian armies in Sicily; Polybios I.19.1 on an epidemic among Roman troops in Sicily in 262 BC; Livy XXV.26.7-15 and Silius Italicus XIV.580-626 for an epidemic striking the Roman and Carthaginian armies at Syracuse in 212 BC; Kermack & MacKendrick (1927) on the Threshold Theorem.

344. T.J. Cornell – Cambridge seminar paper for the estimate of the population of Rome; Polybios II.24, with Brunt (1971) 44-60.

345. Thucydides I.22.4 & II.48.3 on his intentions, I.23.3, II.47.3-54.5, 57, 58.3, 64.1 & III.87.1-3 on the epidemic; Woodman (1988) 32-40 argued that the account of Thucydides is rhetorical and only a limited reflection of reality.

346. Cumston (1903) anticipated the view of Holladay & Poole that the Athenian epidemic may have been caused by a disease which has since become extinct; Page (1953) proposed that Thucydides employed specialised medical terminology, a thesis advocated in much more detail but still unconvincingly by Lichtenthaeler (1965), whose book was unknown to A. Parry (1969); Galen *peri duspnoias* II.7 ed. Kühn vol. VII, p. 854 settles the debate quite conclusively in Parry's favour; Thucydides VII.47.2 employed the popular seasonal explanation of diseases (cf. Herodotos II.77.3), but not in his account of the epidemic of Athens.

347. Thucydides II.51.1; Aristotle *Politics* 1304a4-10 contra Thucydides III.2.3 on Mytilene.

348. Plutarch *Perikles* XXXIV.3-4; Aulus Gellius *NA* II.1.4-5 and Diogenes Laertios II.25 state that Sokrates was the only person not to become infected – this is impossible, as the second phase of the epidemic in 427 BC shows that a significant proportion of the population did not contract the disease during the first phase; Pausanias X.11.5 & VIII.41.7-9 contra Thucydides II.54.5 on the Peloponnese; Plutarch *Perikles* XXXV.3 on Epidauros; Pausanias I.3.4 & II.32.6 contra Thucydides II.48.4 on religious remedies; Diodoros Siculus XII.58.6-7; although the epidemic doubtless inclined the Athenians towards welcoming new divinities of healing, the introduction of the cult of Asklepios to Athens in 420 BC by Telemachos may not have been connected directly to it – IG II² 4960a and Edelstein (1945) vol. 2, p. 120 n. 4, cf. Mikalson (1984); Plato *Symposion* 201d briefly mentions the great epidemic.

349. Diodoros Siculus XII.45.2-4, 46.3-5, 52.2 & 58.1-7; A.W. Gomme *A historical commentary on Thucydides* vol. 2 (1956) 148-149; Lucretius *De rerum natura* VI.1090-1286, with the editions of Ernout & Robin and Bailey on lines 1183-1196 in particular, suggesting Asklepiades or Demetrios of Lakonia as the immediate source used by Lucretius, cf. Commager (1957); Manilius *Astronomica* I.880-895 also mentions the epidemic.

350. Keser (1893/4), H.M. Fisher (1901), Waltz (1914), Hooker (1957) and E. Williams (1962) suggested that plague was responsible for the Athenian epidemic; Shrewsbury (1950) and Page (1953) opted for measles, also considered by Holladay & Poole (1979); the main sources used for smallpox were C. Dixon (1962) esp. 5-14 on fulminating smallpox & 68-71 on differential diagnosis, A.S. Benenson in A. Evans (1984) 541-568, Fenner (1983), and Fenner at al. (1988), the most recent review of smallpox.

351. Littré vol. 1, pp. 39-42, vol. 3, pp. xxxvi-xl on the possibility that the *katastasis* in Hippokrates *Epidemics* III referred to 430 BC, vol. 5, pp. 48-70, vol. 7, pp. xxii-xxviii, and vol. 8, pp. xxii-xxviii; Zinsser (1935) 119-127, also anticipating Littman (1984) on the epidemic of 396 BC in Syracuse, and 135-137 on the Antonine epidemic; Ebbell (1967) 39-52.

352. Blum (1965) 62 on the peasants; Crawfurd (1914) 23-41 & 212-222 and W. MacArthur (1954), (1958) & (1959) opted for typhus, *contra* Zinsser (1935) 122-123; Thucydides II.50.1-2 on dogs and birds, used by (1) Eby & Evjen (1962) to argue the case for glanders, an improbable identification criticised by Holladay & Poole (1982); (2) Wylie & Stubbs (1983) to suggest tularaemia and leptospirosis, improbable ideas criticised by Holladay & Poole (1984); D.R. Hopkins (1983) 187 on cannibals; Chapter III.10 explains the reasons for rejecting the claim of Kobert-Rostock (1899) and Salway & Dell (1955) that ergotism was responsible; Fenner et al. (1988) 47 for secondary bacterial infections of smallpox lesions; Galen *peri chreias tôn en anthrôpou sômati moriôn* III.5 ed. Kühn vol. III, p. 188 noticed gangrene of the extremities during the Antonine epidemic.

353. D.R. Hopkins (1983) esp. 13-21 on antiquity; F.L. Black in A. Evans (1984) 406 and the series of articles in *RID* X.2. (1988) 451-499 on mortality rates of measles epidemics; C. Dixon (1962) 325-326 on mortality rates of smallpox; Fenner et al. (1988) 227 on the Japanese epidemic.

354. Hippokrates *peri nousôn* XXII ed. Littré vol. 6, pp. 182-189 on the differential age-specific effects of various diseases (not smallpox); Willan (1821) 78-79 identified the *ignis sacer* of Lucretius *de rerum natura* V.859 & VI.1167 as smallpox; Marius bishop of Avenches ed. Mommsen *Monumenta Germaniae Historiae* vol. XI s.v. *annus* 570 was the first author to use the word 'variola'; Willan (1821) 86-115 and Shrewsbury (1949) argued that Celtic, Irish & Saxon chronicles suggest that smallpox epidemics were frequent in Britain in the sixth and seventh centuries AD, cf. W. MacArthur (1959); Eusebios *Ecclesiastical History* IX.8.1 ed. Bardy may also mention a smallpox epidemic in AD 302; Rhazes (1848) 27-29, where the discussion of Rhazes on Galen by the translator Greenhill is misguided; Galen *peri tês tôn haplôn pharmakôn kraseôs kai dunameôs* IX.1 ed. Kühn vol. XII, p. 191.

355. Thucydides II.51.6; C. Dixon (1962) 335-336 states that second attacks of smallpox had a mortality rate of about 25 per cent, but Rao cited by Benenson in A. Evans (1984) 555 said that second attacks of smallpox were never fatal, in agreement with Thucydides, although both agree on the frequency of second attacks, also accepted by Fenner et al. (1988) 51-52; Getz & Pickering (1983) criticised the use of density thresholds in relation to smallpox, but as it produces lifelong immunity in most cases it undoubtedly has a high density threshold.

356. Fildes (1986) 179.

357. Delia (1988) on Alexandria; Darwin (1901) 284; the epidemics recorded among the barbarians did not prevent the destruction of the western Roman empire in the long run, e.g. Ambrose *Epistle* XV ed. *Migne Patrologia* Latina vol. 16, col. 957 mentions epidemics among the Goths.

358. J. Preuss (1978) 151, cf. McNeill (1976) 80-81.

359. Lucian *pôs dei historian suggraphein* XV attacked authors who, following Thucydides, placed the origin of epidemics in 'Ethiopia'; later authors falling into this category include Zonaras XII.21b ed. Dindorf on the epidemic of Cyprian (see n. 362 below), Procopius *huper tôn polemôn* II.22-23 on bubonic plague in the reign of Justinian and John VI Cantacuzenus *Historiae* IV.8 ed. Migne *Patrologiae cursus completus* vol. 154, cols. 57-62, discussed by Miller (1976), on the Black Death; Ammianus Marcellinus XIX.4.4 on the epidemic at Amida also

recalled Thucydides; Cicero *De natura deorum* I.36 and Poseidonios F223 eds. Edelstein & Kidd on epidemics in Egypt and Libya, while Theophrastos F159 Wimmer noted how unhealthy the Nile was (owing to schistosomiasis); Regöly-Mérei (1966) and Ebbell (1967) 7-39 on smallpox in ancient Egypt; Fenner et al. (1988) 116-119 on the origins of the variola virus, cf. Cockburn (1963) 197 suggesting that it evolved from the pox viruses of domesticated animals.

360. Littré vol. 3, p. xxxvii cited H. Haeser as having proposed this theory in 1839, taken up again recently by Coughanowr (1985); Livy IV.25.3 on the Apollo temple.

361. Gilliam (1961) attempted to downgrade the importance of the Antonine epidemic, but Littman (1973) rightly reasserted it, cf. Ebbell (1967) 53-59; Galen *peri tôn idiôn biblion* I ed. Kühn vol. XIX, p. 15 for his departure from Rome, *peri melainês cholês* IV vol. V, p. 115, *therapeutikês methodou* V vol. XII, pp. 360-361, *Hippokratous epidêmiôn III kai Galenou eis auto hupomnêma* III.57-58 vol. XVII.1, pp. 709-710, *Hippokratous epidêmiôn VI* ... XXIX vol. XVII.1, pp. 885-886 and *Hippokratous aphorismoi* ... XXI vol. XVII.2, pp. 682-683; Philostratos *VS* ed. Kayser vol. 2, p. 69 for the Antonine epidemic in Athens; *Scriptores Historiae Augustae – Life of Marcus Aurelius* XIII.3 ed. Hohl, cf. Eutropius VIII.12.2 ed. Santini and Orosius VII.15.5-6; Thucydides II.52.4; Pliny *NH* VII.1.170; Willan (1821) 51 on Dio Cassius LXVII.11.6 & LXXIII.14.3-4; Fenner et al. (1988) 245-258 on inoculation; Herodian I.12.1-2 ed. Stavenhagen noted that the epidemic in the reign of Commodus was most severe in Rome because the city was overcrowded and continuously receiving immigrants; Hecker (1857).

362. Cyprian *de mortalitate* XIV ed. Simonetti *Corpus Christianorum* ser. Latina vol. IIIA part II, discussed by Zinsser (1935) 138-140, another epidemic with severe effects in Egypt, cf. Orosios VII.22.1-2, and *SHA Life of Gallienus* V.5 ed. Hohl for its effects on Greece; information on archaeological surveys of early mediaeval Italy derived from B. Ward-Perkins – Cambridge seminar paper.

363. Thucydides II.54.5 and Plutarch *Perikles* XXXIV.3-4, cf. Gomme op. cit. p. 160, while Thucydides III.13.3 suggests that the epidemic did not affect Lesbos; II.52.1-3 on the refugees; E.H. Smith (1797) emphasised the overcrowding factor, suggesting that the epidemic originated locally; Fenner et al. (1988) 118 for the estimate of 200,000; Papadopoulos (1980), Papaevangelou & Halstead (1980) and Stanley (1980) 161-162 on dengue in modern Athens.

364. Matessi & Minozzi (1979); Wood & Smouse (1982); Pearl (1939).

365. Cox & Peel (1972); Vries (1984) 175-198; D.R. Hopkins (1983) 52 & 74 on towns and smallpox in early modern England; Prat (1952) on Albi; Thucydides II.53.1 & III.19.1; *Iustiniani Novellae* CXXII ed. Schoell *idikton peri diatupôseôs technitôn*.

366. Thucydides II.58.3 & III.87.3 on the mortalities, with Strauss (1987) 75-76 and M. Hansen (1988) 14 on the crucial phrase *ek tôn taxeôn*; C. Dixon (1962) 14-20 on malignant confluent smallpox, also Fenner et al. (1988) 1-68.

367. C. Dixon (1962) 317-322 & 325-326, cf. Fenner (1988) 164 & 195-196, on morbidity and mortality rates of smallpox, cites the following estimate of age-specific case mortality:

Age-group	0-4	5-9	10-14	15-19	20-24	25-29	30-40	40-50
% mortality	40	25	20	25	35	35	40	50

368. Thucydides VI.26.2 on the recovery; Le Bras (1969); C. Dixon (1962) 113, Benenson in A. Evans (1984) 557 and Fenner et al. (1988) 54-55 on smallpox and pregnant women; Phadke et al. (1973) on male infertility, a theory criticised by Fenner et al. (1988) 49.

369. McNeill (1976) 103; Pausanias III.9.2 & VII.17.2, cf. VII.10.3; Coale (1972) on ergodicity.

370. Diodoros Siculus XII.58.1-7, cf. Hippokrates *Epidemics* III Constitution II ed. Littré vol. 3, pp. 68-69 associating stifling summer heat with weak etesian winds; Rhazes (1848) 33 on seasonality of smallpox epidemics; Fenner et al. (1988) 47 & 164 on smallpox and malnutrition; Thucydides II.4.2 & II.51.2-3; no one has yet attempted to use possible osteological evidence (osteomyelitis variolosa in children) to confirm the existence of smallpox in antiquity, cf. Jackes (1983).

371. Thucydides II.53.

372. Littré vol. 3, pp. 1-8 & vol. 4, p. 414 pointed out references to very bad illnesses in which the fever preceded or followed formation of a *boubôn* as evidence for plague, e.g. *Aphorismoi* IV.55 ed. Littré vol. 4, pp. 522-523 and *Epidemics* II section III.5 ed. Littré vol. 5, pp. 108-109; Hirst (1953) 36.

373. Hirst (1953) 122-126, J. Rackham (1979), E.M. Davis (1981) 89, Driesch & Boessneck (1983) and Armitage et al. (1984) on archaeological evidence for the rat, cf. R. Robinson in Mason (1984) 284-290; Zinsser (1935) 189-211 is now out of date; Martinet (1986) 247 on *mus*; Aelian *peri zôiôn idiotêtos* XVII.17 citing Amyntas FGH122 F3 Jacoby; Aristotle *HA* 600b13-14 & 632b9 (cf. Pliny *NH* VIII.lv.165) mentions a *mus pontikos ho leukos*, an interesting creature generally understood to be 'a kind of weasel' (as in Liddell & Scott) or a stoat (as in the Budé edition), but (1) there is a white-bellied variety of *R. rattus* and an albino variety of *R. norvegicus* and (2) the words *mus*, *pontiki* 'mouse', and *pontikos* 'rat' refer to mice and rats in modern Greek – perhaps the latter pair indicate that rats were thought to have reached Greece from the Black Sea region; Homer *Iliad* I.39 with scholiast & I.50, Strabo XIII.1.48.604-605c & 64.613c and Aelian *peri zôiôn idiotêtos* XII.5 on Apollo Smintheus, discussed by Bernheim & Zener (1978) whose suggestion of equine encephalomyelitis as the cause of the epidemic in the Trojan War has nothing to recommend it; Grégoire et al. (1949) and Huergon (1952) on the origins of the Apollo Smintheus cult; Pliny *NH* VIII.lxxxii.220-223 on mice.

374. Snyder (1965) describes typhus; Crawfurd (1914), Kiel (1951), Siegel (1960) 80-83 and Mitchel (1964) also argued in favour of typhus as the cause of the Athenian epidemic, contra Zinsser (1935) 117-123, also Grmek (1983) 435-436 criticising Siegel, although elsewhere (p. 494) Grmek states that typhus is attested in the Hippocratic corpus, but does not cite references; Fiennes (1978) 75-83; Hippokrates *peri tôn entos pathôn* XXXIX-XLIII ed. Littré vol. 7, pp. 260-275 describes a variety of different diseases called *tuphos* in antiquity; Kiel (1951) and Davies & Kathirithamby (1986) 168-176 on lice in antiquity, also Busvine (1976), a mine of information on these creatures; Plutarch *Moralia* 208e on Agesilaos; Aristotle *HA* 556b21-557a32 is the most interesting ancient source on lice, also Aristophanes *Eirênê* 740 & *Ploutos* 537 and Euboulos F32 Kock for their frequency in Athens; Edelstein (1945) T423 II.28 for a man with lice at Epidauros.

375. J. Preuss (1978) 152-156 argued that the 'plague' of the Philistines was bubonic plague, rejected by Conrad (1984); E. Williams (1962) argued that a pandemic of plague was the only factor which could have caused the chaos in the eastern Mediterranean and Middle East at the end of the Bronze Age, but this must be dismissed as a ridiculous idea because there is no evidence that plague was active then; Casanova (1984) doubted the existence of plague in the south-eastern Mediterranean in the Hellenistic period, but for some inexplicable reason he only considered Rufus *Iatrika erôtêmata* LXV-LXIX ed. Gärtner, completely overlooking the vital passage of Rufus *peri boubônos* cited by

Oribasios *Coll. Med.* XLIV.14 ed. Raeder which is accepted by experts such as Hirst (1953) 10 and Biraben (1975) vol. 1, pp. 22-25 as a description of plague; Rufus *peri loimôdous helkous*, cited by Oribasios XLIII.41, probably also refers to bubonic plague, as it mentions hard and painful buboes quickly leading to death; Grégoire et al. (1949) 164-168 argued that epizootics among rodents were associated with disease epidemics among humans in antiquity, to be contrasted with the belief of Biraben that this connection was not made in the past; a crucial source on the Black Death is Nikephoros Gregoras, translated by Bartsocas (1966) 395, who associated the characteristic mortality pattern of human plague (whole families wiped out) with an explicit reference to *rats dying in houses*, refuting the human flea hypothesis of Biraben and Ell (1980).

376. On the plague of Justinian see Zinsser (1935) 144-149; J. Russell (1968); Biraben (1975) vol. 1, pp. 25-48; Dols (1977) 15-16 for its origin in east Africa; Patlagean (1977) 85-91; Bratton (1981), the most detailed account, pointing out that Zinsser misinterpreted vesicular plague as smallpox, cf. Mango (1985) emphasising the magnitude of the catastrophe, comparable to the Black Death; J. Russell (1985) tried to use customs regarding the direction of burial in cemeteries to trace the effects of plague in early mediaeval Europe.

377. Bartsocas (1966) translated two Greek descriptions of the Black Death; Panzac (1973) on Ottoman Turkey; Kolodny (1974) vol. 1, pp. 145-147 on Kea and Crete; Biraben (1975) vol. 1, pp. 439-449 listed plague epidemics in the Balkans and Greece.

378. W.D. Tigertt in Evans & Feldman (1982) 403-415 is a general account of plague; McEvedy (1988); Rosqvist et al. (1988) and Lenski (1988) on evolution of plague virulence; Biraben (1975) vol. 1, pp. 10, 12 & 306 on decline of plague virulence during epidemics, 104 & 287 on density dependence, 121 on periodicity in France, 154 on origin of plague epidemics; Brubaker (1972) and Butler (1983) on plague virulence; Boyden (1970) 29-30 suggested that humans have evolved a degree of immunity to plague, cf. Ell (1984); Benedictow (1987), on the demographic effects of plague, concluded that bubonic plague is highly infectious and often caused mortality rates exceeding 50 per cent of those who remained in nucleated settlements and did not flee when news of its imminent arrival was heard, and morbidity was as high in villages as in towns; Hirst (1953) 213-218 on periodicity of plague in wild rodents.

379. A.S. Benenson in Evans & Feldman (1982) 187-206 on cholera; F.L. Ruben & C.W. Norden in Evans & Feldman (1982) 510-524 on staphylococcal infections; Grmek (1983) 179-198; Hippokrates *Epidemics* III Constitution III-IV ed. Littré vol. 3, pp. 76-77 on erysipelas.

380. W.H.S. Jones (1907) & (1909a); for malaria see e.g. Hippokrates *Epidemics* I 2nd Constitution IV ed. Littré vol. 2, pp. 630-631 on children from the age of weaning until puberty dying from semitertian fevers and other causes; Hippokrates *Epidemics* III Constitution XII ed. Littré vol. 3, pp. 92-93 on the prevalence of malarial fevers; Hippokrates *peri pathôn* XIII ed. Littré vol. 6, pp. 220-221.

381. Hippokrates *aphorismoi* III ed. Littré vol. 4, pp. 486-499 on the seasonality of disease incidence, especially III.9-10 on autumn and spring, III.21 for continuous fevers and tertian fevers in summer, III.22 for quartan fevers, irregular fevers (which may arise from multiple infections) and enlarged spleens in the autumn; *aphorismoi* IV.43 & VII.63 ed. Littré vol. 4, pp. 518-519 & 598-599 noted that (falciparum) fevers which became worse every second day were dangerous, while intermittence of any kind (e.g. in quartan malaria) indicated that there was no danger; Siegel (1960) 79-80 on *relapsing fever* in the

Hippokratic corpus, spread by lice in the epidemic form and ticks in the endemic form; Siegel (1960) 86-88 cited Hippokrates *Epidemics* I.3 ed. Littré vol. 2, pp. 610-615 for *brucellosis*, described by E. Young (1983), caused by several members of the genus Brucella in many domesticated and wild animals in the Mediterranean, acquired from infected milk/cheese, especially from goat and sheep, or from contact with infected pigs and cattle, causes abortions in pregnant women, who are most vulnerable, and epidemics of abortions in other animals, with a mortality rate of about 3 per cent in humans in the past; *leishmaniasis*, spread by sandflies from a reservoir in dogs, occurs sporadically in the Mediterranean and is very dangerous if not treated – Rioux et al. (1984) explains how human interference with the environment is spreading it in modern Morocco; Papadopoulos (1980) on an epidemic of *three-day fever* in Athens in 1935; Font-Creus et al. (1985) on *Mediterranean spotted fever*, a mild disease transmitted by dog ticks; Corvisier (1985) 94-96 criticised the interpretation of fevers in the Hippokratic corpus of Littré vol. 2, pp. 538-584.

382. N. Bailey (1982) on the mathematical epidemiology of malaria, cf. Aron & Anderson (1982); Davies & Kathirithamby (1986) 164-167 for ancient sources on mosquitoes; Aristotle *HA* 487b3-6; Hackett (1937) & (1949) described important research on mosquitoes and malaria; Corvisier (1985) 150 argued that there were more cases of malaria among men than among women in the Hippokratic corpus because men spent more time out of doors, but in modern times the mosquito vectors for malaria habitually enter houses (Hackett (1937) 60), so we should consider the alternative explanation, namely that doctors were called to treat men more frequently than they were summoned to treat women, or treated men more effectively, for the reasons spelled out in Hippokrates *Gunaikeiôn* I.52 ed. Littré vol. 8, pp. 126-127, cf. Lloyd (1983) 67-68.

383. McFalls (1984) 99-133 on the effects of malaria on human fertility; McGregor (1982) on malaria in relation to the nutritional status of its victims; Grmek (1983) 409-436 interpreted the case of Philiskos in Hippokrates *Epidemics* I.1 ed. Littré vol. 2, pp. 682-685 as blackwater fever; Hammond & Walbank (1988) 88 n. 1, criticising Borza (1979), maintained that the physical toughness of the soldiers of Alexander the Great was incompatible with a malaria-ridden society, cf. Corvisier (1985) 19-20, but Corvisier's own analysis also requires revision insofar as he regarded drainage schemes such as those undertaken by Philip II in the Macedonian plains as tending to reduce the incidence of malaria, whereas recent experience, summarised by Hackett (1937) 90-91, is that the pioneering phase of land reclamation in the Mediterranean is often *accompanied* by severe malaria epidemics, i.e. the redevelopment programmes of Philip might actually have led to an increased abundance of mosquitoes that act as vectors for malaria, an unintended by-product which might not have yielded its full results until a few years later.

384. On the history of malaria see Laderman (1975); Zulueta (1973); Bruce-Chwatt & Zulueta (1980), who mistakenly denied the existence of falciparum malaria in the fifth century BC; Grmek (1983) 307-436; Jarcho (1987).

385. Angel (1966), also (1972a) & (1984).

386. Walker (1986) on intestinal infections; Kent (1983) 125-126 and Passmore & Eastwood (1986) 117 & 461-463 on iron deficiency anaemia in relation to wheat-based diets (Grmek (1983) 388 only considered nutritional anaemias in relation to maize consumption); Bisel (1980) 54-55 used the zinc content of ancient bones to investigate the level of phytates in consumed cereal products, and Edward et al. (1984) used the same technique to suggest an increase in consumption of coarse unleavened bread at Asine in the Argolid in the Hellenistic

period, as well as an increase in red meat consumption (congruent with animal husbandry assuming greater importance in an epoch of low human population density); Davies & Nightingale (1975); Reinhold (1972) on leavening.

387. Stuart-Macadam (1985) & (1987) on porotic hyperostosis in childhood, cf. Palkovich (1987) and Lallo et al. (1977); G. Clark et al. (1986) on permanent consequences of malnutrition in childhood; Hippokrates *peri aërôn, hudatôn, topôn* IX & *peri nousôn* IV.55 ed. Littré vol. 2, pp. 38-41 and vol. 7, pp. 600-605 respectively, (Aristotle) *Problems* X.43.895a36-b11 and Grmek (1983) 169-170 on bladder stone disease; Edelstein (1945) T423 I.8 mentions a boy of Epidauros who suffered from stones; Darby et al. (1977) vol. 1, p. 84 on iron deficiency anaemia in Egyptian medical papyri.

388. Schoeninger (1982); Passmore & Eastwood (1986) 184 on nutritional deficiencies of wheat; Angel (1972b) 393 on Mycenae, suggesting an average lifespan of 36; differences in average height according to social class were common in the past, e.g. Haviland (1967) on the Maya, probably why *megethos*, tallness, was desired in both sexes according to Aristotle *Rhetoric* 1361a5-6 & 1361b18-21; Dasen (1988) on pathological manifestations of dwarfism in antiquity; May (1963) 233-277 on ecology of malnutrition in modern Greece; Corvisier (1985) 27-47; Ascenzi & Balistreri (1977) and Becker (1982) on skeletal remains from Italy, cf. W.H.S. Jones (1909b), rightly criticised by Brunt (1971) 611-624; there is no evidence for porotic hyperostosis linked to thalassaemia in the human remains from Pompeii (E. Lazer – Cambridge seminar paper); Fornaciari et al. (1981) for iron deficiency anaemia among children and women in the reproductive age groups at Carthage; Wells (1975a).

389. Galen *peri tôn en tais nosois kairôn* VIII and *Hippokratous Epidêmiôn A kai Galênou eis auto hupomnêma* B XXV ed. Kühn vol. VII, p. 435 & XVII.1, p. 121 on Rome; Ammianus Marcellinus XIV.6.23 on frequency of severe illnesses in Rome.

390. Ross (1906) elaborated his ideas in relation to the Lake Kopais region of Boiotia, where all three species of malaria were endemic, with vivax being the commonest, falciparum the second commonest and quartan the rarest, cf. Herakleides Creticus XXV ed. Pfister mentioning *puretos* as characteristic of Onchestos in Boiotia in the Hellenistic period; H. Forbes (1985) 67 on malaria in Troizen; Beaucamp (1988).

391. Ruffié & Sournia (1984) emphasise the relations between epidemiology and population genetics.

392. Grmek (1983) 405; Aristotle *HA* 569b10-12 and Theophrastos *HP* IX.3.1 already regarded Marathon as marshy, but it is probably more marshy in recent times than it was *c.* 300 BC, and the plain of Thermopylae has definitely expanded a lot since 480 BC, when the 300 Spartans with Leonidas were able to block the path of the Persian army; Empedokles 21 A1.70 eds. Diels-Kranz and Timaios FGH566 F7 Jacoby, cited by Diogenes Laertios VIII.70-71, and Delcourt (1938) 83-90; Huntington (1910) 672-674 suggested that climatic change in the first millennium BC permitted the spread of malaria, but the critical comments of other scholars appended to his paper show how difficult it is to prove such a hypothesis (see also Chapter IV).

393. Grmek (1983) 199-225 on STDs; Corvisier (1985) 107-108; McFalls (1984) 350-364 on effects of genital herpes on fertility; Hippokrates *Gunaikeiôn* I.90 ed. Littré vol. 8, pp. 214-218 for genital herpes; E.R. Alexander & H.R. Harrison in Evans & Feldman (1982) 159-185 on chlamydial infections; *RID* VII.6 (1985) 711-786 contains a series of articles on trachoma; Dioskorides *MM* I.64.5 was the first author to use the word *trachôma*; Lucretius *De rerum natura* VI.1116-1117;

Rouse (1902) 212 reported that 40 per cent of the votive offerings at the shrine of Asklepios in Athens were votive eyes; Edelstein (1945) T423 I.4 for an Athenian woman who was blind in one eye at Epidauros; on eye diseases (*ophthalmiai*) in the Hippokratic corpus see e.g. *Epidemics* III Constitution III.7 ed. Littré vol. 3, pp. 84-85, also *peri opsios* IV ed. Littré vol. 9, pp. 156-157 for trachoma; Demosthenes LIV.39 and Aiskhines I.102 mention Athenians with bad eyesight; Pausanias IV.33.7 on Homer; Herodotos VII.229 on Spartans with bad eyesight.

394. Grmek (1983) 214-216 suggested that gonorrhoea is an old disease, but thought that all the passages in ancient medical literature which have been quoted as evidence for it can be interpreted in other ways; Vertue (1953) rejected all the evidence for gonorrhoea in antiquity; McFalls (1984) 258-302 on gonorrhoea and fertility; J. Preuss (1978) 354-357 believed that gonorrhoea did exist in ancient Israel; D. Hrdy (1987).

395. R.H. Kampmeier in Evans & Feldman (1982) 553-588 on treponematoses. D. Ridgway in *Archaeological Reports* 35 (1988/89) 144 reports that 'there is strong evidence that a form of syphilis was widely diffused among the population' buried in the necropolis of Pantanello near Metapontum in southern Italy. If this conclusion appears to be justified when the osteological evidence is published, this is a major discovery in relation to the history of treponematoses. One can only guess that it refers to endemic nonvenereal syphilis; the evidence now suggests that treponemes existed in both the Old and New Worlds before Columbus, cf. Rothschild & Turnbull (1987) on the western hemisphere.

396. Mosley (1978) & (1979) on nutrition and human fertility; Scott & Johnston (1985) criticised the controversial theory of R.E. Frisch that menarche occurs in women when their fat content reaches a certain critical proportion of total body weight.

397. Aristotle *GA* 780a20-22; Sommer (1982); Passmore & Eastwood (1986) 298-302; Antiphanes F161 Kock for sale of stale fish in Athens, also Xenarchos F7 Kock for a law banning fishmongers from pouring water on fish to freshen them, cf. Hadjimarkos & Bonhorst (1962) for fish consumption in Athens; Andrews (1949a) lists the ancient sources on the carrot, the most important being Theophrastos *HP* IX.15.5 (where *daphnoeides* is probably a separate plant rather than an epithet of *daukon*, cf. André (1985) 87), Pliny *NH* XIX.xxvii.89 & XXV.lxiv.110-112, Columella *RR* IX.4.5 and Galen *peri trophôn dunameôn* II.67 ed. Kühn vol. VI, pp. 654-655, but Andrews's article is out of date, as the purple carrots of Afghanistan are now thought to have evolved in a secondary centre of diversity (note also the existence of varieties of wheat with the same purple anthocyanin pigments in Ethiopia, another mountainous secondary centre of diversity) and were not involved in the evolution of the red carrot in Europe (see Chapter III for further discussion of this problem); see Banga (1957) and Heywood (1983) for more recent opinions; Hippokrates *Epidemics* VII.76 ed. Littré vol. 5, pp. 434-435 rightly recommended consumption of green vegetables in cases of eye diseases, but in *peri diaitês hygieinês* I ed. Littré vol. 6, pp. 72-73 abstention from vegetables in winter is recommended.

398. Stephens & Krebs (1986) 117 on herbivores.

399. Galen *peri trophôn dunameôn* II.27 ed. Kühn vol. VI, pp. 608-609 on olives, cf. II.7, p. 570; contrast Passmore & Eastwood (1986) 17 for the modern view; J. Preuss (1978) 564 on Israel; D. Mattingly (1988) on the scale of olive cultivation during the Roman empire.

400. Hippokrates *peri diaitês* II.42 ed. Littré vol. 6, pp. 538-541 on bread, cf. II.40, pp. 536-537 on barley products, also *peri archaikês iatrikês* XIV ed. Littré vol. 1, pp. 600-601 on bread; Diokles of Karystos F141 Wellmann and Galen *peri* *euchumias kai kakochumias trophôn* ed. Kühn vol. VI, pp. 755-757 on fruits; Kiple (1984) 26-27 is a very interesting modern analogy, explaining that vitamin C deficiency leading to scurvy is widespread in west Africa in spite of the ready availability of large quantities of fresh fruit because children are discouraged from eating fruit in case it gives them worms! Hippokrates *peri tôn entos pathôn* XLII ed. Littré vol. 7, pp. 270-273 mentions a type of *tuphos* attributed to a high level of fruit consumption at harvest time.

401. Schoeninger (1979); Klepinger (1984), cf. Runia (1987) pointing out that the strontium/calcium ratio is not constant in plants, and Blakely (1989) observing that in women it is distorted by pregnancy and lactation.

402. Lloyd (1983) 157ff. on dissection; Aristotle *PA* 667b8-10; the author of Hippokrates *peri kardiês* dissected animal hearts, esp. II ed. Littré vol. 9, pp. 79-80 for an experiment on pigs; M. Crawford (1968); Hippokrates *peri diaitês* II.49 ed. Littré vol. 6, pp. 550-553; Galen *peri trophôn dunameôn* III.14 ed. Kühn vol. VI, pp. 680-681; Cato *De agricultura* I.7 placed woodland to provide acorns etc. for animal fodder last in his list of preferences for land use.

403. L. Cohen (1987) 46 on cancer tumour promoters; Retsas (1986) on cancer in antiquity; Grundy (1986).

404. Aristotle *HA* 603a30-604a3 describes three diseases of pigs, 604a4-12 three diseases of dogs, 604a13-21 two diseases of cattle, 604a22-605a15 diseases of horses, 605a16-22 a disease of asses, 605a23-605b5 diseases of elephants, 605b6-21 diseases of bees; Columella *RR* VI.4-18 on diseases of oxen, VI.30-35 diseases of horses, VII.5.1-22 diseases of sheep, VII.7 diseases of goats, VII.10.1-5 diseases of pigs, VII.13.1-2 diseases of dogs, IX.13 diseases of bees; Virgil *Georgics* III.478-566, with Flintoff (1983), cf. the descriptions of epidemics in Ovid *Metamorphoses* VII.523-613, and the less well known *Carmen bucolicum de mortibus boum* eds. Bücheler & Riese *Anthologia Latina* I.2 (1906) no. 893, pp. 334-339 describing an epidemic disease of cattle which spread from Illyria and Pannonia to Italy in the late imperial period; P.S. Brachman in Evans & Feldman (1982) 63-74 describes anthrax.

405. Aristotle *HA* 605a16 for glanders; Hippokrates *Epidemics* VII.36-38 ed. Littré vol. 5, pp. 404-406 describes three cases of tetanus; Aristotle *HA* 604a14-17 for foot-and-mouth disease (Greek *podagra*); Columella *RR* VI.5.1-2 & VII.5.4 and Varro *RR* II.3.9-10 observed the significance of density-dependence in relation to animal diseases.

406. Hubbert et al. (1975) 1118-1138 give a very long list of animal diseases which may infect humans as zoonoses; Aristotle *HA* 604a5-8, Pliny *NH* VIII.lxiii.152-153 and Adamson (1977) on rabies (Greek *lutta*), described by R.E. Shope in Evans (1984) 455-470; Byl (1980) 312-313 interpreted Aristotle's statement that humans do not always develop rabies after a bite by a rabid dog as an a priori expression of human superiority over other animals, but there is no reason why Aristotle, a great reader of books as Byl emphasised, or more probably one of his sources could not have observed this natural phenomenon; Plutarch *Solon* XXIV states that a law of Solon decreed that in a case of dog-bite the dog had to be surrendered wearing a three-cubit long collar.

407. Aristotle *HA* 604b25-27; Herakleitos *Quaestiones Homericae* XIV (eds. Societatis Philologae Bonnensis Sodales, 1910) p. 22, cf. Rufus *peri loimôn* in Oribasios *pros Eustathion* VI.25.3; Thucydides II.50.1-2, cf. the epidemics at Rome described by Livy IV.25.3-6, 26.5, 30.7-9 & Dionysios Hal. *AR* XII.6.

408. Wylie & Stubbs (1983) and Eby & Evjen (1962) devoted their efforts to looking for an epizoötic in 430 BC, cf. Bernheim & Zener (1978) on the epidemic at Troy; in contrast Willan (1821) 70 had already concluded correctly that the diseases of men and animals are in general analogous but not interchangeable; historical sources often mention high mortality among domesticated animals coinciding with plague epidemics among humans, but it is now known that most large domesticated animals are not vulnerable to plague – Hirst (1953) 102 and Biraben (1975) vol. 2, pp. 25-27.

409. (Xenophon) *Athênaiôn Politeia* II.6 on the Athenian empire; Theophrastos *CP* III.22.1-2, IV.14.1 & *HP* VIII.10.2; Pliny *NH* XVIII.xliv.154 & lxix.284-285; Harlan (1976); Orlob (1973) 93-141 on plant pathology in classical antiquity; Vavilov (1914) on the susceptibility of the various wheat species to rust; J. Preuss (1978) 164-167 maintained that *yerakon* was a human disease; Kislev (1982) for the archaeological evidence from Israel, also Stewart & Robertson (1968) for the antiquity of diseases of domesticated plants; (Aristotle) *Problems* I.23.862a25-26 on the climatic conditions that favoured rust; Strabo VIII.3.15.344c on Triphylia; Strabo XIII.1.64.613c mentioned the cult of Apollo *Eruthibios* on Rhodes, apparently a god of cereal rust, although the version of the epithet (*Eremithios*) given by the inscription *SIG*[3] 724 suggests that there is something wrong with Strabo's account; Burdon (1987) on demographic effects of barley mildew; Pliny *NH* XVIII.xx.91 said that *siligo*, bread wheat, had the ear on an erect stalk and so did not get rust, although Theophrastos *CP* III.22.1-2 had stated that varieties of barley with erect stems became infected with rust because dew adhered to the ear, while it dropped off other varieties of barley with drooping heads; Critopoulos (1956) on barley rust in Attica; for *Ornithogalum umbellatum* (Star of Bethlehem), probably ancient Greek *bolbinê*, see Theophrastos *HP* VII.13.9, and André (1985) 230 for *O. pyrenaicum*, possibly the *skilla Epimenideios* of Theophrastos *HP* VII.12.1; André (1985) 225 & 245 lists the scanty direct evidence for the barberry bush in classical antiquity, although it looks as if Pliny *NH* XVIII.xlv.161 must be a reference to it; Xenophon *Oikonomikos* V.18 mentions epidemics of plant and animal diseases; Carefoot & Sprott (1969) 33-52 on the history of wheat rust, especially interesting in relation to the cause of the crop failures leading to the Israelite migration to Egypt, recounted in Genesis 41; Bushnell & Roelfs (1984) 39-77 & (1985) 330-332 on rust evolution and history; Zadoks (1985).

Chapter III

1. Plutarch *Alkibiades* XV.4, Lykourgos *Ag. Leokrates* 77 and Tod *GHI* vol. 2, no. 204 for the oath; Stoianovitch (1967) on the theme of continuity; Theocharopoulos & Georgiadis (1984) on the ecological effects of development in modern Attica; Birot & Dresch (1964), Chevalier (1939), Parain (1936), Semple (1928) & (1932), C.D. Smith (1979) on Mediterranean agriculture, also Nuttonson (1947).

2. Methana – H. Forbes (1985).

3. Bennett (1971) on new varieties; Kayser & Thompson (1964) 302 on 1957.

4. Data taken from Kayser & Thompson (1964).

5. *Greece* (1944) vol. 3, p. 57 and Brumfield (1981) 17-18 & 43-44 on the modern expansion of viticulture.

6. Aymard (1979) 10; Passmore & Eastwood (1986) 71.

7. Kayser & Thompson (1964) 315 on viticulture.

8. Theophrastos *HP* VII.1.1-2 makes it clear that vegetables were grown on a small scale as garden crops; Kayser & Thompson (1964) 309.

9. Brumfield (1981) 18.

10. The mark of the 'free' man was that he did not live under the constraint of or for the sake of another man (Aristotle *Politics* 1317b11-13 & *Rhetoric*

1367a28-33), which has economic connotations, as argued by Ste. Croix (1981) 116, but should not be restricted to purely economic effects.

11. Xenophon *Oikonomikos* XV-XVI on polyculture; his statement of the purpose of agriculture in V.1 is unsophisticated; Philodemos peri *oikonomias* col. VII, lines 26-37 ed. Jensen; (Aristotle) *Oikonomikos* I.1344b31-33 ed. Victor and Philodemos op. cit. col. XI.

12. Plutarch *Perikles* XVI; Andrewes (1978); Wheeler (1955); Veyne (1979).

13. R.A. Gauthier (1951) 73ff. on autarky in Aristotle.

14. Thucydides II.36.3; cf. II.41.1; Demosthenes XX.31; Hicks (1969) 14; (Xenophon) *Athênaiôn Politeia* II.7 & 11-12.

15. Wilson & Russell (1981) 28-47; Xenophon *Poroi* V.

16. Finley (1985a) 131-134.

17. Stoianovitch (1966) and Hémardinquer (1973) on maize; Langer (1975) covers the potato as well.

18. Theophrastos *HP* I.3.1; Kayser & Thompson (1964) 308 show that pulses are not grown on a significant scale as field crops in Attica; on legumes reducing yields of following winter wheat crops see Littlejohn (1946) for experiments on Cyprus, Arnon (1972) vol. 1, p. 465, also noticed by Columella *RR* II.10.5-7; *Geôponika* II.12.2 mentions sowing of legumes after a wheat crop; Hebblethwaite (1983) 265-268 states that beans grown in rotation with cereals in experiments in Britain marginally improve the cereal yields – they behaved differently in the Cyprus experiments because artificial fertilisers were not used there; Arnon (1972) vol. 2, p. 235; Theophrastos *CP* II.12.5; Webb & Hawtin (1981) 112.

19. Theophrastos *HP* VIII.9.1 and Pliny *NH* XVIII.xxx.117 on beans as green manure; Aristotle *HA* 595b6-10 on beans as fodder for cattle.

20. Sinclair & de Wit (1975); Begon et al. (1986) 490-492.

21. Passmore & Eastwood (1986) on the protein content of cereals; Francis (1986) on multiple cropping.

22. The admirable discussion of favism in Grmek (1983) 307-354, extended by Luzzatto & Battistuzzi (1985) and Katz (1987), is to be preferred to the cultural/structuralist interpretation of Lévi-Strauss (1985) 192-200; Andrews (1949) criticised cultural interpretations, but was unaware of the real nature of favism as a biological phenomenon; Blum (1965) 78 on modern Greece; Hebblethwaite (1983) 3-7, 14-17, 25-30 & 48-49 on *V. faba*; Galen peri *trophôn dunameôn* I.19 ed. Kühn, vol. VI, p. 531 on eating beans raw; Pliny *NH* XVIII.xxx.118, Aulus Gellius *NA* IV.11.1-3, Diogenes Laertios VIII.34, Plutarch *Moralia* 729a and Iamblichos *Life of Pythagoras* 109 on the Pythagoreans; Dantuma et al. (1983) on productivity of bean varieties; Chirassi (1968) 39-54 on Greek myths involving the fava bean.

23. Hippokrates *Epidemics* VI ed. Littré vol. 5, pp. 310-311, cf. Stockman (1932) and Galen peri *trophôn dunameôn* I.29 ed. Kühn vol. VI, pp. 546-547; Demosthenes XXII.15; Columella *RR* II.10.34; Plutarch *Moralia* 286d-e; Anaxandrides F41 and Alexis F162 ed. Kock; Galen peri *trophôn dunameôn* I.26 ed. Kühn vol. VI, p. 540; Kroll (1983) 54 on Kastanas, and G.E.M. Jones (1984) and Follieri (1986) on Minoan Crete, for grass pea on prehistoric archaeological sites; Klepinger (1984) and Hastorf & Deniro (1985) on nitrogen isotope analysis.

24. *Résultats du recensement* (1966) 34-37 on the reduction in the proportion of arable land left fallow during the last two generations, also on the spread of irrigation made possible by modern pumps; Kayser & Thompson (1964) 310 report that the cultivation of lucerne and clover has increased six times and of vetch four times since the 1930s.

25. Aristophanes *Hippeis* 606, Aristotle *HA* 595b26-28, Theophrastos *HP*

VIII.7.7, Columella *RR* II.10.24-28 and Pliny *NH* XVIII.xliii.144-148 on lucerne, whose alternative name 'alfalfa' signified 'fodder for horses' in ancient Persian; Meissner (1891) and Postgate in *BSA* 3 (1987) 96-97 for lucerne in cuneiform texts; C.H. Hanson (1972) 5-6 & 98; Simmonds (1976) 165-168; Arnon (1972) vol. 2, pp. 550-551 & 573 states that it is a very good crop for hay, but not so good for actual grazing (cf. Theophrastos *HP* VIII.7.7), and requires abundant moisture for high yields; Laufer (1919) 208-219 on China.

26. Erxleben (1975) found no evidence for Athenian wine exports; Setton (1975b) 196 indicates why the notables of the Byzantine empire disliked Athenian wine.

27. Herodotos V.82.2; Pausanias X.32.19; Loussert & Brousse (1978) 237ff. on irrigation of olive trees; H. Forbes (1985) 320 notes that rainfall on Methana in September and October is vital for a good olive crop, but rainfall in all months in Greece is very variable, which is why irrigation is helpful; Boardman (1976); Raven (1973) and Margaris & Mooney (1981) 21-25 on the evolutionary history of Mediterranean trees; Aristotle *HA* 553a22-23 & 553b23; Wiens et al. (1989) discuss a case of a species of perennial plant apparently being overwhelmed by changing circumstances.

28. Kayser & Thompson (1964) 316 on olives.

29. Gavrielides (1976a & b) on competition between cereals and olives; Theophrastos *HP* II.5.7 said that the plain was the best place for olives, figs and vines, where they would compete with cereals; in *CP* I.18.1-2 he recommended the best soils for cereals and the second best soils for trees; Trenbath (1974), Willey (1979) and Francis (1986) on polycropping; Burdon (1987) 44-48 on disease resistance; Williamson (1981) 246-247 on the Rothamsted experiments, cf. Riebesell (1974); Darwin (1968) 156-157.

30. Theophrastos *CP* I.20.3-5 (cf. (Aristotle) *peri phutôn* 827a39-b5 and Columella *RR* V.8.2) on biennial production in Greece (the one exception that he notes, Olynthos, was probably due to higher rainfall there), cf. *CP* I.19.3-5 on olive ripening; to illustrate the size of the biennial swings the olive oil yield in the census year 1961 was 2½ times the yield of 1960 (Kayser & Thompson (1964) 316), cf. Hartmann & Bougas (1970) 447 and Kolodny (1974) vol. 1, p. 87; Theophrastos *HP* II.5.6 noted that olives had to be planted further apart than other trees, cf. Plutarch *Solon* XXIII.

31. Wijmstra (1969), Greig & Turner (1974), Turner & Greig (1975), Athanasiadis (1975), Bottema (1979), (1980) & (1982), Renault-Miskovsky (1980), Gennett (1982), Huntley & Birks (1983) and Moody (1987) on palynology in Greece; Thiersch vol. 1 (1833) 297 noted that over two-thirds of the olive trees in Greece were destroyed during the War of Independence from the Ottoman Empire, perhaps a parallel for the decrease in olive cultivation during the break-up of the Mycenaean world.

32. Plutarch *Lykourgos* VIII; Dikaiarchos F72 Wehrli; Persaios FGH584 F2 Jacoby; Thucydides I.6.5; Cartledge (1979) 95-96, Buckler (1977) and Figueira (1984) on Peloponnesian agriculture.

33. Dio Chrysostom XXV.3 for Peisistratos; Plutarch *Solon* XXIII-XXIV; Runnels & Hansen (1986) and Hansen (1988) for the paucity of evidence for olive cultivation in mainland Greece before the Late Bronze Age; Amouretti (1986) 44-45 on its spread in archaic Greece; Dittenberger *Syll.*[3] 527, line 47 for the Dreros oath from third-century BC Crete enjoining each ephebe to plant an olive tree.

34. Kroll (1982); Melena (1983); Jasink (1983).

35. Bottema (1980) 214, Gennett (1982) and Moody (1987) on Cretan

palynology; the earliest definite evidence for olive oil production on Cyprus is an oil-press on a Late Cypriot II site, dating to *c.* 1400-1250 BC – *The Times* 28 September 1988.

36. Theophrastos *CP* II.3.6 on the olive's inability to grow in cold regions; Zohary & Spiegel-Roy (1975), Spiegel-Roy (1986) and D. Zohary (1983) 116-118 on fruit-tree evolution; Barker (1985) 259 emphasised human population growth instead; Halstead (1981) 315, with reference to nut trees in Greece, provides a classic example of Darwin's principle that domestication leads to an increase in productivity, cf. Theophrastos *CP* I.15.3-4 & 16.2, II.10.2-3 & 14.1, *HP* III.2.1, IV.13.1 & 14.1-2, also Columella *RR* III.1.2.

37. Foxhall & Forbes (1982) rightly argued that cereals provided a high proportion of the average total calorific intake in antiquity, but suggested that the ancient rations were intended as maxima. Several queries may be raised: (1) there are many parallels for the large ancient rations (e.g. Le Roy Ladurie (1966) vol. 1, pp. 267-268 and Bray (1984) 4, showing cereals as providing a higher proportion of the calorific intake than Foxhall & Forbes think possible, and Stouff (1970) 229-230), cf. L. Gallo (1984b) 38 and Leslie et al. (1984); (2) it is dangerous to use modern Greek data for olive oil consumption as a yardstick for ancient consumption, since the modern Greek consumption level is itself exceptionally high, twice that of any other country, Loussert & Brousse (1978); (3) the standard tables of nutritional requirements have their values set at a level considerably above the estimated minimum requirement, in order to allow for the natural range of variation which occurs in any population; (4) the relationship between wheat and barley *rations*, as well as the *price* ratio between them, probably represents a unit of value, i.e. the ancient 'rations' did not necessarily bear any close relationship to nutritional requirements, cf. Gelb (1965) for the ancient Near East and section 10 below on 'rations' as wages in kind; Hesiod *WD* 559-560 recommended that rations should be increased in winter and reduced in summer.

38. Allbaugh (1953) 71-72 found that 45 per cent of farmers on Crete pruned their olive trees either never or no more frequently than once every 10 years; Columella *RR* V.9.15 recommended pruning once every eight years, but intensive pruning helps to eliminate the alternate off years, cf. Plutarch *Perikles* XXXIII.4, Theophrastos *HP* II.7.2 & *CP* III.10.4; Theophrastos *CP* II.11.3 on Thasos, cf. Aristotle F611.76 Rose on the shame attached to manual labour in farming at Thespiai in Boiotia.

39. Loussert & Brousse (1978) 50 for its growth cycle; cf. Pliny *NH* XV.i.3 (= Hesiod F347 Merkelbach & West), perhaps derived from the complementary agricultural poem *Megala erga*. (In *NH* VII.xlviii.153 Pliny also mentions that Hesiod commented on human longevity, another sign that the surviving portions of Hesiod's poetry do not contain all the observations he made which would be relevant to the subject matter of this book.)

40. IG II^2 1241 & 2492-2499 are the most important surviving examples; Meuvret (1977).

41. (Demosthenes) XLIII.69 mentions a farm with (allegedly) more than a thousand olive trees. At the present density of plantation (190 per ha – Loussert & Brousse (1978) 10) this might represent no more than about 5 hectares, but ancient cultivation was certainly more extensive, as is indicated by Columella *RR* V.9.7, cf. Pliny *NH* XVII.xix.93. Loussert & Brousse (1978) 178 estimate that 100-130 trees per ha. may be planted in a dry farming area with a rainfall of 500-650 mm per annum (applicable to much of Attica), cf. H. Forbes (1985) 82; Krochmal (1955) 228, Hartmann & Bougas (1970) 447 and Aschenbrenner (1976) 163 for olive oil yields per tree. On Hadrian's law see Day (1942) 189-191; Pleket

(1964) no. 15; Graindor (1973) 74-79; Sayas Abengochea (1983).

42. Compare Ph. Gauthier (1982), reinterpreting a Hellenistic inscription recording a disastrous failure of the olive harvest in Attica, with Theophrastos *CP* I.19.5.

43. H. Forbes (1985). The biology of the olive tree led him to argue that the agricultural cycle of the modern Greek peasant is a biennial, not an annual cycle.

44. Erxleben (1975) on the lack of Athenian exports.

45. Pliny *NH* XVIII.vii.38; Columella *RR* V.8.1-2; Loussert & Brousse (1978) 331-333 on labour requirements; Kolodny (1974) vol. 1, p. 91 states that olive cultivation on the Aegean islands only produces a ground-rent of 3 per cent; the scholiast to Pindar *Nemeans* X.64b claims that olive oil export from Athens was banned, except by victors at the Panathenaic Games, but it is not clear what lies behind this tradition; Hartmann & Bougas (1970) 458 for the quotation.

46. H. Forbes (1985) 278-286.

47. Jardé (1925) 52-53; R. Osborne (1985) 225 n. 82 for the guess of 50 per cent; Figueira (1984) 102 n. 48 for the same problem, with an equally uncertain solution, in regard to the Peloponnese.

48. J. Jones et al. (1962) 114 on the Dema House; Bradford (1956) & (1957) 29-33 on Attica; Jameson (1976) on the inability of Halieis to feed its own population; the need for caution in making such claims is shown by van Andel & Lianos (1983), who argue that a rise of sea level since the classical period has flooded much land that was previously cultivatable at Halieis; G. Sanders (1984) destroyed the arguments of Renfrew & Wagstaff (1982) on Melos; Strabo VIII.6.16.375c states that the Aiginetans artificially extended the cultivated area by spreading soil over rocks, cf. Frick (1985) 134 on ancient Israel.

49. Kayser & Thompson (1964) 301; Allbaugh (1953) 276 reported that the cultivated area on Crete included land that would not produce a crop at all without the assistance of chemical fertilisers; Pounds (1976) 68-72 also suggested that over a third of Attica was cultivated in antiquity.

50. A. Harrison (1968) 248 tackled the problem of the absence of anything like Roman *usucapio* in a purely legalistic manner; Didymos *Commentary on Demosthenes* col. XIV eds. Pearson & Stephens for the *Hiera Orgas*; the vinedresser of Philostratos *Hêrôikos* ed. de Lannoy could not cultivate part of his land because it had been dedicated to a hero by a previous owner; Thucydides V.42.1 on Panakton illustrates some of the complexities of mountain pastures.

51. Finley (1952) 246 n. 6; Kayser & Thompson (1964) 319; Plutarch *Solon* XXIII, Suda s.v. *mêlobotos chôra*, Isokrates XIV (*Plataikos*) 31 and Lykourgos *Ag. Leokrates* 145 for Attica as a sheep breeding area; Georgoudi (1974); Hesiod *WD* 405-406, 436-440, 557-561 & 606-607 on oxen.

52. Lysias XX.11 for a shepherd as *penês*; Briant (1982a) 12-32 for Graeco-Roman attitudes towards pastoralists; Xanthakis-Karamanos (1981) for Moschion F6, ed. Nauck[2], linking the development of agriculture to the progress of culture and civilisation; the Arkadians also claimed autochthony (Xenophon *Hellênika* VII.1.23); Justin VIII.5.7-8 on Philip as a shepherd.

53. Xenophon *Memorabilia* III.14; Messer (1984) on approaches to diet besides the purely economic ones; the perceptive comments of Goody (1982) 102-105 provide the starting point for a sociological analysis of Athenaios; Grigg (1982) 70 on the colossal inefficiency of animal husbandry as a means of producing food for humans.

54. Burford (1960) on draught animals; see also Chapter IV for further discussion of the horse; Aristotle *Politics* 1289b33-36 & 1321a11; J. Davies (1971) xxv-xxvi on *hippotrophia*; Herodotos V.63.4 & IX.13.3 on Attica's unsuitability for cavalry warfare.

55. Meuvret (1977) 103-104 & 204, Arnon (1981) 466, Columella *RR* I.3.9 and Pliny *NH* XVIII.vii.35 on small-scale intensive cultivation as more productive than large-scale extensive production; Columella *RR* II.11.6 on weeding to boost yields; H. Forbes (1985) 217 for hand cultivation on Methana. The argument of Spurr (1986) 82 that the highest yields were obtained on the largest farms, rests on a misunderstanding of the nature of arable cultivation. The 200 *iugera* arable farm of Columella *RR* II.12.7-9, far from being an example of 'intensive' farming, represents a very labour extensive system of farming, compared both to the labour requirements per unit area of smallholders cultivating cereals without the plough and to the needs of viticulture and other cash crops. 'Intensive' is only meaningful in relation to something else which is defined as 'extensive', and it is not clear what Spurr's standard of comparison is.

56. Hesiod *WD* 453-454; Isaios VI.33 only mentions mules in connection with an allegedly very large property holding, cf. Isaios V.43; in Lysias IV.1 the yoke of oxen was on an estate large enough to be involved in an *antidosis*; see also H. Forbes (1985) 210-211, Varro *RR* I.20.4-5 & II.6.5, Columella *RR* VII.1.2, Aristotle *HA* 577b29-578a1 and Pliny *NH* VIII.lxviii.167; Jardé (1925) 125-127; Homer *Iliad* X.351-353 and the commentary of Eustathios pp. 810-811 on the summer ploughing.

57. Hippokrates *peri arthrôn* VIII ed. Littré vol. 4, pp. 96-99 on the bone dislocation; Hesiod *WD* 559-562; Xenophon *peri hippikês* IV.4 with Anderson (1961) 93; Duncan (1983) on horses' exploitation of natural pastures.

58. Theophrastos *HP* VIII.7.4 and Pliny *NH* XVIII.xlv.161 on autumn grazing of cereals in Thessaly, cf. Sprague (1954) and Paige & Whitham (1987); Aristotle *HA* 522b12-25 & *peri thaumasiôn akousmatôn* 842b28-33 on Epirus and Illyria; Frayn (1984) 60 for the estimate; Reynolds (1979) 53; Walpole (1817) 141 on sheep and goats in early modern Attica.

59. Mitchell (1975) 236 n. 27, table D1, for Greece in 1860; Jardé (1925) 96 n. 1 quotes sources for a 2:1 wheat:barley ratio in Attica in 1864.

60. Papadakis (1929) 6-9 (now out of date); Walpole (1817) 290-291 for wheat varieties in early modern Greece; Peterson (1965) 2 and Kislev (1984a) 149 on wheat classification – the old classification separating Aegilops and Triticum as two different genera is preferred here because it marks off crop plants and wild plants with potential for domestication from those of no value as crops; Carlson (1980) 16 on the water requirements of durum wheat, bread wheat and barley for photosynthesis.

61. *Greece* (1944) vol. 2, pp. 56-57.

62. Jasny (1944) 28; Le Roy Ladurie (1971) 20; Patlagean (1977) 39 and Rickman (1980) 6 illustrate the almost universal acceptance of Jasny.

63. Grigg (1982) 125 for the effect of chemical fertilisers on modern cereal yields; M. Parry (1978) 72 for the possible effect of climatic change on modern cereal yields.

64. Excluding the distant island cleruchies. IG II^2 1672, lines 263-275 and Jardé (1925) 36-41. Renfrew & Wagstaff (1982) 111 record a barley:wheat ratio of more than 6:1 on Melos as recently as 1971.

65. Isaios XI.43 describes a property holding with barley, wine and fruits in store, but does not mention wheat; (Demosthenes) XLII.20 alleged that his opponent was growing lots of barley, but his mendacity did not stretch as far as suggesting that he was growing lots of wheat as well (the critique of this speech in Ste. Croix (1966) is well justified); the sacred Rharian plain produced the very large rent of 619 *medimnoi* of barley, but again there is no mention of wheat (IG II^2 1672 lines 252-254, Jardé (1925) 96 n. 2 and Pausanias I.38.6); Demosthenes

LV.24 mentions an Athenian family which allegedly had in store three *medimnoi* of barley and half a *medimnos* of wheat flour.

66. Athenaios IV.137e; scholiast to Pindar *Olympians* IX.150; *Homeric Hymn to Demeter* 309 & 452 ed. Richardson; Galen *peri trophôn dunameôn* I.10 ed. Kühn vol. 6, p. 504 on the utility of white barley for making food.

67. Moritz's (1949) denial that *alphita* in Homer and Aristophanes referred to barley is not convincing. The fact that wheat was the most valued cereal does not prove that it was the most frequently consumed cereal. Historians of mediaeval and early modern Europe take it for granted that many people were forced to eat barley, oats or rye even though wheat was the most prestigious cereal. It is not certain that *puros* in Homer always referred to naked wheats, contrary to Moritz, as Galen *peri trophôn dunameôn* I.13 ed. Kühn vol. 6, p. 522 thought that the word sometimes signified *tiphê* (a hulled wheat) in Homer, as in *Iliad* VIII.188 & X.569, cf. Eustathios p. 707.

68. L. Gallo (1983); Isaios X.10 and Kuenen-Janssens (1941) on women's competence; Ste. Croix cited by Rhodes (1981) 141-142.

69. Dionysios of Halikarnassos *AR* II.25; Pliny *NH* XVIII.xiv.72; Porphyry *peri apochês empsuchôn* II.6 ed. Nauck; Plutarch *Moralia* 292bc states that barley constituted the offering of first fruits in the oldest Greek religious rites, exemplified by Philochoros FGH328 F73 Jacoby (with Carlier (1984) 336 for the *parasitoi* involved in this ceremony), cf. Herodotos I.132.1 & 160.5.

70. Garnsey (1985) was right to challenge the old orthodoxy. I agree with him that IG II² 1672 represents the results of a below-average harvest in Attica. However, there are several reasons why a 1:1 comparison between Attica and Lemnos is probably not justifiable:

(1) 34 per cent of Attica and 37 per cent of Lemnos are classified as farm land. Only 24 per cent of Attica but no less than 52.45 per cent of Lemnos is classified as pasture land, suggesting that the proportion of Lemnos that was cultivated in antiquity might have been rather larger than the proportion of Attica that was cultivated (Kayser & Thompson (1964) 319).
(2) Lemnos is very close to the northern limit of olive cultivation in the Aegean and has very few olive trees (Kayser & Thompson (1964) 320). Cereals probably occupied a larger proportion of the total cultivated area on Lemnos than they did in Attica.
(3) Cereal yields may well have been higher on Lemnos than in Attica, because Lemnos has fertile soil derived from an extinct volcano (Tozer (1890) 252-253).

71. Plutarch *Lykourgos* VIII.7 for the rent of 82 *medimnoi* of barley per *klêros*; Plutarch *Lykourgos* XII.3 and Dikaiarchos F72 Wehrli for the contributions in barley to the *sussitia*; Aristotle F611.13 Rose, Herodotos VI.57.3 and Thucydides IV.16.1 for Spartan consumption of barley; Cartledge (1979) 169-171 on cereals in Sparta; Hekataios FGH1 F9 Jacoby regarded barley as the basis of the diet in Arkadia.

72. Xenophon *Lakedaimoniôn Politeia* V.3; Sphairos in Athenaios IV.141cd; Alkman F9 ed. Calame on social class differentiation in diet in Sparta.

73. Farmland is 42-60 per cent of the four eparchies of modern Messenia – Kayser & Thompson (1964); Plutarch *Agesilaos* XXXIV.1 on Messenia's fertility; Van Wersch (1972) 184-185 on agriculture in Messenia wrongly assumed that the modern superiority of wheat over barley in Greece in terms of yields was also true

in antiquity, as it is a consequence of modern scientific selective breeding of wheat.

74. Le Roy Ladurie (1966) vol. 1, pp. 179-184; Neveux & Tits-Dieuaide (1979) reached the following conclusions:

(1) dispersion of yields is greater for wheat than for barley
(2) all cereals tend to vary in the same direction (i.e. do well or badly together)
(3) variance of yields and the absolute level of yields are independent of each other
(4) standardisation of seed types in recent times has sharply reduced the degree of fluctuation of yields, relative to the pre-modern period. (See J. Barrett (1981) for other consequences of the modern reduction in the diversity of cereal varieties grown by farmers.)

75. A consequence of a rough trebling of wheat yields since AD 1900. The elderly informants of Renfrew & Wagstaff (1982) 132 said that 10 stremmata of land were required at the start of the century to obtain the produce now yielded by 3 stremmata. This is confirmed by the official statistics, which show that the average yield had increased to 2,624 kg per ha in 1976 (*Agra Europa* (1979) 85 for recent yields) from the 742 kg per ha of 1901 (Tsouderos (1919) 132), an increase of 354 per cent; Allbaugh (1953) 54-56 for the reduction in average size of property holding on Crete.

76. Cheetham (1981) 85 & 289; Moretti (*Iscrizioni storiche ellenistiche* vol. 1, no. 55, lines 15-16) envisaged the possibility of grain exports from the territory of the Achaian league; Setton (1975b) 197 for mediaeval Attica; Livy XLIII.6.1-3.

77. Watson (1983) 20-23, cf. Bresc & Guichard (1982) 245, revived the thesis generally accepted before Jasny, following Boeuf (1931) 25; Aubaile-Sallenave (1984) critically reviewed Watson (especially p. 249 on durum wheat); Varro *RR* I.57 speaks of long storage of *triticum* in Spain in a very similar way to the later Arabic sources quoted by Watson, cf. Theophrastos *HP* VIII.11.5-6 on Cappadocian wheat; further information strengthening the identification of the Cappadocian wheat as durum wheat is furnished by Basil *Homiliai eis tên Hexaêmeron* V ed. Giet, pp. 290-291, who said that it had solid culms (bread wheat tends to have hollow straw) and prominent awns to fend off predators, another characteristic of tetraploid wheats – the awn (Greek *athêr* as in Hesiod F62 Merkelbach-West) of wheat is also a photosynthetic organ and in wild cereals serves to fix the seed in the ground, cf. Pliny *NH* XVIII.x.53 and Cicero *De senectute* XV.51; Josephos *Ioudaikos Polemos* VII.295-298 on very long preservation of grain at Masada in Palestine, another pointer towards durum wheat, facilitated by its low water content; Jasny (1944) 89-94 on *puros semidalitês*.

78. Szemerényi (1974) 156 and Chantraine (1980) 996 on *semidalis*; Antiphanes F34, Hermippos F63 and Alexis F168 Kock; the Greek language picked up other Semitic words related to cereals when it spread into the Orient in the Hellenistic period (e.g. Hrozny (1914) 60 n. 2 for *zizanion*); note also Langkavel (1866) and Voigt (1876) (useful sources of references although their botanical identifications are no longer of value); Gansiniec (1956); Amouretti (1979); Vavilov (1926) 158-162 on the distribution and diversity of modern varieties of durum wheat; Polomé (1985) for various views on I-E origins; Szemerényi (1985) 39-44 & 50-54 for the *status quaestionis* of possible links between Semitic and Indo-European languages.

79. Grierson (1959) 129.

80. Candolle (1884) 28.
81. Burdon (1987) 22.
82. Jasny (1944) 05-06.
83. Especially the work of Helbaek (1961) 90; J. Renfrew (1973a) and Harlan (1975) did not mention naked tetraploid wheats in relation to prehistoric/early historic periods; Zeven (1980a) also argued for the spread of naked hexaploid wheats in the Neolithic; Kroll (1983) 40, on the problem of differentiating bread wheat and durum wheat caryopses, thought that the naked wheat of Late Bronze Age and Early Iron Age Kastanas in Macedonia was mainly bread wheat, because of the presence of spikelet fragments of another hexaploid, spelt wheat, but durum wheat was cultivated in northern Greece until the 1920s and the spelt of Kastanas was probably an impurity in emmer crops (see section 9 of this chapter), cf. G.E.M. Jones (1983) 39 for naked wheat grains averaging $3.65 \times 2.75 \times 2.25$ mm at Assiros Toumba.
84. D. Zohary (1973); van Zeist (1976); the shift in Harlan's position from his 1975 book to his 1981 article illustrates the uncertainties of palaeobotany; Zohary & Hopf (1988) 44-45.
85. R. Thompson (1949) 89-109 and Ellison (1984) only identified barley, emmer and bread wheat in the cuneiform texts; J. Renfrew (1984) and Powell (1984b) give more recent accounts of the archaeological and documentary evidence respectively from Mesopotamia; arguments, such as those of Vavilov (1926) 161, Kislev (1973) and Zeven (1980a), which depend on extrapolating backwards from the modern distribution of the various wheats, are not necessarily correct.
86. Darby et al. (1977) vol. 2, pp. 489-491 on emmer, barley and the mysterious cereal called *s-w-t* in Dynastic Egyptian sources; Gardiner (1947) 222 described seven varieties of emmer in ancient Egypt; A.B. Lloyd in Trigger et al. (1983) 327 asserted the presence of naked wheat in Egypt before the time of Alexander the Great, but erred in saying that emmer had a lower nutritive value than barley.
87. The interpretation of Lewy (1956), namely that *se* signified wheat, not barley, seems strong because in the texts in question *se* stands in a 5:3 price ratio to another cereal, the normal wheat:barley price ratio throughout later history (see section 10 of this chapter).
88. Kent (1983) 55 on the unsuitability of durum wheat for making good bread, and 86 on Roman rotary grain mills as intended for grinding bread wheat; Konzak (1977) 421 & 475 on the genetics; Pomeranz (1971) 777-796 and D'Egidio et al. (1979) on the manufacture of alimentary pastes; Irvine (1965) 331.
89. Pliny *NH* XVIII.xxix.109-116, discussed by André (1981) 58-59, cf. 52 n. 28, also André (1985) for his identifications of cereals. Gobert (1955) 502-505, on borghol, wrongly equated Pliny's *far, zea* and *semen* with durum wheat rather than with emmer.
90. Pliny *NH* XXII.lxi.128, criticised by Galen *Hippokratous peri diaitês oxeôn nosêmatôn biblion kai Galênou hypomnêma* I.14 ed. Kühn vol. XV, p. 455; the *alica* of Campania is translated into Greek as *chondros* in Strabo V.4.3.242c; Dioskorides *MM* II.96 and Tryphon of Alexandria in Athenaios 109c for the manufacture of *chondros* from emmer; *Geôponika* III.7 ed. Beckh for the recipe; Galen *peri trophôn dunameôn* I.6 ed. Kühn vol. VI, pp. 496-498.
91. Harlan et al. (1976) 171 n. 5 suggested that the Carthaginians grew mainly barley and production of wheat only became important in the Roman period in North Africa, cf. Diodoros Siculus XXI F16.1 for Agathokles trying to prevent Carthaginian wheat imports from Sicily and Sardinia in the late fourth century BC (this could have been caused by a bad harvest in N. Africa); Haudricourt & Hédrin (1943) 115; Hekataios FGH1 F335 Jacoby states that some of the Libyans

grew cereals (*sitos*) *c.* 500 BC; by the time of Massinissa *c.* 200 BC Numidia was able to export large quantities of 'wheat' and barley to Roman armies operating in the Orient (e.g. Livy XXXI.19.4), but Livy says nothing about emmer, grown in North Africa according to Pliny, which may be included in 'wheat'.

92. Vavilov (1951) 198 described the traditional durum wheat of the south Balkans, *Triticum durum expansum* Vav. section *mediterranea*; *Greek agriculture* (1981) 54-55 and Pomeranz (1971) 787 for the EEC; Brumfield (1981) 36-37 on porridge; Pliny *NH* XVIII.xiv.72.

93. Sedlar (1980) for Greek knowledge of India, insignificant before Alexander the Great; Theophrastos *HP* IV.4.2-3, Bretzl (1903) 207-217, Tolkowsky (1938) 39-94, Andrews (1961a) employing the unreliable evidence of Pompeian wall paintings which may depict only exotic imports, Scora (1975), Athenaios III.83-85, Pliny *NH* XII.vii.15-16 and Antiphanes F58 Kock on the citron; Hjelmqvist (1979) 113-114 on Cyprus; Stearn (1977) on the botanical knowledge acquired by Alexander's expedition.

94. Polybios I.3.3-4 & V.105.4-10.

95. Vavilov (1951) 37-39; Hawkes (1983) 86 cites more recent literature; Bertin et al. (1971) did not discuss the various species of wheat separately.

96. Schiemann (1951); Peterson (1965) 93; Harlan (1969), (1975) & (1981).

97. Differing viewpoints expressed by Harlan et al. (1976), Ehret (1979), Harlan and Philippson in J.D. Clark (1982) 647-649 & 801 respectively.

98. Strabo XVII.2.2.821c, Pliny *NH* XVIII.xxiv.100 and Diodoros Siculus I.33.4 only mention barley and 'millet' in 'Ethiopia', while Herodotos III.22.3-4 implies that wheat was absent from 'Ethiopia'. This detail may be correct, even though his account of Cambyses' expedition, in which it occurs, is fiction. The romantic tale of Heliodoros *Aithiopika* X.5.2 eds. Rattenbury & Lumb mentions wheat (*sitos*) in 'Ethiopia' in the late Roman period. See Kobischtschanow (1984) and Shinnie (1984) on agriculture in Meroe; Herodotos I.193.4, Theophrastos *HP* IV.4.9 and Pliny *NH* XVIII.x.55 on sorghum.

99. Galen *peri trophôn dunameôn* I.2 ed. Kühn vol. VI, pp. 480-481 and Oribasios *Collectiones Medicae* I.2.2-3 ed. Raeder should be compared to the brief non-technical descriptions in Peterson (1965) 12 & 15.

100. Hall et al. (1979) 210 record that the average 100-seed weight of bread wheat is 2.5-3.0 g, of durum wheat 3.5-5.2 g, cf. Pomeranz (1971) 23 & 782; Reynolds (1979) 64 for the protein content of various types of wheat.

101. Foxhall & Forbes (1982) 79 n. 123 questioned Jasny's conclusion that durum wheat was the greatly predominant naked wheat of antiquity. Pliny's rule regarding *panis militarius* cannot possibly have applied to the whole Roman empire. If he had in mind Latium, the region around Rome itself, then it should be noted that Jasny (1944) 97-99 identified the *triticum* of Latium as mainly poulard wheat. This wheat produces a weak flour poorly suited to breadmaking, explaining why it has ceased to be an important crop today in spite of its high productivity. Thus Foxhall's experimental results, Jasny's conclusion and Pliny's data are not necessarily incompatible. Amouretti (1986) 117 offers a different approach to the problem, not incompatible with that outlined above.

102. Hippokrates *peri diaitês* XLII ed. Littré vol. 6, pp. 538-542 stated that the largest loaves were the most nourishing and then spoke of *hoi de semidalitai ischurotatoi pantôn toutôn* (*sc. artôn*); Tryphon of Alexandria (first century BC) in Athenaios III.109bc includes *semidalitês* as one *genos* of *artoi*; Archestratos in Athenaios III.112b praised the *semidalis* of Tegea; Diphilos of Siphnos (third century BC) in Athenaios III.115cd regarded *semidalitês* as the most nourishing and best type of bread made from wheat; Philistion of Lokris (fourth-third century

BC?) in Athenaios op. cit. regarded *semidalitês* as the best bread.

103. Archestratos in Athenaios III.112b and Antiphanes in Athenaios III.112cd praised the excellence of Athenian bread; cf. Lynkeus of Samos in Athenaios III.109de.

104. See n. 99 above and Jasny (1944) 60-61.

105. Cited by Setton (1975b) 197.

106. Pepelasis et al. (1980) ch. 1 and McNeill (1978) on Greek agriculture in recent years.

107. Teall (1959) 118 & 136 for insignificance of grain production in the Crimea in the Byzantine period (probably due to political instability) and Constantinople's monopoly on its use; Bisel (1980) 54-55 on zinc.

108. Oribasios *Coll. Med.* I.2.2; see also the interesting discussion of Dieuches F13 in Bertier (1972) 233 n. 1; *Suda* s.v. *semidalis*; Theodore Prodromus eds. D.C. Hesseling & H. Pernot *Poèmes prodromiques en grec vulgaire* (1910) p. 62, line 316 & p. 77, line 101.

109. For the popular usage of *aleura* in connection with wheat in opposition to *alphita* made from barley, see Plato *Republic* II.372b, (Aristotle) *Problems* I.8.863b2-3 & XXI.927-930 and Moritz (1958) 149-150. In Strabo XVI.1.14.742c the date palm is said to have provided *aleura*, *alphita* and much else besides in Babylonia. Moritz cited Galen *tôn Hippokratous glossôn exêgêsis* ed. Kühn vol. XIX, p. 76 to the effect that *alphita* did not refer to barley only in the Hippokratic corpus.

110. Chantraine (1968) 59 and (1980) 959.

111. Vavilov (1951); Kislev (1981), Janushevich (1984) and Lisitsina (1984) placed the origin of bread wheat in Transcaucasia; Strabo XI.4.3.502c on the region's agriculture; Zimansky (1985) 106 n. 21 noted Heer's *Triticum vulgare antiquorum* on Bronze Age sites in Soviet Armenia; Jasny (1944) 72 on bread wheat's supposed lack of winter hardiness in antiquity; Morris & Sears (1967) 28 on spelt wheat.

112. Galen *peri trophôn dunameôn* I.2 ed. Kühn vol. VI, pp. 483-484, paralleled in Latin literature by Celsus *de medicina* II.18 ed. Daremberg; Jasny (1944) 77-79 on *siligo*.

113. Moritz (1958) 159-167 on Greek & Roman sieves; Pliny *NH* XVIII.xxvii.105; Semonides of Amorgos F7 West for the use of sieves in archaic Greece; Amouretti (1986) 144-147 has refined Moritz's chronology recently.

114. Amouretti (1986) 113-131 is a recent survey of cereal products in ancient Greece. The contrast between *panis siligneus* and *panis plebeius* (the latter made from durum wheat or any inferior cereal) in Seneca *Epistulae morales* CXIX suggests that the upper classes mainly consumed bread made from bread wheat in Rome, cf. Pliny *NH* XIX.xix.52-55. See Galen *peri trophôn dunameôn* I.4 ed. Kühn vol. VI, p. 494 on leavened bread and Pliny *NH* XVIII.xxix.113-114 on *alica*.

115. Theophrastos *HP* VIII.1.2-4 (for the quotation) & *CP* IV.11.3-4, also *CP* III.4.1 & III.23.1, *Geôponika* II.14.3, and Aratos *Phainomena* 254-267 ed. Maass for sowing at the setting of the Pleiades.

116. Theophrastos *Metaphysics* 9a16-11a18 eds. Ross & Fobes rejected the teleological explanations of Aristotle *Physics* 199a20-32; Wöhrle (1985); Morton (1981) on Theophrastos as a botanist; for his interest in the concerns of modern economic botany see Chapter II.7 above on plant diseases and Hatch (1938) on insects that prey on crops; Friedrich (1970), Raven et al. (1971), Berlin (1974) and Atran (1985) on folk taxonomies; Stearn (1976) on the path from Theophrastos to the modern 'Flora Graeca'; the theory of the growth and development of plants in Hippokrates *peri phusios paidiou* XXII-XXVI ed. Littré vol. 7, pp. 514-529,

discussed by Lonie (1969), provides an interesting comparison to Theophrastos; Aristotle *GA* 731a29-30 & *HA* 539a18-21 shows that he did write books on plants, which are not extant.

117. Epikrates F11 Kock; Pellegrin (1982) esp. 27 n. 2 on its epistemological significance; the *kolokuntê sensu stricto* was the bottle gourd (*Lagenaria siceraria*), not the pumpkin (*Cucurbita maxima*) of the Loeb Theophrastos and Thiselton-Dyer (1918) 297-299 & 304, a New World plant unknown in Europe before Columbus. Theophrastos *HP* VII.4.6 said that the *kolokuntê* did not have different varieties, but only superior and inferior individuals, perhaps with respect to size. The *sikua* and the *kolokuntê* were different size groups of the same plant (Athenaios II.59a, equated by Theophrastos *CP* II.8.4 & II.11.4). Athenaios II.59c indicates that Attic writers used the word *kolokuntê* in a broad sense to cover all then known cucurbits, which does nothing to clarify the semantic field of the word. See also Chapter I above on the bottle gourd and Whitaker & Bemis (1975) for the origin of the pumpkin in south America. Earlier views concerning other members of the family Cucurbitaceae in antiquity also require revision now. The wild watermelon (*Citrullus colocynthis*, probably ancient Greek *pepôn* as in e.g. Hippokrates *peri diaitês* II.55 & *peri nousôn* III.17 ed. Littré vol. 6, pp. 564-565 & vol. 7, pp. 158-159 respectively), of the Near East and India, was the ancestor of the cultivated watermelon (*Citrullus lanatus*), rather than the wild watermelon of southern Africa (D. Zohary (1983) 114-116; contra Andrews (1956) and Simmonds (1976) 67). Recent archaeological discoveries (Kroll (1983) 75-76) suggest that the melon proper (*Cucumis melo*) had reached Greece by the end of the Mycenaean period, when it turns up in Tiryns, probably as an exotic import from the Orient, alongside rice (see Chapter I above). Wild forms of *Cucumis melo* occur today from India to Israel (D. Zohary (1983) 116). However, the melon was insignificant in classical times, not clearly differentiated from the watermelon in surviving literature until Galen (*melopepôn*, in *peri trophôn dunameôn* II.54-55 ed. Kühn vol. 6, pp. 564-566). This suggests that it was then far inferior in quality to the modern melon. Stol (1987) 92 is a recent attempt to find *Cucumis melo* in classical sources before Galen. Andrews (1956) is now out of date. Note also Zhukovskij (1962) 65-72 on the Cucurbitaceae. Such plants were originally cultivated for their oil-bearing seeds and only later evolved edible flesh. The earliest domesticated melons were probably all green-fruited, and it was only later that the modern sweet-fruited types of melon evolved. Pliny *NH* XIX.xxiii.67 claims that the *melopepôn* had appeared recently in his own time in Campania, as if by a sudden evolutionary development. This is not a likely time or location for the evolution of domesticated *Cucumis melo*. Note also Columella *RR* XI.3.48-53, Pliny *NH* XIX.xxiv.69-74 and C.B. Heiser in Harris & Hillman (1989) 475-478 on the bottle gourd (Latin *cucurbita*).

118. Theophrastos *HP* VIII.4.2 on *genê* of barley; Briggs (1978) 76 on the interfertility of all known forms of barley; Columella *RR* II.9.14-16; *Hordeum irregulare*, an Ethiopian variety with variable fertility of the lateral florets which conceivably could account for Theophrastos' claims, has never been important in Europe; Harlan (1971) on the origin of barley.

119. Theophrastos *HP* VIII.4.5. See section 10 of this chapter and n. 37 above for the price/ration ratio and n. 60 above.

120. The *polla genê* of Theophrastos *HP* VIII.4.3-5 probably subsume both different species and different varieties, although he attributed the differences between them to soils and climates; Dodoens (1978) 309-318 on cereals; Morris & Sears (1967) 21 for the modern research alluded to in the text.

121. On the mutability of cereals see Theophrastos *HP* VIII.8.1 and *CP* I.9.3,

II.13.3 & IV.1.6; Columella *RR* II.9.13; Varro *RR* I.31.5 for *farrago*, an ancient crop mixture; M. Forbes (1977) 54 noted that it was customary to sow wheat and barley together in the same field until about fifty years ago on Methana, cf. G.E.M. Jones (1983) 67 and Turrill (1929) 243; Bible Leviticus XIX.19, Deuteronomy XXII.9-11, Josephos *Jewish Antiquities* IV.8.20, with Mandelbaum (1982), B. Moore (1984) 210 and Newman (1932) 41; Darwin (1968) 123 for the quotation, confirmed by Briggs & Walters (1984) 313-314; Darwin (1875) vol. 1, p. 333 for the experiments, whose results may be compared to: (1) the ancient opinion that cereals took three years to change from one form to another (e.g. Pliny *NH* XVIII.xx.93); (2) the analogous opinion of New World farmers with respect to maize (Mangelsdorf (1974) 123); (3) Cockburn (1963) 74-76 argued that humans and other mammals require a small number of generations to develop some immunity to diseases to which they had not been exposed previously, generalising from the reaction of the rabbit to myxomatosis.

122. Vavilov (1951) 195 & 198 on durum wheat; Kushnir & Halloran (1982) for the evolutionary primacy of winter varieties of wild emmer.

123. Columella *RR* XI.2.20 and Pliny *NH* XVIII.lxv.239 mention the sowing of *trimestre* in February; Plutarch *eis ta Hêsiodou erga* F68 Sandbach observed that *trimeniaios puros* benefited from spring rainfall, cf. Theophrastos *CP* II.2.3; Columella *RR* II.6.2 regarded *trimestre* as a *genus siliginis*; Theophrastos *CP* IV.9.1 & 11.1-3 on the 'productivity' of autumn-sown and spring-sown wheat; Plutarch *Moralia* 915d-e for *puros trimenos* as giving a lower yield and needing less food than autumn-sown wheat; Walpole (1817) 291 for *dimenio*, 'two-month wheat', sown in March in early modern Greece; Hillman (1981) 147 noted that farmers in modern Anatolia sometimes sow seed in the spring for the simple reason that they are unable to complete the sowing during the autumn.

124. Theophrastos *HP* VIII.1.2, Hesiod *WD* 485-490, Columella *RR* II.6.2 & II.9.7-8, and Pliny *NH* XVIII.xii.69, note also *NH* XVIII.xlix.183 & XVIII.lvi.201-205; Plutarch *eis ta Hêsiodou erga* F60 Sandbach suggests that in the archaic period early sowing was the rule; see n. 273 below on emmer and birds; Aelian *peri zôiôn idiotêtos* II.25 & VI.43 on ants as a pest of cereals; Xenophon *Oikonomikos* XVII.1-6 (to be read with D.C. Hopkins (1985) 215-217) and Theophrastos *HP* VIII.6.1.

125. Brumfield (1981) 37 for the absence of spring wheat in modern Attica; Pliny *NH* XVIII.x.49 said that only the autumn sowing season mattered in Greece; Shpiler & Blum (1986) on the yield reduction.

126. Galen *peri trophôn dunameôn* I.6 and his commentary on Hippokrates *peri arthrôn* II.41-42 ed. Kühn vol. VI, p. 496 & vol. XVIII.1, pp. 469-475 respectively; references to *sitanios* occur in the Hippokratic treatises *peri diaitês oxeôn* (*notha*) ed. Littré vol. 2, pp. 500, 518 & 524-526, *gunaikeiôn* I.74, II.110 & 192 ed. Littré vol. 8, pp. 156-157, 236-237 & 372-373 respectively and in Pollux *Onomasticon* VI.73.

127. Columella *RR* II.9.8, cf. II.9.16; Pliny *NH* XVIII.xii.70, whose source, Theophrastos *CP* IV.11.4, is simply wrong.

128. Peterson (1965) 237; Arnon (1972) vol. 2, p. 47; Jasny (1944) 101 did not give due credit to Columella.

129. L. White (1962) 69-76 on the mediaeval north European system; Parain (1936) 122 states that the French colonists tried to introduce it into Algeria but found that it did not work there.

130. Jasny (1944) 77-79; Harlan (1981); Vavilov (1926) 155-158 on the distribution and diversity of naked hexaploid wheats.

131. E.g. J. Renfrew (1979), maintaining her earlier position; Kislev (1981);

Dennell (1983) 161; Barker (1985) 44, 92, 198 & 204.

132. Theophrastos *HP* VIII.4.4 for Achaia & Euboia; *CP* IV.9.6 for Lemnos; Dioskorides *MM* II.101 for *puros sitanios* on Crete; Pliny *NH* XVIII.xvii.76-77 for the manufacture of starch from *trimestre* on Chios and Crete; P. Cairo Zen. 59155, line 6, from the Zenon 'archive', mentions the sowing of *trimênos puros* in Egypt in the third century BC; this wheat in Egypt was also described as 'Syrian wheat' (*puros suriakos*) and distinguished from the local naked wheat (*puros epichôrios*), a tetraploid wheat – H.A. Thompson (1930); a spring-sown variety of durum wheat, *melanathêr* (Hesykhios s.v. and P. Col. Zen. 69, lines 43, 45 & 51), is differentiated from *sitanios puros* in *Geôponika* III.3.11.

133. Theophrastos HP VIII.4.5; Janushevich & Nikolaenko (1979), Pashkevich (1984) and Janushevich (1981), (1984) and in Harris & Hillman (1989) 607-619. This Russian research shows that millets were important crops in the parts of the USSR adjacent to modern Romania (cf. Aelian *poikilê historia* III.39 and Pliny *NH* XVIII.xxv.101), but not in the Crimea, contrary to Jasny (1950) 233. L. Gallo (1984b) 111 n. 138 rightly affirmed that Greek authors sometimes used the word *Pontos* to refer specifically to the Crimea and the adjacent parts of south Russia, rather than to the Black Sea as a whole.

134. Gernet (1909) 320-326, cf. Noonan (1973) and Bravo (1983). The account of the *Pontos* grain trade in Polybios IV.38.5 reflects climatic variability (Parain (1936) 94) rather than political instability, contrary to Préaux (1978) vol. 2, pp. 520-521. Hartog (1980) 210, an otherwise brilliant book, did not realise that Herodotos IV.17-19 was describing an agricultural system in Scythia that became more extensive with increasing distance from the coast, i.e. plough agriculture on permanent farms eventually gave way to plough agriculture on shifting farms which in turn was displaced by shifting cultivation employing the hoe instead of the plough; R.E.F. Smith (1959) 51-87 on shifting cultivation in Russia, esp. 67 for Arabic sources parallel to Herodotos op. cit.

135. Pliny *NH* XVIII.xix.81.

136. Kislev (1979/80), (1980), (1981), (1984a) & (1984b); M. Zohary (1982) 74 regarded the naked wheat of the Bible as durum wheat; see also Turkowski (1969) on the Levant; Kerber (1964) on TetraCanthatch; Costantini (1984) drew attention to the evolutionary significance of small, round seeded forms of fossil naked wheat in prehistoric India, but suggested that *Triticum sphaerococcum* evolved from a tetraploid wheat resembling durum wheat (see also n. 197 below).

137. P.H. Davis (1985) 249-250 on the Transcaucasian wheats.

138. Lewontin & Birch, cited by Briggs & Walters (1984) 215, cf. 229-232.

139. Janushevich & Nikolaenko (1979) 133 on the wheat from the Crimea with small, round grains, some of it doubtless club wheat (*T. compactum*); see section 8 of this chapter on the Crimea; Follieri (1986) studied cereal grains from Minoan Crete well within the size range of *T. parvicoccum*; Hjelmqvist (1976) records an impression on a potsherd from Cyprus in the second millennium BC of a wheat grain with the proportions of modern durum wheat but absolute dimensions closer to those of *T. parvicoccum*, as well as an impression of club wheat; Te-Tzu Chang (1983) 77 on China; Jasny (1944) 79 did not explain the increase in seed size in the course of history.

140. Harper, Lovell & Moore (1970) 337.

141. Darwin (1875) vol. 1, pp. 336-338, a passage of fundamental importance.

142. Heer (1865) & (1878); Jacomet & Schlichtherle (1984) re-examined Heer's conclusions and decided that they were well-founded; Theophrastos *HP* VIII.2.3 and Pliny *NH* XVIII.xxi.95 on wheat with branching ears, cf. Percival (1921) 241-243 & 256 on 'Mummy' wheat, possibly Pliny's *centigranium*; the thick-stemmed varieties called *drakontias, strangias* and *selinousios* by Theophrastos *CP* III.21.2 and Pliny *NH* XVIII.xii.64-65 may also have been poulard wheat; Pliny *NH* XVII.iii.28 regarded a thick stalk in cereals as a sign of a good soil; Vavilov (1926) 160 observed that 'the entire diversity of English wheat (*T. turgidum*) belongs to the Mediterranean' – there was a time in the second millennium AD when poulard wheat was the principal wheat grown in southern England.

143. Boeuf (1931) 13 & 18 on *T. durum var. duro-compactum*; P.H. Davis (1985) 252-253 on *T. carthlicum*.

144. Evans & Dunstone (1970); Darwin (1875) vol. 2, p. 158.

145. Percival (1921) 206, 211 & 266 on the dimensions of *T. vulgare antiquorum*, durum wheat from Egypt in the first century BC, and modern durum wheat, illustrating the increase in seed size in the course of history. Buschan (1895) on seed sizes in antiquity.

146. Consider Mayer (1980) 423 for the emmer of Pompeii, with Percival (1921) 190 for modern emmer – it has changed less than bread wheat and durum wheat since antiquity, when it ceased to be a major crop in most regions; Theophrastos *CP* IV.4.1 and Pliny *NH* XVII.xiv.72.

147. A random series of examples follows: Mangelsdorf (1974) 148-149 on maize; Harlan et al. (1976) 6-7 on sorghum; Arnon (1972) vol. 2, p. 74 on barley; de Candolle (1884) 280 on wild olives (this applies more to the fruit than to the seed inside the fruit); Simmonds (1976) 39 (lettuce), 110 (rye), 158 (chickpeas), 163 (lentils), 181 (field beans), 313 (lupins).

148. Percival (1921) 425 and Kent (1983) 17 on increases in average grain weight of English wheat over the last four centuries; *Barley Genetics* (1981) 97-103 & 112-117 observed that the mean grain weight of English barley has increased by 15 per cent in the course of the twentieth century AD.

149. Allard (1960) 50-60 for mutations leading to splitting of pure lines; Rindos (1984) correctly emphasised that stressing man's role as a propagating agent is the only way of explaining why it was advantageous in terms of natural selection for cereals that were being domesticated to lose the ability to propagate themselves.

150. Costantini (1984) describes barley with a short stem and small seeds in the Caucasus region and the Indian sub-continent *c.* 4000 BC, preserved in mud-brick impressions, cf. Simmonds (1979) 18-19. *T. parvicoccum*, like the synthetic cultivar TetraCanthatch, may also have been a prehistoric cereal with both short stems and small seeds. Similarly the primitive Transcaucasian tetraploid *T. timopheevi*, mentioned earlier, is also a relatively short plant on average (70-90 cm in height).

151. Aristotle *GA* 749b26 & 771b13-14; (Aristotle) *Problems* 927a6-8; Pliny *NH* XVIII.xxix.115; in Arrian *Anabasis* I.4.1 a field of tall cereals provided cover for the troops of Alexander's army; Percival (1921) 242-243 on poulard wheat; Khush (1963) 60 for rye evolution involving increases in seed size and strengthening of the plant's ability to compete for resources; Simmonds (1979) 183.

152. Theophrastos *HP* VII.6.3-4, *CP* IV.4.12 & VI.16; Dioskorides *MM* ed. Wellmann passim; for many individual examples see Pliny *NH* e.g. XIX.lx.184 (general comment); XII.xxxiii.66 (myrrh); XV.vii.24 (on wild olive oil), also XXIII.xxxviii.77; XX.ii.3 (cucumber); XX.viii.14 (bottle gourd); XX.xxviii.72 (beet); XX.l.130 (cress); XX.xlviii.124 (basil (?), but see Laufer (1919) 586-590); XX.xliii.110 (asparagus); XX.xxxvi.92 (cabbage); XX.xxxii.76 (endive); XX.lv.156 (pennyroyal); XX.li.131 (rue); XX.lvii.162 (cummin); XX.lxxvi.202 (poppy); XXI.xvii.31 (saffron); XXI.xviii.35 (general observation); XXII.lxxiv.154 (lupin).

Columella *RR* XI.3.27 & 3.31 mentions a stratagem for artificially increasing the size of the head of certain vegetables.

153. Helsel (1985) on increases in total biomass; Evans & Dunstone (1970) on tillering; Harlan (1967) on the domestication of einkorn increasing its productivity by increasing seed size at the expense of the components of chaff.

154. Baker (1974) and Harlan & de Wet (1975) on weed evolution; Brinton (1946), Aristotle *peri hupnou* 456b29-31 and Soranos *Gunaikologia* II.56.3 on the effects of darnel ingestion; Dioskorides *MM* II.100 for the use of darnel made in medicine in antiquity; Krochmal & Laurentiades (1955) 177 for its distribution in modern Greece; Kroll (1983) 82-86 compared the darnel of Kastanas with that found in the Levant by Kislev (1980), who discussed the archaeological evidence for darnel and its evolution. Theophrastos *CP* IV.4.4-13 on transformations of one plant into another, esp. IV.4.5 for *puros* to *aira* and *zeia* to *bromos* (emmer to oats, cf. n. 205 below) and IV.4.8 for farmers reaping *aira* after sowing *puros*. See also Theophrastos *CP* II.16.2-3 (noting that darnel is favoured by wet weather), V.3.7, *HP* VIII.4.6 (noting that some varieties of wheat were free from darnel, but not including the wheat of the Levant in his list of darnel-free varieties, thus confirming Kislev's research in that area), VIII.7.1 (noting that darnel was an autumn plant, like cereals and unlike other weeds), VIII.8.3 (stating, correctly, that it may be the case that darnel merely likes to grow amongst cereals and is not spontaneously generated from them), VIII.9.3 (describing *aira* as a wild plant). Columella *RR* VIII.4.1 & 8.6 discusses bird food. The parable is in Matthew 13.24-30 & 36-43, with Bainton (1932); Mishnah ed. Danby First Division Zeraim – Kilaim I.1; Basil *Homiliai eis tên Hexaêmeron* V ed. Giet pp. 294-299; (Aristotle) *peri phutôn* 821a31-32 also mentions the transformation; Laurent-Täckholm (1940) 154 for the fungus. Of related interest is the discussion of *aigilôps* (*Aegilops ovata*), a weed of barley, in Theophrastos *HP* VII.13.5, VIII.8.3, 9.2-3 & 11.9; Turrill (1929) 234; Aaronson (1989); Lieber (1970).

155. Stebbins (1950) 123-134 on the genus Camelina, native to the eastern Mediterranean; Knorzer (1978); Theophrastos *HP* VIII.7.1, *CP* II.16.2 & IV.5.4, and (Aristotle) *peri phutôn* 821a31-32 on the transformation of *linon*; Kroll (1983) 58-59 for *C. sativa* at Kastanas; J. Chadwick (1976) 153-156 on the Linear B tablets; Vavilov (1926) 182-194 on varieties of flax; (Xenophon) *Ath. Pol.* II.12 for the Athenian empire; Demosthenes XLVII.20 mentions a shortage of sail-cloth in the Piraeus; cf. section 4 of this chapter on wool production in classical Attica; Helbaek (1959b) & (1960) on evolution of linseed size; Pausanias V.5.2, VI.26.6 & VII.21.14 and Pliny *NH* XIX.iv.20 on cultivation of flax for linen in Elis; Thiselton-Dyer (1918) 81-83 & 312 on *bussos*; Zhukovskij (1962) 82-83 on *L. angustifolium*; Cartledge (1979) 175 and Pliny *NH* XIX.iii.16 on Peloponnese and N. Italy; Hippokrates *peri diaitês* II.45 and *peri diaitês oxeôn (notha)* XVIII ed. Littré vol. 6, pp. 544-545 & vol. 2, pp. 502-503 respectively, and Scribonius Largus *Compositiones* CLXXXVII ed. Sconocchia on linseed in medicine; Galen *peri trophôn dunameôn* I.32 ed. Kühn vol. VI, p. 549; Vavilov (1951) 39; Gill (1987) 12-21; Columella *RR* II.10.17.

156. Aristotle *HA* 608b19-610a35; Harper (1977) esp. ch. 1 and pp. 201 & 664-672: '... seed size may be of much more crucial importance in evolution than seed number' (p. 664); L.T. Evans (1981); Harper, Lovell & Moore (1970); J. White (1979); Theophrastos *CP* I.11.4 on a plant as a collection of parts and *HP* I.2.2 on the difficulty of defining a 'part' in plants.

157. Ventris & Chadwick (1973) 236-238 and J. Chadwick (1976) 110 on the Linear B tablets; Lewy (1944) & (1949) 2-4 and Powell (1984a) on measurement of area by volume of seed sown in Mesopotamia; Kula (1984) 38-54; Xenophon

Oikonomikos XVII.8-11 thought that the seeding rate should depend on soil fertility, cf. Theophrastos *HP* VIII.6.2 & *CP* III.20.5 and Pliny *NH* XVIII.liv.96.

158. See also Columella *RR* II.9.5-6, thinking in terms of the yield per plant he wishes to encourage tillering, and *RR* III.3.4; Pliny *NH* XVIII.x.55 on fertility of sorghum; XXI.xi.24, expressing the same line of thought for other types of plants; XVIII.xl.141 on tillering of rye; Theophrastos *CP* II.12.1 & *HP* VIII.3.4 on millet fertility and Kent (1983) 3 & 21 for millet seed weights; Josephos *Ioudaikos Polemos* IV.470, Menander F96 Kock and Xenophon *Cyropaedia* VIII.3.38 illustrate use of the seed:yield ratio outside botanical and agronomic texts; the statements of ancient authors on the yields of Byzacium are discussed in section 12 of this chapter; the seed:yield ratio was also generally employed in mediaeval England – Titow (1972) 9.

159. Pliny *NH* XVIII.iii.9 on *iugerum*, Chantraine (1980) 913 on *plethron*, Hesiod *WD* 427 & 436, Homer *Iliad* IX.579 on *pentêkontoguos* and Hesykhios s.v. *guês*, McGrew (1985) 34 on *zeugarion* (pp. 83-84 are also relevant), and H. Forbes (1985) 156 n. 20 on Methana; Polybios IX.26a.1, cf. Thucydides VI.1.1-2 and (Demosthenes) XLII.5 (misunderstood by Ste. Croix (1963) 111); (Aristotle) *Athênaiôn Politeia* VII.3-4 and Plutarch *Solon* XVIII on Solon; consider also the divergence between Polybios VI.45.3, who thought that Spartan *klêroi* were equal in area, and Plutarch *Lykourgos* VIII.4 who thought that the *klêroi* produced an equal volume of crops – as Plato *Laws* 745d recommended that the *klêroi* in his proposed Cretan *polis* should vary to take account of differences in soil fertility and so equalise average total production, Plutarch, although a later source, may be more accurate than Polybios.

160. Pomeranz (1971) 782 for durum wheat's being heavier than bread wheat; Evans & Dunstone (1970), Gill, Vear & Barnard (1980) vol. 2, p. 62, Hadjichristodoulou (1982) and Kent (1983) 3 for durum wheat's nevertheless giving a lower yield per unit area than bread wheat; Columella *RR* II.9.13; Pliny *NH* XVIII.xii.63 ranked the wheat of different regions according to its *weight*; Hippokrates *peri pathôn* LX ed. Littré vol. 6, pp. 268-269 also noted that different types of *sitos* differ in density; Theophrastos *HP* VIII.4.2 noted variations in grain size and shape between barley varieties.

161. Sharma & Gandhi (1977) on the correlations, contra Boeuf (1931) 148; Halloran (1976) on the genetics of seed size; Percival (1921) 182 on wild emmer; the theory of Dennell (1973) on the origin of wild emmer, although probably partially correct as wild emmer hybridises freely with durum wheat and such hybridisations may be commoner in hot climates like that of Israel than in cooler climates, does not account for the different seed size groups of modern varieties of wild emmer. For another example of ancient cultivation leading to an increase in the seed size of a modern wild species note Callen (1967) on the prehistoric Mexican cereal *Setaria genuicalata*, which increased its seed size during incipient domestication until it was abandoned in favour of maize, when the latter achieved yet greater increases in average cob size, but the resulting large-seeded forms of this species of millet still exist in the wild today. Ladizinsky et al. (1983) describes another modern wild species, the Mediterranean lentil species *Lens nigricans*, which appears to be descended from an ancient domesticated plant and manifests the increased seed size of an incipient crop.

162. Jardé (1925) 14-16; Varro *RR* I.5.1-2 regarded the works of Theophrastos as unsuitable for practical farmers; Aristotle *Politics* 1258b39-1259a3 testifies to the existence of books *peri geôrgias*, on farming, in the fourth century BC; Columella *RR* I.1.8 lists earlier writers on agriculture from Athens.

163. Columella *RR* II.9.11, cf. *Geôponika* II.16.1-3; Pliny *NH* XVIII.liv.195;

Varro *RR* I.52.1, with Spurr (1986) 40 and Boeuf (1931) 375; Virgil *Georgics* I.197-200; (Aristotle) *peri phutôn* 821b15-18 and Theophrastos *CP* III.24.3; Hunter (1952) 128-129 and Webb & Hawtin (1981) 74 for modern experiments using mass selection, and Allard (1960) chapters 6 & 11 on selection working on spontaneous mutations; contrast Boeuf (1931) 81-88 & 375, a practical plant breeder looking for immediate results, who disparaged mass selection techniques and denied that they could improve a crop plant in any way whatsoever, but experiments of short duration such as his cannot reveal what could happen over centuries and millennia; Nikophon F19 Kock and Kritias F70 eds. Diels-Kranz on the *spermatopôlês*; Plutarch *Demosthenes* XXIII.6; Aristotle *HA* 578a1; Galen *peri phusikôn dunameôn* I.14 ed. Kühn vol. II, pp. 55-56, with Stewart & Robinson (1971), cf. Hopf (1955); compare Bray (1984) 245-251 on seed selection techniques in ancient China; Harlan (1975) 137 said that primitive farmers usually pay great attention to seed selection.

164. Mangelsdorf (1974) 209; Fogg (1983).

165. Vavilov (1926) 238 & 240.

166. Hulse & Spurgeon (1974) on triticale; Darwin (1875) vol. 2, pp. 177 & 200, stating on the latter page, 'We at the present day profit by a course of selection occasionally and unconsciously carried on during thousands of years.'

167. Dennell (1976); Hillman (1978); G.E.M. Jones (1987); cf. Reynolds (1979) 57-58.

168. Barker (1983) vol. 2, pp. 31-38 on Roman Cyrenaica; Parain (1936) 106; Applebaum (1979); Barker, Lloyd & Reynolds (1985) 121-191.

169. D.W. Thomas (1958) 201-203 on Gezer; Newman (1932) 91; Kislev (1986); Josephos *Ioudaikos Polemos* V.427.

170. Ampolo (1980) on prehistoric Latium; Pliny *NH* XVIII.xi.62 and Dionysios of Halikarnassos *AR* II.25 agree with the archaeological evidence; Livy II.5.2-3 & IV.15.6 and Pliny *NH* XVIII.ii.7-8, iii.14, & iv.15-17 on emmer in archaic Rome; Pliny *NH* XVIII.xxix.111 for the importance of emmer in Roman Campania, confirmed by Mayer (1980), who did not find any evidence for naked wheats at Pompeii, although Wittmack (1904) reported durum wheat from earlier excavations there; Carter et al. (1985) argued for the importance of barley and club wheat at Metapontum in southern Italy in the fourth century BC and found no evidence for durum wheat or bread wheat; Vallino & Ventura (1984) claimed the presence of durum and bread wheat at Sybaris, but only on the basis of the unreliable criteria of seed dimensions, like Carter et al. (1985); the oracle in Diodoros Siculus XII.10.5 in connection with the foundation of Thurii on the site of archaic Sybaris *c.* 444 BC testifies to the importance of barley there.

171. Wasylikowa in van Zeist & Casparie (1984) 257-266 on Poland; van der Veen (1985a) 211 on Britain, cf. Greig (1983) for changes in Roman times.

172. Columella *RR* II.6.1 & 3-4; Pliny *NH* XVIII.xix.81-84; cf. Galen *peri trophôn dunameôn* I.13 ed. Kühn vol. VI, p. 518 on emmer and einkorn in Asia Minor (see also section 10 of this chapter).

173. Galen *peri trophôn dunameôn* I.11 ed. Kühn vol. VI, p. 507; Pliny *NH* XVIII.xv.74; Polybios VI.38.3-4 indicates that the Roman army had abandoned barley by the middle of the second century BC, cf. Livy XXVII.13.9 and Suetonius *Augustus* 24; Livy V.47.8, VI.17.5 & VII.37.3 and the *Twelve Tables* III.4 ed. Warmington mention the rations of emmer of the early Republican period.

174. Haudricourt & Hédrin (1943) 99.

175. (Aristotle) *Athênaiôn Politeia* LI.3; Galen *Hippokratous peri diaitês oxeôn nosêmatôn biblion kai Galênou hypomnêma* I.14 ed. Kühn vol. XV, p. 454 on legumes and *sitos*, cf. Pliny *NH* XVIII.xxx.117; L. Gallo (1984b) correctly affirmed,

contrary to Moritz (1955b), that *sitos* still meant grain in general in the fourth century BC, e.g.: (1) Theophrastos still used the word *sitos* to denote all autumn-sown and spring-sown cereals, as in e.g. *HP* VIII.3.1; (2) the *sitos* of Plato *Laws* 849b is identical to the *puroi kai krithai* of 847e; (3) barley is still important in Cyrenaica today and there is no doubt that much of the *sitos* mentioned on the inscription *SEG* IX.2 was barley – Dobias-Lalou in Barker, Lloyd & Reynolds (1985) 175 noted that barley is mentioned before wheat in inscriptions from Cyrene dating to the fourth century BC, but the order is reversed in Hellenistic inscriptions, cf. van der Veen (1985b); (4) (Demosthenes) XLII.15 of *c.* 330 BC equated barley (*krithai*) and *sitos*.

176. Galen *peri trophôn dunameôn* I.11 ed. Kühn vol. VI, p. 507; Cadell (1973) showed that *sitos* displaced *puros* as the word for wheat on Egyptian papyri in the fourth century AD.

177. Reynolds (1979) 51 for the experiments; Amouretti (1976) 29; H. Forbes (1976); Isidorus Hispalensis *Etymologiae* XVII.1.2 & 2.2 for ancient speculation on the origin of the plough; the anecdote cited by Hehn (1976) 437 shows that the conditions of innovation required for the adoption by primitive farmers of a new-fangled idea such as making tools out of iron are more complicated than may be supposed at first sight; D.C. Hopkins (1985) 217-223 and Frick (1985) 169-189 on the insignificance of the introduction of iron technology for early agriculture, contra Zvelebil (1985); Michael Choniates cited by Bryer (1986) 47; McGrew (1985) 5.

178. Jasny (1942) 760-761 & (1944) 153; Percival (1921) 325-327 on spelt; Hoffmann (1965) 278-280 for spelt wheat yields in Germany in the last century.

179. Jasny (1944) 109, Gansiniec (1956) and Brumfield (1981) 46 n. 10 thought that spelt wheat (*T. spelta*) did not appear until the time of the Late Roman Empire, but the views of McFadden & Sears (1946) on its history are preferable, updated by Kerber & Rowland (1974) and Kislev (1984b) 67; G.E.M. Jones (1981) and Kroll (1981), (1982) & (1984a) for archaeological evidence for spelt in Greece. Galen *peri trophôn dunameôn* I.13 ed. Kühn vol. VI, pp. 514-515 is probably one classical reference to spelt (*zeopuron*) in Bithynia in Asia Minor. van Zeist & Buitenhuis (1983) found a solitary spikelet of spelt on a Neolithic site in Anatolia. See also Janushevitch (1978), Lisitsina (1978) and Hajnalová (1978) for finds of spelt in Neolithic Bulgaria, Neolithic Transcaucasia and Iron Age Czechoslovakia respectively. See n. 214 below for Jerome. The type of *zeia* described by Mnesitheos F27 (with Bertier (1972) 48-56) as a plant of cold regions could also have been *T. spelta*, although Galen wrestled inconclusively with the possibility that it was identical to *briza*, rye. The use of the words *speltae* and *scandulae* (the former also occurs in the unsung *Carmen de mensuris et ponderibus* of *c.* AD 400, the latter also in Pliny *NH* XVIII.xi.62) in Diocletian's Price Edict I.7-8 ed. Graser shows the impact of the provincial Latin of the north Balkans, whence Diocletian himself came, upon the official language of the Roman empire. These two words are rare in literary sources which focus on the crops of the Mediterranean lands, with their different climate. Jasny (1944) 137-141 and Andrews (1964) are now out of date.

180. Helbaek (1961) 90.

181. Andrews (1964) 21; Mercer (1981) xix.

182. D. Zohary et al. (1969); Le et al. (1986) showed that the A genome of einkorn contains a gene for winter hardiness; Macchia et al. (1986) for the northward spread of durum wheat cultivation in modern Italy.

183. Papadakis (1929) on durum wheat in Attica; M. Parry (1978) suggests that subsistence farmers cannot tolerate crop failure more than once every five years on average; H. Forbes (1985) 365-370.

184. Hippokrates *peri nousôn* IV.34 ed. Littré vol. 7, pp. 546-547, Theophrastos *HP* VI.3.1-7 and Andrews (1941) on *silphion*.

185. Pliny *NH* XVIII.xii.63 & 67; Jardé (1925) 17-18 for attempts at transplanting cereal varieties; Theophrastos *HP* VI.2.3-4, Pliny *NH* XXI.xxxi.56-57 and Atchley (1938) 36 on Attic thyme; cf. Walpole (1817) 290-291 for adaptation of cereal varieties to local environments in early modern Greece; Theophrastos *HP* IV.4.1, *CP* II.3.3, Pliny *NH* XVI.lxii.144, Plutarch *Alexander* XXXV.15-16 and Bretzl (1903) 234ff. on the efforts of Harpalos to grow plants from Greece in Babylonia, continuing the Persian and Assyrian custom mentioned in Meiggs & Lewis *GHI* no. 12.

186. Harlan (1981) 14; L. White (1962) 69-76 offered the correct interpretation of the Germanic preference for cereals other than naked wheats; Hesiod *WD* 31-32; Galen *peri kakochumias kai euchumias trophôn* I ed. Kühn vol. VI, pp. 549-550; MacArthur & Pianka (1966) and Stephens & Krebs (1986) on optimal foraging theory; Unger-Hamilton (1988) 168-205 on Epi-Palaeolithic harvesting of wild cereals in the Middle East.

187. Pliny *NH* XVIII.xxi.94; Arnon (1972) vol. 2, p. 89.

188. Sharma & Gandhi (1977); Halloran (1976); Chojecki et al. (1986) on genetic control of seed size in hexaploids, cf. Paroda & Joshi (1970); Pliny *NH* XVIII.xx.91; Percival (1921) 309 on the harvesting of club wheat.

189. Pliny *NH* XVIII.lxxii.296, Palladius *Opus agriculturae* VII.2.1-4 & VIII.1.1 ed. Rodgers, K. White (1984) 29-30 & 60-62 and H. Müller (1985) on the Gallic reaping machine; Quisenberry & Reitz (1967) 120 for variations in shattering tendencies of modern bread wheat varieties; Wet & Oelke (1978) and Simpson & Conner-Ogorzaly (1986) 168 on American wild rice; Columella *RR* II.9.15 & 18 on six-row barley and millets, cf. II.20.1-2 on harvesting.

190. Feldman in Simmonds (1976) 126; elsewhere Pliny *NH* XVIII.x.59 speaks of the whole crop of *frumentum*, perhaps having in mind *triticum* rather than *siligo*, flowering at the same time, cf. Theophrastos *CP* IV.10.

191. Cf. Mangelsdorf (1974) 207, quoting Weatherwax on maize in the New World: 'There is no avoiding the conclusion that … the Indian was a good corn breeder. He has, however, failed to pass on to the white man any details as to how he accomplished what he did. It is probable that he had no idea of how he did this or that he even realised what he was doing.'

192. García-Olmeda et al. (1978) on the curvilinear loss of redundant gene expression in bread wheat after its evolution by polyploidy; Pliny *NH* XVIII.xii.69 on the spring wheat; Dunstone et al. (1973).

193. Reynolds (1979) 64 on harvesting; Pliny *NH* XVIII.lxvii.261 on hay-cutting; Columella *RR* II.20.3 on use of the hand, but ancient sources also mention sickles, e.g. Homer *Iliad* XVIII.550-551, cf. Plutarch *Kleomenes* XXVI.1 for use of sickles by soldiers as the standard way of destroying a standing grain crop; Hillman (1981) 151 quoted G.E.M. Jones for primitive harvesting techniques in modern Greece; Diodoros Siculus V.21.5; Xenophon *Oikonomikos* XVIII.2 on reaping in Attica; Zhukovskij cited by Hanelt (1986) 190-191 for *T. timopheevi*; Herodotos V.92 and Aristotle *Politics* 1284a26-30 on Periander; Allard (1960) 401; Xenophon *Oikonomikos* VIII.9 gives storage of wheat, barley and legumes in the same container as an example of disorder; Ampolo (1988) 125 on intercropping of cereals and legumes in archaic Roman agriculture; J. Renfrew (1973a) 26 suggested that cereal and legume crop mixtures were used in Early Bronze Age Thessaly.

194. Klages (1936) on durum wheat-bread wheat mixtures; Columella *RR* II.6.4 and II.20.1-3 on diversification.

195. Columella *RR* II.9.l3; Meuvret (1977) 147 explains by analogy the line of thought that lies behind Columella's preference for the heaviest wheat; the manuscript reading in Pliny *NH* XVIII.xx.85 should be emended to make the meaning identical to that of Columella, and probably derived from his *RR*, as suggested by Martino (1984) 259 – 'siliginem prope dixerim tritici delicias esse candore, sed sine virtute sine pondere'.

196. Janushevich & Nikolaenko (1979) record that farms in the Crimea fell into four categories, respectively 9, 12, 18 and 26.5 ha in area; see also Pecirka (1970).

197. Kulshrestha (1985); Costantini (1984).

198. P.H. Davis (1985) 254-255 for doubts about *T. parvicoccum*; Galinat (1985).

199. Vavilov (1951) 198; Janushevich (1984) 270; Percival (1921) 188 on emmer; Gunda (1983) on cultivation of the primitive cereals in the north Balkans in recent times.

200. Darwin (1968) 90.

201. Halloran (1975).

202. Schiemann (1951) 311-312 offered alternative explanations for the proliferation of varieties in mountainous areas; Theophrastos *HP* III.2.5 on the diversity of environments on great mountains.

203. Bélteky & Kovács (1984); Hondelmann (1984); Hanelt (1986) 179-182; Hopf (1986) 45-46; Hjelmqvist (1977) & (1979) for small-seeded lupins in Bronze Age Greece and Cyprus; Theophrastos *HP* I.3.6, I.7.3, III.2.1, VIII.11.2, 6 & 8, *CP* II.7.7, III.1.5, IV.2.2, IV.5.4 (noting that the lupin did not 'change' into any other plant, unlike flax), IV.7.1-2, IV.15.3; Athenaios II.55c-f; Galen *peri trophôn dunameôn* I.23 ed. Kühn vol. VI, pp. 534-536; Cato *De agricultura* XI, XXXIV & XXXVII; Columella *RR* II.10.1-4; Pliny *NH* XVII.vi.54 & XVIII.xxxvi.133-136; the Romans valued it as green manure – Columella *RR* II.15.5-6; R.C. Thompson (1949) 126 on Babylonia (Greek *thermos* = Akkadian *tarmus*).

204. Hume (1875) vol. 1, p. 411.

205. Theophrastos *HP* VIII.9.2; Pollux *Onomasticon* I.183, mistranslated by Anderson (1961) 94; Pliny *NH* XVIII.xliv.149 (with Knorzer (1981) 33-34 and Körber-Grohne (1981) 168) & XXII.lxxix.161; Cato *De agricultura* XXXVIII; Galen *peri trophôn dunameôn* I.14 ed. Kühn vol. VI, pp. 522-523; Servius *in Vergilii bucolicon librum commentarius* V.37 ed. Thilo; Dieuches F14 ed. Bertier; Eustathios (Odyssey) p. 919; Dioskorides *MM* II.94 & IV.137 on *bromos*; Ladizinsky (1975a) and Pliny *NH* VI.xxxv.188 on Ethiopia, cf. Syme & Bremner (1968); Columella *RR* II.10.24 & 31-32; Pliny *NH* XVIII.xlii.143 on *avena Graeca* – the reasoning behind André's (1985) 30 identification of *avena Graeca* as *Avena nuda* is incomprehensible, as Pliny does not mention naked oats, a crop which has been confined largely to the Far East in recent times; Theophrastos *CP* IV.5.2 on *bromos* and emmer, cf. Vavilov (1926) 211-212 and n. 154 above; Polemon F88 ed. Preller, where *bromos* occurs after *zeia*, also illustrates the close association of oats and emmer; Topping (1977) ch. III, pp. 284-287 for oats in the mediaeval Peloponnese; T.L. Markey in Harris & Hillman (1989) 593-596 on the etymology of Indo-European words for oats; Vavilov (1926) 173-178 & 209-215; Coffmann (1961) 17-22 & 150-157; Zhukovskij (1962) 6-7; Helbaek (1971); Ladizinsky & Zohary (1971); Simmonds (1976) 86-90; Kroll (1982) 483 & (1983) 89-90 for wild oats at Mycenaean Tiryns and Kastanas; Barker (1985) 46.

206. Pritchett (1956) 186-187 for *melinê*, Italian or foxtail millet (*Setaria italica*), also mentioned by Xenophon *Anabasis* II.4.13, and 191-192 for *kengchros*, proso or broomcorn or common millet (*Panicum miliaceum*), also in Hesiod *Aspis* 398-399 and Aristotle *HA* 595a26-29 (as animal fodder); Theophrastos *HP*

VIII.7.3, VIII.11.6 & *CP* IV.15; Columella *RR* II.9.17-19; Hesykhios s.v. *elumor* (a synonym of *melinê*, the Attic word, with rhotacism of final sigma as a development dating to Roman times in the Lakonian dialect of Greek – Bourguet (1927) 120-121 & 148 n. 1) for Spartan consumption of millet, also s.v. *elimar*; Vavilov (1926) 178-181; Prasada Rao et al. (1987); Cavers & Bough (1985) on millet seed size; Harlan et al. (1976); Simmonds (1976) 308-309; Nesbitt & Summers (1988); Spurr (1983), with the following reservations: (1) (p. 1) millet's shorter growing period means that it requires less water in total than other cereals, but *S. italica* is not very resistant to water shortage during that growing period (Arnon (1972) vol. 2, p. 136); (2) (p. 6) excessive vegetative growth under very favourable environmental conditions is common to traditional varieties of all cereals (see n. 254 below for wheat) and does not prove that the wet Po valley is unfavourable for millet (Strabo XV.1.13.690c noted that in India millets were sown in summer at the time of the monsoon rains – cf. Arrian *Indika* VI.4-5); (3) (pp. 6-7) the evolutionary significance of the historical increase in seed size is misunderstood; (4) (p. 8, n. 21) *Geôponika* II.38.2 ed. Beckh, on millet yields, stresses the importance of irrigation for *kengchros*, as does Diodoros Siculus II.36.3-4 – in the main areas of millet cultivation in antiquity, from south-west France to north China where the millets had their greatest historical significance, there are great rivers which facilitate irrigation in warm areas with little summer rainfall; (5) (p. 9) sowing of cereal mixtures by primitive farmers is well documented and advantageous in terms of productivity; (6) Spurr failed to emphasise the low productivity of millets (see n. 158 above); Haudricourt & Hédrin (1943) 194-197 for the Po valley, the most important centre of maize cultivation in modern western Europe, an important millet-growing area in antiquity (Polybios II.15.2, Strabo V.1.12.218c and Pliny *NH* XVIII.xxv.101); Kroll (1983) 100-101 on Kastanas; Apuleius (1979) p. 48r; Diels-Kranz (1956) vol. 1, pp. 254-255 on the debate.

   207. Herodotos I.193.4, Strabo XVII.2.4.743c, Pliny *NH* XV.vii.28 & 30 on sesame in the Orient; Columella *RR* II.10.18; Arnon (1972) vol. 2, p. 383; Ventris & Chadwick (1973) 227 & 582 and Wylock (1972) 115-118 on sesame at Mycenae; Kroll (1983) 59 suggested that *sasama* in the Linear B tablets was *Camelina sativa*, but this idea has little to recommend it; *The Times* 11 August 1988 for Tutankhamun's tomb, with the letter subsequently addressed to the paper by W.T. Stearn; Topping (1977) ch. X, p. 94 and Keatinge et al. (1985) for crop rotation systems in mediaeval Elis and modern Syria in which a fallow year precedes or follows the summer crop.

   208. Pliny *NH* XVIII.xxxix-xl.140-141 is the clearest reference to rye (*Secale cereale*) in a classical source, also the *briza* of Galen *peri trophôn dunameôn* I.13 ed. Kühn vol. VI, p. 514 in Thrace and Macedonia, identified with *sicale* in Diocletian's Price Edict I.3; Aebischer (1953); in Hellanikos FGH4 F66 Jacoby the reading *brizôn* is preferable to the *rizôn* of Jacoby's text; Jasny (1944) 105 on Theophrastos *HP* VIII.4.4; on the origin of rye cultivation see the divergent views of Vavilov (1926) 196-209, Khush (1963), Helbaek (1971), Hillman (1978) and Sencer & Hawkes (1980); T.L. Markey in Harris & Hillman (1989) 593-596 on the etymology of Indo-European words for rye; Kroll (1983) 92-93 & 146 and (1984a) 214-215 for wild rye at Kastanas and Mycenaean Tiryns; Barger (1931) 40-43 refuted the alleged literary evidence for ergotism in antiquity, but Corvisier (1985) 67 & 107 noted one possible case of ergotism in northern Greece in the Hippokratic corpus; Aaronson (1989); Huntley & Birks (1983) 468-485; Matossian (1989).

   209. Theophrastos *HP* VIII.9.2; Aristotle *HA* 603b26; Galen *peri trophôn dunameôn* I.13 ed. Kühn vol. VI, p. 522; Kroll (1984b); van Zeist & Bottema (1971).

   210. Hopf (1978), J. Renfrew in Renfrew & Wagstaff (1982) 156-160 and Lisitsina

& Filipovich (1981) list finds of cereals on prehistoric Greek sites; Demosthenes VIII.45 mentions *olura* and millet in Thrace; Varro *RR* I.2.7, Homer *Iliad* XIV.372 and Kroll (1982) 468 & (1984a) on the Argolid; see also n. 67 above on the meaning of *puros* in the Homeric poems; Gordon (1967) argued that *kunisu*, a word for 'wheat' in Linear A, is derived from a Semitic word for emmer – accepted by J. Chadwick in *ATQ* 33 (1959) 277; J.N. Postgate in *BSA* 1 (1984) 7 and Powell (1984b) 51 for more recent opinions on the identification of *kunisu*.

211. Pliny *NH* XVIII.xix.84; Theophrastos *Characters* IV (*agroikos*) & *HP* VIII.9.2; Pollux *Onomasticon* I.183 on emmer as horse fodder; Vavilov (1926) 163; Artemidoros *Oneirokritikon* I.68 ed. Pack; Jasny (1944) 56; Hesykhios s.v. *olura*.

212. J. Chadwick (1976) 108-110; Cremona (1982) expressed doubts about the meaning of the ideograms; for the price-ratio see Lewy (1956) 204 on ancient Assyria, Teall (1959) 99-100 on Byzantium and Ashtor (1978) (article entitled 'La recherche des prix ...') 113-114 on the Islamic world, Polybios II.15.1, Diocletian's Price Edict I.1-2 ed. Graser; the inscription edited by Ph. Gauthier (1987) is the latest piece of evidence for the wheat:barley price ratio; cf. J. Preuss (1978) 569 for the prescription in the Jewish Talmud that a husband who did not live with his wife had to give her at least two units of wheat or four units of barley, *inter alia*, as sustenance; Killen (1985) on the Mycenaean economy; Fidio (1982) on the equivalencies.

213. Rathbone (1983a) 47 emphasises labour inputs. Brumfield (1981) 15 notes that the labour input for barley cultivation is lower than that required for wheat in modern Attica. Emmer must also be considered. It needed the same labour input as the naked wheats (Columella *RR* II.12.1-2), the sowing rate was double that of the naked wheats in terms of volume (Columella *RR* II.9.1 & XI.2.75; Varro *RR* I.44; Pliny *NH* XVIII.lv.198-199), but as it was sown and stored husked (Columella *RR* II.8.5; Varro *RR* I.53; Pliny *NH* XVIII.x.61 & XVIII.lxxii.298) one unit volume of the husked grain contained a considerably smaller volume of the actual grain (half in the case of one variety from North Africa, according to Pliny *NH* XVIII.xxix.115 – but the proportion is in fact even lower). G.E.M. Jones (1982) and Jones et al. (1986) deduced from palaeobotanical evidence that emmer was stored husked at Geometric Iolkos in Thessaly and Assiros Toumba in Macedonia.

214. Ventris & Chadwick (1973) 41, 130 & 548. The adjective *zeidôros* in Hesiod *WD* 173 and Homer *Odyssey* III.3 means 'zeia-giving', as it was understood by Pliny *NH* XVIII.xix.82 (accepted by Chantraine (1968) 397). However another ancient tradition, exemplified by Empedokles 21 B151 eds. Diels-Kranz and Hesykhios s.v. *zeidôros*, explained it as meaning 'life-giving', from *zaô*. The Indo-European root of the word *zeia* took on a bewildering array of meanings:

(1) *emmer*, in the passages quoted above;
(2) *einkorn*, according to Dioskorides *MM* II.89 (*zeia haplê*; the *zeia dikokkos* could also have been einkorn but more probably was emmer);
(3) *barley*, as the word *deai* in the Doric dialect of Crete – *Etymologicum Magnum* 264, 12-14 (testimony to the importance of barley on classical Crete), a meaning it also bore in Sanskrit;
(4) *millets*, in the Ossetian language of the Black Sea region (Haudricourt & Hédrin (1943) 99);
(5) *spelt wheat*, according to Jerome in J.P. Migne *Patrologiae cursus completus ... Ser. prima, S. Hieronymi Tomi quintus et sextus* (1845) col. 47, a fascinating passage showing that the ancients had the same problems understanding the vocabulary of cereals that modern scholars have;
(6) Columella *De arboribus* XXVIII.1 gives *zeai* as one of the Greek names for

shrub-trefoil, on which see n. 264 below. This word may be derived from the same root;

(7) much more recently, *zeia* has been incorporated into the scientific name of *maize, Zea mays*.

It would be a mistake to try to reduce the first five or six senses to just one meaning. It is in the nature of words for plants to develop in this way in all languages, cf. the shift in meaning from Latin *far*, emmer, to English *barley*.

215. Jasny (1944) 145 & 151; Diocletian's Price Edict I.1 & 7-8.

216. Herodotos II.36.2; Galen *peri trophôn dunameôn* I.13 ed. Kühn vol. VI, p. 518; Hoffner (1974) 53-93 on the cereals of Hittite Anatolia in the second millennium BC.

217. Arnon (1981) 261, 295 & 516 on HYV varieties of wheat in Greece and Turkey; Islamoglu & Faroqhi (1976) on wheat in early modern Anatolia; Planhol (1968) 197-204 on the climate of central Anatolia in the first millennium BC.

218. Pliny *NH* XVIII.xix.84.

219. E.g. Theophrastos *HP* VIII.7.6-7, II.2.7-8 and *CP* III.1.6; cf. Pliny *NH* XVIII.xlvii.170; Mauss cited by Stoianovitch (1967) 71.

220. Theophrastos *HP* VIII.8.2 for Attica as 'the best (land) for bearing barley', *krithophoros aristê*, *HP* VIII.6.4 on wheat as more winter hardy than barley, *CP* IV.8.3 for barley's giving a higher yield than wheat; Regel (1939) 75-76 on the alkaline soils of Attica; Briggs (1978) and Nuttonson (1957) on the climatic requirements of barley; Peterson (1965), Nuttonson (1955) and Baldy (1986) on those of wheat; Hunter (1952) plate facing p. 70 for ancient Greek coins depicting ears of six-row barley; Aristotle *HA* 573b10-11, 595a28-29 & 595b6-10 on barley as fodder for cattle and pigs; J. Hansen (1978) on Franchthi cave; T.L. Markey in Harris & Hillman (1989) 589-593 on the etymology of Indo-European words for barley.

221. Crawford (Thompson) (1979); Rathbone (1983a); Darby et al. (1977) vol. 2, p. 465 and Bible Isaiah 23.2-3 for Egyptian grain exports; in Bakkhylides F16 lines 10-12 ed. Jebb the adjective *purophoroi*, 'wheat-bearing', may refer to emmer.

222. Rostovtzeff (1928), cf. Treister (1985); Jasny (1944) 68.

223. Reekmans (1966); Crawford (Thompson) (1971) 112-117; but emmer did not disappear entirely from Egypt, as Percival (1921) 188 records that it was still grown there in small quantities at the start of the nineteenth century AD.

224. Crawford (Thompson) (1979) 140; Finley (1985b) 36.

225. See section 6 of this chapter; Percival (1921) 206-207 mentions durum wheat grains from XII Dynasty tombs at Kahun in Egypt *c*. 2000 BC, cf. Percival (1936); Helbaek (1955); D. Dixon (1969); Bein & Horowitz (1986) and Theophrastos *HP* IV.8.4 on papyrus in Palestine; the Seleucids then took it to Mesopotamia according to N. Lewis (1974) 10-11 and Pliny *NH* XIII.xxi-xxii.68-73 (see also Chapter I above).

226. Pliny *NH* XVIII.xx.92; Theophrastos *HP* VIII.9.2; Galen *peri trophôn dunameôn* I.13 ed. Kühn vol. VI, p. 517; Herodotos II.36.2.

227. Rathbone (1983b) argued that Egyptian *olura* was oats, not emmer. Listed below are the reasons why his theory is not convincing:

(1) The obvious independent check on it is to consider archaeological evidence. Oats is rare on Egyptian archaeological sites, and the occasional finds could easily be wild oats (cf. Darby et al. (1977) vol. 2, p. 496). No oats at all was found at Karanis, for example, in the Late Roman levels which were roughly contemporaneous with Pap. Oxy. 3455 – see Leighty (1933).

(2) Oats is not well suited to the environment of Egypt, and it is not likely that it was a major crop there.
(3) The hypothesis is also improbable from a philological viewpoint. Oats is called *bromê* in modern Greek, and everything said about *bromos* in the ancient sources (see n. 205 above) is consistent with oats.
(4) Conversely there is no doubt that *olura* was emmer in all the literary sources. Unlike oats, emmer is a very common find on archaeological sites in Egypt.
(5) Rathbone underestimated the semantic variability of words for cereals such as Coptic *bote* (Darby et al. op. cit.) and Arabic *al-dourah* (Portères in Harlan et al. (1976) 416).
(6) Pliny *NH* XVIII.xi.62 does not bear the interpretation which Rathbone put upon it. The Latin word *spica*, in this context, refers to the shape and character of the ear of grain (e.g. Varro *RR* I.48). Again, in Caelius Aurelianus *Chr.* IV.3.48 ed. Drabkin, cited by Cadell (1971) to make the same point, *olura* and *far* are two different 'land-races' of emmer, not two separate species, just as *alica* is a product of *far* and of *olura*, not a separate species of cereal (see n. 90 above). That *olura* was not sharply marked off from other words designating land-races of emmer is shown by e.g. Pliny *NH* XXII.lvii.121 – 'olyram arincam diximus vocari', and Dioskorides *MM* II.91. Emmer, a hulled wheat, is a distinct species from durum wheat or bread wheat, and not just a 'subvariety' of wheat.
(7) The density values for 'wheat' quoted by Rathbone are all for the bread wheat grown in Britain today. According to Percival (1921) 191 the weight of husked emmer is 40-49 kg/hl (about 25 per cent of the weight of modern husked emmer is chaff), cf. Jasny (1944) 142-144 & 154-159. Is the value of 36.43 kg/hl for *olura* derived from Pap. Oxy. 3455 not after all appropriate for emmer? Note also Theophrastos *HP* VIII.9.2, describing *zeia* as the lightest grain, and Homer *Odyssey* IV.222 on Egypt as *zeidôros aroura*.
(8) Cadell's suggestion that *olura* was sorghum is refuted by the fact that *olura* is bracketed with *puros* as an autumn-sown crop, proving that it was a long-day plant like wheat and other temperate cereals and not a short-day plant like sorghum. See e.g. the papyrus discussed by Vidal-Naquet (1967) 26.

228. E.g. Feldman in Simmonds (1976) 125; Percival (1921) 189-190 on modern emmer.
229. Jasny (1944) 130; Kuckuck & Peters (1964) 227 for the second quotation in the paragraph; Vavilov (1926) 162-166 discussed the modern distribution and diversity of emmer.
230. Guiraud (1893) 548-555, criticised by Barbagallo (1904).
231. Vita-Finzi (1969). Herodotos II.10.3, Thucydides II.52.3 and Diodoros Siculus I.39.12-13, Xanthos FGH765 F13 Jacoby mention sediment deposition by rivers in various parts of Greece.
232. Bintliff (1981) defended his interpretation of the Younger Fill against the scepticism of D. Davidson (1981), Renfrew & Wagstaff (1982) and Wagstaff (1981) & (1985); Pausanias VIII.24.11; Forbes & Koster (1976) 120 on labour forces and terrace walls; H. Forbes (1985); Braudel (1972) vol. 1, p. 52 argued that human habitation started high up, not in the plains.
233. Arnon (1972) vol. 1, pp. 58-59, 353-355 & 391; Briggs (1978) 300-301 on barley.
234. Forbes & Koster (1976) and Thirgood (1981) sharply disagree on the extent of deforestation in the course of history; Meiggs (1982) 189-191 and Plato *Kritias* 111c on forests in Attica; Arnon (1972) vol. 1, pp.

353-355 & vol. 2, p. 27.

235. Columella *RR* III.3.4 – the smaller part of Italy excluded from this statement was probably the area of very fertile volcanic soils around Mt Vesuvius; Duncan-Jones (1982) 370-371 used Columella's sowing rate and fourfold seed:yield ratio to calculate a net wheat yield of 402 kg/ha; Arnon (1972) vol. 2, p. 48 for the modern sowing rate; Boeuf (1931) 377 for the damaged grain.

236. Cato *De agricultura* I.7, Varro *RR* I.7.10, Columella *RR* III.3.3-4 on profitability of different types of land use; Toynbee (1965) vol. 2, pp. 289 & 300-301.

237. Columella *RR* V.1.8-V.3.9 on wine yields per unit area; Columella *RR* III.2.24 and Pliny *NH* XIV.iv.25; Theophrastos *HP* II.2.4-6 & *CP* I.9.1 noted that propagation of such trees as olive, vine, apple, pear and fig from seed gives inferior progeny; in *HP* IV.13.5 he said that the olive tree had a lifespan of about 200 years, an underestimate.

238. Titow (1972) on mediaeval England; Slicher van Bath (1963) & (1967) discusses an apparently huge range of evidence, but even the sources for mediaeval and early modern Europe rarely provide data series from which statistically significant results can be derived; Braudel (1981) 120-124.

239. Svoronos (1976) 57-58; Asdrachas (1978) 52 & 285 n. 34; Topping (1977) ch. III, pp. 284-287; Tsouderos (1919) 132 for a yield:seed ratio of 4.8:1 and a yield per unit area of 742 kg/ha in 1901, a good year, shortly before the introduction of chemical fertilisers; McGrew (1985) 165, Walpole (1817) 292-293 and Thiersch (1833) 303 on seed:yield ratios in early modern Greece.

240. Littlejohn (1946) 127; Arnon (1972) vol. l, pp. 462-464 & vol. 2, pp. 29-30 & 81; Briggs (1978) 300-301; Slicher van Bath (1963) 245 and Asdrachas (1970) 40 & n. 9 for high yields in mediaeval Europe and mediaeval Greece as due to exceptional circumstances; Kashdan (1982) 121 for exaggeration (or simply tillering?).

241. E.g. J.K. Evans (1981) 429-431.

242. Cho-yun Hsu (1981) and Bray (1984) on China; see n. 70 above for Lemnos; Theophrastos *HP* VIII.2.8 & *CP* IV.11.8 and G. Sanders (1984) on Melos; H. Forbes (1985) 201 on Methana.

243. Cicero *Verrines* II.3.109-113: the 10:1 return on the *ager Leontinus* in Sicily is very exceptional ('achieved with the help of all the gods') and the 8:1 yield is an above average yield ('if everything goes well'), in which case the average yield should have been lower, say 6:1, comparable to some cereal yields in southern Italy in the early modern period (Aymard (1982) and other papers in the same volume); Strabo V.4.8.247c and Aristotle *HA* 520a31-b2 on the fertility of the volcanic soils of Leontini; Leonardi (1982) on the predominance of durum wheat in Sicily; (Aristotle) *peri thaumasiôn akousmatôn* 836b23-24 mentions an unidentifiable and peculiar kind of wheat at Enna, unlike any other wheat in Sicily.

244. Xenophon *Poroi* I.3.

245. E.g. Pliny *NH* XVII.iii.41 & XVIII.xxi. 94, with the textual reading of K. White (1964); Varro *RR* I.44.2; cf. Columella *RR* III.8.4; Strabo XVII.3.11.831c, to be read with 833c, where Strabo commented on the pastoral/nomadic way of life in such a 'fertile' area (high yield per plant = low yield per unit area – therefore a low human population density); Ammianus Marcellinus XXVIII.1.17 noted the alternation of periods of abundance and scarcity in North Africa; Guiraud (1893) 548-555; J.K. Evans (1981).

246. Arnon (1971) vol. 1, p. 301; Percival (1921) 71-78 on tillering; Theophrastos *CP* I.12.3 (Greek *karkinousthai*), II.12.3, IV.11.3-4 and *HP*

VIII.4.3 noted variations in tillering capacity between different types of wheat; Harper (1977); L.T. Evans & Dunstone (1970); Islam & Sedgley (1981); Mackey (1979) on the roots; Boeuf (1931) 148 & 179 emphasised that tillering is undesirable in North Africa if yields per unit area are to be maximised.

247. Parain (1936) 122 noted that seeding rates of wheat in Tunisia may be as low as 25 kg/ha; Percival (1921) 430; Strabo XV.3.11.731c; Lewy (1944) 70-71; Boeuf (1931) 317; Pliny *NH* XVIII.xii.66; Chevalier (1932) 742-759 discussed cereals found further south, in the Sahara, in modern times – the origin of the bread wheat in certain oases is obscure; Strabo XVII.3.11.831c.

248. Despois (1937); Pissaloux (1955); Valensi (1985) 144-148 independently reached a conclusion similar to the one reached here.

249. Pliny *NH* XVIII.xliii.146, cf. Columella *RR* II.10.27, recommended dense sowing of lucerne, a crop that needs large quantities of water, to crowd out weeds. A high sowing rate in a region with low precipitation inevitably leads to a very high rate of seedling mortality. Theophrastos *HP* VIII.6.7 noted that heavy rain was bad for cereals because it encouraged the growth of weeds, e.g. darnel.

250. Theophrastos *HP* IV.3.7 & *CP* VI.18; Pliny *NH* XVIII.l.186, on the dryness of N. Africa and Cyrene, states that cereals depended on dew for moisture (an exaggeration – Arnon (1972) vol. 1, pp. 32-33), indicating that the climate was similar to today's climate, cf. Houérou (1986).

251. Herodotos IV.198.3; B. Shaw (1984) 160-165; Boeuf (1931) 413; W.M. Murray (1984) for runoff farming in Akarnania in classical Greece; Balcer (1974) for a dam to prevent flooding at Mycenaean Tiryns; Mayerson (1961) 17 and Evenari et al. (1982) 122 on the Nessana yields; B. Shaw (1981) 391 on the human population density; similarly the thirtyfold yield of the Crimea in Strabo VII.4.6.311c does not indicate a high yield per unit area; Pliny *NH* XVII.xix.93 on Mago.

252. Colinvaux (1980) 94, Livy *Periochae* XLIX and Appian *Libykê* LXXXI; Boeuf (1931) 412-413 on modern Tunisian cereal yields; Varro's claim of 100:1 seed:yield ratios at Sybaris (*RR* I.44.2) may be compared with the 5:1 to 7:1 average seed:yield ratios in the same area in the early modern period – Aymard (1982); *Codex Theodosianus* XI.28.13 ed. Mommsen on Byzacena. Commenting on the ancient sources, K. White (1964) 301 stated that 'they do not refer to yields in the modern sense, viz. 30 bushels of grain reaped per bushel sown, but to returns of seeds reaped for seeds sown'. However, the truly significant conceptual difference is not between these two measurements, but between such measurements and modern absolute measurements in terms of the yield per unit area.

253. Darwin (1875) vol. 1, p. 336.

254. Arnon (1972) vol. 1, pp. 360 & 394. Pliny *NH* XVIII.xliv.154; Theophrastos *HP* VIII.7.4; Virgil *Georgics* I.111.

255. Cicero *De senectute* XV.53-54; H. Forbes (1985) 320-321 noted that animal manure was always scarce on Methana in the past, cf. Spurr (1986) 131.

256. Crivelli (1930); contrast Meuvret (1977) 138.

257. Littlejohn (1946) 132-133; Xenophon *Oikonomikos* XVII.10, Pliny *NH* XVII.vi.54, XVIII.xxx.117, Columella *RR* II.13.1-2 and Varro *RR* I.23.3 on green manure.

258. Pauly-Wissowa *RE* vol. 4, col. 59 s.v. *Cloaca*; Theophrastos *HP* II.7.4 and Columella *RR* II.14 on human manure; (Aristotle) *Ath. Pol.* L.2 with Owens (1983); Archilochos F148 ed. Edmonds observed that rotting human corpses could increase soil fertility.

259. Keatinge et al. (1985) describes a modern example of this system; IG I^3 252, lines 12-13; IG II^2 1241, lines 22-24; IG II^2 2493, lines 9-10 for cereal-legume

rotations in classical Attica.

260. Semple (1922) and Skydsgaard (1988) for the older view; Hodkinson (1988), drawing on Halstead (1984), the recent revision, cf. Halstead (1987); see also Chapter II.2 above.

261. Walpole (1817) 141.

262. Briggs & Courtney (1985) 178 on ley-arable systems; Kerridge (1967) esp. 181 & 330-332.

263. Columella *RR* II.16-17, Cato *De agricultura* VIII-IX and Pliny *NH* XVIII.lxvii.258-263 on meadows and watermeadows.

264. Pliny *NH* XIII.xlvii.130-134; Aiskhylides cited by Aelian *peri ·zôiôn idiotêtos* XVI.32; Eupolis F14 Kock, Aristotle *HA* 522b28 and Theokritos V.128 & X.30 mention shrub-trefoil as forage for goats; Theophrastos *HP* IV.16.5 & *CP* V.15.4; Dioskorides *MM* IV.112; Columella *RR* V.12 & *De arboribus* XXVIII, mentioning several different Greek names for it (see n. 214 above); Kroll (1982) 482 for plants, perhaps wild specimens, of the genus Medicago at Mycenaean Tiryns; Kroll (1983) 77-79 on Kastanas; Theophrastos *HP* I.6.1 on laburnum; Atchley (1938) 14-15.

265. Agra Europa (1979) 79 for the modern Greek data; Cox & Atkins (1979) 642 for a sheep's average annual output of 14 kg N; Krentos & Orphanos (1979), Arnon (1981) 261, Hadjichristodoulou (1982) and Gregory et al. (1984) for fertiliser requirements of wheat and barley in semi-arid regions; Hall et al. (1979) 215.

266. Thiersch (1833) vol. 1, p. 294 for reliance on fallow to fertilise the land in early modern Greece; Seligman et al. (1985).

267. Littlejohn (1946) 127-128, followed by Christodoulou (1959) 43.

268. E.g. Boeuf (1931) 312 and Grigg (1974) 125 regarded water conservation as the main function of fallow in the Mediterranean. Halstead (1987) independently reached a similar conclusion to mine on the function of fallow.

269. Fischer & Turner (1978) 280.

270. Theophrastos *HP* VIII.6.3-4; *CP* III.20.7; Columella *RR* II.9.3-4 & 15; Pliny *NH* XVII.iii.40, XVIII.l.187 & XVIII.lii.191; Varro *RR* III.16.33; Suda s.v. *epi kalamei aroun*; Hesiod *WD* 464 as emended by West (1978); Pindar *Nemeans* VI.10-12; Homer *Iliad* XVIII.540-541.

271. Reynolds (1979) 59 & 61 and in Mercer (1981) 104-111 & 163-166.

272. Theophrastos *HP* VIII.9.2 knew that *zeia* was *polukalamos*; Percival (1921) 171 on einkorn; L.T. Evans & Dunstone (1970); Adcock (1985) for the Reading experiments.

273. Reynolds (1979) 63; Hesiod *WD* 469-471, with Amouretti (1976) 34, Xenophon *Oikonomikos* XVII.7, Varro *RR* I.42, Pliny *NH* XVIII.liv.197 on broadcasting seed by hand; Columella *RR* II.4.2 on harrowing, with Spurr (1986) 48-56; Columella *RR* II.8.5 & II.20.1, Theophrastos *HP* VIII.6.1 and Theopompos FGH115 F274(b) Jacoby on birds as pests of cereal crops; Darwin (1968) 122.

274. Ammianus Marcellinus XVIII.2.3 for Britain's grain exports in the reign of Julian; Le Roy Ladurie (1981) 105; Jasny (1944) 133; Pliny *NH* XVIII.xix.81 & xx.92; Margaris & Mooney (1981) 1.

275. Chorley (1981); Kerridge (1967).

276. Helbaek (1960), Jacobsen (1982) 38-47, Herodotos I.193.3, Theophrastos *HP* VIII.7.4, and Strabo XVI.1.14.742c on Mesopotamia, also Powell (1985) arguing for seeding rates of 20-35 kg/ha and seed:yield ratios of 40-50:1; see sections 6 & 11 of this chapter, Pliny *NH* XVIII.xlv.162, Ammianus Marcellinus XXII.15.13, Laurent-Täckholm (1976) and D. Clark & Brandt (1984) 63 on Egypt;

Percival (1936).

277. Pliny *NH* XVIII.xlvii.167-169; Herodotos II.13-14 & (Aristotle) *Problems* XX.20 for water's giving fertility; Theophrastos *HP* VII.1.8, VIII.1.7, *CP* III.6.1-2 & III.20.2; Columella *RR* II.13.3-15.5; Pliny *NH* XVII.iii-viii & XVIII.liii.192-194 on manure; the scholiast to Aristophanes *Hippeis* 658, *Paroem. Gr.* vol. 1, p. 388 App. I.58 eds. Leutsch & Schneidewin and Suda s.v. *bolitou dikê* mention a law of Solon punishing thefts of cow-dung.

278. Diodoros Siculus V.2.4 states that wild wheat grew in Sicily. Wild einkorn and wild emmer are today mainly confined to the Near East, but their geographical range might have been wider in antiquity. Perhaps Diodoros made a mistake, or had in mind wheat-like plants such as Aegilops. Percival (1921) 164 mentions wild einkorn in Greece. See also Berosos FGH 680 F1(2) Jacoby and Diodoros Siculus I.14.1 for wild wheat in Babylonia and Egypt/Syria respectively. For modern wild einkorn see Harlan (1967), cf. Ladizinsky (1975b) who obtained lower yields.

279. For comparative purposes it is interesting to compare:

(1) Flannery (1973) 297-299 on evolution of productivity of maize in prehistoric Mexico and its connection with sedentarisation, urbanisation and population growth, cf. Miksicek et al. (1981).

(2) Ishizuka (1969) 15-16 on increases in rice yields in Japan during the last millennium. In wet-rice cultivation, unlike wheat and barley cultivation, a high degree of tillering (*polustachu,* as noted by Aristoboulos FGH139 F35 Jacoby) is advantageous, because the seedlings must be transplanted individually into the paddy field, labour-intensive work. It therefore pays to try to maximise the yield per rice plant.

(3) Stanhill (1976) on progress in cereal productivity in England over the last 750 years.

280. Darwin (1875) vol. 1, p. 336.
281. Grigg (1974) 135.
282. Finlay cited by McGrew (1985) 220.

Chapter IV

1. Lewin & Lomas (1974); Hadjichristodoulou (1982); Mariolopoulos (1962) on the Parthenon; Kuniholm – Cambridge seminar paper.

2. Eginitis (1908), Philippson (1948), Mariolopoulos (1925) & (1971) and Guinis (1976) on stability of Greek climate, cf. D.C. Hopkins (1985) 99-109 for Early Iron Age Israel.

3. Aristotle *Meteôrologika* 352a6-18, cf. Longo (1984), Shrimpton (1987) and B. Weiss (1982); M. Parry (1978) 156-157 criticised Carpenter (1966).

4. Huntington (1907) on Asia & (1910) on Olympia; Myres (1915/16) 40; Thorndike (1924) argued that Theophrastos *HP* IV.1.3 and *peri anemôn* XIII eds. Coutant & Eichenlaub provides evidence for a cooler climate on Crete, but the attempt to downdate his botanical works to the second half of the third century BC is wholly unsatisfactory; Panessa (1981) & (1982) argued for increasing aridity in Early Hellenistic Greece; Neumann (1985) on ancient ideas about climatic change; Bintliff (1982).

5. Aristotle *Politics* 1330b4-7 on cisterns; Plutarch *Solon* XXIII on wells; Theophrastos *HP* IV.11.3 & VIII.6.6-7; Demosthenes LV.11 & 28; Hippokrates *peri aërôn, hudatôn, topôn* XXIII ed. Littré vol. 2, pp. 82-83 on alternation of rain and drought.

6. Demosthenes L.61 & XX.33; *SEG* IX.2; Dio Chrysostom VI.2 on the aridity of Attica; Garnsey (1988) 134-164, contrast L. Gallo (1984b) 68 who calculated the average cereal production of Attica as a little above the harvest recorded on IG II² 1672 and concluded that the grain imports from Cyrene were not the result of a local harvest failure, but Chapter III.2 above showed that Jardé (1925), upon whom Gallo relied, underestimated the area of cultivatable land in Attica.

7. IG II² 1672; (Aristotle) *Problems* XXVI.56.946b22-23 on the wind; (Demosthenes) XLII.20 & 31, with Ste. Croix (1966); Wrigley (1987) 92-130 on prices and yields; Le Roy Ladurie (1971) 285; Abel (1981) 9-10.

8. P. Gauthier (1982); Theophrastos *CP* I.19.5, V.12.4, *HP* IV.14.11 and Pliny *NH* XVII.xxxvii.232.

9. D. Williams (1977) on archaeological evidence for vine in Britain, esp. at Gloucester, cf. Huntley & Birks (1983) 144; Tacitus *Agricola* XII.5 ed. Ogilvie said that it did not grow there.

10. Bökönyi (1973) on Neolithic Greece; Halstead & Jones (1980b) on decline in cattle size in Thessaly from the Neolithic to the Bronze Age; Payne (1985) surveyed palaeozoology in Greece; Zeuner (1963) pioneered the ecological approach to animal domestication as an unintended, unconscious, gradual process; Mason (1984); Peters (1983) 164-183 on ecological consequences of reduction in body size; Baldwin (1975) 441 on appearance of domestic cat (domesticated as late as *c.* 2000 BC in Egypt) in Greece in the first millennium BC, also Bodson (1987); Herodotus II.66-67 on cat (Greek *aielouros*) in Egypt.

11. Egerton (1968) & (1975) and Louis (1970) on Aristotle on animals; Aristotle *PA* 643b4-8, *HA* 488a30-31 and Pliny *NH* VIII.lxxix.213-214 for all domesticated animals also existing in a wild form, Aristotle *HA* 542a20-b1, 542b30-31, 544a25-34, 558b11-14, 558b24-25 & 572a5-8 on differences in seasonality and rate of reproduction between wild and domesticated animals, 545a23-546b13 for ages at which various animals begin to breed, 596b20-597a30 for the activities of animals following the seasons, 610b22-28 on stupidity of sheep, with Kruska (1988), 624b27-30 on bees, 532a18-19 & 557b8-10 on inhabitants of books, 557b1-6 on the clothes moth; Theophrastos *HP* IX.11.11 and Dioskorides *MM* I.12, I.115 & III.23 on devices for keeping moths out of clothes; Bökönyi (1988) 174 argued that the rate of reproduction of pigs at Late Neolithic/EBA Sitagroi in Macedonia was no higher than that of a wild pig population, suggesting that the evolution of the higher rates of reproduction characteristic of domesticated animals was a slow process.

12. Bökönyi (1987) on Mesopotamia; Ryder (1983) esp. 132-181 on sheep in Greece and Rome, also (1987); Columella *RR* VII.2.3-4 on varieties of sheep & VII.4.1-6 on the Greek or Tarentine 'coated' sheep; Varro *RR* II.2.18 on Athens and Miletus; Xenophon *Memorabilia* II.7.13-14 and 9.2 & 7 for use of dogs to guard sheep from wolves; Pliny *NH* VIII.lxxii-lxxv.187-199 on sheep and wool; N. Russell (1986) 22-38 on animal breeding in classical antiquity; Ryder (1983) connected the Nymphaion fine wool with the legend of the Golden Fleece in the Black Sea region, but there are at least two other rationalising explanations for the golden fleece: (1) T.V. Buttrey suggests that fleeces were used in obtaining gold from the river Pactolus in Lydia; (2) G.J. Smith (1987) suggested that sheep fed on olive leaves (Aristotle *HA* 596a24-25) rich in oleanolic acid may develop liver damage, leading to accumulation of the yellow pigment bilirubin in their skin and wool.

13. Bökönyi (1984) 118 on Pannonia, cf. Lauwerier (1988) 166-169 for increased cattle size in Holland during the Roman period.

14. Anthony (1985), Telegin (1986), Zeuner (1963) 299-337 and Bökönyi in

Mason (1984) 162-173 on horse domestication; Khazanov (1984) 91-92 argued that the pig bones found alongside horse bones at Neolithic Dereivka in the Ukraine indicate a sedentary way of life, contrast Herodotos IV.63 (with Simoons (1961)) for the refusal of the Scythians to keep pigs in the first millennium BC; Anderson (1961) 7-8 & 15-16 on the small size of Greek horses; Xenophon *peri hippikês* XII; Crouwel (1981) on Homer; Herodotos VII.196 for the poor impression of Thessalian horses in the eyes of Xerxes; Arrian *Anabasis* II.11.3 & III.13.4 for more heavily armoured Persian cavalry at the battles of Issos and Gaugamela; Azzaroli (1972) on small horses in Bronze and Early Iron Age Italy; increased body size as a result of domestication and breeding enormously speeded up a natural trend towards evolution of larger body size in *Equus* and most of its ancestors observed in the fossil record over the last twenty-five million years – MacFadden (1986).

   15. R.H.C. Davis (1989) on the mediaeval warhorse; Appleby (1979) on use of spring-sown cereals to eliminate subsistence crises in early modern Europe, cf. Pliny *NH* XVIII.xlix.183 for a successful experiment of this kind in Roman Gaul.

   16. Aristotle *Politics* 1289b35-40; Strabo X.1.12.448c and Brelich (1961a) on the Lelantine War, which originated in inter-tribal initiation rites (see Chapter II.5 above).

   17. Ammianus Marcellinus XXII.15.24, Herodotos II.71 copied by Aristotle *HA* 502a9-15, and Bytinski-Salz (1965) on hippopotamus; Boessneck & Driesch (1981) found hippopotamus teeth in the Heraion of Samos; Plutarch *Solon* XXIII; Nausikrates F3 ed. Kock; Pausanias I.32.1; Theokritos XXV.185 mentions bears, boars and wolves in the Peloponnese; Walpole (1817) 73 on animals in early modern Greece, also 144 and Bairoch et al. (1988) 36 on the human population of early modern Attica.

   18. Herodotos VII.125-126; Aristotle *HA* 579a31-b14, 606b9-11 & 629b5-630b7; Dio Chrysostom XXI.1 ed. Budé; Martinet (1986) 248; Hammond & Walbank (1988) 7-9 for the fresco; Boessneck & Driesch (1979) & (1981) on the bones from Tiryns, cf. Mylonas (1970); the discussion of lion in Homer, e.g. *Odyssey* IX.292, in Finley (1978) 155 is misguided; Pliny *NH* VIII.xvii-xxi.41-58; Stuart (1977) for lion in Ice Age Britain; Ammianus Marcellinus XVIII.7.4-5; Kurtén & Poulianos (1977); Mallory (1982) 208 cites reports in Russian archaeological periodicals of excavations of lion skeletons at the Greek colony of Olbia, dating to the first millennium BC, and at the Neolithic sites of Beograd and Majaki in the south-western corner of the USSR.

   19. Ims & Stenseth (1989) on the conservation debate, including such questions as whether one large reserve is a better saviour from extinction than two small reserves equal in area to the large reserve and connected by a corridor; Sondaar (1971); Dermitzakis & Sondaar (1978) on Megalopolis; Herodotos I.68 & Pausanias III.3.6 on the bones of Orestes, cf. Philostratos *Hêrôikos* VII.9-VIII.16 ed. de Lannoy; Heurtley (1939) 88-93 gives the earliest Holocene evidence for horse in the southern Balkans; Pliny *NH* VIII.lxxxiii.228 on Crete.

   20. Wilson (1978) 97 for the quotation; Aristotle *Politics* 1253a7-18 anticipated Wilson (1971) & (1975) in considering the question of whether there are any analogies between human societies and insect societies, but concluded that humans had a community life to a greater extent than bees or any other gregarious animal for the reason that man possessed the power not only of speech, permitting expression of emotions such as pain and joy, which was shared with other animals, but also of reasoning (*logos*), permitting understanding of moral issues such as right and wrong and good and evil – he went on to argue that common views on moral issues constituted a *polis*; Dio Chrysostom XL.32 & 40

and XLVIII.16 compared ant and human societies – in an age when it was obvious to all and sundry that humans were closer to nature than they appear to be to some people today, such comparisons did not stir up the kind of controversy created by the publication of Wilson's book *Sociobiology* (1975); for the importance of seed size selection at the origins of agriculture, continuing the interaction between humans and grasses, see most recently O. Bar-Yosef & M.E. Kislev in Harris & Hillman (1989) esp. 637-640.

21. Martin & Klein (1984) is the most detailed compilation of material on the Quaternary extinctions, cf. the papers in Soffer (1987) and V. Geist in J. Clutton-Brock (1989) 282-294; S.J.M. Davis (1981), discussing the evidence for worldwide dwarfing of mammals at the end of the last glaciation, noted that, beside the megafauna which became extinct, many other wild mammals (e.g. porcupine, hedgehog, large carnivores, gazelle, fallow deer, fox), which did *not* become extinct then or later on involved in ecological mutualisms with man which initially produced a further reduction in body size (a quite separate and later development), evolved reduced body size – this parallel development cannot be explained by the 'overkill' hypothesis – Davis suggested that temperature changes directly caused reduced body size via the operation of Bergmann's Rule, but this fails to explain other earlier cases of reduction of body size during the Pleistocene (e.g. on the Mediterranean islands, cf. Lister (1989) showing that dwarfing of deer on Jersey during the Eemian Interglacial was not accompanied by dwarfing of the same species on the mainland at the same time, excluding the global operation of Bergmann's Rule at that particular glacial-interglacial transition), consequently changes in environmental carrying capacity remain the best explanation, and the absence of mass extinctions at the ends of earlier glacial periods may be attributed to a lower amplitude of the climatic changes at previous interglacials; beside R. Foley (1987), note also Bailey et al. (1989) in relation to the argument that early hominids were native to semi-arid environments. P.D. Moore in *NAT* 342 (1989) 858 re-evaluates upwards the productivity of tropical grasslands and suggests that they are a larger sink for atmospheric carbon dioxide than had previously been realised, an important conclusion. Herodotus II.32.6, if trustworthy, suggests that pygmies existed in the grasslands north of the rainforest zone in antiquity until they were pushed into the forest by Negroes, cf. Homer *Iliad* III. 3-7 and Aristotle *HA* 597a4-7.

22. Ehret (1971) 45-46 & 64 on E. Africa; Robertshaw (1989) dated the development of pastoralism in E. Africa to the late third and second millennia BC; Herdt (1984) 51-53 on New Guinea.

23. Feil (1987) 191.

24. Dahl (1979); Goody (1982) 210-213 on Ethiopia.

25. Darwin (1901) 854 noted that women are a constant cause of war among savages, cf. E.O. Wilson (1978) 118 for the suggestion that the availability of women limits reproduction; the incongruity of the abduction of Helen as a motive for such an apparently great conflict as the Trojan War was noted in antiquity by Aelian *peri zôiôn idiotêtos* XI.27, cf. Herodotos I.1-5; Thucydides I.5.3-6.2; Rihll (1986) on the absence of fixed social classes in Homer; Bernardi (1985) 27.

26. Timaios FGH566 F11 Jacoby.

27. Mayr (1988) 55-57.

28. Hypereides V (*Against Demosthenes*) col. 21.

29. Plato *Apologia* 24b; Xenophon *Memorabilia* I.2.35; Whitehead (1982/83) argued that the Thirty Tyrants were modelled on the Spartan *gerousia*, which (if correct) emphasises that it is right to interpret their reaction to Sokrates within the framework of age class organisation; Alexis F94 ed. Kock; Plato *Laws* 942c-d.

30. Weber and Hasebroek rejected the modernising interpretation of the ancient economy given by e.g. Meyer, but it has tended to prevail in more recent historiography in spite of the efforts of Finley; Aristotle *Politics* 1253b33-39 observed that if tools could operate themselves like robots, then masters would not need slaves, but such a situation was not seriously imaginable even in the utopias that were dreamed up by ancient authors.

31. Strauss (1987) on the issue of 'parties' v. 'factions'.

32. D.C. Young (1988) on the Olympic Games.

33. Barnola et al. (1987); Genthon et al. (1987); Lindstrom & MacAyeal (1989); Payette et al. (1989).

34. Darwin (1901) 216-217; Galton (1892) 329-332.

35. Aristophanes of Byzantion in IG XIV.1183 on Menander, cf. Quintilian *Institutio Oratoria* X.1.69-72 and Plutarch *Moralia* 853-854; Snodgrass (1987) 13.

36. Aristotle *Politics* 1329b25-31.

Supplements to notes: Chapter II

6. The only information about the size of the population of ancient Persia (only part of modern Iran) is the statement of Xenophon *Cryopaedia* I.2.15 that there were nearly 120,000 (adult male) Persians.

181. Herodotos I.196.1 describes what looks like age class organisation of the marriages of women, at least, among the Enetoi of Illyria. However it is probably wise to be sceptical of this claim in the same passage that similar customs had once existed in Babylonia until it is confirmed by Oriental sources.

345. Dionysios of Halikarnassos *On Thucydides* XLIII-XLVII criticised the speech put into Perikles' mouth in Thucydides II.60-64, when he was on trial during the epidemic, on the grounds that the words were not appropriate to the situation.

Bibliography

This bibliography is, naturally, only a selection of relevant modern scholarship. It includes relevant literature not cited elsewhere in the book. It is biased towards recent publications.

Abbreviations of titles of periodicals

AA	*Archäologischer Anzeiger*
AAA	*Athens Annals of archaeology*
ABN	*Acta Botanica Neerlandica*
ABSA	*Annual of the British School at Athens*
AC	*Antiquité classique*
ACS	*Ancient society*
ADA	*Advances in agronomy*
ADG	*Advances in genetics*
ADH	*Annales de démographie historique*
AESC	*Annales: économies, sociétés, civilisations*
AH	*Agricultural history*
AHG	*Annals of human genetics*
AHR	*American historical review*
AJA	*American journal of archaeology*
AJAH	*American journal of ancient history*
AJBS	*Australian journal of biological sciences*
AJP	*American journal of philology*
AJPA	*American journal of physical anthropology*
AMA	*American anthropologist*
AMQ	*American antiquity*
AN	*American naturalist*
ANT	*Anthropologika*
AP	*Annali della Scuola Normale di Pisa*
ARA	*Annual review of anthropology*
ARC	*Archeologia*
ARES	*Annual review of ecology and systematics*
ARET	*Arethusa*
ARG	*Annual review of genetics*
ARP	*Annual review of plant physiology*
AS	*Anatolian studies*
ATQ	*Antiquity*
BAR	*British archaeological reports*
BCH	*Bulletin de correspondance héllenique*

BDBG	*Berichte der Deutschen Botanischen Gesellschaft*
BHM	*Bulletin of the history of medicine*
BJLS	*Biological Journal of the Linnean Society*
BNYAM	*Bulletin of the New York Academy of Medicine*
BOJL	*Botanical Journal of the Linnean Society*
BSA	*Bulletin on Sumerian agriculture*
BSBF	*Bulletin de la Société Botanique de France*
BTBC	*Bulletin of the Torrey Botanical Club*
CA	*Current anthropology*
CE	*Chronique d'Egypte*
CH	*Chiron*
CJ	*Classical journal*
CJGC	*Canadian journal of genetics and cytology*
CJPS	*Canadian journal of plant science*
CP	*Classical philology*
CQ	*Classical quarterly*
CSHS	*Cold Spring Harbor symposia on quantitative biology*
CT	*Cahiers de Tunisie*
DAE	*Daedalus*
DEM	*Demography*
DHA	*Dialogues d'histoire ancienne*
DOP	*Dumbarton Oaks papers*
DZ	*Der Züchter*
EB	*Economic botany*
ECO	*Ecology*
EFN	*Ecology of food and nutrition*
EHR	*Economic history review*
EIR	*Eirene*
EJEA	*Empire journal of experimental agriculture*
EM	*Ecologia Mediterranea*
EMC	*Echos du monde classique*
ER	*Eugenics review*
ES	*Ethology and sociobiology*
ETH	*Ethnology*
EUP	*Euphytica*
FCA	*Field crops abstracts*
GR	*Greece & Rome*
GRBS	*Greek, Roman and Byzantine studies*
HB	*Human biology*
HE	*Human ecology*
HER	*Heredity*
HEP	*Hesperia*
HES	*Histoire, économie et société*
HIS	*Historia*
HSCP	*Harvard studies in classical philology*
IJB	*Israel journal of botany*
INQ	*Inquiry*
JAE	*Journal of applied ecology*
JAGS	*Journal of agricultural science*
JAN	*Janus*
JAOS	*Journal of the American Oriental Society*

JARS   *Journal of archaeological science*
JASA   *Journal of the American Society of Agronomy*
JATBA   *Journal d'agriculture traditionnelle et de botanique appliquée*
JBS   *Journal of biosocial science*
JE   *Journal of ecology*
JEH   *Journal of economic history*
JESHO   *Journal of the economic and social history of the Orient*
JFA   *Journal of field archaeology*
JG   *Journal of genetics*
JHB   *Journal of the history of biology*
JHE   *Journal of human evolution*
JHM   *Journal of the history of medicine and allied sciences*
JHS   *Journal of Hellenic studies*
JIES   *Journal of Indo-European studies*
JNE   *Journal of animal ecology*
JTB   *Journal of theoretical biology*
KL   *Klio*
LAN   *Lancet*
LCM   *Liverpool classical monthly*
LS   *Libyan studies*
MH   *Medical history*
MMFQ   *Milbank Memorial Fund Quarterly*
MNE   *Mnemosyne*
MYC   *Mycologia*
NAT   *Nature* (London)
NEJM   *New England journal of medicine*
OP   *Opus*
OSI   *Osiris*
PAA   *Praktika tes Akademias Athenon*
PAL   *Palaeohistoria*
PAPS   *Proceedings of the American Philosophical Society*
PB   *Paleobiology*
PCPS   *Proceedings of the Cambridge Philological Society*
PDP   *Parola del passato*
PDR   *Population and development review*
PEO   *Paléorient*
PFNS   *Progress in food and nutrition science*
PHI   *Philologus*
PHO   *Phoenix*
PLSL   *Proceedings of the Linnean Society of London*
POP   *Population* (Paris)
PRSL   *Proceedings of the Royal Society of London*
PRSM   *Proceedings of the Royal Society of Medicine*
PS   *Population studies*
PTRS   *Philosophical Transactions of the Royal Society*
QUCC   *Quaderni Urbinati di cultura classica*
RBAAT   *Revue de botanique appliquée et d'agriculture tropicale*
REA   *Revue des études anciennes*
REG   *Revue des études grecques*
RHM   *Rheinisches Museum für Philologie*
RHS   *Revue d'histoire des sciences et de leurs applications*

RID   Reviews of infectious diseases
RPP   Review of palaeobotany and palynology
SA   Scientific American
SCI   Science (New York)
SE   Studi Etruschi
SMA   Studies in Mediterranean archaeology
SMEA   Studi Micenei ed Egeo-anatolici
SO   Symbolae Osloenses
SWJA   Southwestern journal of anthropology
TAPA   Transactions of the American Philological Association
TPB   Theoretical population biology
WA   World archaeology
ZA   Zeitschrift für Archäologie
ZPE   Zeitschrift für Papyrologie und Epigraphik
ZPZ   Zeitschrift für Pflanzenzüchtung
ZSY   Zeitschrift für Assyriologie

Aaronson, S. (1989) 'Fungal parasites of grasses and cereals: their role as food or
    medicine, now and in the past' ATQ 63:247-257
Abel, W. (1980) Agricultural fluctuations in Europe from the thirteenth to the
    twentieth centuries (Engl. transl.) London
Abramsky, Z. & Tracy, C.R. (1979) 'Population history of a 'noncycling' population
    of prairie voles and a hypothesis on the role of migration in generating
    microtine cycles' ECO 60:349-361
Acker, C.L. & Townsend, P.K. (1975) 'Demographic models and female
    infanticide' Man 10:469-470 (with discussion on pp. 470-472)
Acsádi, G. & Nemeskéri, J. (1970) History of human lifespan and mortality
    Budapest (multiple reviews in CA 15 (1974) 495-507)
Adams, R. McC. (1981) Heartland of cities Chicago
Adamson, D.A., Gasse, F., Street, F.A. & Williams, M.A.J. (1980) 'Late
    Quaternary history of the Nile' NAT 288:50-55
Adamson, P.B. (1976) 'Schistosomiasis in antiquity' MH 20:176-188
—— (1977) 'The spread of rabies in Europe and the probable origin of this disease
    in antiquity' J. of the Royal Asiatic Society 1977:140-144
Adcock, S.D. (1985) 'Variety trials and a feasibility assessment of small-scale
    wheat production' paper cited in FCA 38:370
Aebischer, P. (1953) 'Le 'seigle' dans le latin médiéval' Zeitschrift für Romanische
    Philologie 69:392-402
Agapitidis, S. (1969) 'L'évolution de la population de la Grèce: les facteurs de la
    reproduction' POP 24:1161-1168
Agelarakis, A. (1986/7) 'Report on the Mycenaean skeletal remains at Archontiki,
    Psara' Ossa 13:3-11
Agra Europa special report no. 3 (1979) The agricultural implications of EEC
    enlargement, part 1: Greece
Agyei, W.K.A. (1984) 'Breast-feeding and sexual abstinence in Papua New
    Guinea' JBS 16:451-461
—— (1988) Fertility and family planning in the Third World: a case study of
    Papua New Guinea London
Alcock, S.E. (1989) 'Greek society and the transition to Roman rule:
    archaeological and historical approaches' (Cambridge PhD)

Alessio, G. (1946) 'Relitti mediterranei nel lessico botanico greco e latino' *AP* ser. II 13:24-51

Alivizatos, G.P. (1950) *The early smallpox epidemics in Europe and the plague of Athens according to Thucydides* Athens (in modern Greek with English summary) (*non vidi*) (reviewed by O. Temkin in *BHM* 29 (1955) 81-82)

Allan, J.A. (ed) (1981) *The Sahara: ecological change and early economic history* London

Allan, W.H. (1971) 'The problem of Newcastle disease' *NAT* 234:129-131

Allard, R.W. (1960) *Principles of plant breeding* New York

Allbaugh, L.G. (1953) *Crete: a case study of an underdeveloped area* Princeton

Allison, J.W. (1983) 'Perikles' policy and the plague' *HIS* 32:14-23

Alsina, J. (1989) 'Hippocrate, Sophocle et la description de la peste chez Thucydide' in G. Baader & R. Winau (eds) *Die Hippokratischen Epidemien: Theorie – Praxis – Tradition* (1989) 213-221 (*Sudhoffs Archiv Beiheft* 27)

Ammermann, A.J. & Cavalli-Sforza, L.L. (1984) *The Neolithic transition and the genetics of populations in Europe* Princeton

Amouretti, M.C. (1976) 'Les instruments aratoires dans la Grèce archaïque' *DHA* 2:25-52

—— (1979) 'Les céréales dans l'antiquité : espèces, mouture et conservation, liaison et interférences dans la Grèce classique' in M. Gast & F. Sigaut (eds) *Les techniques de conservation des graines à long terme* (1979) 57-69 Paris

—— (1985) 'La transformation des céréales dans les villes: un indicateur méconnu de la personnalité urbaine. L'exemple d'Athènes à l'époque classique' in P. Leveau (ed.) *L'origine des richesses dépensés dans la ville antique* (1985) 133-146 Aix-en-Provence

—— (1986) *Le pain et l'huile dans la Grèce antique* Paris

Ampolo, C. (1980) 'Le condizioni materiali della produzione: agricoltura e paesaggio agrario' *Dialoghi d'archeologia* 11:15-46

—— (1988) 'Rome archaïque: une société pastorale?' in Whittaker (1988) 120-133

Amundsen, D.W. & Diers, C.J. (1969) 'The age of menarche in classical Greece' *HB* 41:125-132

—— & —— (1970) 'Menopause in Greece and Rome' *HB* 42:79-86

Andelman, S.J. (1987) 'Evolution of concealed ovulation in vervet monkeys (*Cercopithecus aethiops*)' *AN* 129:785-799

Andersen, J.G. (1969) 'Studies in mediaeval diagnosis of leprosy in Denmark: an osteoarchaeological, historical and clinical study' *Danish medical bulletin* 16 (suppl. IX):1-142

Anderson, J.K. (1961) *Ancient Greek horsemanship* Berkeley

Anderson, R.M. & May, R.M. (1979) 'Population biology of infectious diseases' *NAT* 280:361-367 & 455-461

—— & —— (1988) 'Epidemiological parameters of HIV infection' *NAT* 333:514-519

Anderson, R.M., May, R.M. & McLean, A.R. (1988) 'Possible demographic consequences of AIDS in developing countries' *NAT* 332:228-234

André, J. (1956) *Lexique des termes botaniques en Latin* Paris

—— (1958) *Notes de lexicographie botanique grecque* Paris

—— (1981) *L'alimentation et la cuisine à Rome* (2nd ed.) Paris

—— (1985) *Les noms de plantes dans la Rome antique* Paris

Andrejev, V.N. (1974) 'Some aspects of agrarian conditions in Attica in the fifth to third centuries BC' *EIR* 12:5-46

Andreski, S. (1968) *Military organisation and society* (2nd ed.) London

Andrewartha, H.G. & Birch, L.C. (1954) *The distribution and abundance of animals* Chicago

—— & —— (1984) *The ecological web: more on the distribution and abundance of animals* Chicago

Andrewes, A. (1978) 'The opposition to Pericles' *JHS* 98:1-8

Andrews, A.C. (1941) 'The silphium of the ancients' *Isis* 33:232-236

—— (1949a) 'The carrot as a food in the classical era' *CP* 44:182-196

—— (1949b) 'The bean and Indo-European totemism' *AMA* 51:274-292

—— (1952) 'The opium poppy as a food and spice in the classical period' *AH* 26:152-155

—— (1956) 'Melons and watermelons in the classical era' *OSI* 12:368-375

—— (1958) 'Thyme as a condiment in the Graeco-Roman era' *OSI* 13:150-156

—— (1961a) 'Acclimatisation of citrus fruits in the Mediterranean region' *AH* 35:35-46

—— (1961b) 'Marjoram as a spice in the classical era' *CP* 56:73-82

—— (1963) 'Plant symbolism on Greek coins' *EB* 17:317-318

—— (1964) 'The genetic origin of spelt and related wheats' *DZ* 34:17-22

Angel, J.L. (1944) 'Greek teeth: ancient and modern' *HB* 16:283-297

—— (1945) 'Skeletal material from Attica' *HEP* 14:279-363

—— (1950) 'Population size and microevolution in Greece' *CSHS* 15:343-351

—— (1966) 'Porotic hyperostosis, anaemias, malarias, and marshes in the prehistoric eastern Mediterranean' *SCI* 153:760-763

—— (1969a) 'The bases of palaeodemography' *AJPA* 30:427-438

—— (1969b) 'Palaeodemography and evolution' *AJPA* 31:343-354

—— (1972a) 'Ecology and population in the eastern Mediterranean' *WA* 4:88-105

—— (1972b) 'Human skeletons from Grave Circles at Mycenae' in G.E. Mylonas (ed) *Ho taphikos kyklos B tôn Mykênôn* (1972) 379-397 Athens

—— (1975) 'Palaeoecology, palaeodemography and health' in S. Polgar (ed.) *Population, ecology and social evolution* (1975) 167-190 The Hague

—— (1984) 'Health as a crucial factor in the changes from hunting to developed farming in the eastern Mediterranean' in M.N. Cohen & G.J. Armelagos (eds) *Palaeopathology at the origins of agriculture* (1984) 51-73 Orlando

Anthony, D.W. (1985) 'The social and economic implications of the domestication of the horse' (PhD Univ. of Pennsylvania)

Antoniadis, A., LeDuc, J.W., Acritidis, N.N., Alexiou-Daniel, J., Kyparissi, A. & Saviolakis, G.A. (1989) 'Haemorrhagic fever with renal syndrome in Greece: clinical and laboratory characteristics' *RID* XI suppl. IV:891-896

Applebaum, S. (1979) *Jews and Greeks in ancient Cyrene* Leiden

Appleby, A.B. (1975) 'Nutrition and disease: the case of London 1550-1750' *J. of interdisciplinary history* 6:1-22

—— (1979) 'Grain prices and subsistence crises in England and France, 1590-1740' *JEH* 39:865-887

Apuleius (1979) *Herbarium Apulei* vol. 1 (facsimile of 1481 edition, introduced by E. Caprotti & W.T. Stearn) Milan

Armitage, P., West, B. & Steedman, K. (1984) 'New evidence of black rat from Roman London' *The London archaeologist* 4.14:375-383

Arnim, H. von (1905-1924) *Stoicorum veterum fragmenta* (4 vols) Leipzig

Arnon, I. (1972) *Crop production in dry regions* (2 vols) London

—— (1981) *Modernization of agriculture in developing countries* Chichester

Aron, J.L. & Anderson, R.M. (1982) 'The population dynamics of malaria' in R.M. Anderson (ed.) *The population dynamics of infectious diseases: theory and applications* (1982) 139-179 London

Arrigoni, E. (1967) & (1969) 'Elementi per una ricostruzione del paesaggio in Attica nell'epoca classica' *Nuova rivista storica* 51:267-296 & 53:267-322

Ascenzi, A. & Balistreri, P. (1977) 'Porotic hyperostosis and the problem of origin of thalassaemia in Italy' *JHE* 6:595-604

Aschenbrenner, S.E. (1976) 'Archaeology and ethnography in Messenia' in Dimen & Friedl (1976) 158-167

Aschmann, H. (1984) 'A restrictive definition of Mediterranean climates' *BSBF* 131.2-4:21-30

Asdrachas, S. (1970) 'Aux Balkans du XVe siècle: producteurs directs et marchés' *Etudes balkaniques* 61:36-69

—— (1978) *Mêkanismoi tês agrotikês oikonomias stên Tourkokratia* Athens

Ashmead, A. (1978) 'Greek cats: exotic pets kept by rich youths in fifth-century Athens as portrayed on Greek vases' *Expedition* 20.3:38-47

Ashtor, E. (1978) *The mediaeval Near East: social and economic history* London

Atallah, S.I. (1978) 'Mammals of the eastern Mediterranean region: their ecology, systematics and zoogeographical relationships' *Säugetierkundliche Mitteilungen* 26:1-50

Atchley, S.C. (1938) *Wild flowers of Attica* Oxford

Athanasiadis, A. (1975) 'Zur postglazialen Vegetationsentwicklung von Litochoro Katerinis und Pertouli Trikalon (Griechenland)' *Flora* 164:99-132

Atran, S. (1985) 'Pre-theoretical aspects of Aristotelian definition and classification of animals: the case for common sense' *Studies in the history and philosophy of science* 16:113-163

Aubaile-Sallenave, F. (1984) 'L'agriculture musulmane aux premiers temps de la conquête: apports et emprunts, à propos de *Agricultural innovation in the early Islamic world* de Andrew M. Watson' *JATBA* 31:245-264

Austin, R.B., Bingham, J., Blackwell, R.D., Evans, L.T., Ford, M.A., Morgan, C.L. & Taylor, M. (1980) 'Genetic improvements in winter wheat yields and associated physiological changes' *JAGS* 94:675-689

Aymard, M. (1979) 'Toward the history of nutrition: some methodological remarks' in Forster & Ranum (1979) 1-15

—— (1982) 'Production et productivité agricole: l'Italie du Sud à l'époque moderne' in J. Goy & E. Le Roy Ladurie (eds) *Prestations paysannes, dîmes, rente foncière et mouvement de la production agricole à l'époque préindustrielle* (1982) 147-163 Paris

Azzaroli, A. (1972) 'Il cavallo domestico in Italia dall'età del Bronzo agli Etruschi' *SE* 40:273-306

—— (1985) *An early history of horsemanship* Leiden

Baethge, B.A. & West, B.C. (1988) '*Vibrio vulnificus*: did Hippokrates describe a fatal case?' *RID* X.3:614-615

Bailey, N.T.J. (1975) *The mathematical theory of infectious diseases and its applications* (2nd ed.) London

—— (1982) *The biomathematics of malaria* London

Bailey, R.C., Head, G., Jenike, M., Owen, B., Rechtman, R. & Zechenter, E. (1989) 'Hunting and gathering in tropical rain forest: is it possible?' *AMA* 91:59-82

Baillie, M.G.L. & Munro, M.A.R. (1988) 'Irish tree rings, Santorini and volcanic dust veils' *NAT* 332:344-346

Bainton, R.H. (1932) 'The parable of the tares as the proof text for religious liberty to the end of the sixteenth century' *Church history* 1:67-89

Baird, J.R. & Thieret, J.W. (1989) 'The medlar (*Mespilus germanica*, Rosaceae)

from antiquity to obscurity' *EB* 43:328-372

Bairoch, P., Batou, J. & Chèvre, P. (1988) *La population des villes européennes de 800 à 1850: banque de données et analyse sommaire des résultats* Geneva

Bakels, C.C. (1982) 'Der Mohn, die Linearbandkeramik und das westliche Mittelmeergebiet' *Archäologisches Korrespondenzblatt* 12:11-13

Baker, H.G. (1974) 'The evolution of weeds' *ARES* 5:1-24

Baker, J. & Brothwell, D. (1980) *Animal diseases in archaeology* London

Bakhuizen, S.C. (1975) 'Social ecology of the ancient Greek world' *AC* 44:211-218

Balcer, J.M. (1974) 'The Mycenaean dam at Tiryns' *AJA* 78:141-149

Baldwin, J.A. (1975) 'Notes and speculations on the domestication of the cat in Egypt' *Anthropos* 70:428-448

Baldy, C. (1986) 'Comportement des blés dans les climats méditerranéens' *EM* 12.3/4:72-88

Balfet, H. (1975) 'Breads in some regions of the Mediterranean area' in M.L. Arnott (ed.) *Gastronomy: the anthropology of food and food habits* (1975) 305-314 The Hague

Banga, O. (1957) 'Origin of the European cultivated carrot' *EUP* 6:57-63

Banks, J.A. (1954) *Prosperity and parenthood* London

Barbagallo, C. (1904) 'La produzione media relativa dei cereali e della vite nella Grecia, nella Sicilia e nell'Italia antica' *Rivista di storia antica* 8:477-504

Barclay, G.W., Coale, A.J., Stoto, M.A. & Trussell, T.J. (1976) 'A reassessment of the demography of traditional rural China' *Population index* 42:606-635

Barger, G. (1931) *Ergot and ergotism* London

Barigozzi, C. (ed.) (1986) *The origin and domestication of cultivated plants* Amsterdam

Barker, G. (1985) *Prehistoric farming in Europe* Cambridge

—— (1988) 'Archaeology and the Etruscan countryside' *ATQ* 62:772-785

Barker, G. et al. (1983) *Excavations at Sidi Khrebish Benghazi (Berenice) (Libya antiqua suppl.)* (2 vols) Tripoli

Barker, G., Lloyd, J. & Reynolds, J. (eds) (1985) *Cyrenaica in antiquity (BAR* Int. Ser. 236) Oxford

Barkow, J.H. & Burley, N. (1980) 'Human fertility, evolutionary theory and the demographic transition' *ES* 1:163-180

Barlett, P.F. (1980) 'Adaptive strategies in peasant agricultural production' *ARA* 9:245-273

Barley genetics (1981) *Proceedings of the 4th International barley genetics symposium* Edinburgh

Barnola, J.M., Raynaud, D., Korotkevich, Y.S. & Lorius, C. (1987) 'Vostok ice core provides 160,000 year record of atmospheric CO_2' *NAT* 329:408-414

Barrett, J.A. (1981) 'The evolutionary consequences of monoculture' in J.A. Bishop & L.M. Crook (eds) *Genetic consequences of man-made change* (1981) 209-248 London

Barrett, S.C.H. (1983) 'Crop mimicry in weeds' *EB* 37:255-282

Bartsocas, C.S. (1966) 'Two fourteenth century Greek descriptions of the Black Death' *JHM* 21:394-400

Bartsocas, C.S., Karayanni, C., Tsipouras, P., Baibas, E., Bouloukos, A. & Papadatos, C. (1979) 'Genetic structure of the Greek gypsies' *Clinical genetics* 15:5-10

Bates, D.G. & Lees, S.H. (1979) 'The myth of population regulation' in N.A. Chagnon & W. Irons (eds) *Evolutionary biology and human social behaviour: an anthropological perspective* (1979) 273-289 North Scituate

Battisti, C. (1960) 'Il sostrato mediterraneo nella fitonimia greco-latina' *SE* 28:349-384

Baum, B.R. & Savile, D.B.O. (1985) 'Rusts (Uredinales) of Triticeae: evolution and extent of coevolution, a cladistic analysis' *BOJL* 91:367-394

Baumann, H. (1982) *Die griechische Pflanzenwelt in Mythos, Kunst und Literatur* Munich

Baxter, P.T.W. & Almagor, U. (eds) (1978) *Age, generation and time: some features of East African age organisations* London

Beattie, A.J. (1985) *The evolutionary ecology of ant-plant mutualisms* Cambridge

Beaucamp, C. (1988) 'Fièvres d'hier, paludisme d'aujourd'hui: vie et mort d'une maladie' *AESC* 43:249-275

Becker, M.J. (1982) 'Human skeletal analysis and the study of the prehistory and history of southern Italy: the development of a programme of collaborative research between physical anthropology and archaeology' *Studi di antichità* 3:133-153

Bedigian, D. & Harlan, J.R. (1986) 'Evidence for cultivation of sesame in the ancient world' *EB* 40:137-154

Begon, M., Harper, J.L. & Townsend, C.R. (1986) *Ecology: individuals, populations and communities* Oxford

Bein, A. & Horowitz, A. (1986) 'Papyrus – a historic newcomer to the Hula valley, Israel?' *RPP* 47:89-95

Beloch, K.J. (1886) *Die Bevölkerung der griechischen-römischen Welt* Leipzig

—— (1985) 'Die Landwirtschaft Athens 1' *OP* 4:7-28 (edited by C. Ampolo)

Bélteky, B. & Kovács, I. (1984) *Lupin: the new break* Bradford-on-Avon

Benedictow, O.J. (1987) 'Morbidity in historical plague epidemics' *PS* 41:401-431

Bennett, E. (1971) 'The origin and evolution of agroecotypes in south-west Asia' in P.H. Davis et al. (1971) 219-234

Bentley, J.W. (1987) 'Economic and ecological approaches to land fragmentation: in defence of a much maligned phenomenon' *ARA* 16:31-67

Benveniste, E. (1969) *Le vocabulaire des institutions indo-européennes* (2 vols) Paris

—— (1970) 'Deux modèles linguistiques de la cité' in *Echanges et communications. Mélanges offerts à Cl. Lévi-Strauss* vol. 1 (1970) 589-596 The Hague

Bérard, J. (1947) 'Problèmes démographiques dans l'histoire de la Grèce antique' *POP* 2:303-312

Berendt, A.R., Simmons, D.L., Tansey, J., Newbold, C.I. & Marsh, K. (1989) 'Intercellular adhesion molecule-1 is an endothelial cell adhesion receptor for *Plasmodium falciparum*' *NAT* 341:57-59

Berlin, B. (1974) 'Folk systematics in relation to biological classification and nomenclature' *ARES* 4:259-271

Bernal, M. (1987) *Black Athena: the Afroasiatic roots of classical civilization*: vol. 1 *The fabrication of ancient Greece 1785-1985* London

Bernardi, B. (1985) *Age class systems: social institutions and polities based on age* (Engl. transl.) Cambridge

Bernheim, F. & Zener, A.A. (1978) 'The Sminthian Apollo and the epidemic among the Achaeans at Troy' *TAPA* 108:11-14

Berry, R.J. (1981) 'Population dynamics of the house mouse' in R.J. Berry (ed.) *Biology of the house mouse* (Symposium of the Zoological Society of London vol. 47, 1981) 395-425

Bertier, J. (1972) *Mnésithée et Dieuchès* Leiden

Bertin, J., Hémardinquer, J.-J., Keul, M. & Randles, W.G.L. (1971) *Atlas des cultures vivrières* Paris

Dertman, S. (ed.) (1976) *The conflict of generations in ancient Greece and Rome* Amsterdam

Beswick, T.S.L. (1962) 'The origin and use of the word herpes' *MH* 6:214-232

Bethe, E. (1907) 'Die dorische Knabenliebe: ihre Ethik und ihre Idee' *RHM* 62:438-475

Betts, J.H. (1978) 'More Aegean papyrus: some glyptic evidence' *AAA* 11:61-74

Bideau, A. (1984) 'Autoregulating mechanisms in traditional populations' in Keyfitz (1984) 117-131

Bintliff, J.L. (1977a) 'Pedology and land use' *ABSA* 72:24-30

—— (1977b) *Natural environment and human settlement in prehistoric Greece* (*BAR* suppl. ser. 28) Oxford

—— (1981) 'Archaeology and the Holocene evolution of coastal plains in the Aegean and circum-Mediterranean' in P. Brothwell & G. Dimbleby (eds) *Environmental aspects of coasts and islands* (1981) 11-31 (*BAR* Int. Ser. 94) Oxford

—— (1982) 'Climatic change, archaeology and Quaternary science in the eastern Mediterranean region' in A.F. Harding (ed.) *Climatic change in later prehistory* (1982) 143-161 Edinburgh

Bintliff, J.L. & Snodgrass, A.M. (1985) 'The Cambridge/Bradford Boeotian expedition: the first four years' *JFA* 12:123-161

—— & —— (1988) 'Mediterranean survey and the city' *ATQ* 62:57-71

Biraben, J.-N. (1975) *Les hommes et la peste en France et dans les pays européens et méditerranéens* (2 vols) Paris

—— (1979) 'Essai sur l'évolution du nombre des hommes' *POP* 34:13-25

—— (1988) 'Préhistoire' in Dupâquier et al. (1988) vol. 1, pp. 19-64

Biraschi, A.M. (1984) 'L'auxêsis diversa dell'Attica: a proposito di Tucidide I.2.6' *PDP* 39:5-22

Birdsell, J.B. (1957) 'Some population problems involving Pleistocene man' *CSHS* 22:47-69

Birks, H.J.B. & H.H. (1980) *Quaternary palaeoecology* London

Birot, P. & Dresch, J. (1964) *La Méditerranée et le Moyen-Orient* vol. 1 Paris

Biscardi, A. (1984) 'Nota minima sugli "ectemoroi" ' in *Aux origines de l'Héllenisme. Mélanges à H. van Effenterre* (1984) 193-197 Paris

Bisel, S.L.C. (1980) 'A pilot study in aspects of human nutrition in the ancient eastern Mediterranean, with particular attention to trace minerals in several populations from different time periods' (PhD Univ. of Minnesota)

Biswas, S. (1988) *Stochastic processes in demography and applications* New York

Bittles, A.H. & Makov, E. (1988) 'Inbreeding in human populations: an assessment of the costs' in C.G.N. Mascie-Taylor & A.J. Boyce (eds) *Human mating patterns* (1988) 153-167 Cambridge

Black, F.L. (1966) 'Measles endemicity in insular populations: critical community size and its evolutionary implication' *JTB* 11:207-211

—— (1975) 'Infectious diseases in primitive populations' *SCI* 187:515-518

—— (1980) 'Modern isolated pre-agricultural populations as a source of information on prehistoric epidemic patterns' in N. Stanley & Joske (1980) 37-54

Black, J.H., Lewis, H.E., Thacker, C.K.M. & Thould, A.K. (1963) 'Tristan da Cunha: general medical investigations' *British Medical J.* 2:1018-1024

Blake, L.A., West, B.C., Lary, C.H. & Todd IV, J.R. (1987) 'Environmental nonhuman sources of leprosy' *RID* IX.3:562-577

Bloedow, E.F. (1975) 'Corn supply and Athenian imperialism' *AC* 44:20-29

—— (1981) 'The speeches of Archidamus and Sthenelaidas at Sparta' *HIS* 30:129-143

Blum, R. & E. (1965) *Health and healing in rural Greece* Stanford

Blundell, S. (1986) *The origins of civilization in Greek and Roman thought* London

Boardman, J. (1976) 'The olive in the Mediterranean: its culture and use' *PTRS* B 275:187-196

—— (1980) *The Greeks overseas: their early colonies and trade* (3rd ed.) London

Boardman, S. & Jones, G.E.M. (1990) 'Experiments on the effects of charring on cereal plant components' *JARS* 17:1-11

Bocquet-Appel, J. (1985) 'Small populations: demography and palaeoanthropological inferences' *JHE* 14:683-691

Bocquet-Appel, J. & Mosset, C. (1982) 'Farewell to palaeodemography' *JHE* 11:321-333

Boddington, A. (1987) 'From bones to population: the problem of numbers' in A. Boddington, A.N. Garland & R.C. Janaway (eds) *Death, decay and reconstruction: approaches to archaeology and forensic science* (1987) 180-197 Manchester

Boessneck, J. & Driesch, A. von den (1981) 'Reste exotischer Tiere aus dem Heraion auf Samos' *Mitteilungen des Deutschen Archäologischen Instituts: Athenische Abteilung* 96:245-248 (also 98 (1983) 21-24)

Boeuf, F. (1931) 'Le blé en Tunisie' *Annales du service botanique et agronomique de Tunisie* 8:1-454

Bökönyi, S. (1973) 'Stock-breeding' in Theocharis et al. (1973) 165-178

—— (1984) *Animal husbandry and hunting in Tác-Gorsium: the vertebrate fauna of a Roman town in Pannonia* Budapest

—— (1987) 'Horses and sheep in East Europe in the Copper and Bronze Ages' in S.K. Skomal & E.C. Polomé (eds) *Proto-Indo-European: the archaeology of a linguistic problem: studies in honour of M. Gimbutas* (1987) 136-144 Washington

—— (1988) 'Animal breeding on the Danube' in Whittaker (1988) 171-176

Bolkestein, H. (1922) 'The exposure of children at Athens and the *engchutristriai*' *CP* 17:222-239

Bommeljé, S. & Doorn, P.K. (1987) *Aetolia and the Aetolians: towards the interdisciplinary study of a Greek region* Utrecht

Bonatti, E. (1966) 'North Mediterranean climate during the last Würm glaciation' *NAT* 209:984-985

Bongaarts, J. & Potter, R.G. (1983) *Fertility, biology and behaviour: the proximate determinants* New York

Bonneau, D. (1971) *Le fisc et le Nil* Paris

Borza, E.N. (1979) 'Some observations on malaria and the ecology of central Macedonia in antiquity' *AJAH* 4:102-124

Boserup, E. (1965) *The conditions of agricultural growth* London

—— (1981) *Population and technology* Oxford

Bottema, S. (1979) 'Pollen analytical investigations in Thessaly (Greece)' *PAL* 21:19-40

—— (1980) 'Palynological investigations on Crete' *RPP* 31:193-217

—— (1982) 'Palynological investigations in Greece with a special reference to pollen as an indicator of human activity' *PAL* 24:257-289

Boucher, D.H., James, S. & Kesler, K.H. (1982) 'The ecology of mutualism' *ARES* 13:315-347

Boué, A., Boué, J. & Gropp, A. (1985) 'Cytogenetics of pregnancy waste' *AHG*

14:1-57

Boulanger, P.-M. & Tabutin, D. (eds) (1980) *La mortalité des enfants dans le monde et dans l'histoire* Liège

Bourdieu, P. (1980) *Le sens pratique* Paris

Bourguet, E. (1927) *Le dialecte laconien* Paris

Bourriot, F. (1976) *Recherches sur la nature du genos* (2 vols) Paris

Bousquet, B., Dufaure, J.J. & Pecheux, P.Y. (1983) 'Temps historiques et évolution des paysages égéens' *Méditerranée* 48:3-25

Boyaval, B. (1977a) 'Epigraphie antique et démographie: problèmes de méthode' *Revue du Nord* 59:163-191

—— (1977b) 'Tableau générale des indications d'âge de l'Egypte gréco-romaine' *CE* 52:345-351

Boyce, M.S. (1984) 'Restitution of r- and K-selection as a model of density-dependent natural selection' *ARES* 15:427-447

Boyden, S.V. (ed.) (1970) *The impact of civilization on the biology of man* Canberra

—— (1987) *Western civilization in biological perspective: patterns in biohistory* Oxford

Boylan, M. (1983) *Method and practice in Aristotle's biology* Washington

Braccesi, L. (1977) *Grecità adriatica: un capitolo della colonizazzione greca in occidente* (2nd ed.) Bologna

Bradford, J. (1956) 'Fieldwork on aerial discoveries in Attica and Rhodes, part II' *Antiquaries J.* 36:172-180

—— (1957) *Ancient landscapes* London

Bradley, K.R. (1980) 'Sexual relations in wet-nursing contracts from Roman Egypt' *KL* 62:321-325

Bradley, L. (1971) *Smallpox inoculation: an eighteenth century mathematical controversy* Nottingham

—— (1977) 'The most famous of all English plagues: a detailed analysis of the plague at Eyam, 1665-6' in *The plague reconsidered: a new look at its origins and effects in 16th and 17th century England (Local population studies* supplement no. 4) 63-94

Bras, H. Le (1969) 'Retour d'une population à l'état stable après une catastrophe' *POP* 24:861-896

Bratton, T.L. (1981) 'The identity of the plague of Justinian. Parts I & II' *Transactions and studies of the College of Physicians of Philadelphia* ser. 5, 3:113-124 & 174-180

Braudel, F. (1972) *The Mediterranean and the Mediterranean world in the age of Philip II* (Engl. transl. 2 vols) London

—— (1981), (1982) & (1984) *Civilization and capitalism 15th-18th century*: vol. 1 *The structures of everyday life*; vol. 2 *The wheels of commerce*; vol. 3 *The perspective of the world* (Engl. transl.) London

Bräuer, G. & Fricke, R. (1980) 'Zur Phänomenologie osteoporischer Veränderungen bei Bestehen systemischer hämatologischer Affektionen: paläopathologische Analyse eines Skelettes der geometrischen Periode (900-700 v.u.Z.) aus Tiryns (Peloponnes)' *Homo* 31:198-211

Bravo, B. (1983) 'Le commerce des céréales chez les Grecs de l'époque archaïque' in Garnsey & Whittaker (1983) 17-29

Bray, F. (1984) *Science and civilization in China*: vol. 6 *Biology and biological technology*: Part II *Agriculture* Cambridge

Breitinger, E. (1939) 'Die Skelette aus den submykenischen Gräbern' in W.

Kraiker & K. Kübler *Kerameikos. Ergebnisse der Ausgrabungen:* 1. *Die Nekropolen des 12. bis 10. Jahrhunderts* (1939) 223-255 Berlin

Brelich, A. (1961a) *Guerre, agoni e culti nella Grecia arcaica* Bonn

—— (1961b) 'The historical development of the institution of initiation in the classical ages' *Acta Antiqua Academiae Scientiarum Hungaricae* 9:267-283

—— (1969) *Paides e parthenoi*, vol. 1 Rome

Bremmer, J. (1980) 'An enigmatic Indo-European rite: paederasty' *ARET* 13.2:279-298

Bresc, H. & Guichard, P. (1982) 'Le monde des Abbasides: la "réussite" de l'Islam' in R. Fossier et al. *Le Moyen Age*: vol. 1 *Les mondes nouveaux* (1982) 231-282 Paris

Bretzl, H. (1903) *Botanische Forschungen des Alexanderzuges* Leipzig

Briant, P. (1982a) *Etat et pasteurs au Moyen-Orient ancien* Cambridge

—— (1982b) *Rois, tributs et paysans: études sur les formations tributaires du Moyen-Orient ancien* Paris

Briggs, D. (1978) *Barley* London

Briggs, D. & Courtney, F.M. (1985) *Agriculture and environment: the physical geography of temperate agricultural systems* London

Briggs, D. & Walters, S.M. (1984) *Plant variation and evolution* (2nd ed.) Cambridge

Brinton, D. (1946) 'An unusual form of epidemic food poisoning with neurological symptoms' *PRSM* 39:173-175

Briquel, P. (1982) 'Initiations grecques et idéologie indo-européenne' *AESC* 37:454-464

Brothwell, D.R. (1971) 'Palaeodemography' in W. Brass (ed.) *Biological aspects of demography* (1971) 111-130 London

Brothwell, D.R. & Sandison, A.T. (eds) (1967) *Diseases in antiquity* Springfield

Brown, J.P. (1969) 'The Mediterranean vocabulary of the vine' *Vetus Testamentum* 19:146-170

Brown, P. (1978) *Highland peoples of New Guinea* Cambridge

Brubaker, R.R. (1972) 'The genus Yersinia: biochemistry and genetics of virulence' *Current topics in microbiology and immunology* 57:111-158

Bruce-Chwatt, L.J. & Zulueta, J. de (1980) *The rise and fall of malaria: a historico-epidemiological study* Oxford

Brulé, P. (1978) *La piraterie crétoise hellénistique* Paris

Brumfield, A.C. (1981) *The Attic festivals of Demeter and their relation to the agricultural year* New York

Brun, J. (1984) 'L'oléiculture antique en Provence d'après les recherches archéologiques récentes' *EMC* 28:249-262

Brunt, P.A. (1966) 'Athenian settlements abroad in the fifth century BC' in Ehrenberg (1966) 71-92

—— (1971) *Italian manpower 225 BC – AD 14* Oxford

Bryer, A. (1986) 'Byzantine agricultural implements: the evidence of mediaeval illustrations of Hesiod's *Works & Days*' *ABSA* 81:45-80

Buckland, P.C. (1981) 'The early dispersal of insect pests of stored products as indicated by the archaeological record' *J. of stored products research* 17:1-12

Buckler, J. (1977) 'Land and money in the Spartan economy: a hypothesis' *Research in economic history* 2:249-279

Buikstra, J.E. & Konigsberg, L.W. (1985) 'Palaeodemography: critiques and controversies' *AMA* 87:316-333

Burch, T.K. (1970) 'Some demographic determinants of average household size' *DEM* 7:61-69

Burdon, J.J. (1987) *Diseases and plant population biology* Cambridge

Burford, A.M. (1960) 'Heavy transport in classical antiquity' *EHR* (1960) 1-18

—— (1969) *The Greek temple builders at Epidauros: a social and economic study of building in the Asklepian sanctuary in the fourth and early third centuries BC* Liverpool

Burford Cooper, A.M. (1977/8) 'The family farm in ancient Greece' *CJ* 73:162-175

Burkert, W. (1983) *Homo Necans: the anthropology of ancient Greek sacrificial ritual and myth* (Engl. transl.) Berkeley

Burkill, I.H. (1937/8) 'The contact of the Portuguese with African food plants which gave words such as 'yam' to European languages' *PLSL* 150:84-95

—— (1951/2) 'Habits of man and the origins of the cultivated plants of the world' *PLSL* 164:12-42

Burley, N. (1979) 'The evolution of concealed ovulation' *AN* 114:835-858

Burnet, M. & White, D.O. (1972) *Natural history of infectious disease* (4th ed.) Cambridge

Buschan, G. (1895) *Vorgeschichtliche Botanik der Cultur- und Nutzpflanzen der alten Welt auf Grund prähistorischer Funde* Breslau

Bush, A.C. (1971) 'Latin kinship extensions: an interpretation of the data' *ETH* 10:409-432

Bushnell, W.R. & Roelfs, A.P. (1984-5) *The cereal rusts* (2 vols) Orlando

Busvine, J.R. (1976) *Insects, hygiene and history* London

Butler, T. (1983) *Plague and other yersinia infections* New York

Butzer, K.W. (1976) *Early hydraulic civilization in Egypt: a study in cultural ecology* Chicago

—— (1982) *Archaeology as human ecology* Cambridge

Byl, S. (1980) *Recherches sur les grands traités biologiques d'Aristote: sources écrites et préjugés* Brussels

Bytinski-Salz, H. (1965) 'Recent findings of hippopotamus in Israel' *Israel J. of zoology* 14:38-48

Cadell, H. (1971) 'Le vocabulaire de l'agriculture d'après les papyrus grecs d'Egypte: problèmes et voies de recherche' *American studies in papyrology* 7:69-75

—— (1973) 'Papyrologica: à propos de *puros* et *sitos*' *CE* 48:329-338

Cain, M. (1982) 'Perspectives on family and fertility in developing countries' *PS* 36:159-175

Calame, C. (1977) *Les choeurs de jeunes filles en Grèce archaïque* (2 vols) Rome

Caldwell, J.C. (1982) *Theory of fertility decline* London

Caldwell, J.C., P. & B. (1987) 'Anthropology and demography: the mutual reinforcement of speculation and research' *CA* 28:25-43

Callen, E.O. (1967) 'The first New World cereal' *AMQ* 32:535-538

Cambiano, G. (1984) 'La Grecia antica era molta popolata? Un dibattito nel XVIII secolo' *Quaderni di storia* 20:3-42

Camp, J. McK. (1979) 'A drought in the late eighth century BC' *HEP* 48:397-411

—— (1982) 'Drought and famine in the fourth century BC' *HEP* suppl. 20:9-17

Campbell, B.M.S. (1983) 'Arable productivity in mediaeval England: some evidence from Norfolk' *JEH* 43:379-404

Candolle, A. de (1884) *Origin of cultivated plants* (Engl. transl.) London

Canfora, L. (1983) 'Il soggetto passivo della polis classica' *OP* 1:33-51

Cann, R.L., Stoneking, M. & Wilson, A.C. (1987) 'Mitochondrial DNA and human evolution' *NAT* 325:31-36

Carefoot, G.L. & Sprott, E.R. (1969) *Famine on the wind: plant diseases and human history* London

Carlier, P. (1984) *La royauté en Grèce avant Alexandre* Strasbourg

Carlson, P.S. (ed.) (1980) *The biology of crop productivity* New York

Carneiro, R. (1967) 'On the relationship between population size and the complexity of social organisation' *SWJA* 23:234-243

—— (1970) 'A theory of the origins of the state' *SCI* 169:733-738

Carnoy, A. (1959) *Dictionnaire étymologique des noms grecs de plantes* Louvain

Carothers, J. & McDonald, W.A. (1979) 'Size and distribution of the population in Late Bronze Age Messenia: some statistical approaches' *JFA* 6:433-454

Carpenter, R. (1966) *Discontinuity in Greek civilization* Cambridge

Carr, D.H. (1971) 'Genetic basis of abortion' *ARG* 5:65-80

Carrick, P. (1985) *Medical ethics in antiquity: philosophical perspectives on abortion and euthanasia* Dordrecht

Carrier, N.H. (1958) 'A note on the estimation of mortality and other population characteristics given deaths by age' *PS* 12:149-163

Carrière, J.C. (1979) *Le carnaval et la politique: une introduction à la comédie grecque suivie d'un choix de fragments* Paris

Carr-Saunders, A.M. (1922) *The population problem: a study in human evolution* Oxford

Carson, R. (1962) *Silent spring* London

Carter, J.C. et al. (1985) 'Population and agriculture: Magna Grecia in the fourth century BC' in C. Malone & S. Stoddart (eds) *Papers in Italian archaeology IV. The Cambridge conference:* Part I *The human landscape* (*BAR* Int. Ser. 243) 281-312 Oxford

Cartledge, P.A. (1975) 'Early Sparta c. 950-650 BC: an archaeological and historical study' (Oxford doctoral thesis)

—— (1976) 'Did Spartan citizens ever practise a manual *tekhnê*?' *LCM* 1:115-119

—— (1977) 'Hoplites and heroes: Sparta's contribution to the technique of ancient warfare' *JHS* 97:11-27

—— (1978) 'Literacy in the Spartan oligarchy' *JHS* 98:25-37

—— (1979) *Sparta and Lakonia: a regional history 1300-362 BC* London

—— (1981a) 'Spartan wives: liberation or licence?' *CQ* 31:84-105

—— (1981b) 'The politics of Spartan paederasty' *PCPS* 207:17-36

—— (1985) 'Rebels & sambos in classical Greece: a comparative view' in Cartledge & Harvey (1985) 16-46

—— (1987) *Agesilaos and the crisis of Sparta* London

—— (forthcoming) 'Fowl play: a curious lawsuit in fifth century Athens (Antiphon frr. 57-59 Thalheim)' in Cartledge, P.A., Millett, P.C. & Todd, S.C. (eds) *NOMOS. Essays in Athenian law, politics and society* (forthcoming)

Cartledge, P.A. & Harvey, F.D. (eds) (1985) *CRUX: essays presented to G.E.M. de Ste. Croix on his 75th birthday* Exeter

Cartledge, P.A. & Spawforth, A.J.S. (1989) *Hellenistic and Roman Sparta: a tale of two cities* London

Cary, M. (1949) *The geographic background of Greek and Roman history* Oxford

Casanova, G. (1984) 'Epidemie e fame nella documentazione greca d'Egitto' *Aegyptus* 64:163-201

Cavers, P.B. & Bough, M.A. (1985) 'Proso millet (*Panicum miliaceum* L.): a crop and a weed' in J. White (ed.) *Studies on plant demography: a Festschrift for John L. Harper* (1985) 143-155 London

Cazes, M.H. (1980) 'Hasard et sélection dans les populations d'effectif limité ' *POP* 35:417-435

Cazes, M.H. & Bonné-Tamir, B. (1984) 'Genetic evolution of the Samaritans' *JBS* 16:177-187

Chadwick, J. (1976) *The Mycenaean world* Cambridge

Chadwick, N. (1978) *The Celts* Harmondsworth

Chambers, F.M. (1989) 'The evidence for early rye cultivation in north west Europe' in A. Milles, D. Williams & N. Gardner (eds) *The beginnings of agriculture* (1989) 165-175 (*BAR* Int. Ser. 496) Oxford

Chantraine, P. (1956) *Etudes sur le vocabulaire grec* Paris

—— (1968) & (1980) *Dictionnaire étymologique de la langue grecque* (2 vols) Paris

Chatterton, B.A. & L. (1985) 'A hypothetical answer to the decline of the granary of Rome.' *LS* 16:95-99

Chayanov, A.V. (1966) *The theory of the peasant economy* (Engl. transl.) Homewood

Cheetham, N. (1981) *Mediaeval Greece* New Haven

Cherry, J.F. (1981) 'Pattern and process in the earliest colonisation of the Mediterranean islands' *Proceedings of the Prehistoric Society* 47:41-68

Chesnais, J.-C. & Hong, L. (1986) 'Mariage et régulation démographique: le cas de Chine' *POP* 41:979-1004

Chevalier, A. (1932) 'Les productions végétales du Sahara' *RBAAT* 12:668-924

—— (1938) 'Le Sahara, centre d'origine des plantes cultivées' in *La vie dans la région désertique nord tropicale de l'ancien monde. Mémoires de la Société de Biogéographie* 6:307-322

—— (1939) 'Les origines et l'évolution de l'agriculture méditerranéenne' *RBAAT* 19:613-662

—— (1944) 'Le dolique de Chine en Afrique' *RBAAT* 24:128-152

—— (1948) 'L'origine de l'olivier cultivé et de ses variations' *RBAAT* 28:1-25

Chirassi, I. (1968) *Elementi di culture precereali nei miti e riti greci* Rome

Chojecki, A.J.S., Bayliss, M.W. & Gale, M.D. (1986) 'Genetic analysis of grain weight in wheat' *HER* 57:93-99

Chorley, G.P.H. (1981) 'The agricultural revolution in northern Europe, 1750-1880: nitrogen, legumes and crop productivity' *JEH* 34:71-93

Chowdhury, K.A. & Buth, G.M. (1971) 'Cotton seeds from the Neolithic in Egyptian Nubia and the origin of Old World cotton' *BJLS* 3:303-312

Cho-yun Hsu (1981) *Han agriculture: the formation of early Chinese agrarian economy (206 BC – 220 AD)* Seattle

Christodoulou, D. (1959) *The evolution of the rural land use pattern in Cyprus* London

Clark, C. (1977) *Population growth and land use* (2nd ed.) London

Clark, C. & Haswell, M. (1970) *The economics of subsistence agriculture* (4th ed.) London

Clark, G.A., Hall, N.R., Armelagos, G.J., Borkan, G.A., Panjabi, M.M. & Wetzel, F.T. (1986) 'Poor growth prior to early childhood: decreased health and life expectancy in the adult' *AJPA* 70:145-160

Clark, J.D. (ed.) (1982) *Cambridge history of Africa* vol. 1 Cambridge

Clark, J.D. & Brandt, S.A. (eds) (1984) *From hunters to farmers: causes and consequences of food production in Africa* Berkeley

Clark, J.D. & Stemmler, A.B.L. (1975) 'Early domesticated sorghum from central Sudan' *NAT* 254:588-591

Cleuziou, S. & Costantini, L. (1980) 'Premiers éléments sur l'agriculture protohistorique de l'Arabie orientale' *PEO* 6:245-251

Cliff, A., Haggett, P., Ord, J.K. & Versey, G.R. (1981) *Spatial diffusion: an historical geography of epidemics in an island community* Cambridge

Clutton-Brock, J. (ed.) (1989) *The walking larder: patterns of domestication, pastoralism, and predation* London

Clutton-Brock, T.H., Albon, S.D. & Guinness, F.E. (1989) 'Fitness costs of gestation and lactation in wild mammals' *NAT* 337:260-262

Coale, A.J. (1957) 'How the age structure of a human population is determined' *CSHS* 22:83-89

—— (1972) *The growth and structure of human populations: a mathematical investigation* Princeton

—— (1974) 'The history of the human population' *SA* 231.3:40-51

—— (1985) 'Fertility in rural China: a reconfirmation of the Barclay assessment' in S.B. Hanley & A.P. Wolf (eds) *Family and population in east Asian history* (1985) 186-195 Stanford

Coale, A.J. & Demeny, P. (1983) *Regional model life tables and stable populations* (2nd ed.) New York

Coale, A.J. & Watkins, S.C. (eds) (1986) *The decline of fertility in Europe* Princeton

Cochrane, S.H. (1975) 'Children as by-products, investment goods and consumer goods: a review of some micro-economic models of fertility' *PS* 29:373-390

Cockburn, A. (1988) *Social behaviour in fluctuating populations* London

Cockburn, T.A. (1963) *The evolution and eradication of infectious diseases* Baltimore

—— (1971) 'Infectious diseases in ancient populations' *CA* 12:45-62

Coffmann, F.A. (ed.) (1961) *Oats and oat improvement* Madison

Cohen, G.M. (1978) *The Seleucid colonies: studies in founding, administration and organisation* (*HIS* Einzel. 30) Wiesbaden

Cohen, L.A. (1987) 'Diet and cancer' *SA* 257.5:42-48

Cohen, M.N., Malpass, R.S. & Klein, H.G. (eds) (1980) *Biosocial mechanisms of population regulation* New Haven

COHMAP members (1988) 'Major climatic changes of the last 18,000 years: observations and model simulations' *SCI* 241:1043-1052

Cole, S.G. (1984) 'The social function of rituals of maturation: the Koureion and the Arkteia' *ZPE* 55:233-244

Coleman, D. (1986) 'Population regulation: a long-range view' in D. Coleman & R. Schofield (eds) *The state of population theory: forward from Malthus* (1986) 14-42 Oxford

Colinvaux, P.A. (1980) *The fates of nations: a biological theory of history* Harmondsworth

—— (1982) 'Towards a theory of history: fitness, niche and clutch of *Homo sapiens*' *JE* 70:393-412

—— (1986) *Ecology* New York

Collier, S. & White, J.P. (1976) 'Get them young? Age and sex inferences on animal domestication in archaeology' *AMQ* 41:96-102

Commager Jr., H.S. (1957) 'Lucretius' interpretation of the plague' *HSCP* 62:105-118

Connell, J.H. & Sousa, W.P. (1983) 'On the evidence needed to judge ecological stability or persistence' *AN* 121:789-824

Connor, W.R. (1988) 'Early Greek warfare as symbolic expression' *Past and present* 119 (May):3-29

Conrad, L.I. (1984) 'The Biblical tradition for the plague of the Philistines' *JAOS* 104:281-287

Contogiorgis, G.D. (1978) *La théorie des révolutions chez Aristote* Paris

Cook, M., Molto, El & Anderson, C. (1989) 'Fluorochrome labelling in Roman period skeletons from Dakhleh oasis, Egypt' *AJPA* 80:137-143

Cooke, W.T. & Holmes, G.K.T. (1984) *Coeliac disease* Edinburgh

Corvisier, J.N. (1980) 'La démographie historique est-elle applicable à l'histoire grecque?' *ADH* (1980) 161-184

—— (1982) 'Une source sur l'Homme de la Grèce du Nord: le corpus hippocratique' *HES* 1:171-186

—— (1985) *Santé et société en Grèce ancienne* Paris

Costantini, L. (1984) 'The beginning of agriculture in the Kacchi plain: the evidence of Mehrgarh' in B. Allchin (ed.) *South Asian archaeology* 1981 (1984) 29-33 Cambridge

Coughanowr, E. (1985) 'The plague in Livy and Thucydides' *AC* 54:152-158

Cowgill, G.L. (1975) 'On causes and consequences of ancient and modern population changes' *AMA* 77:505-525

Cox, G.W. & Atkins, M.D. (1979) *Agricultural ecology: an analysis of world food production systems* San Francisco

Cox, P.R. (1976) *Demography* (5th ed.) Cambridge

Cox, P.R. & Peel, J. (eds) (1972) *Population and pollution* London

Crawford (Thompson), D.J. (1971) *Kerkeosiris* Cambridge

—— (1973a) 'Garlic growing and agricultural specialization in Graeco-Roman Egypt' *CE* 48:350-363

—— (1973b) 'The opium poppy: a study in Ptolemaic agriculture' in Finley (1973) 223-251

—— (1979) 'Food: tradition and change in Hellenistic Egypt' *WA* 11:136-146

Crawford, M.A. (1968) 'Fatty-acid ratios in free-living and domestic animals: possible implications for atheroma' *LAN* 1:1329-1333

Crawfurd, R.H.P. (1914) *Plague and pestilence in literature and art* Oxford

Creed, G.W. (1984) 'Sexual subordination: institutionalised homosexuality and social control in Melanesia' *ETH* 23:157-176

Cremona, M.V. (1982) 'I cereali nelle tavolette in Lineare B di Cnosso' *SMEA* 23:73-82

Critopoulos, P. (1956) 'Perpetuation of the brown rust of barley in Attica' *MYC* 48:596-600

Crivelli, E. (1930) 'L'uso agricolo dei nitrati e dei fosfati minerali nell'antichità classica' *Historia* 4:726-741

Crosby Jr., A.W. (1972) *The Columbian exchange: biological and cultural consequences of 1492* Westport

—— (1986) *Ecological imperialism: the biological expansion of Europe 900-1900* Cambridge

Crouwel, J.H. (1981) *Chariots and other means of land transport in Bronze Age Greece* Amsterdam

Crumley, C.L. (1987) 'Historical ecology' in C.L. Crumley & W. Marquandt (eds) *Regional dynamics: Burgundian landscapes in historical perspective* (1987) 237-264 San Diego

Cumston, C.G. (1903) 'The plague of Athens' *Boston Medical and Surgical Journal* 149:449-455

Cushing, J.M. (1986) 'Oscillatory population growth in periodic environments' *TPB* 30:289-308

Cutler, W.B., Schliedt, W.M., Friedmann, E., Preti, G. & Stine, R. (1987) 'Lunar influences on the reproductive cycle in women' *HB* 59:959-972

Dahl, G. (1979) 'Ecology and equality: the Boran case' in *Pastoral production and society* (conference proceedings) 261-281 Cambridge

Daniels, D. (1983) 'The evolution of concealed ovulation and self-deception' *ES* 4:69-87

Dansgaard, W., White, J.W.C. & Johnsen, S.J. (1989) 'The abrupt termination of the Younger Dryas climate event' *NAT* 339:532-534

Dantuma, G., Kittlitz, E. von, Frauen, M. & Bond, D.A. (1983) 'Yield, yield stability and measurements of morphological and phenological characters of faba bean (*Vicia faba* L.) varieties grown in a wide range of environments in western Europe' *ZPZ* 90:85-105

Darby, M.J., Ghalioungui, P. & Grivetti, L. (1977) *Food: the gift of Osiris* (2 vols) London

Darwin, C. (1875) *The variation of plants and animals under domestication* (2nd ed. 2 vols) London

—— (1901) *The descent of man and selection in relation to sex* (new edition) London

—— (1968) *The origin of species by means of natural selection* (ed. J.W. Burrows) Harmondsworth

Dasen, V. (1988) 'Dwarfism in Egypt and classical antiquity: iconography and medical history' *MH* 32:253-276

Daube, D. (1977) *The duty of procreation* Edinburgh

Davidson, D.A. (1981) 'Erosion in Greece in the 1st and 2nd millennia BC' in D.A. Davidson, R. Cullingford & J. Lewin (eds) *Timescales in geomorphology* (1981) 143-158 Chichester

Davidson, J.L. & Christian, K.R. (1984) 'Flowering in wheat' in C.J. Pearson (ed.) *Control of crop productivity* (1984) 111-126 Sydney

Davies, J.K. (1971) *Athenian propertied families 600-300 BC* Oxford

—— (1977/8) 'Athenian citizenship: the descent group and the alternatives' *CJ* 73:105-121

—— (1981) *Wealth and the power of wealth in classical Athens* New York

Davies, M. & Kathirithamby, J. (1986) *Greek insects* London

Davies, N.T. & Nightingale, R. (1975) 'The effects of phytate on intestinal absorption and secretion of zinc, and whole body retention of Zn, copper, iron, and manganese in rats' *British J. of nutrition* 34:243-258

Davis, D.E. (1986) 'Regulation of human population in northern France and adjacent lands in the Middle Ages' *HE* 14:246-267

Davis, E.M. (1981) 'Palaeoecological studies at Stobi' in B. Aleksova & J. Wiseman (eds) *Studies in the antiquities of Stobi* vol. 3 (1981) 87-94 Belgrade

Davis, J.H.R. (1973) *Land and family in Pisticci* London

Davis, M.B. (1986) 'Climatic instability, time lags, and community disequilibrium' in J. Diamond & T.J. Case (eds) *Community ecology* (1986) 269-284 New York

Davis, P.H. (ed.) (1985) *Flora of Turkey and the east Aegean islands* vol. 9 Edinburgh

Davis, P.H., Harper, P.C. & Hedge, I.C. (eds) (1971) *Plant life of south-west Asia* Edinburgh

Davis, R.H.C. (1989) *The mediaeval warhorse: origin, development and redevelopment* London

Davis, S.J.M. (1981) 'The effects of temperature change and domestication on the body size of Late Pleistocene to Holocene mammals of Israel' *PB* 7:101-114

Davis, S.J.M. & Valla, F.R. (1978) 'Evidence for domestication of the dog 12,000 years ago in the Natufian of Israel' *NAT* 276:608-610

Deevey, E.S. (1958) 'The equilibrium population' in R.G. Francis (ed.) *The population ahead* (1958) 64-86 Minneapolis

—— (1960) 'The human population' *SA* 203.3:195-204

D'Egidio, M.G. et al. (1979) 'Proteines totales et composition protéïque de semoules de blés durs italiens: correlations avec la qualité des pâtes alimentaires' *Qualitas plantarum: plant foods for human nutrition* 14:333-348

Delbrück, H. (1913) *Numbers in history: how the Greeks defeated the Persians ...* London

Delcourt, M. (1938) *Stérilités mystérieuses et naissances maléfiques dans l'antiquité classique* Liège

Delia, D. (1988) 'The population of Roman Alexandria' *TAPA* 118:275-292

Demont, P. (1983) 'Notes sur la récit de la pestilence athénienne chez Thucydide et sur ses rapports avec la médecine grecque de l'époque classique' in F. Lasserre & P. Mudry (eds) *Formes de pensée dans la collection Hippocratique: Actes du IVème Colloque Int. Hippocratique* (1983) 341-353 Geneva

—— (1988) 'Hérodote et les pestilences' *Revue de philologie* 62:7-13

Dennell, R. (1973) 'The phylogenesis of *Triticum dicoccum*: a reconsideration' *EB* 27:329-331

—— (1983) *European economic prehistory* London

Dermitzakis, M.D. & Sondaar, P.Y. (1978) 'The importance of fossil mammals in reconstructing palaeogeography with special reference to the Pleistocene Aegean archipelago' *Annales géologiques des Pays Helléniques* 29:808-840

Desanges, J. (1978) *Recherches sur l'activité des Méditerranéens aux confins de l'Afrique* Rome

Despois, J. (1937) 'Rendements en grains du Byzacium il y a 2000 ans et aujourd'hui' in *Mélanges de géographie et d'orientalisme offerts à E.-F. Gautier* (1937) 186-193 Tours

Develin, R. (1985) 'Age qualifications for Athenian magistrates' *ZPE* 61:149-159

Devereux, G. (1968) 'Greek pseudohomosexuality and the 'Greek miracle'' *SO* 42:69-92

—— (1976) *A study of abortion in primitive societies* New York

Devine, A.M. (1985) 'The low birth rate in ancient Rome: a possible contributing factor' *RHM* 128:313-317

Dewar, R.E. (1984) 'Environmental productivity, population regulation, and carrying capacity' *AMA* 86:601-615

Diamond, J.M. (1987) 'Aristotle's theory of mammalian teat number is confirmed' *NAT* 325:200

Dickeman, M. (1975) 'Demographic consequences of infanticide in man' *ARES* 6:107-137

Dickison, S.K. (1973) 'Abortion in antiquity' *ARET* 6:159-166

Diels, H. & Kranz, W. (1956) *Die Fragmente der Vorsokratiker* (6th ed.) Berlin

Dimen, M. & Friedl, L. (eds) (1976) *Regional variation in modern Greece and Cyprus: toward a perspective on the ethnography of Greece* (Annals of the New York Academy of Sciences 268)

Divale, M. & Harris, M. (1976) 'Population, warfare and the male supremacist complex' *AMA* 78:521-538

Dixon, C.W. (1962) *Smallpox* London

Dixon, D.M. (1969) 'A note on cereals in ancient Egypt' in P.J. Ucko & G.W. Dimbleby (eds) *The domestication and exploitation of plants and animals* (1969) 131-142 London

Dodoens, R. (1978) *Histoire des plantes* (reproduction by J.-E. Opsomer of the 1557 French translation by Charles de l'Escluse of the Flemish original) Brussels

Dols, M.W. (1977) *The Black Death in the Middle East* Princeton

Dombrowski, D.A. (1985) *Vegetarianism: the philosophy behind the ethical diet* Wellingborough

Donald, C.M. & Hamblin, J. (1983) 'The convergent evolution of annual seed crops in agriculture' *ADA* 36:97-143

Donlan, W. (1980) *The aristocratic ideal in ancient Greece* Lawrence

Doolittle, R.F. (1989) 'Immunodeficiency viruses: the simian-human connection' *NAT* 339:338-339

Doolittle, R.F., Feng, D.-F., Johnson, M.S. & McClure, M.A. (1989) 'Origins and evolutionary relationships of retroviruses' *Quarterly review of biology* 64:1-30

Dover, K.J. (1978) *Greek homosexuality* London

—— (1988) 'Greek homosexuality and initiation' in *The Greeks and their legacy* (1988) 115-134 Oxford

Dowden, K. (1989) *Death and the maiden: girls' initiation rites in Greek mythology* London

Downey, G. (1961) *A history of Antioch in Syria* Princeton

Dreizehnter, A. (1972) 'Die Bevölkerungszahl im Attika am Ende des 4. Jahrhunderts v.u.Z.' *KL* 54:147-151

Drews, R. (1983) *Basileus: the evidence for kingship in Geometric Greece* New Haven

Driesch, A. von den & Boessneck, J. (1983) 'A Roman cat skeleton from Quseir on the Red Sea coast' *JARS* 10:205-211

Dubos, R. & J. (1953) *The white plague: tuberculosis, man and society* Boston

Dugas, C. (1943) 'L'évolution de la légende de Thésée' *REG* 56:1-24

Dumond, D.E. (1975) 'The limitation of human population: a natural history' *SCI* 187:713-721

Duncan, P. (1983) 'Determinants of the use of habitat by horses in a Mediterranean wetland' *JNE* 52:93-109

Duncan-Jones, R.P. (1982) *The economy of the Roman empire: quantitative studies* (2nd ed.) Cambridge

Dunstone, R.L. & Evans, L.T. (1974) 'Role of changes in cell size in the evolution of wheat' *Australian J. of plant physiology* 1:157-165

Dunstone, R.L., Gifford, R.M. & Evans, L.T. (1973) 'Photosynthetic characteristics of modern and primitive wheat species in relation to ontogeny and adaptation' *AJBS* 26:295-307

Dupâquier, J. (1972) 'De l'animal à l'homme: le mécanisme autorégulateur des populations traditionelles' *Revue de l'Institut de Sociologie* 45:177-211

—— (1973) 'Sur une table (prétendument) florentine d'espérance de vie' *AESC* 28:1066-1070

—— (1979) *La population française aux XVIIe et XVIIIe siècles* Paris

—— (1988) 'L'autorégulation de la population française (XVIe-XVIIIe siècle)' in Dupâquier et al. (1988) vol. 2, pp. 413-436

Dupâquier, J. et al. (1988) *Histoire de la population française* (4 vols) Paris

Dupâquier, J., Fauve-Chamoux, A. & Grebenik, E. (eds) (1983) *Malthus past and present* London

Dupâquier, J., Hélin, E., Laslett, P., Livi-Bacci, M. & Sogner, S. (eds) (1981) *Marriage and remarriage in populations of the past* London

Dupont, F. (1984) 'Pestes d'hier, pestes d'aujourd'hui' *HES* 3:511-524

Durling, R.J. (1986) 'Arresting puberty' *RHM* 129:364

Dyke, B. & McCluer, J.W. (eds) (1973) *Computer simulation in human population studies* New York

Dzierzykray-Rogalski, T. (1980) 'Palaeopathology of the Ptolemaic inhabitants of Dakleh oasis (Egypt)' *JHE* 9:71-74

Eaton, J.W. & Mayer, A.J. (1953) 'The social biology of very high fertility among the Hutterites: the demography of a unique population' *HB* 25:206-264

Ebbell, B. (1967) 'Beiträge zur ältesten Geschichte einiger Infektionskrankheiten' *Skrifter utgitt av det Norske Videnskaps-akademi I, Oslo* II. Hist.-Filos. Klasse Ny Serie 6

Ebert, J. & Luppe, W. (1975) 'Zum neuen Archilochos-Papyrus' *ZPE* 16:223-233

Eby, C.H. & Evjen, H.D. (1962) 'The plague of Athens: a new oar in muddied waters' *JHM* 17:258-263

Edelstein, E.J. & L. (1945) *Asclepius: a collection and interpretation of the testimonies* (2 vols) Baltimore

Edelstein, L. (1979) *Hippocrates: the oath, or, the Hippocratic oath* Chicago

Edelstein, S.J. (1986) *The sickled cell: from myths to molecules* Cambridge, Mass.

Edward, J., Fossey, J.M. & Yaffe, L. (1984) 'Analysis by neutron activation of human bone from the Hellenistic cemetery at Asine, Greece' *JFA* 11:37-46

Egerton, F.N. (1968) 'Ancient sources for animal demography' *Isis* 59:175-189

—— (1973) 'Changing concepts in the balance of nature' *Quarterly review of biology* 48:322-350

—— (1975) 'Aristotle's population biology' *ARET* 8:307-330

Eginitis, D. (1908) 'Le climat de l'Attique' *Annales de géographie* 17:413-432

Ehrenberg, V. (1966) *Ancient society and institutions: studies presented to Victor Ehrenberg on his 75th birthday* Oxford

Ehret, C. (1971) *Southern Nilotic history: linguistic approaches to the study of the past* Evanston

—— (1979) 'On the antiquity of agriculture in Ethiopia' *J. of African history* 20:161-177

Eisenstadt, S.N. (1956) *From generation to generation: age groups and social structure* London

Eliade, M. (1958) *Birth and rebirth: the religious meanings of initiation in human culture* (Engl. transl.) New York

Ell, S.R. (1980) 'Interhuman transmission of mediaeval plague' *BHM* 54:497-510

—— (1984) 'Immunity as a factor in the epidemiology of mediaeval plague' *RID* VI.6:866-879

Elliot, K. & Whelan, J. (eds) (1977) *Health and disease in tribal societies* (Ciba Foundation Symposium) Amsterdam

Ellison, E.R. (1984) 'Methods of food production in Mesopotamia (3000-600 BC)' *JESHO* 27:89-98

Elton, C.S. (1925) 'Plague and the regulation of numbers in wild mammals' *J. of hygiene* 24:138-163

—— (1931) 'The study of epidemic diseases among wild animals' *J. of hygiene* 31:435-456

—— (1935) *Animal ecology* London

—— (1942) *Voles, mice and lemmings: problems in population dynamics* Oxford

—— (1958) *The ecology of invasions by animals and plants* London

Engelbrecht, T. (1916) 'Uber die Entstehung einiger feldmässig angebauter Kulturpflanzen' *Geographische Zeitschrift* 22:328-334

Engels, D.W. (1980) 'The problem of female infanticide in the Graeco-Roman world'

CP 75:112-120

—— (1984) 'The use of historical demography in ancient history' *CQ* 34:386-393

Ericksen, J.A., Ericksen, E.P., Hostetler, J.A. & Huntington, G.E. (1979) 'Fertility patterns and trends among the Old Order Amish' *PS* 33:255-276

Erxleben, E. (1975) 'Das Verhältnis des Handels zum Produktionsaufkommen in Attika im 5. und 4. Jhr. v.u.Z.' *KL* 57 (1975) 365-398

Essex, M. & Kanki, P.J. (1988) 'The origins of the AIDS virus' *SA* 259.4:44-51

Etienne, R. (1973) 'La conscience médicale antique et la vie des enfants' *ADH* (1973) 15-61

—— (1988) 'Gaule romaine' in Dupâquier et al. (1988) vol. 1, pp. 65-117

Evans, A.S. (ed.) (1984) *Viral infections of humans: epidemiology and control* (2nd ed.) New York

Evans, A.S. & Feldman, H.A. (eds) (1982) *Bacterial infections of humans: epidemiology and control* New York

Evans, J.K. (1981) 'Wheat production and its social consequences in the Roman world. I.' *CQ* 31:428-442

Evans, L.T. (1981) 'Yield improvement in wheat: empirical or analytical?' in Evans & Peacock (1981) 203-222

Evans, L.T. & Dunstone, R.L. (1970) 'Some physiological aspects of evolution in wheat' *AJBS* 23:725-741

Evans, L.T., Dunstone, R.L., Rawson, H.M. & Williams, R.F. (1970) 'The phloem of the wheat stem in relation to requirements for assimilate by the ear' *AJBS* 23:743-752

Evans, L.T. & Peacock, W.J. (eds) (1981) *Wheat science: today and tomorrow* Cambridge

Evenari, M. (1984) 'Seed physiology: its history from antiquity to the beginning of the 20th century' *Botanical review* 50:119-142

Evenari, M., Shannon, L. & Tadmor, N. (1982) *The Negev: the challenge of a desert* (2nd ed.) Cambridge, Mass.

Eyben, E. (1972) 'Antiquity's view of puberty' *Latomus* 31:677-697

—— (1980/1) 'Family planning in Graeco-Roman antiquity' *ACS* 11/12:5-82

Feen, R.H. (1983) 'Abortion and exposure in ancient Greece: assessing the status of the fetus and "newborn" from classical sources' in W.B. Bondeson, H.T. Engelhardt, S.F. Spicker & D.H. Winship (eds) *Abortion and the status of the foetus* (1983) 283-300 Dordrecht

Feigenbaum, A. (1956) 'Description of Behçet's syndrome in the Hippocratic Third Book of endemic diseases' *British J. of ophthalmology* 40:355-357

Feil, D.K. (1987) *The evolution of highland Papua New Guinea societies* Cambridge

Feliks, Y. (1963) 'Rice in Rabbinic literature' *Bar-Ilan* 1:177-189 (in Hebrew with Engl. summary on pp. xxxix-xli)

Fenner, F.J. (1983) 'Biological control, as exemplified by smallpox eradication and myxomatosis' *PRSL* B 218:259-285

Fenner, F.J., Henderson, D.A., Arita, I., Jezek, Z. & Ladnyi, I.D. (1988) *Smallpox and its eradication* Geneva

Fenner, F.J. & Ratcliffe, F.N. (1965) *Myxomatosis* Cambridge

Ferguson, W.S. (1918) 'The Zulus and the Spartans: a comparison of their military systems' *Harvard African studies* 2:197-234

—— (1973) *Hellenistic Athens* (reprint) London

Feyel, M. (1942) *Polybe et l'histoire de Béotie* Paris

Fidio, P. de (1982) 'Fiscalità, ridistribuzione, equivalenze: per una discussione sull'economia micenea' *SMEA* 23:83-136

Fiennes, R.N. T-W- (1978) *Zoonoses and the origin and ecology of human disease* London

Figueira, T.J. (1984) 'Mess contributions and subsistence at Sparta' *TAPA* 114:87-109

—— (1986) 'Population patterns in late archaic and classical Sparta' *TAPA* 116:165-213

Fildes, V.A. (1986) *Breasts, bottles and babies: a history of infant feeding* Edinburgh

—— (1988) *Wet nursing: a history from antiquity to the present* Oxford

Fine, J.V.A. (1951) *Horoi: studies in mortgage, real security and land tenure in ancient Athens* (*HEP* suppl. 9) Princeton

Finerty, J.P. (1980) *The population ecology of cycles in small mammals: mathematical theory and biological fact* New Haven

Finkel, D.J. (1982) 'Sexual dimorphism and settlement pattern in Middle Eastern skeletal populations' in Hall (1982) 165-185

Finlay, R. (1981) *Population and metropolis: the demography of London 1580-1650* Cambridge

Finley, M.I. (1952) *Studies in land and credit in ancient Athens 500-200 BC: the Horos inscriptions* (also 1985 reprint with introduction by P.C. Millett) New Brunswick

—— (ed.) (1973) *Problèmes de la terre en Grèce ancienne* Paris

—— (1977) *Aspects of antiquity: discoveries and controversies* (2nd ed.) Harmondsworth

—— (1978) *The world of Odysseus* (2nd ed.) Harmondsworth

—— (1980) *Ancient slavery and modern ideology* London

—— (1981a) 'The elderly in classical antiquity' *GR* 28:156-171 (reprinted in *Ageing and society* 4 (1984) 391-408)

—— (1981b) *Economy and society in ancient Greece* London

—— (1985a) *The ancient economy* (2nd ed.) London

—— (1985b) *Ancient history: evidence and models* London

Fischer, R.A. & Turner, N.C. (1978) 'Plant productivity in arid and semi-arid regions' *ARP* 29:277-317

Fix, A.G. (1979) 'Anthropological genetics of small populations' *ARA* 8:207-230

Fisher, H.M. (1901) 'Was the epidemic that raged in Athens BC 430, genuine bubonic plague?' *New York Medical Journal* 74:639-640

Fisher, R.A. (1958) *The genetical theory of natural selection* (2nd ed.) New York

Flandrin, J.-L. (1984) *Un temps pour embrasser: aux origines de la morale sexuelle occidentale (VIe-XIe siècle)* Paris

Flannery, K.V. (1973) 'The origins of agriculture' *ARA* 2:271-310

Flatz, G. (1987) 'Genetics of lactose tolerance in humans' *AHG* 16:1-77

Flavell, R.B., O'Dell, M. & Hutchinson, J. (1981) 'Nucleotide sequence organisation in plant chromosomes and evidence for sequence translocation during evolution' *CSHS* 45:501-508

Flinn, M.W. (1981) *The European demographic system, 1500-1820* Brighton

Flintoff, E. (1983) 'The Noric cattle plague' *QUCC* 13.1:85-111

Fogel, R.W. & Engerman, S.L. (1974) *Time on the cross: the economics of American Negro slavery* London

Fogg, W.H. (1983) 'Swidden cultivation of foxtail millet by Taiwan aborigines: a cultural analogue of the domestication of *Setaria italica* in China' in Keightley (1983) 95-115

Foley, A. (1988) *The Argolid 800-600 BC: an archaeological survey together with an index of sites from the Neolithic to the Roman period* Göteborg

Foley, R. (1987) *Another unique species: patterns in human evolutionary ecology* Harlow

Follieri, M. (1986) 'Provviste alimentari vegetali in una casa minoica ad Haghia Triada (Creta)' *Annuario della Scuola Archeologica di Atene* 57/58:165-172

Foner, N. (1984) *Ages in conflict: a cross-cultural perspective on inequality between old and young* New York

Font-Creus, B. et al. (1985) 'Mediterranean spotted fever: a cooperative study of 227 cases' *RID* VII.5:635-642

Foraboschi, D. (1984) 'Esiodo e i pascoli arcaici' *Athenaeum* 62:275-280

Forbes, C.A. (1933) *NEOI: a contribution to the study of Greek associations* Middletown

Forbes, H.A. (1976) 'The thrice-ploughed field' *Expedition* 18:5-11

—— (1985) *Strategies and soils: technology, production and environment in Methana* Ann Arbor

Forbes, H.A. & Koster, H.A. (1976) 'Fire, axe and plough: human influence on local plant communities in the southern Argolid' in Dimen & Friedl (1976) 109-126

Forbes, M.H.C. (1977) 'Farming and foraging in prehistoric Greece: the nutritional ecology of wild resource use' in T.K. Fitzgerald (ed.) *Nutrition and anthropology in action* (1977) 46-61 Assen

Ford-Lloyd, B.V. & Williams, J.T. (1975) 'A revision of Beta section Vulgares (Chenopodiaceae), with new light on the origin of the cultivated beets' *BOJL* 71:89-102

Formicola, V., Milanesi, Q. & Scarsini, C. (1987) 'Evidence of spinal tuberculosis at the beginning of the fourth millennium BC from Arene Candide Cave (Liguria, Italy)' *AJPA* 72:1-6

Fornaciari, G. & Mallegni, F. (1987) 'Palaeonutritional studies on skeletal remains of ancient populations from the Mediterranean area: an attempt to interpretation' (*sic*) *Anthropologischer Anzeiger* 45:361-370

Fornaciari, G., Mallegni, F., Bertini, D. & Nuti, V. (1981) 'Cribra orbitalia and elemental bone iron, in the Punics of Carthage' *Ossa* 8:63-77

Forrest, W.G. (1975) 'An Athenian generation gap' *Yale classical studies* 24:37-52

Forster, R. & Ranum, O. (eds) (1975) *Biology of man in history* Baltimore

—— & —— (1979) *Food and drink in history* Baltimore

Fortes, J. Fortes (1984) 'Fitonimia griega I: La identificación de los plantas designadas por los fitónimos griegos; II: Las fuentes del vocabulario fitonímico griego' *Faventia* 6.1:7-29 & 6.2:7-15

Fossey, J.M. (1986) *The ancient topography of eastern Phocis* Chicago

Foucault, A. & Stanley, D.J. (1989) 'Late Quaternary palaeoclimatic oscillations in East Africa recorded by heavy minerals in the Nile delta' *NAT* 339:44-46

Foucault, M. (1970) *The order of things* (Engl. transl.) London

—— (1979) 'Governmentality' *Ideology & consciousness* 6:5-21

—— (1984) *Histoire de la sexualité*: vol. 2 *L'usage des plaisirs* Paris

Fowden, G. (1988) 'City and mountain in late Roman Attica' *JHS* 108:48-59

Fowler, N. (1986) 'The role of competition in plant communities in arid and semi-arid regions' *ARES* 17:89-110

Foxhall, L. & Forbes, H.A. (1982) 'SITOMETREIA: the role of grain as a staple food in classical antiquity' *CH* 12:41-89

Franciosi, G. (1978) & (1980) *Clan gentilizio e strutture monogamiche: contributo alla storia della famiglia romana* (2nd ed. 2 vols) Naples

Francis, C.A. (ed.) (1986) *Multiple cropping systems* New York

Francis, E.D. & Vickers, M. (1985) 'Greek Geometric pottery at Hama and its implications for Near Eastern chronology' *Levant* 17:131-138

Franklin, B. (1751) 'Observations concerning the increase of mankind, peopling of countries, etc., written in Pensilvania, 1751' (*sic*) in A.H. Smyth (ed) *The writings of Benjamin Franklin* (1907) vol. 3, pp. 63-73 New York

Franklin, J. (1986) 'Aristotle on species variation' *Philosophy* 61:245-252

Frayn, J.M. (1979) *Subsistence farming in Roman Italy* Fontwell

—— (1984) *Sheep-rearing and the wool trade in Italy during the Roman period* Liverpool

Freris, A.F. (1986) *The Greek economy in the twentieth century* London

Fretwell, S.D. (1972) *Populations in a seasonal environment* Princeton

Frick, F.S. (1985) *The formation of the state in ancient Israel* Sheffield

Friedl, E. (1962) *Vasilika* New York

Friedman, M.J. (1979) 'Oxidant damage mediates variant red cell resistance to malaria' *NAT* 280:245-247

Friedrich, P. (1970) *Proto-Indo-European trees: the arboreal system of a prehistoric people* Chicago

Frier, B.W. (1982) 'Roman life expectancy: Ulpian's evidence' *HSCP* 86:213-251

—— (1983) 'Roman life expectancy: the Pannonian evidence' *PHO* 37:328-344

Fuà, O. (1979/80) 'La dignità dell'anziano negli scrittori greci fino al IV secolo a.C.' *Atti dell'Istituto Veneto di Scienze, Lettere ed Arti* 138:397-414

Fussell, G.E. (1976) *Farms, farmers and society: systems of food production and population numbers* Lawrence

Fustel de Coulanges, N.D. (1980) *The ancient city* (Engl. transl. with introduction by A. Momigliano & S.C. Humphreys) Baltimore

Gaines, M.S., Vivas, A.M. & Baker, C.L. (1979) 'An experimental analysis of dispersal in fluctuating vole populations: demographic parameters' *ECO* 60:814-828

Galinat, W.C. (1985) 'Domestication and diffusion of maize' in R.I. Ford (ed.) *Prehistoric food production in North America* (1985) 245-278 Ann Arbor

Gallant, T.W. (1985) 'The agronomy, production and utilization of sesame and linseed in the Graeco-Roman world' *BSA* 2:153-158

Galle, O.R. & Gove, W.R. (1978) 'Overcrowding, isolation and human behaviour: explaining the extremes in population distribution' in K.E. Taeuber, L.L. Bumpass & J.A. Sweet (eds) *Social demography* (1978) 95-132 New York

Gallo, L. (1979a) 'Una ignorata testimonianza di Aristofane sul numero convenzionale dei cittadini ateniesi' *AP* ser III 9:505-511

—— (1979b) 'Recenti studi di demografia greca' *AP* ser III 9:1571-1646

—— (1980a) 'L'uso demografico delle liste efebiche e una testimonianza di Demostene' *AP* ser III 10:403-412

—— (1980b) 'Popolosità e scarsità di popolazione: contributo allo studio di un topos' *AP* ser III 10:1233-1270

—— (1983) 'Alimentazione e classi sociali: una nota su orzo e frumento in Grecia' *OP* 2:449-472

—— (1984a) 'Un problema di demografia greca: le donne tra la nascita e la morte' *OP* 3:37-62

—— (1984b) *Alimentazione e demografia della Grecia antica* Salerno

Gallo, R.C. & Montagnier, L. (1988) 'AIDS in 1988' *SA* 259.4:25-32

Galloway, P.R. (1986) 'Long-term fluctuations in climate and population in the pre-industrial era' *PDR* 12:1-24

—— (1988) 'Basic patterns in annual variations in fertility, nuptiality, mortality, and prices in pre-industrial Europe' *PS* 42:275-302

Galton, F. (1892) *Hereditary genius: an inquiry into its laws and consequences* (2nd ed.) London

Gansiniec, S. (1956) 'Cereals in early archaic Greece' *ARC* 8:1-48 (in Polish with Engl. summary)

García, F., Carbonera, P., Aragoncillo, C. & Salcedo, G. (1978) 'Loss of redundant gene expression after polyploidization in plants' *Experientia* 34:332-333

Gardiner, A.H. (1947) *Ancient Egyptian onomastica* vol. 2 Oxford

Garlan, Y. (1982) *Les esclaves dans la Grèce ancienne* (also 1988 Engl. transl.) Paris

Garnsey, P.D.A. (1985) 'Grain for Athens' in Cartledge & Harvey (1985) 62-75

—— (1988) *Famine and food supply in the Graeco-Roman world: responses to risk and crisis* Cambridge

Garnsey, P.D.A. & Whittaker, C.R. (eds) (1983) *Trade and famine in classical antiquity* (*PCPS* suppl. 8) Cambridge

Gasse, F., Lédée, V., Massault, M. & Fontes, J.-C. (1989) 'Water-level fluctuations of Lake Tanganyika in phase with oceanic changes during the last glaciation and deglaciation' *NAT* 342:57-59

Gauthier, Ph. (1973) 'A propos des clérouquies athéniennes du Ve siècle' in Finley (1973) 163-178

—— (1974) ' "Générosité" romaine et "avarice" grecque: sur l'octroi du droit de cité' in *Mélanges d'histoire ancienne offerts à W. Seston* (1974) 207-215 Paris

—— (1981) 'La citoyenneté en Grèce et à Rome: participation et intégration' *Ktema* 6:167-179

—— (1982) 'Les villes athéniennes et un décret pour un commerçant (IG II² 903)' *REG* 95:275-290

—— (1987) 'Nouvelles récoltes et grain nouveau: à propos d'une inscription de Gazôros' *BCH* 111:413-418

Gauthier, R.A. (1951) *Magnanimité, l'idéal de grandeur dans la philosophie païenne et dans la théologie chrétienne* Paris

Gauthier-Pilters, H. & Dagg, A.I. (1981) *The camel: its evolution, ecology, behaviour and relationship to man* Chicago

Gavrielides, N. (1976a) 'The impact of olive growing on the landscape in the Fourni valley' in Dimen & Friedl (1976) 143-157

—— (1976b) 'The cultural ecology of olive growing in the Fourni valley' in Dimen & Friedl (1976) 265-274

Gebeyehou, G. & Knott, D.R. (1983) 'Response of durum wheat cultivars to water stress in the field and greenhouse' *CJPS* 63:801-814

Gehrke, H.-J. (1978) 'Das Verhältnis von Politik und Philosophie im Wirken des Demetrios von Phaleron' *CH* 8:149-194

Gejvall, N.-G. (1969) *Lerna: a preclassical site in the Argolid. I: the fauna* Princeton

Gelb, I.J. (1965) 'The ancient Mesopotamian ration system' *J. of Near Eastern studies* 24:230-243

Gennett, J. (1982) 'Three Holocene pollen records from southern Greece' abstract of paper in *Palynology* 6:282

Genthon, C., Barnola, J.M., Raynaud, D., Lorius, C., Jouzel, J., Barkov, N.I., Korotkevich, Y.S. & Kotlyakov, V.M. (1987) 'Vostok ice core: climatic response to CO_2 and orbital forcing changes over the last climatic cycle' *NAT* 329:414-418

Georgi, L. (1982) 'Pollination ecology of the date palm and fig tree: Herodotus

I.193.4-5' *CP* 77:224-228

Germain, L.R.F. (1969) 'Aspects du droit d'exposition en Grèce' *Revue historique du droit français et étranger* 4th ser. 47:177-197

—— (1975) 'L'exposition des enfants nouveau-nés dans la Grèce ancienne: aspects sociologiques' *Recueils Société J. Bodin* 35:211-246

Gernet, L. (1909) 'L'approvisionnement d'Athènes en blé aux Ve et IVe siècles' in G. Bloch (ed.) *Mélanges d'histoire ancienne* (1909) 269-391 Paris

Gervais, A. (1972) 'A propos de la "Peste d'Athènes": Thucydide et la littérature de l'épidémie' *Bulletin de l'Association Guillaume Budé* 1972:395-429

Getz, W.M. & Pickering, J. (1983) 'Epidemic models: thresholds and population regulation' *AN* 121:892-898

Gilbert, R.I. & Mielke, J.H. (eds) (1985) *The analysis of prehistoric diets* Orlando

Gill, K.S. (1987) *Linseed* Delhi

Gill, N.T., Vear, K.C. & Barnard, D.J. (1980) *Agricultural botany* (3rd ed. 2 vols.) London

Gillen, F.D., Reiner, D.S. & Wang, C.S. (1983) 'Human milk kills parasitic intestinal protozoa' *SCI* 221:1290-1292

Gilliam, J.F. (1961) 'The plague under Marcus Aurelius' *AJP* 82:225-251

Giovannini, A. (1978) *Rome et la circulation monétaire en Grèce au IIe siècle avant J.C.* Basle

Girling, M.A. & Greig, J. (1985) 'A first fossil record for *Scolytus scolytus* (F.) (Elm Bark Beetle): its occurrence in elm decline deposits from London and the implications for Neolithic elm disease' *JARS* 12:347-351

Glacken, C.J. (1967) *Traces on the Rhodian shore: nature and culture in western thought from ancient times to the end of the eighteenth century* Berkeley

Gleick, J. (1988) *Chaos: making a new science* London

Glotz, G. (1968) *La cité grecque* (reprint) Paris

Gobert, E.G. (1955) 'Références historiques des nourritures tunisiennes' *CT* 12:501-542

Godwin, H. (1967) 'The ancient cultivation of hemp' *ATQ* 41:42-48 & 137-138

Golden, M. (1979) 'Demosthenes and the age of majority at Athens' *PHO* 33:25-38

—— (1981) 'Demography and the exposure of girls at Athens' *PHO* 35:316-331

—— (1984) 'Slavery and homosexuality at Athens' *PHO* 38:308-324

—— (1985) '*Pais*, "child" and slave' *AC* 54:91-104

—— (1988) 'Did the ancients care when their children died?' *GR* 35:152-163

Goldman, N., Westoff, C.F. & Paul, L.E. (1987) 'Variations in natural fertility: the effect of lactation and other determinants' *PS* 41:127-146

Gomme, A.W. (1933) *The population of Athens in the fifth and fourth centuries* Oxford

—— (1946) 'The slave population of Athens' *JHS* 66:127-129

—— (1959) 'The population of Athens again' *JHS* 79:61-68

Goodall, E.W. (1934) 'On infectious diseases and epidemiology in the Hippocratic collection' *PRSM* 27:525-534

Goody, J. (1976) *Production and reproduction* Cambridge

—— (1982) *Cooking, cuisine and class* Cambridge

—— (1983) *The development of the family and marriage in Europe* Cambridge

—— (1990) *The Oriental, the Ancient and the Primitive: systems of marriage and the family in the pre-industrial societies of Eurasia* Cambridge

Goody, J. & Tambiah, S.J. (1973) *Bridewealth and dowry* Cambridge

Gordon, C.H. (1967) 'Linguistic continuity from Minoan to Eteocretan' *SMEA* 3:89-92

Gottwald, N.K. (1979) *The tribes of Yahweh: a sociology of the religion of liberated Israel 1250-1050 BCE* London

Gould, S.J. (1989) *Wonderful life: the Burgess Shale and the nature of history* New York

Graf, F. (1979) 'Das Götterbild aus dem Taurerland' *Antike Welt* 10.4:33-41

Graindor, P. (1973) *Athènes sous Hadrien* (reprint) New York

Gras, M. (1985) *Trafics tyrrhéniens archaïques* Rome

Graunt, J. (1662) *Natural and political observations made upon the bills of mortality* (ed. W.F. Willcox 1939) Baltimore

Gray, R.H. (1974) 'The decline of mortality in Ceylon and the demographic effects of malaria control' *PS* 28:205-229

—— (1979) 'Biological factors other than nutrition and lactation which may influence natural fertility: a review' in Leridon & Menken (1979) 217-251

Greece (1944) (Geographical Handbook. Naval Intelligence. 3 vols)

Greek agriculture on accession: situation and outlook (1981) (*Agra Europa* ser. no. 9)

Grégoire, H., Goossens, R. & Mathieu, M. (1949) *Asklèpios, Apollon Smintheus et Rudra: études sur le dieu à taupe et le dieu au rat dans la Grèce et dans l'Inde* Brussels

Gregory, P.J., Shepherd, K.D. & Cooper, P.J. (1984) 'Effects of fertiliser on root growth and water use of barley in northern Syria' *JAGS* 103:429-438

Greig, J.R.A. (1983) 'Plant foods in the past: a review of the evidence from northern Europe' *J. of plant foods* 5:179-214

Greig, J.R.A. & Turner, J. (1974) 'Some pollen diagrams from Greece and their archaeological significance' *JARS* 1:177-194

Gressitt, J.L. (ed.) (1982) *Biogeography and ecology of New Guinea* (2 vols) The Hague

Greuter, W. (1979) 'The origins and evolution of island floras as exemplified by the Aegean archipelago' in D. Bramwell (ed.) *Plants and islands* (1979) 87-106 London

Gribbin, J. & M. (1990) *Children of the ice: climate and human origins* Oxford

Grierson, P. (1959) 'Commerce in the Dark Ages: a critique of the evidence' *Transactions of the Royal Historical Society* 5th ser. 9:123-140

Grigg, D.B. (1974) *The agricultural systems of the world* Cambridge

—— (1980) *Population growth and agrarian change: an historical perspective* Cambridge

—— (1982) *The dynamics of agricultural change: the historical experience* London

Grimm, J. (1965) *Die literarische Darstellung der Pest in der Antike und in der Romania* Munich

Grmek, M.D. (1958) *On ageing and old age: basic problems and historic aspects of gerontology* (*Monographiae Biologicae* 5.2) The Hague

—— (1963) 'Géographie médicale et histoire des civilisations' *AESC* 18:1071-1097

—— (1969) 'Maladies et morts: préliminaires d'une étude historique des maladies' *AESC* 24:1473-1483

—— (1979) 'Les ruses de guerre biologiques dans l'antiquité' *REG* 92:141-163

—— (1983) *Les maladies à l'aube de la civilisation occidentale: recherches sur la réalité pathologique dans le monde grec* Paris

—— (1984) 'Les vicissitudes des notions d'infection, de contagion et de germe dans la médecine antique' *Mémoires du Centre Jean Palerne* 5:53-70

Grove, J.M. (1988) *The Little Ice Age* London

Groves, C.P. (1989) 'Feral mammals of the Mediterranean islands: documents of early domestication' in J. Clutton-Brock (1989) 46-58

Guinis, S.C. (1976) 'New evidence on the stability of the Greek climate in historical times' *PAA* 51:323-329 (in modern Greek)

Guiraud, P. (1893) *La propriété foncière en Grèce jusqu'à la conquête romaine* Paris

Gunda, B. (1983) 'Cultural ecology of old cultivated plants in the Carpathian area' *Ethnologia Europaea* 13:145-179

Gwatkin, D. & Brandel, S. (1982) 'Life expectancy and population growth in the Third World' *SA* 246.5:33-41

Gwynn, A. (1918) 'The character of Greek colonization' *JHS* 38:88-123

Gwynne, M.D. (1975) 'The origin and spread of some domestic food plants of Eastern Africa' in N. Chittick & R.I. Rotberg (eds) *East Africa and the Orient: cultural syntheses in pre-colonial times* (1975) 248-271 New York

Hackett, L.W. (1937) *Malaria in Europe: an ecological study* London

—— (1949) 'Conspectus of malaria incidence in northern Europe, the Mediterranean region and the Near East' in M.F. Boyd (ed.) *Malariology* (1949) vol. 2, pp. 788-799 Philadelphia

Hadjichristodoulou, A. (1982) 'The effects of annual precipitation and its distribution on grain yield of dryland cereals' *JAGS* 99:261-270

—— (1987) 'The effects of optimum heading date and its stability on yield and consistency of barley and durum wheat in dry areas' *JAGS* 108:599-608

Hadjimarkos, D.I. & Bonhorst, C.W. (1962) 'Fluoride- and selenium-levels in contemporary and ancient Greek teeth in relation to dental caries' *NAT* 193:177-178

Hagelberg, E., Sykes, B. & Hedges, R. (1989) 'Ancient bone DNA amplified' *NAT* 342:485

Hagen, K.S. (1966) 'Dependence of the olive fly, *Dacus oleae*, larvae on symbiosis with *Pseudomonas savastanoi* for the utilization of olive' *NAT* 209:423-424

Hajnal, J. (1965) 'European marriage patterns in perspective' in D.V. Glass & D.E.C. Eversley (eds) *Population in history: essays in historical demography* (1965) 101-143 London

Hajnalová, E. (1978) 'Funde von Triticum-Resten aus einer hallstattzeitlichen Getreidespeichergrube in Bratislava-Devín/CSSR' *BDBG* 91:85-96

Hall, A. (1985) 'Nutritional aspects of parasitic infection' *PFNS* 9:227-256

Hall, A.E., Cannell, G.H. & Lawton, H.W. (eds) (1979) *Agriculture in semi-arid environments* Berlin

Hall, R.L. (ed.) (1982) *Sexual dimorphism in Homo sapiens: a question of size* New York

Hallock, R.T. (ed.) (1969) *Persepolis fortification tablets* Chicago

Halloran, G.M. (1975) 'Genetic analysis of yield in wheat' *ZPZ* 74:298-321

—— (1976) 'Genetic analysis of hexaploid wheat, *Triticum aestivum*, using intervarietal chromosome substitution lines: protein content and grain weight' *EUP* 25:65-71

Hallpike, C.R. (1986) *The principles of social evolution* Oxford

Halstead, P.L.J. (1981) 'Counting sheep in Neolithic and Bronze Age Greece' in Hodder et al. (1981) 307-339

—— (1984) 'Strategies for survival: an ecological approach to social and economic change in the early farming communities of Thessaly, N. Greece' (Cambridge PhD)

—— (1987) 'Traditional and ancient rural economy in Mediterranan Europe: plus ça change?' *JHS* 107:77-87

Halstead, P.L.J. & Jones, G.E.M. (1980a) 'Bio-archaeological remains from Assiros Toumba' *ABSA* 75:265-267

—— & —— (1980b) 'Early Neolithic economy in Thessaly: some evidence from Prodromos' *ANT* 1:93-117

—— & —— (1989) 'Agrarian ecology in the Greek islands: time stress, scale and risk' *JHS* 109:41-55

Hamilton, A.C. (1982) *Environmental history of East Africa: a study of the Quaternary* London

Hammell, E.A., McDaniel, C.K. & Wachter, K.W. (1979) 'Demographic consequences of incest tabus: a microsimulation analysis' *SCI* 205:972-977

Hammond, N.G.L. & Walbank, F.W. (1988) *A history of Macedonia* vol. 3 Oxford

Hanelt, P. (1986) 'Pathways of domestication with regard to crop types (grain legumes, vegetables)' in Barigozzi (1986) 179-199

Hansen, J.M. (1978) 'The earliest seed remains from Greece: Palaeolithic through Neolithic at Franchthi Cave' *BDBG* 91:39-46

—— (1985) 'Palaeoethnobotany in Greece: past, present and future' in Wilkie & Coulson (1985) 171-181

—— (1988) 'Agriculture in the prehistoric Aegean: data versus speculation' *AJA* 92:39-52

Hansen, J.M. & Renfrew, J.M. (1978) 'Palaeolithic-Neolithic seed remains at Franchthi cave, Greece' *NAT* 271:349-352

Hansen, M.H. (1985) *Demography and democracy* Herning

—— (1988) *Three studies in Athenian demography* Copenhagen

Hanson, V.D. (1981) *Warfare and agriculture in ancient Greece* Pisa

Hare, R. (1967) 'The antiquity of diseases caused by bacteria and viruses, a review of the problem from a bacteriologist's point of view' in Brothwell & Sandison (1967) 115-131

Harlan, J.R. (1967) 'A wild wheat harvest in Turkey' *Archaeology* 20:197-201

—— (1969) 'Ethiopia: a centre of diversity' *EB* 23:309-314

—— (1971) 'On the origin of barley: a second look' in R.A. Nilan (ed.) *Barley genetics II* (1971) 45-50 Washington

—— (1975) *Crops and man* Madison

—— (1976) 'Diseases as a factor in plant evolution' *Annual review of plant phytopathology* 14:31-51

—— (1981) 'The early history of wheat: earliest traces to the sack of Rome' in Evans & Peacock (1981) 1-15

Harlan, J.R. & Wet, J.M.J. de (1973) 'On the quality of evidence for origin and dispersal of cultivated plants' *CA* 14:51-62

—— & —— (1975) 'Weeds and domesticates: evolution in the man-made habitat' *EB* 29:99-107

Harlan, J.R., Wet, J.M.J. de & Stemmler, A.B.L. (eds) (1976) *Origins of African plant domestication* The Hague

Harper, J.L. (1977) *Population biology of plants* London

Harper, J.L., Lovell, P.H. & Moore, J.G. (1970) 'The shapes and sizes of seeds' *ARES* 1:327-356

Harper, R.M.J. (1975) *Evolutionary origins of disease* Barnstaple

Harrell, B.B. (1981) 'Lactation and menstruation in cultural perspective' *AMA* 83:796-823

Harris, D.R. & Hillman, G.C. (eds) (1989) *Foraging and farming: the evolution of plant exploitation* London

Harris, M. & Ross, E.B. (1987) *Death, sex and fertility: population regulation in the preindustrial and developing countries* New York

Harris, W.V. (1982) 'The theoretical possibility of extensive infanticide in the Graeco-Roman world' *CQ* 32:114-116

Harrison, A.R.W. (1968) *The law of Athens*: vol. 1 *The family and property* Oxford

Harrison, G.A. 'Seasonality and human population biology' in I. de Garine & G.A. Harrison (eds) *Coping with uncertainty in food supply* (1988) 26-31 Oxford

Hart, G.D. (1980) 'Ancient diseases of the blood' in M.M. Wintrobe (ed.) *Blood, pure and eloquent: a story of discovery, of people and of ideas* (1980) 33-55 New York

Hartmann, H.T. & Bougas, P.G. (1970) 'Olive production in Greece' *EB* 24:443-457

Hartog, F. (1980) *Le miroir d'Hérodote: essai sur la représentation de l'autre* Paris

Hasebroek, J. (1965) *Trade and politics in ancient Greece* (reprint of Engl. transl.; German original 1928) London

Hassan, F.A. (1981) *Demographic archaeology* New York

Hastings, R.C. (ed.) (1985) *Leprosy* Edinburgh

Hastorf, C.A. & Deniro, M.J. (1985) 'Reconstruction of prehistoric plant production and cooking practices by a new isotopic method' *NAT* 315:489-491

Hatch, M.H. (1938) 'Theophrastos of Eresos as an economic entomologist' *J. of the New York Entomological Society* 46:223-227

Haudricourt, A.G. (1939) 'De l'origine de quelques céréales' *Annales d'histoire sociale* 1:180-182

Haudricourt, A.G. & Hédrin, L. (1943) *L'homme et les plantes cultivées* Paris

Haviland, W. (1967) 'Stature at Tikal: implications for ancient Maya demography and social organisation' *AMQ* 32:316-325

Hawkes, J.G. (1983) *The diversity of crop plants* Cambridge, Mass.

Hawley, A.H. (1986) *Human ecology: a theoretical essay* Chicago

Hebblethwaite, P.D. (ed.) (1983) *The faba bean (Vicia faba L.)* London

Heer, D. & Smith, D.O. (1968) 'Mortality level, desired family size and population increase' *DEM* 5:104-121

Heer, O. (1865) *Die Pflanzen der Pfahlbauten* Zurich

—— (1878) 'Abstract of the "Plants of the lake dwellings" ' in F. Keller (ed.) *The lake dwellings of Switzerland and other parts of Europe* (2nd ed. 1878) vol. 1, pp. 513-536 (Engl. transl.) London

Hehn, V. (1976) *Cultivated plants and domesticated animals: historico-linguistic studies* (ed. J.P. Mallory, Engl. transl.) Amsterdam

Helbaek, H. (1955) 'Ancient Egyptian wheats' *Proceedings of the Prehistoric Society* 2:93-95

—— (1959a) 'Domestication of food plants in the Old World' *SCI* 130:365-372

—— (1959b) 'Notes on the evolution and history of Linum' *Kuml. Ärbog for Jysk Arkaeologisk Selskab* (1959) 103-129

—— (1960) 'The ecological effects of irrigation in ancient Mesopotamia' *Iraq* 22:186-196

—— (1961) 'Late Bronze Age and Byzantine crops at Beycesultan in Anatolia' *AS* 11:77-97

—— (1962) 'Late Cypriot vegetable diet at Apliki' *Opuscula Atheniensia* 4:171-186

—— (1964) 'The Isca grain, a Roman plant introduction to Britain' *New phytologist* 63:158-164

—— (1971) 'The origin and migration of rye, *Secale cereale*: a palaeoethnobotanical study' in P.H. Davis et al. (1971) 265-280

Heligman, L. (1983) 'Patterns of sex differentials in mortality in less developed countries' in Lopez & Ruzicka (1983) 7-32

Helsel, D.B. (1985) 'Grain yield improvement through biomass selection in oats (*Avena sativa* L.)' *ZPZ* 94:298-306

Hémardinquer, J.J. (1973) 'Les débuts du maïs en Méditerranée (premier aperçu)' in *Mélanges ... F. Braudel* (1973) vol. 1, pp. 227-244 Toulouse

Hemmer, H., Kadel, B. & Kadel, K. (1981) 'The Balearic toad (*Bufo viridis balearicus* (Boettger, 1881)), human bronze age culture, and Mediterranean biogeography' *Amphibia-Reptilia* 2:217-230

Hendry, G.W. (1923) 'Alfalfa in history' *JASA* 15:171-176

Hengeveld, R. (1989) *Dynamics of biological invasions* London

Henige, D.P. (1974) *The chronology of oral tradition: quest for a chimaera* Oxford

—— (1982) *Oral historiography* London

Henry, L. (1961) 'Some data on natural fertility' *Eugenics quarterly* 8.2:81-91

—— (1976) *Population: analysis and models* London

Henry, L. & Vincent, P. (1947) 'Rythme maximum d'accroissement d'une population' *POP* 2:663-680

Herdt, G.H. (ed.) (1982) *Rituals of manhood: male initiation in Papua New Guinea* Berkeley

—— (ed.) (1984) *Ritualised homosexuality in Melanesia* Berkeley

Herlihy, D. (1975) 'Life expectancies of women in mediaeval society' in R.T. Morewedge (ed.) *The role of woman in the Middle Ages* (1975) 1-22 Albany

—— (1985) *Mediaeval households* Cambridge, Mass.

Herman, G. (1987) *Ritualised friendship and the Greek city* Cambridge

Herrmann, B. & Bergfelder, T. (1978) 'Über den diagnostischen Wert des sogenannten Geburtstrauma am Schambein bei der Identifikation' *Zeitschrift für Rechtsmedizin* 81:73-78

Heurtley, W.A. (1939) *Prehistoric Macedonia* Cambridge

Heywood, V.H. (1983) 'Relationships and evolution in the *Daucus carota* complex' *IJB* 32:51-65

Hillmann, G.C. (1978) 'On the origins of domestic rye, *Secale cereale*: the finds from aceramic Can Hasan III in Turkey' *AS* 28:157-174

—— (1981) 'Reconstructing crop husbandry practices from charred remains of crops' in Mercer (1981) 123-162

Hillmann, G.C. et al. (1985) 'The use of electron spin resonance spectroscopy to determine the thermal histories of cereal grains' *JARS* 12:49-58

Himes, N.E. (1936) *Medical history of contraception* New York

Hinman, C.W. (1986) 'Potential new crops' *SA* 255.1:24-29

Hirst, L.F. (1953) *The conquest of plague: a study of the evolution of epidemiology* Oxford

Hjelmqvist, H. (1973) 'Some economic plants from ancient Cyprus' in V. Karageorghis *Excavations in the necropolis of Salamis III* (text) (1973) 231-255 Nicosia

—— (1976) 'Grain impressions from Hala Sultan Tekke, Cyprus' *SMA* 45.1:120-122

—— (1977) 'Some economic plants from the Greek Bronze Age' in P. Åstrom *The cuirass tomb from Dendra and other finds* (1977) 123-135 Göteborg

—— (1979) 'Some economic plants and weeds from the Bronze Age of Cyprus' *SMA* 45.5:110-133

Hobcraft, J.N., McDonald, J.W. & Rutstein, S.O. (1985) 'Demographic determinants of infant and early child mortality: a comparative analysis' *PS* 39:363-385

Hodder, I. et al. (eds) (1981) *Pattern of the past: studies in honour of David Clarke* Cambridge

Hodkinson, S.J. (1983) 'Social order and the conflict of values in classical Sparta' *CH* 13:239-281

—— (1986) 'Land tenure and inheritance in classical Sparta' *CQ* 36:378-406

—— (1988) 'Animal husbandry in the Greek polis' in Whittaker (1988) 35-74

—— (1989) 'Inheritance, marriage and demography: perspectives upon the success and decline of classical Sparta' in A. Powell (ed.) *Classical Sparta: techniques behind her success* (1989) 79-121 London

Hodkinson, S.J. & H. (1981) 'Mantineia and the Mantinike: settlement and society in a Greek polis' *ABSA* 76:239-296

Hoeppli, R.J. (1959) *Parasites and parasitic infections in early medicine and science* Singapore

—— (1971) 'Early navigation and the spread of parasitic diseases' *Episteme* 5:201-217

Hoffmann, W.G. (1965) *Das Wachstum der Deutschen Wirtschaft seit der Mitte des 19. Jahrhunderts* Berlin

Hoffner, H.A. (1974) *Alimenta Hethaeorum: food production in Hittite Asia Minor* New Haven

Högberg, V., Iregren, E., Siven, C.-H. & Diener, L. (1987) 'Maternal deaths in mediaeval Sweden: an osteological and life table analysis' *JBS* 19:495-503

Höhn, C. & Mackensen, R. (eds) (1982) *Determinants of fertility trends: theories re-examined* Liège

Holden, C. (1987) 'Why do women live longer than men?' *SCI* 238:158-160

Holladay, A.J. (1987) 'Thucydides and the recognition of contagion: a reply' *Maia* 39:95-96

Holladay, A.J. & Poole, J.C.F. (1979) 'Thucydides and the plague of Athens' *CQ* 29:282-300

—— & —— (1982) 'Thucydides and the plague: a footnote' *CQ* 32:235-236

—— & —— (1984) 'Thucydides and the plague: a further footnote' *CQ* 34:483-485

Hollingsworth, T.H. (1968) 'The importance of the quality of the data in historical demography' *DAE* 97:415-432

Hombert, M. & Préaux, Cl. (1945) 'Note sur la durée de la vie dans l'Egypte gréco-romaine' *CE* 39/40:139-146

Hondelmann, W. (1984) 'The lupin: ancient and modern crop plant' *Theoretical and applied genetics* 68:1-9

Hopf, M. (1955) 'Formveränderungen von Getreidekörnern beim Verkohlen' *BDBG* 68:191-193

—— (1961) 'Pflanzenfunde aus Lerna/Argolis' *DZ* 31:239-247

—— (1978) 'Frühe Kulturpflanzen in Südeuropa' *BDBG* 91:31-38

—— (1986) 'Archaeological evidence of the spread and use of some members of the Leguminosae family' in Barigozzi (1986) 35-60

Hopkins, D.C. (1985) *The highlands of Canaan: agricultural life in the Early Iron Age* Sheffield

Hopkins, D.R. (1983) *Princes and peasants: smallpox in history* Chicago

Hornblower, J. (1981) *Hieronymus of Cardia* Oxford

Horowitz, A. & Gat, J.R. (1984) 'Floral and isotopic indications for possible summer rains in Israel during wetter times' *Pollen et Spores* 26:61-68

Horowitz, M.C. (1976) 'Aristotle and women' *JHB* 9:183-213

Houérou, H.N. Le (1981) 'Impact of man and his animals on Mediterranean vegetation' in F. di Castri, D.W. Goodall & R.L. Specht (eds) *Mediterranean-type shrublands* (1981) 479-521 Amsterdam

—— (1986) 'The desert and arid zones of northern Africa' in M. Evenari, I. Noy-Meir & D.W. Goodall (eds) *Hot deserts and arid shrublands*, B (1986) 101-147 Amsterdam

Howard, D.H. (1963) 'Friedrich Loeffler and the Thessalian field mouse plague of 1892' *JHM* 18:272-281

Howell, N. (1979) *Demography of the Dobe !Kung* New York

—— (1986) 'Demographic anthropology' *ARA* 15:219-246

Howes, F.N. (1950) 'Age old resins of the Mediterranean regions and their uses' *EB* 4:307-316

Hrdy, D.B. (1987) 'Cultural practices relating to the transmission of human immunodeficiency virus in Africa' *RID* IX.6:1109-1119

Hrdy, S.B. (1979) 'Infanticide among animals: a review, classification, and examination of the implications for the reproductive strategy of females' *ES* 1:13-40

Hrozny, Fr. (1914) *Das Getreide im alten Babylonien. I Teil* Vienna

Hubbard, R.N.L.B. (1980) 'Development of agriculture and the Near East: evidence from quantitative studies' *EB* 34:51-67

Hubbert, W.T., McCulloch, W.F. & Schnurrenberger, P.R. (eds) (1975) *Diseases transmitted from animals to man* (6th ed.) Springfield

Huergon, J. (1952) 'D'Apollon Smintheus à P. Decius Mus: la survivance du dieu au rat, *'Sminth-'*, dans le monde étrusco-italique' *Atti del I Congresso Internazionale di Preistoria e di Protostoria Mediterranea* (1952) 483-488 Florence

Hughes, J.D. (1975a) 'Ecology in ancient Greece' *INQ* 18:115-125

—— (1975b) *Ecology in ancient civilizations* Albuquerque

—— (1980) 'Early Greek and Roman environmentalists' in L.J. Bilsky (ed.) *Historical ecology: essays on environment and social change* (1980) 45-59 Port Washington

—— (1983a) 'Gaia: an ancient view of our planet' *The Ecologist* 13:54-60

—— (1983b) 'How the ancients viewed deforestation' *JFA* 10:437-445

—— (1988) 'Theophrastos as ecologist' in W.W. Fortenbaugh & R.W. Sharples (eds) *Theophrastean studies* vol. 3 (1988) 67-75 New Brunswick

Hughes, J.D. & Thirgood, J.V. (1982) 'Deforestation in ancient Greece and Rome: a cause of collapse' *The Ecologist* 12:196-208

Hulse, J.H. & Spurgeon, D. (1974) 'Triticale' *SA* 231.2:72-80

Hume, D. (1875) *Essays, moral, political and literary* (2 vols, ed. T.H. Green & T.J. Grose) London

Humphreys, S.C. (1983) *The family, women and death* London

Hunter, H. (1952) *The barley crop* London

Huntington, E. (1907) *The pulse of Asia: a journey in central Asia illustrating the geographic basis of history* London

—— (1910) 'The burial of Olympia: a study in climate and history' *Geographical Journal* 36:657-686

Huntley, B. & Birks, H.J.B. (1983) *An atlas of past and present pollen maps for Europe: 0-13,000 years ago* (2 vols) Cambridge

Huntley, B. & Prentice, I.C. (1988) 'July temperatures in Europe from pollen data 6000 years before present' *SCI* 241:687-690

Hutchinson, G.E. et al. (1970) *Ianula: an account of the history and development of the Lago di Monterosi, Latium, Italy* (Trans. Amer. Philos. Soc. vol. 60)

Hutter, H. (1978) *Politics as friendship: the origins of classical notions of politics in the theory and practice of friendship* Waterloo, Ont.

Huxley, A. & Taylor, W. (1989) *Flowers of Greece and the Aegean* London

Huxley, G.L. (1971) 'Crete in Aristotle's Politics' *GRBS* 12:505-515

Ims, R.A. & Stenseth, N.C. (1989) 'Divided the fruitflies fall' *NAT* 342:21-22

Isager, S. (1981/2) 'The marriage pattern in classical Athens: men and women in Isaios' *Classica et mediaevalia* 33:81-96

Isager, S. & Hansen, M.H. (1975) *Aspects of Athenian society in the fourth century BC* (Engl. transl.) Odense

Ishizuka, Y. (1969) 'Engineering for higher yields' in J.D. Eastin et al. (eds) *Physiological aspects of crop yield* (1969) 15-25 Madison

Islam, T.M.T. & Sedgley, R.H. (1981) 'Evidence for a "uniculm effect" in spring wheat (*Triticum aestivum* L.) in a Mediterranean environment' *EUP* 30:277-282

Islamoglu, H. & Faroqhi, S. (1979) 'Crop patterns and agricultural production trends in sixteenth century Anatolia' *Review* 2:401-436

Jackes, M.K. (1983) 'Osteological evidence for smallpox: a possible case from seventeenth century Ontario' *AJPA* 60:75-81

Jackson, M. (1985) 'Comparing the Balkan demographic experience, 1860 to 1970' *J. of European economic history* 14:223-272

Jacobsen, T. (1982) *Salinity and irrigation agriculture in antiquity: Diyala basin archaeological report on essential results, 1957-58* Malibu (review by M.J. Geller in *Bulletin of the School of Oriental and African Studies. University of London* 47 (1984) 331-332)

Jacoby, F. (1923-1958) *Die Fragmente der griechischen Historiker* (16 vols) Berlin

Jacomet, S. & Schlichtherle, H. (1984) 'Der kleine Pfahlbauweizen Oswald Herrs – neue Untersuchungen zur Morphologie neolithischer Nacktweizen-"Ähren" ' in van Zeist & Casparie (1984) 153-176

James, P.J., Thorpe, I.J., Kokkinos, N. & Frankish, J.A. (1987) *Studies in ancient chronology I* London

James, S. (1984) *The content of social explanation* Cambridge

James, W.H. (1987) 'The human sex ratio. Part 1: a review of the literature' *HB* 59:721-752

Jameson, M.H. (1976) 'The southern Argolid: the setting for historical and cultural studies' in Dimen & Friedl (1976) 74-91

—— (1977/8) 'Agriculture and slavery in classical Athens' *CJ* 73:122-145

—— (1980) 'Apollo Lykeios in Athens' *Archaiognosia* 1:213-236

—— (1983) 'Famine in the Greek world' in Garnsey & Whittaker (1983) 6-16

Janushevitch, Z.V. (1978) 'Prehistoric food plants in the south-west of the Soviet Union' *BDBG* 91:59-66

—— (1981) 'Die Kulturpflanzen Skythiens' *ZA* 15:87-96

—— (1984) 'The specific composition of wheat finds from ancient agricultural centres in the USSR' in van Zeist & Casparie (1984) 267-276

Janushevitch, Z.V. & Nikolaenko, G.M. (1979) 'Fossil remains of cultivated plants in the ancient Tauric Chersonese' in Körber-Grohne (1979) 115-134

Janushevitch, Z.V., Nikolaenko, G.M. & Kuzminova, N. (1985) 'La viticulture à Chersonèse de Tauride aux IVe-IIe s. av. n. è. d'après les recherches archéologiques et paléoethnobotaniques' *Revue archéologique* (1985) 115-122

Jarcho, S. (1967) 'The longevity of the ancient Greeks' *BNYAM* 43:941-943

—— (1987) 'A history of semitertian fever' *BHM* 61:411-430

Jardé, A. (1925) *Les céréales dans l'antiquité grecque. I. La production* Paris

Jasink, A.M. (1983) 'Le "tavolette dell'olio" di Pilo: nuove proposte d'interpretazione' *QUCC* 15.3:119-145

Jasny, N. (1942) 'Competition among grains in classical antiquity' *AHR* 47:747-764

—— (1944) *The wheats of classical antiquity* Baltimore

—— (1950) 'The daily bread of the ancient Greeks and Romans' *OSI* 9:228-253

Jeanmaire, H. (1913) 'La cryptie lacédémonienne' *REG* 26:121-150

—— (1939) *Couroi et Courètes* Lille

—— (1951) *Dionisos: histoire du culte be Bacchus* Paris

Jennings, P.R. (1976) 'The amplification of agricultural production' *SA* 235.3:180-194

Jerphagon, L. (1981) 'Les mille et un morts des philosophes antiques: essai de typologie' *Revue belge de philologie et d'histoire* 59:17-28

Johansson, S.R. & Horowitz, S. (1986) 'Estimating mortality in skeletal populations: influence of the growth rate on the interpretation of levels and trends during the transition to agriculture' *AJPA* 71:233-250

Johnston, F.E. (1974) 'Control of age at menarche' *HB* 46:159-171

Jolly, C.J. (1970) 'The seed-eaters: a new model of hominid differentiation based on a baboon analogy' *Man* 5:5-26

Jones, A.H.M. (1957) *Athenian democracy* Oxford

Jones, G.E.M. (1981) 'Crop processing at Assiros Toumba: a taphonomic study' *ZA* 15:105-111

—— (1982) 'Cereal and pulse remains from Protogeometric and Geometric Iolkos, Thessaly' *ANT* 3:75-78

—— (1983) 'The use of ethnographic and ecological models in the interpretation of archaeological plant remains: case studies from Greece' (Cambridge PhD)

—— (1984) 'The LM II plant remains' in M.R. Popham et al. *The Minoan unexplored mansion at Knossos.* Text (1984) 303-306 London

—— (1987) 'A statistical approach to the archaeological identification of crop processing' *JARS* 14:311-323

Jones, G.E.M., Wardle, K.A., Halstead, P.L.J. & Wardle, D. (1986) 'Crop storage at Assiros' *SA* 254.3:84-91

Jones, J.E., Sackett, L.H. & Graham, A.J. (1962) 'The Dema House in Attica' *ABSA* 57:75-114

Jones, W.H.S. (1907) *Malaria: a neglected factor in the history of Greece and Rome* Cambridge

—— (1909a) *Malaria and Greek history* Manchester

—— (1909b) 'Dea Febris: a study of malaria in ancient Italy' *Annals of archaeology & anthropology* 2:97-124

—— (1947) *The medical writings of Anonymus Londinensis* Cambridge

Jongman, W. (1988) *The economy and society of Pompeii* Amsterdam

Jutikkala, E. & Kauppinen, M. (1971) 'The structure of mortality during catastrophic years in a pre-industrial society' *PS* 25:283-285

Kashdan, A. (1982) 'Two notes on Byzantine demography of the eleventh and twelfth centuries' *Byzantinische Forschungen* 8:115-122

Katsas, A.G. (1975) 'Starvation disease in Greece' *NEJM* 293:881

Katz, S.H. (1987) 'Fava bean consumption: a case for the co-evolution of genes and culture' in M. Harris & E.B. Ross (eds) *Food and evolution: toward a theory of human food habits* (1987) 133-159 Philadelphia

Kauffmann, M.L. & McFadden, A.D. (1963) 'The influence of seed size on the results of barley trials' *CJPS* 43:51-58

Kayser, B. & Thompson, K. (1964) *Economic and social atlas of Greece* Athens

Keatinge, J.D.H., Dennett, M.D. & Rodgers, J. (1985) 'The influence of precipitation regime on the management of three-course crop rotations in northern Syria' *JAGS* 104:281-287

Keegan, W., Johnson, A. & Earle, T. (1985) 'Carrying capacity and population regulation: a comment on Dewar' *AMA* 87:659-663

Keightley, D.N. (ed.) (1983) *The origins of Chinese civilization* Berkeley

Keller, P.R. & Rupp, D.W. (eds) (1983) *Archaeological survey in the Mediterranean* (*BAR* Int. Ser. 155) Oxford

Kelley, J.O. & Angel, J.L. (1987) 'Life stresses of slavery' *AJPA* 74:187-211

Kelly, R.C. (1976) 'Witchcraft and sexual relations: an exploration in the social and semantic implications of the structure of belief' in P. Brown & G. Buchbinder (eds) *Man and woman in the New Guinea highlands* (1976) 36-53 Washington

Kent, N.L. (1983) *Technology of cereals* (3rd ed.) Oxford

Kerber, E.R. (1964) 'Wheat: reconstitution of the tetraploid component (AABB) of hexaploids' *SCI* 143:253-255

Kerber, E.R. & Rowland, G.G. (1974) 'Origin of the free-threshing character in hexaploid wheat' *CJGC* 16:145-154

Kermack, W.O. & MacKendrick, A.G. (1927) 'A contribution to the mathematical theory of epidemics' *PRSL* A 115:700-721

Kerridge, E. (1967) *The agricultural revolution* New York

Kertzer, D.I. & Keith, J. (eds) (1984) *Age and anthropological theory* Ithaca

Keser, J. (1893/4) 'The plague of Athens' *The medical magazine* 2:911-925

Keyfitz, N. (1971a) 'Changes of birth and death rates and their demographic effects' in *Rapid population growth: consequences and policy implications* (US National Academy of Sciences) (single volume edition) 639-680

—— (1971b) 'On the momentum of population growth' *DEM* 8:71-80

—— (1977) *Introduction to the mathematics of population* (2nd ed.) Reading, Mass.

—— (ed.) (1984) *Population and biology* Liège

Khazanov, A.M. (1984) *Nomads and the outside world* (Engl. transl.) Cambridge

Khush, G.S. (1963) 'Cytogenetic and evolutionary studies in Secale III: cytogenetics of weedy ryes and origin of cultivated rye' *EB* 17:60-71

Kiel, H. (1951) 'The louse in ancient Greece, with comments on the diagnosis of the Athenian plague as recorded by Thucydides' *BHM* 25:305-323

Killen, J.T. (1985) 'The Linear B tablets and the Mycenaean economy' in A. Morpurgo-Davies & Y. Duhoux (eds) *Linear B: a 1984 survey* (1985) 241-305 Louvain

Kingsland, S.E. (1985) *Modelling nature: episodes in the history of population ecology* Chicago

—— (1988) 'Evolution and debates over human progress from Darwin to sociobiology' in M.S. Teitelbaum & J.M. Winter (eds) *Population and resources in Western intellectual traditions* (*PDR* suppl. 14, 1988) 167-198 Cambridge

Kinsey, A.C., Pomeroy, W.B., Martin, C.E. & Gebhard, P.H. (1953) *Sexual behaviour in the human female* Philadelphia

Kiple, K.F. (1984) *The Caribbean slave: a biological history* Cambridge

Kislev, M.E. (1973) 'HITTA and KUSSEMET, notes on their interpretation'

Leshonenu 37.4 (in Hebrew with Engl. summary)

—— (1979/80) '*Triticum parvicoccum* sp. nov., the oldest naked wheat' *IJB* 28:95-107

—— (1980) 'Contenu d'un silo à blé de l'époque du fer ancien' in J. Briend & J.-B. Humbert *Tell Keisan (1971-1976): une cité phénicienne en Galilée* (1980) 361-379 Fribourg

—— (1981) 'The history of evolution of naked wheats' *ZA* 15:57-64

—— (1982) 'Stem rust of wheat 3300 years old found in Israel' *SCI* 216:993-994

—— (1984a) 'Botanical evidence for ancient naked wheats in the Near East' in van Zeist & Casparie (1984) 141-152

—— (1984b) 'Emergence of wheat agriculture' *PEO* 10.2:61-70

—— (1986) 'A barley store of the Bar-Kochba rebels (Roman period)' *IJB* 35:183-196

—— (1989) 'Origins of the cultivation of *Lathyrus sativus* and *L. cicera* (Fabaceae)' *EB* 43:262-270

Klages, K.H.W. (1936) 'Changes in the proportion of seeded and harvested cereal mixtures in abnormal seasons' *JASA* 28:935-940

Klapisch-Zuber, C. (1983) 'Parents de sang, parents de lait: la mise à nourrice à Florence (1300-1530)' *ADH* 1983:33-64

Klein, A.E. (1932) *Child life in Greek art* New York

Klepinger, L.L. (1984) 'Nutritional assessment from bone' *ARA* 13:75-96

Knodel, J. (1977) 'Breast-feeding and population growth' *SCI* 198:1111-1115

Knorzer, K.-H. (1966) 'Uber Funde römischer Importfrüchte in Novaesium (Neuss am Rhein)' *Bonner Jahrbucher* 166:433-443

—— (1978) 'Entwicklung und Ausbreitung des Leindotters (*Camelina sativa* s.l.)' *BDBG* 91:187-195

—— (1981) *Römerzeitliche Pflanzenfunde aus Xanten* Cologne

Knox, B.M.W. (1956) 'The date of the *Oedipus Tyrannus* of Sophokles' *AJP* 67:133-147

Kobert-Rostock, R. (1899) 'Über die Pest des Thucydides' *JAN* 4:240-251 & 289-299

Kobischtschanow, Y.M. (1984) 'Agriculture and economic-cultural types in mediaeval Nubia: on the cultural heritage of Meroe in the Middle Ages' in *Meroitica 7. Meroitistische Forschungen 1980* (1984) 472-482

Kolendo, J. (1960) 'Techniques rurales: la moissonneuse antique en Gaule romaine' *AESC* 15:1099-1114

—— (1980) *L'agricoltura nell'Italia romana* Rome

Kolodny, E.Y. (1974) *La population des îles de la Grèce: essai de géographie insulaire en Méditerranée orientale* (3 vols) Aix-en-Provence

Konzak, C.F. (1977) 'Genetic control, amino acid composition, and processing properties of proteins in wheat' *ADG* 19:407-582

Körber-Grohne, U. (ed.) (1979) *Festschrift Maria Hopf* (*Archaeo-physika* 8) Cologne

—— (1981) 'Pflanzliche Abdrücke in eisenzeitlicher Keramik: Spiegelbild damaliger Nutzpflanzen?' *Fundberichte aus Baden-Württemberg* 6:165-211

Kot, M. & Schaffer, W.M. (1984) 'The effects of seasonality on discrete models of population growth' *TPB* 26:340-360

Kothe, H. (1975) 'Der Hesiodpflug' *PHI* 119:1-26

Kraft, J.C., Aschenbrenner, S.E. & Rapp Jr., G. (1977) 'Palaeogeographic reconstructions of coastal Aegean archaeological sites' *SCI* 195:941-947

Kraft, J.C., Kayan, I. & Erol, O. (1980) 'Geomorphic reconstructions in the environs of ancient Troy' *SCI* 209:776-782

Krenkel, W.A. (1971) 'Erotica 1: Der Abortus in der Antike' *Wissenschaftliche Zeitschrift der Universität Rostock* 20:443-452

Krentos, V.D. & Orphanos, P.I. (1979) 'Nitrogen and phosphate fertilisers for wheat and barley in a semi-arid region' *JAGS* 93:711-717

Kritikos, P.G. & Papadaki, S.P. (1967) 'The history of the poppy and of opium and their expansion in antiquity in the eastern Mediterranean area' *Bulletin on narcotics* 19.3:17-38 & 19.4:5-10

Krochmal, A. (1955) 'Olive growing in Greece' *EB* 9:228-232

Krochmal, A. & Laurentiades, G. (1955) 'Poisonous plants of Greece' *EB* 9:175-189

Kroll, H. (1981) 'Thessalische Kulturpflanzen' *ZA* 15:97-103

—— (1982) 'Kulturpflanzen von Tiryns' *AA* (1982) 467-485

—— (1983) *Kastanas. Ausgrabungen in einem Siedlungshügel der Bronze- und Eisenzeit Makedoniens 1975-1979. Die Pflanzenfunde (Prähistorische Archäologie in Südosteuropa* vol. 2) Berlin

—— (1984a) 'Zum Ackerbau gegen Ender der mykenischen Epoche in der Argolis' *AA* (1984) 211-222

—— (1984b) 'Bronze Age and Iron Age agriculture in Kastanas, Macedonia' in van Zeist & Casparie (1984) 243-246

Kruska, D. (1988) 'Mammalian domestication and its effect on brain structure and behaviour' in H.J. & I. Jerison (eds) *Intelligence and evolutionary biology* (1988) 211-250 Berlin

Krzywicki, L. (1934) *Primitive society and its vital statistics* London

Kuckuck, H. & Peters, R. (1964) 'Experimentelle Untersuchungen zur Entstehung der Kulturweizen. II. Induzierte Mutationen bei *Triticum aestivum ssp. macha* (Dek. et Men.) Mackey und *Triticum dicoccum* Schübl. und ihre phylogenetische Bedeutung' *ZPZ* 51:215-228

Kudlien, F. (1971) 'Galens Urteil über die Thukydideische Pestbeschreibung' *Episteme* 5:132-133

Kuenen-Janssens, L.J. (1941) 'Some notes on the competence of the Athenian woman to conduct a transaction' *MNE* 3rd ser. 9:199-214

Kula, W. (1984) *Les mesures et les hommes* (French transl.) Paris

Kullmann, W. (1984) 'Equality in Aristotle's political thought' in I. Kajanto (ed.) *Equality and inequality of man in ancient thought* (1984) 31-44 Helsinki

Kulshrestha, V.P. (1985) 'History and ethnobotany of wheat in India' *JATBA* 32:61-71

Kuniholm, P.I. & Striker, C.L. (1983) 'Dendrochronological investigations in the Aegean and neighbouring regions, 1972-1982' *JFA* 10:411-420

—— & —— (1987) 'Dendrochronological investigations in the Aegean and neighbouring regions, 1983-1986' *JFA* 14:385-398

Kuper, A. (1982) 'Lineage theory: a critical retrospect' *ARA* 11:71-95

—— (1988) *The invention of primitive society: transformations of an illusion* London

Kurtén, B. & Poulianos, A.N. (1977) 'New stratigraphic and faunal material from Petralona Cave with special reference to the carnivora' *Anthropos* 4:47-130

Kushnir, U. & Halloran, G.M. (1981) 'Evidence for *Aegilops sharonensis* Eig as the donor of the B genome in wheat' *Genetics* 99:495-512

—— & —— (1982) 'Variation in vernalization and photoperiod response in tetraploid wheat (*Triticum dicoccum dicoccoides*) ecotypes' *JAE* 19:545-554

—— & —— (1983) 'Evidence on the origin of the G genome in wheat: cytology and fertility of a *T. timopheevi*-like mutant' *CJGC* 25:651-661

Kuznets, S. (1974) *Population, capital and growth* London

Lack, D. (1954) *The natural regulation of animal numbers* Oxford

Lacoste, Y. (1969) *Ibn Khaldoun: naissance de l'histoire passé du tiers-monde* (2nd ed.) Paris

Laderman, C. (1975) 'Malaria and progress: some historical and ecological considerations' *Social science and medicine* 9:587-594

Ladizinsky, G. (1975a) 'Oats in Ethiopia' *EB* 29:238-241

—— (1975b) 'Collection of wild cereals in the Upper Jordan valley' *EB* 29:264-267

Ladizinsky, G., Braun, D. & Muehlbauer, F.J. (1983) 'Evidence for domestication of *Lens nigricans* (M. Bieb.) Godron in S Europe' *BOJL* 87:169-176

Ladizinsky, G. & Zohary, D. (1971) 'Notes on species delimitation, species relationships and polyploidy in Avena L.' *EUP* 20:380-395

Laiou-Thomadakis, A. (1978) *Peasant society in the Late Byzantine empire* Princeton

Lallo, J.W., Armelagos, G.J. & Mensforth, R.P. (1977) 'The role of diet, disease and physiology in the origin of porotic hyperostosis' *HB* 49:471-483

Lampe, J.R. & Jackson, M.R. (1982) *Balkan economic history 1550-1950: from imperial borderlands to developing nations* Bloomington

Landry, A. (1936) 'La dépopulation dans l'antiquité gréco-romaine' *Revue historique* 167:1-33

Lane Fox, R. (1985) 'Aspects of inheritance in the Greek world' in Cartledge & Harvey (1985) 208-232

—— (1986) *Pagans and Christians* Harmondsworth

Lang, H. & Göhlen, R. (1985) 'Completed fertility of the Hutterites' *CA* 26:395

Lange, O.L. (1988) 'Ecophysiology of photosynthesis: performance of poikilohydric lichens and homoihydric Mediterranean sclerophylls' *JE* 76:915-937

Langer, W.L. (1972) 'Checks on population growth: 1750-1850' *SA* 226.2:92-99

—— (1975) 'American foods and Europe's population growth 1750-1850' *J. of social history* (Winter 1975) 51-66

Langkavel, B. (1866 & 1964 reprint) *Botanik der späteren Griechen vom 3. bis zum 13. Jahrhunderte* Berlin & Amsterdam

Langmuir, A.D., Worthen, T.D., Solomon, J., Ray, C.G. & Petersen, E. (1985) 'The Thucydides syndrome: a new hypothesis for the cause of the plague of Athens' *NEJM* 313:1027-1030

Laslett, T.P.R. (1977) *Family life and illicit love in earlier generations* Cambridge

—— (1978) 'Measuring patriline extinction for modelling social mobility in the past' in K.W. Wachter et al. *Statistical studies in historical social structure* (1978) 113-135 New York

—— (1983) *The world we have lost further explored* (1971 edition also cited) London

Laslett, T.P.R. & Wall, R. (eds) (1972) *Household and family in past time* Cambridge

Laufer, B. (1919) *Sino-Iranica* Chicago

Laumont, P. & Berbigier, A. (1953) 'L'alfa et l'expérimentation alfatière en Algérie' *RBAAT* 33:125-140

Laurent-Täckholm, V. (1940) 'A mummy coffin in the Egyptian Museum, Stockholm, and its plant remains' *Svensk Botanisk Tidskrift* 34:141-161

—— (1976) 'Ancient Egypt: landscape, flora and agriculture' in J. Rzóska (ed.) *The Nile, biology of an ancient river* (1976) 51-68 The Hague

Lauwerier, R.C.G.M. (1988) 'Animals in Roman times in the Dutch eastern river area' (PhD Univ. of Groningen)

Le, H.T. et al. (1986) 'Freezing hardiness of some accessions of *Triticum tauschii* and *T. turgidum L. var. durum' CJPS* 66:893-899

Le Roy Ladurie, E. (1966) *Les paysans du Languedoc* (2 vols) Paris

—— (1971) *Times of feast, times of famine* (Engl. transl.) London

—— (1975) 'Famine amenorrhoea (seventeenth-twentieth centuries)' in Forster & Ranum (1975) 163-178

—— (1978) *Montaillou* (Engl. transl.) London

—— (1981) *The mind and method of the historian* (Engl. transl.) Brighton

Leach, D. (1981) 'Re-evaluation of the logistic curve for human populations' *J. of the Royal Statistical Society* A 144:94-103

Leach, G. (1976) *Energy and food production* Guildford

Leakey, L.S.B. (1930) 'Some notes on the Masai of Kenya colony' *J. of the Royal Anthropological Institute* 60:185-210

Lee, R.B. (1972) 'Population growth and the beginnings of sedentary life amongst the !Kung bushmen' in B. Spooner (ed.) *Population growth: anthropological implications* (1972) 329-342 Cambridge, Mass.

—— (1980) 'Lactation, ovulation, infanticide, and women's work: a study of hunter-gatherer population regulation' in M. Cohen et al. (eds) (1980) 321-348

Lee, R.D. (1987) 'Population dynamics of humans and other animals' *DEM* 24:443-465

Legesse, A. (1973) *Gada: three approaches to African society* New York

Lehner, T. & Barnes, C.G. (eds) (1986) *Recent advances in Behçet's disease* London

Leighty, C.E. (1933) 'Cereals' in A.E.R. Boak (ed.) *Karanis: the temples, coin hoards, botanical and zoological reports. Seasons 1924-1931* (1933) 87-88 Ann Arbor

Lelley, J. (1976) *Wheat breeding: theory and practice* Budapest

Lello-Finuoli, A.L. di (1984) 'Donne e matrimonio nella Grecia arcaica' *SMEA* 25:275-302

Lenschau, T. (1936) 'Forschungen zur griechischen Geschichte im VII e VI Jahr. v. Chr. IV: Die Siegerliste von Olympia' *PHI* 91:396-411

Lenski, R.E. (1988) 'Evolution of plague virulence' *NAT* 334:473-474

Lenski, R.E. & Service, P.M. (1982) 'The statistical analysis of population growth rates calculated from schedules of survivorship and fecundity' *ECO* 63:655-662

Leonardi, S. (1982) 'Sulla produttività primaria in colture erbacee della Sicilia' *EM* 8.4:143-164

Lerat, L. (1943) 'Un loi de Delphes sur les devoirs des enfants envers leurs parents' *Revue de philologie* 17:62-86

Leridon, H. (1977) *Human fertility: the basic components* Chicago

—— (1984) 'Selective effects of sterility and fertility' in Keyfitz (1984) 83-97

Leridon, H. & Menken, J. (eds) (1979) *Natural fertility* Liège

Leslie, P.W., Bindon, J.R. & Baker, P.T. (1984) 'Calorie requirements of human populations: a model' *HE* 12:137-162

Lesthaeghe, R. (1971) 'Nuptiality and population growth' *PS* 25:415-432

—— (1980) 'On the social control of human reproduction' *PDR* 6:527-548

Levin, D.A. (1976) 'The chemical defences of plants to pathogens and herbivores' *ARES* 7:121-159

Lévi-Strauss, Cl. (1985) *The view from afar* (Engl. transl.) Oxford

Lévy, E. (1978) 'Notes sur la chronologie athénienne au VIe siècle' *HIS* 27:513-521

Lewin, J. & Lomas, J. (1974) 'A comparison of statistical and soil-moisture modelling techniques in a long-term study of wheat yield performance under semi-arid conditions' *JAE* 11:1081-1090

Lewis, D.M. (1955) 'The diatêtai of 330-329' *ABSA* 50:27-36

Lewis, N. (1974) *Papyrus in classical antiquity* Brussels

—— (1989) *Papyrus in classical antiquity: a supplement* (Pap. Brux. 23)

Lewy, H. (1944) 'Assyro-Babylonian and Israelite measures of capacity and rates of seeding' *JAOS* 64:65-73

—— (1949) 'Origin and development of the sexagesimal system of numeration' *JAOS* 69:1-11

—— (1956) 'On some Old Assyrian cereal names' *JAOS* 76:201-204

Lichtenthaeler, C. (1965) *Thucydide et Hippocrate vus par un historien-médecin* Geneva

Lidicker, W.Z. (1975) 'The role of dispersal in the demography of small mammals' in F.B. Golley, K. Petrusiewicz & L. Ryszkowski (eds) *Small mammals: their productivity and population dynamics* (1975) 103-128 Cambridge

Lincoln, B. (1981) *Emerging from the chrysalis: studies in rituals of women's initiation* Cambridge, Mass.

Lincoln, R.J., Boxshall, G.A. & Clark, P.F. (1982) *A dictionary of ecology, evolution and systematics* Cambridge

Lindstrom, D.R. & MacAyeal, D.R. (1989) 'Scandinavian, Siberian, and Arctic Ocean glaciation: effect of Holocene atmospheric CO_2 variations' *SCI* 245:628-631

Liphschitz, N. (1987) '*Ceratonia siliqua* in Israel: an ancient element or a newcomer?' *IJB* 36:191-197

Liphschitz, N. & Biger, G. (1989) '*Cupressus sempervivens* in Israel during antiquity' *IJB* 38:35-45

Lisitsina, G.N. (1978) 'Main types of ancient farming in the Caucasus on the basis of palaeo-ethnobotanical research' *BDBG* 91:47-57

—— (1984) 'The Caucasus: a centre of ancient farming' in van Zeist & Casparie (1984) 285-292

Lisitsina, G.N. & Filipovich, L. (1981) 'Kulturpflanzenfunde des 7.-2. Jahrtausends v.u.Z. auf dem Balkan' *ZA* 15:77-86

Lister, A.M. (1989) 'Rapid dwarfing of red deer on Jersey in the Last Interglacial' *NAT* 342:539-542

Little, M.A. & Haas, J.D. (eds) (1989) *Human population biology: a transdisciplinary science* Oxford

Littlejohn, L. (1946) 'Some aspects of soil fertility in Cyprus' *EJEA* 14:123-134

Littman, R.J. (1984) 'The plague at Syracuse, 396 BC' *MNE* 37:110-116

Littman, R.J. & M.L. (1969) 'The Athenian plague: smallpox' *TAPA* 100:261-275

—— & —— (1973) 'Galen and the Antonine plague' *AJP* 94:243-255

Littré, E. (ed.) (1839-1861) *Oeuvres complètes d'Hippocrate* (10 vols) Paris

Livi-Bacci, M. (1977) *A history of Italian fertility during the last two centuries* Princeton

Livingstone, D.A. (1975) 'Late Quaternary climatic change in Africa' *ARES* 6:249-280

Livingstone, F.B. (1967) *Abnormal haemoglobins in human populations* Chicago

—— (1971) 'Malaria and human polymorphisms' *ARG* 5:33-64

—— (1984) 'The Duffy blood groups, vivax malaria, and malaria selection in human populations: a review' *HB* 56:413-425

—— (1985) *Frequencies of haemoglobin variants: thalassaemia, the glucose-6-phosphate dehydrogenase deficiency, G6PD variants, and ovalocytosis in human populations* Oxford

—— (1987) 'Simulation of the founder effect and its role in the determination of the polymorphic frequency of deleterious genes in human populations' *HB* 59:59-75

Lloyd, G.E.R. (1983) *Science, folklore and ideology* Cambridge

—— (1987) *The revolutions of wisdom: studies in the claims and practice of ancient Greek science* Berkeley

Loizides, P.A. (1958) 'Fertilizer experiments in Cyprus: II. Cereals' *EJEA* 26:25-33

Longo, O. (1984) 'Micene/Argo: un modello aristotelico di interpretazione geostorica' *Studi italiani di filologia classica* ser. 3, 2:202-216

Longrigg, J. (1980) 'The great plague at Athens' *History of science* 18:209-225

Loomis, R.S. et al. (1971) 'Agricultural productivity' *ARP* 22:431-468

Lopez, A.D. & Ruzicka, L.T. (eds) (1983) *Sex differentials in mortality: trends, determinants and consequences* Liège

Loraux, N. (1981) *L'invention d'Athènes: histoire de l'oraison funèbre dans la cité classique* Paris

Lorimer, F. et al. (1954) *Culture and human fertility* (UNESCO)

Lotka, A.J. (1934) & (1939) *Théorie analytique des associations biologiques. I. Principes. II. Analyse démographique avec application particulière à l'espèce humaine* (*Actualités scientifiques et industrielles* 187 & 780) Paris

Loudon, I. (1986) 'Deaths in childbed from the eighteenth century to 1935' *MH* 30:1-41

Louis, P. (1970) 'La domestication des animaux à l'époque d'Aristote' *RHS* 23:189-201

Loussert, R. & Brousse, G. (1978) *L'olivier: techniques agricoles et productions méditerranéennes* vol. 1 Paris

Louw, G.N. & Seely, M.K. (1982) *Ecology of desert organisms* London

Lovelock, J. (1988) *The ages of Gaia: a biography of our living earth* Oxford

Luzzatto, L. & Battistuzzi, G. (1985) 'Glucose-6-phosphate dehydrogenase' *AHG* 14:217-329

MacArthur, R.H. & Pianka, E.R. (1966) 'On optimal use of a patchy environment' *AN* 100:603-609

MacArthur, R.H. & Wilson, E.O. (1967) *The theory of island biogeography* Princeton

MacArthur, W. (1954) 'The Athenian plague: a medical note' *CQ* 4:171-174

—— (1958) 'The plague of Athens' *BHM* 32:242-246

—— (1959) 'The medical identification of some pestilences of the past' *Transactions of the Royal Society of Tropical Medicine and Hygiene* 53:423-439

Macchia, M., Benvenuti, A. & Balardi, M. (1986) 'Temperature requirements of Italian *Triticum durum* cultivars in the germination stage' *Seed science and technology* 14:41-48

MacDowell, D.M. (1986) *Spartan law* Edinburgh

MacFadden, B.J. (1986) 'Fossil horses from "*Eohippus*" (*Hyracotherium*) to *Equus*: scaling, Cope's Law, and the evolution of body size' *PB* 12:355-369

Mackey, J. (1979) 'Wheat domestication as a shoot:root interrelation process' in S. Ramanujam (ed.) *Proceedings of the 5th Int. Wheat Genetics Symposium* vol. 2 (1979) 875-890 New Delhi

Maggiani, A. (1972) 'Aska eleivana' *SE* 40:183-187

Magioris, S.N. (1987) 'Check-list of the bird species have been observed in Cyclades, Aegean-Greece, during 19th and 20th century' (*sic*) *EM* 13.1/2:15-22

Magrath, W.T. (1975) 'The Athenian king-list and Indo-European trifunctionality' *JIES* 3:173-194

Makler, P.T. (1980) 'New information on nutrition in ancient Greece' *KL* 62:317-319

Mallory, J.P. (1982) 'Indo-European and Kurgan fauna I: wild mammals' *JIES* 10:193-222

Mallwitz, A. (1988) 'Cult and competition locations at Olympia' in Raschke (1988) 79-109

Malthus, T.R. (1970) *Essay on the principle of population* (ed. A. Flew) Harmondsworth

Manchester, K. (1984) 'Tuberculosis and leprosy in antiquity: an interpretation' *MH* 28:162-173

Mandelbaum, I. (1982) *A history of the Mishnaic law of agriculture: Kilayim* Chico

Mangelsdorf, P.C. (1974) *Corn: its origin, evolution and improvement* Cambridge, Mass.

Mango, C. (1985) *Le développement urbain de Constantinople (IVe-VIIIe siècles)* Paris

Mansfeld, J. (1971) *The pseudo-Hippocratic tract PERI HEBDOMADON ch. 1-11 and Greek philosophy* Assen

Marcy, P.T. (1981) 'Factors affecting the fecundity and fertility of historical populations' *J. of family history* 6:309-326

Margaris, N.S. & Mooney, H.A. (eds) (1981) *Components of productivity of Mediterranean-climate regions: basic and applied aspects* The Hague

Mariolopoulos, E.G. (1925) *Etude sur le climat de la Grèce* Paris

—— (1962) 'Fluctuation of rainfall in Attica during the years of the erection of the Parthenon' *Geofisica pura e applicata* 51:243-262

—— (1971) 'Has the climate changed?' *PAA* 46:38-53 (in modern Greek)

Marrou, H.-I. (1946) 'Les classes d'âge de la jeunesse spartiate' *REA* 48:216-230

Martin, P.F. (1913) *Greece in the twentieth century* London

Martin, P.S. & Klein, R.G. (eds) (1984) *Quaternary extinctions: a prehistoric revolution* Tucson

Martinet, A. (1986) *Des steppes aux océans: l'indo-européen et les 'Indo-Européens'* Paris

Martino, F. de (1984) 'Ancora sulla produzione di cereali in Roma arcaica' *PDP* 39:241-263

Marx, J.L. (1988) 'Sexual responses are – almost – all in the brain' *SCI* 241:903-904

Masnick, G.S. (1979) 'The demographic impact of breastfeeding: a critical review' *HB* 51:109-125

Mason, I.L. (ed.) (1984) *Evolution of domesticated animals* London

Masson, E. (1967) *Recherches sur les plus anciens emprunts sémitiques en grec* Paris

Masson, M. (1988) 'A propos de quelques mots grecs relatifs à l'alimentation' *Revue de philologie* 62:25-39

Matessi, C. & Menozzi, P. (1979) 'Environment, population size and vital statistics: an analysis of demographic data from 18th century villages in the province of Reggio Emilia (Italy)' *ECO* 60:486-493

Mattingly, D.J. (1988) 'Oil for export? A comparison of Libyan, Spanish and Tunisian oil production in the Roman empire' *J. of Roman archaeology* 1:33-56

Mattingly, P.F. (1983) 'The palaeo-geography of mosquito-borne disease' *BJLS* 19:185-210

May, J.M. (1963) *The ecology of malnutrition in five countries of eastern and central Europe* New York

May, R.M. (1976) 'Simple mathematical models with very complicated dynamics' *NAT* 261:459-467

—— (1977) 'Thresholds and breakpoints in ecosystems with a multiplicity of stable states' *NAT* 269:471-477

—— (1981) 'Models for single populations' & 'Models for two interacting populations' in R.M. May (ed.) *Theoretical ecology: principles and applications* (2nd ed., 1981) 6-29 & 78-104 Oxford

—— (1989a) 'Chaos: detecting density dependence in imaginary worlds' *NAT* 338:16-17

—— (1989b) 'An inordinate fondness for ants' *NAT* 341:386-387

Mayer, F.G. (1980) 'Carbonised food plants of Pompeii, Herculaneum, and the villa at Torre Annunziata' *EB* 34:401-437

Mayerson, P. (1961) *The ancient agricultural regime of Nessana and the central Negev* London

Mayr, E. (1988) *Toward a new philosophy of biology: observations of an evolutionist* Cambridge, Mass.

McClelland, D. & Zeckhauser, R.J. (1982) *Demographic dimensions of the New Republic: American interregional migration, vital statistics, and manumissions, 1800-1860* Cambridge

McCluer, J.W. & Dyke, B. (1976) 'On the minimum size of endogamous populations' *Social biology* 23:1-12

McConnell, C. & M. (1987) *The Mediterranean diet: wine, pasta, olive oil and a long healthy life* London

McCracken, R.D. (1971) 'Lactase deficiency: an example of dietary evolution' *CA* 12:479-517

McCullagh, C.B. (1984) *Justifying historical descriptions* Cambridge

McDonald, W.A. & Rapp, G.R. (eds) (1972) *The Minnesota Messenia expedition* Minneapolis

McEvedy, C. (1988) 'The bubonic plague' *SA* 258.2:74-79

McFadden, E.S. & Sears, E.R. (1946) 'The origin of *Triticum spelta* and its free-threshing relatives' *J. of heredity* 37:81-89 & 106-116

McFalls Jr., J.A. & McFalls, M.H. (1984) *Disease and fertility* Orlando

McGeorge, P.J.P. (1988) 'Health and diet in Minoan times' in R.E. Jones & H.W. Catling (eds) *New aspects of archaeological science in Greece* (1988) 47-54 Athens

McGrath, D.G. (1987) 'The role of biomass in shifting cultivation' *HE* 15:221-242

McGrath, J.W. (1988) 'Multiple stable states of disease occurrence: a note on the implications for the anthropological study of human disease' *AMA* 90:323-334

McGregor, I.A. (1982) 'Malaria: nutritional implications' *RID* IV.4:798-804

McGrew, W.W. (1985) *Land and revolution in modern Greece, 1800-1881* Kent, OH

McIntosh, R.P. (1985) *The background of ecology: concept and theory* Cambridge

McIntosh, S.K. & R.J. (1983) 'Current directions in West African prehistory' *ARA* 12:215-258

McKeown, T. (1976) *The modern rise of population* London

—— (1988) *The origins of human disease* Oxford

McNeill, W.H. (1976) *Plagues and peoples* Garden City, NY

—— (1978) *The metamorphosis of Greece since World War II* Oxford

—— (1984) 'Human migration in historical perspective' *PDR* 10:1-18

Meiggs, R. (1982) *Trees and timber in the ancient Mediterranean world* Oxford

Meiggs, R. & Lewis, D.M. (1969) *A selection of Greek historical inscriptions to the end of the fifth century BC* Oxford

Meindl, R.S., Lovejoy, C.O. & Mensforth, R.P. (1983) 'Skeletal age at death: accuracy of determination and implications for human demography' *HB* 55:73-87

Meindl, R.S., Lovejoy, C.O., Mensforth, R.P. & Carlos, L.D. (1985) 'Accuracy and direction of error in the sexing of the skeleton: implications for palaeodemography' *AJPA* 68:79-85

Meinecke, B. (1927) 'Consumption (tuberculosis) in classical antiquity' *Annals of medical history* 9:379-402

Meissner, B. (1891) 'Babylonische Pflanzennamen' *ZSY* 6:289-298

Meister, R. (1963) 'Die spartanischen Altersklassen vom Standpunkt der Entwicklungspsychologie betrachtet' *Sitzungsberichte der Österreichischen Akademie der Wissenschaft in Wien* 241.5:3-24

Melena, J.L. (1983) 'Olive oil and other sorts of oil in the Mycenaean tablets' *Minos* 18:89-123

Mercer, R. (ed.) (1981) *Farming practice in British prehistory* Edinburgh

Mercier, L. (1974) 'Essai d'interprétation de *steriskomenoi* et de la "Peste" d'Athènes' *Bulletin de l'Association Guillaume Budé* 1974:223-226

Merlin, M.D. (1984) *On the trail of the ancient opium poppy* Rutherford

Messer, E. (1984) 'Anthropological perspectives on diet' *ARA* 13:205-249

Meuvret, J. (1977) *Le problème des subsistances à l'époque Louis XIV* vol. 1 Paris

Mikalson, J.D. (1976) 'Erechtheus and the Hyakinthia' *AJP* 97:141-153

—— (1984) 'Religion and the plague in Athens, 431-423 BC' in A.L. Boegehold et al. (eds) *Studies presented to Sterling Dow on his eightieth birthday* (1984) 217-225 (*GRBS* monographs no. 10)

Miksicek, C.H. et al. (1981) 'Preclassic lowland maize from Cuello, Belize' *NAT* 289:56-59

Mill, J.S. (1973) *A system of logic ratiocinative and inductive* (ed. J.M. Robson) vol. 1 Toronto

Miller, T.S. (1976) 'The plague in John VI Cantacuzenus and Thucydides' *GRBS* 17:385-395

Millett, P.C. (1984) 'Hesiod and his world' *PCPS* 30:84-115

Milner, G.R., Humpf, D.A. & Harpending, H.C. (1989) 'Pattern matching of age-at-death distributions in palaeodemographic analysis' *AJPA* 80:49-58

Mindel, A. (1989) *Herpes simplex virus* London

Minois, G. (1989) *History of old age from antiquity to the Renaissance* (Engl. transl.) Oxford

Mitchel, F.W. (1964) 'The Athenian plague: new evidence inviting medical comment' *GRBS* 5:101-112

Mitchell, B.R. (1975) *European historical statistics 1750-1970* London

Mitrakos, K. (1982) 'Winter low temperatures in Mediterranean-type ecosystems' *EM* 8.1/2:95-102

Möbius, M. (1933) 'Pflanzenbilder der minoischen Kunst in botanischer Betrachtung' *Jahrbuch des deutschen archäologischen Instituts* 48:1-39

Moïssides, M. (1913/14) 'La puériculture et l'eugénique dans l'antiquité grecque' *JAN* 18:413-422 & 643-649 and 19:289-311

—— (1922) 'Contribution à l'étude de l'avortement dans l'antiquité grecque' *JAN* 26:59-85 & 129-145

—— (1932) 'Le malthusianisme dans l'antiquité grecque' *JAN* 36:169-179

Mollesen, I. (1981) 'The archaeology and anthropology of death: what the bones tell us' in S.C. Humphreys & H. King (eds) *Mortality and immortality: the anthropology and archaeology of death* (1981) 15-32 London

Mols, R. (1972) 'Population in Europe 1500-1700' in C.M. Cipolla (ed.) *Fontana economic history of Europe* vol. 2 (1972) 15-82 London

Moody, J.A. (1987) 'The environmental and cultural prehistory of the Khania region of west Crete: Neolithic through Late Minoan III. Part 1.' (PhD Univ. of Minnesota)

Moore Jr., B. (1984) *Privacy: studies in social and cultural history* Armonk, NY

Moore, J.C. (1815) *The history of the smallpox* London

Moore, P.D. (1989) 'Ancient climate from fossils' *NAT* 340:18-19

—— (1990) 'Palaeoecology: ups and downs in the Sahel' *NAT* 343:414-415

Moreau, J. (1949) 'Les théories démographiques dans l'antiquité grecque' *POP* 4:597-614

Morgan, C.A. (1986) 'Settlement and exploitation in the region of the Corinthian Gulf c. 1000-700 BC' (Cambridge PhD)

Morgenstern, O. (1963) *On the accuracy of economic observations* (2nd ed.) Princeton

Moritz, L.A. (1949) 'ALPHITA: a note' *CQ* 43:113-117

—— (1955a) 'Husked and "naked" grain' *CQ* 49:129-134

—— (1955b) 'Corn' *CQ* 49:135-141

—— (1958) *Grain-mills and flour in classical antiquity* Oxford

Morris, I. (1987) *Burial and ancient society: the rise of the Greek city state* Cambridge

Morris, L.N. (ed.) (1972) *Human populations, genetic variation and evolution* London

Morris, R. & Sears, E.R. (1967) 'The cytogenetics of wheat and its relatives' in Quisenberry & Reitz (1967) 19-87

Morsink, J. (1979) 'Was Aristotle's biology sexist?' *JHB* 12:83-112

Morton, A.G. (1981) *History of botanical science: an account of the development of botany from ancient times to the present day* London

—— (1986) 'Pliny on plants: his place in the history of botany' in R. French & F. Greenaway (eds) *Science in the early Roman empire: Pliny the Elder, his sources and his influence* (1986) 86-97 London

Mosley, W.H. (ed.) (1978) *Nutrition and human reproduction* New York

—— (1979) 'The effects of nutrition on natural fertility' in Leridon & Menken (1979) 83-105

Mossé, Cl. (1962) *La fin de la démocratie athénienne* Paris

Mosset, Cl. & Parzysz, B. (1985) 'Démographie des cimetières? Incertitude statistique des estimateurs en paléodémographie' *L'Homme* 94:147-154

Mugler, Ch. (1967) 'Démocrite et les dangers de l'irradiation cosmique' *RHS* 20:221-228

Mulder, C. (1988) 'Human AIDS virus not from monkeys' *NAT* 333:396

Mulhern, J.J. (1975) 'Population and Plato's Republic' *ARET* 8:265-281

Müller, C. (1841-1872) *Fragmenta historicorum graecorum* (5 vols) Paris

Müller, F. (1899) review of W. Ebstein (1899) *Die Pest des Thukydides* in *Berliner Philologische Wochenschrift* 19:453-460

Müller, H.-H. (1985) 'Zur Rekonstruktion der gallorömischen Erntemaschine' *ZA* 19:191-196

Murray, A.C. (1983) *Germanic kinship structure* Toronto

Murray, W.M. (1984) 'The ancient dam of the Mytikas valley' *AJA* 88:195-203

Musgrave, J.H. (1980) 'The human remains from the cemeteries' in M.R. Popham et al. *Lefkandi I. The Iron Age. Text. The settlement* (1980) 429-446 London

Musgrave, J.H. & Evans, S.P. (1981) 'By strangers honor'd: a statistical study of ancient crania from Crete, mainland Greece, Cyprus, Israel and Egypt' *J. of Mediterranean anthropology and archaeology* 1:50-107

Muthuri, F.M. & Kinyamario, J.I. (1989) 'Nutritive value of papyrus, a tropical emergent macrophyte' *EB* 43:23-30

Myres, J.L. (1915/16) 'The causes of rise and fall in the population of the ancient world' *ER* 7:15-45

Nag, M. (1962) *Factors affecting human fertility in nonindustrial societies: a cross-cultural study* New York

—— (ed.) (1975) *Population and social organisation* The Hague

Nardi, E. (1971) *Procurato aborto nel mondo greco-romano* Milan

—— (1980) 'Aborto e omicidio nella civiltà classica' in H. Temporini (ed.) *Aufstieg und Niedergang der römischen Welt* II.13 (1980) 366-385 Berlin

Nash, L.L. (1978) 'Concepts of existence: Greek origins of generational thought' *DAE* 107.4:1-21

Navajas y Navarro, M. & Britton-Davidian, J. (1989) 'Genetic structure of insular Mediterranean populations of the house mouse' *BJLS* 36:377-390

Nayar, N.M. (1973) 'Origin and cytogenetics of rice' *ADG* 17:153-292

Nayar, N.M. & Mehra, K.L. (1970) 'Sesame: its uses, botany, cytogenetics, and origin' *EB* 24:20-31

Negbi, M. (1989) 'Theophrastos on geophytes' *BOJL* 100:15-43

Nelson, H.E. (1971) 'Disease, demography and the evolution of social structure in highland New Guinea' *J. of the Polynesian Society* 80:204-216

Nesbitt, M. & Summers, G.D. (1988) 'Some recent discoveries of millet (*Panicum miliaceum* L. and *Setaria italica* (L.) P. Beauv.) at excavations in Turkey and Iran' *AS* 38:85-97

Nesteroff, W., Olive, P. & Vergnaud-Grazzini, C. (1982) 'After the deluge: Mediterranean stagnation and sapropel formation' *NAT* 295:105-110

Neumann, J. (1985) 'Climatic change as a topic in classical Greek and Roman literature' *Climatic change* 7:441-454

Neveux, H. & Tits-Dieuaide, M.J. (1979) 'Etude structurelle des fluctuations courtes des rendements céréaliers dans l'Europe du Nord-Ouest (XIV-XVIe siècles)' *Cahiers des Annales de Normandie* 11:17-42

Newman, J. (1932) *The agricultural life of the Jews in Babylonia between the years 200 CE and 500 CE* London

Newsome, A.E. (1969) 'A population study of house-mice temporarily inhabiting a south Australian wheat field' & 'A population study of house-mice permanently inhabiting a reed bed in south Australia' *JNE* 38:341-359 & 361-377

Noonan, T.S. (1973) 'The grain trade of the northern Black Sea in antiquity' *AJP* 94:231-242

Noy-Meir, I., Gutman, M. & Kaplan, Y. (1989) 'Responses of Mediterranean grassland plants to grazing and protection' *JE* 77:290-310

Nriagu, J.O. (1983) *Lead and lead poisoning in antiquity* New York

Nuttonson, M.Y. (1947) *Ecological crop geography of Greece* Washington

—— (1955) *Wheat-climate relationships* ... Washington

—— (1957) *Barley-climate relationships* ... Washington

Ober, J. (1985) *Fortress Attica: defence of the Athenian land frontier* Leiden

Oka, H.I. (1988) *Origin of cultivated rice* Amsterdam

Oldenziel, R. (1987) 'The historiography of infanticide in antiquity: a literature stillborn' in J. Blok & P. Mason (eds) *Sexual asymmetry: studies in ancient society* (1987) 87-107 Amsterdam

Ordish, G. (1972) *The great wine blight* London

—— (1976) *The constant pest: a short history of pests and their control* London

Orlob, G.B. (1973) 'Ancient and mediaeval plant pathology' *Pflanzenschutz-Nachrichten Bayer* 26.2:65-294

Osborne, M.J. (1981-83) *Naturalization in Athens* (4 vols) Brussels

Osborne, R.G. (1985) *Demos: the discovery of classical Attika* Cambridge

—— (1987) *Classical landscape with figures: the ancient city and its countryside* London

—— (1988) 'Social and economic implications of the leasing of land and property in classical and Hellenistic Greece' *CH* 18:279-323

Owens, E.J. (1983) 'The *koprologoi* at Athens in the fifth and fourth centuries BC' *CQ* 33:44-50

Page, D.L. (1953) 'Thucydides' description of the great plague at Athens' *CQ* 3:97-119

Paige, K.N. & Whitham, T.G. (1987) 'Overcompensation in response to mammalian herbivory: the advantage of being eaten' *AN* 129:407-416

Paine, H.R. (1989) 'Model life table fitting by maximum likelihood estimation: a procedure to reconstruct palaeodemographic characteristics from skeletal age distributions' *AJPA* 79:51-61

Palkovich, A.M. (1987) 'Endemic disease patterns in palaeopathology: porotic hyperostosis' *AJPA* 74:527-537

Panessa, G. (1981) 'Oscillazioni e stabilità del clima nella Grecia antica: introduzione ad una ricostruzione paleoclimatologica' *AP* n.s. III 10:123-158

—— (1982) 'Recenti studi di interesse paleoclimatologico riguardanti la Grecia' *AP* n.s. III 12:1601-1614

Pantelakis, S.N., Papadimitriou, G.C. & Doxiadis, S.A. (1973) 'Influence of induced and spontaneous abortions on the outcome of subsequent pregnancies' *American J. of obstetrics and gynaecology* 116:799-805

Panzac, D. (1973) 'La peste à Smyrne au XVIIIe siècle' *AESC* 28:1071-1093

Papadakis, J.S. (1929) *Les formes grecques du blé* Salonica

Papadopoulos, O. (1980) 'Arbovirus problems in Greece' in J. Vesenjak-Hirjak et al. (eds) *Arboviruses in the Mediterranean countries* (1980) 117-121 Stuttgart

Parain, C. (1936) *La Méditerranée, les hommes et leur travaux* Paris

Parke, H.W. (1933) *Greek mercenary soldiers from the earliest times to the battle of Ipsos* Oxford

—— (1945) 'The deposing of Spartan kings' *CQ* 39:106-112

Paroda, R.S. & Joshi, A.B. (1970) 'Correlations, path-coefficients and the implication of discriminant function for selection in wheat (*Triticum aestivum*)' *HER* 25:383-392

Parry, A. (1969) 'The language of Thucydides' description of the plague' *Bulletin of the Institute of Classical Studies* 16:106-118

Parry, M.L. (1978) *Climatic change, agriculture and settlement* Folkestone

Pashkevich, G.A. (1984) 'Palaeoethnobotanical examination of archaeological sites in the Lower Dnieper region, dated to the last centuries BC and the first centuries AD' in van Zeist & Casparie (1984) 277-283

Passmore, R. & Eastwood, M.A. (1986) *Davidson and Passmore: human nutrition and dietetics* (8th ed.) Edinburgh

Patlagean, E. (1977) *Pauvreté économique et pauvreté sociale à Byzance* Paris

Patrick, A. (1967) 'Disease in antiquity: ancient Greece and Rome' in Brothwell & Sandison (1967) 238-246

Patterson, C. (1981) *Pericles' citizenship law 451-450 BC* New York

—— (1985) ' "Not worth the rearing": the causes of infant exposure in ancient

Greece' *TAPA* 115:103-123

Payette, S., Fillon, L., Delwaide, A. & Bégin, C. (1989) 'Reconstruction of tree-line vegetation response to long-term climatic change' *NAT* 341:429-432

Payne, S. (1985) 'Zoo-archaeology in Greece: a reader's guide' in Wilkie & Coulson (1985) 211-244

Pearl, R. (1924) 'The curve of population growth' *PAPS* 63:10-17

—— (1925) *The biology of population growth* New York

—— (1939) *The natural history of population* London

Pecirka, J. (1970) 'Excavations of farms and farmhouses in the chora of Chersonesus in the Crimea' *EIR* 8:123-174

Peel, D.A. (1989) 'Ice-age clues for warmer world' *NAT* 339:508-509

Pélékides, Ch. (1962) *Histoire de l'éphébie attique des origines à 31 avant J.C.* Paris

Pellegrin, P. (1982) *La classification des animaux chez Aristote: statut de la biologie et unité de la aristotélisme* Paris

—— (1988) 'L'imaginaire de la fièvre dans la médecine antique' *History and philosophy of the life sciences* 10:109-120

Pepelasis, A. et al. (1980) *The Mediterranean challenge* Brighton

Percival, J. (1921) *The wheat plant: a monograph* London

—— (1927) 'Wheat in 3500 BC' *NAT* 119:280-281

—— (1936) 'Cereals of ancient Egypt and Mesopotamia' *NAT* 138:270-273

Peristiany, J.G. (ed.) (1976) *Mediterranean family structures* Cambridge

Perry, I. & Moore, P.D. (1987) 'Dutch elm disease as an analogue of Neolithic elm decline' *NAT* 326:72-73

Peters, R.H. (1983) *The ecological implications of body size* Cambridge

Petersen, W. (1975) 'A demographer's view of prehistoric demography' *CA* 16:227-245

Peterson, R.F. (1965) *Wheat: botany, cultivation and utilization* London

Petropoulakou, M. & Pentazos, E. (1973) *Attika. Oikistika stoicheia: prôtê ekthesis* Athens

Phadke, A.M., Samant, N.R. & Dewal, S.D. (1973) 'Smallpox as an etiologic factor in male infertility' *Fertility and sterility* 24:802-804

Philippson, A. (1948) *Das Klima Griechenlands* Bonn

Pianka, E.R. (1988) *Evolutionary ecology* (4th ed.) New York

Piault, C. (ed.) (1985) *Familles et biens en Grèce et à Chypre* Paris

Pinault, J.R. (1986) 'How Hippokrates cured the plague' *JHM* 41:52-75

Pissaloux, R. (1955) 'Production agricole et alimentation humaine' *CT* 12:543-614

Planhol, X. de (1968) *Les fondements géographiques de l'histoire de l'Islam* Paris

Pleket, H.W. (ed.) (1964) *Epigraphica* vol. 1 Leiden

Plucknett, D.L. & Smith, N.J.H. (1986) 'Historical perspectives on multiple cropping' in Francis (1986) 20-39

Poinsot-Balaguer, N. (1984) 'Comportement des microarthropodes du sol en climat méditerranéen français' *BSBF* 131.2-4:307-318

Polignac, F. de (1984) *La naissance de la polis grecque* Paris

Pollard, J.H. (1973) *Mathematical models for the growth of human populations* Cambridge

Polomé, E.C. (ed.) (1985) series of papers on the origins of the Indo-Europeans in *JIES* 13.1-2

Polunin, O. (1980) *Flowers of Greece and the Balkans: a field guide* Oxford

Polunin, O. & Huxley, A. (1987) *Flowers of the Mediterranean* (3rd ed.) London

Pomeranz, Y. (ed.) (1971) *Wheat: chemistry and technology* (2nd ed.) St. Paul

Pomeroy, S.B. (1983) 'Infanticide in Hellenistic Greece' in A. Cameron & A. Kuhrt (eds) *Images of women in antiquity* (1983) 207-222 London

Pool, R. (1989a) 'Is it chaos, or is it just noise?' *SCI* 243:25-28

—— (1989b) 'Ecologists flirt with chaos' *SCI* 243:310-313

Pope, K.O. & van Andel, T.H. (1984) 'Late Quaternary alluviation and soil formation in the southern Argolid: its history, causes and archaeological implications' *JARS* 11:281-306

Porceddu, E. & Lafiandra, D. (1986) 'Origin and evolution of wheats' in Barigozzi (1986) 143-178

Post, J.D. (1977) *The last great subsistence crisis in the western world* Baltimore

—— (1985) *Food shortage, climatic variability and epidemic disease in pre-industrial Europe: the peak in the early 1740s* Ithaca

Postan, M.M. (1972) *The mediaeval economy and society* Harmondsworth

Pounds, N.J.G. (1976) *An historical geography of Europe 450 BC – AD 1330* Cambridge

Powell, M.A. (1984a) 'Late Babylonian surface mensuration: a contribution to the history of Babylonian agriculture and arithmetic' *Archiv für Orientforschung* 31:32-66

—— (1984b) 'Sumerian cereal crops' *BSA* 1:48-72

—— (1985) 'Salt, seed, and yields in Sumerian agriculture: a critique of the theory of progressive salinization' *ZSY* 75:7-38

—— (1987) 'Classical sources and the problem of the apricot' *BSA* 3:153-156

Power, J.F. & Follett, R.F. (1987) 'Monoculture' *SA* 256.3:56-64

Prandi, L. (1982) *Ricerche sulla concessione della cittadinanza ateniese nel V secolo a.C.* Milan

Prasada Rao, K.E., Wet, J.M.J. de, Brink, D.E. & Mengesha, M.H. (1987) 'Infraspecific variation and systematics of cultivated *Setaria italica*, foxtail millet (Poaceae)' *EB* 41:108-116

Prat, G. (1952) 'Albi et le peste noire' *Annales du Midi* 64:15-25

Préaux, Cl. (1939) *L'économie royale des Lagides* Brussels

—— (1965) 'Réflexions sur l'entité hellénistique' *CE* 40:129-139

—— (1978) *Le monde hellénistique* (2 vols) Paris

Preston, S.H. (ed.) (1978) *The effects of infant and child mortality on fertility* New York

—— (ed.) (1982) *Biological aspects of mortality and the length of life* Liège

—— (1986) 'The relation between actual and intrinsic growth rates' *PS* 40:343-351

Preuss, A. (1975) 'Biomedical techniques for influencing human reproduction in the fourth century BC' *ARET* 8:237-263

Preuss, J. (1978) *Biblical and Talmudic medicine* (Engl. transl.) New York

Price, T.D. (ed.) (1989) *The chemistry of prehistoric human bone* Cambridge

Pritchard, J.B. (ed.) (1969) *Ancient Near Eastern texts relating to the Old Testament* (3rd ed.) Princeton

Pritchett, W.K. (1956) 'The Attic stelai, part II' *HEP* 25:178-328

Pulliam, H.R. (1988) 'Sources, sinks and population regulation' *AN* 132:652-661

Quiller, B. (1981) 'The dynamics of the Homeric society' *SO* 56:109-155

Quisenberry, K.S. & Reitz, L.P. (eds) (1967) *Wheat and wheat improvement* Madison

Rackham, J. (1979) '*Rattus rattus*: the introduction of the black rat into Britain' *ATQ* 53:112-120

Rackham, O. (1980) *Ancient woodland: its history, vegetation and uses in England*

London
—— (1982) 'Land-use and the native vegetation of Greece' in M. Bell & S. Limbrey (eds) *Archaeological aspects of woodland ecology* (*BAR* Int. Ser. 146, 1982) 177-198 Oxford
—— (1983) 'Observations on the historical ecology of Boiotia' *ABSA* 78:291-351
Radt, S.L. (1978) 'Zu Thukydides' Pestbeschreibung' *MNE* 31:233-245
Raepsaet, G. (1971a) 'Les motivations de la natalité à Athènes aux Ve et IVe siècles avant notre ère' *AC* 40:80-110
—— (1971b) 'Etude d'un comportement sociale: les relations entre parents et enfants à Athènes à l'époque classique' *AC* 40:589-606
—— (1973) 'A propos de l'utilisation des statistiques en démographie grecque: le nombre d'enfants par famille' *AC* 42:536-543
Rao, M.R. (1986) 'Cereals in multiple cropping' in Francis (1986) 96-132
Raphael, D. (1984) 'Weaning is always: the anthropology of breastfeeding' *EFN* 15:203-213
Raschke, W.J. (ed.) (1988) *The archaeology of the Olympics* Madison
Rathbone, D.W. (1983a) 'The grain trade in the Hellenistic east' in Garnsey & Whittaker (1983) 45-55
—— (1983b) 'The weight and measurement of Egyptian grains' *ZPE* 53:265-275
Raven, P.H. (1973) 'The evolution of Mediterranean floras' in F. di Castri & H.A. Mooney (eds) *Mediterranean type ecosystems: origins and structure* (1973) 213-224 London
Raven, P.H., Berlin, B. & Breedlove, D. (1971) 'The origins of taxonomy' *SCI* 174:1210-1213
Rawski, E.S. (1972) *Agricultural change and the peasant economy of south China* Cambridge, Mass.
Reekmans, T, (1966) *La sitométrie dans les archives de Zénon* (Pap. Brux. 3)
Regel, C. (1939) 'Pflanzengeographisches von der Balkanhalbinsel' *Repertorium specierum novarum regni vegetabilis* Beiheft 111:74-84
Regöly-Mérei, G. (1966) 'Paläopathologische und epigraphische Angaben zur Frage der Pocken in Altägypten' *Sudhoffs Archiv: Vierteljahrsschrift für Geschichte der Medizin und der Naturwissenschaften, der Pharmazie und der Mathematik* 50:411-417
Reich, C.V. (1987) 'Leprosy: cause, transmission, and a new theory of pathogenesis' *RID* IX.3:590-594
Reinhold, J.G. (1972) 'Phytate concentrations of leavened and unleavened Iranian breads' *EFN* 1:187-192
Reinhold, M. (1970) 'The generation gap in antiquity' *PAPS* 114:347-365
Reinmuth, O.W. (1971) *The ephebic inscriptions of the fourth century BC* Leiden
Renault-Miskovsky, J. (1980) 'Analyse pollinique des sédiments néolithiques de la grotte de Kitsos (Lavrion – Grèce)' *Mémoires du Museum National d'histoire naturelle* B 27:98-107
Rendine, S., Piazza, A. & Cavalli-Sforza, L.L. (1986) 'Simulation and separation by principal components of multiple demic expansions in Europe' *AN* 128:681-706
Renfrew, C. (1972a) 'Patterns of population growth in the prehistoric Aegean' in P.J. Ucko, R. Tringham & G.W. Dimbleby (eds) *Man, settlement and urbanism* (1972) 383-399 London
—— (1972b) *The emergence of civilization: the Cyclades and the Aegean in the third millennium BC* London
Renfrew, C. & Wagstaff, J.M. (eds) (1982) *An island polity: the archaeology of exploitation on Melos* Cambridge

Bibliography

Renfrew, J.M. (1973a) *Palaeoethnobotany* New York
—— (1973b) 'Agriculture' in Theocharis et al. (1973) 147-164
—— (1976) 'Carbonised seeds from Anza' in M. Gimbutas (ed.) *Neolithic Macedonia as reflected by excavation at Anza, southeast Yugoslavia* (1976) 300-312 Los Angeles
—— (1979) 'The first farmers in southeast Europe' in Körber-Grohne (1979) 243-265
—— (1984) 'Cereals cultivated in ancient Iraq' *BSA* 1:32-44
Retsas, S. (ed.) (1986) *Palaeo-oncology: the antiquity of cancer* London
Reynolds, P. (1979) *Iron Age Farm* London
Rhazes (1848 edition) *A treatise on the small-pox and measles* by Abú Becr Mohammed Ibn Zacaríyá Ar-Rází (commonly called Rhazes) (transl. by W.A. Greenhill) London
Rhodes, P.J. (1980) 'Epheboi, bouleutae and the population of Athens' *ZPE* 38:191-201
—— (1981) *A commentary on the Aristotelian Athênaiôn Politeia* Oxford
Richardson, J.B. III (1972) 'The pre-Columbian distribution of the bottle gourd (*Lagenaria siceraria*): a re-evaluation' *EB* 26:265-273
Rickert, H. (1986) *The limits of concept formation in natural science: a logical introduction to the historical sciences* (abridged Engl. transl.) Cambridge
Rickman, G.E. (1980) *The corn supply of ancient Rome* Oxford
Riddle, J.M. (1985) *Dioscorides on pharmacy and medicine* Austin
Riebesell, J.F. (1974) 'Paradox of enrichment in competitive systems' *ECO* 55:183-187
Riele, G.-J.-M.-J. te (1987) 'Hélisson entre en sympolitie avec Mantinée: une nouvelle inscription d'Arcadie' *BCH* 111:167-190
Rihll, T.E. (1986) ' "Kings" and "commoners" in Homeric society' *LCM* 11:86-91
Rindos, D. (1984) *The origins of agriculture: an evolutionary perspective* Orlando
Rioux, J.-A., Rispail, P., Lanotte, G. & Leport, J. (1984) 'Relations phlébotomes-bioclimats en écologie des leishmanioses: corollaires épidémiologiques: l'exemple du Maroc' *BSBF* 131.2-4:549-557
Ripinsky, M. (1983) 'Camel ancestry and domestication in Egypt and the Sahara' *Archaeology* 36.3:21-27
Ripley, S. (1980) 'Infanticide in langurs and man: adaptive advantage or social pathology' in M. Cohen et al. (eds) (1980) 349-390
Ritchie, J.C. & Haynes, C.V. (1987) 'Holocene vegetation zonation in the eastern Sahara' *NAT* 330:645-647
Robert, L. (1949) 'Epitaphe d'un berger à Thasos' *Hellenika* 7:152-159
—— (1969) in J. des Gagniers et al. *Laodicée du Lykos. Campagnes 1961-8: la Nymphée* (1969) 328ff. Paris
Roberts, D.F. (1971) 'The demography of Tristan da Cunha' *PS* 25:465-479
Roberts, D.F., Luttrell, V. & Pasternak Slater, C. (1965) 'Genetics and geography in Tinos' *ER* 56:185-193
Robertshaw, P. (1989) 'The development of pastoralism in East Africa' in J. Clutton-Brock (1989) 207-214
Robinson, D.M. (1942) *Excavations at Olynthus: Part XI Necrolynthia: a study in Greek burial customs and anthropology* Baltimore
Robinson, V. (1938) 'The nurse of Greece' *BHM* 6:1001-1009
Rodman, J. (1976) 'The other side of ecology in ancient Greece: comments on Hughes' *INQ* 19:108-112
Rook, A. & Dawber, R. (1982) *Diseases of the hair and scalp* Oxford

Rose, M.R. (1987) *Quantitative ecological theory: an introduction to basic models* London

Rosenberg, E.M. (1980) 'Demographic effects of sex-differential nutrition' in N.W. Jerome, R.F. Kandel & G.H. Pelto (eds) *Nutritional anthropology: contemporary approaches to diet and culture* (1980) 181-203 New York

Rosqvist, R., Skurnik, M. & Wolf-Watz, H. (1988) 'Increased virulence of *Yersinia pseudotuberculosis* by two independent mutations' *NAT* 334:522-525

Ross, R. (1906) 'Malaria in Greece' *J. of tropical medicine* 9:341-347

Rossignol-Strick, M. & Planchais, N. (1989) 'Climate patterns revealed by pollen and oxygen isotope records from a Tyrrhenian sea core' *NAT* 342:413-416

Rostovtzeff, M. (1928) 'Greek sightseers in Egypt' *J. of Egyptian archaeology* 14:13-15

—— (1941) *The social and economic history of the Hellenistic world* (3 vols) Oxford

Roth, M.T. (1987) 'Age at marriage and the household: a study of Neo-Babylonian and Neo-Assyrian forms' *Comparative studies in society and history* 29:715-747

Rothschild, B.M. & Turnbull, W. (1987) 'Treponemal infection in a Pleistocene bear' *NAT* 329:61-62

Rouse, W.H.D. (1902) *Greek votive offerings: an essay in the history of Greek religion* Cambridge

Roussel, D. (1976) *Tribu et cité* Paris

Roussel, P. (1943) 'L'exposition des enfants à Sparte' *REA* 45:5-17

—— (1951) 'Etude sur le principe de l'ancienneté dans le monde hellénique du Ve siècle av. J.-C. à l'époque romaine' *Mémoires de l'Institut National de France. Académie des Inscriptions et Belles-Lettres* 43.2:123-227

Rudhardt, J. (1963) 'Sur quelques bûchers d'enfants découverts dans la ville d'Athènes' *Museum Helveticum* 20:10-20

Ruffié, J. (1982) *Traité du vivant* Paris

Ruffié, J. & Sournia, J.C. (1984) *Les épidémies dans l'histoire de l'homme: essai d'anthropologie médicale* Paris

Runia, L.T. (1987) 'Strontium and calcium distribution in plants: effect on palaeodietary studies' *JARS* 14:599-608

Runnels, C.N. & Hansen, J.M. (1986) 'The olive in the prehistoric Aegean: the evidence for domestication in the Early Bronze Age' *Oxford J. of archaeology* 5:299-308

Runnels, C.N. & van Andel, T.H. (1987) 'The evolution of settlement in the southern Argolid, Greece: an economic explanation' *HEP* 56:303-334

Ruschenbusch, E. (1979) 'Die soziale Herkunft der epheben um 330' *ZPE* 35:173-176

—— (1981) 'Epheben, Bouleuten und die Bürgerzahl von Athen um 330 v. Chr.' *ZPE* 41:103-105

—— (1982) 'Die Diaitetenliste IG II-III² 1927, zugleich ein Beitrag zur sozialen Herkunft der Schiedsrichter und zur Demographie Athens' *ZPE* 49:268-281

—— (1984a) 'Die Diaiteteninschrift vom Jahre 371 v. Chr., IG II² 143 frg. a, b, c, d und Hesperia 7 (1938) 278f. Nr. 13a' *ZPE* 54:247-252

—— (1984b) 'Zum letzten Mal: Die Bürgerzahl Athens im 4. Jh. v. Chr.' *ZPE* 54:253-270

Russell, C.E. & Felker, P. (1987) 'The prickly pears (Opuntia spp., Cactaceae): a source of human and animal food in semi-arid regions' *EB* 41:433-445

Russell, J.C. (1958) 'Late ancient and mediaeval population' *Transactions of the American Philosophical Society* 48.3

—— (1960) 'Late mediaeval Balkan and Asia Minor population' *JESHO* 3:265-274

—— (1968) 'That earlier plague' *DEM* 5:174-184

—— (1985) *The control of late ancient and mediaeval population (Memoirs of the American Philosophical Society* vol. 160)

Russell, N. (1986) *Like engend'ring like: heredity and animal breeding in early modern England* Cambridge

Russell, W.M.S. (1983) 'The palaeodemographic view' in G.D. Hart (ed.) *Disease in ancient man* (1983) 217-253 Toronto

Russell, W.M.S. & C. (1968) *Violence, monkeys and man* London

—— & —— (1983) 'Evolutionary and social aspects of disease' *Ecology of disease* 2:95-106

Ruzicka, L.T. (ed.) (1981) *Nuptiality and fertility* Liège

Ruzicka, L.T. & Hansluwka, H. (1983) 'Sex differences in mortality: effects on the family life cycle and fertility' in Lopez & Ruzicka (1983) 311-333

Ryder, M.L. (1983) *Sheep and man* London

—— (1987) 'The evolution of the fleece' *SA* 256.1:100-107

Sabatier, R. & Campo, M. van (1984) 'L'analyse en composantes principales de variables instrumentales appliquée à l'estimation des paléoclimats de la Grèce, il y a 18,000 ans' *BSBF* 131.2-4:85-96

Sabbah, G. (1982) 'La 'Peste d'Amida' (Ammien Marcellin, 19.4)' in G. Sabbah (ed.) *Médecins et médecine dans l'antiquité* (1982) 131-157 (*Mémoires du Centre Jean Palerne* III) St. Etienne

Saïd, S. (1983) 'Féminin, femme et femelle dans les grands traités biologiques d'Aristote' in E. Lévy (ed.) *La femme dans les sociétés anciennes* (1983) 93-123 Strasbourg

Ste. Croix, G.E.M. de (1966) 'The estate of Phaenippos (Ps. Demosthenes XLII)' in Ehrenberg (1966) 109-114

—— (1972) *The origins of the Peloponnesian War* London

—— (1981) *The class struggle in the ancient Greek world* London

Salmon, J. (1984) *Wealthy Corinth* Oxford

Salmon, P. (1955) 'La population de la Grèce antique' *Bulletin de la Société Royale Belge de Géographie* 79.1-2:34-61

—— (1959) 'La population de la Grèce antique (essai de démographie appliquée à l'antiquité)' *Bulletin Association G. Budé. Supplément* 18:448-476

Salway, P. & Dell, W. (1955) 'Plague at Athens' *GR* 2nd ser. 2:62-70

Sambursky, S. (1956) 'On the possible and the probable in ancient Greece' *OSI* 12:35-48

Sanders, G.D.R. (1984) 'Reassessing ancient populations' *ABSA* 79:253-261

Sattenspiel, L. & Harpending, H. (1983) 'Stable populations and skeletal age' *AMQ* 48:489-498

Sayas Abengochea, J.J. (1983) 'La ley de Adriano sobre el aceite ático' in *Producción y comercio del aceite en la antigüedad. 2nd Congr. Int. 1982* 441-464 Seville

Scarborough, J. (1970a) 'Diphilos of Siphnos and Hellenistic medical dietetics' *JHM* 25:194-201

—— (1970b) 'Thucydides, Greek medicine, and the plague at Athens: a summary of possibilities' *Episteme* 4:77-90

—— (1978) 'Theophrastos on herbals and herbal remedies' *JHB* 11:353-385

Schacht, R.M. (1980) 'Two models of population growth' *AMA* 82:782-798

—— (1981) 'Estimating past population trends' *ARA* 10:119-140

Schaffer, W.M. (1984) 'Stretching and folding in lynx fur returns: evidence for a strange attractor in nature' *AN* 124:798-820

Schaffer, W.M. & Kot, M. (1985) 'Nearly one-dimensional dynamics in an epidemic' *JTB* 112:403-427

Schaps, D. (1975) 'Women in Greek inheritance law' *CQ* 25:53-57

—— (1977) 'The woman least mentioned: etiquette and women's names' *CQ* 27:323-330

—— (1979) *Economic rights of women in ancient Greece* Edinburgh

Schiemann, E. (1951) 'New results on the history of cultivated cereals' *HER* 5:305-320

Schiller, W. (1921) 'Das Hungerödem bei Hesiod' *JAN* 25:37-44

Schmidt, J.W. & Johnson, V.A. (1963) 'A sphaerococcum-like tetraploid wheat' *Crop science* 3:98-99

Schneider, E.L. & Reed, J.D. (1985) 'Life extension' *NEJM* 312:1159-1168

Schoen, R. (1983) 'Measuring the tightness of a marriage squeeze' *DEM* 20:61-78

Schoeninger, M.J. (1979) 'Diet and status at Chalcatzingo: some empirical and technical aspects of strontium analysis' *AJPA* 51:295-310

—— (1982) 'Diet and the evolution of modern human form in the Near East' *AJPA* 58:37-52

Schofield, R.S. (1986) 'Did the mothers really die? Three centuries of maternal mortality in "The world we have lost"' in L. Bonfield, R.M. Smith & K. Wrightson (eds) *The world we have gained: histories of population and social structure* (1986) 231-260 Oxford

Scholten, C.M. (1985) *Childbearing in American society: 1650-1850* New York

Schönert-Geiss, E. (1974) 'Die Geldzirkulation Attikas im 4. Jahrhundert v.u.Z.' in E.C. Welskopf (ed.) *Hellenische Poleis* (1974) vol. 1, pp. 531-550 Berlin

Schrire, C. & Steiger, W.L. (1974) 'A matter of life and death: an investigation into the practice of female infanticide in the Arctic' *Man* 9:161-184

Schrödinger, E. (1944) *What is life? The physical aspect of the living cell* Cambridge

—— (1954) *Nature and the Greeks* Cambridge

Schuhl, P.-M. (ed.) (1968) *Aristote: cinq oeuvres perdues* Paris

Scobie, A. (1986) 'Slums, sanitation and mortality in the Roman world' *KL* 68:399-433

Scora, R.W. (1975) 'On the history and origin of citrus' *BTBC* 102:369-375

Scott, E. & Johnston, F.E. (1985) 'Science, nutrition, fat, and policy: tests of the critical fat hypothesis' *CA* 26:463-473

Seager, R. (1986) review of Cartledge & Harvey (1985) in *LCM* 11.8:140-141

Sealey, R. (1984) 'Lawful concubinage in Athens' *Classical antiquity* 3:111-133

Sécond, G. (1986) 'La domestication en régime autogame: exemple des Riz (Oryza spp.)' *BSBF* 133.1:35-44

Sedlar, J.W. (1980) *India and the Greek world: a study in the transmission of culture* Totowa

Segalen, M. (1986) *Historical anthropology of the family* Cambridge

Seligman, N.G., Feigenbaum, S., Benjamin, R.W. & Feinerman, D. (1985) 'Efficiency of fallow as a store for fertiliser nitrogen in a semi-arid region' *JAGS* 105:245-249

Semple, E.C. (1922) 'The influence of geographic conditions upon ancient Mediterranean stock-raising' *Annals of the Association of American Geographers* 12:3-38

—— (1928) 'Ancient Mediterranean agriculture' *AH* 2:61-98 & 129-156

—— (1932) *The geography of the Mediterranean region: its relation to ancient history* Cambridge

Sencer, H.A. & Hawkes, J.G. (1980) 'On the origin of cultivated rye' *BJLS* 13:299-313

Sergent, B. (1979) 'Les trois fonctions des Indo-Européens dans la Grèce ancienne' *AESC* 34:1155-1186

—— (1980) 'L'utilisation de la trifonctionnalité d'origine indo-européenne chez les auteurs grecs' *ARET* 13.2:233-278

—— (1984) *L'homosexualité dans la mythologie grecque* Paris

—— (1986) *L'homosexualité initiatique dans l'Europe ancienne* Paris

Setton, K.M. (1975a) *Catalan domination of Athens* London

—— (1975b) *Athens in the Middle Ages* London

Shackleton, N.J. (1970) 'Stable isotope study of the palaeoenvironment of the Neolithic site of Nea Nikomedeia, Greece' *NAT* 227:943-944

Sharma, T.R. & Gandhi, S.M. (1977) 'Variation and various agronomical characters in common and durum wheats' *ZPZ* 79:40-46

Sharp, P.M. & Wen-Hsiung Li (1988) 'Understanding the origins of AIDS viruses' *NAT* 336:315

Sharpe, W.D. (1962) 'Lung disease and the Graeco-Roman physician' *American review of respiratory diseases* 86:178-192

Shaw, B.D. (1976) 'Climate, environment and prehistory in the Sahara' *WA* 8:133-149

—— (1979) 'The camel in Roman North Africa: history, biology and human economy' *Bulletin de l'Institut Fondamental d'Afrique Noire* sér. B, 41:663-721

—— (1981) 'Climate, environment and history: the case of Roman North Africa' in T.M.L. Wigley, M.J. Ingram & G. Farmer (eds) *Climate and history: studies in past climates and their effect on man* (1981) 379-403 Cambridge

—— (1982/83) ' "Eaters of flesh, drinkers of milk": the ancient Mediterranean ideology of the pastoral nomad' *ACS* 13/14:5-31

—— (1984) 'Water and society in the ancient Maghrib: technology, property and development' *Antiquités africaines* 20:121-173

—— (1987) 'The age of Roman girls at marriage: some reconsiderations' *J. of Roman studies* 77:30-46

Shaw, R.F. (1961) 'The effect of polygamy and infanticide on the sex ratio' *AJPA* 19:79-83

Sheehan, M.C. & Whitehead, D.R. (1981) 'The late-postglacial vegetational history of the Argolid peninsula, Greece' *National Geographic Society Research Reports* 13:693-708

Shepard, P. & McKinley, D. (eds) (1969) *The subversive science: essays toward an ecology of man* Boston

Shepherd, K.D., Cooper, P.J.M., Allan, A.Y., Brennan, D.S.H. & Keatinge, J.D.H. (1987) 'Growth, water use and yield of barley in Mediterranean type environments' *JAGS* 108:365-378

Sherratt, A. (1981) 'Plough and pastoralism: aspects of the secondary products revolution' in Hodder et al. (1981) 261-305

Shinnie, P.L. (1984) 'The main lines of socio-economic development in the Sudan in post-Neolithic times' in L. Krzyzaniak & M. Kobusiewicz (eds) *Origin and early development of food-producing cultures in north-eastern Africa* (1984) 109-115 Poznań

Shipley, D.G.J. (1987) *A history of Samos 800-188 BC* Oxford

Short, R.V. (1976) 'The evolution of human reproduction' *PRSL* B 195:3-24

—— (1984) 'Breast feeding' *SA* 250.4:23-29

Shpiler, L. & Blum, A. (1986) 'Differential reaction of wheat cultivars to hot environments' *EUP* 35:483-492

Shrewsbury, J.F.D. (1949) 'The yellow plague' *JHM* 4:5-47

—— (1950) 'The plague of Athens' *BHM* 24:1-25

Shrimpton, G. (1987) 'Regional drought and the economic decline of Mycenae' *EMC* 31:137-176

Siegel, R.E. (1960) 'Epidemics and infectious diseases at the time of Hippocrates' *Gesnerus* 17:77-98

Simmonds, N.W. (ed.) (1976) *Evolution of crop plants* London

—— (1979) *Principles of crop improvement* London

Simoons, F.J. (1961) *Eat not this flesh: food avoidances in the Old World* Westport

—— (1979) 'Dairying, milk use and lactose malabsorption in Eurasia: a problem in culture history' *Anthropos* 74:61-80

Simpson, B.B. & Conner-Ogorzaly, M. (1986) *Economic botany* New York

Sinclair, T.R. & de Wit, C.T. (1975) 'Photosynthetic and nitrogen requirements for seed production by various crops' *SCI* 189:565-567

Sindiga, I. (1987) 'Fertility control and population growth among the Masai' *HE* 15:53-66

Skydsgaard, J.E. (1988) 'Transhumance in ancient Greece' in Whittaker (1988) 75-86

Slater, W.J. (1986) *Aristophanis Byzantii Fragmenta* Berlin

Slicher van Bath, B.H. (1963) *The agrarian history of western Europe AD 500-1850* London

—— (1967) 'The yields of different crops (mainly cereals) in relation to the seed c. 810-1820' *Acta historiae neerlandica* 2:26-106

Smartt, J. & Hymowitz, T. (1985) 'Domestication and evolution of grain legumes' in Summerfield & Roberts (1985) 37-72

Smith, C.D. (1979) *Western Mediterranean Europe: a historical geography of Italy, Spain and southern France since the Neolithic* London

Smith, D.G. & Guinto, R.S. (1978) 'Leprosy and fertility' *HB* 50:451-460

Smith, E.H. (1797) 'The plague of Athens. Sections I & II' *The medical repository* (New York) I.1:3-29

Smith, G.F. (1987) 'Jason's Golden Fleece explained?' *NAT* 327:561

Smith, R.E.F. (1959) *The origins of farming in Russia* Paris

Smith, T.E. (1960) 'The Cocos-Keeling islands: a demographic laboratory' *PS* 14:94-130

Snaydon, R.W. (1980) 'Plant demography in agricultural systems' in O.T. Solbrig (ed.) *Demography and evolution in plant populations* (1980) 131-160 Oxford

Snodgrass, A.M. (1971) *The Dark Age of Greece: an archaeological survey of the eleventh to the eighth century BC* Edinburgh

—— (1974) 'An historical Homeric society?' *JHS* 94:114-125

—— (1977) *Archaeology and the rise of the Greek state* Cambridge

—— (1980) *Archaic Greece: the age of experiment* London

—— (1983a) 'Two demographic notes' in R. Hägg (ed.) *The Greek renaissance of the eighth century BC* (1983) 167-171 Stockholm

—— (1983b) 'The Greek Early Iron Age: a reappraisal' *DHA* 9:73-86

—— (1987) *An archaeology of Greece: the present state and future scope of a discipline* Berkeley

Snyder, J.C. (1965) 'Typhus fever rickettsiae' in F.L. Horsfall & I. Tamm (eds) *Viral and rickettsial infections of man* (4th ed. 1965) 1059-1094 Philadelphia

Soffer, O. (ed.) (1987) *The Pleistocene Old World: regional perspectives* New York

Solomon, J. (1985) 'Thucydides and the recognition of contagion' *Maia* 37:121-123

Sommer, A. (1982) *Nutritional blindness: xerophthalmia and keratomalacia* Oxford

Sondaar, P.Y. (1971) 'Palaeozoogeography of the Pleistocene mammals from the Aegean' *Opera botanica* 30:65-70

—— (1977) 'Insularity and its effect on mammal evolution' in M.K. Hecht, P.C. Goody & B.M. Hecht (eds) *Major patterns in vertebrate evolution* (1977) 671-707 New York

Sorensen, T.I.A., Nielsen, G.G., Andersen, P.K. & Teasdale, T.W. (1988) 'Genetic and environmental influences on premature death in adult adoptees' *NEJM* 318:727-732

Sourvinou-Inwood, C. (1988) *Studies in girls' transitions: aspects of the arkteia and age representation in Attic iconography* Athens

Spiegel-Roy, P. (1986) 'Domestication of fruit trees' in Barigozzi (1986) 201-211

Sprague, M.A. (1954) 'The effect of grazing management on forage and grain production from rye, wheat and oats' *Agronomy journal* 46:29-33

Spruytte, J. (1983) *Early harness systems: experimental studies* (Engl. transl.) London

Spurr, M.S. (1983) 'The cultivation of millet in Roman Italy' *Papers of the British School at Rome* 51:1-15

—— (1986) *Arable cultivation in Roman Italy* London

Stanhill, G. (1976) 'Trends and deviations in the yield of the English wheat crop during the last 750 years' *Agro-ecosystems* 3:1-10

Stanley, N.F. (1980) 'Man's role in changing patterns of arbovirus infections' in Stanley & Joske (1980) 151-173

Stanley, N.F. & Joske, R.A. (eds) (1980) *Changing disease patterns and human behaviour* London

Stanley, S.M. (1973) 'An explanation for Cope's Rule' *Evolution* 27:1-26

Stearn, W.T. (1976) 'From Theophrastos and Dioskorides to Sibthorp and Smith: the background and origin of the "Flora Graeca" ' *BJLS* 8:285-298

—— (1977) 'The earliest European acquaintance with tropical vegetation' *The Gardens' Bulletin, Singapore* 29:13-18

Stebbins Jr., G.L. (1950) *Variation and evolution in plants* New York

Steele, W.M., Allen, D.J. & Summerfield, R.J. (1985) 'Cowpea' in Summerfield & Roberts (1985) 520-583

Steensberg, A. (1980) *New Guinea gardens: a study of husbandry with parallels in prehistoric Europe* London

Steinbock, R.T. (1976) *Palaeopathological diagnosis and interpretation: bone diseases in ancient human populations* Springfield

Stephens, D.W. & Krebs, J.R. (1986) *Foraging theory* Princeton

Stewart, A.B. & Robertson III, W. (1968) 'Fungus spores from prehistoric potsherds' *MYC* 60:701-704

—— & —— (1971) 'Moisture and seed carbonisation' *EB* 25:381

Stickel, L.F. (1979) 'Population ecology of house mice in unstable habitats' *JNE* 48:871-887

Stini, W.A. (1982) 'Sexual dimorphism and nutrient reserves' in Hall (1982) 391-419

Stirling, P. (1965) *Turkish village* London

Stockman, R. (1932) 'Historical notes on poisoning by leguminous foods' *JAN* 36:180-189

Stoianovitch, T. (1966) 'Le maïs dans les Balkans' *AESC* 21:1026-1040

—— (1967) *A study in Balkan civilization* New York

—— (1976) 'The Balkan domestic family: geography, commerce, demography' *Revue des études sud-est européennes* 14:465-475

Stol, M. (1987) 'The Cucurbitaceae in the cuneiform texts' *BSA* 3:81-92

Stopes, M.C. (1931) 'Positive and negative control of conception in its various technical aspects' *J. of state medicine* 39:354-360

Stouff, L. (1970) *Ravitaillement et alimentation en Provence aux XIVe et XVe siècles* Paris

Strauss, B.S. (1987) *Athens after the Peloponnesian War: class, faction and policy 403-386 BC* Ithaca

Street, F.A. (1981) 'Tropical palaeoenvironments' *Progress in physical geography* 5:157-185

Stuart, A.J. (1977) 'The vertebrates of the Last Cold Stage in Britain and Ireland' *PTRS* B 280:295-312

Stuart-Macadam, P. (1985) 'Porotic hyperostosis: representative of a childhood condition' *AJPA* 66:391-398

—— (1987) 'New evidence to support the anaemia theory' *AJPA* 74:521-526

—— (1989) 'Porotic hyperostosis: the relation between orbital and vault lesions' *AJPA* 80:187-193

Suchey, J.M., Wiseley, D.V., Green, R.F. & Noguchi, T.T. (1979) 'Analysis of dorsal pitting in the os pubis in an extensive sample of modern American females' *AJPA* 51:516-523

Summerfield, R.J. & Roberts, E.H. (eds) (1985) *Grain legume crops* London

Sutcliffe, A.J. (1985) *On the track of Ice Age mammals* London

Svoronos, N. (1976) 'Remarques sur les structures économiques de l'empire byzantin au XIe siècle' *Travaux et mémoires* 6:49-67

Swedlund, A.C. (ed.) (1975) *Population studies in archaeology and biological anthropology: a symposium* Washington

—— (1978) 'Historical demography as population ecology' *ARA* 7:137-173

Swee-Hock, S. (1980) *Population control for zero growth in Singapore* Oxford

Syme, J.R. & Bremner, P.M. (1968) 'Growth and yield of pure and mixed crops of oats and barley' *JAE* 5:659-674

Symeonoglou, S. (1985) *The topography of Thebes from the Bronze Age to modern times* Princeton

Szemerényi, O. (1974) 'The origins of the Greek lexicon: ex Oriente lux' *JHS* 94:144-157

—— (1977) *Studies in the kinship terminology of the Indo-European languages* Teheran

—— (1985) 'Recent developments in Indo-European linguistics' *Transactions of the Philological Society* (1985) 1-71

Tabutin, D. (1978) 'La surmortalité féminine en Europe avant 1940' *POP* 33:121-148

—— (1981) 'Nuptiality and fertility in Maghreb' in Ruzicka (1981) 101-122

Talbert, R.J.A. (1974) *Timoleon and the revival of Greek Sicily 344-317 BC* Cambridge

Talbot, A.-M.M. (1984) 'Old age in Byzantium' *Byzantinische Zeitschrift* 77:267-278

Tamarin, R.H. (1977) 'Dispersal in island and mainland voles' *ECO* 58:1044-1054

Tammaro, F. & Xepapadakis, G. (1986) 'Plants used in phytotherapy, cosmetics and dyeing in the Pramanda district (Epirus, north-west Greece)' *J. of ethnopharmacology* 16:167-174

Tavenner, E. (1918) 'The Roman farmer and the moon' *TAPA* 49:67-82

Tazelaar, C.M. (1967) '*Paides kai epheboi*: some notes on the Spartan stages of youth' *MNE* 20:127-153

Teall, J.L. (1959) 'The grain supply of the Byzantine empire' *DOP* 13:87-139

—— (1971) 'Byzantine agricultural tradition' *DOP* 25:33-59

Telegin, D.Y. (1986) *Dereivka: a settlement and cemetery of Copper Age horse keepers on the middle Dneiper* (*BAR* Int. Ser. 287, Engl. transl.) Oxford

Testart, A. (1982) 'Les tubercules sont-ils aux céréales comme la sauvagerie est à la civilisation?' *JATBA* 29:349-354

Te-Tzu Chang (1976) 'The origin, evolution, cultivation, dissemination and diversification of Asian and African rices' *EUP* 25:425-441

—— (1983) 'The origins and early cultures of the cereal grains and food legumes' in Keightley (1983) 65-94

Thapa, S., Short, R.V. & Potts, M. (1988) 'Breast feeding, birth spacing and their effects on child survival' *NAT* 335:679-682

Theide, J. (1978) 'A glacial Mediterranean' *NAT* 276:680-683

Theocharis, D.R. et al. (1973) *Neolithic Greece* Athens

Theocharopoulos, M. & Georgiadis, Th. (1984) 'Contribution à l'étude de la végétation de l'Attique orientale (Nea Makri) en Grèce (prise en compte des impacts urbains et touristiques)' *EM* 10.3/4:133-157

Thiersch, F. (1833) *De l'état actuel de la Grèce et des moyens d'arriver à sa restauration* (2 vols) Leipzig

Thirgood, J.V. (1981) *Man and the Mediterranean forest* London

Thiselton-Dyer, W.T. (1918) 'On some ancient plant names. II and III' *J. of philology* 34:78-96 & 290-312

Thomas, D.W. (ed.) (1958) *Documents from Old Testament times* London

Thomas, K.D. (1983) 'Agricultural and subsistence systems of the third millennium BC in north-west Pakistan: a speculative outline' in M. Jones (ed.) *Integrating the subsistence economy* (*BAR* Int. Ser. 181) 279-314 Oxford

Thompson, D'A.W. (1940) *Science and the classics* London

Thompson, H.A. (1930) 'Syrian wheat in Hellenistic Egypt' *Archiv für Papyrusforschung und verwandte Gebiete* 9:207-213

Thompson, W.E. (1967) 'The marriage of first cousins in Athenian society' *PHO* 21:273-282

—— (1972) 'Athenian marriage patterns: remarriage' *California studies in classical antiquity* 5:211-225

Thomson, G. (1943) 'The Greek calendar' *JHS* 63:52-65

Thomson, M.H. (1955) *Textes grecs inédits relatifs aux plantes* Paris

Thorndike, L. (1924) 'Disputed dates, civilization and climate, and traces of magic in the scientific treatises ascribed to Theophrastos' in C. Singer & H.E. Sigerist (eds) *Essays on the history of medicine presented to Karl Sudhoff* (1924) 73-86 Zurich

Thunnell, R.C. (1979) 'Eastern Mediterranean sea during the last glacial maximum: an 18,000-years BP reconstruction' *Quaternary science* 11:353-372

Thunnell, R.C. & Williams, P.F. (1989) 'Glacial-Holocene salinity changes in the Mediterranean sea: hydrographic and depositional effects' *NAT* 338:493-496

Thüry, G.E. (1977) 'Zur Infektkette der Pest in hellenistisch-römischer Zeit' in *Festschrift 75 Jahre Anthropologische Staatssammlung München 1902-1977* (1977) 275-283

Tien, H.Y. (1984) 'Induced fertility transition: impact of population planning and socio-economic change in the People's Republic of China' *PS* 38:385-400

Tisdale, S.L., Nelson, W.L. & Beaton, J.D. (1985) *Soil fertility and fertilizers* (4th ed.) New York

Titow, J.Z. (1972) *Winchester yields: a study in mediaeval agricultural productivity* Cambridge

Tolkowsky, S. (1938) *Hesperides: a study of the culture and use of citrus fruits* London

Toole, H. (1978) 'The plague of Athens and its description by Thucydides' (in modern Greek) *PAA* 53:225-247

Topping, P. (1977) *Studies in Latin Greece, AD 1205-1715* London

Toynbee, A.J. (1965) *Hannibal's legacy* (2 vols) London

Tozer, H.F. (1890) *The islands of the Aegean* Oxford

Treister, M.J. (1985) 'Bosporus and Egypt in the third century BC' *Vestnik drevnei istorii* 172:126-139 (in Russian with Engl. summary)

Trenbath, B.R. (1974) 'Biomass productivity of mixtures' *ADA* 26:177-210

Trigger, B.G., Kemp, B.J., O'Connor, D. & Lloyd, A.B. (1983) *Ancient Egypt: a social history* Cambridge

Trussell, J., Menken, J. & Coale, A.J. (1981) 'A general model for analysing the effect of nuptiality on fertility' in Ruzicka (1981) 7-27

Trussell, J. & Wilson, C. (1985) 'Sterility in a population with natural fertility' *PS* 39:269-286

Tsouderos, E.-J. (1919) *Le relèvement économique de la Grèce* Paris

Turkowski, L. (1969) 'Peasant agriculture in the Judaean hills' *Palestine exploration quarterly* 101:21-33 & 101-112

Turner, J. & Greig, J.R.A. (1975) 'Some Holocene pollen diagrams from Greece' *RPP* 20:171-204

Turrill, W.B. (1929) *Plant life of the Balkan peninsula: a phytogeographical study* Oxford

—— (1958) 'The evolution of floras with special reference to those of the Balkan peninsula' *J. of the Linnean Society of London. Botany* 56 (1958) 136-152

Uchitel, A. (1984) 'Women at work: Pylos and Knossos, Lagash and Ur' *HIS* 33:257-282

Udachin, R.A. (1986) 'Possible existence of *Triticum antiquorum* Heer in our day' article in Russian cited in *FCA* 39:123

Ullmann, M. (1975) 'Die Schrift des Rufus "De infantium curatione" und das Problem der Autorenlemmata in den "Collectiones Medicae" des Oreibasios' *Medizinhistorisches Journal* 10:165-190

Ullrich, H. (1975) 'Estimation of fertility by means of pregnancy and childbirth alterations at the pubis, the ilium, and the sacrum' *Ossa* 2:23-39

Underwood, J.H. (1979) *Human variation and human microevolution* London

Unger-Hamilton, R. (1988) *Method in microwear analysis: prehistoric sickles and other stone tools from Arjoune, Syria* (*BAR* Int. Ser. 435) Oxford

Utida, S. (1957) 'Population fluctuation, an experimental and theoretical approach' *CSHS* 22:139-151

Valaoras, V.G. (1936) 'A comparative study of the mortality of the population of Greece' *HB* 8:553-564

—— (1938) 'The average duration of life in ancient Greece' *PAA* 13:401-409 (in modern Greek)

—— (1946) 'Some effects of the famine on the population of Greece' *MMFQ* 24:215-234

—— (1960) 'A reconstruction of the demographic history of modern Greece' *MMFQ* 38:115-139

Valaoras, V.G., Polychronopoulou, A. & Trichopoulos, D. (1965) 'Control of family size in Greece' *PS* 18:265-278

——, —— & —— (1969) 'Greece: postwar abortion experience' *Studies in family planning* 46:10-16

Valensi, L. (1985) *Tunisian peasants in the eighteenth and nineteenth centuries* (Engl. transl.) Cambridge

Vallet, G. (1962) 'L'introduction de l'olivier en Italie centrale d'après les données de la céramique' in M. Renard (ed.) *Hommages à Albert Grenier* vol. 3 (1962) 1554-1563 Brussels

Vallino, F.O. & Ventura, G. (1984) 'Dati archeobotanici dal Broglio: semi ed altri reperti' in R. Peroni (ed.) *Nuove ricerche sulla protostoria della Sibaritide* (1984) 272-284 Rome

Vallois, H.V. (1960) 'Vital statistics in prehistoric populations as determined from archaeological data' in R.F. Heizer & S.F. Cook (eds) *The application of quantitative methods in archaeology* (1960) 186-204 (with discussion on pp. 205-222) Chicago

van Andel, T.H. & Lianos, N. (1983) 'Prehistoric and historic shorelines of the southern Argolid peninsula' *International J. of nautical archaeology* 12:303-324

van Andel, T.H. & Runnels, C.N. (1987) *Beyond the acropolis: a rural Greek past* Stanford

van Andel, T.H., Runnels, C.N. & Pope, K.O. (1986) 'Five thousand years of land use and abuse in the southern Argolid, Greece' *HEP* 55:103-128

van de Walle, E. (1980) 'Motivations and technology in the decline of French fertility' in R. Wheaton & T. Hareven (eds) *Family and sexuality in French history* (1980) 135-178 Philadelphia

van der Veen, M. (1985a) 'Evidence for crop plants from north-east England: an interim overview with discussion of new results' in N.R.J. Fieller, D.D. Gilbertson & N.G.A. Ralph (eds) *Palaeobiological investigations: research designs, methods and data analysis* (*BAR* Int. Ser. 266) 197-219 Oxford

—— (1985b) 'The UNESCO Libyan valleys survey X: botanical evidence for ancient farming in the pre-desert' *LS* 16:15-28

van Gennep, A. (1960) *The rites of passage* (Engl. transl.) London

van Gerven, D.P. & Armelagos, G.J. (1983) ''Farewell to palaeodemography?' Rumours of its death have been greatly exaggerated' *JHE* 12:353-360

van Ness, G.B. (1971) 'Ecology of anthrax' *SCI* 172:1303-1307

van Valen, L. (1973) 'A new evolutionary law' *Evolutionary theory* 1:1-30

van Wersch, H.J. (1972) 'The agricultural economy' in McDonald & Rapp (1972) 177-187

van Zeist, W. (1976) 'Macroscopic traces of food plants in south-western Asia' *PTRS* B 275:27-41

—— (1987) 'Some reflections on prehistoric field weeds' in J.A. Coetzee (ed.) *Palaeoecology of Africa and the surrounding islands* 18 (1987) 405-427

van Zeist, W. & Bottema, S. (1971) 'Plant husbandry in Early Neolithic Nea Nikomedeia, Greece' *ABN* 20:524-538

van Zeist, W. & Buitenhuis, H. (1983) 'A palaeobotanical study of Neolithic Erbaba, Turkey' *Anatolica* 10:47-89

van Zeist, W. & Casparie, W.A. (eds) (1984) *Plants and ancient man* Rotterdam

Vandier, J. (1936) *La famine dans l'Egypte ancienne* Cairo

Vartigian, H. (1983) 'Attic Greek kinship terminology' (PhD Iowa Univ. microfilm)

Vavilov, N.I. (1914) 'Immunity to fungus diseases as a physiological test in genetics and systematics, exemplified in cereals' *JG* 4:49-65

—— (1922) 'The law of homologous series in variation' *JG* 12:47-89

—— (1926) *Studies on the origin of cultivated plants* (Engl. transl.) Leningrad

—— (1951) *The origin, variation, immunity and breeding of cultivated plants* (Engl. transl. in *Chronica botanica* 13) Waltham

Veblen, Th. (1970 edition) *The theory of the leisure class* London

Velitzelos, E. & Gregor, H.-J. (1990) 'Some aspects of the Neogene floral history of Greece' *RPP* 62:291-307

Vernant, J.-P. (1989) 'Entre la honte et la gloire: l'identité du jeune Spartiate' in *L'individu, la mort et l'amour: soi-même et l'autre en Grèce ancienne* (1989) 173-209 Paris

Vertue, H. StH. (1953) 'An enquiry into venereal disease in Greece and Rome' *Guy's Hospital Reports* 102:277-302

Veyne, P. (1979) 'Mythe et réalité de l'autarcie à Rome' *REA* 81:261-280

—— (1982) 'Critique d'une systématisation: les lois de Platon et la réalité' *AESC* 37:883-908

Vial, Cl. (1984) *Délos indépendante 314-167 avant J.C.* (*BCH* suppl. 10) Athens

Vidal-Naquet, P. (1967) *Le bordereau de l'ensemencement dans l'Egypte ptolemaique* (Pap. Brux. 5)

—— (1981) *Le chasseur noir* Paris

Vincent, P. (1947) 'Guerre et population' *POP* 2:9-30

Vita-Finzi, C. (1969) *The Mediterranean valleys: geological changes in historical times* Cambridge

Voigt, M. (1876) 'Die verschiedenen Sorten von Triticum, Weizen-Mehl und Brod bei den Römern' *RHM* 31:105-128

Vokou, D., Kokkini, S. & Bessière, J.-M. (1988) '*Origanum onites* (Lamiaceae) in Greece: distribution, volatile oil yield, and composition' *EB* 42:407-412

Vollmer, H. (1959) 'Infant-mother relations in ancient Greece' *Pediatrics* 23:419-420

Vries, J. de (1984) *European urbanisation 1500-1800* London

Wagstaff, J.M. (1981) 'Buried assumptions: some problems in the interpretation of the Younger Fill raised by recent data from Greece' *JARS* 8:247-264

—— (1985) *The evolution of the Middle Eastern landscapes* London

Walker, P.L. (1986) 'Porotic hyperostosis in a marine-dependent California Indian population' *AJPA* 69:345-354

Wall, R., Robin, J. & Laslett, P. (eds) (1983) *Family forms in historic Europe* Cambridge

Walpole, R. (1817) *Memoirs relating to European and Asiatic Turkey* (2nd ed.) London

Walsh, J. (1986) 'Return of the locust: a cloud over Africa' *SCI* 234:17-19

Waltz, P. (1914) 'Note sur Thucydide, II.49' *REG* 27:39-43

Ward, A.G. et al. (1970) *The quest for Theseus* London

Warren, P. (1976) 'Did papyrus grow in the Aegean?' *AAA* 9:89-95

Wasson, R.G., Hofmann, A. & Ruck, C.A.P. (1978) *The road to Eleusis: unveiling the secret of the Mysteries* New York

Watson, A.M. (1983) *Agricultural innovation in the early Islamic world* Cambridge

Weaver, J. (1960) 'Grape growing in Greece' *EB* 14:207-224

Webb, C. & Hawtin, G. (eds) (1981) *Lentils* Farnham Royal

Webb, S.D. & Barnosky, A.D. (1989) 'Faunal dynamics of Pleistocene mammals' *Annual review of earth and planetary sciences* 17:413-438

Weber, M. (1968) *Economy and society* (2 vols, Engl. transl.) New York

—— (1976) *The agrarian sociology of ancient civilizations* (Engl. transl.) London

Weber, N.A. (1972) *Gardening ants: the attines* (*Memoirs American Philosophical Society* vol. 92)

Weidauer, K. (1954) *Thukydides und die Hippokratischen Schriften: der Einfluss der Medizin auf Zielsetzung und Darstellungsweise des Geschichtswerks* Heidelberg

Weinberg, E.D. (1984) 'Pregnancy-associated depression of cell-mediated immunity' *RID* VI.6:814-831

Weiss, B. (1982) 'The decline of Late Bronze Age civilization as a possible response to climatic change' *Climatic change* 4:173-198

Weiss, K.M. (1972) 'On the systematic bias in skeletal sexing' *AJPA* 37:239-249

—— (1973) *Demographic models for anthropology* (*AMQ* 38.2, part 2)

—— (1975a) 'The application of demographic models to anthropological data' *HE* 3:87-103

—— (1975b) 'Demographic disturbance and the use of life tables' in Swedlund (1975) 46-56

—— (1988) 'In search of times past: gene flow and invasion in the generation of human diversity' in C.G.N. Mascie-Taylor & G.W. Lasker (eds) *Biological aspects of human migration* (1988) 130-166 Cambridge

Welinder, S. (1979) *Prehistoric demography* Bonn

—— (1983) *The ecology of long-term change* Bonn

Wells, C. (1975a) 'Prehistoric and historical changes in nutritional diseases and associated conditions' *PFNS* 1:729-779

—— (1975b) 'Ancient obstetric hazards and female mortality' *BNYAM* 51:1235-1249

Weser, U., Miesel, R., Hartmann, H.-J. & Heizmann, W. (1989) 'Mummified enzymes' *NAT* 341:696

West, B. & Ben-Xiong Zhou (1988) 'Did chickens go north? New evidence for domestication' *JARS* 15:515-533

West, M.L. (1978) *Hesiod Works and Days* Oxford

Wet, J.M.J. de & Oelke, E.A. (1978) 'Domestication of American wild rice (*Zizania aquatica* L., Gramineae)' *JATBA* 25:67-84

Weyl, N. (1968) 'Some possible genetic implications of Carthaginian child sacrifice' *Perspectives in biology and medicine* 12:69-78

Wheeler, J.M. (1955) 'Self-sufficiency and the Greek city' *J. of the history of ideas* 16:416-420

Whitaker, T.W. & Bemis, W.P. (1975) 'Origin and evolution of the cultivated Cucurbita' *BTBC* 102:362-368

White, J. (1979) 'The plant as a metapopulation' *ARES* 10:109-145

White, K.D. (1964) 'The parable of the sower' *J. of theological studies* 15:300-307

—— (1970a) *Roman farming* London

—— (1970b) 'Fallowing, rotation and crop yields' *AH* 44:281-290

—— (1984) *Greek and Roman technology* London

White Jr., L. (1962) *Mediaeval technology and social change* Oxford

Whitehead, D. (1982/83) 'Sparta and the Thirty Tyrants' *ACS* 13/14: 105-130

—— (1986) *The demes of Attica 508/7-ca. 250 BC: a political and social study* Princeton

Whitley, A.J.M. (1987) 'Style, burial and society in Dark Age Greece: social, stylistic and mortuary change in the two communities of Athens and Knossos between 1100 and 700 BC' (Cambridge PhD)

Whittaker, C.R. (ed.) (1988) *Pastoral economies in classical antiquity* (*PCPS* suppl. 14) Cambridge

Wiens, D., Nickrent, D.L., Davern, C.I., Calvin, C.L. & Vivrette, N.S. (1989) 'Developmental failure and loss of reproductive capacity in the rare palaeoendemic shrub *Dedeckera eurekensis*' *NAT* 338:65-67

Wiesenfeld, S.L. (1967) 'Sickle cell trait in human biological and cultural evolution' *SCI* 157:1134-1140

Wijmstra, T.A. (1969) 'Palynology of the first 30 metres of a 120 m deep section in northern Greece' *ABN* 18:511-527

Wilcox, A.J. et al. (1988) 'Incidence of early loss of pregnancy' *NEJM* 319:189-194

Wilkes, I.G. (1953) 'A history of infant feeding. Part I. Primitive peoples: ancient works: Renaissance writers' *Archives of disease in childhood* 28:152-158

Wilkie, N.C. & Coulson, W.D.E. (eds) (1985) *Contributions to Aegean archaeology: studies in honour of W.A. McDonald* Minneapolis

Wilkinson, L.P. (1979) *Classical attitudes to modern issues* London

Wilkinson, T.J. (1982) 'The definition of ancient manured zones by means of extensive sherd-sampling techniques' *JFA* 9:323-333

Willan, R. (1821) 'Inquiry into the antiquity of the smallpox, measles and scarlet fever' in *Miscellaneous works* (ed. Ashby Smith) 1-115 London

Willcox, G.H. (1977) 'Exotic plants from Roman waterlogged sites in London' *JARS* 4:269-282

Willey, R.W. (1979) 'Intercropping: its importance and research needs. I. Competition and yield advantages' *FCA* 32:1-10

Williams, D. (1977) 'A consideration of the sub-fossil remains of *Vitis vinifera* L. as evidence for viticulture in Roman Britain' *Britannia* 8:327-334

Williams, E.W. (1957) 'The sickness at Athens' *GR* 4:98-103

—— (1962) 'The end of an epoch' *GR* 9:109-125

Williamson, M. (1981) *Island populations* Oxford

Wilson, E.O. (1971) *The insect societies* Cambridge, Mass.

—— (1975) *Sociobiology: the new synthesis* Cambridge, Mass.

—— (1978) *On human nature* Cambridge, Mass.

Wilson, N.G. & Russell, D.A. (eds) (1981) *Menander Rhetor* Oxford

Wiseman, J. (1973) 'Gods, war and plague in the time of the Antonines' in J. Wiseman (ed.) *Studies in the antiquities of Stobi* vol. 1 (1973) 143-183 Belgrade

Wittfogel, K. (1957) *Oriental despotism* New Haven

Wittmack, L. (1904) 'Die in Pompeji gefundenen pflanzlichen Reste' *Botanischer Jahrbücher für Systematik, Pflanzengeschichte und Pflanzengeographie* 33 Beiblatt no. 73, pp. 38-66

Wöhrle, G. (1985) *Theophrasts Methode in seinen botanischen Schriften* Amsterdam

Wolfe, A.B. (1932) 'The economics of population in ancient Greece' in *Facts and factors in economic history: articles by former students of E.F. Gay* (1932) 18-39 Cambridge, Mass.

Wolff, K.H. (ed.) (1950) *The sociology of Georg Simmel* Glencoe

Wood, E.M. (1983) 'Agricultural slavery in classical Athens' *AJAH* 8:1-47

—— (1988) *Peasant-citizen and slave: the foundations of Athenian democracy* London

Wood, J.W. & Smouse, P.E. (1982) 'A method of analyzing density-dependent vital rates with an application to the Gainj of Papua New Guinea' *AJPA* 58:403-411

Wood, J.W., Johnson, P.L. & Campbell, K.L. (1985) 'Demographic and endocrinological aspects of low natural fertility in highland New Guinea' *JBS* 17:57-79

Wood, J.W., Smouse, P.E. & Long, J.C. (1985) 'Sex-specific dispersal patterns in two human populations of highland New Guinea' *AN* 125:747-768

Woodman, A.J. (1988) *Rhetoric in classical historiography: four studies* London

Worster, D. (1985) *Nature's economy: a history of ecological ideas* (2nd ed.) Cambridge

Wrightson, K. & Levine, D. (1979) *Poverty and piety in an English village: Terling, 1525-1700* New York

Wrigley, E.A. (1969) *Population and history* London

—— (1978) 'Fertility strategy for the individual and the group' in C. Tilly (ed.) *Historical studies in changing fertility* (1978) 135-154 Princeton

—— (1987) *People, cities and wealth: the transformation of traditional society* Oxford

Wrigley, E.A. & Schofield, R.S. (1981) *The population history of England 1541-1871: a reconstruction* London (also 1989, Cambridge, with a new introduction)

Wylie, J.A.H. & Stubbs, H.W. (1983) 'The plague of Athens 430-428 B.C.: epidemic and epizoötic' *CQ* 33:6-11

Wylock, M. (1972) 'Les aromates dans les tablettes Ge de Mycènes' *SMEA* 15:105-146

Wyse, W. (1904) *The speeches of Isaios* Cambridge

Xanthakis-Karamanos, G. (1981) 'Remarks on Moschion's account of progress' *CQ* 31:410-417

Yasuda, N., Cavalli-Sforza, L.L., Skolnick, M. & Moroni, A. (1974) 'The evolution of surnames: an analysis of their distribution and extinction' *TPB* 5:123-142

Youmans, G.P. (1979) *Tuberculosis* Philadelphia

Young, D.C. (1988) 'How the Amateurs won the Olympics' in Raschke (1988) 55-75

Young, E.J. (1983) 'Human brucellosis' *RID* V.5:821-842

Young, G.L. (1974) 'Human ecology as an interdisciplinary concept: a critical inquiry' *Advances in ecological research* 8:1-105

Zadoks, J.C. (1985) 'Cereal rusts, dogs and stars in antiquity' *Cereal rusts bulletin* 13:1-9

Zawadski, T. (1960) & (1961) 'L'agriculture de la Grèce antique' *ARC* 11:104-127 & 12:19-47 (in Polish)

Zeuner, F.E. (1963) *A history of domesticated animals* London

Zeven, A.C. (1980a) 'The spread of bread wheat over the Old World since the Neolithicum as indicated by its genotype for hybrid necrosis' *JATBA* 27:19-53

—— (1980b) 'Polyploidy and domestication: the origin and survival of polyploids in cytotype mixtures' in W.H. Lewis (ed.) *Polyploidy: biological relevance* (1980) 385-407 New York

Zhukovskij, P.M. (1962) *Cultivated plants and their wild relatives* (Engl. transl.) Farnham Royal

Zimansky, P.E. (1985) *Ecology and empire: the structure of the Urartian state* Chicago

Zimmermann, M.R. & Angel, J.L. (eds) (1986) *Dating and age determination of biological materials* London

Zinsser, H. (1935) *Rats, lice and history* (1985 reprint London)

Zivanovich, S. (1982) *Ancient diseases: the elements of palaeopathology* (Engl. transl.) London

Zohary, D. (1973) 'The origin of cultivated cereals and pulses in the Middle East' *Chromosomes today* 4:307-321

—— (1983) 'Wild genetic resources of crops in Israel' *IJB* 32:97-127

Zohary, D., Harlan, J.R. & Vardi, A. (1969) 'The wild diploid progenitors of wheat and their breeding value' *EUP* 18:58-65

Zohary, D. & Hopf, M. (1988) *Domestication of plants in the Old World* Oxford

Zohary, D. & Spiegel-Roy, P. (1975) 'Beginnings of fruit-growing in the Old World' *SCI* 187:319-327

Zohary, M. (1982) *Plants of the Bible* Cambridge

Zulueta, J. de (1973) 'Malaria and Mediterranean history' *Parassitologia* 15:1-15

Zvelebil, M. (1985) 'Iron Age transformations in northern Russia and the northeast Baltic' in G. Barker & C. Gamble (eds) *Beyond domestication in prehistoric Europe: investigations in subsistence archaeology and social complexity* (1985) 147-180 London

Supplementary bibliography

Allen, P. (1979) 'The Justinianic plague' *Byzantion* 49:5-20

Avezzù, E. (1983) 'Stilemi associativi e rappresentazioni della parentela nell'Iliade' *Quaderni di storia* 17:69-97

Barton, C.M., Rubio Gomiz, F., Miksicek, C.A. & Donaghue, D.J. (1990) 'Domestic olive' *NAT* 346:518-519

Blakely, R.L. (1989) 'Bone strontium in pregnant and lactating females from archaeological samples' *AJPA* 80:173-185

Bodson, L. (1978) 'Données antique de zoogéographie: l'expansion des léporidés dans la Méditerranée classique' *Les naturalistes belges* 59:66-81

Bodson, L. (1987) 'Les débuts en Europe du chat domestique' *Ethnozootechnie* 40:13-38

Boessneck, J. & Driesch, A. von den (1979) 'Ein Löwenknochenfund aus Tiryns' *AA* 94:447-449

Boessneck, J. & Driesch, A. von den (1981) 'Ein Beleg für das Vorkommen des Löwen auf der Peloponnes in "Herakleischer" Zeit' *AA* 96:257-258

Borza, E.N. (1987) 'Malaria in Alexander's army', *The ancient history bulletin* (Calgary) 1:36-38

Brunner, T.F. (1973) 'Evidence of marijuana use in ancient Greece and Rome?' *BHM* 47:344-355

Byl, S. (1988) 'Rheumatism and gout in the Corpus Hippocraticum' *AC* 57:89-102

Chappellaz, J., Barnola, J.M., Raynaud, D., Korotkevich, Y.S. & Lorius, C. (1990) 'Ice-core record of atmospheric methane over the past 160,000 years' *NAT* 345:127-131

Conophagos, C.E. (1980) *Le Laurium antique et la technique grecque de la production de l'argent* Athens

Day, J. (1942) *An economic history of Athens under Roman domination* New York

Dennell, R. (1976) 'The economic importance of plant resources represented on archaeological sites' *JARS* 3:229-247

Desborough, V.R. (1964) *The last Mycenaeans and their successors: an archaeological survey c. 1200 – c. 1000 B.C.* Oxford

Duncan-Jones, R.P. (1990) 'Roman life-expectancy' in *Structure and scale in the Roman economy* (1990) 93-104 Cambridge

Georgoudi, S. (1974) 'Quelques problèmes de la transhumance dans la Grèce ancienne' *REG* 87:155-185

Gill, D.W.J. (1988) 'Silver anchors and cargoes of oil: some observations on

Phoenician trade in the western Mediterranean' *Papers of the British School at Rome* 56:1-12

Golden, M. (1990) *Children and childhood in classical Athens* Baltimore

Grmek, M.D. (1989) *Histoire du sida: début et origine d'une pandémie actuelle* Paris

Grundy, S.M. (1986) 'Comparison of monounsaturated fatty acids and carbo-hydrates for lowering plasma cholesterol' *NEJM* 314:745-748

Habs, H. (1982) *Die sogenannte Pest des Thukydides: Versuch einer epidemiologi-schen Analyse Sitzungsberichte der Heidelberg Akademie der Wissenschaften, Mathematisch-Naturwissenschaftliche Klasse* Abhandlung 6:1982

Haeser, H. (1882) *Lehrbuch der Geschichte der Medicin und der epidemischen Krankheiten* vol. 3, pp. 3-53 Jena

Hanson, C.H. (ed.) (1972) *Alfalfa science and technology* Madison

Hecker, J.F.K. (1857) *La peste Antoniniana* Berlin

Hemmer, H. (1990) *Domestication: the decline of environmental appreciation* (2nd. ed., Engl. transl.) Cambridge

Hicks, J. (1969) *A theory of economic history* Oxford

Holladay, A.J. (1988) 'New developments in the problem of the Athenian plague' *CQ* 38:247-250 (cf. *NEJM* 314 (1986) 855-856 and 315 (1986) 1170-1173)

Hortsmanshoff, H.F.J. (1979) 'Epidemieën in de antieke wereld' *Hermeneus* 51:58-80

Hoyle, F. & Wickramasinghe, C. (1977) 'Does epidemic disease come from space?' *New scientist* 76:402-404

Katsouyanni, K., Trichopoulos, D., Boyle, P., Xirouchaki, E., Trichopoulou, A., Lisseos, B., Vasilaros, S. & MacMahon, B. (1986) 'Diet and breast-cancer: a case-control study in Greece' *International J. of cancer* 38:815-820

Kemp, D.J., Cowman, A.F. & Walliker, D. (1990) 'Genetic diversity in *Plasmodium falciparum*' *Advances in parasitology* 29:75-149

Klein, R., Loya, Y., Gvirtzman, G., Isdale, P.J. & Susic, M. (1990) 'Seasonal rainfall in the Sinai desert during the late Quaternary inferred from fluorescent bands in fossil corals' *NAT* 345:145-147

Koehl, R.B. (1986) 'The Chieftain Cup and a Minoan rite of passage' *JHS* 106:99-110

Kreager, P. (1982) 'Demography *in situ*' *PDR* 8:237-266

Kutzbach, J.E. & Street-Perrott, F.A. (1985) 'Milankovitch forcing of fluctuations in the level of tropical lakes from 18 to 0 Kyr BP' *NAT* 317:130-134

Lieber, E. (1970) 'Galen on contaminated cereals as a cause of epidemics' *BHM* 44:332-345

Littré, E. (1872) *Médecine et médecins* (2nd. ed.) Paris

Longo, O. (1980/81) 'Rapporti di riproduzione, "sacrifici" di adolescenti e controllo demografico nella Grecia antica' *Atti. Centro ricerche e documentazione sull' antichità classica* 11:127-163

Lonie, I.M. (1969) 'On the botanical excursus in *De natura pueri* 22-27' *Hermes* 97:391-411

Matossian, M.K. (1989) *Poisons of the past: moulds, epidemics, and history* New Haven

Mensink, R.P. & Katan, M.B. (1987) 'Effect of monounsaturated fatty acids versus complex carbohydrates on high density lipoproteins in healthy men and women' *LAN* 1:122-124

Mooney, H.A. (1988) 'Lessons from Mediterranean-climate regions' in E.O. Wilson & F.M. Peters (eds) *Biodiversity* (1988) 157-165 Washington, D.C.

Mylonas, G.E. (1970) 'The lion in Mycenaean times' *AAA* 3:421-425

Osborne, R.G. (1989) 'A crisis in archaeological history? The seventh century B.C. in Attica' *ABSA* 84:297-322

Paabo, S., Higuchi, R.G. & Wilson, A.C. (1989) 'Ancient DNA and the polymerase chain reaction: the emerging field of molecular archaeology' *J. of biological chemistry* 264.17:9709-9712

Panessa, G. (1987) 'Recenti studi sulla problematica paleoclimatologica ed ambientale della Grecia nell'antichità *ASNP* 17:1163-1171

Papaevangelou, G. & Halstead, S.B. (1980) 'Transmission of dengue 1 and 2 viruses in Greece in 1928' *American J. of tropical medicine and hygiene* 29:635-637

Paraskevaides, E.C., Pennington, G.W. & Naik, S. (1988) 'Seasonal distribution in conceptions achieved by artificial insemination by donor' *British medical J.* 297:1309-1310 (cf. *BMJ* 297:1611)

Ping-ti Ho (1959) *Studies on the population of China, 1368-1953* Cambridge, Mass.

Rackham, O. (1978) 'The flora and vegetation of Thera and Crete before and after the great eruption' in *Thera and the Aegean world, I: papers presented at the 2nd. International Scientific Congress, Santorini, Greece* (1978) 755-764 London

Résultats du recensement 1961 (1966) Athens

Reyment, R.A. (1971) *Introduction to quantitative palaeoecology* Amsterdam

Ruschenbusch, E. (1988) 'Demography and democracy: Doch noch einmal die Bürgerzahl Athens im 4. Jh. v. Chr.' *ZPE* 72:139-140

Scarrow, G.D. (1988) 'The Athenian plague: a possible diagnosis' *The ancient history bulletin* 2:4-8

Skoda, F. (1988) *Médecine ancienne et métaphore: le vocabulaire de l'anatomie et de la pathologie en grec ancien* Paris

Thompson, R.C. (1949) *A dictionary of Assyrian botany* London

Valverde, V., Martorell, R., Mejia-Pivaral, V., Delgado, H., Lechtig, A., Teller, C. & Klein, R.E. (1977) 'Relationship between family land availability and nutritional status' *EFN* 6:1-7

Vandermeer, J. (1989) *The ecology of intercropping* Cambridge

Ventris, M.G.F. & Chadwick, J. (eds.) (1973) *Documents in Mycenaean Greek* (2nd. ed.) Cambridge

Weiss, R.F. (1988) *Herbal medicine* (Engl. transl.) Beaconsfield

Willis, K.J. (1989) 'Late Quaternary vegetational history of Epirus, northwest Greece' (Cambridge PhD)

Index

abortion, in ancient Greece, 148, 154-155, 444-445, during illness, 131-132, 439, in modern Greece, 78, 154-155, in Sparta, 446, spontaneous, 130, 396, 438

aceramic hypothesis, 65

acetysalicylic acid, 13

Achaia, Early Hellenistic population, 106, grain exports, 479, LHIIIC population, 61, little affected by epidemic of 430 BC, 260, wheat, 485

adoption, in Athens, 195

adultery, non-existent in Sparta, 169, in Athens, 141

Aegilops, *ovata* as a crop mimic, 339, 487, *A. searsii*, 343, *A. sharonensis*, 343, *A. squarrosa*, and bread wheat evolution, 325, 356, small seeded, 343, 354, susceptible to rust, 292, tillering capacity, 376

Africa, Ice Age climate, 236

Africa, North, cereal yields, 376-380, 497-498, locusts, 27, olive, 17, 379, wheat, 324-325, 334, 338, 347, 357, 480-481

age class systems, 84-85, 160-192, basis for chronology, 452, citizenship, 200, and economy, 383, generational, 453, history, 404-407, 409-410, 417-418, not homeostatic, 213-214, kinship, 200-201

age of death, difficult to assess, 111, sex-differential, 129-133, 435-436

age, old, in Greece, 177-179

agriculture, definition, 11-12, labour inputs in Mediterranean, 56-57, 82-83, 297, 309, 427-428, on smallholdings, 55-56, origins, 17-18, 403-404, productivity, 14-15, productivity in relation to fallow, 105-106, role of child labour, 142-143, slavery, 55-57, women, 83, 220, 431, see also entries for individual crop plants

AIDS, 8, 223-224, 262, 422, 458, evolution, 26, 223-224, 290, and promiscuity, 262, 282, 443

Aigina, artificial extension of cultivated area, 179, 476, slavery, 58

Ainos, famine, 302

Aitolia, Early Hellenistic population, 106, land erosion, 373, 375, rainfall, 392, raw meat eaten, 226

Akanthos, skeletal population, 435

Akarnania, runoff farming, 498

Akragas, export of olive oil, 33

alcohol, nutritional value, 297

Alexandria, epidemic of Cyprian, 465, population, 88-89, 464, smallpox, 251, vivisection, 286

almond, 28, 423

amenorrhoea, lactational, 137-140, 440-441, famine, 230

Amida, epidemic, 464

Amorgos, muteness, 235, 461

Amphipolis, 96

anachronism, in historiography, 13-14, 399, 410-413

anaemia, sickle-cell, 235-236, 461, iron deficiency, 275-277, 283-284, 468

Anaphe, invasion of partridges, 39

Anatolia, chickpea, 30, cereal rust, 293, invaded by Celts, 67, 129, lucerne, 303, oats, 361, rice, 22, rye, 364, spring sowing, 484, wheat, 334, 353, 357, 367, 495

animals, diseases, 287-290, 471-472, see also entries for individual animals and husbandry, animal

anthrax, 288, 290, 471

Antioch, Athenian colonists, 434

ants, ancient views, 420, 503, as farmers, 11-12, prey on wheat, 329, 384, slavery, 212

apple, 29, 423

apricot, 32, 424

arbitrators, in Athens, 119-122, 178, 438

arboriculture, 32-34, absence in early Greece, 85, and fallow periods, 83

ard, see plough

area, methods of measuring, 342

Argolid, spelt wheat, 349, population of southern, 103-105, eighth-century colonisation, 90-91

Argos, patriline discontinuity, 456, rivalry with Mycenae, 391-392, ritual wars with Sparta, 242, 449, Temenid kings, 182,

wheat, 365, 494
aristocracy, 205-206, 412
Arkadia, barley, 478, claims autochthony, 476, legend of Euanthes, 452, no olive, 306, population decline in Hellenistic, 106, role of music in age class systems, 453
Artemisia steppe, 402
Asine, Hellenistic, 468-469
Asklepios, and blindness, 470, god of healing, 104-105, and infertility, 148, introduction to Athens, 463
Askra, 106, 140
asparagus, Bath, 292
asphodel, 230-231, 459
Assiros Toumba, emmer, 494, rye scarce, 364
Assyria, 47, attacks Samaritans, 234, cotton, 26, development of cavalry, 399, rice, 22
astronomy, 9, theories of Hipparchos, 34
Astypalaia, invasion of hares, 39, 426, good snails but no snakes, 426
Athens, age class organisation in Dark Age, 184-185, age classes in classical, 175-176, aristocracy, 205-206, 412, citizenship, 188, compared to Sparta, 128, dengue, 256-257, no evidence for grain imports in archaic period, 94, or during *Pentêkontaëtia*, 97, grain imports in fourth century BC, 332, epidemic in 430 BC, 6-7, 207-208, 244-262, 264-265, execution of Sokrates, 410, eye diseases, 470, inheritance, 202-208, 214-217, marriage, 148-151, 218-221, little iron in mediaeval, 348, kinship, 195-204, nineteenth-century historiography, 411-413, old age, 178, role of olive, 296, 304-309, as a peasant society, 214-217, paederasty, 167-168, population growth in eighth century, 86-91, 125-126, population in fifth century, 95-99, 126, population in fourth century BC, 52-60, 73, population in Hellenistic period, 107, population in late antiquity, 108, population tied to countryside, 98, refuse disposal, 257, 382, seed selection, 344, self-sufficiency, 298-300, slavery, 53-60, 209-211, Solonian classes, 342, 488, water supply, 392-393, wool production, 313
Attica, animal husbandry, 310-313, 383-385, barley and wheat, 313-316, 328, 368, 477-478, bees, 423, cereal yields, 376-389, darnel and flax, 339-340, einkorn, 365, emmer, 365, forests, 35-36, gout, 227, land use in ancient, 309-313, in modern, 295-303, locusts, 27-28, millets, 363, oats, 361-362, olive, 56, 304-309, partridge, 426, rye, 364, settlement history, 63, shrub-trefoil, 385, sheep, 312-313, soils, 401,

sowing, 330, thyme, 352, no tapeworms, 226, wheat in early modern, 313, wolf, 400, yields in early modern, 389
Australopithecus, 403
autarkeia, 298-299
Avena abyssinica, byzantina, sativa, see oats
awn, of wheat, 479

baboon, and treponematoses, 283
bachelors, in Athens, 157, in Sparta, 170, within age class systems, 171
badger, in Greece, 400
baldness, on Mykonos, 234-235
Balearic Islands, and rabbit, 40
balsam, in Judaea, 29
barberry, 293
barley, 470, 483, 489, 491, 495, diseases, 292, 472, gruel supplement to breast milk, 276, in modern Attica, 296, in ancient Attica, 79, 313-316, 324, 364, 367-368, 477-478, in Britain, 347, 350, in Crete, 317, 494, in Cyrene, 490, in Israel, 347, in Linear B tablets, 366, labour inputs, 494, in Meso-potamia, 318, naked, 368, at origins of agriculture, 353, in Peloponnese, 314, pre-ferred for porridge, 321, price, 394, rapid shattering, 356, in religious rites, 478, in three-field rotation, 331, 352, 399, types, 327, wild, 337, 362, 368
Bassai, temple, 246
bathing, and conception, 156
bats, in Athens, 400
bean (*Vicia faba*), broad and field, 300-302, 473
bee, in Attica, 423, diseases, 471, absent from Mykonos, 460, and olives, 304, social, 503, and thyme, 352, wild and domesticated, 397, 501
beet, sugar, 28
Behçet's disease, 234
'big-men', in Greece and New Guinea, 406
biology, models, 7-8, in Aristotle, 408-409
birds, prey on cereals, 329, 484, in Athenian epidemic, 249, 289-290
bladder stone disease, 276, 284, 469
blindness, caused by trachoma, 281-282, 469-470, night, 284
Boiotia, 295, ephebes, 438, family structure, 196, heavy rainfall, 393, partridge, 426, population history, 158-160, 204-205, 429, defeats Sparta, 173, survey, 106, tapeworms, 226, wheat, 328
bones, see osteological evidence
Brauron, 131, 186, 453
bread, in Greece, 321-323, iron deficiency anaemia associated with wholemeal,

275-276, leavened, 326, nutritional value, 285-286

bread wheat, see wheat

breastfeeding, in Greece, 137-140, 231, 440, energetic costs in mammals, 152-153

bridewealth, 218-219, 458

Brill-Zinsser's disease, 265

Britain, animal husbandry, 383, lentil, 30, peach, 423, ploughing, 348, barley, 347, 350, cereal yields, 386-387, rat, 263, vine, 395-396, 501, wheat, 350, 355, 357, 386-388

brucellosis, 271, 468

burial, formal, 126-127, in Athens, 108-109, 255, in Sparta, 127-128

Butser Ancient Farm Project, 386-388

Byzacium, 376-380

Byzantion, see Constantinople

cactus, prickly pear, 32, 424

camel, 27, 422

Camelina sativa var. linicola, 340-341, 487, 493

cancer, breast, 287, 471, in pregnant women, 131

canine distemper, 288

Cappadocia, durum wheat, 479

carbonisation, of cereals, 335, 344

carnivores, 400-404

carob, 29, 423

carrot, evolution, 284, 470

carrying capacity, 73-84, of Attica, 79-80, in relation to natural fertility, 213-214, and diseases, 285

Carthage, 100, arboriculture reaches, 33, colonisation from, 212-213, epidemics, 243, 463, exports wine to Cyrene, 424, iron deficiency anaemia, 469, political institutions, 455, struggle with Rome, 27, 72, 380, 400, population size in Roman period unknown, 252

cassava, 81

cat, wild, in Greece, 400, size decrease under domestication, 396

cattle, badly nourished, 312, diseases, 471, size decrease under domestication, 396, size increase later under selective breeding, 398

causality, 2-3

census, Demetrios of Phaleron, 52-54, in modern Greece, 158

cereals, diseases, 291-293, 387, 472, in Greece, 313-316, 361-368, productivity increased in modern Greece, 78, 294-295, 367, r-selected, 70, 336, sowing seasons, 326-332, 484-485, yields, 372-389, see also individual entries

chaos, deterministic, 71-72, 416, 430, and diseases, 223, 251, 458

cherry, 29-30, 423

chestnut, 29, 423

chicken, eats darnel, 339, history, 233, 320, 460, increase in size, 398

chickenpox, 228-229, 254, 259, 459, confused with smallpox, 248

chickpea, 301-302, origin of plant and name, 30, from Byzantion, 103

children, obliged to support parents in Greece, 140-141, 441, sale in Athens and Thebes, 94, 209, 444

Chios, 242, three-month wheat in, 485, vine in, 375

cholera, absent from ancient Greece, 241, 270

chufa, in Egypt, 26, 422

citizenship, 176, block grants in fifth-century Athens, 95-96, in Greece, 188-189, in Rome, 189-190

citron, 32, 321, 481

citrus fruits, 32, 54, 321, in modern Attica, 296-297

class struggle, 163, 416

Claviceps purpurea, see ergotism

climate, variation and variability, 390-396, 413-414, 500-501

cockspur grass, 363

coeliac disease, 13

co-evolution, 12, 396

coinage, invention, 366, small volume in Athens, 57-58, 457

coitus, see intercourse

coitus interruptus, in antiquity, 156, in modern Greece, 78

cold, common, 21

colonisation, archaic Greek, 91-92, Athenian in fifth century, 96, Greek in fourth century, 100-101, 107, 212, 434, and genetics, 236

commensalism, 12

community, ecological, 18, 225

Constantinople, chickpea, 103, good harbour, 92, plague, 131, 258, 266, population, 252, wheat from Crimea, 482

consumer city, 89, 162-163, 191

contagion, absent from Hippokratic corpus, 225, in epidemic of Athens, 245, 289

contraception, 156, drugs, 434-435, rhythm method, 146, see also family, limitation and amenorrhoea

Cope's Rule, 398

Corinth, 100, League, 50, 244, skeletal population of, 109, 438, slavery, 58, urban development, 88

Corsica, rabbit, 426

cotton, evolution, 25-26, 422, in modern Attica, 396

cowpea, 25

cowpox, 290, 422

crambe, 32, 424

Crete, age class systems restrict population growth in, 169, age of death, 435, age grades, 166, *apetairoi*, 457, barley, 317, 494, bread in Minoan, 326, climate, 500, in Dark Ages, 185, emmer in Linear A tablets, 494, grass pea, 473, mediaeval export of wheat, 316, fauna, 402, flora, 40, 426, infanticide, 442, inheritance, 217, last age class society in Europe, 192, literacy, 448, marriage, 149, 176, natural fertility, 145, old age, 178, olive cultivation, 306-307, 474-475, paederasty, 169, plague, 267, Plato's ideal *polis*, 48-49, population history, 169-170, regulation of access to food, 173, respect for elderly, 450, poisonous spider, 402, segregation of sexes, 145, sesame, 363, sheep, 313, three-month wheat, 485

cribra orbitalia, 275

Crimea, wheat, 323-325, 331-332, 352, 355, 358-359, 367, 377, 498, wool, 397, viticulture, 33, 358, farm sizes, 492

crisis, Malthusian, 106

criticism, literary, 37, 135, 152, 417

cummin, 31

cypress, 29-30, 423

Cyprus, cereals, 348, 485, citron, 321, flora, 40, 426, lupin, 361, 492, olive, 475

Cyrene, barley, 346, 489, colonisation, 91, 431-432, donates grain, 393, dryness, 498, expedition against Carthage, 100-101, 434, land use, 378, locust, 27, plague, 266, no rice, 24, *silphion*, 32, 352, 424

cystic hydatid disease, 227, 459

cytomegalovirus, 228

Dark Ages, 64

darnel, history and evolution, 338-340, 487, 498

defences, chemical, 13, 302, 338, 360

deforestation, 35-36, 425, 496-497

Delos, family size, 193, purification, 246

Delphi, 39, 67, 242, 407, 441

democracy, historical origins, 181-182, 406

demography, see fertility, life expectancy, lifespan, life tables, mortality, population

Dendra, suit of armour, 398

dendrochronology, 391

dengue, 271, exclusive with yellow fever, 239, in modern Athens, 256-257, 465

descent, group, 197, 200, 202-203

devolution, diverging, 217

diarrhoea, 231

diffusionism, 19, 67

dimorphism, seasonal, 35, sexual, 130, 439

dinosaurs, extinction of, 9

diphtheria, 232, 460

diseases, see individual entries and also see epidemics and fever

dog, carries cystic hydatid disease, 227, size decrease under domestication, 396, canine distemper, 288, diseases, 471, eaten in antiquity, 459, in epidemic of 430 BC, 249, 289-290, used to hunt hares, 39, 426

Dorians, 128-129, 452

dowry, 218-219

Dreros, olive, 474

durum wheat, see wheat

Dutch Elm Disease, 71, 430

dysentery, amoebic, 228, 230, 441, 460

Echinochloa crus-galli, see millets

ecology, definition of, 4-6, etymology, 3,

economy, concept of, 3, market, 213-214, 411, 424

ecosystem, boundaries of, 16, 18

educational system, in Britain, 6, 414

Egypt, age of death, 435-436, antibiotics, 420, cereals, 318-319, 368-372, 388, 485, darnel, 340, daughters support parents, 441, epidemics, 229, 254, epidemic of 430 BC, 253-254, flood-basin agriculture, 23, hippopotamus, 400, infant exposure, 134, iron deficiency anaemia, 469, leprosy, 240, papyrus and chufa, 26, 422, plague, 266, population density, 102, office of pharaoh, 182, poppy, 421, schistosomiasis, 26, 465, sesame, 363-364, smallpox, 465, starvation, 77, wet-nursing, 440

eicosapentaenoic acid, 287

einkorn, 487, in Anatolia, 367, at Butser Farm, 386-387, diploid, 335, genetics of seed size, 343, domesticated and wild similar, 337, 358, in Greece, 365, 493, at origins of agriculture, 353, wild, 388, 500

elephant, diseases, 471, longevity, 437, at Megalopolis, 401

Eleusis, 256, 453, barley, 314, first fruits, 394, heavy rain, 393, Mysteries, 186, 364, *kukeôn*, 364, no chicken, 233

Elis, crop rotation, 493, cultivation of flax, 133, 340, 487, old age, 178, paederasty, 167, age grades for women, 172

emmer, 493-496, at Butser Farm, 386-387, confused and mixed with spelt, 349, 357, in Crimea, 331, 359, 367, and darnel, 339, evolution, 329, in Britain, 347, 350, in Egypt, 370-372, 495-496, in Ethiopia, 359, in Italy, 347, in N. Africa, 338, in Pompeii, 486, history, 365-367, 370-372, 493-496, oats as a weed, 362, 492, at origins of agriculture, 353, photoperiodic and temperature requirements of, 430, sowing, 329, tetraploid, 335, tillering, 386, preferred for *alica*, 320, 326, wild, 329, 333, 337, 362, 388, 430, 488, 500

encephalomyelitis, equine, 290, 466

endogamy, 203-204

environment, of an animal, 4

ephebes, in Athens, 119-122, 177, 192, 437-438, oath, 294, in Boiotia, 438

Ephesos, regulation of marriage, 149, 168, 192, sale of infants, 459-460

Epidauros, epidemic, 246, 263, eye diseases, 281, infertility, 443, lice, 466, parasitic worms, 226, skilled labour, 58, sanctuary of Asklepios, 104

epidemics, Antonine, 38, 248, 255, 425, 465, ancient definition, 225, 252-253, create prosperity, 258, modern definition, 225, in Athens in 430 BC, 6-7, 96-98, 207-208, 244-262, 264-265, 463-466, in Dark Age Greece, 229-230, 459, in Sicily, 243, in Italy, 243-244, and urbanisation, 256-258, see also entries for individual diseases

epiklêros, function, 195, marriage, 149, 157, 445, sexual intercourse, 146, 169, inheritance, 214-16

Epirus, animal husbandry, 312, 477, malaria, 274

equilibrium, assumption of, 5, 152, 225, 414

ergodicity, 261, 466

ergotism, absent or rare in Greece, 248, 464, history, 364, 493

erucic acid, 32

erusibê, 291

erysipelas, 232, 467

esparto, 20, 421

Ethiopia, 26, 405, cereals, 321-322, 481, 483, emmer, 359, 362, epidemics, 253-254, 464-465, flax as cereal, 340, oats, 362, 492, wheat, 321-322, 334, 357, 359

Etruria, commencement of olive cultivation, 32-33, 424

eucalyptus, 32

exogamy, 203-204

Failaka, 100, 434

falciparum, see malaria

fallow, 81, 303, 309, 385-386

family, size, in Athens and Delos, 135-136, 193, 196-197, variations, 123, 137, limitation, 94, 133, 145, 151-159, 166, maximum possible size, 133-134, 439-440, optimum size, 147, and age-specific nuptiality, 150

family, structure, at Athens, 195-196, in relation to fertility, 141

famine, 230-231, 459-460, as a cause of death, 431, oedema, 231, 459-460, amenorrhoea, 230

fats, and cancer and heart disease, 287, in olive oil, 285-287

favism, 301-302, 473

ferret, Libyan, 40

fertility, affected by baths, 156, and coitus, 150, and education, 143, influence on age structure of population, 123-125, and age-specific nuptiality, 150-151, genetic component, 95, 194, and malaria, 273, motives for high, 140-144, natural, 91, 123, 134-137, 145-146, 150, 194, 211, relation to family structure, 141, and sedentarisation, 115

fever, blackwater, 273, 468, as a discrete 'disease', 225, 242, Mediterranean spotted, 271, 468, puerperal, 130, 232, relapsing, 231, 241, 271, 467-468, sandfly, 271, 468, scarlet, 232, 248, typhoid, 228, 230, 254, undulant (brucellosis), 271, 468, yellow, 236, 239, 257

fig, 30, 423

fire, naturally occurring in Mediterranean ecosystems, 35, 425

fish, 284, 287, 470

flax, evolution and history, 340-341, 487, *L. angustifolium*, 15, 30, 32, 340, processed at Patrai, 133

flea, transmits murine typhus, 264, transmits plague, 265-267

foetus, ancient attitudes, 155, and smallpox, 259

foot-and-mouth disease, 288, 471

foraging theory, (optimal), 284-285, 353, 362, 491

founder effect, 234

fox, in Greece, 400

Franchthi cave, wild barley, 368

fruit, ancient attitudes, 286, trees in modern Attica, 296, domestication of fruit trees, 307

Garamantes, 27

garlic, in Lycia, 103, and shrub-trefoil, 385

Gaul, population of Roman, 224, smallpox, 250, 255, thyme, 491, wheat, 355, 377, 387

genos, in Athens, 197-203, 455, in botanical terminology, 326-328, 339

gestation, 147, 152-153

gift exchange, in Homeric Greece, 219, 415-417

glaciations, see Ice Age

glanders, 288, 290, 471

glottochronology, 404

glucose-6-phosphate dehydrogenase, 235, 279, 301

goat, 382, 385, decreased in size under domestication, 396, diseases, 471, number in modern Attica, 297, 312-313, wild, in Greece, 400

gold of pleasure, 340-341

gonorrhoea, 281-282, 470

Gordion, hemp, 20

Gortyn, civil war, 174, inheritance, 217

gourd, bottle, 25, 327, 483

gout, 227, 458

grafting, 29-30, 308, 375, 423

Greece, area of land cultivated, 80, 373, malaria in early modern, 278, marriage in early modern, 151, plague in early modern, 267-268, population growth in nineteenth century, 75-79, 85 see also entries for individual regions and towns in antiquity

Greek, influence of demographic processes on language, 93-94

Greeks, origins of, 30-31

greenhouse effect, 4, 280, 413-414

gunaikonomoi, 83

Gyara, epidemic of mice, 426

Haliartos, 106

Halieis, disappearance, 103, sea level rise, 476, tuberculosis, 435

hare, 20, 39-40, 400

harrow, 387

hazel, 423

head-hunting, in Sparta, 172, among Proto-Indo-Europeans, 448

heart, disease, 286-287, 471, failure in small-pox, 258

heirship, strategies of, 204-205

hektêmoroi, in Attica, 56, 94, 208-209, 456-457

Helisson, absorbed into Mantinea, 453

Helots, status, 454

hemlock, used on Keos, 451

hemp, used at Gordion, 20

hen, see chicken

hepatitis A and B, 227

heredity, ancient concepts, 37, 425

herpes, genital and simplex, 228, 234, 281-282, 459, 469, zoster, see chickenpox

hexaploid, see wheat

hippopotamus, on Aegean islands, 402, in

Egypt and Israel, 400, at Megalopolis, 401, on Samos, 502

hoe, 55, 82, 142-143

Homer, date, 365, 407, gift exchange, 406-407, *polis*, 409, warfare, 398-399, wheat, 478, 494

homeostasis, dilatory, 115, 210, 212-213

homosexuality, see paederasty

hoplite, 52, 100, 120-121, 258-260, 428, 433, farm, 358

horse, in Americas, 87, for chariot racing, 384, and disease, 26, 289-290, 471, domestication, 20-21, and emmer, 494, evolution and history, 398-400, 402-403, 502, and lucerne, 303, number in modern Attica, 297, and oats, 361-362, in ancient Attica, 311-312, in Athenian cavalry, 290, in Sahara, 27, used by Mongols, 67

hubris, 448

husbandry, animal, 36, 75, 476-477, and age class systems, 184-185, in Arkadia, 106, in Attica, 310-313, 382-385, in Italy, 375

Hutterites, 89, 131, 134, 137

hyacinth, 30, retards puberty, 423

hybridisation, of mammals, 37, plant, 36

hyperostosis, porotic, 275-277, 279, 469

Ice Age, Little, 19, 391, Quaternary, 17, 71-72, 307, 401-404, 503, and Greek flora, 350, and malaria, 274, 280

Illyricum, animal husbandry, 477, epidemic, 242, marriage, 504, pre-marital intercourse, 169

Imbros, Athenian cleruchy, 96

inbreeding, in Sparta, 235

incest, 203-204, 235

Indo-European, Anatolian branch, 30, head-hunting, 448, institutionalised paederasty, 448, social organisation, 199-201

infanticide (infant exposure), 48, in Egypt, 134-135, in Greece, 151-157, in Hellenistic Athens, 443-444, and population growth, 152-153, in Sparta, 165-166

infants, deaths ignored by orators, 193, deformed, 444, feeding, 138-139, malnutrition, 276, mortality, 117, 123-124, 134, 153, named after seven or ten days, 117-118, 193, sale, 444, swaddling, 139

infertility, see sterility

influenza, 241, 245, 248, 254, 262, 462, in pregnant women, 131

inheritance, customs in Athens, 136, 195-196, 198, 214-217, and marriage, 218-219, in Sparta, 217, and wealth, 206-208

inoculation, defeated smallpox, 232, in

Roman empire, 255
intercourse, sexual, abstention during lactation, 138, abstention in Messenian War, 174-175, anal, 146, 156, 447, fellatio, 447, frequency, 146-147, 149-150, 169, 442, penalty in Athens for illegitimate heterosexual, 168, pre-marital, 168-169, vaginal, 146
invasions, ecological, 38-41, 87
Iolkos, emmer, 494
Ionian migration, 91, kinship, 201
iron, and anaemia, 275-276, technology, 348, 490
island biogeography, 38-40, 402-403
isouramil, 301
Israel, age of marriage, 221, balsam, 29, barley, 347, cereal rust, 292, 472, coitus interruptus, 156, darnel, 339, 487, extension of cultivated area, 476, hippopotamus, 400, papyrus, 370, paederasty, 453, plague, 266, population, 60, prohibition of crop mixtures, 328, 484, rice, 22, as segmentary society, 188, 453, wet-nursing, 153, wheat, 333, 347, 485
Italy, animal husbandry, 375, bread wheat, 355, emmer, 346-347, epidemics, 243-244, 462-463, gout alien to, 458, locusts, 27, population decline at end of empire, 256, porotic hyperostosis, 277, 469, tuberculosis in Neolithic, 461, wheat yields, 374-375, 380
ivy, 30

jackal, in Greece, 400

'K' species, 69, 336
Kastanas, cereals, 363-364, darnel, 487, gold of pleasure, 487, grass pea, 473, millet, 363, shrub-trefoil, 499, wheat, 480, wild oats, 492, wild rye, 364, 493
Keos, agriculture, 385, constitution, 451, marriage, 149, 179, 443, old age, 179, 451, plague, 267, 467, population decline, 106, shrub-trefoil, 384-385
Khalkedon, compulsory sex for women, 433, no good harbour, 92, 432
Khalkis, 96, 99, 395, 431, 451
kindred, bilateral, 195
kingship, in Greece, 170, 178-183, 451
kinship, among Germans, 199, in Greece, 195-204, 455-456, in Rome, 198-200
Kition, epidemic, 462
Kleonai, epidemic, 246
Knossos, sheep, 313
Kolophon, rich citizens outnumber poor, 440

Kopais, Lake, malaria, 435, 469, heavy rain, 393
kouros, in art and linguistics, 187
kutisos, see shrub-trefoil
Kylon, conspiracy, 175, 183, 209, 229, 409, 449
Kythnos, shrub-trefoil, 384

labour, demographic consequences of wage and slave, 210-211, division of, and population density, 65, 256, inputs in farming, 56-57, 82-83, 297, 309, 427-428, sexual division, 83, related to fertility, 141-143, wage, in Athens, 138-139, wage, as slavery, 457, wage labour in Mediterranean agriculture, 55, 431
laburnum, 385
lactation, see breastfeeding
lactose, intolerance, 139, 238, 441
land, not a commodity, 207
Laodicea on the Lykos, Athenian colonists, 434
lathyrism, 302
Laurion, silver and lead mines, 35, 57-58, 425
lead, ointment as a contraceptive, 156, poisoning, 34, 425
leases, of land, 142, 308, 310
Lefkandi, small population, 228, skeletal remains, 435, 437
legumes, 300-303, 473-474, in bread, 348, see also individual entries
leishmaniasis, 271, 468
leisure, conspicuous, 59
lemmings, 65
Lemnos, Athenian cleruchy, 96, 432, 445, epidemic, 253, fertility, 376, land use, 478, locusts, 27, wheat, 331, 485
lentil, 30, 301, 423, 428, wild, 488
leprosy, 226, 228, 239-241, 461-462
leptospirosis, 290, 464
Lerna, chicken, 460
ley-arable systems, 384, 499
lice, transmit epidemic typhus, 264-265, 466
life expectancy, associated with varying fertility levels, 90, 108 in classical Greece, 114, in family of Ausonius, 114, and malnutrition, 276, in mediaeval Greece, 122, relation to age of death, 116-117, sex-specific, 129-133, 438-439
lifespan, maximum, 116, in Georgia, 117, determinants of, 221
life tables, from Angel's data, 109-115, models, 112-113, 436, sex-specific, 129, influence of tuberculosis, 237, of Ulpian, 437, a euphemism, 416
linoleic acid, 287

linseed, 340-341, 487
lion, in Greece, 401, 404, 502
literacy, in Sparta, 171
literature, origin of concept, 3
liturgical class, 58, 193, 204-206
locust, desert, 27-28, 39, 69, 422
lodging, in cereals, 381
logistic equation, 74-75, 80, 97, 137, 142
Lotka-Volterra prey-predator cycles, 39, 43, 65-66, 70, 222
louse, in antiquity, 265, 466
lucerne, 32, 303, 311, 382, 473-474, 498
lupins, 28, 360-361, 492
lynx, in Greece, 400
lysine, in short supply in wheat, 300

Macedonia, 445, beans as green manure, 300, initiation rites, 448, lion, 401, malaria, 273-274, 468, no olive, 306, pre-marital intercourse, 169, 447, compulsory procreation, 161, rye, 364, 493, spelt wheat, 349
maize, 32, 319, 468, 495, history, 344, 358-359, 500, in modern Attica, 296, 300, 363
malaria, 271-281, 467-469, evolution, 26, and favism, 301-302, mortality, 226, in pregnant women, 131, genetic traits resistant to, 235-236, 461, synergistic with salmonella, 231
malnutrition, 283-286, in childhood, 276, in epidemic of 430 BC, 261, and population growth, 101
mammoth, woolly, 401
manioc, 81
Mantinea, pressure on carrying capacity, 106, 435
manure, animal, 382-385, green, 382, human, 257, 382, 498
Marathon, animals, 400, burial of Persians, 108, malaria, 280, 469
marriage, age, 8, 148-151, 177, 443, and age class organisation, 150, 191, in Israel and Mesopotamia, 221, regulated by age class system in Sparta and Crete, 165, 176, squeeze, 157-158, history of types, 217-221
marten, in Greece, 400
meadows, 382-384, 499
measles, 227, 229, 254, 263, density-dependent and chaotic, 222-223, absent from ancient Greece, 232, evolution, 288, more infectious than smallpox, 256, 259, mortality, 250, 464, not responsible for epidemic of 430 BC, 247-248, and wet-nurses, 252
meat, consumption of raw in Aitolia, 226, from dog, 227, and heart disease, 287, a

luxury in Athens, 311
Medicago arborea, see shrub-trefoil
Mediterranean, as a biogeographical region, 16-18, consequences of summer drought, 35, 105, 300-303, history of climate, 17-18, 20, 44-45, 390-396, and malaria, 271-273, wetlands, 22, 280
megafauna, extinction, 9-10, 401-404
Megalopolis, census, 53, 427, megafauna, 401
Megara, 106, 295, 310, 435, 449
melon, water and sweet, 483, origin, 25, 32, in modern Attica, 296
Melos, 96, barley, 477, carrying capacity, 476, fertility, 376, 497
menarche, 144-145, 169, 442, 470, in New Guinea, 137
menopause, 144-145, 442
mercenary service, 57, 162, 434, demographic consequences, 100, 153
Meroe, sorghum in, 21-22, 322
Mesopotamia, age of marriage, 221, animal breeding, 397, Antonine epidemic, 255, cereals, 317-319, 322, 334, 347, 360, cereal yields, 388, 500, date palm, 482, lion, 401, lupin, 361, 492, measurement of area, 487, papyrus, 495, plants transplanted from Greece, 491, rapid population growth, 432, sesame, 363-364, tillering, 379, wild wheat, 500
Messenia, 62, 91, 434, barley, 314, 478
Metapontum, cereals, 489, syphilis, 470
Methana, emigration, 431, fertility, 376, 497, hand cultivation, 477, influence of olive harvest on marriage rate, 103, measurement of area, 342, 488, olive, 474, polyculture, 294, 484, scarcity of animal manure, 498, storage of surpluses, 353
metics, in Athens, 60, 427
migration, see colonisation
mildew, barley, 292
Miletos, abortion, 155, mercenaries, 152-153, 444, wool, 397
militarism, in Crete and Sparta, 172-173
milk, 153, animal and human, 139, and tuberculosis, 237-238, 288
millets (*S. italica* and *P. miliaceum*), 319, 363, 492-493, a sign of poverty, 365, rapid shattering, 356, spread, 20, small seeded, 342, in USSR, 485, *Echinocloa crus-galli*, 363, finger and teff millets, 321-322, 422, *Setaria genuicalata*, 488
mint, 30
mixtures, of crops, boost productivity, 298, 304-305, 349, 357, 362, 384-385, impact of diseases on, 292
mobility, social, 206-207, 215

momentum, of population growth, 101
monkey (*Cercopithecus aethiops*), 147,
     442-443
monkeypox, related to smallpox, 253, 290
moon, and menstrual cycle, 452
morphine, 20
mortality, differential, 118, infant, 117-118,
     124, 134, 153, maternal, 104, 130-133,
     237, 439, caused by measles and smallpox,
     250, 258-260, 464-465, caused by malaria,
     226, caused by plague and AIDS, 223-224,
     in Old Testament, 252-253, slave, 118-119,
     at weaning, 231
mosquito, and dengue, 256, and malaria,
     271-272, 274, 276, 280-281, 468
moth, clothes, 397, 501
mountains, and wheat, 360
mouse, evolution of domesticated, 21, genetic
     differentiation of populations, 460,
     population dynamics, 39, 69, 77-78, and
     rat, 263-264, 466
mule, fertility, 425, in ancient Attica, 312,
     477, modern Attica, 297
mumps, chaotic, 223, epidemic, 232-233, 460
mushroom, 458
mutations, neutral, 36
muteness, on Amorgos, 235
mutualism, ecological, 11-14, 21, 396
Mycenae, collapse, 15-16, 185, crops, 15, life-
     span, 469, lion, 401, measurement of area,
     342, rivalry with Argos, 391-392, sesame,
     363, 493, stature of inhabitants, 277
Mykonos, baldness, 234-235, 460
myrtle, 28, 423
Mytilene, 246
myxomatosis, 40-41, 224, 269, 484

narcissus, 30
Naxos, 96, 426
neoteny, in animals, 396
Nessana, 378, 498
Newcastle disease, of poultry, 233, 460
New Guinea, age class systems, 404-407,
     417-418, land clearance, 348, languages,
     93-94, motives for high fertility, 140,
     natural fertility, 137, sugar cane, 28,
     sweet potato, 70, 405, taboos on heter-
     osexual intercourse, 450
Nile, origin, 26, 422, fertility, 388,
     unhealthiness, 465
nitrogen, 81, 300, 302, 373, 381-384
nomadism, 21, population dynamics, 66-69,
     and milk, 238
nursing, wet, in Greece, 137-140, in Egypt,
     440, in Israel, 153, in Rome, 138, and
     smallpox and measles, 252

nutrition, sex-specific, 130, 439

oats, evolution, 311, 361-363, 492, in Britain,
     350, native to Balkans, 28, in modern
     Attica, 296, not in Egypt, 495-496, in
     three-field rotation system, 331, 352, 399
oedema, famine, 230-231, 459-460
oikos, 197
Olbia, citizenship grants, 427
oleic acid, 287
olive, in Attica, 56, 304-309, 474-476, and
     bees, 304, competition with linseed and
     sesame, 340-341, 363, and Greek colo-
     nisation, 92, in Etruria, 424, etymology,
     30, evolution, 304-309, 375, fleas sensitive
     to oil, 267, fly, 12, grafting, 30, harvest and
     marriage on Methana, 103, historical dis-
     tribution, 17-18, 32-33, in India, 421,
     leaves fed to sheep, 501, leaves in Spartan
     tombs, 127, rare on Lemnos, 478, lifespan,
     497, low labour input, 54, in North Africa,
     379, nutritional value, 34, 285, oil and
     cancer and heart disease, 287, oil as a
     contraceptive, 156, 445, origin in Levant,
     85, pollen, 306, 424-425, population den-
     sity, 379, 475, on Samos, 424, in Sicily,
     425, variability of harvests, 395, vege-
     tative propagation, 30, 375
olura, see emmer
Olympia, Olympic Games, 412, 452, 459, sedi-
     ment deposition, 392, water supply, 231
Olynthos, infant mortality, 135, 437, olive,
     474, skeletons, 109
Oman, sorghum, 22
Onchestos, malaria, 469
oregano, 35, 425
Orchomenos (Boiotia), qualification for
     citizenship, 438
orthopoxviruses, 290
osteological evidence, for decreasing fertility,
     94, age- and sex-differential preser-
     vation, 111, for disease ecology, 225-226,
     for fertility, 115, for nutritional status,
     101, 275-277, for sex-differential age at
     death, 129, for smallpox, 466, for social
     organisation, 184-185, age structure in
     cemeteries, 122-126
osteoporosis, 111, 436
otter, in Boiotia, 400
overshoot, of carrying capacity, 101-102, 159
ovulation, concealed, 146-147, 442

paederasty, institutionalised, distinct from
     prostitution, 141, antiquity, 453, on Crete,
     145, 169, in Sparta and Crete, 166-167, in
     Elis and Thebes, 167, in Athens, 167-168,

447, in Ionia, 168, absent from Israel, 188, female, 171-172, in modern sense, 446

Paestum, chicken, 233

paideia, 165

pallakai, in Athens, 157, 218-219, 458

palynology, 374, 391, 474, chestnut and walnut, 423, olive, 306, 424-425, pine, 425, rye, 365, of southern Argolid, 103-105, of Thessaly, 106

Panakton, mountain pasture, 476

Pannonia, animal breeding, 398, epidemic of animal disease, 471, skeletal population, 436

papyrus, 26, 32, 370, 422, 495

parainfluenza, 233, 460

Parthenon, temple in Athens, 391, 393

partridge, 39, 426

pastoralism, see husbandry, animal, and nomadism

pathocoenosis, 225

Patrai, sex ratio, 133

patriline, discontinuity, 136, 140, in Argos, 456, in Athens, 194-195, 204-206, 454-455, in Boiotia, 159, 205, in Sparta, 216-217, 456

pea, grass, 28, 302, 473

peach, 29, 423

peacock, 28, 38, 426

pear, 29, 423

Peloponnese, barley, 314, 316, cereal rust, 292, epidemic of 430 BC, 246, 260, 463, flax, 340, flora, 19, olive, 424, *silphion*, 352, see also entries for individual towns and regions

periodisation, of ancient history, 46

Persia, empire, 47-48, size of population, 504, in Xenophon's *Cyropaedia*, 189

Phigalia, in epidemic, 246

philosophy, of biology, 7

Phoenicia, 25, 85, exports olive oil to Spain, 424, exports *semidalis* to Athens, 317

Phokis, disruption of age class system, 407

phosphorus, 373, 381-382, 388

Phylloxera vitifolii, 76-77

phytic acid, 275-277, 285

pig, decreased in size under domestication, 396, diseases, 471, number in modern Attica, 296, parasitic worms, 458, at Sitagroi, 501, in Ukraine, 502

pine, in Attica, 35-36, 425

Piraeus, epidemic, 253, 256, grain merchants, 344, emmer, 365

pistachio, 29

plague (*Y. pestis*), 26, 241, 263-271, 458, 466-467, and Black Death, 223, 258, 467, exclusive with yersiniosis, 239, generation

length, 71, in pregnant women, 131, lacks G6PD, 235, pneumonic, 223, 254, not responsible for epidemic of 430 BC, 247, not truly adapted to man, 290, septicaemic, 223

'plague of Athens', 244, see epidemic, in 430 BC

Plataia, 261

plough, 54, 82-84, 348, 477, 485, 490

plum, 29, 423

poliomyelitis, 241

polis, 3, 161-164, 181, 207, 409

pollution, environmental, 4, 35

poluanthrôpia, 59

polyculture, see mixtures

polyploidy, 340, in humans, 396

Pompeii, population, 61, 436-437, no porotic hyperostosis, 469, rat, 263-264, sex ratio, 439, wall paintings, 481, wheat, 486, 489

poppy, opium, 20, 364, 421

population, age structure of rapidly growing, 124-125, growth and malnutrition, 101, as a transient structure, 44, concept, 37, cycles, 10, 43-44, 65-73, cycles and migration, 77, demography of cities, 88-89, 257-258, density in desert, 28, density and social stratification, 99, geometric increase, 87, growth and family structure, 196-197, growth and landlessness, 208-209, in Greece in nineteenth century, 75-79, 85, irregular rates of growth, 42-43, maximum rate of growth, 86, 89-90, 134, momentum of growth, 101, of Athens in Dark Ages, 86-91, of Athens in fifth century, 95-99, 126, of Athens in fourth century BC, 52-60, 73, shifting, 18, sink, 89, size, 48, size and division of labour, 65, stability, 152

potato, 32, in modern Attica, 296, 300, sweet, 70, 405

Potidaia, 96, epidemic, 258-259

pottery, chronology of styles, 63-64

prasis epi lusei loans, 457

pregnancy, at very early age, 104, death during, 130-132, smallpox in, 259

primogeniture, 196

probability, ancient concept, 37-38, and smallpox, 232

productivity, cereal, 372-389, concepts of cereal, 299, 341-343, individual plant, 335-338, in Mediterranean and Britain, 105-106

prostitutes, female, 155, male, 141

proteins, 300-301, 322, 384, 459, 473

psoriasis, 240

puberty, 144, 442, retarded by hyacinth, 423

pumpkin, native to south America, 32, 483
Punic Wars, 27, 244, 375, 379-380, 400
Pylos, lost, 62, cereals, 366, Ethiopians, 236

quantification, in science, 7-10
quartan, see malaria

'r' species, 68-69, 336
rabbit, spread, 20, population dynamics, 39-41, 426, syphilis, 282-283
rabies, 288-289, 335
rainfall, summer in Neolithic, 17, at start of Peloponnesian War, 261, variation and variability, 390-395
rat, in antiquity, 263-266, 466, and plague, 268, 467
rations, cereal, 301, 475, or wages in kind, 366, sex-specific, 439
reconstitution, family, 50, for Athens, 135-136
reference group theory, 207
refuse, disposal in Athens, 257, 382
regulation, of population as distinct from family, 152
religion, Greek, 3, and age class systems, 186-188
remarriage, in Athens, 148, 157-158, 443
research, comparative, 10-11, 151, 164, 190, 417
retrovirus, 26, 224, 262
Rharian plain, at Eleusis, 477
rhinoviruses, 21
Rhodes, carob, 29, census, 53, 427, cult of Apollo Eruthibios, 472
rice (Oryza spp.), evolution and diffusion of African and Oriental, 22-24, 32, 338, 421, irrigation, 83, labour inputs, 56, 500 and malaria, 280, mimicked by cockspur grass, 363, wild (*Zizania aquatica*), 355-356, 491
rickets, in Greece and Rome, 139, 284, 441
rinderpest, of cattle, 288
ripening, differential, 354-356
Rome, age grades, 454, as population sink, 88-89, cereals in, 489, citizenship, 190, Gaulish attack, 67, demography, 43, 61, density-dependent diseases, 243-244, 252, 254-255, 462-463, epidemic of 430 BC, 254, early growth of population, 243-244, 463, incommensurable with Greece, 11, infanticide, 154, 444, kinship, 198-200, 455-466, malaria, 278, marriage, 149, olive and vine, 32-33, 424, polyculture, 491, population of empire, 229, 252, poulard wheat cultivated in vicinity, 481, reproduction of urban population, 257, rickets, 139, seed selection, 343-344, slave demography, 118-119, sorghum, 322,

unhealthiness, 278, 432, upper class eat bread wheat, 482, wet-nursing, 138
rotaviruses, 231
rubella, chaotic, 223, absent from Greece, 232, confused with smallpox, 248
rust, cereal, 291-293, 364, 472
rye, 315, 332, 352, 364-365, 399, 486, 490, 493, in modern Attica, 296

Sahara, 17, 21, 24, 26-28, cereals in, 377-380, 498
Salamis, Athenian cleruchy, 96, 433, 449
salmonella, 231, 460, synergistic with malaria, 273
salt, 285
Samaritans, genetics of, 234, 460
Samos, Athenian cleruchy, 99, exports olive oil, 424, hippopotamus, 502
schistosomiasis, in Egypt, 26, 274, 465
seed, size, 302, 317-318, 320, 333-346, 371, 481, factors affecting, 317-318, hominids adapted to collection, 403
selection, natural, acts on individuals, 93, works on differential reproduction, 114, 222, and population genetics, 234-236, of seeds, 343-346, 488-489
selection, sexual, 133, 157
Selinus, epidemic, 280, no good harbour, 92, wheat in, 486
Semitic, languages, 31, 317
semidalis, 31, 317-325, 329, 333, 370, 479, 481-482
semolina, 319-320
Seriphos, insignificant, 47, 427
sesame, 24, 31, 363-364, 493
sex, see intercourse
sex ratio, evolution, 132-133, 439, imbalance in Athens late in Peloponnesian War, 98-99, in skeletal populations, 109-111, in classical Greece, 133
sheep, 382, 385, 501, decreased in size under domestication, 396, and disease, 289, in ancient Attica, 312-313, in modern Attica, 297, evolution of fleece, 397-398, stupidity, 397
shifting cultivation, in tropics, 81-82
shigellosis, 230-231, 460
shingles, see chickenpox
shrub-trefoil, 30, 410-411, 438, 442, labour inputs for, 300
Sicily, cereal yields, 376, 497, difficulty of farming, 421, epidemics, 243, locusts, 27, olive, 425, extra-urban sanctuaries, 187, wheat, 480, 497
sickle, 491
Sikyon, olive cultivation, 304

silphion, 32, exported from Cyrene to Carthage, 424, unsuccessfully transplanted to Greece, 352

slavery, among ants, 212, burial in Athens, 108, children sold in archaic Athens, 209, in agriculture, 55-57, 209, 428, in classical Athens, 53-60, demographic consequences, 210-211, as a mode of production, 164, natural, 210-211, rarely mentioned on *horoi* inscriptions, 428, in silver mining, 57-58, 428, and mortality, 118-119, in paederasty, 144, skilled labour, 58, manumitted slaves in wet-nursing, 139

smallpox, 227, density-dependent, 229-230, in early mediaeval period, 464, in epidemic of Athens, 246-262, 463-466, in recent times, 257-258, 262-263, inoculation, 232, 255, 465, peaks in infancy and old age, 237, occurrence with other diseases, 245, and pregnant women, 131, 259, not in Hippokratic corpus, 232, specific to man, 290, and wet-nurses, 252

Sokrates, 408, bigamy, 99, not infected in epidemic, 246, 463, as social revolutionary, 410

sorghum, 21-22, 32, 338, 481, 488

Sparta, abortion, 446, no adultery, 169, bachelorhood, 157, burial customs, 127-128, 438, citizenship, 189, compared to Athens, 128, conquers Messenia, 91, a democratic system, 181, family limitation, 154, 165, *gerousia*, 451, hare, 426, hostility to innovation, 445, *Hyakinthia* festival, 423, inbreeding, 235, infant care, 139, 440, inheritance, 217, kinship, 200-202, 455-456, *klêroi*, 435, 478, 488, literacy, 171, 448, marriage, 149, 151, 165, 176, 443, 450, meaning of word *loimos* in Spartan dialect, 459, millet, 493, old age, 178, olive consumption, 305-307, outside League of Corinth, 51, paederasty, 166, payments to *sussitia* for citizenship, 170, poppy, 421, population decline, 47, 72, 170-171, 447, population instability, 213-214, posthumous honours for maternal mortality, 131, preference for tall women, 37-38, professionalism in war, 162, Roman, 192, same amount of food for both sexes, 130, no sex during Messenian War, 174-175, status of Helots, 454, treaty with Argos, 242, wheat and barley, 314, 478, wife-sharing, 169, wolf, 400

spelt wheat, see wheat

spider, poisonous, on Crete, 402

spina bifida, at Tiryns 154

splenomegaly, in malaria, 273, 467

spondylarthritis, 267

squash, 32

squirrel, in Greece, 400

staphylococcus, 245, 270

state, definition, 406, subject to cyclical development, 72

stature, 276

sterility, adolescent, 144, 169, 442, caused by disease, 233, 237, 241, 260, 465, natural, 148, 443, in Troizen, 104

Stobi, bitter vetch, 423, rat, 263

Stoics, 36, 298, 420

succession, 198

sugar, beet, 28, cane, 24, 28, 32, 56, 421, 423

survey, archaeological, 15, in Crete, 169-170, in Greece, 60-65, 99, on Keos, 179, urban, 106

sussitia, 170, 172-174

Switzerland, wheat in prehistoric, 374

Sybaris, cereals, 489, fertility, 376, 498

syphilis, 241, 281-283, 462, 470

Syracuse, age of eligibility for office, 449, Athenian expedition, 175, 259-260, epidemics, 251, 463-464, a large *polis*, 99

Syria, diphtheria, 232, plague, 266, wheat, 485

tapeworms, 226

Tarentum, *Partheniai*, 174, 449

taro, 32, 405, 424

taxonomy, folk, 327, 482

technology, in agricultural history, 81, in antiquity, 13-14, 368, 414

teeth, 277

teleology, 327, 408, 416, 482

tetanus, 288, 471

Tethys Sea, 17

TetraCanthatch, 333

tetraploid, see wheat

thalassaemia, 154, 235, 275-277, 279

Thapsia garganica, 420

Thasos, mumps, 233, 460, olive, 307-308, tuberculosis, 461, vine, 375

Thebes (Boiotia), 106, 435, paederasty, 167-168, sale of children, 444

Thera, date of volcanic eruption of, 63

thermodynamics, 5, 311

Thermopylae, malaria, 280, 469

Thespiai, 106, farming regarded as shameful, 475

Thessaly, animal husbandry, 383, beans as green manure, 300, cattle, 501, grazing on cereal crops, 312, palynology, 106, polyculture, 491, spelt wheat, 349

thetes, as emigrants, 100-101, as labourers employed for a year, 209, in naval service,

52, 427, thetic *epiklêroi*, 157
Thrace, Athenian colonists, 433, healthiness, 432, millet, 494, oats, 362, premarital intercourse, 169, 447, rye, 364
Thurii, 96, 489
thyme, in Attica and Gaul, 352, 491
tillering, in wheat, 341, 343, 354, 374, 376-379, 488, 497-498
Tiryns, dam to prevent flooding, 498, lion, 401, 502, Medicago spp., 499, melon and rice, 23, 483, olive, 306, spina bifida, 154, wild oats, 492, wild rye, 493
tomato, 32, 54, 297
trachoma, 228, 281-282, 284, 469-470
transition, demographic, 118, 143, 147, 156, 159, 239
treponematoses, endemic, 282-283
Triphylia, cereal rust epidemics, 292, 472
triticale, 345-346, 356
Triticum, aestivum, compactum, durum, spelta, turgidum, see wheat, *T. boeoticum, T. monococcum,* see einkorn, *T. dicoccum, T. dicoccoides,* see emmer, *T. araraticum, T. timopheevi,* 333, 486, *T. parvicoccum,* 333, 343, 358-359, 485-486, *T. carthlicum,* 335, *T. compactum vars. griseovavilovianum & vavilovianum,* 335, *T. durum var. duro-compactum,* 334, 486, *T. sphaerococcum,* 358, 485, *T. urartu,* 343, *T. vulgare antiquorum,* 333-335, 482
Troad, currant vine, 76
Troizen, diseases of feet, 458, epidemic, 246, unhealthiness and infertility, 104, 435, 439, malaria in modern, 469, marriage, 149, modern agriculture, 303, 373
trypanosomiasis, 82
tryptophan, 300
tuberculosis, 226, 228, 236-241, 258, 461-462, in pregnant women, 131, 461, in autumn, 271, bovine, 237-238, 288-289
tularaemia, 254, 290
typhus, epidemic, 241-242, 248-250, 254, 264-265, 466, murine, 264

uniformitarianism, 10

vaccinia, 255
variance, in reproductive performance, 132-133
varicella, see chickenpox
variola, major and minor, see smallpox
vegetables, ancient attitudes towards, 284, in modern Attica, 296-297
vegetarianism, 34, 425
Vergina, 401
vernalisation, 307, 329-330
vetch, bitter, consumed in famine, 302, native

to Aegean, 28, at Stobi, 423
vine, currant, 76-77, 431, diversification, 357, evolution, 375, in Britain, 395-396, high labour input, 54, in modern Attica, 296-297, 303-304, productivity of individual, 338, 375, spread, 32-33, 424, raised carrying capacity, 297, use of harvest dates to study climatic variation, 391
vivax, see malaria

walnut, 28, 423
'wave-of-advance' model, in demography, 430, 432
weaning, secondary peak of mortality, 231
weeds, diffusion, 30, and cereals, 378, and lucerne, 498, sometimes ignored by farmers, 428
weevil, grain, 30
wheat, in ancient and modern Attica, 79, 296, 313-316, breeding, 9, 294-295, chemical defence, 13, club wheat, 331, 355, 485, 491, consumed by wet-nurses, 139, density, 377, diseases, 291-293, 387, 472, bread wheat, 139, 313, 324-332, 335, 343, 347, 350-51, 354-358, 488-489, 491, 498, durum wheat, 275, 292, 313, 319, 316-331, 333-335, 343, 347, 350-352, 357, 368-369, 380, 386, 480, 485, 488-489, 491, hybridisation, 36, in Homer, 478, 494, and iron deficiency anaemia, 275-277, nutritional deficiencies, 285-286, poulard wheat, 320, 334-335, 338, 350, 377, 481, 485-486, selection for plant height, 336-338, selection for seed size, 343-346, spelt wheat, 325, 332, 335, 348-350, 362, 386, 490, yields, 372-389, see also einkorn, emmer, Triticum
whooping cough, 232, 460
willow tree, 13, 420
wine, 231, 375, Athenian, 303, 474, for children, 139, 231, 297, 440, price, 394, at Troizen, 104, yields, 375
wolf, 396, 400, 446
wool, 313, 340, 397-398, of Golden Fleece, 501

xerophthalmia, 284

yersiniosis, exclusive with plague, 239, inhibited by plague, 269
yields, cereal, 372-389
Younger Fill, 45, 103, 105, 372-373, 392, and malaria, 280

zeia, see emmer
zinc, 275-276, 324, 468
zoonoses, 288-290, 471